The ULTIMATE CRAFTS COMPENDIUM

The ULTIMATE CRAFTS COMPENDIUM

300 BEAUTIFUL, EASY-TO-MAKE CRAFT PROJECTS FOR THE HOME,
PHOTOGRAPHED STEP BY STEP

HERMES
HOUSE

This edition is published by Hermes House

Hermes House is an imprint of Anness Publishing Ltd
Hermes House, 88–89 Blackfriars Road, London SE1 8HA
tel. 020 7401 2077; fax 020 7633 9499; info@anness.com

© Anness Publishing Ltd 1998, 2002

Published in the USA by Hermes House, Anness Publishing Inc.
27 West 20th Street, New York, NY 10011; fax 212 807 6813

A CIP catalogue record for this book is available from the British Library.

Publisher: Joanna Lorenz
Project Editor: Judith Simons
Assistant Editor: Kathrin Henkel
Designers: Hannah Attwell, Dean Hollowood,
Siân Keogh, Patrick McLeavey

Printed and bound in Hong Kong / China

1 3 5 7 9 10 8 6 4 2

CONTENTS

INTRODUCTION

*T*his book contains over 300 step-by-step projects using a variety of exciting crafts, both traditional and new. You can select a project at any level of skill, from the simplicity of paper cut-outs to the more detailed art of soldering tin. Or, use a needlework craft to create soft furnishings for the home and complement them with some beautiful painted glassware. Children, in particular, will love the salt dough ideas, and anyone wanting to cheer up walls and furniture should look no further than the stamping projects.

Whatever your preferred style of craft, you're bound to find inspiration in this collection. You could also try out a craft new to you and discover hidden talents. Just pick your project, experiment with the materials, follow the clear instructions and enjoy the result.

USING TEMPLATES

There are easy-to-use templates at the back of the book for a lot of the projects. For tracing templates, you will need tracing paper, a pencil, card or paper and a pair of scissors. The templates can be traced on to tracing paper and cut out to use as pattern guides. If a pattern is to be used a number of times, the template tracing should be transferred to thin card. To do this, trace the template on to tracing paper, using a pencil, then place the tracing paper face down on the card. Re-draw the motif on the back of the tracing and it will appear on the card.

To enlarge the templates to the required size, either use a grid system or a photocopier. For the grid system, trace the template and draw a grid of evenly spaced squares over your tracing. To scale up, draw a larger grid on to another piece of paper. Copy the outline on to the second grid by taking each square individually and drawing the relevant part of the outline in the larger square.

PAPERCRAFTS AND PAPIER-MACHE

Experiment with paper to create some memorable gifts, such as this charming Sunburst Bowl.

STENCILLING,
STAMPING AND
PRINTING

*A marvellously easy
and effective method to
make individual pieces,
such as this Mexican
Citrus Tray.*

EMBROIDERY

*Embroider beautiful
effects on to fabrics, as
illustrated in this
Underwater Picture.*

APPLIQUE, PATCHWORK AND CROSS STITCH

Follow the step-by-step instructions to make exciting projects, such as this pretty Seashell Beach Bag.

MODELLING AND SALT DOUGH

Get stuck into the wonderful texture of salt dough and clay, and create some amazing end results, such as these Salt and Pepper Pots.

WOOD, WIRE AND TINWORK

This section includes fun ideas such as this wood Grasshopper on a Stick, as well as exciting wire and tin projects.

DECORATING GLASS AND CERAMICS

Re-vamp old china and glass and your crockery cupboard will soon be transformed with projects such as this Fruit Bowl.

PAPERCRAFTS AND PAPIER-MACHE

*W*orking with paper is a truly satisfying and creative craft, and the bonus is that it can also be good for the environment, if you recycle old and used papers in your projects. There is such a wealth of colours, textures and sizes available in paper that the scope for producing wonderful decorations and gifts really is endless.

The projects in this book should inspire you to experiment with paper whatever your tastes and ability. Steps are provided to take you through the process of creating a traditional paper cut-out, which you can easily adapt to make as simple or intricate as you like. Or, if you prefer a more weighty project, you could get involved in the art of papier-mâché – and explore the delights you can make from the simplest of materials.

MATERIALS AND EQUIPMENT

Paper comes in many different weights, textures, patterns and colours. Before you embark on the projects here, explore some possible paper sources. Art and hobby shops, printers, office stationers and specialist suppliers are all good starting points. And don't forget to look around your own home – you'll be amazed at how many pieces of paper and card you have got already. You just need to view the material in a different light, and recognize that those old newspapers on the coffee table can be transformed into an exciting new creation.

A craft knife and a cutting mat or a pair of paper scissors are vital when working with paper, and so too is masking tape as it won't tear the paper. Paper glue or spray adhesive are also useful to have at hand if you want to attach pieces of paper to each other.

Painting and colouring your paper projects presents no problem, and there is a wide range of crayons, pens, paints and varnishes available that are suitable for paper. Just check the manufacturer's instructions before you apply the material to paper, and if you like, you can always do a test run on a scrap of paper first, just to make sure.

RIGHT *The equipment necessary for papercrafts is very simple and straightforward.*

Working with different papers

There are so many varieties of paper available that you will have to let your personal taste dictate what you use for your projects. Here are a few of the more exciting papers you could try.

Tissue and crepe paper are cheap papers sold at stationers and craft suppliers. Tissue paper needs to be layered to build up intense colour. Crepe paper is thicker and crinkly and its only drawback is that adhesive tape doesn't stick to it well.

Hand-printed paper is the perfect way to personalize gift wrap. All you need is plain paper and a spark of inspiration. Potato cuts, rubber stamps, stencils, rollers or brushstrokes will all produce unique patterned papers. Use lightweight paper, or cheap brown wrapping paper for the best results.

Corrugated card gives projects a unique texture and depth, and it is also very cheap to buy.

Natural papers are environmentally friendly handmade papers usually imported from the East; the selection really is enormous. It is possible to buy paper made from banana skins or recycled Bombay newsprint inlaid with rose petals. The colours are often hotter and spicier than home-produced papers, so it is well worth seeking out a specialist paper outlet and stocking up for future use.

LEFT *Papers are available in every kind of colour and texture from art suppliers and craft shops.*

BASIC TECHNIQUES

Tearing newspaper

Sheets of newsprint are laid and have a definite grain, usually running from the top to the bottom of the newspaper.

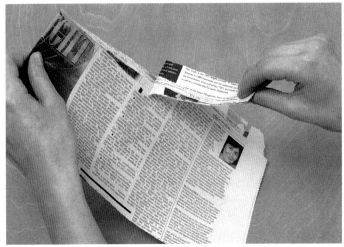

1 If you try to tear a sheet of newspaper against the grain – from side to side – it is impossible to control.

2 If newspaper is torn along the grain it is possible to produce very regular strips, as wide or narrow as you need.

Making papier-mâché pulp

MATERIALS

*5 sheets newspaper
45 ml/3 tbsp PVA (white) glue
20 ml/ 4 tsp wallpaper paste
10 ml/2 tsp plaster of Paris
10 ml/2 tsp linseed oil*

1 Tear the newspaper into pieces about 2.5 cm/1 in square and put them in an old saucepan with water to cover. Simmer for about half an hour.

2 Spoon the paper and any water into a blender or food processor and liquidize it. Pour it into a suitable container with a lid.

3 Add the PVA (white) glue, wallpaper paste, plaster of Paris and linseed oil. Stir vigorously and the pulp is ready to use.

Preparing the surface for papier-mâché painting

The surface of the papier-mâché should be primed before painting to conceal the newsprint and to provide a good ground for decoration.

MATERIALS

*fine sandpaper
paintbrush
white emulsion (latex) paint*

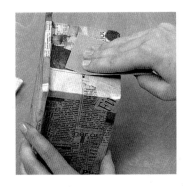

1 Gently smooth the surface of the papier-mâché using fine sandpaper.

2 Apply a coat of white emulsion (latex) paint and leave the object to dry.

3 Rub down the dry paint lightly using fine sandpaper, and apply a second coat of paint. Once this has dried, the papier-mâché may be decorated.

PAPER CUT-OUTS

*G*emini – the twins – is the chosen motif for this effective paper card decoration: the two halves of the card are identical in design, yet one is the negative image of the other. These cut-outs are a traditional skill in Poland, where they are usually deftly cut freehand using a pair of scissors.

YOU WILL NEED

MATERIALS	EQUIPMENT
tracing paper	*pencil*
thin card or paper in two	*craft knife*
colours	*cutting mat*
all-purpose glue	*scissors*

1 Trace the template from the back of the book, enlarging if necessary. Attach the tracing to the wrong side of one piece of coloured card with a few dabs of glue.

2 Using a craft knife, cut out through the template and reserve all the shapes.

3 Remove the tracing paper, turn the card over and then back it with some card in a contrasting colour.

4 Cut the backing card twice the size of the cut-out card and fold down the centre. Stick a piece of the contrast card or paper to one side of the fold and arrange cut-out pieces on it to match the original design. Stick the cut-out card on the opposite side.

DECOUPAGE ROSE EGGS

Re-use old wrapping paper when you are making these patterned eggs.

YOU WILL NEED

MATERIALS

rose scrapbook motifs or rose-decorated wrapping paper
PVA (white) glue
wooden or blown eggs
clear nail varnish

EQUIPMENT

small scissors
paintbrush

1 Cut out a selection of small rose motifs. You may find other motifs you can use, such as butterflies or forget-me-nots. Look out for interesting shapes and cut them out carefully around the outlines.

2 Using PVA (white) glue, stick the cut-out flowers to the wooden or blown eggs, making sure you overlap the edges to give a densely patterned surface. Make sure that all the wood or shell is covered.

3 Once the glue is dry, coat the eggs with three or four coats of clear nail varnish, allowing each coat to dry thoroughly before adding the next one.

CHRISTMAS TREE STAR

*P*ersuade the fairy to take a well-earned rest this
year, and make a magnificent gold star to take
pride of place at the top of the Christmas tree.

YOU WILL NEED

MATERIALS	EQUIPMENT
tracing paper	*pencil*
thin card or paper	*scissors*
corrugated card	*craft knife*
newspaper	*cutting mat*
PVA (white) glue	*metal ruler*
gold spray paint	*bowl*
gold relief or puff paint	*paintbrush*
gold glitter	
thin gold braid	

1 Trace the template from the back of the book, enlarging if necessary, then transfer it to thin card or paper. Cut it out and draw around it on the corrugated card. Cut it out using a craft knife and metal ruler. Tear the newspaper into small strips. Thin the PVA (white) glue with some water and brush it on to both sides of the newspaper, coating it thoroughly. Stick it on the star, brushing it down with more glue to get rid of any air bubbles. Work all over the star in a single layer, covering the edges and points neatly. Allow the star to dry thoroughly, then apply a second layer.

2 If the star begins to buckle, place it under a heavy weight. When it is thoroughly dry, spray both sides of it gold and allow to dry.

3 Draw the design on one side of the star in gold relief paint and sprinkle it with glitter while it is still wet. Allow to dry thoroughly before repeating the design on the other side. Attach thin gold braid with which to hang the star from the top of the Christmas tree.

PAPIER-MACHE PLATE

F or this papier-mâché plate, the colour is incorporated into the paper pulp before the plate is moulded, rather than applied as a decoration once the papier-mâché has dried.

YOU WILL NEED

MATERIALS	EQUIPMENT
acrylic paints	*fork*
paper pulp (see Basic	*pencil*
Techniques)	*plate*
strong card	*craft knife*
PVA (white) glue	*cutting mat*
crepe paper	*paintbrush (optional)*
wallpaper paste	
tracing paper	
thin card or paper	
chalk or white pencil	
black emulsion (latex) paint	
and gold paint (optional)	

1 Using a fork, mash acrylic paint into the paper pulp until the colour is evenly mixed. Cut out two circles of card the same size, using an old plate as a template. Cut a smaller circle from one and glue the rim to the front of the other circle and the centre to the back. Cover with crepe paper soaked in wallpaper paste.

2 Press coloured pulp on to the edge of the plate, building it up in thin layers, and adding more when dry. Trace the template from the back of the book, enlarging if necessary. Transfer to thin card or paper. Cut it out and draw around it with chalk or white pencil on to the plate. Build up the body with pulp, covering the outline.

3 Add finer details such as legs and claws with more thin layers of paper pulp. Allow to dry thoroughly. To add some definition, take a dry brush with some black emulsion (latex) paint and wipe lightly over the scorpion and the rim of the plate. Repeat with gold paint.

GILDED BOOKMARK

*L*ook for pictures of old engravings and heraldic devices for this découpage: the clearly defined images will photocopy perfectly and look great once they've been cunningly aged with tea. Use stiff card so that the bookmark isn't too bulky.

YOU WILL NEED

MATERIALS	EQUIPMENT
stiff card	*craft knife*
acrylic gesso	*cutting mat*
acrylic paints: red, orange	*metal ruler*
and green	*paintbrush*
gold paint	*bowl*
tea bags	*scissors*
photocopied images	
PVA (white) glue	
velvet ribbon	

1 Using a craft knife and metal ruler, cut a rectangle of card 15 x 5 cm/6 x 2 in, and cut off the corners diagonally.

2 Paint it with acrylic gesso. Mix a red oxide colour using red, orange and green acrylics and paint this all over the bookmark. When dry, cover with gold paint, leaving some of the red oxide showing through.

3 Make a very strong solution of tea and paint the photocopies with this to create an aged appearance. Allow to dry, then cut out.

4 Stick on the cut-outs with PVA (white) glue and varnish with diluted PVA (white) to seal. Glue a length of velvet ribbon to the back of the bookmark.

GARLAND TRAY CUT-OUTS

*T*he simple leaf design for this pretty découpage tray is folded and cut out like a row of dancing paper dolls. When drawing the design, make sure that your outline continues to the folds so that your paper garland stays in one piece when it is opened out.

YOU WILL NEED

MATERIALS
wooden tray
emulsion (latex) paint
large sheet of green paper
PVA (white) glue
clear gloss acrylic varnish

EQUIPMENT
paintbrushes
pencil
scissors
scrap paper

1 Paint the tray with two coats of yellow emulsion (latex) paint and allow to dry. Place the tray on the green paper and draw around it. Cut out the shape just inside the line.

2 Fold the paper in half, then in half again. Draw a series of connecting leaf shapes on to scrap paper and cut them out. When you are happy with the design, draw around it on to the green paper, making sure that it reaches the folded edges. Cut along the pencil line.

3 Open out the garland carefully and glue it on to the tray. Allow to dry.

4 Protect the tray with up to four coats of varnish.

BEAMING SUN WALL PLAQUE

A cheerful sunny face looking down at you is sure to cheer you up, so put this wall plaque where it will do you most good — perhaps over the breakfast table! The plaque is made from sandwiched layers of corrugated card and mounted on card in the same way, so it is very easy to make. There is also an alternative idea, using papier-mâché pulp to mould the face.

YOU WILL NEED

MATERIALS	EQUIPMENT
corrugated card	*pair of compasses*
PVA (white) glue	*pencil*
masking tape	*craft knife*
white undercoat paint	*scissors*
acrylic paints: red, yellow and blue	*paintbrushes*
matt varnish	

1 Draw and cut out five equal circles of card to the size required. Glue together three circles. Bind the edges with masking tape.

2 Glue the remaining two circles together and cut out a circle from the centre. Trim this smaller circle so that there will be a gap all around it when it is replaced.

3 On the circle with the hole, draw the rays of the sun and cut them out. Bind the edges inside and out and also the edges of the small circle.

4 Glue the prepared sun rays and the face on to the backing circle, centralizing the face in the slightly larger area left for it.

5 Draw the features on card freehand and cut them out. Glue them on to the face.

6 Prime the whole of the plaque with white undercoat and allow to dry.

7 Decorate with acrylic paints. When dry, apply two coats of varnish.

8 Alternatively, make the sun shape from papier-mâché pulp (see Basic Techniques), moulding it by hand on the backing circle. Use fine string to delineate the features and give relief detail to the rays. Coat the face in primer and paint as before.

DECORATIVE NAPKIN RING

*T*his practical project recycles old card to create *something special for the dinner table. You could decorate the ring with a design of your choice, or use this stylish heraldic motif.*

YOU WILL NEED

MATERIALS	EQUIPMENT
tracing paper	*hard and soft pencils*
thick card	*craft knife*
poster tube	*cutting mat*
newspaper	*bowl*
wallpaper paste	*fine and medium*
acrylic gesso	*paintbrushes*
acrylic paints: blue, red,	*glue gun or epoxy resin glue*
yellow, light gold, black	
and white	
gloss acrylic varnish	

1 Trace the template from the back of the book, enlarging if necessary. Cut out a card diamond. Cut a 4 cm/1½ in section from the poster tube. Coat strips of newspaper with wallpaper paste. Cover the ring, with the edges, with several layers. Cover the diamond with about ten layers.

2 When the papier-mâché is dry, prime it with three coats of acrylic gesso. Transfer the traced design on to the diamond by rubbing over the back with a soft pencil, then drawing over the outlines.

3 Paint the background diamonds in blue and red and the lion and fleur-de-lys in yellow. Highlight the design in light gold paint and outline the shapes in black. Pick out details in red and white. Paint the ring with two coats of blue. Seal the diamond and ring with acrylic varnish and, when dry, glue the two parts together.

ORANGE BOWL

*H*oard your old magazines so that you can assemble a good collection of orange and yellow papers for this papier-mâché bowl. It is designed to look like half an orange – plain on the outside and beautifully textured inside.

YOU WILL NEED

MATERIALS
petroleum jelly
newspaper
wallpaper paste
*old magazine pages that
are predominantly orange
and yellow*
orange wrapping paper
gloss varnish
gold paint

EQUIPMENT
large bowl
scissors
*medium and fine
paintbrushes*

1 Coat the inside of the bowl with a layer of petroleum jelly. Soak strips of newspaper in wallpaper paste. Cover the inside of the bowl with at least ten layers of strips. Allow to dry thoroughly, then gently ease the bowl from the mould.

2 Tear the magazine pages into long, narrow triangles and paste them around the inside of the bowl so that they taper towards the bottom.

3 Cover the outside of the bowl with torn strips of plain orange and yellow wrapping paper, carefully overlapping the edges.

4 Leave the bowl to dry thoroughly, then trim the top edge with scissors. Coat the bowl with a protective layer of varnish. Paint a thin line of gold paint along the top edge to complete the bowl.

SUNBURST BOWL

*T*his spectacular sun seems to burst out of the bowl towards you. Use all your creativity to make the design as exuberant as possible. Papier-mâché gives you the ability to make graceful vessels without the skill and equipment needed for making ceramics. This bowl is ideal for fruit, nuts or small display items, but you might well want to leave it empty to show it off.

YOU WILL NEED

MATERIALS
petroleum jelly
newspaper
paper pulp (see Basic Techniques)
PVA (white) glue
white undercoat paint
gouache or acrylic paints: yellow, blue and red
gold "liquid leaf" paint or gold gouache paint
fixative spray
gloss varnish

EQUIPMENT
bowl
medium and fine paintbrushes
paint-mixing container
pair of compasses
pencil

1 Coat the inside of the bowl with a layer of petroleum jelly. Dip strips of newspaper in water, then lay them over the inside of the bowl.

2 Press the paper pulp into the mould so that it is about 1 cm/½ in thick. Allow to dry in an airing cupboard, for about five days.

3 Release the dried paper pulp from the mould and cover it in strips of newspaper dipped in PVA (white) glue. Allow to dry thoroughly.

4 Give the bowl two coats of white undercoat, allowing each coat to dry.

5 Use the pair of compasses to locate the sun shape accurately, then draw a small circle for the centre and a larger one to contain the rays. Draw the rays freehand.

6 Fill in the yellow and gold areas first of all. Then paint the rim in gold. Fill in the blue background, leaving a white band below the gold rim.

7 Paint the red border and allow to dry. Seal the bowl with fixative spray and protect it with a coat of varnish.

PALMISTRY

Stars, spirals and rings spring from this mystical hand. The vibrant decoration is enhanced with light-reflecting mirror glass.

YOU WILL NEED

MATERIALS	EQUIPMENT
tracing paper	*pencil*
thin card	*craft knife*
newspaper	*cutting mat*
masking tape	*wire-cutters*
galvanized wire	*round-nosed pliers*
wallpaper paste	*hammer*
mirror glass	*paintbrushes*
chemical metal filler	
PVA (white) glue	
white acrylic primer	
liquid gold leaf paint	
gloss polyurethane varnish	
small brass screw hooks	
epoxy resin glue	
gouache paints	
small brass jump rings	
picture wire	

1 Trace the templates from the back of the book, enlarging if necessary, and cut out all the shapes from card. Crumple small pieces of newspaper and tape them to each shape to create the form. Leave the wings of the hand and the small stars flat. Using round-nosed pliers, coil and bend a piece of wire, following the template, and tape to the sun shape.

2 Using wallpaper paste, cover each shape in several layers of newspaper. Allow to dry.

3 Break the mirror by placing it between several layers of newspaper and hitting it gently with a hammer. Mix the chemical filler according to the manufacturer's instructions. Apply to one side of each wing and along the top of the hand, then carefully press in the pieces of mirror. Allow to dry, then repeat on the other side of the wings. If you like, stick one small piece of mirror on to each of the small star shapes.

4 Cut five lengths of wire and coil into elaborate "S" shapes, following the template. Coat with PVA (white) glue, white acrylic primer and gold paint, then varnish, leaving to dry between each coat. Screw one small hook into each of the papier-mâché shapes, into the tip of each finger and into each wing of the hand. Screw four hooks into the sun piece. Secure the hooks with epoxy resin glue. Coat the shapes with PVA (white) glue, then with white acrylic primer.

5 Paint each shape with gouache paints, then decorate with gold paint and allow to dry.

6 Varnish with gloss and allow to dry. Suspend the smaller shapes from the hand using the jump rings. Suspend the larger shapes from three of the wire coils and hang these from the hand. Attach the remaining wire coils to the wings. Attach the small stars to the sun piece. Thread a length of picture wire through the two coils on the wings for hanging.

TWISTED PAPER FRAME

*T*his frame is made from unravelled twisted paper, which is available from most gift shops. It is simple to make, and provides the ideal frame for your favourite photo or picture.

YOU WILL NEED

MATERIALS
card
twisted paper
PVA (white) glue
emulsion (latex) paints:
white and gold
fabric star motifs
backing card (optional)

EQUIPMENT
plate and saucer
pencil
scissors
craft knife
cutting mat
old toothbrush
paint-mixing containers

1 Draw around the plate on to the card. Place the saucer in the centre of the circle and draw around it. Cut out the outer circle with scissors and then the inner circle using a craft knife, so you are left with a card ring.

2 Unwind the twisted paper and wind it carefully around the ring until it is fully covered. Stick the end down with PVA (white) glue.

3 Dip an old toothbrush into the white paint and run your finger along the bristles so that a fine spray of paint lands on the card frame. Repeat with the gold paint.

4 Stick the star motifs all over the frame with PVA (white) glue. If you like, stick a card backing circle on the back, leaving a gap in which to insert a picture.

PAPIER-MACHE JUG

*T*his jug looks like a modern Italian ceramic, with its elegant shape and brilliant colours, but in fact it is made from papier-mâché shaped round a blown-up balloon.

YOU WILL NEED

MATERIALS	EQUIPMENT
balloon	*scissors*
newspaper	*medium and fine*
wallpaper paste	*paintbrushes*
thin card	*paint-mixing container*
masking tape	
round margarine container	
fine string	
paper pulp (see Basic Techniques)	
acrylic paints: blue, yellow, red and green	
clear varnish	

1 Blow up the balloon and tie a knot in it. Soak strips of newspaper in wallpaper paste, and cover the balloon with at least eight layers of them. Allow to dry. Cut slits in the top of the balloon at the knot end and remove the balloon. Cut out a V-shape in one side. Cut a piece of card to form a spout and tape in position.

2 Tape the rim of a margarine container to the bottom for the base. For the handle, roll up some glued newspaper sheets and curve them to fit the jug. Allow to dry. Cover the handle with string, leaving about 1–2.5 cm/½ –1 in at each end uncovered. Cut two slits in the side and insert the handle.

3 Model the paper pulp on the side of the jug in the shape of sunflowers and leaves. Allow to dry overnight. Paint the background, flowers and details and allow to dry, before giving the jug a coat of varnish.

PAPIER-MACHE FRAME

*T*his frame provides a beautiful three-dimensional background to a picture or painting. You can experiment as much as you like with the frame: try using softer colours instead of the strong ones here, or replace the heart motifs with a design of your choosing to create a truly individual frame.

YOU WILL NEED

MATERIALS	EQUIPMENT
tracing paper	*pencil*
card	*craft knife*
masking tape	*cutting mat*
wire	*paintbrushes*
newspaper	*clay modelling tool*
wallpaper paste	
white emulsion (latex)	
paint	
self-hardening clay	
poster paints: royal-blue,	
violet and yellow	
clear varnish	
photo or picture	
PVA (white) glue (optional)	

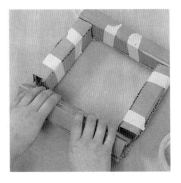

1 Trace the template from the back of the book, enlarging if necessary. Cut out the centre square. Score along the dotted lines using a craft knife, taking care not to cut right through.

2 Fold each flap inwards along the scored edges and tape the frame together with masking tape.

3 Fix a piece of wire to the back, using masking tape.

4 Tear the newspaper in small squares, measuring about 2.5 x 2.5 cm/ 1 x 1 in. Dip them in wallpaper paste and stick them on to the frame until both the front and the back of the frame are well covered.

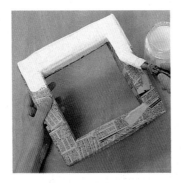

5 Prime the covered frame with a coat of white paint and allow to dry. Apply a second coat of paint to make sure that the surface is opaque. Allow to dry thoroughly.

6 Form heart shapes out of clay by hand and push these on to the front of the frame for decoration. Fix the hearts in place by smoothing down the sides with a clay modelling tool.

7 Paint the frame with poster paints and allow to dry. Seal with a coat of varnish. Once dry, stick your chosen photo or picture on to the card (set aside in step 1) and glue or tape it in place.

CRACKLE-GLAZED PRINT

*A*ntique prints are expensive, but with this technique you can create your own thoroughly original design very cheaply. Use a photocopier to enlarge or reduce motifs and practise arranging them until you have a design that appeals.

1 Cut out the prints and lightly coat them on the back with spray adhesive. Arrange the prints until you are happy with the result. By using spray adhesive, you can reposition the designs as many times as you like. Photocopy the final result.

YOU WILL NEED

MATERIALS

*selection of black and white cupid prints
spray adhesive
tea bags and instant coffee
PVA (white) glue
hardboard or card
acrylic medium
clear acrylic gloss varnish
burnt umber acrylic paint*

EQUIPMENT

*scissors
large soft Chinese paintbrush
household and fine paintbrushes
paint-mixing container*

2 Make a "cocktail" of one tea bag and three teaspoons of coffee and let it cool. Apply to the print with a Chinese paintbrush. You can experiment with brews of different strengths and apply the mixture several times, to create depth. Allow to dry.

3 Mix equal parts of PVA (white) glue and water and apply the mixture to the back of the print with a household paintbrush. Smooth the print on to the hardboard or card backing. (You can also apply the print directly to a wall or a piece of furniture.) Brush the PVA (white) mixture on top of the print and backing and allow to dry.

4 Cover the print and backing with acrylic medium in the same way. This may cause the paper to wrinkle, but don't worry: once dry, the wrinkles will vanish.

5 Coat with acrylic varnish, to give a shiny finish and add an antique look.

6 Mix burnt umber acrylic paint into the varnish and paint cracks with a fine paintbrush. Add more shadows and blend them in softly. Finally, apply another coat of acrylic varnish and allow to dry.

WATER BEARER'S SHRINE

*A*quarius, the water bearer, carries the waters of creation and symbolizes death and renewal. An original tribute to him is this charming wall plaque.

YOU WILL NEED

MATERIALS

thin card or paper
corrugated card
masking tape
paper pulp (see Basic
    Techniques)
newspaper
wallpaper paste
PVA (white) glue
white acrylic primer
gouache paints: pale blue,
dark blue, orange and red
gloss varnish
gold enamel paint
epoxy resin glue
mirror-hanging plate

EQUIPMENT

pencil
craft knife
cutting mat
bowl
paintbrushes

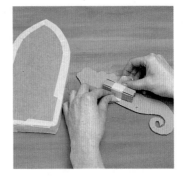 

1 Draw templates for the shrine, its sides and figure, and transfer them to corrugated card. Cut them out and assemble them using masking tape. Make a small rectangular "step" from card and fix it to the figure's back.

2 Apply paper pulp to the front of the figure to give a rounded shape. When dry, cover the figure and plaque in several layers of newspaper strips soaked in wallpaper paste. Allow to dry.

3 Paint on a coat of PVA (white) glue followed, when dry, by a coat of white acrylic primer. Decorate the plaque and figure with gouache paints.

4 Varnish, then, when dry, highlight the details with gold enamel paint. Use epoxy resin glue to secure the figure in place and fix a mirror-hanging plate to the back.

GOLD-RIMMED BOWL

This attractive bowl is delicately hand-painted and decorated with gold paint. Its cheerful, sunny design will brighten up any dull corner. Use it purely as decoration, or to hold trinkets, nuts or sweets.

YOU WILL NEED

MATERIALS
*petroleum jelly
newspaper
paper pulp (see Basic Techniques)
PVA (white) glue
white undercoat paint
gold "liquid leaf" paint
acrylic paints: white, yellow, ochre, turquoise and brown
paper tissue
fixative spray
gloss varnish*

EQUIPMENT
*bowl
scissors
large, medium and fine paintbrushes
pair of compasses
pencil
paint-mixing container*

1 Apply a coat of petroleum jelly to the inside of the bowl. Line it with strips of wet newspaper. Put the paper pulp into the bowl in an even layer about 1 cm/½ in deep. Allow to dry in an airing cupboard for about five days. Release the bowl from the mould. Dip strips of newspaper in PVA (white) glue and cover the bowl.

2 Give the bowl two coats of white undercoat. Use a pair of compasses to help you centralize the flower motif. Draw the flower freehand.

3 Paint the rim with gold "liquid leaf". Decorate the bowl with the acrylic paints. Mix white into all the colours to lighten them and, before the paint dries, dab some off with a paper tissue so that the undercoat shows through in places. Allow to dry. Spray with fixative spray, then give the bowl a coat of varnish.

FLOATING LEAVES MOBILE

*F*eatherlight paper leaves will flutter delicately in the merest whiff of air. Use a variety of textures for the cut-outs – look out for handmade paper incorporating leaves and flower petals.

YOU WILL NEED

MATERIALS	EQUIPMENT
thick silver florist's wire	*wire-cutters*
tracing paper	*round-nosed pliers*
thin card or paper	*pencil*
selection of coloured and	*scissors*
textured papers	*needle*
matching sewing thread	

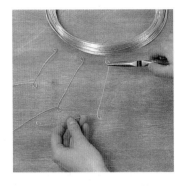

1 Cut two lengths of wire 20 cm/8 in and one length 30 cm/12 in. Twist each piece of wire in the middle to make a loop. Make a small loop, pointing downwards, at each end of each length.

2 Trace the templates from the back of the book, enlarging if necessary. Transfer them to card or paper and cut out. Draw round them on coloured and textured papers, then cut out the shapes.

3 Use a needle to attach an assortment of leaves on to a length of thread to hang from each wire loop.

4 Use thread to hang the two shorter wires from the ends of the longer one. Tie the leaves to each wire loop. Fasten a length of thread to the top loop to hang the mobile.

MIRRORED KEEPSAKE BOX

*T*his box is made from an old poster tube decorated with mirror shards. It is an original idea for storing jewellery.

YOU WILL NEED

MATERIALS

section of poster tube
card
masking tape
PVA (white) glue
newspaper
4 marbles
wallpaper paste
epoxy resin glue
chemical metal filler
(i.e. car-body repair filler)
mirror fragments
white acrylic primer
selection of gouache paints
glossy varnish
gold enamel paint

EQUIPMENT

pencil
scissors
pair of compasses
small and fine paintbrushes
paint-mixing containers

1 Draw around the poster tube end on card, cut it out and tape it to the tube. Cut out a slightly larger lid and another circle 1 cm/½ in less in diameter. Glue together. Bend a roll of newspaper into a heart shape and tape it to the lid. Cover the marbles with masking tape.

2 Cover the box, lid and marbles with several layers of newspaper strips soaked in wallpaper paste. When dry, glue the marbles to the box base with epoxy resin glue. Mix up the filler, spread it on to the lid, and carefully push in the mirror fragments.

3 Paint the box, excluding the mirror pieces, with PVA (white) glue. When dry, prime the box and paint the design with gouache paints.

4 Coat the box with several layers of glossy varnish, and allow to dry thoroughly. Add detail in gold enamel.

DECORATED BOX

This mirror box has a wonderful corrugated texture. The mirror is hidden behind doors, which can be closed when not in use.

1 Cut out the box pieces from corrugated card. The back is 26 cm/10 in high and 13 cm/ 5 in wide at the base. The sides are 3.5 cm/1½ in deep. Create a recess 3.5 cm/1½ in deep and 8 cm/3 in square, for the mirror to sit in. Cut a 13 cm/5 in flat square frame for the outside of the recess. Cut a 7 cm/2¾ in square piece of card in half for the doors. Cut out the petals for the sides of the box. Cut out the sunflowers and the stems, bulking out the middles by gluing on scrunched-up newspaper with PVA (white) glue. Assemble the box, using masking tape. Leave off the doors.

YOU WILL NEED

MATERIALS	EQUIPMENT
corrugated card	*craft knife*
PVA (white) glue	*cutting mat*
newspaper	*metal ruler*
masking tape	*pencil*
white undercoat paint	*fine paintbrushes*
gouache paints: red, blue,	*paint-mixing container*
orange, yellow and white	
gloss varnish	
gold "liquid leaf" paint	
mirror	
epoxy resin glue	
2 small brass door hinges	

2 Cover the box with layers of newspaper soaked in diluted PVA (white) glue. Allow to dry. Paint with undercoat.

3 Paint all the pieces with gouache paints. When dry, apply several coats of varnish. Add details in gold and glue on the mirror. Pierce three holes in the shelf and glue in the sunflowers with epoxy resin glue. Glue the hinges and doors in position.

LOVE TOKEN BOWL

*T*his delightful container for a Valentine's gift uses a simple but very decorative technique.

YOU WILL NEED

MATERIALS	EQUIPMENT
petroleum jelly	*bowl*
newspaper	*medium and fine*
paper pulp (see Basic	*paintbrushes*
Techniques)	*pencil*
PVA (white) glue	*scissors*
white acrylic primer	*paint-mixing container*
tracing paper	
masking tape	
gouache or acrylic paints:	
blue, white, red, yellow	
and gold	
clear gloss varnish	

1 Coat the inside of the bowl with a layer of petroleum jelly, followed by strips of newspaper. Press a layer of paper pulp into the bowl. When dry, release from the bowl. Cover the pulp with newspaper strips dipped in PVA (white) glue.

2 When dry, cover with white primer. Trace the template from the back of the book, enlarging if necessary. Snip the edges so the template can be taped flat inside the bowl, and transfer the outline.

3 Paint the background pale blue, dabbing on lighter shades for a mottled effect.

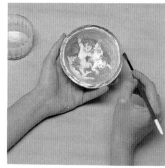

4 Paint the design, mixing the colours to achieve subtle shades. Paint the rim gold. When dry, give the bowl a coat of varnish.

SCHERENSCHNITTE

Intricately cut paper designs existed for many centuries in the Middle and Far East before they became popular in Europe and America. This papercraft technique is also known by the German term "Scherenschnitte".

YOU WILL NEED

MATERIALS	EQUIPMENT
tracing paper	*pencil*
paper	*craft knife*
thin black paper	*metal ruler*
spray adhesive	*cutting mat*
mounting paper	

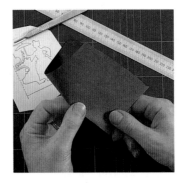

1 Trace the template from the back of the book, enlarging if necessary. Transfer it to paper. Fold the thin black paper in half.

2 Cut along the centre edge of the design using a craft knife and a metal ruler.

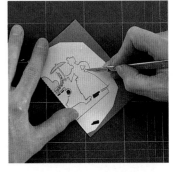

3 Give the reverse side of the tracing a very light coat of spray adhesive and stick it to the back of the black paper. Cut out the shapes using the tip of the craft knife. Move the paper around as you cut, so that you always cut at the easiest angle.

4 Very carefully, separate the black paper from the tracing, making sure that the picture does not tear. Unfold the picture and display it on mounting paper.

WALL PLAQUE

Although the heart and farm animal motifs call to mind folk art, the strong pastel colours used to paint this plaque give it a more contemporary feel. It would be at home in a light, modern interior.

YOU WILL NEED

MATERIALS
galvanized wire, from a coat hanger
card, 13 x 13 in/5 x 5 in
masking tape
newspaper
wallpaper paste
white emulsion (latex) or poster paint
self-hardening clay
acrylic or poster paints: pink, mauve, blue, green and yellow
clear varnish

EQUIPMENT
scissors
medium and small paintbrushes
clay-modelling tools
paint-mixing containers

1 Shape a hook from the wire and tape it on to the back of the card with masking tape.

2 Tear the newspaper into small strips. Dip them into the wallpaper paste and cover both sides of the card with a layer of newspaper.

3 Prime both sides of the plaque with white paint and allow to dry. Mould decorative borders, heart shapes and a central chicken motif in the self-hardening clay. Allow to dry thoroughly.

4 Decorate with the paints and allow to dry. Finish with a coat of varnish.

CARDBOARD GIFT BOXES

*I*t is simple to transform a flat sheet of thin card into an attractive gift box to make an ideal receptacle for that special present. Stamp rows of scampering dogs diagonally on to your box before folding it to add a frivolous touch, or select your own motif for an individualized look. The box can be scaled up or down, depending on the size you require, and the surface can be decorated with different designs to suit the occasion.

YOU WILL NEED

MATERIALS	EQUIPMENT
thin coloured card	*pencil*
piece of paper (optional)	*ruler*
stamp pad	*craft knife*
double-sided tape	*cutting mat*
	rubber stamp
	set square (optional)
	blunt knife

1 Follow the design from the back of the book, scaling it up or down to the required size, but taking care to keep the proportions the same.

2 Cut out the box from coloured card using a ruler and craft knife to ensure that you make neat and accurate lines for it.

3 Using a straight-edged piece of paper or a ruler as a guide, stamp rows of motifs diagonally across the card.

4 Make sure that you extend the pattern over the edges by stamping partial motifs at the ends of each alternate row.

5 On the wrong side of the card, hold a set square or ruler against the fold lines and score along them with a blunt knife. Make sure that you do not break the surface of the card at all.

6 Fold along the score lines, making sure that all the corners are square. Apply double-sided tape to the joining edges, then peel off the backing paper and press the sides of the box together.

7 Continue folding and sticking the card in this way, ensuring that all the edges fit together neatly. Finally, fold in the end pieces to complete the card box.

CREPE PAPER BAGS

These bags can be decorated with any motif – use stickers of cartoon characters, cars, animals or planes to decorate gift bags for children's parties.

YOU WILL NEED

MATERIALS

bright crepe paper
contrasting thread
metallic stick-on stars
gold or silver cord

EQUIPMENT

pinking shears
sewing machine, with zigzag attachment

1 Decide on the size of your bag and, using pinking shears, cut out two rectangles from the crepe paper.

2 Set the sewing machine to a large zigzag stitch. Place the triangles together and sew along the three edges.

3 Place the stars randomly over the bag, then fill it with your gifts, and tie up the bag with gold or silver cord.

CARRIER BAGS

It really is great fun making bags, and they can be used for all sorts of objects – buttons, sweets, jewellery and, of course, for presenting gifts.

YOU WILL NEED

MATERIALS

tracing paper
stiff coloured paper
double-sided tape
cord or ribbon

EQUIPMENT

pencil
blunt knife or scissors
ruler
hole punch

1 Trace the template from the back of the book, enlarging if necessary. Transfer it to stiff paper. The dotted lines indicate mountain folds and the dashed lines are valley folds. Use a blunt knife or scissors and a ruler to score along the fold lines. Cut out the shape.

2 Stick the bag together using double-sided tape along the seams. Using the hole punch, carefully make two sets of holes opposite each other on the top seam.

3 Place a square of tape below each hole. Thread the cord or ribbon through the holes, peel off the backing paper and press together to hold the handles in place between the bag and the overlapping seam.

PAPIER-MACHE MIRROR

*T*his jolly papier-mâché herald is blowing a fanfare for your reflection – he's swapped his traditional banner for a miniature mirror. Paint his part-coloured costume in plenty of cheerful, bright shades to suit the mood of the piece.

YOU WILL NEED

MATERIALS

tracing paper
thin card
PVA (white) glue
newspaper
mirror, 5.5 cm/2¼ in square
white acrylic or matt emulsion (latex) paint
acrylic paints: red, purple, black, white, brown, green, permanent rose, blue, ivory and gold
gloss varnish
narrow red ribbon, 50 cm/½ yd
picture ring

EQUIPMENT

pencil
ruler
scissors
paintbrushes

1 Trace the template from the back of the book, enlarging it to 32 cm/12½ in high and cut it out of thin card. Using diluted PVA (white) glue, cover it with several layers of newspaper, building up the cheeks, nose, wavy hair and legs to create a relief effect. Allow to dry.

2 Cut two 6.5 cm/2½ in squares of card and glue the mirror in the centre of one. Cut out the centre of the second square, leaving a 1 cm/½ in frame. Cover with newspaper strips. When dry, stick the frame to the mirror and backing, and build up with more layers of newspaper. Pierce two holes in the top of the frame with a pair of scissors.

3 Prime the herald and the mirror frame with white acrylic or emulsion (latex) paint. When this is dry, decorate with acrylic paints. When the paint is dry, protect with gloss varnish. With the ribbon, tie the mirror on to the trumpet. To complete, screw the picture ring into the back of the herald's shoulder.

SEASHELL MIRROR

This pretty papier-mâché mirror is decorated with paints and pieces of glass.

YOU WILL NEED

MATERIALS

tracing paper
strong card
paper pulp
newspaper
wallpaper paste
PVA (white) glue
white acrylic primer
glass "globs"
epoxy resin glue
gouache paints: deep yellow, cadmium-yellow, deep cobalt, pale blue, Cyprus-green, grenadine, indigo and white
gold enamel paint
clear gloss and matt varnishes
mirror and fixing-tabs
plate-hanging fixture

EQUIPMENT

pencil
craft knife
cutting mat
small and fine paintbrushes
screwdriver

1 Trace the template from the back of the book, enlarging if necessary. Transfer it to the card and cut it out. Add the paper pulp to the card, to build up a 3-D form. Allow to dry.

2 Cover the whole mirror frame with three or four layers of newspaper, soaked in wallpaper paste. Allow to dry.

3 Coat with PVA (white) glue and add a coat of primer. When it is dry, attach the glass "globs" with epoxy resin glue. Decorate the frame with gouache paints, adding detail with the gold enamel paint.

4 Paint the frame with several coats of gloss varnish, using matt varnish in places to provide contrast. Allow to dry. Secure the mirror with fixing-tabs. Attach the plate-hanging fixture, securing all screws with epoxy glue.

GLITTERING BROOCH

This delightful brooch is cleverly made from the humblest of materials: corrugated card and newspaper.

YOU WILL NEED

MATERIALS

paper
corrugated card
newspaper
wallpaper paste
PVA (white) glue
white acrylic primer
gouache paints: light blue,
yellow and red
gloss varnish
gold enamel paint
brooch pin
epoxy resin glue

EQUIPMENT

pencil
craft knife
cutting mat
bowl
paintbrushes

1 Draw a star shape freehand on to paper and transfer the design to the corrugated card. Cut out the star shape. Soak some newspaper in wallpaper paste, scrunch it up and mound it in the centre of the star.

2 Cover the whole brooch in layers of newspaper pieces soaked in wallpaper paste and allow to dry.

3 Give the brooch a coat of PVA (white) glue, then one of white acrylic primer. Allow to dry, then paint on the design and protect the brooch with a coat of clear gloss varnish.

4 Add gold enamel paint details. Finally, fix a brooch pin to the back using epoxy resin glue.

FRUITY BRACELET

Paint a summery bracelet with pretty oranges and lemons. This example is decorated with many slices of different citrus fruits.

YOU WILL NEED

MATERIALS
tracing paper
thin card
large hook and eye
masking tape
paper pulp
strong clear glue
gold foil (from a chocolate wrapper)
acrylic paints: white, yellow, red and orange
gold paint
clear gloss varnish

EQUIPMENT
pencil
scissors
paintbrushes
paint-mixing container

1 Trace the template from the back of the book, enlarging it to fit your wrist, and cut out of thin card. Tape a large hook and eye to either end.

2 Cover the card with several layers of paper pulp, making sure the masking tape and all the edges are neatly covered. Allow to dry. Use strong, clear glue to stick a sheet of gold foil to the inside of the bracelet. Trim the edges.

3 Prime the outside of the bracelet with a coat of white acrylic paint to smooth the surface. Decorate with slices of citrus fruit using acrylic paints. Add touches of gold paint around the edges, pips and dimples.

4 When the paint is dry, protect it with a coat of clear gloss varnish.

HERALDIC SYMBOLS MOBILE

*T*here are plenty of strong, simple shapes in heraldry, just right for cutting out to hang on this fascinating mobile. The small motifs on a heraldic shield are called "charges". Pick out the raised detailing on each shape in gold to catch the light subtly.

YOU WILL NEED

MATERIALS

tracing paper
stiff card
newspaper
wallpaper paste
acrylic gesso
acrylic paints: cobalt-blue,
yellow, orange, red, purple
and black
28 earring pins
super glue
gold magic marker
fine thread
1 cm/½ in wooden dowel,
36 cm/14 in long
2 large wooden beads
2 brass screws
gold paint
3 red tassels
length of red cord

EQUIPMENT

pencil
craft knife
cutting mat
metal ruler
scissors
glue gun and glue sticks
paintbrushes
fine- and coarse-grade
sandpaper
drill
screwdriver
needle

1 Trace the template from the back of the book to measure 30 cm/12 in across, and transfer the design to card. Use a craft knife and metal ruler to cut out the main shapes.

2 Cut out the charges with scissors. Tear strips of newspaper and coat them with wallpaper paste. Cover the banner with a layer of papier-mâché, using tiny strips of paper for the small charges.

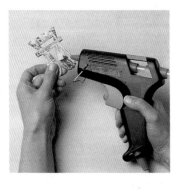

3 Allow to dry, then apply a second layer of newspaper strips. Once this is dry, create the raised designs on the motifs using a glue gun.

4 Paint the pieces with two coats of acrylic gesso, sanding lightly between layers. Mark diagonal stripes on the banner with a pencil and paint alternate stripes in cobalt-blue.

5 Insert an earring pin in the centre top of each charge and secure with a few drops of super glue. Attach an earring pin at each corresponding point on the banner in the same way.

6 Paint the charges in different heraldic colours. Highlight the raised design with a gold pen. Once the pieces are dry, assemble the mobile using fine thread. Apply a drop of glue to each knot.

7 Drill a hole in each end of the wooden dowel. Flatten one end of each bead by rubbing with coarse sandpaper, then screw the beads to each end of the dowel. Coat with gesso and paint gold.

8 Stick three earring pins on the top of the banner and tie to the dowel. Sew a tassel to each end of the cord and slip the loops over the beads. Glue to the dowel. Pin a third tassel to the bottom of the banner.

DRESSING TABLE MIRROR

*T*his beautiful dressing-table mirror is made of papier-mâché pulp. Give free rein to your imagination and creativity by hand-painting it in the brightest and most beautiful colours.

YOU WILL NEED

MATERIALS	EQUIPMENT
corrugated card	*pencil*
round mirror,	*craft knife*
8 cm/3 in diameter	*cutting mat*
epoxy resin glue	*paintbrushes*
paper pulp	*paint-mixing container*
newspaper	
wallpaper paste	
PVA (white) glue	
white acrylic primer	
selection of gouache paints	
clear gloss and clear matt	
varnish	
gold enamel paint	

1 Draw your chosen design on to the corrugated card. Cut it out carefully with a sharp craft knife using a cutting mat to protect the work surface.

2 Glue the mirror in position with epoxy resin glue.

3 Carefully build up paper pulp on the card all around the mirror. Do not place any pulp over the mirror, but ensure the pulp butts up to the edge. Allow to dry thoroughly.

4 Apply several layers of newspaper dipped in wallpaper paste over the dried pulp, just overlapping the edges of the mirror. Allow to dry.

5 Coat with a layer of PVA (white) glue and then with some white acrylic primer. Allow the paint to dry between each stage.

6 When the paint is dry, cut away the excess paper that overlaps the edge of the mirror, to create a neat finish.

7 Paint on your design in gouache paints; note that the back of the mirror is as important as the front.

8 When dry, coat in three or four layers of gloss varnish, adding matt varnish as a contrast in some areas. Allow to dry between each stage. Finish with gold enamel detail.

LEMON MIRROR FRAME

*H*unt around for interesting printed material to combine with the lemon motif on this very striking papier-mâché frame. You could use a photocopier to reproduce graphics from books, or you could produce an ancient manuscript of your own choice.

YOU WILL NEED

MATERIALS

corrugated card
mirror, 15 x 18 cm/6 x 7 in
wallpaper paste
newspaper
acrylic paints: black, yellow and green
paperclip
acrylic gesso
lemon motif wrapping paper
scraps of printed paper or manuscript
white tissue paper
matt acrylic varnish

EQUIPMENT

craft knife
metal ruler
cutting mat
mixing bowl
paintbrush
natural sponge

1 Cut two rectangles, each 17 x 20 cm/6½ x 8 in, from the corrugated card. Lay the mirror centrally on one piece and cut strips of card to fit around it down two sides and across the bottom. Cut a window out of the centre of the other rectangle of card, leaving a 4 cm/1½ in border.

2 Coat all the pieces of card with wallpaper paste and allow to dry. Coat strips of newspaper with wallpaper paste and cover the front of the frame. Paste the spacer strips in position on the sides and bottom of the back panel, cover with papier-mâché strips and allow to dry before applying a second layer.

3 When the papier-mâché is dry, paint the inside surfaces of the frame black to minimize any possible reflection they might give in the mirror.

4 Open out the paperclip and thread one end through the papier-mâché at the centre back of the frame. Paste strips of newspaper over the clip, leaving the top section showing to act as a hook.

5 Join the front of the frame to the back with more strips of pasted newspaper. Paste folded strips over the top of the frame to either side of the opening for added strength. Once dry, paint the frame with acrylic gesso.

6 Sponge the entire frame with thin yellow paint, then with green paint to create an all-over mottled effect.

7 Tear the lemon motifs from the wrapping paper in interesting shapes and then arrange them over the frame. Fill the gaps between the lemons with small pieces of printed paper. Paste in position.

8 To soften the design, tear small pieces of white tissue paper and paste them on to the frame, crinkling them slightly and overlapping the edges of some of the motifs. When the paste is dry, paint the frame with two coats of matt acrylic varnish and insert the mirror into the top slit to finish.

GILDED TIMEPIECE

*T*his clock, decorated with a découpaged print of an antique map of the heavens, combines practicality with a reminder of the timeless mystery of the stars. The luxurious gilded finish enhances the atmosphere created by the map; hang the clock where it will catch the light and create a mood of serenity and contemplation.

YOU WILL NEED

MATERIALS	EQUIPMENT
hardboard, 30 x 30 cm/ 12 x 12 in	pencil
celestial map print	ruler
all-purpose glue	scissors
Japanese gold size	drill, with size 10 bit
Dutch gold leaf transfer book	paintbrush
clock movement and hands	

1 Using a pencil and ruler, draw two diagonals across the hardboard, to find the centre of the square. Cut out the celestial map and find its centre in the same way. Place the map on the hardboard, draw around the outside of the map, and remove it.

2 Drill a hole in the centre of the hardboard to fit the width of the clock mechanism. Paint a coat of size around the edge, up to the pencil line. Leave until touch-dry. Lay strips of gold leaf on top of the size to cover. Trim off any excess by rubbing with a finger.

3 Pierce a hole in the centre of the map for the hands. Stick the map in position.

4 Add the hands and the clock movement.

ASTROLOGICAL CLOCK

The passing of time is the real essence of astrology, as the stars make their regular courses around the heavens: you can reflect their progress with this stylish clock. Simple battery-run movements are now readily available: all you really have to supply is the clockface.

YOU WILL NEED

MATERIALS
sheet of thick white card
set of zodiac signs
PVA (white) glue
black acrylic paint
quartz clock movement
and hands

EQUIPMENT
ruler
scissors
pair of compasses
pencil
craft knife
cutting mat
paintbrush

1 Cut a square of card measuring 20 cm/8 in. Draw a circle slightly smaller than the square. Cut out a small circle in the centre of the card to fit the clock spindle. Photocopy a set of zodiac symbols or draw your own using the templates at the back of the book. Cut them out.

2 Arrange the 12 star signs around the clockface, in the correct order (as shown in the picture). Position those corresponding to 12, 3, 6 and 9 o'clock first, then space the rest equally. Stick down with PVA (white) glue.

3 Paint the area around the clockface black. Allow the paint to dry, then seal the whole clock with two coats of diluted PVA (white) glue. Attach the clock movement to the back and fit the hands to the spindle. Insert a battery.

NIGHT AND DAY MOBILE

*G*olden *suns and moody blue moons contrast with each other in this attractive mobile. Although mobiles are usually associated with children's rooms, this one is sophisticated enough to hang up as a decoration in any room in the house.*

YOU WILL NEED

MATERIALS

*corrugated card
newspaper
masking tape
wallpaper paste
small brass screw hooks
epoxy resin glue
PVA (white) glue
white undercoat paint
gouache paints: blue, silver,
orange and gold
gloss and matt varnishes
gold enamel paint
small jewellery jump rings
picture-hanging wire*

EQUIPMENT

*pencil
craft knife
cutting mat
paintbrushes*

1 Draw all the freehand shapes on the corrugated card and cut them out with a sharp craft knife.

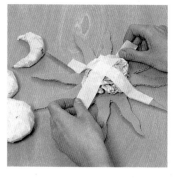

2 Bulk out the shapes by scrunching up pieces of newspaper and wrapping masking tape around them to secure them in place.

3 Cover the pieces in several layers of newspaper strips soaked in wallpaper paste. Allow to dry overnight, or longer if necessary.

4 Screw in the hooks in the appropriate places for hanging, securing them with epoxy resin glue.

5 Coat the shapes with PVA (white) glue and allow to dry. Coat with white undercoat and allow to dry again.

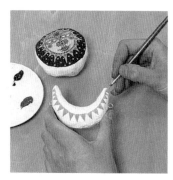

6 Use gouache paints to decorate the shapes.

7 Give the shapes several coats of gloss varnish, picking out some areas in matt varnish to contrast. Allow to dry. Add details in gold enamel, painted on with a fine brush.

8 Assemble all the pieces, using the hooks and jump rings to join them together. Suspend the mobile from a length of picture wire threaded through the hook and ring in the topmost shape.

GILDED LAMPSHADE

*T*he delicate laciness of filigree work inspired the
elegant design for this lampshade. The success
depends on arranging cut-out motifs pleasingly, so keep
an eye out for decorative paper with suitable designs.
You need two papers, one of a lighter weight than the
other, such as tissue paper and wrapping paper.

YOU WILL NEED

MATERIALS	EQUIPMENT
cupid-patterned wrapping paper	*paintbrushes*
gold-patterned tissue paper	*paint-mixing container*
PVA (white) glue	*clean cloth (optional)*
lampshade	
gold acrylic paint	

1 Carefully tear around the cupid shapes in the wrapping paper. Tear smaller areas from the gold-patterned tissue paper, for contrast.

2 Mix equal parts PVA (white) glue and water. Coat the lampshade with this to seal it. Paint the PVA (white) glue on to the reverse of the cupid shapes and stick them around the shade. The glue may stretch the paper, so smooth out any wrinkles with a clean cloth (or leave them for added texture). Fill in the areas that are left with gold-patterned paper, overlapping to make sure the shade is completely covered. Finally, seal the paper with more diluted PVA (white) glue.

3 When dry, decorate the edge of the lampshade with gold paint.

PINPRICKED LAMPSHADE

This is a satisfying way to turn a plain paper lampshade into something special. Switching on the light transforms the delicate pricked design into a magical pattern of stars.

YOU WILL NEED

MATERIALS
tracing paper
paper
lampshade
masking tape

EQUIPMENT
pencil
scissors
towel
darning needle
cork (optional)

1 Trace the templates from the back of the book, enlarging if necessary. Copy them several times and cut out roughly from paper.

2 Arrange the motifs in a repeating pattern on the outside of the lampshade and secure with masking tape. Trace the shape of the stuck-on motifs on the inside of the shade.

3 Rest the shade on a towel and, working from the inside, gently pierce the design with a needle. You can bind the needle with masking tape or stick it into a cork to make it easier to hold. Finish the design with a scalloped edging.

CREPE PAPER GIFT BOX

*T*o make a gift seem even more special, present it in this decorated box. The romantic roses make it perfect for a wedding present.

YOU WILL NEED

MATERIALS	EQUIPMENT
single- and double-sided	*scissors*
crepe paper in soft colours	*ruler*
adhesive tape	*glue gun and glue sticks*
round card box, with lid	
wire-edged ribbon	

1 To make a rose, cut through folded crepe paper to make two strips about 5 cm/2 in wide. Tape two strips at right angles to each other. Fold one over the other to make a concertina.

2 Holding the ends, stretch the concertina to its fullest extent and wind it up, twisting to get a rose shape. Tape the ends of the strips into a "stalk". Make several roses of different colours and sizes.

3 Cover the box and lid with crepe paper, neatly pleating the fullness and sticking it down so it is as flat as possible in the centre of the lid.

4 Glue the roses on top and finish with a ribbon.

CONFETTI BOX

This sweet little paper box makes a much prettier holder for confetti than a shop-bought one, and can be kept after the wedding as a reminder of a special day.

YOU WILL NEED

MATERIALS	EQUIPMENT
tracing paper	*pencil*
stiff paper or card	*scissors*
pink paint	*paintbrush*
gold ink	*ruler*
double-sided adhesive tape	*blunt knife*
ribbon	*craft knife*
rose-petal confetti	*cutting mat*

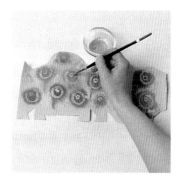

1 Trace the template from the back of the book, enlarging if necessary. Lay it on the card, draw around it and cut it out. Wet the card and paint rough, round pink shapes, so that the colour bleeds out. Allow to dry. With gold ink, paint circles and leaf shapes. Allow to dry.

2 With a ruler and blunt knife, score the fold lines.

3 With a craft knife, cut the slits for the ribbon.

4 Cut a piece of double-sided tape and stick it to one side of the tab. Peel off the backing, overlap the tab and stick in place. Fold under the bottom edge and thread the ribbon through the slits. Fill with rose confetti and then tie the ribbon in a bow.

PAPIER-MACHE WALL PLAQUE

*T*his engaging crab relief is easily made from moulded papier-mâché and it looks very effective as a hanging decoration.

YOU WILL NEED

MATERIALS	EQUIPMENT
strong card	scissors
wire, for hanging	ruler
masking tape	wire-cutters
newspaper	clay-modelling tool
wallpaper paste	paintbrushes
paper pulp	
white emulsion (latex) paint	
self-hardening clay	
acrylic or poster paints:	
turquoise-blue, navy blue,	
pink and yellow	
gloss varnish	

1 Cut out a piece of card about 13 cm/5 in square. Cut a short piece of wire and bend it into a hook shape. Attach to one side of the card with masking tape.

2 Soak 2.5 cm/1 in squares of newspaper in wallpaper paste and apply to both sides of the card. When dry, apply paper pulp to the border area. Allow to dry thoroughly.

3 Apply a coat of white emulsion (latex) paint. When dry, use self-hardening clay to make relief decorations and a frame, shaping it with a modelling tool. Leave to harden.

4 Paint the crab and the border in acrylic or poster paints, then seal with several coats of varnish.

EMBOSSED CARDS

Embossed paper has a subtle, expensive and specialist look about it, but it is in fact not at all difficult to make. Just follow the steps below to find out how it's done.

YOU WILL NEED

MATERIALS
tracing paper
thin card
coloured paper, card and envelopes
PVA (white) glue
ribbon (optional)

EQUIPMENT
pencil
blunt and smooth-end plastic embossing tools
scissors
hole punch (optional)

1 Trace the template from the back of the book, enlarging if necessary, and transfer to thin card. Cover it with the paper.

2 Holding down firmly, begin rubbing the paper gently over the cut-out area to define the shape. Increase the pressure until the shape shows up as a clear indentation. Turn the paper over.

3 Trim the paper shape and stick it to a card background. Pair it up with a contrasting envelope or punch a hole in it and thread a ribbon through to use as a gift tag.

WOODLAND GIFT WRAP

*L*ook out for interestingly textured card and paper in complementary colours to make a whole range of greetings cards, postcards, gift wrap and gift tags for beautiful seasonal or birthday presents.

YOU WILL NEED

MATERIALS	EQUIPMENT
tracing paper	pencil
thin card or paper	scissors
selection of coloured and	craft knife
textured papers and card	cutting mat
corrugated paper	brush
PVA (white) glue	ruler
stencil card	cotton wool or stencil brush
selection of acrylic paints	paint-mixing container
narrow paper ribbon	hole punch
sealing wax	safety matches
fresh leaves	

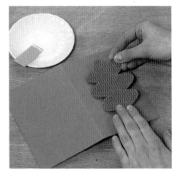

1 Trace the template from the back of the book, enlarging if necessary, and transfer to thin card or paper. Cut out. Cut a rectangle of coloured card and fold in half to make a greetings card. Draw around a leaf template on the front and cut out the shape with a craft knife. Cut a contrasting paper to the same size as the card and stick it on the inside.

2 Fold a second card, and draw around the template of the oak leaf on the reverse of the corrugated paper. Cut out the shape and glue it to the front of the card.

3 For the stencilled card, tear a square of coloured paper and glue it to the front of a piece of card. Draw around a leaf template on to stencil card and cut it out with a craft knife. Place the stencil on the coloured square and dab paint on to it with a ball of cotton wool or a stencil brush.

4 Use the same leaf stencil on a large sheet of coloured paper to make some co-ordinating gift wrap.

5 Make a selection of gift tags and postcards in the same way. Cut some leaf shapes out of coloured paper to make simple tags. Punch a hole in the tags and thread with ribbon.

6 Make your own simple envelopes by folding a piece of coloured paper to fit around a greetings card. Secure the flaps with melted sealing wax and decorate while it is still sticky with a small fresh leaf.

SPONGE-PRINTED SHELF EDGING

*S*helf edgings are a lovely decorative detail for a *country-style kitchen or breakfast room. Even if you do not possess the perfect heirloom dresser, you can make the plainest of shelves beautiful in this way.*

YOU WILL NEED

MATERIALS	EQUIPMENT
tracing paper	*pencil*
thin card or paper	*scissors*
sponge	*felt-tipped pen*
13 cm/5 in strip	*ruler*
unbleached calico, length	*paintbrush*
of shelf	*iron*
spray fabric stiffener	*dressmaker's pins*
fabric paints: red, yellow	*sewing machine*
and green	*needle*
6 cm/2½ in strip green print	
cotton fabric, length of shelf	
matching sewing thread	
double-sided tape	

1 Trace the templates from the back of the book, enlarging them so that the triangular shape measures about 13 cm/5 in across. Transfer the fruit and leaf outlines to thin card or paper and cut them out. Draw around them on to the sponge and cut out the shapes.

2 Mark a row of triangles along one edge of the calico, spray with fabric stiffener and allow to dry. Cut along the pencil lines. Use the sponge blocks to print the design. Print a leaf on each side of the fruit.

3 Stipple darker areas on the fruit and leaves.

4 With wrong sides facing, press the green fabric in half lengthways, then press under 5 mm/¼ in along one long edge. With right sides facing, sew the other raw edge to the top of the shelf edging with a 5 mm/¼ in allowance. Fold the green fabric over to cover the top and slip stitch the folded edge to the back of the seam. Neaten the corners and then tape to the shelf.

COLLAGE GIFT WRAP

Look along the racks of newspaper stands for interesting foreign scripts to incorporate in this special gift wrap. The newspaper is painted with translucent watercolour inks so that the print shows through.

YOU WILL NEED

MATERIALS
*foreign language
newspapers
watercolour inks
tracing paper
stencil card
white cartridge paper or
coloured card
stencil paints: gold and
black
corrugated card
plain gold gift wrap
glue stick*

EQUIPMENT
*pencil
paintbrush
craft knife
cellulose kitchen sponge
scissors*

1 Paint sections of the newspaper in bright inks. Trace the template from the back of the book, enlarging if necessary, and transfer to stencil card. Cut out.

2 Paint cartridge paper in different coloured inks or use coloured card. Stencil the paper in black and gold.

3 Cut a Christmas tree from sponge and stick it to a piece of corrugated card. Stamp some of the coloured newsprint with gold trees.

4 Tear strips, rectangles and simple tree shapes from the newsprint. Tear around the stamped and stencilled motifs and cut out some with scissors. Glue in place on the gift wrap.

XMAS TREE GIFT TAGS

*S*pend some time making yourself a selection of
*stamped, stencilled and painted motifs before you
begin to assemble these gift tags.*

YOU WILL NEED

MATERIALS	EQUIPMENT
tracing paper	pencil
thin card	scissors
cellulose kitchen sponge	paintbrush
corrugated card	hole punch
glue stick	
coloured and textured papers	
stencil card	
stencil paints: black and gold	
white cartridge paper	
watercolour inks	
white oil crayon	
brown parcel wrap	
gift tags	
hole punch	
fine gold cord	

1 Trace the template from the back of the book, enlarging if necessary, transfer to paper and cut out. Draw around the template on sponge and cut out so you have a positive and a negative image to use as stamps. Glue each stamp on card. Stamp both motifs in gold on to a selection of papers.

2 Trace the branch pattern and transfer it to a piece of stencil card. Cut out and stencil in black and gold on to a selection of papers and on some of the stamped motifs.

3 Paint cartridge paper in bright inks and cut out a star motif. Scribble spots on parcel wrap with a white oil crayon to make snowflakes. Tear them out individually, leaving a border of brown paper around each one.

4 Assemble the tags. Cut or tear out a selection of motifs and arrange them on the cards. Glue in place. Punch a hole in the top and thread each with a loop of fine gold cord.

WINGED CUPID BROOCH

This exotic piece of jewellery is made from paper pulp, hand-painted in gorgeous colours, then decorated.

YOU WILL NEED

MATERIALS

tracing paper
thin card
paper pulp
wallpaper paste
newspaper
PVA (white) glue
white acrylic primer
flat-backed glass gems
epoxy resin glue
eye-hook pins
selection of gouache paints
clear matt varnish
gold enamel paint
small glass tear-drop beads
small jump-rings
brooch fixing

EQUIPMENT

pencil
craft knife
cutting mat
paintbrushes
dressmaker's pin
paint-mixing container
round-nosed jewellery pliers

1 Trace the template from the back of the book, enlarging if necessary, and transfer to card. Cut it out and cover with paper pulp. Apply several layers of wallpaper paste and newspaper strips. Allow to dry.

2 Coat with PVA (white) glue and then white primer. Allow to dry between each stage. Glue the glass gems on with epoxy resin. Make holes with a pin and insert the eye-hook pins, securing them with epoxy resin.

3 Paint on your design with gouache paints. When dry, coat with matt varnish. Allow to dry again, then add the gold enamel details.

4 Assemble all the brooch pieces and tear-drop beads, joining them with jump-rings, using the pliers. Glue the brooch fixing into position.

PAPIER-MACHE MOBILE

This colourful mobile is made from papier-mâché, elaborately painted with gouache colours. The more individual you make the decoration, the more charming it becomes.

YOU WILL NEED

MATERIALS
newspaper
masking tape
tracing paper
corrugated card
wallpaper paste
screw eyes
epoxy resin glue
chemical metal filler
mirror fragments
PVA (white) glue
white acrylic primer
gouache paints
gloss varnish
gold enamel paint
galvanized wire
jewellery jump rings

EQUIPMENT
pencil
scissors
craft knife
cutting mat
small and fine paintbrushes
paint-mixing container
wire-cutters
round-nosed pliers

1 Roll up some newspaper, bend it in the centre and then bend the ends over, to make a heart shape. Secure the ends with masking tape. Trace the template for the wings and stars from the back of the book, enlarging if necessary, and cut them out from corrugated card. Cut two slits in the side of the biggest heart, slot in the wings, and secure with tape.

2 Tear more newspaper into strips. Cover all the hearts and stars with several layers of newspaper strips dipped in wallpaper paste. Allow to dry.

3 Screw small screw eyes in place, securing them with epoxy glue. Allow to dry. Then mix up the filler, according to the manufacturer's instructions. Spread filler on the wings and carefully push in pieces of broken mirror. Allow to dry. Repeat the process on the back of the wings.

4 Coat all the shapes (except the wings) in PVA (white) glue and allow to dry. Paint on a layer of white acrylic primer, using a fine brush to fill between the pieces of mirror.

5 Paint on the design using gouache paints.

6 Coat with several layers of gloss varnish. When dry, add detail in gold enamel.

7 Cut a 40 cm/16 in length of wire and two lengths of 28 cm/11 in. Using the round-nosed pliers, coil the wire into shape, following the outlines given with the templates. Coat in turn with white glue, primer, and gold enamel, allowing each coat to dry before applying the next one.

8 Assemble the mobile using small jump rings and round-nosed pliers.

DECOUPAGE OAK LEAF BOX

Find one pretty motif and you can create lovely repeat patterns with it instantly, using a photocopier. Copies of old engravings are perfect for this technique: here they were delicately hand-coloured in a selection of autumnal shades.

YOU WILL NEED

MATERIALS	EQUIPMENT
wooden box	*paintbrushes*
cream emulsion (latex) paint	*paint-mixing container*
black and white leaf motif	*scissors*
acrylic paints: yellow-ochre	*craft knife*
and red oxide	*cutting mat*
PVA (white) glue	
clear gloss acrylic varnish	

1 Paint the box with two or three coats of cream paint. Make copies of the leaf motif in two sizes for the sides and lid. Hand-tint the copies with a thin wash of yellow-ochre and then red oxide.

2 Use scissors to cut around the outside of the leaf shapes. Cut away any small spaces within the design with a craft knife.

3 Arrange the leaves on the lid and sides of the box. Glue them on with PVA (white) glue and allow to dry.

4 Protect the box with two or three coats of clear gloss varnish.

FOLK ART BOX

The cupid motif is very popular in traditional folk art designs. Here, it has been used to embellish an oval Shaker-style box. The distressed hand-painted finish gives it a timeless quality that will ensure it is treasured for ever.

YOU WILL NEED

MATERIALS
oval card box
corrugated card
PVA (white) glue
newspaper
wallpaper paste
white acrylic primer
acrylic paints: dark green,
brick-red, yellow-ochre,
pale blue and brown

EQUIPMENT
craft knife
cutting mat
paintbrushes
paint-mixing container
sandpaper

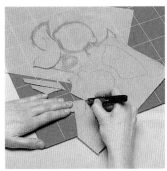

1 Trace the templates from the back of the book, enlarging them to fit the lid of your box. Trace the shapes on to the card, cut them out and glue them to the lid of the box.

2 Soak small strips of newspaper in wallpaper paste. Stick three layers over the edges of the card shapes. Allow to dry. Paint the lid and box with white acrylic primer.

3 Paint the box and the background of the lid with a coat of dark green. When it is dry, paint with brick-red and allow to dry. Sand down for a distressed finish.

4 Paint the cupid, mixing the colours to create subtle shades. Use a fine paintbrush for the border and the decoration. Stipple the cheeks with a dry brush.

OCTOPUSSY

This is an inexpensive and easy way to make a mobile – brightly coloured paper is simply torn and stuck together to form the bold sea creatures. This mobile is bound to delight children and will certainly brighten up a bedroom or bathroom.

YOU WILL NEED

MATERIALS	EQUIPMENT
tracing paper	*pencil*
thin card	*scissors*
papers, brightly coloured on	*hole punch*
one side	
PVA (white) glue	
thread	

1 Trace the octopus template from the back of the book, enlarging if necessary. Transfer to card and cut out two of them. Draw freehand and cut out eight fish, squid and starfish shapes in varying sizes.

2 Fold the paper with the coloured side innermost. Draw around each of the card shapes and tear out slightly outside the pencil line. As you have folded the paper, you will tear two copies of each shape.

3 Glue the paper to both sides of each card shape. Tear out eyes, fins, tails and scales. Glue on. Cut a slot in each octopus body, as shown. Punch a hole at the end of each arm and two holes in the head. Punch a hole at the top edge of each sea creature.

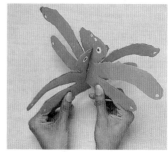

4 Slot together the octopus pieces. Assemble the pieces with thread and suspend the mobile from the top of the octopus's head.

BEETLE STATIONERY

*H*unt *through nineteenth-century natural history books for engravings of weird and wonderful beetles, which you can use to decorate a matching set of greetings cards, envelopes, gift tags and postcards.*

YOU WILL NEED

MATERIALS	EQUIPMENT
thin card and writing paper	*craft knife*
in various colours and	*ruler*
white	*cutting mat*
ready-made envelopes	*scissors*
photocopies of beetles	*hole punch*
matt gold paper	
glue stick	
gold cord	

1 For postcards, use a craft knife and ruler to cut the coloured card to a suitable size. Measure your envelopes and cut the greetings cards to fit neatly inside when folded. Score down the centre with the blunt edge of the scissors. Use the scraps for gift tags and punch a single hole in the top.

2 Cut round the beetle motifs with the craft knife and ruler, making neat rectangles. Tear squares and rectangles of various sizes from the coloured card and gold paper.

3 Arrange the beetle shapes in a pleasing design on the paper or card. Glue each piece in place. Make sure the glue reaches right to the edges so that they don't curl up. Stick single motifs on the flaps of the envelopes and at the top of the writing paper. To complete the tags, thread a length of gold cord through each hole.

CONTEMPLATIVE CUPID CARD

This elaborate hand-made card isn't difficult to make and will tell someone special that they are in your thoughts. Some ordinary pencils are water-soluble, so try what you have before buying pencils specially!

YOU WILL NEED

MATERIALS
tracing paper
masking tape
heavy watercolour paper
thin card
water-soluble pencils:
dark and light green, dark
and light blue, red, pink
and grey
watercolour or drawing
inks: pink and orange
all-purpose glue
glitter glue

EQUIPMENT
pencil
cutting mat
craft knife
scissors
fine paintbrush
heavy book

1 Trace the templates from the back of the book, enlarging if necessary. Tape the background and cupid tracings to the watercolour paper and go over the outlines with a pencil, leaving an indentation on the paper. Fold along the fold lines.

2 Transfer the design for the frame to the thin card in the same way. Cut out the card and frame and fold them.

3 Colour in the background and cupid, using water-soluble pencils, and cut out the cupid. On spare pieces of watercolour paper, draw and colour in some simple flowers and stems. Go over the pencil work with a wet paintbrush to blend the colours.

4 Decorate the outside of the card with watercolour or drawing ink, mixing the colours for a patchy effect.

5 Cut out the flowers, stick them together and apply a little glitter glue on to the centres. Apply glitter glue to the wings of the cupid.

6 Line up the edges of the cupid with the edges of the background at points A and C. Stick on some flowers.

7 Stick the frame to the front of the card at point D. Attach a few more flowers to the inside of the frame. Outline the leaves.

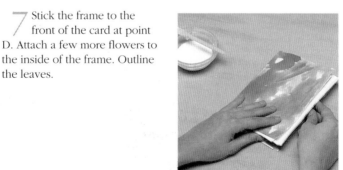

8 Finally, stick the background and cupid into the card, taking care to line up points B. Stick flap A to join the card together and fold up the card. Press it under a book before sending.

SUN HATBOX

*T*his hatbox positively glitters with gold decoration, creating an effect that seems to glow like the heavenly bodies to which it pays tribute.

YOU WILL NEED

MATERIALS	EQUIPMENT
carpet roll tube	*saw (optional)*
card	*tape measure*
masking tape	*pair of compasses*
newspaper strips	*pencil*
PVA (white) glue	*ruler*
white undercoat paint	*craft knife*
acrylic paints: blue, deep	*paintbrushes*
violet and red	*scissors*
gold paint	
sun-face motif print	
glitter glue	

 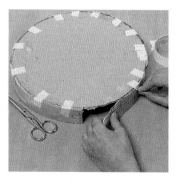

1 Using a section of a carpet tube, cut with a saw for the cylindrical part of the box, or bend a piece of card into a cylinder. Draw and cut a circle of card for the base and another slightly larger circle for the lid. To make the lid, cut a long narrow strip of card the length of the circumference of the lid, plus a small overlap. Bend the strip and fix it in position with masking tape. Bind the edge and the join with strips of newspaper and slightly watered-down PVA (white) glue.

2 Assemble the base and sides, fix with masking tape and bind the edge and joins with newspaper strips in the same way as the lid. Allow to dry.

3 Prime the base and lid with white undercoat paint.

4 Mark the stripes on the side of the box and paint them in different colours. Allow to dry. Use gold paint to add fine stripes.

5 Paint the details with gold paint and a fine brush.

6 Paint the lid violet. Photocopy the motif about 18 times. Cut the photocopied motifs out and stick them to the lid and the side of the box, using watered-down PVA (white) glue.

7 Paint the faces of the motifs to highlight all the features. Add glitter glue squiggles.

INSECT STORAGE BOX

If you have access to a photocopier you can make up striking and original designs on paper. Before you begin this project, it's a good idea to measure your box carefully and keep a note of all the dimensions to be sure that your design will fit well.

YOU WILL NEED

MATERIALS

insect images
white A3 paper
glue stick
shoe box
white acrylic or poster paint (optional)
PVA (white) glue
black paper
clear matt varnish

EQUIPMENT

scissors
paintbrush

1 Photocopy the images to the desired size. Arrange them on A3 paper and secure in place with a glue stick. When you are happy with your arrangement, make enough copies of it to cover the box, plus a few spares in case you go wrong. Two designs have been used here: one with a large central motif for the top of the box, and the other with insects scattered all over the paper.

2 If the box is printed, give it a coat of white paint and allow to dry. Brush a thin layer of PVA (white) glue over the top and sides of the lid. Position your covering paper carefully and smooth out from the centre to exclude air bubbles. Make a straight cut to each corner of the lid top and trim the overlap at the corners and edges to 2 cm/¾ in. Smooth the paper over the sides, gluing each flap under the next side piece to make neat corners, and tucking the overlap inside the lid.

3 Measure the sides of the box, adding 2 cm/¾ in to each dimension, and cut four pieces of paper. Glue and cover the inner sides.

4 From the paper you used for the lid, cut the lining for the bottom to the exact size of the box and glue in place.

5 Cut a rectangle from the black paper large enough to cover the bottom and sides of the box with a 2 cm/¾ in overlap all round. Cut out a wavy edge 1 cm/¼ in deep. Make straight cuts to the corners of the box and trim the flaps, as before. Glue the paper to the box, turning in the edge.

6 Measure the inside of the box lid and cut a piece of black paper to fit, again allowing a 2 cm/¾ in overlap. Cut the wavy edge, trim the corners as before and glue.

7 Dilute some PVA (white) glue with water and brush all over the box and lid. This will go on cloudy but will clear as it dries. Finally, seal the box with a coat of varnish.

ROLLER PLAIDS

*T*his project borrows materials from the home decorator, using two paint rollers with emulsion (latex) paint to form the basic checkered pattern. The plaid effect is added in two stages, with drying time in between.

YOU WILL NEED

MATERIALS
terracotta-pink emulsion (latex) paint
white paper
olive-green watercolour paint
white acrylic, poster or gouache paint
adhesive tape
red string

EQUIPMENT
small paint roller, with integral paint tray
2 saucers
square-tipped and fine paintbrushes
scissors

1 Put pink paint in the tray and coat the roller. Begin just in from the edge and run parallel stripes down the length of the paper.

2 Allow to dry, then do the same horizontally. Leave to dry thoroughly.

3 Put the olive-green paint in a saucer and paint stripes on the paper that cross through the centres of the white squares.

4 Dilute the white paint in a saucer and paint fine lines that cross through the centres of the solid pink squares.

5 Place your gift on the paper and wrap it carefully.

6 Wrap the red string around the gift and tie it in a knot at the centre. Unravel the individual threads of the string to make a crinkly bow.

BEADED VELVET FRAME

*T*he luxurious texture and glowing colour of velvet
*is highlighted with the jewel-like colours of glass
and metallic beads, to produce an effect of considerable
sophistication and style.*

YOU WILL NEED

MATERIALS	EQUIPMENT
card	*pencil*
velvet square	*ruler*
matching thread	*craft knife*
metallic beads	*cutting mat*
glass beads	*sharp-pointed scissors*
self-adhesive felt	*needle*
PVA (white) glue	*dressmaker's pins*

1 Cut out a square from the card at least 1 cm/½ in smaller than the velvet square. Cut out a square from the middle to make a frame. Place the velvet right-side down and put the frame on top. On the outside edge, leave a 1 cm/½ in seam allowance and mitre the corners. Cut away the middle section of velvet leaving a 1 cm/½ in seam allowance and snipping into the corners. Sew large stitches along the velvet and pull the sides together over the back of the frame.

2 Thread the beads on to the pins, first a metallic and then a glass one on each pin. Push the beaded pins firmly into the inside and outside edges of the card.

3 Cut a backing square from the card at least 1 cm/½ in smaller than the finished frame. Cover it on both sides with felt. Glue it on the back of the frame on three sides.

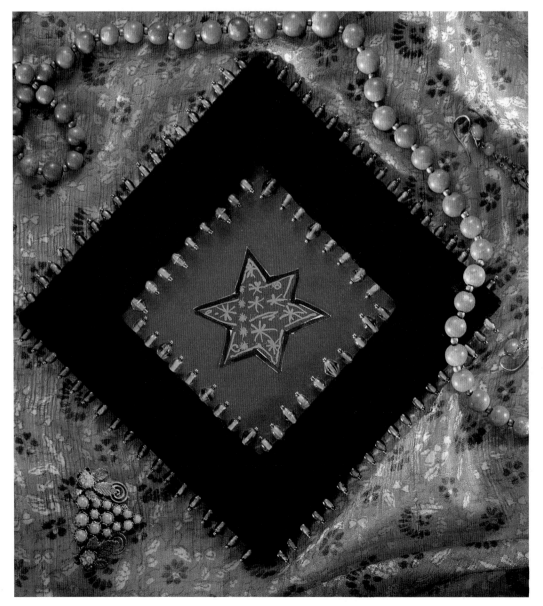

EMBOSSED PAPER FRAME

*T*his opulent frame is made from watercolour paper
coated with poster paint and PVA (white) glue.
The decorative pattern is achieved by scoring through
the glue with the end of a paintbrush.

YOU WILL NEED

MATERIALS

paper
tracing paper
*300 lb rough watercolour
paper*
crimson poster paint
PVA (white) glue
4 red glass nuggets
gold wax
silk tassel with bead
strong thread
mirror tile
masking tape
strong paper, for backing
strong glue

EQUIPMENT

pencil
scissors
craft knife
cutting mat
paintbrush
brush for glue
jeweller's pliers
thick, sharp needle

2 Cover the frame with a thin
layer of PVA (white) glue.
Working quickly, use a
paintbrush handle to mark
decorative patterns in the
surface of the glue so that the
paint shows through.

1 Draw a heart shape on to
paper, trace on to the
watercolour paper and cut out.
Use scissors for the outside and
a craft knife and cutting mat on
the inside. Paint the frame with
crimson poster paint.

3 Stick the red glass nuggets
on to the glue at the top
and bottom of the heart shape.
When the glue is dry and
transparent, crimp the edges
using jeweller's pliers.

4 Gently rub on gold wax
with your fingertip to cover
the whole frame. Be sparing
with the wax as you just want to
highlight the pattern, not fill in
the grooves.

5 With a thick, sharp needle,
make a hole in the bottom
of the frame and fasten on the
tassel and bead with strong
thread. Place the mirror tile
behind the frame and stick it on
to the frame, using masking
tape around the edge. Use the
heart-shaped template to cut
out the backing paper. Cover
one side of the backing paper
with strong glue and fix it to the
back of the frame.

DECOUPAGE VALENTINE BOX

A romantic gift for Valentine's Day, or any time of year. The combination of cut-out flowers and gold hearts creates a really strong, graphic impression, quite different from the usual whimsical "Victoriana" look. Découpage is an easy technique that gives truly spectacular results, making it possible to cover relatively large areas with a repeat pattern.

1 Paint the box red inside and out. Cut out flower images of various sizes from the paper. Trace the template from the back of the book, enlarging if necessary. Transfer to card and place on the gold paper. Draw around it. Repeat seven times and cut out the gold hearts.

2 Arrange the hearts on the box, two on the lid and on each long side and one on each end. Glue in place. Position the flowers around the hearts and glue them, pushing out any air bubbles. Allow to dry.

3 Add a coat of antique varnish, and rub it off with a cloth, to give an old, soft look. Finish with three or four coats of polyurethane varnish, letting each one dry before adding the next one.

YOU WILL NEED

MATERIALS

plain wooden box
red emulsion (latex) paint
floral wrapping paper
tracing paper
thin card
gold paper
glue
antique oak varnish
polyurethane varnish

EQUIPMENT

paintbrushes
scissors
pencil
cloth

DANCING BEES BOX

*T*he bees encircling this painted box have been cut out of folded paper like a row of dancing dolls. Measure the lid before you begin and enlarge or reduce the template so that the ring of bees will fit well. This box would make a wonderful gift filled with pots of honey or some beeswax cosmetics.

YOU WILL NEED

MATERIALS
tracing paper
thin card
circular painted box
black paper
yellow acrylic paint
all-purpose glue
clear varnish

EQUIPMENT
pencil
craft knife
cutting mat
white marker pencil
scissors
paintbrushes

1 Trace the template from the back of the book, enlarging to fit your box. Transfer to card and cut out. Fold some black paper in half, then in half again. Position the template across the folded corner so the tips of the wings touch the folds, and draw around it with a white pencil.

2 Cut out, making sure that the bees are joined by their wings. Unfold the bees carefully. Make two sets. Draw the bees' stripes on each circle and paint their stripes and wings in yellow acrylic paint.

3 Glue the bees to the lid of the box. Cut the second set in half and stick them on the sides of the box. Protect the box with a coat of varnish.

PRESSED FLOWER GIFT TAG

*G*ive ordinary brown paper designer status with the simple addition of a few pressed flowers. Make the gift tag to fit neatly into the envelope, sealed with a scrap of flower petal.

YOU WILL NEED

MATERIALS	EQUIPMENT
scrap card	*scissors*
brown paper	*ruler or straight edge*
small brown envelope	*small paintbrush*
PVA (white) glue	*craft knife*
pressed flowers	

1 Working on a piece of scrap card, cut a gift tag out of the brown paper so that it fits the envelope when folded in half. Score along the fold line with the scissors.

2 Using a small paintbrush, apply a tiny amount of glue to the faces of the flowers, holding each flower steady as you work. Press the flowers on to the gift tag, so that they overlap the edges of the tag. Leave to dry.

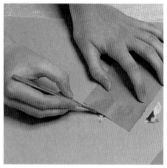

3 Working on a piece of scrap card, and using a craft knife, carefully cut away the overlapping edges of the petals.

4 Glue one of the petal offcuts on to the envelope flap, so that it overlaps the edge. Write the gift tag, then put it in the envelope and glue the rest of the petal offcut on to the envelope to seal.

SEASHORE CARDS

*R*eceiving a card that has been made for you is so special that it makes the card a gift in itself. Use it as the base in which to frame shells found at the seaside. The envelope completes the gift, stitched together with raffia and held closed by a feather threaded through a limpet shell.

YOU WILL NEED

MATERIALS
assorted handmade papers
raffia
PVA (white) glue
seaweed
assorted shells
double-sided tape
fine sandpaper
weathered limpet shell with hole
feather

EQUIPMENT
darning needle
scissors

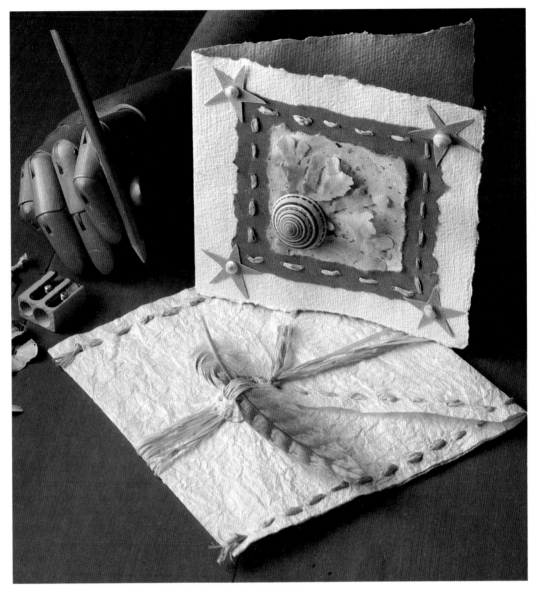

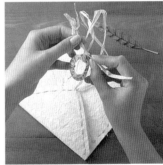

1 Fold a sheet of paper in half to make a card. Tear two squares from paper in contrasting colours, one smaller than the other. Thread a darning needle with raffia and sew the larger square on to the card with running stitch.

2 Glue the smaller square on top. Glue on seaweed and a shell. Back a piece of sandpaper with double-sided tape. Cut out starfish shapes and stick one in each corner. Glue a small shell in the centre of each starfish.

3 Cut a rectangle of paper with a triangular flap at one end, large enough to hold the card when folded. Stitch the sides together with raffia. Start stitching at the bottom and continue to the point of the flap, leaving a loose end.

4 Tie the limpet shell on to the end of the two loose strands of raffia. Wrap the raffia around the envelope and thread the feather through the raffia under the shell to hold the envelope closed.

HOLIDAY ALBUM

Make a photograph album with shells, raffia matting and postcards. The cover is made from polyboard and the pages from recycled card, bound with raffia.

YOU WILL NEED

MATERIALS

*polyboard
double-sided carpet tape
fine raffia matting
rust-coloured raffia
thin recycled card
tissue paper
glue stick
postcards or photos
assorted shells
PVA (white) glue
ribbon*

EQUIPMENT

*craft knife
metal ruler
cutting mat
pencil
bradawl
scissors
pins
darning needle
table knife
hole punch*

1 Using a craft knife, metal ruler and a cutting mat, cut a rectangle of polyboard 61 x 21.5 cm/24 x 8½ in. Mark the centre line on both sides, then mark a line 2 cm/¾ in on each side. Partially cut through the board along these two lines.

2 Turn the board over and stick double-sided carpet tape around all the edges. Mark a line 5.5 cm/2⅛ in from each side of the centre line. Partially cut through the board along these two lines as before.

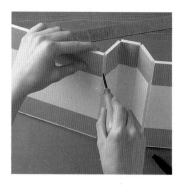

3 Fold the board along the partially cut lines to form the spine and hinges. Using a bradawl, pierce holes along both hinges 5.75 cm/2¼ in in from the top and bottom edges, and at 2 cm/¾ in intervals between these holes.

4 Cut a piece of raffia matting slightly larger than the board. Lay the board on top and remove the backing from the tape. Fold the matting around the board and stick to the tape. Mitre the corners.

5 Cut another piece of matting to line the inside, allowing for a small hem. Fold the edges under and pin in place. Thread a darning needle with raffia and overstitch around the outside edge.

6 Cut 20 sheets of card 31 x 18.5 cm/12¼ x 7¼ in and 20 of tissue paper 28 x 17.5 cm/ 11 x 7 in. Using a table knife, score lines 3 cm/1¼ in and 4 cm/1½ in from one edge of each piece of card.

7 Fold each piece of card along the first scored line. Run the glue stick inside the fold and insert a piece of tissue paper. Press firmly to seal.

8 Using a hole punch, make holes just above the folded edge, 4.25 cm/1¾ in from the top and bottom edges, and at 2 cm/¾ in intervals between.

9 Place the pages inside the cover. Using raffia, stitch the pages to the cover through the punched holes, making a criss-cross pattern.

10 Decorate the front with old postcards or photos and shells, sticking them in place with glue. Tie a piece of ribbon around the album.

GOTHIC CANDELABRA

*A*s if rooted in the base of this graceful candelabra, sinuous ivy entwines its stem and arms. The basic structure consists of just three wire coathangers and some corrugated cardboard, coated with several layers of papier-mâché. The handmade paper adds weight to the candelabra and tensile strength.

YOU WILL NEED

MATERIALS

3 wire coathangers
heavy corrugated cardboard
thin garden wire
gummed paper tape
thin card
newspaper
PVA (white) glue
handmade paper
masking tape
spray acrylic varnish
gold and silver gouache paints

EQUIPMENT

pliers
jam jar
pencil
pair of compasses
ruler
craft knife
cutting mat
sponge
mixing bowl
fine sandpaper
paintbrushes
paint-mixing container

1 Using pliers, bend two wire coathangers to make two curved arms. Bend the wire around a jam jar to get a smooth shape. Cut off the hooks.

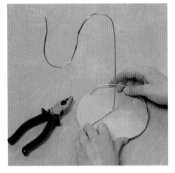

2 Draw a 15 cm/6 in circle on corrugated cardboard and cut out. Bend the lower end of each arm into a semicircle to fit around the edge.

3 Bind the arms together with thin garden wire to make the stem. Attach the cardboard base to the wires with gummed paper tape.

4 Cut two 9 cm/3½ in circles of thin card. Make a slit to the centre of each, then twist into cone-shaped candle-holders. Secure with tape. Soak newspaper strips in diluted glue and cover the cones. Push one on to the end of each wire arm and secure with tape.

5 Twist long strips of newspaper and wrap them around the wire frame. Secure the twists with garden wire. Soak strips of handmade paper in diluted glue and cover the structure with a further layer of papier-mâché.

6 Bend the third coathanger to make the ivy stem. Draw 8–10 ivy leaf shapes on card, cut out and tape each one to a short length of garden wire. Attach the leaves to the stem and secure with masking tape. Cover the stem and stalks with handmade paper strips.

7 Using garden wire, attach the ivy stem to the main frame of the candelabra. Twist the stem around the candelabra in an attractive shape and wire it in place.

8 Cover the whole candelabra in a layer of papier-mâché. Leave to dry completely in a warm place. Using fine sandpaper, carefully smooth over the papier-mâché.

9 Spray the candelabra with a coat of acrylic varnish to seal it. Decorate with gold and silver gouache paints, then varnish again.

TABLE LAMP

*C*reate an unusual and stylish lamp by binding together rectangles of thick, plain grey chipboard with small knots of string. The shade is designed to sit over the lamp fitting and will cast a warm glow.

YOU WILL NEED

MATERIALS
thick unlined chipboard
string
two-core flex
two-core flex switch
plug
candle lightbulb
pendant lampholder
suitable for two-core flex
13 cm/5 in wire lampshade
holder

EQUIPMENT
pencil
metal ruler
craft knife
cutting mat
revolving hole punch
eraser
scissors

1 Draw a rectangle on the chipboard: the base is 14.5 cm/5¾ in wide, the height 25 cm/10 in and the top 11 cm/4½ in wide. Using a metal ruler, craft knife and cutting mat, cut out. You will need four identical pieces.

2 With a pencil and ruler, mark a line 8 mm/⅜ in from the edge along both long sides of each of the four pieces. Then mark a dot every 1 cm/½ in along each line.

3 Using a hole punch, make a hole on every mark, then erase the marks. Hold two sides together. Using a short length of string, tie a double knot through the topmost holes, cutting the ends very short. Repeat at every alternate hole.

4 Ease each knot so that it sits flat against one side of the shade. Repeat with all four pieces. To assemble the table lamp, place the lampshade over the lamp, guiding the flex gently between two sides so that it sits flat on a surface.

JAM POT COVERS

*P*retty paper circles like these are perfect for dressing up your home-made jams and chutneys to give as presents. With their imitation lace edgings, they make an assortment of unmatching recycled jars into a set that will stand out from all the rest.

YOU WILL NEED

MATERIALS

handmade paper
jam jar
ribbon

EQUIPMENT

scissors – small, pointed pair and a larger pair
pencil
small hole punch
small hammer

1 Cut out a circle of handmade paper that is roughly twice the diameter of the jam jar lid. Fold the circle of paper in half four times.

2 Lightly pencil in half-hearts on the edges and cut them out with small scissors. Mark dotted hearts – one whole one in the middle and two half-hearts either side along the folded edges.

3 Place the folded paper on a hard surface and use the hole punch and hammer to tap out the dotted holes.

4 Using the small scissors, cut a scalloped edge by snipping out triangles between the bases of the hearts. Unfold and flatten the cover. Place it over the jam jar and secure it with ribbon tied in a bow.

SILHOUETTE

Before the camera was invented, people who could not afford to have a portrait painted would use the services of the silhouette artist. The subjects would sit by a screen with a light to project the shadow of their profile, or the skilled artist might cut freehand just from looking at his subject. Our method produces a very accurate likeness using all the tricks of modern technology to make a charming old-fashioned portrait.

YOU WILL NEED

MATERIALS

*profile photograph
oval photo mount
spray adhesive
cream paper
red paper
glue*

EQUIPMENT

*pencil
craft knife and cutting mat
or small, sharp scissors
black permanent marker
pen
pinking shears*

1 Enlarge the photograph on a photocopier to fit your photo mount.

2 Select the best photocopy. Use a pencil to draw in the "bust" shape that is typical on old silhouettes.

3 Using a craft knife and cutting mat, cut very carefully around the face and cut a bit extra around the hair. You may find it easier to cut the profile with small, sharp scissors – it's a personal preference.

4 Turn the cut-out over and colour it with a black marker pen. Be careful not to overwork the edges as every dent will show.

5 Add the finishing touches to the edges of the hair – this is where the extra allowance is useful. Spray the back of the profile with adhesive and position it in the centre of the cream paper.

6 To make the decorated border, place the oval mount on the back of a sheet of red paper and draw around the inside edge.

7 Cut out the red paper and fold it in quarters.

8 Cut inside the line, using pinking shears to give a decorative edge.

9 Glue the red paper mount on to the cream paper. Leave the silhouette as it is or you can add the black photo mount on top.

STENCILLING, STAMPING AND PRINTING

In this section you can find projects which, in their different ways, all involve transferring an image or motif to a surface, which can be anything from paper to plaster, floors to fabric. Stamping – whether using commercial stamps or the home-made kind – is probably the easiest method there is of transforming a plain surface. You can use the techniques to cover large areas, such as the walls of a room, or small, such as notepaper or gift wrapping.

In addition to stamping, there are exciting print projects for linocuts and potato prints, and a great selection of stencilling ideas from cork tiles to curtains. All the projects are easily adaptable to suit your needs and will inspire you to make up your own motifs and patterns!

BASIC STAMPING TECHNIQUES

Stamping is a simple and direct way of making a print. The variations, such as they are, come from the way in which the stamp is inked and the type of surface to which it is applied. It is a good idea to experiment and find a method and effect that you find most pleasing.

RIGHT *Printing is fun as well as decorative. Here is a selection of the materials you may find yourself using.*

OPPOSITE *You can buy ready-made commercial stamps, or make them yourself from plastic foam, linoleum blocks – and, of course, the humble potato.*

Stamping with a brush

The advantage of this technique is that you can see where the colour has been applied. This method is quite time-consuming, so use it for smaller projects. It is ideal for inking an intricate stamp with more than one colour.

Stamping with a foam roller

This is the very best method for stamping large areas, such as walls. The stamp is evenly inked and you can see where the colour has been applied. Variations in the strength of printing can be achieved by only re-inking the stamp after several printings.

Stamping with a stamp pad

This is the traditional way to ink rubber stamps, which are less porous than foam stamps. The method suits small projects, particularly printing on paper. Stamp pads are more expensive to use than paint, but they are less messy and produce very crisp prints.

Stamping by dipping in paint

Spread a thin layer of paint on to a plate and dip the stamp into it. This is the quickest way of stamping large decorating projects. As you cannot see how much paint the stamp is picking up, you will need to experiment.

Stamping with fabric paint

Spread a thin layer of fabric paint on to a plate and dip the stamp into it. Fabric paints are quite sticky and any excess paint is likely to be taken up in the fabric rather than to spread around the edges. Fabric paint can also be applied by brush or foam roller, and is available with integral applicators.

Stamping with several colours

A brush is the preferred option when using more than one colour on a stamp. It allows greater accuracy than a foam roller because you can see exactly where you are putting the colour. Two-colour stamping is very effective for giving a shadow effect or a decorative pattern.

BASIC STAMPING TECHNIQUES

Potato

Commercial

Foam

Lino

Surface applications

The surface on to which you stamp or stencil your design will greatly influence the finished effect. This page gives hints and tips for best results.

Rough plaster

You can roughen your walls before stamping or stencilling by mixing the filler to a fairly loose consistency and spreading it randomly on the wall. When dry, roughen it with coarse sandpaper, using random strokes.

Fabric

As a rule, natural fabrics are the most absorbent, but to judge the painted effect, experiment first on a small sample. Fabric paints come in a range of colours, but to obtain the subtler shades, you may need to combine the primaries with black or white. Card behind the fabric will protect your work surface.

Tiles

Wash tiles in hot water and detergent to remove any dirt or grease, and dry thoroughly. If the tiles are already on the wall, avoid printing in areas which require a lot of cleaning. The paint will only withstand a gentle wipe with a cloth. Loose tiles can be baked to add extra strength and permanence to the paint. Always read the manufacturer's instructions before you do this.

Smooth plaster or lining paper

If you are using a stamp, ink it with a small foam roller to achieve the crispest print. Re-create perfect repeats by re-inking with every print, or give a more hand-printed effect by making several prints between inkings.

Wood

Rub down the surface of any wood to give the paint a better "key" to adhere to. Some woods are very porous and absorb paint, but you can intensify the colour by over-printing later. If you stamp or stencil on wood lightly, the grain will show through. Seal your design with matt varnish.

Glass

Wash glass in hot water and detergent to remove any dirt or grease, and dry it thoroughly. It is best to print on glass for non-food uses, such as vases. Practise on a spare sheet of glass first. As glass has a slippery, non-porous surface, you need to apply your print with a direct on/off movement.

SUNS AND MOONS NAPKIN

*T*ransform plain napkins by decorating them with
golden suns and blue moons. To achieve the best
result, cut the stencils carefully and register them
accurately, with the help of the cross-points you draw
on the napkin.

YOU WILL NEED

MATERIALS

tracing paper
*2 sheets of thin card, size of
the napkins*
spray adhesive
napkins
fabric paints: gold and blue

EQUIPMENT

pencil
ruler
craft knife
cutting mat
iron
fabric marker
sponge or stencil brush

1 Trace the template from the
back of the book, enlarging
it if necessary. Rule grids on the
card to help you position the
motifs. Transfer the motifs on to
the thin card; you will need to
make one stencil for the suns
and one for the moons. Cut out
the stencils.

2 Spray adhesive on the sun
stencil. Iron a napkin and
lay it on the stencil, smoothing
it outwards from the centre.
With a fabric marker, draw the
registration marks on the
napkin, parallel to the edges.
The lines should cross at the
centre of the corner sun motif.

3 Spray adhesive on the
reverse of the sun stencil
and register the stencil on the
cross-points. Using a sponge or
stencil brush, apply the gold
paint. Remove the stencil, then
allow to dry. Repeat with the
moon stencil and blue paint,
registering the stencil as before.
Fix the paints according to the
manufacturer's instructions.

STENCILLED SPRIG CURTAIN

This regular repeat pattern is easy to achieve by ironing the curtain fabric to mark a grid before you start to stencil. Alternatively, the leaf motif could be stencilled randomly across the fabric for a more informal look. Wash and iron the fabric before you start work.

YOU WILL NEED

MATERIALS

tracing paper
thin card or paper
cotton voile, to fit window
newspaper
masking tape
spray adhesive
fabric paints: green, blue, brown and pink
matching sewing thread
curtain wire

EQUIPMENT

pencil
craft knife
cutting mat
iron
thick and thin stencil brushes
paint-mixing container
sewing machine

1 Trace the template from the back of the book, enlarging it to 17 cm/6½ in high. Transfer it to thin card and cut it out. Fold the fabric into 20 cm/8 in vertical pleats and 25 cm/10 in horizontal pleats, then iron it lightly to leave a grid pattern. Cover your work surface with newspaper and tape the fabric down so that it is fairly taut.

2 Spray the back of the stencil with adhesive and place it in the first rectangle. Mix the paints to achieve subtle shades. Paint the leaves in green, adding blue at the edges for depth. Paint the stem in brown and the berries in a brownish pink. Repeat the design in alternate rectangles.

3 Turn the stencil upside-down and paint the top leaf in the centre of the plain rectangles pink. Add a darker shade at the tip and mark the stalk in brown. Fix the paints according to the manufacturer's instructions. Hem the sides and lower edge of the curtain. Make a 2.5 cm/1 in channel at the top and insert the curtain wire.

STYLISH LAMPSHADE

*U*nusual lampshades can be very expensive, so the
solution is to take a plain lampshade and apply
some surface decoration that will transform it from a
utility object into a stylish focal point. This design,
which resembles a seedpod, is easy to cut from high-
density foam and it makes a bold, sharp-edged print
that is highly effective.

YOU WILL NEED

MATERIALS	EQUIPMENT
tracing paper	pencil
card	craft knife
spray adhesive	cutting mat
high-density foam	2 plates
thinned emulsion (latex)	small rubber roller
paints: cream-yellow and	
pale blue	
plain lampshade	

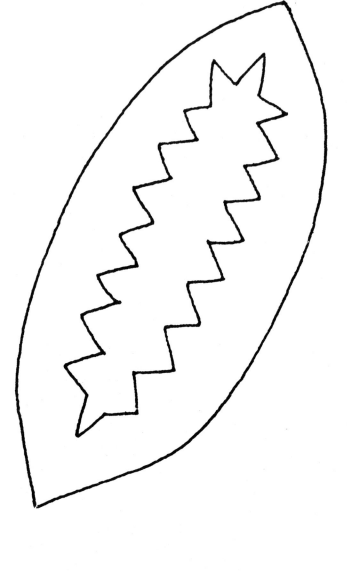

1 Trace the template on this
page, enlarging it if
necessary. Transfer it to a piece
of card and cut it out. Lightly
spray the shape with adhesive
and place it on the foam. Cut
around the outline, going all the
way through the foam. Then cut
around the centre detail to a
depth of about 1 cm/½ in.
Undercut and scoop this section
away before cutting away the
background.

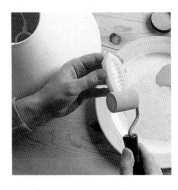

2 Spread some cream-yellow
paint on to a plate and coat
a small roller evenly. Use it to
apply a coat of paint to the
foam stamp.

3 Make the first print a
partial one, using only the
top end of the stamp. Continue
to print at random angles,
leaving plenty of spaces for the
second colour. Wash the stamp
to remove all traces of yellow.

4 Spread some pale blue
paint on to a second plate
and coat the roller evenly. Use it
to apply a coat of paint to the
foam stamp.

5 Stamp pale blue shapes at
random angles in between
the cream-yellow ones. Be sure
to make some partial prints so
that the pattern continues over
the edges.

SEASHORE SPONGEWARE SET

*I*magine the effect of a whole tea-set of this seashore design. Painting your own is an inexpensive way of transforming white china, and the end result is unique.

YOU WILL NEED

MATERIALS	EQUIPMENT
cellulose kitchen sponge	*ballpoint pen*
all-purpose glue	*scissors*
corrugated card	*plate*
ceramic paints: dark blue	*rag*
and dark green	*fine black magic marker*
paper towels	*stencil brush*
white china	*cosmetic sponge (optional)*
white spirit	

1 Draw your crab shape freehand on the sponge. Cut the crab out and glue it to a small square of corrugated card. Trim the card as close to the crab as possible. Pour a small amount of dark blue ceramic paint on to a plate. Lightly press the sponge into the paint and blot off any excess paint with paper towels. Gently apply even pressure to stamp the crab on to the china. Carefully lift off the sponge, in a single movement. Repeat the pattern as often as necessary for your design. Remove any mistakes with white spirit on a rag. Fix the paint according to the manufacturer's instructions.

2 With the magic marker, draw the border freehand around the bottom of the mug. Fill in the waves using a stencil brush and fix the paint again.

3 Alternatively, use the cosmetic sponge to sponge the border around the mug. Use both the blue and green paints, to give depth to the border. Fix the paint.

CREEPY CRAWLY HANDKERCHIEF

A handkerchief full of little bugs sounds alarming, but these prints adapted from nineteenth-century folk art woodcuts are anything but! If the handkerchief has a self-weave pattern, use it as a guide for the prints; if not, scatter them about but make sure they are evenly spaced over the fabric. Practise first on a spare piece of fabric.

YOU WILL NEED

MATERIALS

*lino tile, 15 x 15 cm/6 x 6 in
tracing paper
fabric paints in various
colours
fabric paint medium
laundered white
handkerchief*

EQUIPMENT

*lino tools
craft knife
pencil
paintbrush*

1 Cut the lino tile into six pieces, each measuring 5 x 7.5 cm/2 x 3 in. Trace the templates from the back of the book and transfer them to the lino pieces.

2 Using a V-shaped lino tool, carefully cut around the outlines of the bug templates. Then use a wider lino tool to cut away the remainder of the background.

3 Apply fabric paints to the blocks. Using a paintbrush, blend the colours to achieve interesting paint effects. Dilute the paint as necessary with fabric medium.

4 Place the block on the fabric, press evenly over the back and lift it up carefully to avoid smudging the print. Fix the paints according to the manufacturer's instructions.

CHECKERBOARD POTATO PRINT

*P*otato prints are one of the easiest and most satisfying ways of creating a personalized repeat design. Here, one potato half is cut into a square stamp and the other half is given the same treatment with a cross shape added to make a checkerboard design.

YOU WILL NEED

MATERIALS
potato
acrylic paints: cadmium-
yellow and cobalt-blue
sheet of white paper
thin blue ribbon
florist's wire (optional)

EQUIPMENT
chopping board
sharp knife or craft knife
2 plates
paper towels
scissors

1 On the chopping board, cut the potato in half with one smooth movement. Cut the sides of one half to make a plain square.

2 Cut the other potato half into a square, then cut out a cross shape by removing triangular sections around the edge and squaring off the corners of the cross.

3 Put the paints on separate plates and have some paper towels handy. Print the yellow squares first on a sheet of paper, starting in one corner and working down and across the sheet.

4 Print the blue crosses in the white squares and allow to dry thoroughly.

5 Wrap a gift in the paper and use a thin blue ribbon, set off-centre, as a trimming.

6 If you like, make a separate bow, securing loops of ribbon with some florist's wire.

ZODIAC CAFE CURTAIN

*U*se gold fabric paints to dramatize a plain muslin (cheese-cloth) curtain. Stencil the shapes at random all over the curtain, but try to plan your design so that they all appear fairly regularly. Add variety by blending the two shades of gold on some of the designs that you make.

YOU WILL NEED

MATERIALS
tracing paper
thin card or paper
scrap fabric
fabric paints: light and dark gold
paper towels
newspaper
white muslin (cheesecloth), to fit window
masking tape
spray adhesive
matching sewing thread
curtain clips and metal rings

EQUIPMENT
pencil
craft knife
cutting mat
2 stencil brushes
iron
needle

1 Trace the templates from the back of the book, enlarging if necessary. Transfer on to 12 rectangles of thin card or paper and cut out the shapes with a craft knife. Before working on your curtain, practise your stencilling technique on some spare fabric. Don't overload your brush and wipe off any excess paint on paper towels before you begin.

2 Cover your work table with newspaper. Iron the muslin (cheesecloth), then fix one corner to the table with masking tape, keeping it flat. Coat the back of each stencil lightly with spray adhesive before positioning it on the fabric. Start with the light gold, then paint over the edges of the motif with dark gold to give depth. Allow to dry, then gently peel the card off.

3 Cover the rest of the fabric with the motifs, repositioning it on the work table as necessary and stencilling one section at a time. Fix the paint according to the manufacturer's instructions. Iron, then hem the edges and attach the curtain clips to the upper edge.

CUPID LINOCUT

*L*inocut images have a pleasing graphic simplicity. Here, the marvellous texture and light-enhancing qualities of gold metallic organza are contrasted with the solidity of the image. The beauty of linocuts is that the lino block can be used lots of times, so this idea can be adapted for making, for example, your own greetings cards.

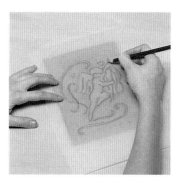

1 Trace the template from the back of the book, enlarging if necessary, and transfer to the lino block. Cut the design with the lino cutting tools: use the scoop to cut out large background areas and the nib for the fine details.

2 Squeeze the printing inks on to a plate and use the roller to mix the colours to get a deep burgundy shade. Coat the roller evenly, then roll over the surface of the linocut.

3 Tape the corners of the metallic organza to scrap paper to ensure the fabric is wrinkle free. Put the linocut over the organza and press evenly to ensure a crisp print. Use the decorative paper to create a mount, then frame.

YOU WILL NEED

MATERIALS

tracing paper
printing inks: red and blue
masking tape
gold metallic organza
scrap paper
decorative paper
picture frame

EQUIPMENT

pencil
lino block
lino cutting tools:
U-shaped scoop and
V-shaped nib
plate
paint roller

STAMPED BEDLINEN

*M*atching bedlinen is the last word in luxury. The white pillowcases have an all-round border of horse chestnuts and the top sheet folds back to reveal a matching pattern. Smooth cotton with straight edging is a dream to work with because the stamps can be confidently lined up with the edges and the sheeting absorbs the paint well to give a very crisp print.

YOU WILL NEED

MATERIALS

fabric paints: dark green and blue
scrap paper
sheet and pillowcase
thin card
scrap fabric

EQUIPMENT

rubber stamp
scissors

1 To plan your design, stamp out several motifs on scrap paper and cut them out. Arrange these along the sheet edge or the pillowcase border to work out the position and spacing of your pattern.

2 Place a sheet of card under the sheet or inside the pillowcase to prevent the paint from soaking through.

3 Follow the manufacturer's instructions and apply green paint to half of the stamp.

4 Apply blue paint to the other half of the stamp.

5 Test the distribution of the paint by making a print on a scrap of fabric. Re-apply and test the paint until you feel confident enough to make the first print on the bedlinen.

6 Check the arrangement of the paper-stamped motifs, then lift one at a time and stamp the fabric in its place. Press quite firmly to give the fabric time to absorb the paint.

7 Continue to re-coat and test the stamp as you print all the way around the edges to complete a matching bedlinen set. Fix the paint according to the manufacturer's instructions.

STENCILLED SEA WALL

*T*his unusual idea for a wall decoration capitalizes on the shininess of ordinary kitchen foil. The effect is shimmering and glittering, with an underwater feel that is ideal for a bathroom wall. It can also be done directly on a wall surface.

YOU WILL NEED

MATERIALS

sheet of hardboard
emulsion (latex) paint
gloss paints: dark blue and olive-green
tracing paper
thin card
aluminium foil
clear gloss varnish
artist's oil colours: dark blue and chrome-yellow

EQUIPMENT

decorator's paintbrush
sponge or rag
pencil
scissors
dressmaker's pins
fine paintbrush

1 Paint the hardboard with an undercoat of emulsion (latex) paint. Paint the surface with dark blue gloss paint. When it is dry, sponge or rag roll the green paint in blotches all over the hardboard surface.

2 Trace the templates from the back of the book, enlarging if necessary. Cut out the templates very roughly on thin card and lay them, face-up, on one or two pieces of foil, slightly larger than the templates. Pin the layers together, then cut out the shapes and separate the layers.

3 Brush some varnish on to the hardboard and apply foil shapes to the surface. Tint some of the varnish with the artist's colours. Add detail and texture with varnish tinted with artist's colours, using a fine paintbrush. When the varnish is dry, give the whole design a further coat of tinted varnish.

FLEUR-DE-LYS TILES

This design is based on some original tiles from a medieval flooring. The modern version can quickly be stencilled on to plain tiles using a little imagination and some acrylic paint. Experiment with different colours and sizes to come up with an individual design for your tiles.

YOU WILL NEED

MATERIALS
*tracing paper
thin card
unglazed terracotta tiles,
13 x 13 cm/5 x 5 in
detergent
spray adhesive
cream acrylic paint
clear matt acrylic spray
varnish*

EQUIPMENT
*pencil
craft knife
cutting mat
stencil brush*

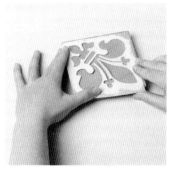

1 Trace the template from the back of the book, enlarging if necessary to fit on to a tile leaving a narrow border. Transfer it to thin card and cut out with a craft knife.

2 Wash the tiles with detergent to remove grease and dust. Allow to dry. Spray the back of the stencil lightly with adhesive and smooth in place on the first tile.

3 Paint in the design with small circular movements of the brush. Be careful not to overload the brush with paint.

4 Peel off the stencil and leave the paint to dry thoroughly. Then seal with several coats of clear matt acrylic spray varnish.

LEAFY ESPRESSO CUPS

*B*rowsing around antique stalls, you sometimes come across coffee cups hand-painted with broad brush strokes and lots of little raised dots of paint. It is simple to decorate your own coffee service in this style.

YOU WILL NEED

MATERIALS	EQUIPMENT
white ceramic cup and saucer	acetone or other grease-dispersing alcohol
thin card or paper	cotton buds
sticky-backed plastic	pencil
green acrylic ceramic paint	scissors
pewter acrylic paint with nozzle-tipped tube	paintbrush
	hair dryer (optional)
	craft knife

1 Clean any grease from the surface of the china to be painted, using the acetone or alcohol and a cotton bud.

2 Draw leaves and circles freehand on to thin card or paper. Cut them out and draw around them on the backing of the sticky-backed plastic. Cut out. Peel away the backing paper and stick the pieces on the cup and saucer.

3 Paint around the shapes with the ceramic paint, applying several coats to achieve a solid colour. Leave each coat to air-dry or use a hair dryer for speed.

4 To ensure a clean edge, cut around each sticky shape with a craft knife, then peel off.

5 Clean up any smudges with a cotton bud dipped in acetone or water.

6 Using pewter paint and the nozzle-tipped paint tube, mark the outlines and details of the leaves with rows of small dots. Allow to dry for 36 hours. Fix the paints according to the manufacturer's instructions. The paint should withstand general use and gentle washing up, but not the dishwasher.

STENCILLED PICTURE FRAME

*T*he stylish raised leaf patterns around these frames are simple to create using ordinary white interior filler instead of paint to fill in the stencilled shapes.

YOU WILL NEED

MATERIALS

2 wooden frames
dark green acrylic paint
fine-grade sandpaper
tracing paper
thin card
ready-mixed interior
filler

EQUIPMENT

paintbrush
pencil
scissors
stencil brush

1 Paint the wooden frames dark green. When dry, gently rub them down with sandpaper to create a subtle distressed effect.

2 Trace the templates from the back of the book, enlarging to fit the frames. Transfer the designs to thin card and cut them out.

3 Position a stencil on the first frame and stipple ready-mixed filler through the stencil. Reposition the stencil and continue all around the frame. Allow to dry.

4 Repeat with a different combination of motifs on the second frame. When the filler is completely hard, gently smooth the leaves with fine-grade sandpaper.

SGRAFFITO EGGS

*T*he familiar scraper-
board technique has
a wonderful new delicacy
when it is applied to
the fragile surface of a
real eggshell.

YOU WILL NEED

MATERIALS

blown egg
acrylic paints: purple-
brown and dark blue

EQUIPMENT

pencil
paintbrush
craft knife
white marker pencil

1 Draw a cameo outline on
the front and back of the
eggshell in pencil. Paint the
two oval shapes in purple-
brown acrylic paint, allowing
one side to dry before you turn
the egg over. You may need
two coats. Paint the band
around the egg in dark blue,
again using two coats if
required. Allow to dry.

2 Use the point of a craft
knife blade to scratch
double lines between the
purple-brown and blue
sections. Make a criss-cross
pattern across the blue section
and mark a dot in each
diamond. Scratch a series of
dots between the double lines
of the borders.

3 Using a white marker
pencil, very lightly sketch
the outline of an insect in each
purple-brown oval. You can
copy the moth in the
photograph or use a natural
history print as a reference.
Engrave the design following
the white pencil line, adding in
more intricate details.

MEXICAN CITRUS TRAY

*B*reakfast in bed will really wake you up if it is *presented on this flamboyant fruit tray, painted in zingy, sunny colours.*

YOU WILL NEED

MATERIALS
sandpaper
wooden tray
matt emulsion (latex) paints:
dark emerald, lime-green
and turquoise
tracing paper
acrylic gouache paints
matt polyurethane varnish

EQUIPMENT
medium and fine
paintbrushes
hard and soft pencils

1 Sand the tray to remove any varnish. Paint the whole tray a dark emerald-green colour, then paint the inside of the tray lime-green, and the base turquoise. Allow to dry thoroughly.

2 Trace the templates from the back of the book, enlarging to fit the base and sides of the tray. Rub over the outlines on the reverse of the tracing with a soft pencil, then transfer the designs to the tray.

3 Paint the oranges, lemons and leaves on the base of the tray, and the flower motif on the sides, using acrylic gouache. When dry, add the details in white.

4 Paint a pink wavy border around the edge and the base of the tray. Paint the handle holes in bright orange. When the paint is dry, protect with several coats of varnish.

LEAFY PENCIL POT

This useful pencil pot is stencilled with a simple leaf motif over a dark green background which is painted with a "dragged" effect.

YOU WILL NEED

MATERIALS

*pine slat, 8 x 45 mm/
⅓ x 1¾ in
pine slat, 8 x 70 mm/
⅓ x 2¾ in
wood glue
masking tape
sandpaper
white undercoat paint
thin card
acrylic paints: green, blue
and yellow
PVA (white) glue*

EQUIPMENT

*ruler
fretsaw
paintbrushes
pencil
craft knife
cutting mat
paint-mixing container*

1 Cut two 9 cm/3½ in lengths of each pine slat. Glue with wood glue to form the sides of the pot. Hold with masking tape until the glue is dry.

2 Sand all the rough edges. Measure the inside dimensions of the pot and cut a piece of wood to make the base. Glue it in place and allow to dry.

3 Paint with two coats of white undercoat, sanding lightly between coats. Cut a piece of thin card the same size as the broad side of the pot. Draw a leaf design and cut out with a craft knife.

4 Mix the paints to blue-green and yellow-green. Apply blue-green paint with a stiff brush to show the brush strokes. Stencil the leaf pattern in yellow-green. Finish with a coat of diluted white glue.

MEDIEVAL CORK TILES

*T*ransform ordinary unsealed cork tiles to look like medieval terracotta by using a variety of wood stains. They give just the right range of muted shades, and you can mix them together to add further subtlety. Use the template provided for all of your tiles or find other mythical beasts in heraldic books to create a variety of designs.

YOU WILL NEED

MATERIALS	EQUIPMENT
unsealed, unstained cork tiles, 30 x 30 cm/12 x 12 in	*pencil*
wood stains: pine-yellow, red and brown-mahogany	*ruler*
tracing paper	*brown crayon*
thin card or paper	*fine and medium paintbrushes*
permanent black ink	*scissors*
waterproof gold ink (optional)	*dip pen*
matt polyurethane varnish	

1 Mark the geometric pattern on a tile: use a brown crayon which will merge in with the design. Paint with the various wood stains. They spread on the cork, so don't overload the brush and start in the middle of each area, working outwards. A narrow gap between each colour looks very effective.

2 Scale up the animal template from the back of the book as required, transfer to thin card or paper and cut out. Position it in the centre of the tile and draw around it with permanent black ink, using a dip pen.

3 Use a fine brush to fill in the animal design in black. Highlight the design with gold ink, if you wish, then seal the tile with several coats of polyurethane varnish.

GILDED WALL BORDER

*T**his simple version of stencilling produces an extremely effective and eye-catching border. Buy a cheap roll of wallpaper border paper and use the wrong side, then stick the completed design in place. This gets over the problem of stencilling on to a vertical surface.*

YOU WILL NEED

MATERIALS

*tracing paper
paper glue
thin card
aerosol gloss paint
wallpaper border paper
emulsion (latex) paints:
warm-blue and white
masking tape
silver acrylic paint
rub-on gold paint*

EQUIPMENT

*pencil
craft knife
cutting mat
scissors
paintbrush
paint-mixing container
sponges*

1 Trace the template from the back of the book, enlarging if necessary. Using a few dabs of paper glue, stick the template on to the card for the stencil.

2 Cut out the stencil and remove the template.

3 Spray both sides of the stencil with gloss paint.

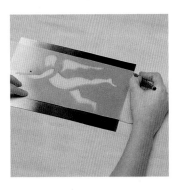

4 In order to line up the design on the border, cut a strip of tracing paper to the width of the border paper. Trace the cupid design on to it, placing it centrally. Place this tracing over the stencil, lining up the cupids. Mark the edges of the stencil at the edges of the tracing paper. Cut notches in the stencil to mark the top and bottom edges of the border. Use these to line up the stencil on the border paper.

5 Paint a background colour of warm-blue emulsion (latex) on the border paper. Place the stencil over the border, lining up the notches with the top and bottom, and fix it in place with masking tape. Dip a sponge into the silver paint and apply it sparingly over the whole stencil. Allow to dry. Repeat along the length of the border. You can use the stencil several times before it becomes clogged, then you will have to cut a new one.

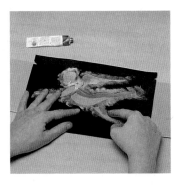

6 Use your finger to apply the gold paint to give depth to the body.

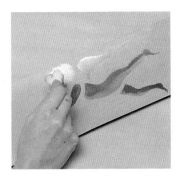

7 Remove the stencil template and sponge hair on to the cupids.

8 Apply the doves randomly between the cupids, using white emulsion (latex) paint and a second sponge.

FROSTED FLOWER VASE

*T*his is a magical way to transform a plain glass vase into something stylish and utterly original. Check the vase all over to make sure that it is evenly frosted before you peel off the leaf shapes: it may be necessary to paint on another coat of etching cream.

YOU WILL NEED

MATERIALS	EQUIPMENT
coloured glass vase	*pencil*
tracing paper	*scissors*
sticky-backed plastic	*paintbrush*
etching cream	

1 Wash and dry the vase. Trace the templates from the back of the book, enlarging if necessary. Cut them out and draw around them on to the backing of the plastic and draw small circles freehand.

2 Cut out the shapes and peel off the backing paper. Arrange the shapes all over the vase, then smooth them down carefully to avoid any wrinkles.

3 Carefully paint the etching cream all over the cleaned vase and leave it in a warm place to dry, following the manufacturer's instructions.

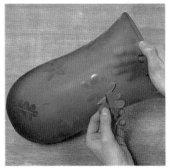

4 Wash the vase in warm water to remove the cream. If the frosting looks smooth, you can remove the shapes. If not, repeat with another coat of etching cream, then wash before removing the shapes.

STELLAR TABLECLOTH

The tablecloth used here has a scalloped edging which makes for very even stamping – just count the scallops and then decide to stamp on, say, every third one.

YOU WILL NEED

MATERIALS

*tablecloth and napkins
scrap of fabric
navy blue fabric stamping ink*

EQUIPMENT

large and small star rubber stamps

1 Plan the position of your motifs. Coat the smaller stamp with fabric ink and make a test print on to a scrap of fabric first to ensure the stamp is not overloaded.

2 Make the first print by positioning a small star in one corner.

3 Stamp a large star on either side of it and continue along the edges, alternating the size of stars.

4 Stamp one widely spaced square of small stars about 10 cm/4 in from the first row, and another square of large stars 10 cm/4 in closer to the centre. It should look like an all-over pattern with a border.

COUNTRY-STYLE SHELF

Simple in shape but conveying a universally understood message, the heart has been used in folk art for centuries. Here, the outline of a heart is drawn in four positions on a foam block, then cut out to make a stamp that resembles a four-leafed clover. The smaller heart is a traditional solid shape that fits neatly along the edges of the shelf supports.

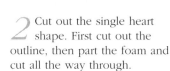

YOU WILL NEED

MATERIALS	EQUIPMENT
tracing paper	*pencil*
spray adhesive	*craft knife*
high-density foam	*plate*
country-style shelf	*paintbrush (optional)*
deep-red acrylic or	
emulsion (latex) paint	
scrap paper	

1 Trace the templates from the back of the book, enlarging if necessary. Lightly spray the shapes with adhesive and place them on the foam. Cut around the outline of the shapes with a craft knife.

2 Cut out the single heart shape. First cut out the outline, then part the foam and cut all the way through.

3 Use the foam stamp as a measuring guide to estimate the number of prints to fit along the back of the shelf. Mark the positions with a pencil. Spread some deep-red paint on to a plate.

4 Coat the clover-leaf stamp evenly and make a test print on scrap paper to ensure that it is not overloaded with paint. (You may find it easier to apply the paint to the stamp with a paintbrush.) Using the pencil guidelines, make the first print on the shelf.

5 Continue until you have completed all of the clover-leaf shapes. Try not to get the finish too even; this is a rustic piece of furniture and an uneven effect is more suitable.

6 Finish off the shelf with a row of small hearts along the support edges, then add one heart between each of the larger motifs.

FOAM-BLOCK PRINTING

*P*rinting with cut-out foam blocks must be the easiest possible way to achieve the effect of hand-painted wallpaper. A special feature of this project is the paint used – a combination of wallpaper paste, PVA (white) glue and gouache colour. This is not only cheap, but it also has a wonderful translucent quality all of its own that really does produce a unique finish.

YOU WILL NEED

MATERIALS

tracing paper
thin card
high-density foam
paper, 15 x 15 cm/6 x 6 in
wallpaper paste
PVA (white) glue
gouache paints: viridian,
deep-green and off-white
clear matt varnish
(optional)

EQUIPMENT

pencil
scissors
felt-tipped pen
craft knife
plumb-line
plate
paintbrush (optional)

1 Trace the templates on this page, enlarging if necessary. Transfer them to thin card and cut them out. Trace the design on to the foam, outlining it with a felt-tipped pen.

2 Cut out the shapes. First cut around the pattern and then part the foam slightly and carefully cut through the entire thickness.

3 Prepare the wall for decorating. Attach the plumb-line to the wall or ceiling in one corner of the room. Turn the paper square on the diagonal and let the plumb-line fall through the centre. Make pencil dots on the wall at each corner of the paper. Move the paper down the plumb-line, marking the corner points each time. Then move the plumb-line along sideways and continue marking dots until the wall is covered in a grid of dots.

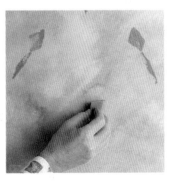

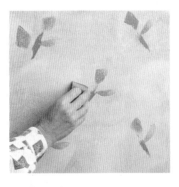

4 Mix the wallpaper paste according to the instructions. Add PVA (white) glue, in the proportion three parts paste to one part glue. Add a squeeze of viridian and deep-green paint and blend.

5 Put some paint mixture on to a plate and dip the first sponge into it. Wipe off any excess paint and then print on the wall, using a light rolling motion. Use the dots to position the stamp.

6 Use the second sponge to complete the sprig design with leaf shapes, varying the angle slightly to add life.

7 Use the dot-shaped sponge and off-white to complete the design with berries, adding the colour to the PVA (white) mixture as before. If liked, protect the wall with a coat of varnish.

CELESTIAL WRAPPING PAPER

*R*ed and gold suns grace a midnight-blue
background to create wrapping paper that will be
as special as the present you wrap in it. If you can't bear
to part with the paper when you've finished making it,
use it to cover a box such as a hatbox.

YOU WILL NEED

MATERIALS	EQUIPMENT
acrylic paints: gold and red	*2 plates*
white paper	*small paint roller*
acetate sheet	*sun-motif rubber stamp*
masking tape	*cutting mat*
plain blue wrapping paper	*craft knife*
newspaper	*stencil brush*

1 Put a little gold paint on a plate and roll the paint on to the stamp. Stamp a sun on the white paper, being careful to leave a clear impression. Put the paper on the cutting mat, place the acetate on top and secure with masking tape. Cut out the sun outline when dry with a craft knife. Place the stencil on the wrapping paper and secure with masking tape.

2 Put some red paint on another plate and dip in the stencil brush, dabbing off any excess on newspaper. Stipple the paint on the wrapping paper through the stencil. Repeat, moving the acetate and re-securing it, until the whole paper is covered in an orderly and spacious pattern of suns.

3 Put some more gold paint on the plate and roll the paint on to the stamp. Stamp the design on top of the red suns, as closely as possible to the original outline, to give a three-dimensional effect.

FLOWER-STENCILLED WRAP

If you have taken trouble to find a really special gift, home-made wrapping paper is the perfect finishing touch. Once the stencil is cut, this design doesn't take long to do and its effect is truly magnificent.

YOU WILL NEED

MATERIALS
tracing paper
acetate sheet
green crepe paper
acrylic or stencil paints:
raw umber, white and
yellow

EQUIPMENT
pencil
indelible black magic
marker
craft knife
cutting mat
paint-mixing container
stencil brush

1 Trace the template from the back of the book, enlarging if necessary, and transfer to the acetate sheet. The design is made from two pieces: the petals and the centre. Cut each part out separately.

2 Using the flower centre stencil, apply raw umber paint to the crepe paper. Position the stencil at random, covering the paper; be sure to allow enough room between the centres for the petals.

3 Lighten the raw umber with white paint, and apply as a highlight.

4 Take the second stencil and, taking care to align it properly over the first, stencil the petals in yellow.

SPRIGGED CALICO CURTAINS

*N*atural calico has a lovely creamy colour, especially when the sun shines through it. A stamped floral sprig adds a delicate decorative touch.

YOU WILL NEED

MATERIALS	EQUIPMENT
calico fabric	*linocut stamp*
fabric stamping inks: green	*craft knife*
and dark blue	*cutting mat*
paper	*ruler*
card	*pencil*
scrap of fabric	

1 Lay the fabric out on a flat surface. Make several prints of the stamp on scrap paper and cut them out. Plan the design on the fabric.

2 Decide on the distance you want between sprigs and cut out a square of card to act as a measuring guide. Use it diagonally, marking with a pencil at each corner all over the fabric.

3 Put green ink on the edges of the linocut and fill the centre with dark blue. Make an initial print on a scrap of fabric to determine the density of the stamped image.

4 Stamp the floral sprig on to the calico, using the pencil marks to position the base of the stamp. You need to apply gentle pressure to the back of the stamp and allow a couple of seconds for the ink to transfer.

ART NOUVEAU ROSE BOX

*I*nspired by the motifs of early 20th-century art nouveau, this design for a simple wooden box combines sinuous lines, swirling leaf shapes and stained-glass-style roses to dramatic effect.

YOU WILL NEED

MATERIALS

*fine-grade sandpaper
oval wooden craft box,
with lid
white primer paint
tracing paper
acrylic paints: rose-pink,
green, yellow, white, black
and blue
clear acrylic or
crackle varnish*

EQUIPMENT

*thick bristle and fine hair
paintbrushes
hard and soft pencils
paint-mixing container*

1 Sand the box and lid and give them three layers of primer. Trace the template from the back of the book, enlarging if necessary, to fit the lid of the box. Transfer it to the lid, with a soft pencil and tracing paper.

2 Paint the rose petals and the leaves as solid blocks of colour.

3 Paint the stems and thorn ring; add shade and tone to the flowers. Paint the veins on the leaves. Paint a black outline around the rose petals.

4 Colour-wash the outside rim of the lid with watered-down rose paint. Paint the box blue in the same way. Seal the surface with a coat of varnish (crackle varnish will give an antique effect).

PICTURE FRAME

*T*his project combines all the creative possibilities of stamping. It involves four processes: painting a background, stamping in one colour, over-printing in a second colour and rubbing back to the wood.

YOU WILL NEED

MATERIALS	EQUIPMENT
picture frame	*paintbrush*
emulsion (latex) paints:	*plate*
sky-blue, red-brown and	*foam roller*
gold	*small and large star stamps*
	fine wire wool or sandpaper

1 Paint the frame sky-blue and leave it to dry.

2 Spread a small amount of red-brown paint on to a plate and run the roller through it until it is evenly coated. Ink the first stamp and print it in the middle of each side.

3 Using the red-brown paint, stamp a large star over each corner. Allow to dry.

4 Ink the large stamp with gold and over-print the red-brown corner stars. Allow to dry before rubbing the frame gently with fine wire wool or sandpaper. Experiment with dropped shadow effects and some other designs as well.

PRIMITIVE FRAMES

*S*imple *wooden frames can be transformed into a richly patterned, colour-matched set with acrylic paint and pre-cut rubber stamps. The three frames used here are all different, but they have enough in common to be treated as a group.*

YOU WILL NEED

MATERIALS

*3 wooden frames
acrylic paints: sienna, sea-
blue, stone and
maize-yellow
clear matt varnish
(optional)*

EQUIPMENT

*fine-grade sandpaper
paintbrushes
3 plates
3 rubber stamps*

1 Follow the same procedure for all frames, using different colours and rubber stamps. Sand down and paint each frame. Allow to dry, then apply a second coat for a really solid covering of colour.

2 Mix some sienna paint into the sea-blue to produce an olive-green colour. Spread an even coating of the other colours on to separate plates.

3 Dip a stamp into the paint to make a test print on scrap paper to ensure that the stamp is not overloaded. Print closely-spaced motifs on to the background colour.

4 Stamp the design over every visible surface, going over the edges and around the sides. When the paint is dry, give each frame a coat of clear matt varnish, if you like.

GILDED LAMP

A silver gilded lamp base and a golden shade form a light source that will be a glowing focal point in any room. When lit, the gilded lamp seems to shimmer; the effect in a dark corner is magical.

YOU WILL NEED

MATERIALS

turned-wood lamp base
red oxide primer
3-hour oil size
aluminium leaf
white card
parchment coolie shade,
45 cm/18 in
PVA (white) glue
Dutch gold leaf transfer
book
black watercolour paint
methylated spirits-based
varnish

EQUIPMENT

paintbrushes
large stencil brush
craft knife
cutting mat
pencil
cotton wool

1 Prime the lamp base with red oxide and allow to dry. Paint the lamp base with size and allow to dry for three hours. When the size is "squeaky", it is ready for gilding. Lay the aluminium leaf on the base and rub with a stencil brush so it adheres to the base. Repeat until the lamp base is covered.

2 Draw the sunflower motif freehand on to white card. Carefully cut out a stencil from the card with the craft knife. Trace the outline on to the base, through the stencil, with a sharp pencil.

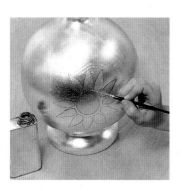

3 Paint the size on to the stencilled sunflower shapes and leave it to dry for three hours, until "squeaky".

4 Meanwhile, paint a small area of the lampshade with slightly diluted PVA (white) glue. Straight away, lay a sheet of Dutch gold on top and rub with the stencil brush, so it adheres. Quickly brush off any excess, so the effect is slightly patchy.

5 Repeat with another small area, applying Dutch gold as before.

6 Continue until the shade is covered. Seal the shade with another coat of diluted PVA (white) glue.

7 When the size on the base is "squeaky", cover the design with a sheet of Dutch gold and rub gently with the stencil brush, so that the gold adheres to the size. Brush off any excess.

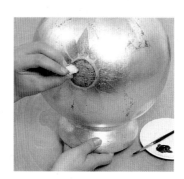

8 Put a little watercolour paint on a piece of cotton wool and rub it into the centre of the sunflower, to give a mottled or stippled effect. Finally, give the whole base a coat of varnish.

BUTTERFLY GIFT WRAP

*O*riginal, handprinted wrapping paper can make any present seem extra special.

YOU WILL NEED

MATERIALS

tracing paper
acetate sheet
coloured paper
masking tape
acrylic paints: red and black

EQUIPMENT

pencil
indelible black magic marker
craft knife
cutting mat
stiff brush

1 Trace the template from the back of the book, enlarging if necessary. Place a piece of acetate over it and use a magic marker to draw the wings for the first stencil. Use a second piece of acetate to make a second stencil of the body and the wing markings.

2 Cut out both stencils. Secure the first stencil lightly to the paper with masking tape and stipple on the red paint. Do not overload the brush. Reposition the acetate and repeat to cover the paper.

3 When the red paint is dry, secure the second stencil in place with masking tape. Stipple on the black paint and repeat the process to complete the butterflies.

TAURUS GIFT WRAP

*P*ersonalize a gift by creating some of this original gift wrap that is stencilled with the appropriate star-sign. Strong dark red and black have been used here to match the energetic, earthy character of the Taurean. Don't overfill the brush when stencilling: blot any excess paint on paper towels before you begin. If paint does seep under the edges of the stencil, wipe it away carefully before repositioning the acetate.

YOU WILL NEED

MATERIALS
thin card or paper
acetate sheet
plain deep red gift wrap
masking tape
black acrylic paint

EQUIPMENT
pencil
black magic marker
craft knife
cutting mat
stencil brush
paper towels

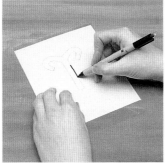

1 Draw a template following the finished picture above on card or paper. Place the acetate over the template and trace the outline with a magic marker.

2 Carefully cut out the stencil using a craft knife.

3 Decide on the positioning of the motifs on the paper, marking lightly with a pencil if necessary. Position the stencil and use a little masking tape to hold it in place. Stipple the design with the stencil brush. Lift the stencil off carefully and repeat to cover the paper.

STENCILLED CHAIR

*I*t is usually easy to find an old chair at a reasonable price, and with a stencil pattern like the one used here, it can soon be transformed into a charming piece of furniture fit for any room in the house.

YOU WILL NEED

MATERIALS	EQUIPMENT
chair	paintbrush
matt emulsion (latex)	paint-mixing container
paints: pumpkin-yellow,	cloth
white and brick-pink	pencil
(optional)	stencil brush
tracing paper	pale-coloured chalky pencil
stencil card	long-haired artist's brush
spray adhesive	fine-grade steel wool
various artist's acrylic or	
stencil paints	
paper	
clear water-based varnish	
small tubes of raw umber	
and raw sienna artist's	
acrylic paint	

1 If your chair is bare wood, apply a coat of light pumpkin-yellow (add a touch of white to lighten it); if you are covering old paint, first apply a coat of brick-pink paint as a base for the chair.

2 Thin the pumpkin-yellow with equal parts water and apply to the chair. Use a damp cloth to wipe some of it off. It will remain in the grain to emphasize the mouldings. Trace the template from the back of the book, enlarging if necessary, and transfer to stencil card.

3 Spray the back of the stencil lightly with adhesive and position it centrally on the chair back. Apply the colours sparingly, rubbing the paint through the stencil with circular strokes.

4 Use a chalky pencil to draw radiating guidelines in the centre of the lower chair back. Practise the strokes on paper, using a long-haired brush. Starting with the tip of the brush in the centre, draw it towards you, pressing down in the middle of the stroke to make a teardrop shape. Support your hand with your ring finger on the brush hand.

5 Line the chair with thick and thin stripes. Add water until the paint flows easily off your brush.

6 When drawing lines, try to complete the whole line with a single brushstroke. Begin with the shortest and least conspicuous lines, progressing to the more obvious ones as your skill grows. Add rings of colour to highlight any turned features in the chair.

7 Rub back the paint with steel wool to simulate wear and tear. Don't overdo it and just concentrate your efforts on the edges. Tint the clear varnish with a small amount of raw umber and raw sienna and apply two coats, leaving to dry between coats. Apply one final layer of tinted varnish.

STENCILLED ROLLER BLIND

Stylized, almost abstract oranges and lemons on this stencilled blind give it a fifties feel. It would look great in a kitchen decorated with strong, fresh vibrant colours.

YOU WILL NEED

MATERIALS	EQUIPMENT
tracing paper	*pencil*
stencil card	*craft knife*
plain white cotton fabric, to	*cutting mat*
fit window	*scissors*
masking tape	*stencil brush*
acrylic gouache paints:	*large paintbrush*
orange, yellow, lime-green,	*paper towels*
black and red	
roller blind fabric stiffener	
roller blind kit	

1 Trace the template from the back of the book, enlarging it so that the repeat design will fit across the width of your blind, and trace it. Transfer it three times to stencil card. Using a craft knife, cut out only the areas you will need for each stencil: 1) the lemons, oranges and red spots; 2) the leaves; 3) the black details.

2 Lay out the white fabric on a smooth flat surface and secure with masking tape. Using gouache paints, stencil the oranges and lemons motif all over the fabric. Keep the stencil brush as dry as possible, blotting off any excess paint on paper towels and cleaning the stencil if paint starts to bleed under the edges.

3 Leave the orange and lemon motifs to dry, then proceed with the remaining colours. Paint the leaves next, then the red spots (using the first stencil) and finally the black details. When dry, paint the fabric with fabric stiffener following the manufacturer's instructions. Hang the fabric on a washing line to dry, keeping it very straight. Make up the blind using the blind kit.

IVY STOOL

*T**his very delicately painted little seat would look charming in the leafy surrounds of a garden room.***

YOU WILL NEED

MATERIALS

*wooden stool
white emulsion (latex) paint
tracing paper
acetate sheet
masking tape
acrylic paints: sap-green
and white
clear gloss acrylic varnish*

EQUIPMENT

*sandpaper
paintbrushes
pencil
permanent magic marker
craft knife
cutting mat
stencil brush
paint-mixing container*

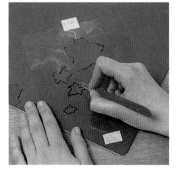

1 Sand the stool and paint it with two or three coats of white emulsion (latex) paint. Trace the templates from the back of the book, enlarging if necessary. Tape the acetate over the design and draw the outlines of the leaves with a magic marker.

2 Cut out the stencil carefully using a craft knife.

3 Using sap-green acrylic paint mixed with a little white, stencil the leaves all over the stool. Allow to dry.

4 Using sap-green acrylic paint and a fine brush, paint the tendrils, outlines and veining on the leaves. Finally, protect the stool with two or three coats of gloss varnish.

TOY BOX

This project gives instant appeal to the most ordinary of wooden boxes. It works just as well on old as new woods, but if you are using an old box, give it a good rub down with sandpaper first.

YOU WILL NEED

MATERIALS

hinged wooden box or chest, with lid
rust-red emulsion (latex) paint
emulsion (latex) or acrylic paints: maroon, sap-green, bright green and dark blue
small, large and trellis heart stamps
matt varnish

EQUIPMENT

paintbrushes
plate
foam roller
fine-grade sandpaper

1 Paint the box with rust-red paint, applying two coats to give a good matt background. Allow to dry between coats.

2 Spread some maroon paint on a plate and run the roller through it until it is evenly coated. Use the roller to apply a border around the edge of the lid and allow to dry.

3 Spread some sap-green paint on to the plate and coat the roller. Ink the small stamp and print a few hearts randomly over the lid.

4 Ink the large and trellis stamps with sap-green paint. Print some hearts close together and others on their own to create a random pattern. Cover the whole lid in this way.

5 Clean all three stamps and ink with the bright green paint. Build up the pattern by adding this colour in the gaps, leaving enough space for the last two colours.

6 Using the dark blue paint, continue stamping the three hearts over the lid.

7 Fill in the remaining background space with maroon paint and the three heart stamps. No large spaces should remain. Allow to dry.

8 Use sandpaper to rub down the lid where you think natural wear and tear would occur.

9 You can preserve the comfortable "weathered" look of the toy box by applying two coats of varnish.

STENCILLED TABLECLOTH

*T*wo stencils are arranged here to decorate a square tablecloth; the same motifs could be used in many different combinations and scales. Use two or three shades with each stencil shape to achieve a rounded, three-dimensional look on the roses and branches.

YOU WILL NEED

MATERIALS

tracing paper
stencil card
heavy white cotton fabric,
76 x 76 cm/30 x 30 in
stencil paints: dark and
pale pink, yellow, dark and
light green and warm
brown
white sewing thread

EQUIPMENT

pencil
craft knife
cutting mat
iron
spray adhesive
3 stencil brushes
vanishing fabric marker
long ruler
set square
needle

1 Trace the rose template from the back of the book, enlarging to 15 cm/6 in across. Enlarge the branch template so it is 30 cm/12 in long. Transfer both to stencil card and cut out the stencils.

2 Fold the fabric in half each way to find the centre. Press lightly along the creases. Spray the back of the rose stencil lightly with adhesive and place it in the middle of the cloth. Paint dark pink in the corner petals and around the outer edge of the inner petals.

3 Fill in the rest of the petals with pale pink and colour the centre dots yellow. Keep the brush upright and use a small circling motion to transfer the paint. Be careful not to overload the bristles. Peel off the stencil and allow the paint to dry.

4 Work a branch motif on each side of the rose, using the crease as a placement guide, to form a cross. Spray the back of the card with adhesive, as before. Stencil yellow paint in the centre of each leaf.

5 Blend dark and light green paints and finish painting the leaves.

6 Work a small amount of brown around the base of the leaves and the outside edge of the branches. Stencil a rose at the end of each branch. With a fabric marker, and using the ruler and set square to get a perfectly accurate square, draw a line about 15 cm/6 in from each edge, so that it is on the same level as the outer edge of the roses. Stencil a rose in each corner and then work a branch between the roses.

7 When the paint is dry, fix it according to the manufacturer's instructions. Turn under, press and stitch a narrow double hem along the outside edge.

CUPID WRAPPING PAPER

This wrapping paper design, with its dropped-shadow image, can be achieved by stencilling or stamping. Home-made wrapping paper would be the perfect finishing touch for a Valentine's Day present or even for a Christmas present; choose colours to suit the occasion.

YOU WILL NEED

MATERIALS

cupid motif
acetate sheet
plain wrapping paper
acrylic paints: red oxide and gold

EQUIPMENT

black magic marker
craft knife
cutting mat
stencil brush
tile
paint roller
cupid rubber stamp

1 If you are using the stencil method, place a cupid motif (or a freehand sketch) under a sheet of acetate. Draw the image on the acetate with a magic marker. Cut it out with the craft knife to create the stencil.

2 Stencil the cupid on to the wrapping paper, using red oxide paint and a stencil brush. Allow to dry. Using gold paint, stencil the cupid slightly off-centre, to give a dropped-shadow effect.

3 If you are using the rubber stamp method, put some red oxide paint on to the tile and use the roller to coat the stamp. Stamp the images, then over-print using the stamp and the gold paint as before.

GLORIOUS GIFT WRAP

If you want to make a gift extra special, why not print your own wrapping paper, designed to suit the person to whom you are giving the present? Home-made gift wrap shows that you wanted to make your gift memorable.

YOU WILL NEED

MATERIALS

plain paper

EQUIPMENT

rubber stamps in a variety of motifs
stamp pads

1 To make a non-regimented design, first stamp on one edge of the paper. Then rotate the stamp in your hand to change the direction of each print. Re-charge the stamp with ink as required.

2 Turn the paper and continue stamping the shapes. The end result should have roughly an even amount of background pattern.

3 To achieve a more formal pattern, begin by stamping a row of shapes along the bottom edge.

4 Build up the design, alternating between two colours if you like, to make an all-over pattern of closely spaced shapes.

OAK LEAF BOX

*T*his *dressing table box uses a charming oak leaf motif for its decoration. The design is completed with hand-painted brushstrokes.*

YOU WILL NEED

MATERIALS	EQUIPMENT
round wooden box, with lid	*paintbrush*
emulsion (latex) paints:	*plates*
deep blue-green, deep red	*foam rollers*
and dusky-pink	*square-tipped artist's brush*
leaf stamp	*fine lining brush*
clear satin varnish	

1 Paint the box and lid in deep blue-green and allow to dry. Spread some deep red paint on a plate and run the roller through it until it is evenly coated. Ink the leaf stamp and stamp evenly spaced leaf motifs around the sides of the box.

2 Stamp two leaves in the centre of the box lid, side by side and facing in opposite directions. Use the square-tipped brush to paint a border around the top edge of the lid. Paint the sides of the lid in the same colour.

3 Using a fine lining brush and dusky-pink, paint veins on the leaves and a fine line around the inside edge of the red border.

4 When the paint is completely dry, seal the box with a coat of satin varnish.

DRAGONFLY PRINT BOX

*T*he *background of this bold dragonfly print has been roughly cut to give it the look of a primitive woodcut. If you haven't tried lino-cutting before, practise on a scrap. Make sure the tools are very sharp and always keep your free hand out of the way of the cutting edge. Don't dig too deep.*

YOU WILL NEED

MATERIALS

tracing paper
thick yellow paper
water-based block printing paints: red, green and black
lino tile
PVA (white) glue
wooden box
clear varnish

EQUIPMENT

pencil
paintbrushes
lino cutters
craft knife
cutting mat
glass sheet
lino roller

1 Trace the template from the back of the book, enlarging if necessary. Transfer to yellow paper and paint in red and green. Trace the completed dragonfly motifs, turn the tracing over and transfer to the lino, giving a reverse image.

2 Cut out the design on the lino, cutting a criss-cross pattern freehand on the wings to give a lacy effect. Cut out the background roughly, leaving some areas untouched to give texture to the design. Trim the lino round the design to make positioning easier.

3 Spread the black paint on the glass sheet with the roller and roll it evenly on to the lino cut. Position the lino cut carefully on the paper and apply even pressure to make the print. Leave the print to dry, then glue it to the top of the box. Seal and protect it with a coat of varnish.

PEG BAG

*T*his peg bag is made from practical unbleached calico. The sunflowers are worked in dry stencil fabric paint. Once they are fixed, the stencils will be hand-washable.

YOU WILL NEED

MATERIALS	EQUIPMENT
tracing paper	*soft and hard pencils*
stencil card	*craft knife*
unbleached calico,	*cutting mat*
50 x 75 cm/20 x 30 in	*dressmaker's scissors*
child's wooden coat hanger,	*dressmaker's pins*
30 cm/12 in	*vanishing fabric marker*
dry stencil fabric paints:	*2 stencil brushes*
yellow and brown	*iron*
matching machine	*sewing machine*
embroidery thread	*needle*
yellow ribbon, 1 m/1 yd	

1 Trace the template from the back of the book, enlarging if necessary. Transfer the outline to stencil card and cut out. From the unbleached calico, cut two 36 cm/14 in squares.

2 Pin the squares together, place the hanger along one edge and draw round it with the marker. Cut this curve. Stencil a sunflower in each corner of one piece of fabric. Allow the paint to dry and fix it, according to the manufacturer's instructions.

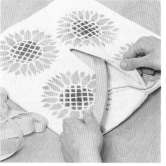

3 Cut a 10 x 25 cm/4 x 10 in piece of calico facing for the front opening. Tack (baste) the facing on to the centre top of the stencilled fabric. Sew two 20 cm/8 in lines of straight stitch, 5 mm/¼ in away from both sides of the centre. Cut in between these lines, and turn the facing to the wrong side. Press and top stitch around the opening. With right sides together, stitch the back to the front. Turn right sides out, fit the coat hanger in place and finish off with a yellow bow.

ROMANTIC GIFT WRAP

*W*hat better way to present the perfect Valentine's Day gift than wrapped in this hand-stencilled paper with bold hearts? This is an easy stencil to cut out and use. Your finishing touch won't take you long to complete, and you are sure to end up with a really professional result.

1 Trace the template from the back of the book, enlarging if necessary, and transfer to acetate sheet. Carefully cut out the design.

2 Stencil burnt umber hearts randomly across the paper. Allow to dry.

3 Stencil gold hearts on top and slightly to the right. The finished effect should be that the umber hearts look like the shadows of the gold hearts.

YOU WILL NEED

MATERIALS

tracing paper
acetate sheet
crepe paper
acrylic paints: burnt umber and gold

EQUIPMENT

pencil
indelible black magic marker
craft knife
cutting mat
stencil brush
paint-mixing container

PRIVATE CORRESPONDENCE

*T*his personalized stationery makes a statement before you even put pen to paper. Although there are many ways of making stationery using pre-cut rubber stamps, this project goes one step further and shows you how to make your own rubber stamp from an eraser. Choose images that express something about your character.

YOU WILL NEED

MATERIALS
drawings of chosen motif
plain paper
new eraser
liquid lighter fuel
embossing ink and powder
(optional)

EQUIPMENT
craft knife
cutting mat
lino-cutting tool
stamp pad

1 Cut out and arrange your motifs on a piece of paper so they will fit on to the eraser.

2 Photocopy the motif arrangement and cut out the shape to fit the eraser.

3 Place this squarely on the eraser, with the drawing face down.

4 Spread about three drops of liquid lighter fuel over the back of the paper. Make sure that the paper does not slide across the eraser as you do this.

5 Remove the paper to reveal the transferred design. This will be reversed, but the stamping process will reverse it again, bringing it back to the original image.

6 Use a fine lino-cutting tool and a craft knife to cut around the outline and the pattern details. Scoop out any excess to leave the design standing proud of the eraser – look at a pre-cut rubber stamp to judge the depth of the cut-away pieces.

7 Press the eraser stamp into a coloured stamp pad and print your stationery. For a raised image, stamp the motif with some embossing ink and then sprinkle with embossing powder.

ROSE-STAMPED STATIONERY

*H*and-printed stationery sends its own message, even before you have added your greetings or invitation. This golden rose would be particularly suitable for wedding stationery, making a welcome change from the usual mass-produced cards.

YOU WILL NEED

MATERIALS	EQUIPMENT
tracing paper	*pencil*
lino square	*lino-cutting tools*
gold paint	*cutting mat*
blank stationery, such as	*small paint roller*
deckle-edged notepaper	*paper towels*
and envelopes	*fine paintbrush*
stationery box	
Japanese paper, cut into strips	
glue stick	
ribbon	

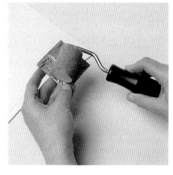

1 Trace the template from the back of the book, enlarging if necessary, and transfer to lino. Using a narrow-grooved tool, cut out the motif, keeping your free hand behind the blade at all times. With a wide tool, cut away the excess lino. Indicate with an arrow which edge is the top, on the back.

2 Ink the lino stamp with gold paint and stamp the stationery, re-inking the roller each time. Wipe away any build-up of paint with paper towels.

3 Edge the envelopes, cards and the top edge of the notepaper with a fine line of gold paint. Glue the box with strips of Japanese paper. Arrange the notepaper and cards in the box. Bind the envelopes with more Japanese paper and ribbon and add them to the box. Decorate the box lid with ribbon.

VALENTINE'S CARD

*H*and-made cards really do convey your feelings. This special card captures the spirit of some elaborate Victorian Valentine's cards, with its combination of gold and silver lace, soft, velvety pink background and central cupid motif.

YOU WILL NEED

MATERIALS
paper glue
dark pink paper,
15 x 15 cm/6 x 6 in
gold card,
20 x 20 cm/8 x 8 in
decorative gold cake band
silver, white and gold
paper doilies
lilac and dark green
paper scraps
Victorian-style cupid motif

EQUIPMENT
scissors

1 Glue the pink paper to the gold card, leaving an equal margin all around. Trim the edges with narrow strips of gold foil lace, cut from the cake band. Cut out a small silver flower for each corner from the silver doilies.

2 Cut out four white petals and two flower shapes from a white doily and back them with lilac paper. Choose a larger rectangular shape for the centre and back it with dark green paper. Stick the backed shapes on to the background.

3 Cut out silver flowers and white leaves and glue them around the edges of the main shape, in an interesting pattern.

4 Finish by fixing the cupid to the centre and adding more cut-out gold flowers.

STARPRINT WRAPPING PAPER

*C*omplete *an original gift by dressing it up in original, hand-decorated wrapping paper. It's not only pretty, but fun to print. This star pattern printed in festive colours makes great Christmas wrapping.*

YOU WILL NEED

MATERIALS	EQUIPMENT
thin card	*pair of compasses*
plain wrapping paper	*pencil*
water-based block printing	*scissors*
paints: red, green and	*white chalk*
white	*star-motif rubber stamp*
water-based gold paint	*paintbrush*

1 Cut a circular template out of card and draw around it in chalk on the wrapping paper, spacing the circles evenly on the sheet.

2 Print alternate circles with red and green stars, brushing the paint evenly on the stamp between each print.

3 Print white stars in the middle of each circle, between the circles and in each of the corners.

4 Following the chalk circle between the stars, make rings of gold dots and dot the point of each star with gold.

SEAWEED GIFT WRAP

*S*wirling seaweed shapes in watery shades of green *and blue on a blue-green background produce an underwater effect that makes a really unusual wrapping paper. Vary the colours of the paints depending on the colour of the background paper you choose.*

YOU WILL NEED

MATERIALS
tracing paper
acetate sheet
blue-green wrapping paper
acrylic paints: sap-green,
white and blue

EQUIPMENT
pencil
fine black magic marker
craft knife
cutting mat
paint-mixing container
stencil brushes

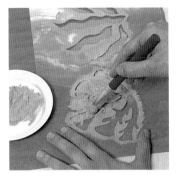

1 Trace the template from the back of the book, enlarging if necessary. Go over the outline with the magic marker. Lay the acetate on top and carefully cut the stencil.

2 Position the stencil on the wrapping paper. Mix sap-green paint with a little white. Stencil motifs A and B side by side in rows across the paper, leaving space for a row of motif C between.

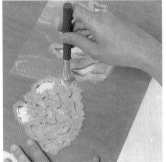

3 With white, add highlights to the seaweed tips.

4 Mix blue paint with white and stencil C in rows, leaving a stencil space in between for lighter coloured seaweed shapes.

EMBROIDERY

*E*mbroidering detail on to fabric – whether by hand or by machine – is a beautiful method of decoration, and it can be applied to a wide range of materials and objects, including clothes, linens and pictures. The wealth of threads available today means that your embroidery can be bright and vivid or muted and subtle – whatever mood you wish to evoke, there will be a thread available for you. The range of fabrics in varying colours, textures and strengths is quite astounding, and you can choose to work on a small square of fabric to create a purse, or enhance a baby's outfit with fine stitching.

Whatever project you choose to embark on, you will soon find that your embroidery skills increase with practice and experimentation. So, gather needle and thread together and enjoy one of the most rewarding of decorative crafts.

MATERIALS AND EQUIPMENT

Most of the materials used for embroidery can be purchased from craft suppliers or department stores. The range of fabrics available is immense, so consider how the texture will affect your finished piece when making your fabric choice. Cotton and silk are easy to handle, and felt, plastic and leather produce interesting results. Some key materials and pieces of equipment to help you with your embroidery are given below.

Bobbins are useful to have in a fair quantity so that you don't have to unwind and rewind them with each different thread colour.

Buttons and beads come in a range of shapes and sizes and a variety of materials, such as plastic, glass, wood and bone.

Dressmaker's carbon is used to transfer designs to fabric.

Embroidery hoops A wooden hand embroidery hoop can also be used for machine embroidery if the inner ring is wrapped with strips of cotton to improve tautness.

Specialized **machine embroidery hoops** with spring closures are more convenient.

Fabric glue can be used instead of fusible bonding web.

Fabric paints are water-based non-toxic paints that are fixed by ironing.

Feet For most machine embroidery, a foot should be used, although a presser foot will give a cleaner satin stitch.

You can work without a foot, but the thread will tend to snap more often.

Fusible bonding web is used to bond appliqué fabrics to the ground fabric temporarily during stitching. Templates can be marked out on the paper backing.

Hand embroidery threads are available in skeins and can be couched or stitched to enhance machine embroidery.

Machine embroidery threads are available in every imaginable colour and in different strengths. They are more lustrous than sewing threads.

Metallic embroidery threads are very popular and are available in many colours as well as shades of gold, silver and bronze. Be careful when stitching at high speeds, as occasionally the thread will snap.

Scissors Use dressmaker's scissors for cutting fabrics and embroidery scissors for cutting threads and trimming.

Sewing machine The machine should have a free arm and a detachable bed for ease of movement. Take care of the machine and oil and clean it regularly to prevent stitch problems.

ABOVE *Equipment required for embroidery – whether by hand or by machine – can be easily obtained from crafts suppliers. Each embroidery project in this section tells you exactly what you will need for best results.*

Stabilizers should be used to prevent the fabric from puckering and distortion. Water-soluble polythene will stabilize open-work and sheer fabrics, and is easily dissolved in cold water.

Vanishing fabric markers are available in pink and purple and will fade with exposure to air or water.

WORKING WITH DIFFERENT STITCHES

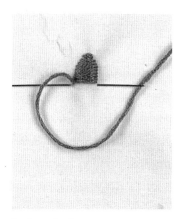

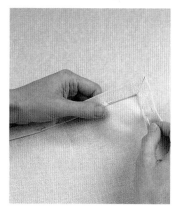

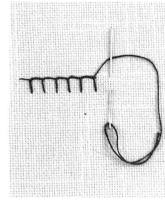

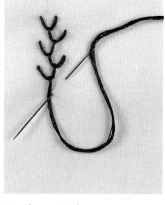

Satin stitch

Satin stitch is used for filling in and outlining. Ensure the fabric is held tautly in a frame to prevent puckering. Carry the thread across the area to be filled, then return it back underneath the fabric as near as possible to the point from which the needle emerged.

Slip stitch

Slip stitch is used to join together two folded edges, and for flat-hemming a turned-in edge. It should be nearly invisible. Pick up two threads of the single fabric and slip the needle through the fold for about 5 mm/1/4 in. Draw the thread through to make a tiny stitch.

Blanket stitch

Blanket stitch can be used for finishing hems and, when the stitches are worked closely together, for buttonholes. It is used decoratively for scalloped edging. Working from left to right, bring the needle down vertically and loop the thread under its tip before pulling it through.

Feather stitch

Feather stitch is a looped stitch, traditionally used for smocking and decorating crazy patchwork. It can be worked in straight or curved lines. Bring the thread through the fabric and make slanting stitches, working alternately to the right and left of the line to be covered.

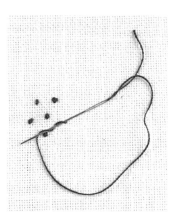

French knot

French knots are used sparingly as accents, or worked more closely together to produce a texture. The stitch should be worked with the fabric in a frame, leaving both hands free. Bring the thread through and hold down. Twist the thread around the needle a few times and tighten. Holding the thread taut, insert the needle back into the fabric with the other hand, at the point from which it emerged. Pull the needle through the thread twists to form the knot.

Tacking

This is a temporary stitch, used to hold seams together before sewing by machine. The stitches should be between 0.5–1 cm/1/4–3/8 in long and evenly spaced. Use a contrasting thread to make the stitching easy to unpick.

RIGHT *For machine embroidery projects, keep a number of bobbins ready-wound with threads of different colours.*

EMBROIDERED ORGANZA SCARF

*U*se muted, autumnal colours for this delicate, sheer scarf. The painted and embroidered leaves create an almost abstract pattern.

YOU WILL NEED

MATERIALS	EQUIPMENT
laundered silk organza	*embroidery hoop*
or chiffon	*fine paintbrush*
fabric paints: green	*paint-mixing container*
and blue	*iron*
machine embroidery	*sewing machine, with*
threads: orange and red	*darning foot*
matching sewing thread	*dressmaker's scissors*
	needle

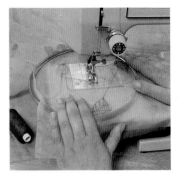

1 Stretch the fabric taut in an embroidery hoop. Paint the leaf shapes freehand in greens and blues, mixing the paints to achieve subtle shades. Allow to dry. Iron the silk to fix the paint, according to the manufacturer's instructions.

2 Select the darning or free stitch mode on the sewing machine and attach a darning foot. With the fabric in an embroidery hoop, stitch the details on the design in orange and red thread over the painted leaves.

3 Trim and roll the raw edges of the scarf and slip stitch the hems in place.

EMBROIDERED INSECT DISPLAY

This pretty design is inspired by old Victorian display cases containing rows of beetles and bugs. It's ecologically sound, however, because these stylish black bugs are embroidered on calico.

YOU WILL NEED

MATERIALS
thick tracing paper
natural calico,
30 x 30 cm/12 x 12 in
embroidery threads: black,
ochre, emerald and yellow
thick card, 20 x 20 cm/
8 x 8 in
strong button thread
3 small labels
wooden frame, to fit
20 x 20 cm/8 x 8 in

EQUIPMENT
transfer pencil
iron
embroidery hoop
embroidery needle
large needle
pen

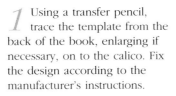

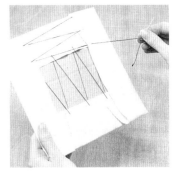

1 Using a transfer pencil, trace the template from the back of the book, enlarging if necessary, on to the calico. Fix the design according to the manufacturer's instructions.

2 Stretch the calico in an embroidery hoop and work over the design outlines using two strands of black embroidery thread in simple straight and satin stitches. Work legs and antennae in small chain stitch and pick out a few details in colour. Iron lightly from the wrong side.

3 To mount the embroidery, place the card centrally on the back of the work and fold two opposite sides over it. Lace together with strong thread, then repeat with the other two sides. Write labels for the three orders of insects: Hymenoptera (bees and wasps), Lepidoptera (butterflies) and Coleoptera (beetles). Fix these to the fabric and insert it in the frame.

LEMON SLICE NAPKINS

These lovely yellow napkins embroidered with cool lemon slices would look delightful on a table set for a summer lunch in the garden.

YOU WILL NEED

MATERIALS

*tracing paper
large yellow napkin
embroidery threads: dark
and pale yellow, off-white
and dark green*

EQUIPMENT

*soft and hard pencils
dressmaker's pins
embroidery needle
iron*

1 Trace the template at the back of the book, enlarging if necessary. Rub over the lemon motif on the reverse of the tracing with a soft pencil. Pin the tracing in the corner of the napkin and transfer the motif on to it.

2 Using dark yellow thread, work French knots in the centre of the lemon. Fill the segments in stem stitch using pale yellow. Fill the pith in stem stitch using off-white, and fill the skin area with dark yellow French knots.

3 Work dark green blanket stitch around the hem of the napkin. The stitches can be worked over the existing machine stitching. Work a row of dark yellow stem stitch around the edge of the lemon pith and another row outside that in green. Work a dark green running stitch around the edge of the French knots and add some small dark green stitches as shading in the segments to complete the design. Iron the embroidery on the reverse side.

FLEUR-DE-LYS SHOE BAG

Rich purple velvet and opulent gold braid suit the regal motif on this luxurious bag for your best party shoes. The appliquéd braid technique could easily be adapted to other items such as cushions and throws.

YOU WILL NEED

MATERIALS	EQUIPMENT
cotton velvet fabric, 53 x 38 cm/21 x 15 in	dressmaker's scissors
tracing paper	dressmaker's pins
thin card or paper	pencil
gold embroidery thread	needle
gold braid	sewing machine
matching sewing thread	safety pin
black satin ribbon, 4 cm/1½ in wide	
elastic, 1 cm/½ in wide	

1 Cut the velvet in half across the width and mark the centre of one piece with a pin. Trace the template from the back of the book on to thin card and pin it to the centre of the velvet towards the lower edge. Use gold thread to sew on the gold braid, pinning it around the template as you stitch. Work in a continuous pattern around the outline. Add the swirls.

2 Machine stitch the sides and hem, leaving a seam allowance of 1 cm/½ in. Neaten the raw edges. Fold down the top edge, leaving a generous cuff. Cover the raw edge with satin ribbon, stitching along both edges to form a casing. Fold under the ends of the ribbon and butt them together. With a safety pin, thread some elastic through the casing and stitch the ends together.

3 Complete the bag by making a tie with another length of braid, coiling and stitching the ends. Attach to one side seam and tie around the neck of the bag.

BEADED ORANGE PURSE

This luxurious purse is embroidered to look like slices of fruit with tiny beads to echo the texture.

YOU WILL NEED

MATERIALS

*velvet or brocade pieces,
1 orange and 1 yellow,
15 cm/6 in
2 pieces yellow silk,
15 cm/6 in
tracing paper
embroidery threads: white,
crimson, orange, yellow
and lime-green
small glass beads: yellow,
orange and clear
tacking (basting) thread
zip, 12 cm/4¾ in
matching sewing thread*

EQUIPMENT

*dressmaker's scissors
pencil
tailor's chalk
embroidery needle
dressmaker's pins
needle*

1 Cut circles, 14 cm/5½ in in diameter: one each of orange and yellow velvet and two of silk. Trace the template from the back of the book, enlarging to fit the circle, and transfer it to the velvet with tailor's chalk. Sew chain stitch in white for the pith. On the orange side, sew crimson segments and orange flesh; on the lemon side, sew yellow segments and lemon and lime flesh. Use chain stitch for the segments and back stitch for flesh. Add coloured beads for the skin and clear beads for moisture. With right sides together, pin and tack (baste) the zip, leaving a 1 cm/½ in allowance.

2 Stitch along the zip. Open it and complete the seam around the rest of the circle.

3 With right sides together, sew the two pieces of silk halfway round. Turn to the right side. Put the purse, inside out, inside the lining. Turn in the lining seam allowance and slip stitch it to the zip.

HEAVENLY BAG

T his delicate and pretty bag is ideal for lingerie.

YOU WILL NEED

MATERIALS

*2 rectangles silver metallic organza, 65 x 28 cm/ 26 x 11 in
2 circles silver metallic organza, 18 cm/ 7 in in diameter
2 rectangles gold metallic organza, 24 x 26 cm/ 7 x 11 in
contrasting metallic machine threads
tacking (basting) thread
tracing paper
ribbon*

EQUIPMENT

*sewing machine, with darning foot
tape measure
needle
dressmaker's scissors
fabric marker*

1 Fold the rectangular pieces of fabric in half widthways. Stitch an 8 cm/3 in seam from the folded edge on both side edges. Turn the rectangles right sides out. To make the ribbon casing, stitch two parallel lines 8 and 10 cm/3 and 4 in from the folded edge. Make a grid of tacking (basting) lines to attach a gold rectangle to a silver rectangle, matching the bottom edges.

2 Using a fabric marker, trace the template from the back of the book, enlarging if necessary, and transfer it to the gold side of the two silver and gold pieces. On the sewing machine, set the dial to the darning or free embroidery mode. Work the circles in straight stitch, with contrasting thread in the top and bobbin.

3 Cut away the gold organza inside the stitched line. Work the remaining signs in contrasting colours. Cut away and discard the organza again. Top stitch 1.5 cm/⅝ in from the top edge and pull away the weft threads, to produce a gold fringe. Remove the tacking (basting). Lay the two embroidered sides right sides together.

4 Stitch the sides to make a tube-shaped outer, embroidered bag, with a lining formed by the folded half. Stitch one silver circle to the bottom of the outside tube, and the other to the bottom of the lining. Turn right sides out. Tuck the lining inside the bag and slip stitch the gap. Thread a ribbon through the casing.

SPARKLING IVY GARLAND

*M*ake this beautiful jewelled crown of leaves for a midsummer night's party, or perhaps for a summer wedding.

YOU WILL NEED

MATERIALS

water-soluble fabric
paper or thin card
fine green wool or green embroidery thread
metallic threads: silver and blended gold and silver
sewing threads: dark and light green
paper towels
fine silver or brass wire: 0.6 mm for circlet, 0.4 or 0.2 mm for leaves
selection of beads

EQUIPMENT

embroidery hoop
fabric marker
large-eyed needle
sewing machine, with size 11 needle
dressmaker's scissors

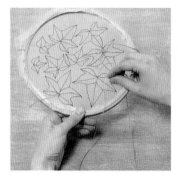

1 Stretch the water-soluble fabric on to the embroidery hoop. Using a fabric marker, trace the template from the back of the book, enlarging if necessary, on to the fabric. For the first style of leaf, hand stitch the central veins in fine green wool or embroidery thread. Use a running stitch and a thicker thread for the larger leaves.

2 For the second style of leaf, work the veins and outlines on the machine with a straight stitch, using silver metallic thread in the bobbin and dark green sewing thread in the needle. Fill in between the veins with the lighter green. For the first style of leaf, fill in with blended gold and silver thread in the bobbin and silver thread in the needle.

3 Sew randomly across the machined lines within each section of leaf to make the tiny veins. (This also holds the embroidery together.)

4 Work a zigzag stitch up the central veins and around the outer edge of each leaf to stiffen it.

5 Cut the leaves off the hoop and dissolve the fabric of each one in turn in water. Pat dry on paper towels. While still damp, fold each leaf in half and press with your fingers to make a crease along the central vein. Open out and allow to dry.

6 Continue to embroider more leaves in both styles to make enough for the whole garland. Sew each leaf on to fine wire.

7 Twist a piece of thicker wire into a band to fit your head. Twist on more wire to make loops for attaching the leaves. Make the loops higher at the front of the garland.

8 Wind the wired leaves on to the loops on the band, using the larger leaves at the front. Add beads threaded with more wire. Bend and arrange the leaves into shape.

TUDOR ROSE BUTTONS

*T*hese buttons take up the theme of the Tudor Rose, a famous heraldic union of the red rose of Lancaster and the white rose of York.

YOU WILL NEED

MATERIALS	EQUIPMENT
water-soluble fabric	*embroidery hoop*
machine embroidery	*fine magic marker*
threads: green, red	*embroidery needle*
and white	*sewing machine*
fine metallic thread	*dressmaker's scissors*
a few small pearl beads	*fine paintbrush*
self-cover buttons,	
22 mm/¾ in	
piece of metallic fabric	
piece of sheer organza	
PVA (white) glue	

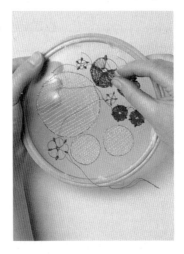

1 Stretch the water-soluble fabric on to the embroidery hoop. Trace the template from the back of the book on to the fabric using a fine magic marker. Hand or machine embroider the leaf detail in green, using straight stitch and sewing back and forth to link the stitches. Cut off the trailing green threads and hand or machine embroider in red or white over the flower, making sure that you interlock the stitches. To make the mesh, thread the machine with metallic thread and sew straight rows, first one way then the other, to make a net. Remove the embroidery from the hoop.

2 Cut around the flowers and mesh and sew them together, adding a few beads, before you dissolve the water-soluble fabric.

3 Follow the manufacturer's instructions to cover the buttons. Cut circles of metallic and sheer fabrics and dab a little glue in the centre of each button before covering with the layers of fabric.

UNDERWATER PICTURE

*T*he effect of the layers of delicate blue and green chiffon is marvellously evocative of an undersea scene. This tranquil picture would be ideal in a bedroom, where its calm, reflective quality is bound to induce plenty of sweet dreams.

YOU WILL NEED

MATERIALS

shot organza in shades of green and blue
white paper
metallic organza
shot velvets
shot silk
shot organza
pearlized lamé
metallic embroidery threads

EQUIPMENT

dressmaker's scissors
dressmaker's pins
embroidery hoop
sewing machine, with embroidery foot

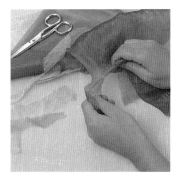

1 Use one sheet of organza as the base of the sea. Tear strips of organza to form the sea background.

2 Assemble all the strips, pin them together, and fit them into the embroidery hoop. Pin them in place.

3 Make shell, fish and starfish paper templates. Cut out shells from the metallic organza, fish from the velvets and silk, and starfish from the shot organza and lamé. Pin and machine stitch to the sea base, using metallic threads.

4 Build up the design with texture and colour. Remove the embroidery from the hoop and stretch it back into shape, ready for framing.

UNICORN PENNANT

*T*his richly embroidered pennant uses the unicorn as its motif. Cool colours are used to great effect to reflect his elusive nature.

YOU WILL NEED

MATERIALS

4 toning cotton fabrics,
15 x 21.5 cm/6 x 8½ in
matching sewing thread
tracing paper
fusible bonding web
unbleached calico,
25 x 25 cm/10 x 10 in
gold machine
embroidery thread
1.5 m/1½ yd wire-edged
fleur-de-lys ribbon
tacking (basting) thread
cotton backing fabric,
28 x 40 cm/11 x 16 in
wooden pole, 36 cm/14 in
dark blue craft-paint

EQUIPMENT

sewing machine
iron
pencil
dressmaker's scissors
needle
dressmaker's pins
paintbrush

1 Join the fabric rectangles in pairs along the long edges. Iron the seams open, then join the two pairs to form a large rectangle. Iron the seams open.

2 Trace the template from the back of the book, enlarging it to 23 cm/9 in across. Transfer it, in reverse, to the backing paper of the fusible bonding web. Iron it on to the calico, then cut it out along the outline. Peel off the backing paper and iron it on to the centre of the patchwork. Draw on the features.

3 Using a narrow satin stitch and gold thread, sew around the outside edge of the motif and over the various details of the design.

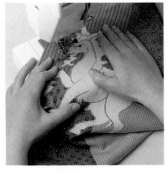

4 Embroider the eye, tongue and nostril by hand or with a machine.

5 Cut three 15 cm/6 in lengths of ribbon, that match the design, and remove the wire from the edges. Fold each piece in half, then pin and tack (baste) in place on the upper edge of the banner so that the loops are facing downwards.

6 With right sides facing, pin the backing fabric to the banner and sew around the edge leaving a 1 cm/½ in seam allowance. Leave a 10 cm/4 in gap at the lower edge for turning. Trim the corners and turn. Iron.

7 Paint the pole and allow to dry, then thread the banner on to the pole.

8 Tie each end of the remaining ribbon to the pole in a bow. Secure with a few stitches and pull the wired edges of the loops into shape.

WILD ROSE CHIFFON SCARF

*S*himmering silk chiffon or organza and glittering silver metallic paint combine here to make a ravishing scarf that would completely transform a plain outfit. You do not have to wear this, though; it is a technique that could equally well be used to make beautiful fabric wall hangings.

YOU WILL NEED

MATERIALS
silk chiffon or organza,
30 x 50 cm/12 x 20 in
tracing paper
silver metallic fabric paint
metallic paint with nozzle-
tipped dispenser

EQUIPMENT
iron
wooden frame
drawing pins
pencil
paintbrush
fabric marker
needle

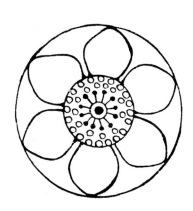

1 Wash, dry and iron the silk. Fold it in half and iron twice. Fold diagonally and iron. Unfold and stretch the fabric taut on the frame using drawing pins. Trace the template on this page, enlarging if necessary, on to the back of the silk at the centre. Trace eight more motifs around it, using the pressed folds as a guide.

2 Turn the frame over and go over the outlines of the design with silver paint on the front of the fabric. Allow to dry. Unpin the scarf and fix the paint according to the manufacturer's instructions. Stretch the fabric again.

3 Using the nozzle-tipped tube, make dots of metallic paint around the outer edges of each rose and fill in the details. Mark lines of dots 5 cm/2 in from the edges of the scarf, with the marker. To fray the edges, work one side at a time. Use a needle to separate and remove threads from the raw edges, then pull away up to the dotted edges.

HEAVENLY HAT

*T*his richly coloured hat is made from a circle and a rectangle. Measure your head and add a 5 cm/2 in seam and shrinkage allowance. The height of the hat shown is 12 cm/4¾ in plus a 2.5 cm/1 in seam allowance. Cut a circle for the top, according to the size required, and add on a seam allowance of 2.5 cm/1 in.

YOU WILL NEED

MATERIALS

3 colours of dupion silk heavy iron-on interfacing velvet, 10 x 10 cm/4 x 4 in paper contrasting cotton threads contrasting metallic machine embroidery threads metallic fabric paints

EQUIPMENT

dressmaker's scissors tape measure iron pencil dressmaker's pins sewing machine, with darning foot paintbrush

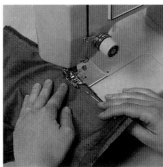

1 Cut three rectangles of silk and one of interfacing to the correct size. Iron the interfacing on to the back of the bottom layer of silk. Stitch around the edge of the rectangles, leaving a gap in one long seam. Insert the square of velvet slightly larger than the moon template through the gap, on top of the top layer of silk.

2 Draw and cut out the sun and moon shapes and pin on to the silk. With the machine in embroidery mode, stitch on top of the moon template, then stitch the features. Stitch the stars and outline stitching in the same way, using different coloured threads. Go over all the stitching twice, then tear away the paper.

3 Next, cut out the fabric layers to reveal your desired colours. Random whip stitch in a loop fashion inside the moon, with metallic thread. Paint areas of the hat with metallic fabric paints. Stitch the crown and top of the hat together and clip into the seam allowances.

DRAGONFLIES

*T*hese beautiful irid-escent creatures look almost ready to fly away! If you've never tried free machine embroidery, look in your sewing machine manual for detailed instructions.

YOU WILL NEED

MATERIALS

water-soluble fabric
tracing paper
opalescent cellophane
(or cellophane sweet
wrappers)
small pieces of sheer
synthetic organza: brown
and green
fine metallic thread
thicker metallic thread
paper towels
piece of card
spray varnish
glitter pipecleaners
fine wire and a few glass
beads, for the butterflies

EQUIPMENT

embroidery hoop
fine magic marker
dressmaker's pins
sewing machine, with
fine needle
dressmaker's scissors
needle

1 Stretch the fabric on to the hoop. Trace the template from the back of the book on to the fabric with the magic marker. Sandwich the cellophane between the sheer fabrics and pin under the hoop. Machine around the wing details in straight stitch with fine thread.

2 Remove the hoop from the machine and trim away the spare fabric and cellophane with scissors.

3 With fine metallic thread in the needle and the thicker metallic thread on the bobbin, machine all round the outlines of the insects in ordinary straight stitch.

4 Put the fine thread on the bobbin and fill in between the outlines, joining all of the design. To stiffen the edges, go over the outlines in zigzag.

5 Hold the work to the light to check that the outlines are linked. Remove from the hoop and dissolve the fabric in water. Dry on paper towels.

6 Pin the insects out flat on a piece of card and spray with varnish. Allow to dry.

7 Cut a piece of glitter pipecleaner longer than the dragonfly body and sew it to the underside of the body part as far as the head. Trim it.

8 Bend the rest of the embroidery under the head and upper body to cover the pipecleaner. Stitch in place. Finally, fold the wings together and secure with a few stitches near the body so that the wings are raised.

9 Thread some small glass beads on to fine gold wire and twist into two antennae for the butterfly. Thread these on to the head, and then complete it as for the dragonfly.

CONTEMPORARY TABLEMAT

*H*ere, a very traditional and popular motif is
depicted in bright and bold modern colours.

YOU WILL NEED

MATERIALS	EQUIPMENT
light grey Zweigart Annable	*tape measure*
evenweave fabric,	*dressmaker's scissors*
38 x 56 cm/ 15 x 22 in	*dressmaker's pins*
matching and black	*sewing machine*
sewing thread	*iron*
tacking (basting) thread	*needle*
tracing paper	*pencil*
Anchor "Marlitt": 836, 815,	
801 and 1032	

1 Cut two fabric rectangles,
28 x 38 cm/11 x 15 in. Pin
them together and stitch around
the edges, 1.5 cm/⅝ in from the
edge, with matching thread and
leaving a gap on one side. Mitre
the corners, turn right side out
and iron. Top stitch 1 cm/½ in
from the edge. Tack (baste)
guides around the edge of the
mat, 2.5 cm/1 in and 4 cm/1½ in
from the edge. Machine zigzag
stitch over the top of the
guidelines, using black thread.
Use the presser foot as a guide
to stitch the crossways lines.
Stitch in the thread ends on the
reverse side.

2 Trace the template from the
back of the book, enlarging
if necessary. Pin in position.
Tack (baste) around the lines,
then tear the tracing paper
away. Machine zigzag along the
lines and sew in the ends.

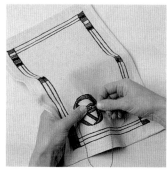

3 Fill in the coloured areas of
the border in satin stitch,
using two strands of Marlitt.
Ease the satin stitches on the
rose to fit round the curves, and
fill in the centre to complete.

EMBROIDERED DRESS

*S*eashore motifs make for a pleasing decoration on this denim dress. Shown here as a repeat pattern, the shell and starfish shapes are appliquéd, then decorated with embroidery; the embroidered detail helps to unify the design as a whole.

YOU WILL NEED

MATERIALS

ironed white cotton
lining paper or newspaper
selection of fabric paints
tracing paper
dress
fabric glue
embroidery threads

EQUIPMENT

paintbrush
paint-mixing container
iron
pencil
embroidery scissors
selection of needles
towel

1 Lay the cotton on a larger sheet of paper and paint separate pieces of fabric in different colours. Allow to dry for 24 hours, then fix them, according to the manufacturer's instructions. Draw starfish and shell shapes on tracing paper.

2 Transfer the shapes several times on to the painted fabric. Cut them out, leaving a 5 mm/¼ in border outside the outlines. Lay the shapes on the hem of the dress and work out a pleasing pattern. Glue the shapes down sparingly.

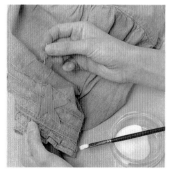

3 Embroider a running stitch, or a continuous double running stitch, around the template outlines.

4 Embroider details to represent sand, stones, etc. Tidy loose threads and iron on the wrong side, over a towel.

MIDNIGHT SKY PICTURE

Glittering metallic threads against shimmering dark blue shot silk create a real feeling of the night sky in this machine-embroidered picture.

YOU WILL NEED

MATERIALS
thin card
pearlized chiffon and lamé
dark blue shot silk,
23 x 23 cm/9 x 9 in
embroidery threads:
metallic silver, gold and
blue
wadding (batting)
thick card
all-purpose glue

EQUIPMENT
pencil
scissors
fabric marker
embroidery hoop
ruler
dressmaker's pins
sewing machine, with
darning foot

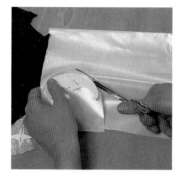

1 Draw the moon and stars freehand on to thin card and cut out to use as templates. Draw round the templates on the pearlized fabrics, using the fabric marker, and cut them out.

2 Stretch the silk in an embroidery hoop. Mark out a 10 cm/4 in square in the centre, using the fabric marker. Position the pearlized shapes and pin them in place.

3 Using metallic thread and with the machine on the darning or free embroidery mode, define the shapes with machine embroidery. Continue building up colours and layers. Take the piece out of the hoop. Cut 10 cm/4 in squares of wadding (batting) and thick card. Lay the embroidery face down and place the wadding (batting) and card on top. Glue the edges of the card and then stretch the silk over and press it down firmly. Add a few stitches to hold the silk.

BABY SUIT

This ribbonwork decoration for a ready-made romper or sunsuit is easy to achieve and it looks really delightful. This type of ribbonwork is simple, because you can follow the existing oversewn garment seams, which act as sewing lines. Choose a plain, not patterned, suit, without any motifs.

YOU WILL NEED

MATERIALS

chocolate-brown ribbon,
6 m/6 yd
romper or sunsuit
tracing paper
rust ribbon, 3 m/3 yd
sewing threads: orange and
chocolate-brown
salmon or peach ribbon,
3 m/3 yd

EQUIPMENT

needle
pencil
fabric marker
dressmaker's scissors

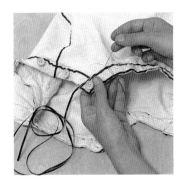

1 Use running stitch to attach chocolate-brown ribbon to the seams of the suit. Turn under, and finish the ends.

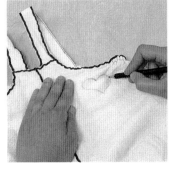

2 Trace the template from the back of the book, enlarging if necessary. Transfer to the suit four times. As an alternative, draw your own motifs with a pencil or marker.

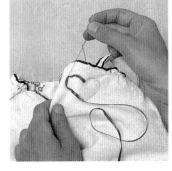

3 Turn under the end of the rust ribbon. Working anti-clockwise from the top of the heart, sew in place with running stitch in orange thread.

4 Repeat the process with the salmon or peach ribbon, using chocolate-brown or orange thread.

VELVET SCARF

*T*his sinuous velvet scarf is encrusted down its full length with the "sigils", or abstract symbols, of the twelve signs of the zodiac. The shiny metallic decorations contrast deliciously with the silky smooth fabric. Choose some darkly glowing colours to wear on a starry evening. Before sewing the seams, make sure that the pile of each piece of velvet is running in the right direction.

YOU WILL NEED

MATERIALS

velvet in main colour,
1.5 m x 64 cm/60 x 26 in
velvet in toning colour,
36 x 64 cm/14 x 26 in
matching sewing thread
tracing paper
metallic organza
matching embroidery
thread

EQUIPMENT

dressmaker's scissors
tape measure
sewing machine
pencil
tailor's chalk
embroidery hoop
needle

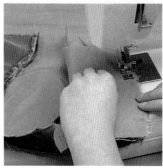

1 Cut two lengths of velvet to 1.5 m x 32 cm/ 60 x 13 in in the main colour, and four pieces 18 x 32 cm/7 x 13 in in the toning velvet. With right sides together and a 1 cm/½ in seam allowance, machine stitch one toning panel to each end of each scarf length.

2 Mark out the positions for the astrological signs along the side of the scarf length, placing them 2 cm/¾ in from the seam line and at 13 cm/5 in intervals. Trace the templates from the back of the book, enlarging if necessary. Copy on to the velvet using tailor's chalk.

3 Place the velvet in a hoop. Cut 2 cm/¾ in strips of metallic organza. Stitch one end of the organza to the marked line, twist the strip tightly and stitch in place. Work all the designs in the same way. With right sides together, join the two scarf lengths, leaving a small opening. Turn to the right side and slip stitch the opening.

SILVER MOTH SCARF

*E*thereal silver moths flutter delicately over one side of this lovely silk scarf, their glitter reflected in the pleated organza on the other side. Your sewing machine manual will provide details of how to do free machine embroidery.

YOU WILL NEED

MATERIALS

tracing paper
fusible bonding web
small amounts of contrasting silk, velvet and organza
silk satin,
142 x 30 cm/56 x 12 in
matching fine machine embroidery thread
pleated metallic organza,
142 x 30 cm/56 x 12 in
matching sewing thread

EQUIPMENT

pencil
iron
dressmaker's scissors
embroidery hoop
sewing machine
dressmaker's pins
needle

1 Trace the templates from the back of the book, enlarging if necessary. Lay the bonding web over the templates and trace the moths. Iron the bonding to the wrong side of the silk. Trace the same number of body shapes on the bonding and iron to the wrong side of the velvet. Cut out the shapes.

2 Remove the backing paper and iron the shapes to the right side of the silk satin. Place the satin in a hoop. Cut some pieces of organza slightly larger than the moths and machine stitch them to the satin along the wing outlines. Trim the organza close to the line of stitching round each motif.

3 Work two or three lines of stitching around each moth to conceal the raw edges. Pin the pleated organza to the satin with right sides together, and stitch all around the edge, leaving a gap of 10 cm/4 in on one side. Turn the scarf to the right side and slip stitch the gap.

FISHY ORNAMENTS

*T*hese charming fish are quickly made and would be a rewarding project for children. The symbol of Pisces represents coming and going, past and future, so hang them to swim in different directions!

YOU WILL NEED

MATERIALS	EQUIPMENT
scrap paper	*pencil*
thin card or paper	*dressmaker's pins*
scraps of woollen fabric	*dressmaker's scissors*
mother-of-pearl buttons	*needle*
embroidery cotton in	
contrasting colours	
scraps of polyester wadding	
(batting), 5 mm/¼ in thick	

1 Draw a fish motif on to scrap paper and transfer it on to thin card or paper to make a template. Pin it to two layers of the fabric and cut out the fish. (No seam allowance is required for these shapes.)

2 Separate the pieces and sew on the buttons to make eyes. Embroider each side of the fish, using three strands of embroidery cotton, in cross stitch, stem stitch and feather stitch as shown in the picture.

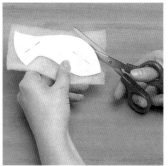

3 Cut a piece of wadding (batting) using the template, then trim it so that it is slightly smaller all round than the fish.

4 Sandwich the wadding (batting) between the two sides and attach a length of thread for the hanger. Blanket stitch round the edge to join the sides together.

DECORATIVE PINCUSHION

*A*n essential item on Victorian dressing tables, pincushions are still as useful as they are decorative. There is no more appropriate way to personalize them than with the pins themselves. The symbols used here are Capricorn and Taurus.

YOU WILL NEED

MATERIALS
plain velvet,
28 x 14 cm/11 x 5½ in
brass-headed pins,
1 cm/½ in long
matching sewing thread
polyester wadding (batting)
fine white tissue paper

EQUIPMENT
dressmaker's scissors
tailor's chalk
sewing machine
needle
pencil
tracing paper
dressmaker's pins

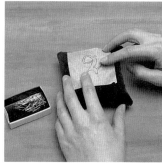

1 Cut the velvet into two 14 cm/5½ in squares and pin them together with right sides facing. Mark a 1 cm/½ in seam allowance with tailor's chalk. Machine around all four sides, leaving a 5 cm/2 in gap in the centre of one side.

2 Trim the seam allowance at the corners of the cushion and turn it to the right side, easing out the corners with the points of the scissors. Stuff very firmly with polyester wadding (batting). Sew up the opening neatly by hand along the seam.

3 Trace the signs you want from the templates in the back of the book, enlarging if necessary, and transfer them to fine white tissue paper. Centre and pin a motif on the pincushion.

4 Work the motif with the brass-headed pins. When complete, tear away the tissue, gently pulling any bits from between the pins.

CUPID CAMISOLE

*T*his *beautiful camisole will make you feel like a million dollars. You will need a commercial paper pattern for a camisole, which you can then embellish with machine embroidery. You can embroider over the tissue paper pattern first and then tear away the paper, leaving an outline to be filled in with colour.*

YOU WILL NEED

MATERIALS
*satin fabric, 1 m x 90 cm/
1 x 1 yd
tissue paper
machine embroidery
threads: cream, white,
gold and grey*

EQUIPMENT
*commercial camisole
pattern
dressmaker's scissors
dressmaker's pins
embroidery hoop
sewing machine, with
darning foot*

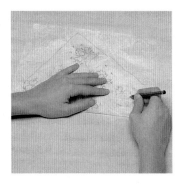

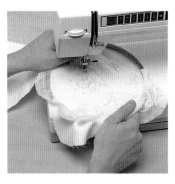

1 Cut out the pattern from the satin, with 1 cm/½ in extra all around to allow for any shrinkage during embroidery. Make a tissue paper duplicate of the front pattern piece. Trace the template from the back of the book, enlarging if necessary, and trace it on to the tissue paper duplicate, rotating it each time and avoiding the darts.

2 Use the tissue paper duplicate for embroidering by pinning it to the satin. Place the satin in the embroidery hoop. Set the machine to darning mode and attach the darning foot. With cream thread, stitch along the outline of the design.

3 Remove the tissue paper and fill in the design. Use white thread for the face, body and hearts, gold for the hair and features and grey for the wings and cloud. Make up the camisole according to the pattern instructions.

BRIDAL HEART

*P*ink satin and lace are the essence of femininity; this delicate bridal favour would be the perfect loving touch for the wedding day of a daughter, sister or friend. The decoration of sequins, pearls and motifs can be as simple or elaborate as you like, and you can be sure that no two of these will ever be the same.

YOU WILL NEED

MATERIALS

tracing paper
pink satin fabric,
40 x 20 cm/16 x 8 in
lace fabric or mat,
20 x 20 cm/8 x 8 in
contrasting tacking
(basting) thread
ready-made silk flowers
(optional)
matching sewing thread
flat sequins
seed pearls
polyester wadding (batting)
narrow lace edging,
60 cm/24 in
short lengths of matching
satin ribbon

EQUIPMENT

pencil
dressmaker's scissors
dressmaker's pins
very fine needle
sewing machine (optional)

1 Trace the heart template from the back of the book, enlarging if necessary. Cut out two hearts from pink satin. Place one under the lace fabric or mat, and move it about to find the most attractive pattern area. Pin and then tack (baste) through both layers. Cut the lace, carefully following the outline of the satin heart.

2 From the remaining lace, cut flowers and motifs. Sew to the centre of the lace heart. (Or use silk flowers.) Add sequins and pearls. Pin the hearts together, right sides facing. Stitch 1 cm/½ in from the edges, leaving a 5 cm/2 in gap. Trim seams and clip curves. Turn right side out. Fill the heart with wadding (batting) and slip stitch the gap.

3 Run a gathering thread along the straight edge of the lace edging and pin one end to the top of the heart. Adjusting the gathers evenly, continue to pin the lace around the outside edge and then slip stitch it firmly in place with small, invisible stitches. Remove the gathering thread. Finish with a hanging loop, small ribbon bows and additional beads and sequins.

CUSHION WITH SEASHELLS

With this lovely cushion cover, the fluid curves of the seashells contrast strikingly with the regularity of the checks.

YOU WILL NEED

MATERIALS

tracing paper
fusible bonding web,
20 x 20 cm/8 x 8 in
3 shades beige cotton scraps
light-tone cotton gingham,
25 x 25 cm/10 x 10 in
embroidery threads
medium-tone cotton
homespun check,
25 x 35 cm/10 x 14 in
matching sewing thread
unbleached calico,
60 x 100 cm/24 x 40 in
dark-tone cotton homespun
check, 20 x 20 cm/8 x 8 in
24 buttons
cushion pad

EQUIPMENT

pencil
dressmaker's scissors
fabric marker (optional)
iron and pressing cloth
needle
dressmaker's pins
sewing machine

1 Trace the template from the back of the book, enlarging as required. Place the bonding web on top and trace the motifs on to the fabric with a pencil. Cut them out roughly. Iron each shell on to a different scrap of plain cotton fabric. Cut out neatly round each outline.

2 Using a fabric marker or sharp pencil, mark the curves and spirals on the right side of the shells. Peel off the backing paper and arrange the three shapes on the gingham square, using the finished picture as a guide. Fuse by pressing with a cool iron and a pressing cloth.

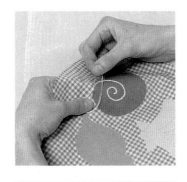

3 Using three strands of embroidery thread and, working with small, regular stitches, embroider a line of chain stitches around the shell shapes, to cover the raw edges and pick out the marked details.

4 Cut two strips of medium-tone cotton measuring 7 x 25 cm/3 x 10 in. With right sides facing and leaving a seam allowance of 1 cm/½ in, sew them to opposite sides of the gingham square. Press the seams open. Cut two strips, each 7 x 38 cm/3 x 15 in. Pin and then sew them to the remaining two sides. Press the seams open.

5 Cut four strips of calico 10 x 38 cm/4 x 15 in and four squares of dark-tone cotton 10 cm/4 in. Stitch two strips to opposite sides of the main square, leaving a 1 cm/½ in seam allowance and press the seams open. Sew a square to each end of the other strips and press the seams open. With right sides facing, sew in place and press the seams open.

6 Cut two rectangles of unbleached calico to make the back of the cushion, each 30 x 45 cm/12 x 18 in. Hem one long side of each. With right sides facing, pin one rectangle to two opposite sides of the cushion front. Sew around the four edges, leaving a 1 cm/½ in seam allowance. Clip the corners and turn the cover right side out.

7 Sew the buttons securely along the calico strips at 5 cm/2 in intervals, using embroidery thread.

S W E E T   H E A R T S

*T*he heart is the ultimate symbol of devotion, so
heart-shaped gifts have a special significance,
whether they are given to friends and family, or
exchanged by lovers. These padded hearts are made
from leftovers of old lace fabric, embellished with tiny
beads and gauze ribbons. The golden versions are filled
with pot-pourri and edged with metallic lace.

YOU WILL NEED

MATERIALS

*silk backing fabric
small pieces of lace fabric
matching sewing thread
polyester wadding (batting)
rocaille embroidery beads
lace, 50 x 2.5 cm/20 x 1 in
gauze ribbon, 1 m x 4 cm/
1 yd x 1½ in*

EQUIPMENT

*dressmaker's scissors
dressmaker's pins
needle*

1 Cut out two hearts from the
backing fabric and one
from lace, leaving a 1 cm/½ in
seam allowance all around.

2 Pin the hearts together,
sandwiching the lace heart
between the two layers of silk.
Sew together along one straight
edge, leaving a 4 cm/1½ in gap
for turning through.

3 Turn the heart the right
way out and stuff it firmly,
ensuring that the wadding
(batting) fills out the point of
the heart. Slip stitch the sides,
making sure that the fabric lies
flat and has no wrinkles.

4 Sew the beads on to the
lace, picking out and
highlighting the various designs
within the pattern of lace itself.

5 Gather the length of lace
to fit around the outside
edge of the heart, then stitch it
in place.

6 Cut a 30 cm/12 in length of
gauze ribbon and sew it to
the top of the heart to form a
hanging loop. Make a bow from
the rest of the ribbon and sew it
to the base of the loop.

EMBROIDERED JEWELLERY

*G*littering embroidery, *I*ridescent paper, and shimmering beads combine to make this very special jewellery.

YOU WILL NEED

MATERIALS

water-soluble fabric
tracing paper
iridescent paper
metallic sewing threads
paper towels
modelling clay
blue-green watercolour inks
metallic paints
spray varnish
selection of small beads
2 jewellery split rings
2 earring wires or posts
2 jewellery jump rings

EQUIPMENT

embroidery hoop
dressmaker's pins
pencil
vanishing fabric marker
sewing machine
scissors
iron
stiff wire
paintbrush
card
felt
plastic sheet
beading needle
flat-nosed jewellery pliers

CRAFT TIP

You need a sewing machine that can be used without a foot for free embroidery (most can). Sewing through the iridescent paper does blunt needles, so have some spares ready. You can buy water-soluble fabric from good craft shops.

1 Stretch a layer of the fabric in the hoop and pin another layer to the back. Trace the template from the back of the book, enlarging if necessary. Trace them on to the fabric with the vanishing marker. For the centres, pin iridescent paper to the back of the fabric. Thread the machine with metallic thread and experiment with sewing without a foot, using different thicknesses of thread, to achieve the right tension. Consult the manufacturer's instructions for more help. Machine around the heart centres and cut away any excess paper from the back.

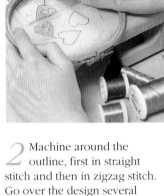

2 Machine around the outline, first in straight stitch and then in zigzag stitch. Go over the design several times, so it is quite stiff.

4 Make small balls of clay for the beads, and push them on to a stiff wire. Allow to dry, stuck into a piece of clay.

6 Cover a piece of card with felt and plastic, to make a soft backing sheet. Pin the motifs to the sheet and spray the clay beads and motifs with the varnish.

3 Dissolve the fabric in some water according to the manufacturer's instructions. Iron dry between paper towels.

5 Paint the beads with watercolour inks. When dry, add dots of metallic paint, to highlight them.

7 Attach metallic thread to the top of the earring. Thread on two small beads, then a clay bead, and two small beads. Take the thread through a split ring and then down again through the beads and into the motif. Fasten off. Sew small beads on to the centres of the motifs, in a ring.

8 To join the earring fixings, open up a jump ring with pliers and thread through the split ring. Join it to the ring on the earring. For a pendant, thread a machine-embroidered chain through the slip ring.

QUILTED CUSHION

*T*he classic Tudor rose motif is picked out in quilting lines on this vibrant silk cushion; the traditional rosy red colour makes a perfect complement for the motif.

YOU WILL NEED

MATERIALS

tracing paper
red silk taffeta,
100 x 90 cm/40 x 36 in
calico,
100 x 90 cm/40 x 36 in
wadding (batting),
50 x 50 cm/20 x 20 in
tacking (basting) thread
red sewing thread
piping cord, 1.5 m/1½ yd
polyester stuffing
(batting)

EQUIPMENT

fine black felt-tipped pen
tape measure
dressmaking scissors
quilter's pencil
needle
dressmaker's pins
sewing machine
iron

1 Trace the template from the back of the book, enlarging it as necessary. Outline the rose in black pen. Cut a 50 cm/20 in square of silk. Lay the silk on top and trace the rose directly on to the fabric with a quilter's pencil. Cut a 50 cm/20 in square of calico. Layer the wadding (batting) between the calico and the silk. Tack (baste) the layers together with lines of stitches radiating from the centre. Using red thread, quilt along the lines of the outline of the design, working from the centre out. Once complete, draw a five-sided shape around the design and trim the cushion along the lines.

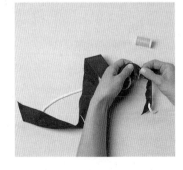

2 Cut and join 5 cm/2 in bias strips from red silk. Press the seams open and trim. Fold the strip over the piping cord and tack (baste) along it. Next, pin and tack (baste) the piping around the cushion edge, with raw edges together. Machine stitch along one side, close to the piping. Lay a square of silk and then calico on the right side of the cushion. Pin, tack (baste) and stitch round the edges, leaving a small gap. Trim the seams and corners and turn through. Fill with stuffing (batting) and slip stitch the gap closed.

SEA PILLOWCASE

*R*ainbow yarn, in which a variety of beautifully toning shades are combined in one length, is couched with embroidery thread to create lovely sea-toned shell shapes on this special pillowcase.

YOU WILL NEED

MATERIALS
tracing paper
pillowcase, with flanges
and decorative
embroidery line
rainbow yarn
stranded embroidery
threads: pale blue , blue-
green and dark blue
iron-on interfacing

EQUIPMENT
dressmaker's pins
transfer pen
small, fine embroidery and
tapestry or large-eyed
needle
iron

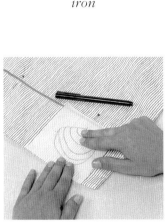

1 Trace the template from the back of the book, enlarging if necessary. Mark the positions of the shell motifs on the pillowcase with pins. Transfer to the pillowcase.

2 Cut the rainbow yarn into separate colours. Use a single strand of pale blue to couch the blue threads, and the same of blue-green for the green-blue shades. Couch a single pale blue thread between the bands of colour.

3 Using a large-eyed or tapestry needle, pull the ends through to the wrong side. Iron interfacing on to secure.

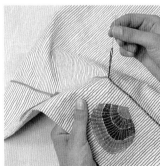

4 Weave a thread of dark blue thread through the decorative stitching.

SUNBURST CLOCK

*T*his luxurious clock takes its inspiration from the styles that were favoured by Louis XIV, the Sun King.

YOU WILL NEED

MATERIALS

tracing paper
bronze-coloured velvet,
36 x 36 cm/14 x 14 in
2 pieces of metallic organza
in dark gold and cream,
36 x 36 cm/14 x 14 in
tacking (basting) thread
sewing machine
machine embroidery
threads: gold and black
mounting board
fabric glue
clock movement and hands

EQUIPMENT

pencil
tape measure
dressmaker's pins
needle
dressmaker's scissors
pair of compasses
craft knife
cutting mat
paintbrush

1 Trace the template from the back of the book, enlarging to a diameter of 30 cm/12 in. Lay the dark gold, then the cream organza on top of the velvet. Pin the template in the centre and tack (baste) in place.

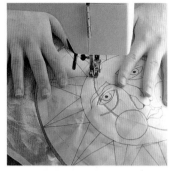

2 Using gold thread and the widest setting, satin stitch around the outer circle of the sun, joining all the layers of fabric together. Outline the main facial outline, the nostrils and the areas under the eyes in medium satin stitch with gold.

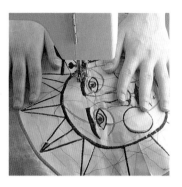

3 Using black thread and a single line of medium satin stitch, outline all the other features, apart from the upper mouth and eyebrows as these need a double line.

4 Still working in black, outline the inner circle on the widest satin stitch setting. Change the setting to medium and outline the sun's rays.

5 Unpick the tacking (basting) and cut away the loose threads. Cut away the tracing paper.

6 Following the main picture, cut away one or two layers of the fabric to reveal the colours beneath.

7 Using a pair of compasses, draw a circle 30 cm/12 in in diameter on mounting board, and cut out.

8 Stick the fabric cloth on to the board with fabric glue.

9 Cut a hole with a craft knife through the centre of the clockface. Push through the clock movement and attach the hands.

FLEUR-DE-LYS BOX

*T*his design makes the most of the bold colours and geometric patterns of heraldry. The crunchy textures of the materials used are as eye-catching as the brilliant colours.

YOU WILL NEED

MATERIALS

*fusible bonding web,
13 x 13 cm/5 x 5 in
calico,
25 x 25 cm/10 x 10 in
1 cm/½ in wide corded
ribbon, 1 m/1 yd each of
red and green
bright yellow felt
embroidery threads: black
and yellow
tracing paper
gold bullion, size 2:
38 cm/15 in each of rough
and smooth
gold metallic embroidery
thread
dark oak trinket box with
lid for 10 cm/4 in padded
insert*

EQUIPMENT

*iron
cork board
scissors
dressmaker's pins
sewing machine
embroidery hoop
needle
large-eyed needle*

1 Iron the bonding web in the centre of the calico square. Lay the square on a cork board. Cut the red ribbon into strips and lay these diagonally across the bonding web and pin in place.

2 Weave strips of green ribbon diagonally through the red strips in the opposite direction. Press with an iron to bond and remove the pins. Stitch around the edge to secure the strips.

3 Trace the template from the back of the book, enlarging if necessary. Cut three graduated fleur-de-lys shapes out of the felt. Place the smallest in the middle of the square and lay the larger pieces on top. Pin.

4 Stretch the panel in an embroidery hoop. Stitch around the felt with small hemming stitches, bringing the needle up close to the felt and down through the edge.

5 Cut the bullion into small pieces. Thread alternate types on to the needle, one at a time, and stitch down like beads in a random pattern all over the felt.

6 Couch two strands of gold metallic thread around the edge of the fleur-de-lys, leaving 5 cm/2 in ends on the right side. Couch the strands separately at the corners.

7 Use a large-eyed needle to pull the ends through to the reverse side. Trim and stitch securely. Trim the edge of the panel close to the machine stitching.

8 Lay the panel on top of the padded box insert. Ensure that it is straight and pin on all sides. Stitch two opposite edges together using a double thread and pull up tightly. Repeat with the two remaining edges. Insert in the lid and screw in position.

SPARKLING BROOCH

*L*ayers of contrasting fabrics and glittering machine embroidery make this a spectacular item of jewellery. The rough texture of the felts is wonderfully highlighted by the shimmering organza and metallic machine embroidery.

YOU WILL NEED

MATERIALS	EQUIPMENT
thin card or paper	*scissors*
purple felt	*dressmaker's pins*
rust felt	*tailor's chalk*
shot organza	*sewing machine, with*
metallic embroidery threads	*embroidery foot*
sewing thread	*needle*
brooch findings: back plate	
and pin	

1 Draw two freehand starfish shapes, one larger than the other, on to thin card or paper. Cut the templates out roughly. Pin the large starfish template to the purple felt and draw around it with tailor's chalk.

2 Cut out irregular pointed shapes from the purple and the rust felt. Pin them down into the points of the starfish outline. Cut out the small starfish shape from the shot organza and pin it on top of the felt starfish.

3 Thread the machine with metallic thread and stitch over the edges of the organza. Build up layers of texture and colour with different threads.

4 Cut out the starfish brooch shape and stitch a small felt circle on to the centre-back. Stitch on the brooch findings.

EMBROIDERED HATPIN

A decorated hatpin is an easy way to jazz up a plain hat. This one features an elaborately embroidered velvet sun backed with beaten brass.

YOU WILL NEED

MATERIALS	EQUIPMENT
yellow velvet	*scissors*
fine strong fabric	*embroidery hoop*
contrasting cotton threads	*sewing machine, with*
contrasting metallic	*darning foot*
machine-embroidery	*tin snips*
threads	*metal file*
brass sheet	*small, round-nosed*
brass wire	*hammer*
epoxy resin glue	*small anvil*
beads	*wire-cutters*
hatpin	*round-nosed jewellery pliers*

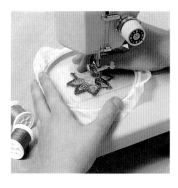

1 Cut out a yellow velvet sun. Place a piece of fine fabric in an embroidery hoop and machine stitch the sun to it. Thread the machine with contrasting threads in the top and bobbin and whip stitch around the edge. Then make a deeper band of stitching around the edge. Stitch spirals in contrasting metallic threads, then stitch the face.

2 Cut a sun from the brass sheet with tin snips and file the edges smooth. Hammer to give texture. Bend a spiral at each end of a piece of wire and hammer flat. Position the wire spirals in the centre front of the sun shape and glue a circle of brass just in the centre, over the ends of the wire.

3 Trim the velvet sun away from the fine fabric and glue it in the centre of the brass sun. Thread some beads on the hatpin and glue them in place. To assemble, bend the spirals slightly backwards and slide the hatpin through the top and bottom spirals.

ASTROLOGICAL CUSHION

*T*his cover achieves its effect with a combination of metallic fabric and embroidery. The fabric creates a rich impression, but machine embroidery makes the cover quite straightforward to achieve. This cushion is bound to induce a feeling of tranquillity when you settle down for a nap.

YOU WILL NEED

MATERIALS	EQUIPMENT
brown velvet	tape measure
cushion pad	dressmaker's scissors
matching thread	sewing machine, with
matching zip	darning foot
gold metallic organza	vanishing fabric marker
matching machine	embroidery hoop
embroidery thread	needle
tracing paper	
press (snap) fasteners	

1 For the front, cut one piece of velvet to the size of the cushion pad plus 2 cm/¾ in all round. For the back, cut two pieces of velvet each to half the width of the front piece, plus a 2 cm/¾ in allowance on both centre back edges. Join the two pieces and insert a zip. Lay the front and back right sides together and stitch all round the outside. Cut one front and two back pieces of organza as before. Turn under and stitch a double hem of 1 cm/½ in on each centre edge of the back pieces. Trace the template from the back of the book, enlarging if necessary. Put the front organza piece over the design and trace it on the fabric with a fabric marker.

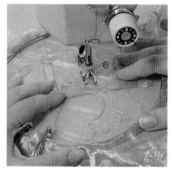

2 Select the darning or free embroidery mode on the sewing machine and place the organza in a hoop. Stitch around the shapes with gold embroidery thread.

3 With right sides facing, stitch the organza pieces together. Stitch on the press (snap) fasteners. Insert the cushion pad in the velvet and insert the cushion in the organza.

ENGLISH LION CUSHION

*C*hoose toning velvets in glowing "antique" colours for this sumptuous cushion, which will add a touch of historic grandeur to a room. A glittering metallic organza has been used for the lion.

YOU WILL NEED

MATERIALS	EQUIPMENT
tracing paper	*pencil*
tissue paper	*needle*
tacking (basting) thread	*embroidery hoop*
cotton velvet fabrics:	*sewing machine, with*
32 x 43 cm/12½ x 17 in	*darning foot*
deep red,	*scissors*
32 x 88 cm/12½ x 34½ in	*dressmaker's pins*
orange	
metallic organza,	
32 x 43 cm/12½ x 17 in	
metallic machine	
embroidery thread	
matching sewing thread	
70 cm/28 in fringing	
cushion pad,	
28 x 55 cm/11 x 21½ in	

1 Trace the template from the back of the book and transfer to tissue paper. Tack (baste) the tissue to the wrong side of the red velvet and the right side of the organza. Stretch in an embroidery hoop. Using the free embroidery mode and metallic thread, machine stitch the design. Remove the tissue and tacking (basting). On the right side, trim away the organza from the outer edge of the motif. Put the piece back in the hoop, right side up, and sew a narrow zigzag stitch to cover the edges.

2 Cut two strips of orange velvet 32 x 11 cm/12½ x 4¼ in. With right sides together, stitch these to either end of the panel. Cut two pieces of orange velvet, 32 x 48 cm/12½ x 19 in and 32 x 18 cm/12½ x 7 in for the back. Stitch a narrow double hem on the overlapping edges. Position the fringing along both short ends of the embroidered panel and pin in place. With right sides together, pin the backing pieces to the front, overlapping the hemmed edges. Stitch, trim, turn to the right side and insert the pad.

DIAMOND EARRINGS

*T*hese earrings are made from appliquéd silk and organza pieces, embroidered in a combination of colours and textures to give a jewel-like quality.

YOU WILL NEED

MATERIALS

thin card
small pieces of calico,
organza and silk
coloured and metallic
machine embroidery
threads
wadding (batting)
PVA (white) glue
metallic acrylic paint
2 eye pins
2 metallic beads
2 glass beads
2 ear wires

EQUIPMENT

scissors
fabric marker or pen
dressmaker's pins
sewing machine, with
darning foot
needle, size 80/12
embroidery hoop
paintbrush
needle
jewellery pliers

1 Draw two diamond shapes on card and cut out. Cut out two of the diamond shapes from calico. Draw four horizontal lines inside each diamond. Cut two slightly larger organza diamonds and pin them over the marked shapes. Place the fabric in a hoop. With matching thread, stitch the horizontal lines and several lines around the design. Trim away the excess organza close to the stitched outline.

2 Cut two small pieces of silk in a contrasting colour and pin over the diamond shapes. Place the piece in a hoop and stitch several lines around the horizontal stripes with matching thread. Trim away any excess fabric close to the stitch line. Work several stitch lines around the appliquéd stripes to cover the raw edges. Work more stitch lines around the design with metallic thread.

3 Pin a a second piece of calico to the wrong side of the embroidery. Place it in the hoop, and stitch around three sides of each diamond. Stuff both shapes with wadding (batting), poking it into the corners. Stitch the fourth side to close the gap. Cut out the shapes close to the stitched outline. With a small brush, apply glue to the edges of the shapes to varnish and stiffen the piece. Allow to dry, then paint in a metallic acrylic paint. Allow to dry. Make a hole at the top of each diamond with a needle. Thread each eye pin through a small metallic bead, a glass bead and then the diamond. Twist the wire at the back and attach the ear wires and eye pins.

JEWELLERY POUCH

The intense dark red of the velvet here provides a suitable setting for your most precious jewels but it also evokes the softness and tonal contrasts of rose petals, which are stylized into a free-embroidered motif to decorate the pouch.

YOU WILL NEED

MATERIALS

wadding (batting)
dark red velvet
taffeta lining fabric
tracing paper
matching sewing thread
paper
velvet ribbon
small button

EQUIPMENT

tape measure
dressmaker's scissors
dressmaker's pins
sewing machine, with darning foot
pencil
fabric marker
needle

1 Cut pieces of wadding (batting) and lining fabric, 38 x 25 cm/15 x 10 in. Assemble and pin together with the velvet in the middle. Stitch seams across the top and bottom. Turn right sides out so the wadding (batting) is inside, and pin the top and bottom seams. Trace the template from the back of the book, enlarging if necessary. Transfer the rose and leaf motifs to the fabric. Select the darning or free embroidery mode on the machine. Stitch the design.

2 With right sides together, stitch the two short edges together to form a tube, leaving the lining unstitched. Fold under the lining and slip stitch the edges together. Make a paper template for a circle with a 7.5 cm/3 in radius. Use it to cut pieces of velvet and taffeta to this size. With right sides together, stitch around the seam allowance, leaving a 4 cm/1½ in gap. Clip the seam allowance and turn the circle the right way out. Hand stitch the circle to the bottom edge of the tube. Cut a 40 cm/16 in length of ribbon. Stitch the centre point to the side seam of the bags, and sew a small button in place.

DECORATIVE BATH MAT

Stitch this plain cotton bath mat in colours to co-ordinate with your bathroom.

YOU WILL NEED

MATERIALS

natural cotton bath mat
tacking (basting) thread
soft cotton embroidery
thread, in a variety of
colours

EQUIPMENT

needle
large, sharp needle
embroidery scissors

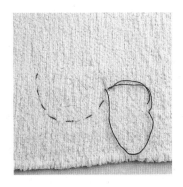

1 Stitching the lines about 2.5 cm/1 in apart, tack (baste) 12 large swirls spaced evenly over the bath mat. Leaving a 5 cm/2 in end of soft cotton on the reverse side, stitch each spiral using 2.5 cm/1 in running stitches. When you reach the end of the spiral, work back along the stitching line to fill in the spaces.

2 Work two spirals in each colour. Tie the ends of the embroidery thread together with a secure knot.

3 Work cross stitches in between the spirals, beginning and finishing the thread in the same way. Finish the mat with a row of different coloured cross stitches along each end.

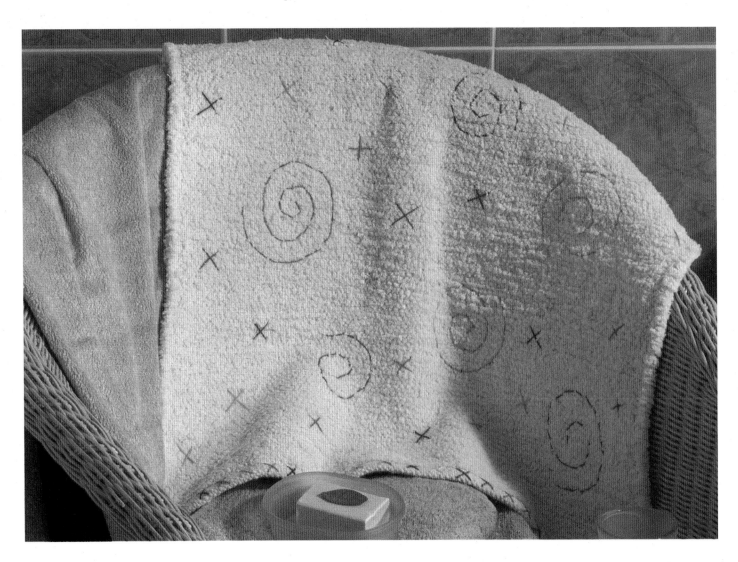

EMBROIDERED TABLECLOTH

Choose a fine white or cream linen, lawn or cambric for this cloth. The birds are painted with fabric paints and fixed by ironing; the cut-work is finished with a zigzag stitch in a contrasting colour.

YOU WILL NEED

MATERIALS

tracing paper
graph paper
stencil card
cotton or linen fabric, to fit table
water-based fabric paints
card
contrasting thread

EQUIPMENT

pencil
magic marker
iron
paintbrush
fabric marker
sewing machine
small, sharp scissors

1 Trace the templates from the back of the book, enlarging on graph to size. Redraw it with a magic marker on stencil card. Wash, dry and press the fabric.

2 Mark the position of the birds, spacing them evenly around the edge of the cloth. Position the template under the fabric and smooth out the fabric. Apply fabric paint to the cloth, tracing the design.

3 Fix the paint by ironing on the wrong side of the fabric, following the manufacturer's instructions. Draw around the scallop template along the edge of the cloth with a fabric marker.

4 With contrasting thread, stitch along the marked line and then machine stitch a close zigzag around the scallops. Trim the excess fabric down to the stitched edge using small, sharp scissors.

SCENTED CUSHION

A regal little cushion fit for a Leo. When stuffing the cushion, you can either scent the wadding (batting) with a few drops of essential oil, or pack a small amount of pot-pourri in among the filling.

YOU WILL NEED

MATERIALS

tracing paper
cream cotton fabric,
23 x 23 cm/9 x 9 in
tear-off interfacing,
23 x 23 cm/9 x 9 in
stranded embroidery
cotton: black and 5
graduated shades of yellow
and gold
dark blue velvet,
34 x 17 cm/13 x 6½ in
matching sewing thread
gold cord, 38 cm/15 in
polyester toy wadding
(batting)
essential oil or pot-pourri
4 gold tassels

EQUIPMENT

pencil
transfer pen
needle
embroidery hoop
iron
scissors

1 Trace the template from the back of the book, enlarge it to the size required, and transfer it to the cotton fabric. Tack (baste) the tear-off interfacing to the back and mount in a hoop. Using two strands of embroidery thread, work the two circles in split stitch in dark gold, then outline the lion and zodiac symbols in black using straight and split stitch. Fill in the background with long and short stitch, blending the colours from light to dark gold.

2 Remove the hoop and press the embroidery lightly on the wrong side. Cut out, leaving a 5 mm/¼ in seam allowance. Clip the curves and tack (baste) the allowance to the back.

3 Cut the velvet into two 17 cm/6½ in squares. Tack (baste) and stitch the motif to the centre front of one square. Slip stitch the gold cord around the circle. Make a small slit in the velvet and push the two ends to the wrong side. Sew over the slit and unpick the tacking (basting) threads.

4 With right sides together, join three sides. Clip the corners and turn. Fill with scented polyester wadding (batting). Slip stitch the opening and sew a tassel to each corner.

NURSERY CUSHION

*T*his is a delightful cushion that would lend a touch of jollity to any nursery and would also make a lovely accessory for a bedroom chair.

YOU WILL NEED

MATERIALS

tracing paper
dressmaker's carbon paper
white sprigged cotton fabric,
42 x 42 cm/16½ x 16½ in
3 skeins dark red stranded
embroidery thread
4 strips darker patterned
cotton fabric,
1 m x 14 cm/1 yd x 5½ in
matching and contrasting
sewing threads
2 rectangles plain cotton,
30 x 42 cm/12 x 16½ in
dark red velvet ribbon,
120 cm/48 in
cushion pad,
40 x 40 cm/16 x 16 in

EQUIPMENT

pencil
embroidery hoop
needle
sewing machine
dressmaker's pins

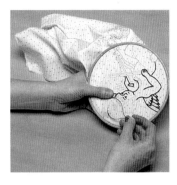

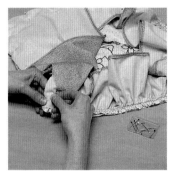

1 Trace the template from the back of the book. Transfer to the sprigged cotton fabric, using dressmaker's carbon paper. Stretch the fabric in a hoop and embroider the outline in chain stitch. To make the frill, join the darker fabric strips together and hem one long edge.

2 Run a gathering thread along the edge opposite the hem. With right sides together, pin the gathers to the embroidered cushion front, matching the four joins to the four corners. Draw up the gathering thread until the frill fits the cushion, pin and stitch.

3 For the backing, stitch a double hem along one long side of each rectangle of plain fabric. With right sides together, place one rectangle at each end of the embroidered front, so that the hemmed edges lie to the centre. Pin and stitch around the outer edge, leaving a small seam allowance. Turn the cushion the right way out. Make four bows from the velvet ribbon. Sew to the corners of the cushion and insert the pad.

APPLIQUE, PATCHWORK AND CROSS STITCH

Appliqué, patchwork and cross stitch are crafts requiring only a modicum of skills that nevertheless produce individual and stunning results. The techniques can be used to give an extra sparkle to a whole range of items such as cards, bags, towels and mats as well as bed linen and clothes. The materials needed are all readily available, and most needleworkers will probably already have most of the equipment required. Once you have mastered the techniques, you will be able to experiment fully to create your own designs and projects on fabrics of your choice.

There are few constraints with these needlework techniques, as even the most unassuming scraps of fabric and old clothes can be rejuvenated given a little imagination and some basic know-how. In addition there is a selection of cross-stitch projects for enthusiasts of this most popular of needlecrafts!

BASIC TECHNIQUES

The materials and equipment required for appliqué, patchwork and cross stitch are more or less the same as those for hand and machine embroidery.

ABOVE *Appliqué and patchwork projects make full use of any fabric remnants.*

Using fusible bonding web

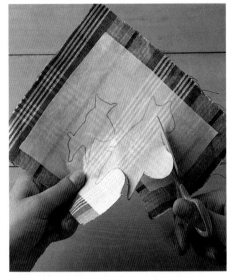

1 Fusible bonding web is useful for stabilizing appliqué pieces, as it binds on to the fabric when pressed with an iron. You can then cut around the shape to be appliquéd, with the bonding web in place to act as a stiffener.

2 Fusible bonding web has a backing paper that can be peeled off. The pieces can then be pressed in place on the ground fabric.

Basic cross stitches

Cross stitch can either be worked as a single stitch or in a row that is completed in two journeys. Irrespective of which method is used, the top stitch should always face in the same direction. If working a border or a detailed piece of cross stitch, it is helpful to put a pin in the work showing the direction that the top stitch should face.

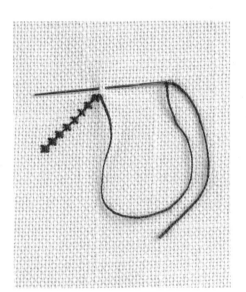

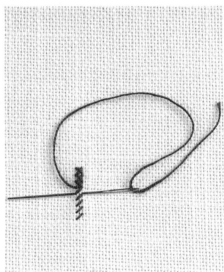

Single cross stitch

This produces a slightly raised cross and should be used for individual stitches and small details. It is also ideal when stitching with tapestry wool.

Row of cross stitches

First work a row of cross stitches either diagonally or in a straight line. Complete the cross stitches by stitching the other half on the way back.

BASIC TECHNIQUES

Simple appliqué

Embroidered appliqué pieces

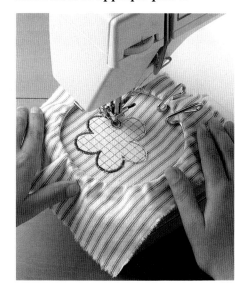

Draw the shape on the fabric with a fabric marker and embroider the pattern over the edges of the outline.

Straight stitch appliqué

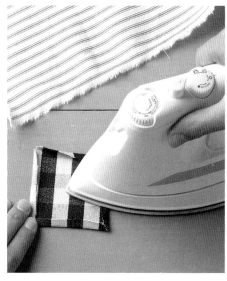

1 Cut out the shape, making sure to leave a 1 cm/½ in allowance all round. Press the allowance to the wrong side, snipping away corners and curves.

2 Pin the piece to the fabric and work a straight stitch all round.

Zigzag or satin stitch appliqué

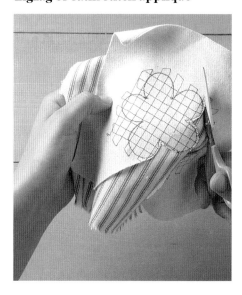

Pin the appliqué piece to the ground fabric and stitch around the outline. Trim away the excess fabric close to the stitched line. Work a zigzag stitch around the outline, covering raw edges. This can be followed by a second line of satin stitch.

Shadow appliqué

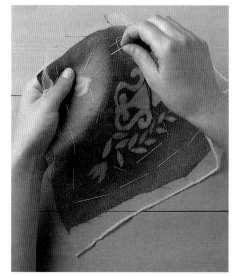

1 Work the appliqué pieces using one of the methods described before, then pin and tack a piece of sheer fabric over the design.

2 Use matching thread to stitch over the sheer fabric, close to the stitches on the appliquéd pieces.

HERALDIC TABLEMAT

*M*edieval retainers used to wear circular badges with a distinctive family motif on their clothes to identify them with their feudal overlord: such emblems were much simpler designs than armorial bearings and were often animals or flowers. For this project, you could create your own heraldic design.

YOU WILL NEED

MATERIALS	EQUIPMENT
PVC (vinyl) coated cotton fabric: plain blue, plain red and co-ordinating print	pair of compasses
	pencil
PVA (white) glue	scissors
tracing paper	paintbrush
thin card or paper	sheet of plastic
baize or felt, for backing	sewing machine, with
quilting thread	leather needle

1 Decide on the diameter of your mat, then draw and cut out a rim of plain blue fabric. Glue this to the background print fabric, to secure it while you sew.

2 Trace an animal template from the back of the book, enlarging if necessary, and transfer it to thin card or paper. Cut it out and draw around it on the reverse of the plain red fabric. Cut it out.

3 Glue the animal in the centre of the mat, and glue a piece of baize or felt to the back. Cover with a sheet of plastic and leave under a weight until it is dry.

4 Using quilting thread, machine stitch around the edges of the motif and in rows around the border. Use a long, straight stitch. Trim the edge of the mat and wipe off any glue.

OAK LEAF POTHOLDER

Many quilt patterns are inspired by natural images. This oak-leaf pattern is based on a block from an appliqué quilt made in 1850.

YOU WILL NEED

MATERIALS

thin card or paper
fusible bonding web
green felt,
15 x 15 cm/6 x 6 in
checked cotton fabric,
22 x 30 cm/9 x 12 in
2 polyester wadding
(batting) squares,
22 cm/9 in
thick cotton backing fabric,
18 x 18 cm/7 x 7 in
tacking (basting) thread
matching sewing thread
small eyelet screw
wooden toggle

EQUIPMENT

pencil
tape measure
fabric marker
iron
dressmaker's scissors
dressmaker's pins
needle

1 Trace the template from the back of the book, enlarging it to 14 cm/5½ in across. Transfer the outline to the bonding web with a fabric marker and iron it on to the green felt. Cut out the shape.

2 Cut a 22 cm/9 in square from the checked cotton fabric. Peel off the backing paper from the felt square and iron it centrally on to the cotton fabric square. Iron under a hem of 1 cm /½ in.

3 Pin the polyester wadding (batting) squares between the backing fabric and the decorated square. Pin, tack (baste) and slip stitch the turned edge over the backing square to conceal the raw edges.

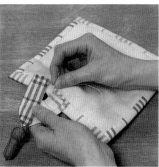

4 For the hanger, sew together the long sides of the remaining checked cotton fabric. Screw the eyelet into the toggle and thread the hanger through. Fold it in half and sew it in place.

MATISSE OUTFIT

*T*he artist Henri Matisse spent his later years creating dynamic and exciting paper collages, characterized by bold colours and strong graphic shapes. They were the inspiration behind this collection of clothes, which shows just how easy it is to customize a ready-made garment and so transform it into something really individual.

YOU WILL NEED

MATERIALS

*tracing paper
plain white T-shirt
fusible bonding web
scraps of plain cotton fabric
in bright colours
matching sewing threads
plain white long-sleeved
shirt
coloured buttons
denim jacket*

EQUIPMENT

*pencil
fabric marker
dressmaker's scissors
iron
sewing machine
needle*

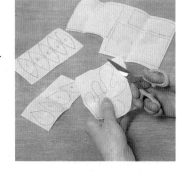

1 Trace the template from the back of the book, enlarging it to fit your T-shirt, and transfer each element of the design, in reverse, on to fusible bonding web with a fabric marker. Cut out roughly.

2 Choose three colours for the background shapes and iron one rectangle on to each. Cut out along the outline, peel off the backing paper and iron in place. Stitch around the outside edge with a narrow zigzag stitch in matching thread.

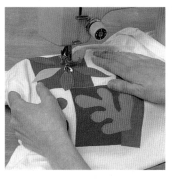

3 Cut out the branched and single leaf shapes in the same way and iron them on to the T-shirt.

4 Sew each shape in place with zigzag stitch, working accurately around the curves. Iron lightly.

5 Finish off on the reverse of the work, knotting the ends of the threads together and clipping close to the surface.

6 Customize a plain white shirt by removing the buttons and pocket. Wash and iron. Sew appliqué motifs to each side of the front, as you did for the T-shirt.

7 Replace the white buttons with brightly coloured ones, chosen to match the appliquéd design.

8 Decorate the back of the denim jacket in the same way; again, use coloured buttons to add the final detail.

APPLIQUED SUNFLOWER CARD

A home-made card is much nicer than a bought one, and this cheery sunflower design would be perfect for someone with a high-summer birthday.

YOU WILL NEED

MATERIALS	EQUIPMENT
tracing paper	*pencil*
yellow and brown fabric	*fabric marker*
scraps	*dressmaker's scissors*
fabric glue	*needle*
background fabric	
embroidery thread	
green paper scraps	
blank card and envelope	
paper glue	

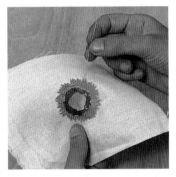

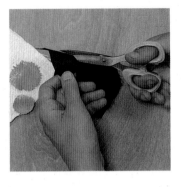

1 Trace the template from the back of the book, enlarging if necessary. Using the fabric marker, transfer the outline to the yellow fabric first and cut it out. Then cut out the smaller centres from brown fabric.

2 Stick the yellow piece on to the background fabric and the brown one on top. Then stick the third piece on top. Sew from the edge of the inner ring, using a running stitch on the centre piece.

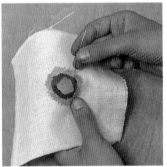

3 On the dark brown ring, sew from the outer to the inner edge in one large stitch, like a very loose, random satin stitch, to give a textured effect. Continue all the way round.

4 On the centre piece, sew running stitches at random, to give the effect of seeds. Sew on green paper leaves. Check for any loose threads on the back and tie them in. Trim the fabric to the correct size for the aperture of the card. Stick the appliqué in position cleanly.

STAR PATCHWORK SACHET

*P*atchwork stars made out of diamond shapes appear on many early American quilts; this one is based on the eight-point Lone Star motif. Lining the patches with backing paper is the traditional English way of making patchwork. It keeps the shapes sharp and accurate when joining the points of the star.

YOU WILL NEED

MATERIALS
*tracing paper
thin card
mustard-yellow
cotton fabric,
12.5 x 20 cm/5 x 8 in
green and white check
cotton fabric,
12.5 x 20 cm/5 x 8 in
dark orange cotton fabric,
20 x 40 cm/8 x 16 in
backing paper
tacking (basting) thread
matching sewing thread
dried herbs or pot-pourri
1 small pearl button*

EQUIPMENT
*pencil
scissors
dressmaker's scissors
ruler
needle
iron
dressmaker's pins*

1 Trace the templates from the back of the book, enlarging if necessary. Cut eight diamonds, four squares and four triangles from thin card. Add a 5 mm/¼ in allowance and cut out four yellow and four check diamonds, four orange squares and four orange triangles. Lay the backing paper in the centre of each shape, turn the seam over the paper, folding at the points, and tack (baste) in place.

2 Stitch a yellow and a check diamond together along one edge, then sew an orange square into the right angle. Make four of these units, then join together to form a star. Sew the orange triangles into the remaining spaces to complete the square. Iron lightly and remove all the tacking (basting) threads.

3 Cut a 19 cm/7½ in square from the remaining orange fabric and iron a 5 mm/¼ in seam allowance all round. With wrong sides together, pin this square to the patchwork and overstitch around the outside edge leaving a 7.5 cm/3 in gap on one side. Fill with herbs or pot-pourri and sew up the opening. Sew the button to the centre of the star.

APPLIQUE THROW

*T*his appliqué throw *recycles an old blanket as its background fabric and is pleasingly quick to put together, using fusible bonding web. Old buttons and bold woollen embroidery stitches add detail and colour.*

YOU WILL NEED

MATERIALS

cream blanket
matching and contrasting crewel wool
tracing paper
thin card or paper
four pieces of flannel fabric, 25 x 50 cm/10 x 20 in
green, rust and brown felt, 30 x 30 cm/12 x 12 in
fusible bonding web, 1.5 m/1½ yd
assorted shirt buttons (optional)
65 larger brown buttons (optional)

EQUIPMENT

dressmaker's scissors
tape measure
tapestry needle
pencil
fabric marker
iron
pressing cloth

1 Cut a rectangle measuring 1 x 1.3 m/40 x 50 in from the blanket. Fold a 1 cm/½ in hem around the outside edge and sew with a large blanket stitch worked in cream wool.

2 Trace the template for the diamond from the back of the book, carefully enlarging it to 20 cm/8 in high. Use this as a guide for cutting 25 diamonds of different colours from the flannel fabric.

3 Enlarge the leaf templates to fit within the diamonds. For each motif, choose a felt colour that tones with the background fabric. Trace the various leaf outlines, in reverse, on to fusible bonding web with a fabric marker. Cut out roughly and iron on to the felt, then cut out neatly. Peel off the backing paper and iron a leaf to the centre of each diamond.

4 Sew the leaves down using a single strand of crewel wool and a running stitch or blanket stitch – follow the picture as a guide. Some of the leaves have an extra appliquéd motif or a cut-out shape; you can make your own variations on these ideas.

5 Use straight stitch to embroider a vein pattern on some leaves and sew on the extra motifs using a cross or straight stitch.

6 Sew on tiny shirt buttons as a finishing touch, or add embroidered stars. (If the throw is for a small child, do not use buttons.) Each leaf can be different, or you could make several in the same colours.

7 Iron fusible bonding web on to the back of each diamond. Peel off the backing paper and arrange them in five rows of five, leaving an even border all around. Iron in place using a pressing cloth.

8 If desired, sew a large button over each diamond intersection, using wool in a contrasting colour.

ROSE APPLIQUE BAG

*T*his *attractive shopping bag recycles old table linen, fabric remnants and buttons. Look for unworn areas of old tablecloths or damask napkins to combine with other kinds of material.*

YOU WILL NEED

MATERIALS

*rose-print furnishing
fabric remnant
fusible bonding web
tracing paper
striped or checked table
napkins, cloths or remnants
calico, 60 x 83 cm/
24 x 33 in
matching sewing threads
6 old buttons*

EQUIPMENT

*dressmaker's scissors
iron
pencil
sewing machine
ruler
fabric marker
safety pin
needle*

1 Pick out five interesting rose motifs and eight single leaf motifs from the fabric and cut them out roughly.

2 Iron the wrong side of the roses and leaves to the bonding web. Cut around the edges, simplifying the outlines to make them easier to sew.

3 Trace the template from the back of the book, enlarging if necessary, and trace six flower shapes on to the paper side of more bonding web. Cut them out roughly and iron them on to the striped or checked fabrics. Cut around the outlines. Make ten leaves in the same way and one large blue and white jug.

4 Cut a 50 x 83 cm/20 x 33 in calico rectangle and fold it in half widthways. Peel the backing paper from the jug and iron in place on the centre front. Using matching thread and a narrow satin stitch, sew in place. Remove the backing paper from the leaves and flowers and arrange them around the jug. Iron in place.

5 Sew the shapes in place with satin stitch, using matching thread and working over the outside edges of the fabric. Finish off all the threads on the wrong side.

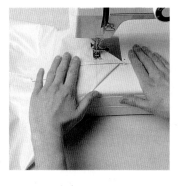

6 Join the bottom and side edges with French seams, for strength. Turn inside out and flatten one corner, to make a right-angled point at the end of the bottom seam. Measure 5 cm/2 in down from the end and mark a line across the corner. Sew across this line. Repeat for the other corner, to make a flat base for the bag.

7 Turn under, press and stitch a double hem of 2.5 cm/1 in around the top of the bag. Cut the remaining calico into two equal strips and fold each in half lengthways. Join 1 cm/½ in from the outside edge and, using a safety pin, turn inside out. Top stitch both sides and sew one handle to each side of the bag.

8 Sew a button to the centre of each plain flower, as a finishing touch.

FLEUR-DE-LYS TIEBACK

*M*ake *this smart tieback with a beautifully stylized lily to add restrained elegance to a plain or striped curtain.*

YOU WILL NEED

MATERIALS
tracing paper
white cotton poplin,
20 x 90 cm/ 8 x 36 in
navy cotton poplin,
30 x 90 cm/ 12 x 36 in
navy-white striped poplin,
50 x 90 cm/20 x 36 in
wadding (batting),
thin card or paper
fusible bonding web,
20 x 90 cm/ 8 x 36 in
tacking (basting) thread
matching sewing thread
two white "D" rings

EQUIPMENT
pencil
dressmaker's scissors
dressmaker's pins
fabric marker
iron
needle
sewing machine

1 Trace the tieback template from the back of the book, enlarging it to fit the width needed for your curtain. Cut out the shape in each of the fabrics and the wadding (batting). Mark the positions of the motifs on the white fabric.

2 Trace the fleur-de-lys motif and cut it out on card or paper. Draw around it seven times on the backing paper of the bonding web and iron on to the remaining navy fabric. Cut out the shapes carefully.

3 Iron the motifs on to the white fabric. Layer the wadding (batting) between the striped and navy fabrics, lay the white fabric on top and tack (baste). Quilt around the motifs. Cut two 6 cm/2¼ in bias strips from the striped fabric. Pin one piece along the top edge and stitch, leaving a 1.5 cm/⅝ in allowance. Fold the binding to the back, turn in the raw edge, pin and hem. Stitch the second strip along the bottom edge. Loop each end of the binding through a "D" ring, turn in the raw edge neatly and stitch.

ORANGE SAMPLER

The fruit basket, piled high with oranges and lemons, was a popular cross-stitch motif in the nineteenth century. You can use the colours suggested here, or experiment with your own shades of embroidery threads to make a more personalized design.

YOU WILL NEED

MATERIALS

tacking (basting) thread
white cross stitch fabric,
15 x 20 cm/6 x 8 in
stranded embroidery
threads: orange, light
orange, yellow, ochre, dark
olive, light olive and
chocolate-brown
mount board
plain wooden frame, with
9 x 14 cm/3½ x 5½ in
opening

EQUIPMENT

needle
tapestry needle
embroidery scissors
iron
craft knife
cutting mat

1 Using tacking (basting) thread, mark guidelines vertically and horizontally across the centre of the fabric. Follow the chart at the back of the book; the sampler is worked with three strands of embroidery thread throughout, and one square of the chart represents one cross stitch. Using orange thread, work the centre orange of the bottom row of fruit.

2 Stitch the other oranges, then work the leaves around them and the basket. Use the guidelines to establish the position of the other motifs and count the squares between them carefully. When the design is complete, unpick the tacking (basting) threads and iron lightly from the back of the work.

3 Cut a piece of mount board to fit the finished piece, using the lining paper from the frame as a guide. Place the board centrally on the back of the work and lace the two long sides together using long stitches. Repeat the process with the two short sides, then insert in the frame.

CRADLE QUILT

*W*ith its contrast-ing patchwork squares and heart motifs reminiscent of American folk art, this embroidered quilt will look really special in a cradle or crib.

YOU WILL NEED

MATERIALS

blue cotton chambray,
140 x 90 cm/54 x 36 in
white cotton fabric,
15 x 60 cm/6 x 24 in
graph paper,
20 x 20 cm/8 x 8 in
tracing paper
dressmaker's carbon paper
stranded embroidery
threads: white, red
and blue
fusible bonding web,
25 x 37 cm/10 x 15 in
5 scraps of checked or
striped cotton shirting
matching sewing thread
iron-on wadding (batting),
60 x 60 cm/24 x 24 in
tacking (basting) thread
strips of chambray,
5 x 65 cm/2 x 26 in

EQUIPMENT

iron
dressmaker's scissors
pen or hard pencil
dressmaker's pins
sewing machine
needle

1 Iron the fabric. Using the graph paper as a template, cut four squares of blue chambray and five of white cotton. Make sure that you cut all the squares exactly in line with the grain of the fabric.

2 Trace the heart template from the back of the book, enlarging if necessary. Using dressmaker's carbon paper, transfer it on to the centre of one blue square, using a pen or hard pencil and pressing firmly to achieve a strong line.

3 Using three strands of white thread, work over the lines in a small, regular running stitch. Work a red whipstitch over the inner and outer heart outlines. Work a blue whipstitch over the parallel lines inside the heart. Repeat the process with the three remaining blue squares.

4 Trace just the outline of the heart template on to the paper side of the bonding web. Cut out roughly around the edge and then iron the heart on to a piece of shirting, following the manufacturer's instructions. Make sure that the centre line matches the stripes or checks. Cut out carefully around the outline. Repeat with the remaining fabric scraps.

5 Remove the backing paper and iron the heart on to the centre of a white square. With three strands of embroidery thread, work a row of feather stitching around the outside of the heart, to conceal the raw edges. Repeat with the remaining four pieces of shirting and white squares.

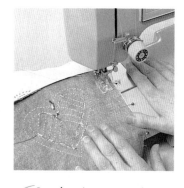

6 Lay the nine squares in three rows of three, with alternating colours. Machine stitch along each row, with right sides facing, and allowances of 1 cm/½ in. Iron with the allowances lying on the blue squares. Pin the rows together, matching the joins. Sew along the long edges with 1 cm/½ in allowances. Clip the seams where the squares meet. Iron the seams towards blue squares.

7 Cut a square of iron-on wadding (batting) the same size as the completed quilt. Secure it to the back of the quilt, following the manufacturer's instructions. Cut a square of chambray the same size for the backing. Tack (baste) it to the back of the wadding (batting).

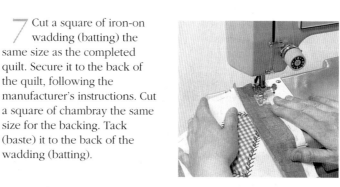

8 Fold the cambray strips in half lengthways and iron the folds. Iron 5 mm/¼ in under each long edge. Pin in the first strip with the raw edge lying 1 cm/½ in from the quilt edge. Sew 2 cm/¾ in from the edge. Fold the facing over, turn in the hem and slip stitch. Repeat for each side. Neaten each corner and remove the tacking (basting).

PATCHWORK CUBE

*T*his soft baby's toy is a perfect project for a beginner to patchwork. Experiment with a different pattern for each side of the cube.

YOU WILL NEED

MATERIALS	EQUIPMENT
7 x 90 cm/2¾ x 36 in fabric strips, in five colours matching threads wadding (batting)	dressmaker's scissors dressmaker's pins sewing machine needle

PREPARATION

Cut each strip into thirteen 7 cm/2¾ in squares. Arrange the squares into six blocks, cutting some to make triangles.

1 Pin and stitch the squares together. Right sides facing, pin and stitch four blocks to a central one. Join the top block to one side block. Stitch the sides in pairs, leaving a small gap to turn through.

2 Fill with wadding (batting) and slip stitch the gap. Make a small rouleau loop and stitch to one corner.

TABLEMAT AND NAPKIN RING

A design adapted from the yoke of a dress worn by the Baluchi people of western Pakistan.

YOU WILL NEED

MATERIALS

tacking (basting) thread
25 x 36 cm (10 x 14 in)
black 18 count Aida for
each tablemat
8 x 22 cm (3 x 8½ in) black
18 count Aida for each
napkin ring
stranded cotton DMC: 349,
352, 3731, 3733
sewing thread

EQUIPMENT

needle
scissors
embroidery hoop (frame)
tapestry needle

TABLEMAT

Tack (baste) a guideline round the bottom righthand corner of the Aida 5 cm (2 in) from the edge. Work three complete diamonds using two strands of cotton.

1 To make up: mitre the corners and turn a small 5 mm (¼ in) hem to the reverse side. Tack (baste), then machine or hand stitch to finish.

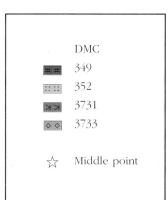

	DMC
▨	349
⋯	352
⊳⊲	3731
◇	3733
☆	Middle point

NAPKIN RING

Tack (baste) a guideline down the centre of the Aida. Using two strands of cotton, work three full diamonds in cross stitch, with a half diamond at each end.

1 To make up: turn under the top and bottom edges by 5 mm (¼ in) and oversew invisibly on the wrong side. Trim the ends of the band to 5 mm (¼ in), turn under and slip stitch together from the right side.

SEASHELL BEACH BAG

*C**risp cream and navy give this smart beach bag a*
nautical feel. The charm of the project lies in
combining colours to give a three-dimensional feel.

YOU WILL NEED

MATERIALS

cream cotton drill or denim,
55 x 75 cm/21½ x 30 in
tracing paper
stencil card
spray adhesive
2 lengths blue cotton drill or
denim, 15 x 38 cm/6 x 15 in
dry fabric stencil paints:
dark yellow, dark red and
navy blue
sewing threads: white, dark
orange and blue
cream cord, 2 m/2 yd
masking tape

EQUIPMENT

dressmaker's scissors
craft knife
cutting mat
3 stencil brushes
iron
sewing machine
dressmaker's pins
ruler or tape measure

1 Cut the cream cotton drill in two lengthways. Trace the template from the back of the book, enlarging if necessary. Transfer it to stencil card and cut out. Spray the back lightly with adhesive and stencil five shells on to each piece of fabric, using two or three colours. When thoroughly dry, fix the paint according to the manufacturer's instructions.

2 With right sides together, sew a blue strip to the top edge of each cream piece, leaving a 1 cm/½ in seam allowance. Press the seam upwards. Pin rectangles right sides together and stitch around the main bag. Press under the seam allowances on the open sides of the blue fabric and top stitch in orange. Fold in half lengthways. Machine stitch parallel to the top stitch.

3 Cut the cord in half and bind the ends with masking tape. Thread both pieces through the bag. Remove the tape and bind the ends with blue thread, 5 cm/2 in from the ends. Fringe and comb the cord to make tassels. Trim neatly.

YELLOW ROSES LAMPSHADE

A hand-decorated lampshade makes the perfect finishing touch to any room scheme. This particularly charming one has roses made from textured paper that are enhanced when the light is switched on.

YOU WILL NEED

MATERIALS	EQUIPMENT
tracing paper	*soft and sharp pencils*
yellow and green textured	*fine black felt-tipped pen*
paper	*scissors*
fabric lampshade	*paintbrush*
PVA (white) glue	
matt water-based acrylic	
varnish	

1 Trace the templates from the back of the book, enlarging if necessary. Go over the lines again with a black pen.

2 Lay the yellow paper over the motif and trace the outline showing through, using a sharp pencil. Cut carefully along the lines and lay the pieces out on a flat surface. Trace and cut out the green pieces in the same way.

3 Stick the shapes on to the shade, spreading a thin layer of glue on the reverse of each piece as you go. Using the traced rose as a guide, stagger the motifs over the lampshade.

4 Glue the calyx and stem under each rose. Once the glue has dried, paint the shade with two coats of varnish.

BAROQUE VELVET CUSHION

*U*se richly coloured
velvets and gold
braid to create a gorgeous
baroque cushion.

YOU WILL NEED

MATERIALS

*2 coloured paper cupid
motifs
white cotton fabric,
30 x 40 cm/12 x 16 in
image transfer fluid
fabric glue
blue velvet,
42 x 62 cm/16½ x 25 in
metallic machine
embroidery threads: gold
and red
red velvet scraps
1 cm/½ in wide gold braid,
40 cm/16 in
2 pearl-drop beads
gold cord, 50 cm/20 in
matching sewing threads
2 squares matching taffeta,
42 x 42 cm/16½ x 16½ in
3 cm/1¼ in wide wire-edged
red ribbon, 2 m/2 yd
cushion pad
40 x 60 cm/16 x 24 in*

EQUIPMENT

*dressmaker's scissors
sewing machine
needle*

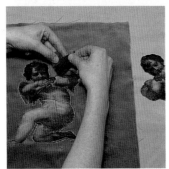

1 Follow the manufacturer's
instructions to transfer the
cupid motifs to the cotton fabric
with image transfer fluid. Cut
out each cupid and glue in
place on the velvet. Machine
stitch the edges with zigzag
stitch using gold thread. Cut one
large and two small hearts from
the red velvet. Stitch as before,
using red metallic thread.

2 Stitch gold braid around
the larger heart. Sew a
pearl-drop bead to the top and
bottom of the heart and trim
with gold cord, looping it
around the beads. Stitch the
cord in place.

3 Make the backing for the
cushion with the two
squares of taffeta, as described
in the Nursery Cushion project.
Clip the corners and turn the
work the right way out. Cut the
wire-edged ribbon into four
equal lengths and tie them into
bows. Trim the ends to
V-shapes and stitch one to each
corner. Insert the cushion pad.

STAR-SPANGLED SCARF

A lavish scattering of gold appliqué and beads on dark velvet creates a luxurious scarf for winter evenings.

YOU WILL NEED

MATERIALS

*burgundy velvet,
23 x 63 cm/9 x 25 in
gold velvet,
23 x 63 cm/9 x 25 in
tracing paper
fusible bonding web,
23 x 30 cm/ 9 x 12 in
gold machine
embroidery thread
translucent gold
rocaille beads
matching sewing thread
black velvet,
32 x 122 cm/12½ x 48 in
black glazed cotton,
56 x 89 cm/22 x 34½ in*

EQUIPMENT

*dressmaker's scissors
pencil
iron
pressing cloth
sewing machine
needle
dressmaker's pins*

1 Cut the burgundy velvet into two rectangles 23 x 32 cm/9 x 12½ in. From the gold velvet cut two 4 x 32 cm/ 1½ x 12½ in strips and two 6 x 32 cm/2½ x 12½ in strips.

Trace the templates from the back of the book, enlarging if necessary. Draw and cut out each star twice on the fusible bonding. Iron on to the wrong side of the remaining gold velvet. Cut out each star neatly along the outline. Peel off the backing paper and arrange eight stars on each burgundy rectangle. Iron in place using a pressing cloth. Using gold thread, machine around the edge of each appliqué star and work a spiral over the centres of the three largest shapes. Sew a thick sprinkling of beads to the background with double thread.

2 Join one wide and one narrow gold velvet strip to the long sides of each burgundy panel, using a 1 cm/½ in seam allowance. Attach a panel to each end of the black velvet,

joining the narrow gold strip to the main scarf. Iron all seams open lightly, using a cloth. Cut the lining fabric in half lengthways and join to form one long strip. Press the seam open, then pin the cotton lining to the scarf along the long edges with right sides facing. Stitch, leaving a 12.5 cm/5 in opening in the centre of one seam. Remove the pins and adjust the ends so that an equal amount of velvet lies on each side of the lining. Pin, then stitch across the ends. Clip the corners and turn the scarf to the right side. Press lightly and slip stitch the opening.

STAR-SPANGLED BANNER

Make a bold statement with this cheerful wall hanging, based on an American bed quilt from 1876.

YOU WILL NEED

MATERIALS

tracing paper
fusible bonding web,
76 x 142 cm/30 x 56 in
white cotton fabric,
30 x 40 cm/12 x 16 in
blue cotton fabric,
76 x 40 cm/30 x 16 in
matching sewing thread
dark red cotton fabric,
76 x 38 cm/30 x 15 in
medium weight wadding
(batting), 66 x 66 cm/
26 x 26 in
6 curtain rings, 2.5 cm/1 in
curtain pole with decorative
finials, 86 cm/34 in
acrylic paints: dark red
and cream
red cord, 130 cm/50 in

EQUIPMENT

pencil
dressmaker's scissors
iron
dressmaker's pins
sewing machine
needle
tacking (basting) thread or
safety pins
paintbrush

1 Trace the star template from the back of the book, enlarging if necessary. Transfer it to fusible bonding nine times and cut out. Iron them on to white fabric, then cut out and peel off the backing paper. Cut nine 14 cm/5½ in blue cotton squares and fuse a star to the centre of each.

2 Neaten the edges of the stars by stitching over them with a narrow satin stitch in white thread. Cut out four red and four white rectangles, each 7.5 x 14 cm/3 x 5½ in. Press all seams flat and join the red and white pieces in pairs along the longer sides.

3 Lay the squares alternating with the blue star squares as a border around the central star. Pin and sew together in three rows of three, then join the rows to form a square. Cut out four red and four white rectangles, each 7.5 x 40 cm/3 x 15½ in, and join in pairs along the longer sides.

4 With right sides together, stitch a blue square to each end of two of the rectangles. Stitch the remaining pieces to opposite sides of the central panel, with the white sides on the inner edge, then stitch the longer strips to the other two sides.

5 Cut 66 cm/26 in squares of wadding (batting) and blue cotton and tack (baste) to the patchwork with tacking (basting) thread or safety pins. Machine or hand quilt along the seam lines, then stitch all round the outside, 3 mm/⅛ in from the edge. Trim.

6 From the remaining blue cotton, cut four strips, each 3 x 66 cm/1¼ x 26 in for the binding. Iron in half lengthways, then press under 5 mm/¼ in along one edge. Pin each strip along one side of the quilted square, raw edges even, and stitch. Turn the folded edge to the back and slip stitch in place. Neaten the corners.

7 Sew the curtain rings to the top of the banner, spacing them evenly.

8 Remove the finials from the curtain pole and paint dark red, using a dry brush for a dragged effect. Paint cream stripes or details on the turned ends. Thread the pole through the rings and replace the finials. Attach the cord to one end of the pole and wrap it round, securing with matching cotton. Do the same with the other end, then make a loop in the centre.

SPICE-SCENTED POT STAND

The lovely homespun look of this pot stand is achieved by tinting all the fabrics with tea. Placing a hot pot on the mat releases a rich, spicy scent of cloves.

YOU WILL NEED

MATERIALS

calico, 18 x 18 cm/7 x 7 in
red gingham,
22 x 44 cm/9 x 18 in
blue ticking,
6 x 22 cm/2½ x 9 in
small blue check cotton,
6 x 22 cm/2½ x 9 in
tea bags
tracing paper
stencil card
masking tape
yellow-ochre stencil crayon
paper towels
stranded embroidery
threads: yellow-ochre and
beige
4 buttons
matching sewing thread
whole cloves

EQUIPMENT

bowl
iron
pencil
craft knife
cutting mat
metal ruler
masking tape
stencil brush
dressmaker's pins
needle
sewing machine

1 Wash all the fabrics to remove any dressing. Brew some strong tea and soak the fabrics until you are satisfied with the colour. It is best to do this in stages, re-dipping if you need to make them darker. Allow to dry and press well.

2 Trace the star template from the back of the book, enlarging if necessary. Transfer it to stencil card. Cut out the star using a craft knife and a ruler.

3 Tape the stencil in the centre of the calico. Work around the card with the stencil crayon, scribbling the paint near the edges of the shape, avoiding getting any on the fabric. Work the stencil brush into the crayon and gently ease the paint from the stencil on to the fabric with a light scrubbing action. Add more paint if necessary. Do not try to get an even coverage as this adds to the "antique" effect.

4 Iron the calico on the wrong side between sheets of paper towels to fix the motif and blot excess paint. Fold under the edges of the calico fabric until it measures 11.5 x 12 cm/4½ x 4¾ in. Press.

5 Pin the calico in the centre of one gingham square. With your fingers, gently fray one long edge of the ticking and check strips and pin them to opposite sides of the gingham, with the frayed edges pointing inwards.

6 Using three strands of yellow thread, stitch the strips to the gingham with a running stitch near the frayed edges. Using beige thread and running stitch, attach the calico square and sew a button in each corner. With wrong sides together, machine stitch the second gingham square to the decorated square, leaving an opening in one side.

7 Turn the holder to the right side and fill it with cloves. Do not overfill or the pot will be unsteady when resting on the mat. Neatly sew up the opening by hand.

ORANGES TEA TOWEL

Appliquéd shapes and machine embroidery make a hard-wearing decoration for bright tea towels. Choose a strong base shade to match your own kitchen colour scheme, or use these motifs on a set of towels in different colours.

YOU WILL NEED

MATERIALS	EQUIPMENT
tracing paper	*pencil*
thin card or paper	*scissors*
fusible bonding web	*iron*
scraps of yellow, orange	*tailor's chalk*
and green cotton fabric	*embroidery hoop*
tea towel	*sewing machine, with*
black machine embroidery	*darning foot*
thread	*needle*

1 Trace the template from the back of the book, enlarging if necessary. Transfer it to thin card or paper and cut out the orange and lemon motifs. Draw around each motif several times on the paper backing of fusible bonding web. Cut out roughly. Iron the web on to the wrong side of the fabric scraps and cut neatly around the outlines.

2 Arrange the shapes along the bottom of both ends of the tea towel until you are happy with your design. Remove the paper backing from the fusible bonding web and iron the motifs on to the towel.

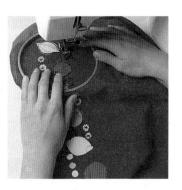

3 Use tailor's chalk to join up the motifs with a series of parallel lines. Put the work in an embroidery hoop. Select the darning or free embroidery mode on the sewing machine and work several lines of black stitching around each fruit. Work down the chalk lines with a series of small embroidered motifs. Hand sew French knots on the oranges.

SHAKER TOWEL

Cross-stitched hearts and initials conjure up the art of the Shakers, for whom the heart was a well-loved decorative image. Hearts denoted not the traditions of romantic love, but the spiritual devotion of the movement's followers, summed up in the saying "Hands to work, hearts to God."

YOU WILL NEED

MATERIALS

*homespun cotton gingham, 20 x 90 cm/8 x 36 in
cotton seersucker towel
tacking (basting) thread
stranded embroidery
threads: dark and light
crimson and dark turquoise
matching sewing thread*

EQUIPMENT

*dressmaker's scissors
tape measure
needle
embroidery hoop
iron
dressmaker's pins
sewing machine (optional)*

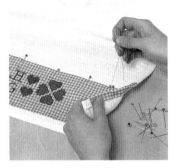

1 Wash the gingham and towel. Cut the gingham 5 cm/2 in wider than the towel. Mark the centre with two intersecting lines of tacking (basting) thread. Stretch the fabric in a hoop. Using the charts at the back of the book, embroider four initials in three strands of dark crimson thread. Work the second diagonal in the same direction each time.

2 Again, following the charts, embroider the four dark turquoise hearts in cross stitch on each side of the monogram. Then work the light crimson hearts. These are given extra definition with an outline of running stitch, worked in dark crimson thread. Press the embroidery lightly.

3 Trim the long edges so that there is 3.5 cm/1½ in of fabric on each side of the embroidery and press under 1 cm/½ in along each side. Fold the towel in half to find the centre point and pin the gingham along the bottom edge. Turn the sides of the gingham to the back of the towel and tack (baste) in place. Then stitch with matching thread.

245

NEEDLEPOINT MAT

*I*n *the 1950s, leaves were a great inspiration to designers, who turned them into almost abstract shapes. The muted colours of this needlepoint are also expressive of the period.*

YOU WILL NEED

MATERIALS	EQUIPMENT
tacking (basting) thread	*needle*
needlepoint canvas square	*fabric marker*
tapestry wools: 3 shades of	*tapestry needle*
cream, 2 shades of green,	*scissors*
yellow, gold and black	*metal ruler*
card	*craft knife*
black velvet, for backing	*cutting mat*
PVA (white) glue	

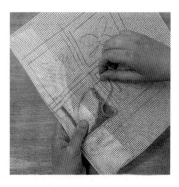

1 Tack (baste) vertically and horizontally across the canvas to mark the centre. Mark the design on to the canvas, following the chart at the back of the book; each square represents a stitch. Work the pattern in half cross stitch.

2 When the half cross stitch is complete, use black wool to embroider the details. Work the straight lines in back stitch and use French knots for the dots.

3 Measure the needlepoint and cut out a piece of card to the same size. Cut out a piece of velvet to this size plus a 2 cm/¾ in turning allowance all round. Spread glue on the card and stick it centrally on to the back of the velvet. Clip the corners, fold over the turning allowance and glue in place. Trim the canvas and clip the corners; turn the allowance to the wrong side. Spread glue on the wrong side of the card and press the needlepoint in place.

APPLIQUE STAR CARD

A beautiful birthday card to treasure, in which the traditional craft of tin-punching is combined with appliqué and embroidery.

YOU WILL NEED

MATERIALS

*light blue check cotton,
16 x 12 cm/6 x 4¾ in
medium blue check cotton,
10 x 12 cm/4 x 4¾ in
blue stranded embroidery
thread
dark blue check cotton,
4 x 16 cm/1½ x 6 in
tacking (basting) thread
silver embroidery thread
plain, unridged tin can,
14 x 24 cm/5½ x 9½ in
tracing paper
small piece of wood
all-purpose glue
silver card, folded in half*

EQUIPMENT

*dressmaker's scissors
dressmaker's pins
needle
can opener
tin snips
pencil
hammer
bradawl or large nail*

1 Cut the light blue fabric into four 4 cm/1½ in strips. Fold under the raw edge along the long side of each strip and pin it to the medium blue fabric. Using blue embroidery thread, sew small running stitches close to the fold line on both edges.

2 Cut out four 4 cm/1½ in squares of dark blue fabric. Turn under the edges of each square and pin in each corner of the panel. Turn under the remaining edges and tack (baste). Sew small running stitches in silver thread around the edges of the corner squares and embroider a simple star in the centre.

3 Remove the top and bottom of the tin can, cut down the back seam with tin snips and flatten. Trace the template from the back of the book, enlarging if necessary. Cut three tin stars and hammer the points flat. Lay the stars right side up on the wood and punch a star shape using the hammer and bradawl. Embroider three stars in silver thread. Glue the panel to the front of the card. Glue the tin stars in position.

APPLIQUE NOTEBOOK

*S*titch a delicate appliquéd cover for a special diary, address book or birthday book. This design is appropriate for a gardening or cookery notebook.

YOU WILL NEED

MATERIALS

scraps of plain cream, green check and orange patterned cotton fabrics
hardback notebook
tracing paper
fusible bonding web
stranded embroidery threads: green, orange and cream
green cotton fabric
tacking (basting) thread
matching sewing thread
orange, yellow and green buttons

EQUIPMENT

dressmaker's scissors
pencil
iron
embroidery needle
needle
sewing machine

1 Cut a rectangle of cream fabric slightly smaller than the front of your notebook. Trace the template from the back of the book, enlarging it to fit the notebook. Trace the shapes on to the backing paper of the fusible bonding web and cut out roughly. Iron the pieces on to their respective fabrics, then cut out.

2 Peel off the backing paper and iron on to the cream fabric. Chain stitch around the leaves in green. Work the urn handles in orange, and chain stitch around it. Cut the green fabric for the cover: the width is four times that of the book and the depth 2.5 cm/1 in more. Press under a 2.5cm/1 in fold at each short edge.

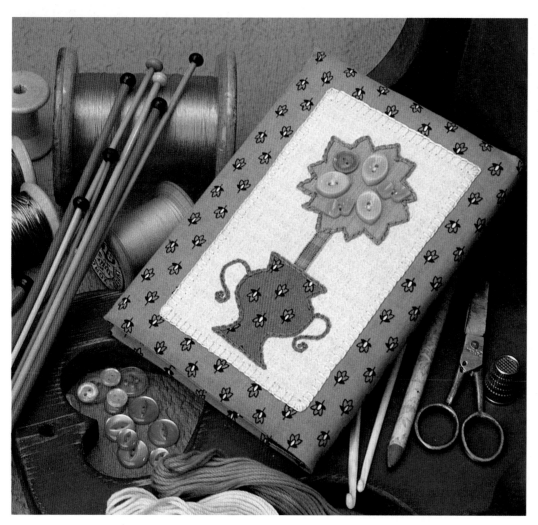

3 Fold in half, wrong sides together, and wrap around the book. Tuck the loose fabric under the front cover and stitch the embroidered panel on the centre front. Fold all the flaps underneath the book covers and loosely tack (baste) the raw edges together at top and bottom. Slip the cover off and machine stitch along the tacked lines. Turn the cover right side out and press. Sew the buttons on to the tree.

HAND TOWEL AND WASHCLOTH

*T*ransform a plain white hand towel and washcloth into an individual gift set, by adding appliquéd pansies in velvet and cotton prints.

YOU WILL NEED

MATERIALS	EQUIPMENT
tracing paper	*pencil*
velvet, 20 x 15 cm/8 x 6 in	*iron*
medium-weight iron-on	*fabric marker*
interfacing	*dressmaker's scissors*
3 different cotton floral	*dressmaker's pins*
print fabrics	*needle*
tacking (basting) thread	*sewing machine*
matching embroidery	
thread	
white cotton tea towel and	
washcloth	
matching machine	
embroidery threads	

1 Trace the templates from the back of the book, enlarging if necessary. Back the velvet with interfacing. Transfer the pansy to the interfacing and cut out three large and one small petal shape from the backed velvet. Cut one large flower shape from each of the three floral prints and one small flower from one of them.

2 Pin and tack (baste) the shapes to the flowers. With matching thread and satin stitch, stitch around the edge of the inner petals. Embroider details on to the flowers. Fill in the centre of each pansy with satin stitch and sew the petal markings with two lines of stem or back stitch. Iron the interfacing on to the back of each flower.

3 Tack (baste) flowers on the towel and cloth. Using matching thread on top and a white spool, appliqué in place.

4 Cover the towel borders with strips of floral fabric. Cut a piece 4 cm/1½ in wide to fit from the edge to the pansies with an allowance of 1 cm/½ in at each end. Press, pin and tack (baste) in place. Zigzag to finish.

APPLIQUED SHEET AND PILLOWCASE

*T*his bold design gives bedlinen a unique appeal. The shapes can be cut from either patterned or checked fabrics, according to your personal taste.

YOU WILL NEED

MATERIALS

tracing paper
graph paper
fusible bonding web
coloured or patterned fabrics
sheet and pillowcase
matching machine embroidery thread

EQUIPMENT

pencil
dressmaker's scissors
tape measure
iron
dressmaker's pins
sewing machine

1 Trace selected fabric patterns (or use the template from this book), enlarging as necessary for your design. Cut a piece of bonding web 25 x 25 cm/ 10 x 10 in. Lay it over the designs, and, with paper side facing, trace along the outlines.

2 Cut four or five pieces of the fabric to squares, each about 20 x 20 cm/8 x 8 in. Iron the bonding web on to the wrong side of the fabric and cut the shapes out.

3 Peel away the backing paper and arrange the cut-outs on the sheet and pillowcase, parallel to the fabric edge. Pin in place, then iron over the pieces, removing the pins as you go.

4 Work a zigzag machine stitch all around the fused edges to complete the design.

CHILD'S T-SHIRT

*A*n ordinary T-shirt is transformed, with appliquéd fabric scraps, machine embroidery and beads, into something really special. There's no reason why the same idea couldn't be used for an adult-size T-shirt.

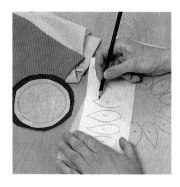 

YOU WILL NEED

MATERIALS

tracing paper
unbleached cotton T-shirt
fusible bonding web,
30 x 30 cm/12 x 12 in
yellow, orange and brown
cotton fabric scraps
machine embroidery
threads: light orange and
brown
small orange beads

EQUIPMENT

pencil
dressmaker's scissors
iron
pressing cloth
sewing machine

1 Trace the template from the back of the book, enlarging it to fit the T-shirt. Number the petals consecutively 1–12. Trace the even-numbered petals on to the paper side of the bonding and cut out. Iron the bonding to the yellow cotton. Repeat with the other petals in orange, and with brown for the centre.

2 Cut out all the shapes around the outlines and remove the backing paper. Place the petals in a circle on the front of the T-shirt, using the template as a guide. Iron them in place, using a cool iron and a pressing cloth.

3 Thread the sewing machine with orange thread and set it to a closely spaced medium-size zigzag. Stitch around the edges of all the petals to conceal the raw edges. Iron the flower centre in position and sew around its circumference with brown thread. Using brown thread, sew the beads on to the flower centre, making sure they are evenly scattered.

INITIAL CUSHION

A dapt this design by using the initials of a special *person or a couple as the centrepiece. It would make an ideal wedding gift, and a larger version could even include the couple's full names and the date and location of their wedding.*

YOU WILL NEED

MATERIALS

stranded embroidery threads
cream cross stitch fabric,
15 x 15 cm, 8 holes per cm/
6 x 6 in, 18 holes per in
cream silk backing fabric
thread
polyester wadding (batting)
cream cotton lace,
1 m x 6 cm/1 yd x 2½ in
4 mother-of-pearl buttons

EQUIPMENT

needle
dressmaker's scissors
dressmaker's pins
tape measure

1 Following the chart at the back of the book, or using an alphabet of your own, embroider the initials on to the cross stitch fabric. Work in cross stitch, using two strands of thread. Make sure that the four letters are squared up.

2 Cut the backing fabric to the same size as the front piece of the cushion. Pin with right sides together. Allowing a seam of 1 cm/½ in, stitch together, leaving a 5 cm/2 in gap at one edge. Trim the seam allowance and clip the corners. Turn inside out and stuff firmly. Slip stitch the opening.

3 Join the ends of the lace together and run a neat gathering thread along the straight edge. Gather the thread to fit around the outside of the cushion and pin it in place, allowing for extra fullness at the corners. Oversew the lace on to the cushion with matching thread, using small, neat stitches. Finish off by sewing a button to each corner.

MUSLIN (CHEESECLOTH) CURTAIN

*F*elt stars are caught in the deep hem of this unusual, sheer curtain. When machining them in, match the sewing thread to each of the colours of the felt.

YOU WILL NEED

MATERIALS

tracing paper
thin card or paper
felt squares: purple, light,
medium and dark blue,
light and dark pink
white muslin (cheesecloth),
to fit window, plus
36 cm/14 in
matching machine
embroidery threads
curtain tape

EQUIPMENT

pencil
scissors
tailor's chalk
iron
dressmaker's pins
tacking (basting) thread
needle
sewing machine

1 Trace the template from the back of the book, enlarging if necessary, transfer to thin card or paper and cut out. Using tailor's chalk, draw two stars on each felt colour and cut out.

2 Make a 25 cm/10 in hem in the muslin (cheesecloth) and press along the fold. Open it out and arrange the felt stars above the fold line and within the depth of the hem.

3 Carefully pin the hem back over the stars, turning under 1 cm/½ in along the raw edge. Pin the stars in position and tack (baste) around the edges 5 mm/¼ in outside the felt.

4 Machine stitch around each star using matching sewing thread. Sew the ends under the muslin (cheesecloth) and trim. Stitch the hem and add curtain tape at the top of the curtain.

FELT APPLIQUE FRAME

*F*elt is a great material because it does not fray when cut and it can be either sewn or glued in place. It comes in vivid colours, so it is ideal for a bright, modern interior. Copy the fluid outline of the frame shown here or experiment with your own ideas.

YOU WILL NEED

MATERIALS	EQUIPMENT
medium-density fibreboard (MDF)	pencil
emulsion (latex) paint	dust mask
selection of felt sheets	jigsaw
fabric glue	paintbrush
	ballpoint pen
	scissors

1 Copy your chosen design on to MDF and, wearing a dust mask, cut out the frame with a jigsaw. Apply a coat of paint and allow to dry. Place the frame on a sheet of felt and draw around it with a pen.

2 Snip the centre diagonally and cut out the felt. Glue the piece of felt on to the front of the frame. Glue the centre flaps back over the rebate on to the back of the frame.

3 Cut out a zigzag felt border and stick it to the inner edge of the frame. Glue narrow strips of felt in a contrasting colour around the rebate of the frame.

4 Cut out the felt shapes for decoration and stick them all over the frame.

COUNTRY-STYLE PILLOWCASE

Customize some plain bedlinen and give it a country appeal with this charming heart design. Emphasize the hearts and raise the design with a halo of multi-coloured running stitches.

YOU WILL NEED

MATERIALS

iron-on interfacing, 25 x 25 cm/10 x 10 in brightly coloured fabric scraps tacking (basting) thread pillowcase matching and contrasting threads

EQUIPMENT

pencil or fabric marker dressmaker's scissors iron needle dressmaker's pins crewel needle

1 Draw 17 hearts on to the interfacing and cut them out. Iron the interfacing to the fabric scraps and cut out the shapes, leaving a 5 mm/¼ in seam allowance.

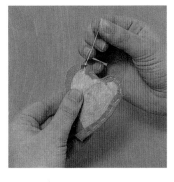

2 Clip the seam allowance around the curves, fold over and tack (baste) in place.

3 Arrange the hearts randomly over the pillowcase. Pin, tack (baste) and then slip stitch them in place. Using an assortment of coloured threads in one strand, work lines of tiny stitches around each heart in halos. Iron to finish the design.

PATCHWORK THROW

*T*his patchwork throw is an ideal way to use up odd remnants of furnishing fabrics. Your local upholsterer may sell off old sample books, which are a good source of different rose prints and contrasting weaves and textures.

YOU WILL NEED

MATERIALS

selection of rose-printed and plain fabrics
matching sewing thread
dusky red heavyweight Jacquard-weave fabric, 1.4 m/1 yd 16 in square
25 small buttons
woven furnishing braid, 4.75 m/5 yd 29 in

EQUIPMENT

iron
dressmaker's scissors
rotary cutter
quilter's square rule
cutting mat
sewing machine
dressmaker's pins and tacking (basting) thread, or safety pins
needle

1 Press the fabrics and cut out 18 plain and 18 patterned squares, each 20 cm/8 in square. For accuracy, use a rotary cutter and quilter's square for this.

2 Lay the pieces on the floor, to form a checkerboard of alternate plain and printed squares. Take time to find a pleasing pattern and balance of colours.

3 Sew rows of three squares together, leaving seam allowances of 1 cm/½ in. Press the seams open.

4 Sew three rows together, with the same seam allowances, carefully matching the joins to assemble four blocks of three by three squares. Join the four blocks together, to form a large square.

5 Square up the edges of the backing fabric. Fringe the edges by pulling away threads from each side.

6 Place the patchwork square in the centre of the backing fabric. Pin and tack (baste) or safety pin it in place.

7 Fix the patchwork in place by firmly sewing a button at each intersection point. Make sure that you sew through all the layers of fabric.

8 Slip stitch the braid on to the backing to attach and conceal the raw edges. Mitre the corners as you sew.

NEEDLEPOINT CUSHION

*T*his cushion would be perfect for an easy chair in the kitchen. The cushion is worked in simple stitches, but they produce a really stylish effect.

YOU WILL NEED

MATERIALS

12-count, single-thread canvas, 25 cm/10 in square
masking tape
tracing paper
2 skeins each 3-strand yarn: dark brown, 2 shades of mid-blue and light cream
1 skein each 3-strand yarn: light brown, light and dark yellow and warm light brown
velvet polyester wadding (batting),
19 cm/7½ in square
matching sewing thread

EQUIPMENT

pencil
scissors
felt-tipped pens
ruler
tapestry needle
dressmaker's pins
needle
drawing pins

1 Bind the edges of the canvas with masking tape. Trace the template from the back of the book, enlarging as required. Place the canvas over the tracing. Trace the main outline on the centre of the canvas, then fill in the detailed lines.

2 All the stitches are sewn with two strands of yarn. Work the main outline in dark brown tent stitch, and then fill in the petals with tent stitch and the flower centre with upright cross stitch. Rule a 16.5 cm/6½ in square around the flower and fill in the background with cushion stitch. Work with two different strands of blue together, and alternate blue and cream squares.

3 Block the canvas by spraying it lightly with water. Stretch and pin it squarely. When dry, trim the canvas to leave 1 cm/½ in all around the edge. Pin velvet to the backing, with right sides together. Stitch around three sides and turn right sides out. Insert the wadding (batting) and slip stitch the gap closed.

GARDEN APRON

F or this project you may need access to a colour photocopier. A collection of prints of old botanical paintings would make a beautiful apron for a horticulturally minded friend.

YOU WILL NEED

MATERIALS	EQUIPMENT
selection of colour images of leaves	*scissors*
cotton apron	*paintbrush*
masking tape (optional)	*soft cloth*
image transfer gel	

1 Make a selection of images and photocopy them in colour if you want to create a repeat pattern.

2 Cut around each leaf shape until you have enough to cover the apron.

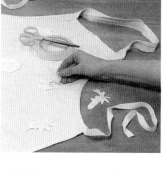

3 Plan your design by positioning the leaves on the apron, face down. Secure with masking tape if required. Paint a thick layer of transfer gel on to the first motif. Replace the image face down on the apron and rub with a soft cloth. Repeat with all the images and leave to transfer overnight. Soak the cloth with clean water and rub away the paper.

CHILD'S STRIP PATCHWORK RUCKSACK

Young girls will love to carry their lunch to school in this practical rucksack. Floral and gingham fabrics are sewn into a patched piece, which is then quilted along the seams.

YOU WILL NEED

MATERIALS

*paper
60 cm x 1 m/24 in x 1 yd
wadding (batting)
1 m x 90 cm/1 yd x 36 in
gingham fabric
assorted floral and
gingham cotton scraps
matching thread
tacking (basting) thread
1 m/1 yd rope
wooden toggle*

EQUIPMENT

*pencil
dressmaker's scissors
sewing machine
needle
dressmaker's pins*

PREPARATION

Enlarge the templates on to paper. Make a template for the straps measuring 50 x 4 cm/20 x 1½ in. Cut a rectangle 36 x 85 cm/14 x 34 in and a base, a flap and two straps in both wadding (batting) and gingham. Cut a gingham casing for the rope tie 1 m x 10 cm/1 yd x 4 in, and a gingham bias strip 1.5 m x 4 cm/1½ yd x 1½ in. Cut the scraps into strips 6 x 36 cm/2½ x 14 in. Leaving a 5 mm/¼ in seam allowance, stitch the strips into a patched piece.

Cut a rectangle, a base, a flap and two straps. Lay the patchwork on top of the matching wadding (batting) and gingham pieces, tack (baste) through all layers, then quilt along the seamlines. Join the two short ends to make a tube. Centre the wadding along the gingham straps and fold the fabric round it. Turn under the raw edge and stitch along the centre. Layer the patchwork, wadding and gingham base and flap pieces, and quilt diagonally.

1 Wrong sides facing, pin the base to the tube. Insert the straps at either end, centred 5 cm/2 in apart, and pin to the bag. Bind the raw edges with the gingham bias strip.

2 Bind the top edge with the casing strip so that the ends meet at the centre front of the bag. Fold the binding over to the right side, turn under a hem and top stitch below the previous seam.

3 Bind the shaped edge of the flap with the gingham bias strip. Right sides facing, pin the flap to the back of the bag just below the casing. Stitch two rows, 1 cm/½ in apart, close to the edge. Thread the rope through the casing and knot the ends. Make a narrow fabric rouleau and sew to the flap. Sew on the toggle.

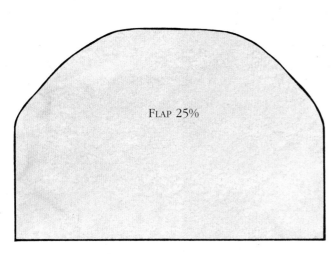

FLAP 25%

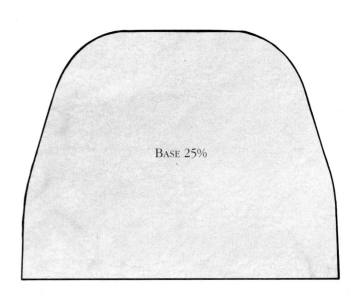

BASE 25%

CHILD'S BLANKET

Small children will love to snuggle up under this cosy blanket.

YOU WILL NEED

MATERIALS

blanket fabric
contrasting tapestry wool
assorted scraps of coloured
woollen or blanket fabric
large buttons

EQUIPMENT

dressmaker's scissors
crewel needle
saucer

1 Cut the blanket to the size required, turn under a small hem and blanket stitch the edge with tapestry wool.

2 Draw around a saucer on to the scraps of fabric and cut out circles. Hand appliqué to the blanket in running stitch.

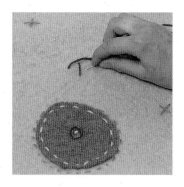

3 Sew a button very securely to the centre of each circle. Work large cross stitches in a contrasting colour to fill the background fabric.
SAFETY NOTE: Not for use with very young children, who may be tempted to chew on the buttons.

MOSAIC VELVET CUSHION

*T*his rich velvet cushion cover is a clever way to use scraps of fabric. The triangular shapes and decorative embroidery are reminiscent of crazy patchwork, which was very popular in the Victorian era. To create a mosaic effect, the pieces are arranged more regularly.

YOU WILL NEED

MATERIALS	EQUIPMENT
cushion pad	*dressmaker's scissors*
velvet	*needle*
scraps of contrasting velvet	*dressmaker's pins*
basting thread	*embroidery needle*
matching sewing threads	*embroidery scissors*
embroidery threads	
backing fabric	

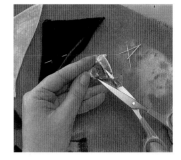

1 Measure the cushion pad. For the cushion front, cut a piece of velvet to the size plus 2 cm/¾ in all around. Cut triangles in different sizes from scraps of velvet in contrasting colours. Press under the edges of the triangles by 8 mm/⅜ in, making sure that all the edges are straight.

2 Trim the excess fabric at the corners. Tack (baste) around the edge of each triangle. Arrange the triangles on the background velvet and pin in place.

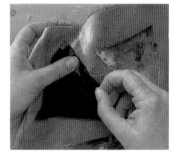

3 Slip stitch neatly around the edge of each triangle, then remove the tacking (basting) threads.

4 Outline some of the triangles with feather stitch, using contrasting threads.

5 Stitch around the edge of other triangles with blanket stitch and other decorative embroidery stitches. Make the backing for the cushion, as described in the Nursery Cushion project. Make up the cushion and insert the pad.

FRUITY APPLIQUE CUSHION

A bright, graphic cushion which would be ideal for a kitchen, a sunny garden bench or conservatory.

YOU WILL NEED

MATERIALS

*orange cotton fabric,
60 x 15 cm/24 x 6 in
yellow cotton fabric,
45 x 15 cm/18 x 6 in
green cotton fabric,
30 x 15 cm/12 x 6 in
matching sewing thread
tracing paper
fusible bonding web
craft felt: orange, yellow
and 4 shades of green
blue and white cotton,
60 x 90 cm/24 x 36 in
5 self-cover buttons
50 cm/20 in cushion pad*

EQUIPMENT

*dressmaker's scissors
sewing machine
iron and pressing cloth
pencil
dressmaker's pins
needle*

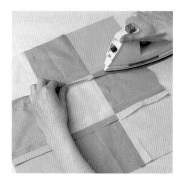

1 Cut the cotton fabric into 15 cm/6 in squares: four orange, three yellow and two green. Machine stitch together in three rows of three, with a 1 cm/½ in seam allowance. Press the seams open. Join the three strips into a square, carefully matching the seams, and press the long seams open.

2 Trace the template from the back of the book, enlarging it as necessary. Transfer the leaf and fruit to the backing paper of the bonding web. Cut the shapes out roughly and iron on to the different coloured felts, then cut out accurately along the outlines.

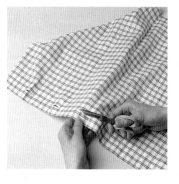

3 Peel off the backing paper and place the shapes on the coloured squares, arranging the leaves so that they lie under the orange and yellow circles. Iron in place following the manufacturer's instructions.

4 Trace the shapes for the second layer of appliqué shapes – the orange slices, leaf veins and the star-shaped trim for the whole oranges – on to the bonding web. Cut out from felt as before and press in place.

5 From the check fabric, cut two 53 x 45 cm/21 x 18 in rectangles and two strips of 8 x 40 cm/3¼ x 16 in. Sew the two strips along opposite sides of the appliqué square. Turn under and stitch a double hem along one long side of each large rectangle. Make five evenly spaced buttonholes along one hemmed edge, then, with right sides facing, sew the unfinished long edges to the other two sides of the square.

6 Following the button manufacturer's instructions, cover each of the five buttons in a different coloured felt.

7 Fold the two back panels to the wrong side, leaving a 6 cm/2½ in check border at the front of the cushion cover. Pin and stitch the seams, leaving a 1 cm/½ in seam allowance. Turn to the right side and press. Sew the buttons in place, insert the pad and do up the buttons.

APPLIQUED CACTI FRAME

*T*his frame is a mixture of appliqué, collage and embroidery. Much of the work is glued so that it is quick to make, and the stitching is mostly decorative.

YOU WILL NEED

MATERIALS	EQUIPMENT
velvet, enough to cover the front and sides of the frame	*pen*
MDF (medium-density fibreboard) frame	*dressmaker's scissors*
tacking (basting) thread	*needle*
paper	*pencil*
selection of fabric scraps	*scissors*
fabric glue	
embroidery threads	
felt	

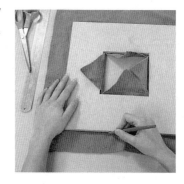

1 Lay the velvet face down and place the frame in the centre. Draw around the outside edges and around the central opening. Mark diagonal lines across the opening, then cut along the diagonal lines. These triangles will fold back.

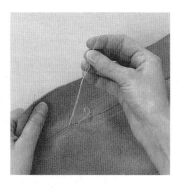

2 Tack (baste) along the marked outline of the frame. These stitches will clearly indicate the outer edges of the frame.

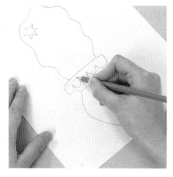

3 Draw several different cacti designs on paper and then cut them out with scissors to make templates.

4 Cut out the shapes from the fabric scraps and arrange them on the velvet. Stick them in position with fabric glue.

5 Add various decorative embroidery stitches to outline the cacti shapes.

6 Stretch the velvet around the frame, matching the tacking (basting) lines to the edges of the frame. Glue the overlap down at the back, all around the outside and the inside of the frame.

7 Cut out a piece of felt to fit over the back of the frame. Glue it into position, making sure to cover all the unsightly joins at the back.

SPECTACLE CASE

Your spectacles will never be lost again if they are kept in this attractive case, which can be hung around your neck on a tasselled cord.

YOU WILL NEED

MATERIALS

23 x 28 cm/9 x 11 in 12 count single-thread canvas
tacking (basting) thread
coton perlé: DMC no. 5, 3 skeins of 930, 1 skein each of 310, 321, 783, 796, 972
coton à broder: DMC 745
gold thread: DMC Art. 284
sewing thread
23 x 28 cm/9 x 11 in heavy-duty iron-on interfacing
23 x 28 cm/9 x 11 in tie silk or similar fabric
1 m/1 yd of 5 mm/¼ in cord

EQUIPMENT

needle
tapestry needle
embroidery scissors

DMC	
▨▨	310
1 1	783
4 4	972
▶▶	796
◥◥	930
O O	321
⊠⊠	coton à broder 745

Backstitch
DMC Art. 284 ——

☆ Middle point

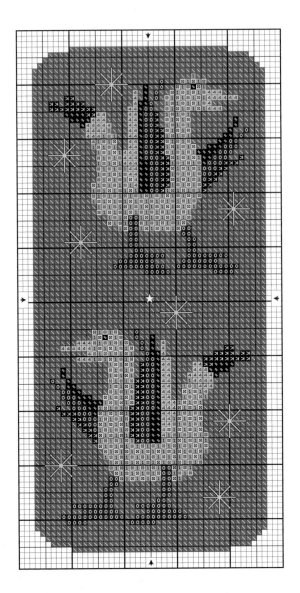

WORKING THE CROSS STITCH

Tack (baste) guidelines across the centre of the canvas in both directions. Work the coton perlé cross stitch on the birds first, then use the coton à broder to fill in. Work the background then add the gold stars in back stitch. Press the embroidery on the wrong side and trim the canvas to 1 cm/½ in. Snip into the curves, turn the edges in and tack (baste).

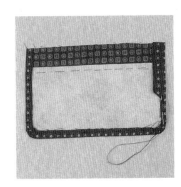

1 To make up: cut two pieces of iron-on interfacing 8.3 x 17.2 cm/3¼ x 6¾ in and round off the corners. Iron these on to the silk and cut out, leaving a 1 cm/½ in seam allowance. Turn the edges over and tack (baste) carefully, easing in the fullness at the corners.

2 Place the canvas and lining pieces together with right sides facing out and oversew the edges. Once both are stitched round, put the spectacle case together and oversew with coton perlé 930, starting and finishing 5 cm/2 in down from the top edge.

3 Tie a knot in the cord 4 cm/1½ in from the end and tease out the end. Take the frayed ends over the knot and tie tightly, then pull the ends back down over the knot and wrap with thread. Repeat at the other end, trim and stitch to each side of the spectacle case.

268

SHOO FLY COVER

*I*t's a frivolous idea, but why not decorate a gauzy food cover with the very insects you are trying to keep out! Or perhaps just the more attractive-looking ones. A sheer curtain could be given the same treatment.

YOU WILL NEED

MATERIALS

mesh food cover
Anchor stranded cotton: 1 skein each of 1, 189, 238, 281, 290, 335, 403, 410, 1014
non-woven tear-off backing fabric

EQUIPMENT

tapestry needle
embroidery scissors

PREPARATION

Decide on the position of the insects, remembering that the angle of the finished motifs will depend on the grain of the mesh fabric. For each motif, cut a piece of non-woven tear-off backing fabric between 5 cm/2 in and 10 cm/4 in square. Pin and securely tack (baste) a square to the wrong side of the mesh.

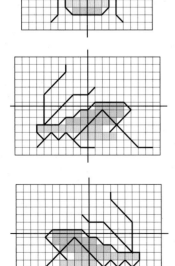

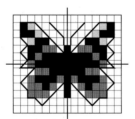

Anchor stranded cotton
410 blue
290 yellow
335 red
1014 rust
281 olive green
238 emerald green
403 black
1 white
189 dark green

1 Using three strands of cotton and, starting in the centre, stitch the design from the chart through both the mesh and the backing fabric. If starting in the usual way is difficult, leave an end of about 8 cm/3 in before making the first stitch and darn it in later.

2 When the cross stitch has been completed, remove the tacking (basting) threads and gently tear away the backing fabric. Now work the double running stitch using one strand of 403, except for the veins on the dragonfly's wings which are worked with two strands of 189. Double running stitch returns the needle to the starting point for darning in ends. That is, a line of running stitch is worked back along the same line, filling in the spaces between stitches.

NEEDLEPOINT BEETLE

*T*his *delightful beetle on its subtly coloured background is easy to work in tent stitch. Measure the frame you have chosen and work enough of the background to ensure that no bare canvas will be visible when the picture is framed.*

YOU WILL NEED

MATERIALS	EQUIPMENT
needlepoint canvas,	*waterproof magic marker*
25 x 25 cm/10 x 10 in	*dressmaker's scissors*
with 24 holes per 5 cm/	*tapestry needle*
12 holes per 1 in	*iron*
picture frame	*damp cloth*
masking tape	*dressmaker's pins*
tapestry wools: as listed in	*(optional)*
key at the back of the book	

1 To prepare the canvas, mark a vertical line down the centre and a horizontal line across the centre using a magic marker. Mark the edges of the aperture in the frame you intend to use, positioning it centrally over the marked lines.

2 Bind the edges of the canvas with masking tape to keep it straight and prevent the yarn catching as you sew.

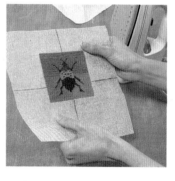

TENT STITCH Begin with a knot on the right side of the canvas, bringing the needle up again about 2.5 cm/1 in away. Work the first few stitches over this thread to secure it; the knot can then be cut away neatly. To work tent stitch, insert the needle one row up and one row to the right, bringing it back up through the hole to the left of your starting point. All the stitches must slant in the same direction – at the end of a row, turn the canvas upside down in order to work the next row.

VERTICAL TENT STITCH Tent stitch is worked horizontally, but it can be worked vertically where necessary. Always keep the stitches on the reverse side longer and more sloping than those on the front to avoid distorting the fabric. Try to keep an even tension and do not pull too tightly.

3 Cut a 45 cm/18 in length of tapestry wool and work the design from the chart at the back of the book in tent stitch. Start from the centre and work outwards to help keep the piece from distorting as you sew. When the design is completed and the background is large enough to fill the frame, remove the masking tape.

4 Use a hot iron and a damp cloth to steam the work gently, pulling it into shape as you go. If the canvas is very distorted, pin it into shape on the ironing board before steaming it. Dry the canvas thoroughly and quickly.

5 Cut away the excess canvas and mount your picture into the frame.

SHADOW-APPLIQUE SCARF

*T*his delicate, floaty scarf is made of layers of chiffon, with squares of fabric appliquéd at random with a leaf-like motif. Chiffon is a rather slippery fabric, so it pays to tack (baste) the layers securely together before machine stitching. The raw edges of the appliqué are finished with embroidery stitches, and the edges of the scarf are rolled and stitched by hand.

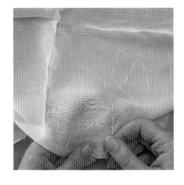

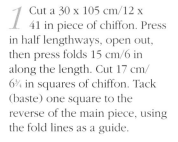

YOU WILL NEED

MATERIALS
chiffon, in three different colours
tacking (basting) thread
matching sewing threads
paper or thin card

EQUIPMENT
dressmaker's scissors
iron
dressmaker's pins
needle
sewing machine
fabric marker pen
embroidery scissors

1 Cut a 30 x 105 cm/12 x 41 in piece of chiffon. Press in half lengthways, open out, then press folds 15 cm/6 in along the length. Cut 17 cm/6¾ in squares of chiffon. Tack (baste) one square to the reverse of the main piece, using the fold lines as a guide.

2 Following the fold lines, machine stitch the square in place. Trim the excess fabric 3 mm/⅛ in outside the stitch line. Repeat along the scarf.

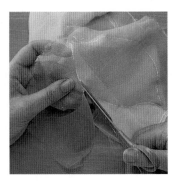

3 Make leaf and circle templates. Using a fabric marker, draw around the templates several times on different squares of chiffon.

4 Pin each appliqué square on to a contrasting square on the scarf, choosing squares at random. Tack (baste), then stitch around the shape. Trim the excess fabric 3 mm/⅛ in outside the stitch line.

5 Using doubled sewing thread, stitch along all the machine-stitched lines in feather stitch to cover the raw edges.

6 Using your forefinger and thumb, carefully roll each edge of the scarf until the raw edges are concealed. Stitch in place with slip stitch.

Tablemat

*T*his versatile mat would look marvellous on any shape or size of table. You could change the colours to match your own decor.

You Will Need

MATERIALS	EQUIPMENT
50 cm (20 in) square of white 36 count linen	needle
	scissors
tacking (basting) thread	embroidery hoop (frame)
Anchor Marlitt stranded	tapestry needle
cotton: 852, 816, 879, 897,	sewing machine
881	
sewing thread	

Anchor Marlitt
▽▽ 852   ▲▲ 816   ◇◇ 879
╱╱ 897   ♥♥ 881   ☆ Middle point

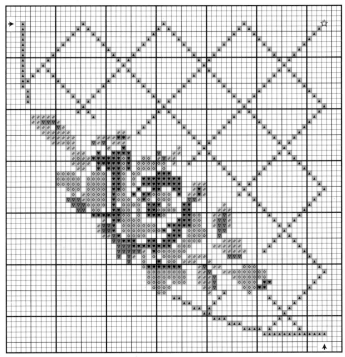

WORKING THE CROSS STITCH

Tack (baste) guidelines in both directions across the centre of the linen. Beginning in the centre, work one quarter of the design using two strands of Marlitt over three threads. Once complete, turn the fabric through 90 degrees and work the next section of the cross stitch. The design on each quarter is identical and is not a mirror image. Work the other section in the same way.

1 To make up: press on the reverse side with a damp cloth. Trim the linen to 40 cm (16 in) diameter. Turn under a narrow hem and tack (baste) in position.

2 Stitch close to the folded edge, slip stitch the corners and tack (baste) in position. Press carefully as Marlitt is a synthetic thread and may be damaged by a hot iron.

BEDSIDE TABLECLOTH

This versatile geometric border design could be stitched on to a set of napkins or across each corner of a much larger tablecloth. Or for a co-ordinated look, it could be used to embellish a special set of white cotton bed linen.

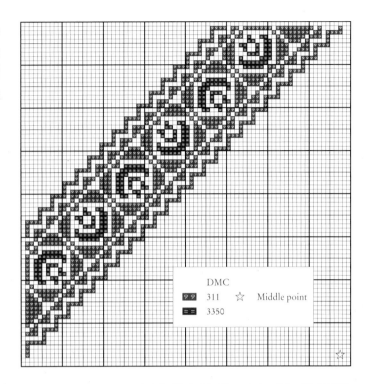

DMC			
9 9	311	☆	Middle point
= =	3350		

YOU WILL NEED

MATERIALS

46 cm (18 in) square of antique white 28 count Cashel linen
tacking (basting) thread
stranded cotton DMC: 3 skeins of 311, 1 of 3350
sewing thread
8 cm (3 in) square of cardboard

EQUIPMENT

scissors
needle
embroidery hoop (frame)
tapestry needle

WORKING THE CROSS STITCH

Tack (baste) a guideline round a corner of the linen 2.5 cm (1 in) from the edge. The design begins 90 threads from the corner of the guideline. Work the cross stitch and back stitch over two threads using two strands of cotton.

1 To make up: trim the square to leave a 1.5 cm (⅝ in) seam allowance outside the cross stitch. Mitre the corners and turn a narrow hem. Slip stitch the corners and the hem.

2 Work the same design in the corner diagonally opposite and press on the reverse side when complete.

3 Wrap blue thread (311) around the cardboard and make four tassels. Stitch one securely to each corner of the tablecloth.

MODELLING AND SALT DOUGH

*M*odelling is a craft particularly suitable for children of any age, as it is soft, safe and a lot of fun to do. The modelling projects in this section use polymer clay, self-hardening clay and salt dough. Working with salt dough has the added attraction that children can take an active part in preparing and baking the dough, as well as shaping it as they wish. When buying commercial modelling materials for use by children, look particularly for non-toxic varieties.

Children and adults alike will find plenty of inspiration within these next pages. There are projects to suit all abilities, ranging from simple and effective motifs that can be stamped on to clay or salt dough using pastry cutters, to more technically challenging three-dimensional creations.

MATERIALS AND EQUIPMENT

Modelling with self-hardening clay or salt dough requires very little in the way of materials and equipment, and you will probably already have the basic items at home. You should work on a clean, smooth, flat surface, and take care to keep sharp implements, glues, paints and varnish well out of the reach of children. Polymer clay (see picture) is a highly adaptable modelling medium that comes in a dazzling array of colours.

RIGHT *Salt dough is economical to make and easy to use - yet produces wonderfully decorative results. Here you can see a selection of special pastry cutters from the wide range now available.*

Tinting dough and clay

Food colouring is ideal for use on salt dough, and it is available in liquid and paste form. The paste is easier to use and more than one colour can be added to the dough to produce the shade required. Self-hardening clay can be bought from craft suppliers in a variety of colours, or you can colour it with paints and varnishes. Salt dough, too, can be decorated with paints and varnishes.

LEFT *Polymer clay is a versatile, easy-to-handle medium that can be used to make objects as diverse as picture frames and jewellery. Once shaped, it can be baked hard at low temperature in a domestic oven.*

SALT DOUGH RECIPE

Salt dough recipe

Simply follow the method below, adjusting the quantities to make the amount of salt dough you need. The quantities given here are sufficient to make a bowl with a diameter of about 23 cm/9 in.

The addition of 15 ml/1 tbsp vegetable oil to the recipe adds suppleness, while 10 ml/1 tbsp wallpaper paste gives the dough elasticity.

INGREDIENTS

230 g/8 oz/2 cups plain flour
200 g/7 oz/1 cup salt
250 ml/8 fl oz/1 cup water

Raw dough

Once the dough has been kneaded, it is pliable and easily manipulated, suitable for even intricate details.

Remember that salt dough is susceptible to steam and damp, so always keep your creations in a dry atmosphere to prevent deterioration.

1 Mix together the flour, salt and half the water in a mixing bowl. Knead the mixture, gradually adding more water until the dough has a smooth, firm consistency. Be careful not to add too much water or the dough will sag and become sticky.

2 Remove the dough from the bowl and continue to knead for 10 minutes. The dough can be modelled immediately, but is best left to rest for 30 minutes in an airtight container. Bake the salt dough in an oven at 120°C/250°F/Gas 1/2 until the dough is completely hardened all over.

Working with salt dough and clay

Dough and clay can be rolled out flat with a rolling pin. Work directly on baking parchment if you are using salt dough, otherwise work on a clean, flat surface. A small craft knife or clay modelling tool is indispensable for cutting dough and clay and indenting details. A cocktail stick, knitting needle or thick sewing needle is also useful, and can be used to pierce holes for hanging or decorating models. Make any holes about 3 mm/1/8 in wider than needed to allow for any distortion during painting and varnishing.

Various bowls, plates and dishes make suitable moulds for modelling (if the dough is to be baked, then the mould must be heat-resistant). Also, there is an exciting range of beautiful pastry moulds, biscuit cutters and icing cutters that can all be used to great effect.

LEFT *Rolling out salt dough on baking parchment.*

GINGERBREAD HEARTS

*T*he designs of these Germanic hearts are based on edible gingerbread and fondant cakes. They are formed from a salt dough base with painted motifs applied in contrasting and complementary patterns.

YOU WILL NEED

MATERIALS	EQUIPMENT
tracing paper	*pencil*
paper or thin card	*scissors*
salt dough (see Salt Dough Recipe)	*rolling pin*
	craft knife
baking parchment	*aspic cutters*
metal eyelet loop	*baking tray*
acrylic gesso or matt emulsion (latex) paint	*paintbrushes*
acrylic or craft paints	
polyurethane matt varnish	
paper ribbon	

1 Trace the gingerbread heart template from the back of the book, enlarging if necessary. Transfer it to paper or thin card and cut out. Roll an orange-size ball of salt dough out flat on baking parchment to 1 cm/½ in thick. Place the template on the dough and cut around the edge. Pat the raw edges to round them. Roll some more dough to 5 mm/¼ in thick and cut out shapes with aspic cutters. Moisten the border of the main heart shape and apply the small shapes. Fix the eyelet loop to the top of the heart. Place the model, on the baking parchment, on a tray and bake at 120°C/250°F/Gas ½, for nine hours. Allow to cool.

2 Paint on an undercoat of acrylic gesso or matt emulsion (latex) and allow to dry. Pick out the applied decoration with bright acrylic or craft paints, using a fine paintbrush to avoid getting paint on the base heart. When dry, apply five layers of matt varnish, allowing each coat to dry between layers. Cut a 40 cm/16 in length of paper ribbon, thread it through the eyelet and tie in a reef knot about 10 cm/4 in from the heart. Unravel the ribbon and cut out a chevron shape from each end.

WHEATSHEAF

*T*he wonderful golden colour of baked salt dough lends itself beautifully to the theme of a sheaf of wheat. This makes an ideal decoration for a kitchen wall, but keep it away from steam.

YOU WILL NEED

MATERIALS

tracing paper
salt dough (see Salt Dough Recipe)
baking parchment
polyurethane satin varnish

EQUIPMENT

pencil
rolling pin
craft knife
clay modelling tool (optional)
baking tray
paintbrush

1 Trace the template from the back of the book, enlarging if necessary. Roll out the dough flat on baking parchment to a thickness of 1 cm/½ in. Use the template to cut the wheatsheaf shape. To make the stalks, roll out thin spaghetti-like strands of dough to a length of about 12 cm/5 in and build them up into a bundle as shown. Moisten the strands with a little water to prevent them from drying out.

2 To make the tie for the bundle, roll four strands of dough to a length of 12 cm/5 in. Join the ends together with a little water and gently separate out the strands. Lay the first strand over the second, and the third over the fourth. Then lay what is now the third strand back over the second strand. Repeat these two steps until the plait (braid) is complete. Pinch the bottom ends together, using a little water to moisten and stick in place.

3 Moisten one side of the plait (braid) and place it over the stalks at the narrowest point. Tuck the ends of the plait (braid) neatly under to conceal them. Reserve sufficient salt dough to make the "ears" of the wheatsheaf.

4 Roll sausages from the salt dough, measuring 3 x 1 cm/ 1¼ x ⅜ in. Taper the rolls at one end and flatten them slightly. Use a knife or modelling tool to mark separate grains, curving the edges of each one. Moisten and apply the ears of wheat in overlapping layers. Place the wheatsheaf, on the baking parchment, on a tray and bake at 120°C/250°F/ Gas ½, for 10 hours. Allow to cool. Apply five layers of the satin varnish.

HANGING SHAPES

*A*bstract astrological symbols are combined to create *an original mobile, decorated with glass panels and beads that will catch the light as the pieces swing in the breeze.*

YOU WILL NEED

MATERIALS	EQUIPMENT
tracing paper	*pencil*
thin card or paper	*scissors*
1.5 kg/3 lb modelling clay	*rolling pin*
5 glass circles, 5 mm/¼ in	*clay modelling tools*
thick, 5 cm/2 in diameter	*polythene bag*
1 glass circle, 5 mm/¼ in	*wire-cutters*
thick, 3 cm/1¼ in in	*jewellery pliers*
diameter	*needle*
0.8 mm copper wire	
glass beads in a mixture of	
colours and sizes	
sandpaper	
10 cm/4 in thin wire,	
2 m/2 yd	
2 mm galvanized wire	

1 Trace the templates from the back of the book, enlarging if necessary. Transfer to thin card or paper and cut out. Roll out the modelling clay to a flat sheet 5 mm/¼ in thick.

2 Place one shape on to the clay sheet and cut around it with a modelling tool. Return any excess clay to a polythene bag to keep moist. With wet fingers, smooth all the surfaces and edges of the shape.

3 Lift up the circular part of the clay shape and hold it gently while positioning a circle of glass centrally underneath. (Use the damp mark left by the clay on the work surface as a guide.) Press the clay around the glass circle with wet fingers.

4 Cut out a circle of clay to reveal the glass, leaving a 3 mm/⅛ in border.

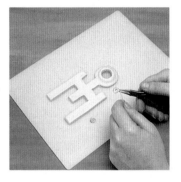

5 Cut the copper wire in half and twist it into two small spirals using pliers. Press gently into the surface of the clay.

6 Use a needle to help you lift and position the coloured glass beads and press them into the clay.

7 Pierce a small hole in the top and bottom of the piece and allow to dry thoroughly. Repeat the process with the other shapes.

8 Once the pieces have fully dried and hardened, sand down all the edges.

9 Use thin wire to join all the shapes together and then hang them from a galvanized wire hanger.

STAR FRAME

A plain frame can be transformed by decorating it with brightly painted cut-out shapes. The result is guaranteed to cheer up any wall.

YOU WILL NEED

MATERIALS

tracing paper
salt dough (see Salt Dough Recipe)
baking parchment
fine-grade sandpaper
acrylic gesso
emulsion (latex) paints
PVA (white) glue
wooden frame
polyurethane satin varnish

EQUIPMENT

pencil
rolling pin
craft knife
baking tray
paintbrushes

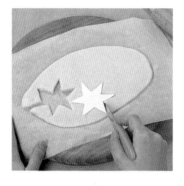

1 Trace the template from the back of the book, enlarging if necessary. Roll out the dough and cut out the star shapes. Place the stars, on baking parchment, on a tray and bake at 120°C/250°F/Gas ½, for five hours. Allow to cool.

2 Sand all of the baked stars with fine-grade sandpaper.

3 Paint each star with gesso and allow to dry. Decorate the stars with a coat of emulsion (latex) paint as a base colour. Allow to dry thoroughly.

4 Paint patterns in other colours on the stars. Glue the stars to the frame. Finish with a coat of satin varnish.

SPIDER BUTTONS

Brighten up a child's coat (or your own!) with these friendly spiders. Use the metal buttons that are sold for covering in fabric, and match the size to your buttonholes. Snap the fronts on to the button backs before you start to decorate them. You can coat the baked buttons with a gloss varnish, if you wish.

YOU WILL NEED

MATERIALS
polymer clay: bright green, black and white
set of metal buttons
clear gloss varnish (optional)

EQUIPMENT
rolling pin
craft knife
cutting mat
paintbrush (optional)

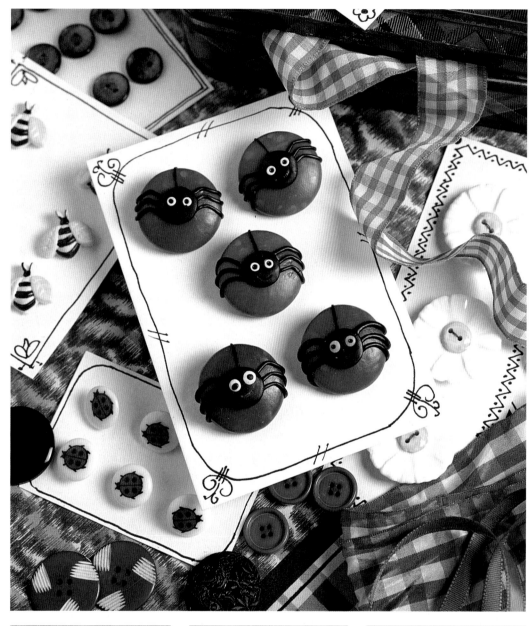

1 Roll the green clay out thinly and cut a circle large enough to cover the button. Mould the clay over the button.

2 Using black clay, roll very thin strands for the legs and press them on to the button. Roll a finer strand for the spider's thread.

3 Roll a pea-size ball of black clay and press it into the centre of the button for the spider's body.

4 Roll two small balls of white clay and press in position to make the eyes. Make the pupils from tiny black balls. Bake in a low oven, following the manufacturer's instructions.

ENGRAVED MIRROR FRAME

*T*he zodiac stands for the wheeling of the seasons as the sun appears to circle the earth, and astrologers draw it as a circle, with each of the twelve sections presided over by its familiar sign. Here, the ancient calendar is the inspiration for a stunning engraved frame. Secure the hook firmly to the back of the frame to support the weight of the mirror.

YOU WILL NEED

MATERIALS

pencil
thin card or paper
1 kg/2¼ lb modelling clay
3 mm/⅛ in thick circular
mirror, cut to
15 cm/6 in diameter
acrylic paints: deep
turquoise, white,
lemon-yellow and purple
matt varnish
hook
epoxy resin glue

EQUIPMENT

plate
rolling pin
clay modelling tools
paint-mixing container
paintbrushes

1 Draw around a plate on to thin card or paper to make a template. Roll out the clay to a large flat sheet 5 mm/¼ in thick. Cut two circles of clay.

2 Place the mirror on one of the circles and cut around it. Fit the mirror between the two frames, stretching the clay over the edge of the mirror.

3 Bond the frame by pressing down through both layers with wet fingers at intervals around the outer edge, then smooth the inner and outer edges to leave a neat finish.

4 Trim the inner edge of the frame to leave an overlap of 5 mm/¼ in around the mirror. Neaten with a modelling tool.

5 Wet and smooth the surface, then divide it into 12 equal sections by engraving straight lines with a wet modelling tool, working from the raised inner border to the edge of the frame.

6 Engrave an astrological sign in each section of the frame, following the correct order as shown in the photograph. Allow to harden.

7 Mix turquoise, white and lemon paint, adding water to get a creamy consistency, and paint the frame in two thin coats, allowing the brush strokes to show through. Allow the first coat to dry before applying the second.

8 Mix purple and white paint, this time to a thicker texture, and apply with a wide dry brush so that the engraved figures and raised inner edge remain green. When dry, coat with a layer of clear varnish and attach the hook to the back with epoxy resin glue.

MODELLED MIRROR

A *magical frame that uses up little odds and ends you have lying about the house. Use old buttons, beads, shells and even keys.*

YOU WILL NEED

MATERIALS

copper wire
strong glue
odds and ends to decorate,
such as shells, glass and
plastic nuggets
modelling clay
card template, outer
diameter 18 cm/7 in, inner
diameter 20 cm/4½ in
mirror, 9 cm/3½ in
in diameter
2 pieces of aluminium
tubing, 1 cm/½ in in
diameter, 20 cm/8 in long
small plastic drinks bottle
plaster of Paris
acrylic paints

EQUIPMENT

wire-cutters
round-nosed pliers
rolling pin
acetate sheet
clay modelling tool
craft knife
paintbrushes

1 Cut the wire into lengths and curl into shapes. Glue odds and ends on one end of each wire. Bend the other ends to make a hook.

2 Roll out pieces of clay on the acetate sheet. Use the template to cut two circles, 18 cm/7 in in diameter. Cut a circle with a diameter of 11.5 cm/4½ in from one centre.

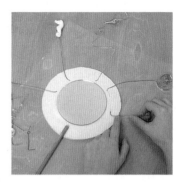

3 Place the mirror in the middle of the circle and arrange the wires around the edge, with the decorated ends outwards. Push the hooked ends into the clay. Put one aluminium tube in the position which you want to become the bottom of the mirror frame.

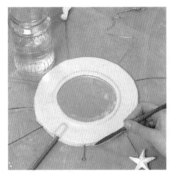

4 Place the clay ring on top and smooth off the overlap around the mirror and the tube with your finger and a little water. Smooth off the sides with the modelling tool. Decorate the front of the frame with small circles of clay. Allow to dry for several days.

5 Cut the bottle in half and make four 5 cm/2 in cuts around the top half of the bottle. Make a hole in the lid. Mix enough plaster of Paris to half-fill the bottle base and pour it in. Push the top of the bottle part-way into the base and push the second aluminium tube through the hole in the bottle lid down into the plaster.

6 When dry, remove the plastic from the plaster. Remove the tube and fit the real tube and mirror into the plaster base. Paint the base, stand and frame with acrylic paints.

ANTIQUE WALL TILE

*T*he subtle look of this charming tile is achieved very simply by staining it with tea; wiping the design with colour accentuates the relief, and you can repeat it as many times as you like until you get the shade you desire.

YOU WILL NEED

MATERIALS	EQUIPMENT
tracing paper	*pencil*
450 g/1 lb modelling clay	*rolling pin*
tea bag	*clay modelling tools*
matt varnish	*paintbrush*

1 Trace the template from the back of the book, enlarging if necessary. Roll out the clay to a flat sheet 1 cm/½ in thick.

2 Place the tracing on top of the clay and mark all the lines using a modelling tool.

3 Wet the clay surface thoroughly to make it easier to manipulate. Indent the lines of the design, moulding the figure's body to raise it above the background area.

4 Smooth the surface with wet fingers as you work to keep the clay moist.

5 Cut out the tile shape and engrave a double border around the edge to frame the central motif.

6 Stipple the background with the point of a wet modelling tool to create texture. Then leave the tile to harden completely before staining.

7 Brew a strong cup of tea with a tea bag and use it to stain the clay, wiping over the design with the tea bag. When you are satisfied with the colour, allow to dry, then protect the tile with a coat of matt varnish.

DISPLAY CASE

This purpose-made unit suits the scale of shells and echoes their sinewy curves in its shape. It is the perfect way of displaying beautiful shells, as the aquamarine colour sets off the tints of the shells and is a reminder of the water that is their natural setting. The gold decoration, like sunlight on water, is the perfect finishing touch.

YOU WILL NEED

MATERIALS

tracing paper
thin card or paper
modelling clay
acrylic paints: turquoise,
white and lemon-yellow
gold powder
clear matt varnish
selection of seashells
epoxy resin glue

EQUIPMENT

pencil
rolling pin
polythene sheet (optional)
clay modelling tools
paint-mixing container
small flat-bristled and fine
paintbrushes

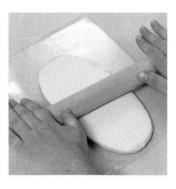

1 Trace the template from the back of the book, enlarging if necessary, and transfer to thin card or paper. Roll out the clay in an approximation of the swirl shape, to 8 mm/⅓ in thick. You may find it helpful to work on a sheet of polythene.

2 Lay the template on the clay and, with a wet modelling tool, cut out the shape for the back of the unit.

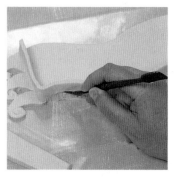

3 Roll out long clay snakes and cut them into rectangles about 2.5 cm/1 in wide, with perfectly straight edges, to make the side walls. Attach the walls to the back, moulding, smoothing the join with a wet modelling tool. Make a hole for hanging in the middle "wave" at the top.

4 Roll out and cut shorter rectangles, for the shelves, and attach them to the back and the walls. Use a small piece of clay, smoothed over the joins, to strengthen them. Allow to dry for several days.

5 Mix the acrylic paints to make a sea-green colour. To achieve a slight verdigris effect, do not mix the colours too thoroughly. Paint the inside and outside of the display unit and allow to dry.

6 Mix the gold powder with varnish, varying the amount of varnish depending on the consistency you wish to achieve. Paint the edges of the display case and the waves gold, using a fine paintbrush.

7 Working from the top down, arrange the shells in the compartments and glue them in position.

SALT DOUGH BASKET

*M*ake this delightful wall decoration from simple ingredients you are bound to have in your kitchen already. Salt dough is quite durable once it is varnished, but remember not to hang it anywhere damp or steamy as this may make it crumble slightly.

YOU WILL NEED

MATERIALS

salt dough (see Salt Dough Recipe)
paper bowl
paperclip
aluminium foil
4 cloves
baking parchment
acrylic paints: green, white, yellow, orange, burnt sienna and black
polyurethane satin varnish

EQUIPMENT

rolling pin
craft knife
fork
scissors
cheese grater
heart-shaped pastry cutter
baking tray
paintbrushes

1 Roll out some salt dough to a thickness of 5 mm/¼ in. Cut out a large oval and a half oval. Mark a basket pattern on the dough with a fork.

2 Cut the paper bowl in half and trim to fit the large oval. Place the half dough oval on top of the bowl, moisten the edges and stick to the large oval. Cut 2 cm/¾ in slits along the rim for the ribbon.

3 Use a thinly rolled piece of dough to attach a paperclip to the top of the basket on the reverse side.

4 Roll out two long thin sausages of dough to fit down the side of the basket. Twist them together, moisten the surfaces and stick them to the edge. Make another twist for the other side. Trim and join invisibly at the top and overlap in a "knot" at the bottom of the basket. Make a smaller twisted length for the handle at the top.

5 Roll four walnut-size balls of aluminium foil. Mould some dough over the foil and make two lemon shapes and two oranges. Roll the fruit over a fine grater to simulate the texture of the skin, and insert a clove at the top. Arrange the fruit inside the basket.

6 Roll out some more dough thinly. Cut small rectangles to fit between the slits to look like ribbon. Cut out four heart shapes, then cut them in half and trim to make leaves. Mark the veins with the point of the knife and shape them. Moisten and arrange around the fruit. Place the basket, on baking parchment, on a tray and bake at 120°C/250°F/Gas ½, for eight hours, or until the basket is hardened. Allow to cool.

7 Paint the fruit with acrylic paints. Thin the green paint slightly and paint the leaves. Brush off some of the paint with a stiff, dry brush to add highlights. Paint the ribbon white, then allow to dry thoroughly. Paint in a gingham pattern with yellow, orange and green stripes.

8 Paint the basket with a thin wash of burnt sienna mixed with a little black paint. Brush off the excess with a dry brush. Paint the completed basket with at least two coats of polyurethane satin varnish.

FOLK ANGEL

*T*his plaque-style angel is a perfect model to create from salt dough. On flat pieces of dough, the baking process takes place evenly through the sheet of dough, thus avoiding any hardening inconsistencies.

YOU WILL NEED

MATERIALS	EQUIPMENT
tracing paper	*pencil*
salt dough (see Salt Dough Recipe)	*scissors*
baking parchment	*rolling pin*
watercolour paints	*craft knife*
polyurethane matt varnish	*dressmaker's pin*
coloured string or fine ribbon	*wire-cutters*
	paperclip
	baking tray
	paintbrushes

1 Trace the template from the back of the book, enlarging if necessary, and cut out. Roll out the salt dough on baking parchment to 1 cm/½ in thick. Place the template on the dough and cut out the shape. Remove the template and pat the cut edges with a moistened finger to neaten them. Replace the template and transfer the details of the design by pricking along the lines with a pin, working on one layer at a time. Lightly moisten the pricked line, then draw along it with the tip of the knife, leaning the blade towards you then away from you to make an inverted division. Prick and indent all the lines.

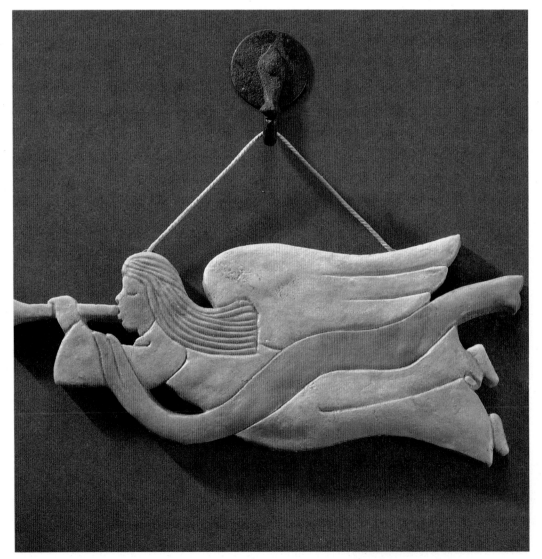

2 Cut a paperclip in half and insert the two outer halves into the edges at the crosses, leaving the loops visible. Bake at 120°C/250°F/Gas ¼, for ten hours. Allow to cool.

3 Apply the paint thinly to the model, lightening the colours with white. Leave the flesh areas unpainted, but highlight the cheek in pink. Allow to dry. Apply five coats of varnish. Hang up the angel.

SHAKER HAND

*T*he unpainted salt dough of this open, friendly hand gives it an amazingly lifelike appearance. The bordered heart motif is typical of the influential Shaker style founded in 18th-century America.

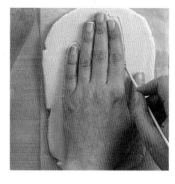

YOU WILL NEED

MATERIALS

*salt dough (see Salt Dough
Recipe)
baking parchment
eyelet loop
polyurethane matt varnish*

EQUIPMENT

*rolling pin
knitting needle
craft knife
heart-shaped cutter
(optional)
clay modelling tool
baking tray
paintbrush*

1 Roll out the salt dough on to baking parchment to a thickness of 1.5 cm/⅝ in. Lay your hand flat on to the dough with your fingers together. Use a knitting needle to trace around the edge and mark your fingers, then cut out the outline with a craft knife. Pat the cut edges with a moistened finger to round them.

2 Cut out a heart shape from the palm, either cutting freehand or using a pastry cutter. Turn the hand over and insert an eyelet loop for hanging it up. Bake at 120°C/250°F/Gas ½, for ten hours. Allow to dry, then apply five coats of varnish.

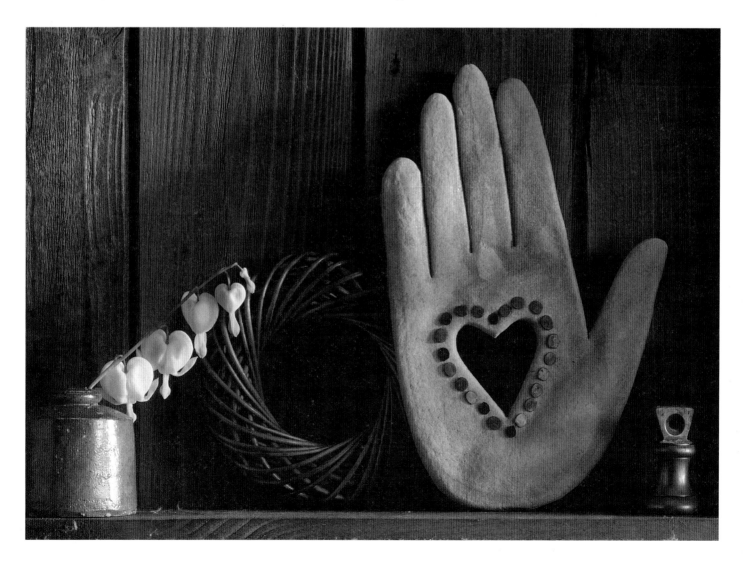

SALT AND PEPPER POTS

A request to pass the salt will be the starting signal for these eager mobile ladybirds to wheel their way down the table to you. They're based on toy trucks with a friction drive, and are sure to be a big hit at family mealtimes.

YOU WILL NEED

MATERIALS	EQUIPMENT
pair of matching toy trucks	*screwdriver*
stiff card	*pencil*
matching salt and	*scissors*
pepper pots	*rolling pin*
polymer clay: black,	*craft knife*
red and white	*pliers*
coloured paperclips	*paintbrushes*
epoxy resin glue	
clear gloss varnish	
enamel paints: red and	
black	

1 Undo the fixing screws and remove the body from each toy truck.

2 Mark out two matching templates on card which will fit over the truck chassis and around the bases of the salt and pepper pots, leaving a rim of about 5 mm/¼ in. Cut them out.

3 Roll a piece of black clay thinly to cover the template. Cut to shape. Stand the salt cellar in position on the base and mould a sausage of clay around it.

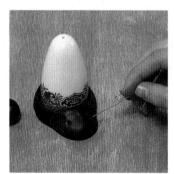

4 Press a ball of clay on to the front of the template and mould it into shape for the head of the ladybird. Make two holes for the feelers with the end of a paperclip. Remove the pot and template carefully. Make a matching base for the pepper pot in the same way.

5 Straighten out the paperclips and trim to length to make the feelers. Roll out four small balls of red clay and make a hole in each one with a paperclip. Mould two pairs of eyes from white and black clay.

6 Roll a ball of red clay for each truck wheel and press it on, moulding it into a dome shape. Remove carefully.

7 Bake the clay elements in a low oven, following the manufacturer's instructions. Fix everything in place with epoxy resin glue, avoiding the drive mechanism in the truck chassis. Varnish the wheel hubs and allow to dry.

8 Paint the salt and pepper pots in bright red. Allow to dry, then add ladybird spots in black. Allow to dry.

WINGED HEART

*T*his salt dough wall decoration is a charming way to tell someone absent that you are thinking of them – with a heart that has, literally, taken wing.

YOU WILL NEED

MATERIALS

salt dough (see Salt Dough Recipe)
baking parchment
aluminium foil
2 screw eyes
acrylic paints: red, white, black, green, blue and gold
clear varnish
length of cord

EQUIPMENT

pencil
scissors
rolling pin
craft knife
clay modelling tools
sponge
paint-mixing container
small and fine paintbrushes

1 Follow the instructions to make the salt dough (see Salt Dough Recipe). Trace the template from the back of the book, enlarging if necessary, on to baking parchment and cut it out.

2 Roll about two-thirds of the dough on to a sheet of baking parchment so that it is about 5 mm/¼ in thick. Put the template on the dough and cut around it with a craft knife. Make a thin roll of dough to fit each side of the background. Moisten the edges and put the rolls in place. Smooth the joints with a modelling tool and finish by moulding a small dough heart for each corner.

3 Using the template as a guide, mould a solid heart shape from foil. Roll out some dough to 5 mm/¼ in thick and place it over the foil heart. Trim the edges and place the heart in the centre of the background. Smooth with a damp sponge. Roll out some more dough to 5 mm/¼ in thick. Cut out the wing templates from the baking parchment and place them on the dough. Cut around the edges with a modelling tool and make the feather divisions. Moisten the backs and then put them on to the background and smooth the edges.

4 Bake the clay heart at 120°C/250°F/Gas ½, for two hours and then remove it and carefully insert the screw eyes on the back, one at each side. Return to the oven for at least six hours, or until it is completely hard. Allow to cool. Paint the heart red, the wings white and background black.

Following the template and picture, decorate the heart with a painted daisy chain and add feathery markings to the wings. Highlight with gold paint and then finish with at least two coats of varnish, to protect the dough. When dry, thread the cord through the screw eyes, so you can hang it on the wall.

LOVE BUG

A most lovable insect, with a heart-shaped body – this is perfect for giving a friend as a token of your affection.

YOU WILL NEED

MATERIALS

*copper wire
tracing paper
thin copper sheet
modelling clay
red acrylic paint
clear varnish
gold powder*

EQUIPMENT

*round-nosed pliers
pencil
tin snips
rolling pin
acetate sheet
clay modelling tools
small paintbrushes*

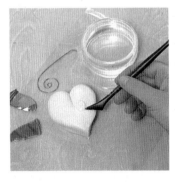

1 Curl the wire. Trace the templates from the back of the book, enlarging if necessary. Trace two wings on to the copper sheet and cut out with tin snips. Roll out the clay on the sheet. Cut out a heart with a wet modelling tool and model the face.

2 Stick the wings and wire curl into the clay and allow to dry for several days.

3 Paint the love bug red and allow to dry. Then give it a coat of varnish.

4 With a dry brush, apply gold powder mixed with a little varnish, to finish.

WALL DECORATION

Salt dough is a great medium for making architectural-style reliefs. This charming "bronze" wall plaque can easily be incorporated into an interior scheme – or simply used for decoration.

YOU WILL NEED

MATERIALS

baking parchment
salt dough (see Salt Dough Recipe)
paperclip
white acrylic primer
acrylic paints: verdigris and bronze

EQUIPMENT

pencil
clay modelling tools
flat pliers
scissors
medium and fine paintbrushes
small sponge

1 Trace the template from the back of the book, enlarging if necessary, on to baking parchment. For the outer wings, make ten thin rolls of salt dough. Moisten the edges and press them gently together on the template. Use a flat-edged modelling tool to make some "feathers".

2 Shape the inner wing to fit the parchment outline. Moisten the back of the wing and press it gently in place. Make the face and hair in the same way, shaping the pieces separately and pressing them in place. Cut the paperclip in half with the pliers. Press one piece into the top of the cupid's head for hanging.

3 Bake the decoration at 120°C/250°F/Gas ½, for at least eight hours. Trim the baking parchment and allow to cool. Leaving to dry between each stage, paint with white acrylic primer, then with the verdigris paint. To complete, burnish the raised details with bronze paint.

CORNUCOPIA

*T*his harvest cornucopia follows the traditional salt dough theme of natural objects used to decorate the home.

YOU WILL NEED

MATERIALS	EQUIPMENT
tracing paper	*pencil*
salt dough (see Salt Dough	*scissors*
Recipe)	*rolling pin*
baking parchment	*craft knife*
2 cloves	*dressmaker's pin*
eyelet loop	*clay modelling tools*
watercolour inks	*knitting needle*
polyurethane matt varnish	*baking tray*
	paintbrushes

1 Trace the template from the back of the book, enlarging if necessary. Roll the dough out on baking parchment to a thickness of 8 mm/⁵⁄₁₆ in. Place the template on the dough and cut around it. Prick out the design with a pin.

2 Shape a pear, plum and apple from dough, following the template. Moisten with water and press into place. Shape the leaves, with veins, moisten them with water and press into position.

3 Mould grapes, blackberries, cherries, nuts, redcurrants and strawberries. Use a knitting needle to add detail. Moisten each shape and press in place. Make stalks as shown and insert a clove into the bases of the apple and pear.

4 Attach four leaves to the underside of the cornucopia. Press an eyelet loop into the back and bake at 120°C/250°F/Gas ½, for 20 hours. Cool, then paint. When dry, apply five coats of varnish.

CHECKERED HEART

*T*his heart takes its inspiration from traditional Scandinavian folk art. Although seeming to be separate pieces, the salt dough "squares" are actually formed by deep indentations.

YOU WILL NEED

MATERIALS

tracing paper
salt dough (see Salt Dough Recipe)
baking parchment
gold paperclips
acrylic gesso or matt emulsion (latex) paint
cherry-red acrylic or craft paint
polyurethane matt varnish
coloured raffia

EQUIPMENT

pencil
rolling pin
dressmaker's pin
craft knife
wire-cutters
baking tray
paintbrushes

1 Trace the template from the back of the book, enlarging if necessary, and cut out. Roll the dough out on baking parchment to 1 cm/½ in thick. Cover with the template and mark the squares with a pin.

2 Neaten the cut edge by patting it with a moistened finger to round and smooth it. Indent lines on the heart, following the pricked marks, leaning the knife first towards you and then away.

3 Cut a paperclip in half and insert it into the top of the heart. Make two or three more hearts in the same way. Bake on the parchment paper on a tray at 120°C/250°F/ Gas ½, for nine hours.

4 Paint with acrylic gesso or emulsion (latex), then paint in cherry-red, leaving alternate squares plain. Allow to dry. Apply five coats of varnish. Thread some raffia through each loop and tie in a bow.

COOKIE HEARTS

*D*elicious to eat – or you can double-bake them to
use as decorations.

YOU WILL NEED

MATERIALS	EQUIPMENT
dough (see Gingerbread	*rolling pin*
Cupids)	*selection of heart-shaped*
baking parchment	*cookie cutters*
white royal icing	*baking tray*
garden twine	*piping bag, with fine icing*
homespun cotton	*nozzle*
checked fabric	*bradawl or skewer*
clear glue or glue gun	*scissors*
cotton gingham fabric	
buttons and ribbons	
picture-hanging hook	
card (optional)	

1 Make the dough as for Gingerbread Cupids. Roll out the dough thinly and evenly on a floured board. Cut out the shapes and place on baking parchment on a baking tray. Bake at 180°C/350°F/Gas 4 for 10–15 minutes. Make a hole for hanging while warm, then allow to cool completely.

2 For edible cookies, decorate them with white royal icing, using a piping bag and a fine icing nozzle.

3 If the cookies are not to be eaten, put them back in a low oven for a couple of hours to dry them out. String some together with garden twine. Make bows for tying from checked fabric for some; cut out heart motifs and glue them on others. Do the same with the gingham. Decorate the ties with buttons and ribbons. Use the bradawl to decorate the cookies with a pattern of holes (or do this with a skewer before baking). If the cookie breaks, repair the damage with glue. To make a cookie for hanging on the wall, glue a picture-hanging hook on the back. Large cookies need careful handling and you can glue pieces of card on to the backs, to reinforce them.

GINGERBREAD CUPIDS

What better token of your affection than a gift of these gilded cherubs? They taste as delicious as they look, and they make excellent decorations.

YOU WILL NEED

MATERIALS

350 g/12 oz/3 cups plain white flour
15 ml/1 tbsp ground ginger
7.5 ml/½ tbsp ground cinnamon
2.5 ml/½ tsp grated nutmeg
75 g/3 oz/6 tbsp butter, cut into small pieces
50 g/2 oz/4 tbsp soft brown sugar
225 g/8 oz/1 cup black treacle
baking parchment
powdered food colouring: silver and gold

EQUIPMENT

mixing bowl
wooden spoon
rolling pin
pencil
scissors
craft knife
baking tray
saucer
spoon
fine paintbrush

1 Place the dough between two sheets of parchment and roll out very thinly. Trace the templates from the back of the book on to baking parchment, cut out and place on the dough, then cut out. Join the sections and mark on details. Place on baking parchment on a baking tray. Bake at 180°C/350°F/Gas 4 for 10–15 minutes. Leave to cool.

2 Mix each food colouring with water, to make a paste. The easiest way is to tip some on to a saucer, add a drop of water and grind into a paste with the bowl of a spoon. Paint the wings and the centre of the arrows silver.

3 Paint the body, the hearts and the flights of the arrows with gold paste. Allow to dry thoroughly.

TO MAKE THE DOUGH

Sieve the flour and spices into a mixing bowl. Add the butter and rub it in with your fingers, until the mixture looks like fine breadcrumbs. Stir in the sugar. Make a well in the centre and pour in the treacle. Mix well and beat until the mixture comes away from the sides of the bowl. Knead until smooth.

METAL EMBEDDED BOWL

*T*hese rustic bowls have the appearance of weather-worn stone. The heat-resistant qualities of metal provide an exciting source of decorative materials to use with salt dough – here, coins, bronze decorations, jewellery, wire and copper motifs are all embedded in the dough.

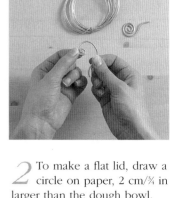

YOU WILL NEED

MATERIALS

cooking fat or vegetable oil
salt dough (see Salt Dough Recipe)
baking parchment
fine copper sheet
metal for embedding, such as jewellery accessories, coins and bonsai wire
paper
watercolour paints
metallic craft paints
polyurethane satin varnish
PVA (white) glue
jewellery stones

EQUIPMENT

2 ovenproof bowls
rolling pin
craft knife
old pair of scissors
baking tray
pair of compasses
pencil
ruler
paintbrushes
paint-mixing container
natural sponge

1 Smear the upturned bowls with cooking fat or oil. Roll two pieces of dough on baking parchment to 1 cm/½ in thick. Lift each piece of dough over a bowl and smooth it down. Cut the edges level. To make spirals, cut rough circles from a sheet of copper, then cut into spirals. Press your chosen metal pieces into the dough. Bake at 120°C/250°F/Gas ½, for nine hours, removing the bowls once the dough has dried completely.

2 To make a flat lid, draw a circle on paper, 2 cm/¾ in larger than the dough bowl. Cut out the circle to use as a template. Roll some more dough out to 1 cm/½ in thick and cut a circle with the template. Roll a ball of dough, moisten it and press to the centre. Smooth the edges and join it to the lid. Coil two lengths of bonsai wire and bend the ends downwards to form two halves of a heart for the handle.

3 Insert the metal handle ends into the centre of the lid. Transfer the lid, on the parchment paper, to a tray and bake as before for five hours, until it is almost hardened. Measure across the dough bowl between the inner edges. Draw a circle on paper with a diameter 1 cm/½ in less than that of the measurement. Cut out and use as a template to cut a circle from dough.

4 Upturn the baked lid and support it on the ovenproof bowl. Moisten the back of the lid and place the smaller circle on top. Return to the oven for five hours until completely hardened.

5 Paint the bowls and lid, blending your chosen colours with black or white to dull the colours. Lightly dab the bowls with metallic paints, using a sponge. Allow to dry, then apply five coats of varnish. Glue jewellery stones to the metal decorations.

GOTHIC STAR MIRROR

*U*se curly sausages of clay and cut out simple, freehand star shapes to decorate the frame of this mirror. To make sure the frame is symmetrical, fold a sheet of paper in half, draw a simple template and transfer it to the card before you cut.

YOU WILL NEED

MATERIALS
thick card
mirror,
12.5 x 7.5 cm/5 x 3 in
masking tape
short length of thin wire
newspaper
PVA (white) glue
white emulsion (latex) paint
self-hardening clay
acrylic paints
varnish

EQUIPMENT
craft knife
cutting mat
paintbrushes
clay-modelling tools

1 Draw the shape of the frame on to the card twice and cut it out with a craft knife. Cut out the central shape from the front piece of the frame. Fix the mirror to this piece with masking tape. Make a hook from wire and fix it securely to the back section of the frame. Put the two pieces of card together, sandwiching the mirror, and tape securely.

2 Tear the newspaper into squares about 2.5 cm/1 in across and use PVA (white) glue to stick them in a single layer on both sides and around the edges of the frame. Allow to dry.

3 Prime with white emulsion (latex) paint and allow to dry. Roll some clay into long sausages and use to make an edging for the mirror, and decorative scrolls and curls. Press on to the frame with the help of a modelling tool. Cut star shapes out of the clay and fix on. Allow to dry. Decorate the frame with acrylic paints. Varnish when dry.

GOLDEN MIRROR

The contrasts of gold paint and metallic copper combine to flattering effect in this mirror frame. The curvaceous shapes in twisted wire set off the graphic copper triangles to create a stylish effect that will be at home in any contemporary decor.

YOU WILL NEED

MATERIALS

copper sheet
copper wire
modelling clay
small round mirror
terracotta acrylic paint
gold powder
matt varnish

EQUIPMENT

tin snips
ruler
wire-cutters
jeweller's pliers
rolling pin
clay-modelling tools
paint-mixing container
paintbrushes

1 Cut out six triangles from the copper sheet. Cut the wire into twelve 25 cm/10 in lengths. With the pliers, bend six wires into zigzags and six wires into spirals.

2 Roll the clay to 5 mm/¼ in thick. Cut two circles, each 13 cm/5 in. From the centre of one, cut a 6 cm/2½ in circle. Place the mirror in the centre of the other and the wires and triangles around the edge.

3 Place the second clay circle on top and smooth the edges together with a wet modelling tool. Allow to dry for several days.

4 Paint the clay with terracotta acrylic paint and allow to dry. Mix the gold powder with the varnish and paint a coat of the mixture over the terracotta.

313

SEAHORSE FRAME

*T*his frame-decorating idea would complement a picture with a seashore subject. It would be equally suited to a mirror, perhaps in a bathroom with a blue and white colour scheme. Shells are popular motifs for bathroom fabrics and wallpapers, and this frame would co-ordinate perfectly.

YOU WILL NEED

MATERIALS

*modelling clay
seashells and seahorse
ready-made frame
epoxy resin glue
acrylic paints: blue, white
and lemon-yellow
gold powder
clear matt varnish*

EQUIPMENT

*rolling pin
polythene sheet (optional)
clay-modelling tools
paint-mixing container
small flat-bristled and
fine paintbrushes*

1 Take a lump of clay and roll it into a ball. Use a polythene sheet to protect the work surface, if you like. Roll the ball into a thick sheet. Press a shell into the clay, to create a negative impression. Repeat with the other shells and the seahorse. Allow to dry for several days.

2 Take another ball of clay and roll it out in the same way. Press it into the moulds, filling the shell and seahorse impressions. Carefully lift off the clay and place it face-up on the work surface.

3 Cut away the excess clay from around each shape. Set aside and allow to dry for several days.

4 Arrange the shell and seahorse shapes around the frame and glue them carefully in position.

5 Mix the acrylic paints to make a turquoise colour. To achieve a slight verdigris effect do not mix the colours too thoroughly. Paint the shapes and allow to dry.

6 Mix the gold powder with varnish, varying the amount of varnish depending on the consistency you want to achieve. Highlight and decorate the shapes with gold.

MINIATURE BROOCH

*P*olymer clay is a marvellous medium for moulding: it is much easier to use than clay and can be baked hard in an ordinary oven. The colours are jewel-like in their intensity and yet this hand-made brooch has a charming naïvety, reminiscent of folk art.

YOU WILL NEED

MATERIALS	EQUIPMENT
polymer clay: carmine, green and golden-yellow	*rose nail*
earring posts	*kitchen foil*
epoxy resin glue	*small rolling pin*
brooch pin	*kitchen knife*
	trefoil-shaped aspic cutter

1 Roll three small balls of carmine clay for each rose. Flatten a ball between your finger and thumb and wrap it around the rose nail. Overlap the petals as you work and gently open out the bud with your finger. Ease off the nail and insert an earring post. Push into a ball of foil. Make another four roses in the same way. Bake in a preheated oven at 110°C/225°F/Gas ¼ for about 10–15 minutes. Roll out the green clay thinly. With a kitchen knife, cut small squares and fringe one edge. Wrap this around the base of the rose to form the calyx. Cut out several trefoil shapes, using the cutter. Cut three leaves from each and mark veins with the knife.

2 Roll out a 2 x 5 cm/¾ x 2 in rectangle of yellow clay for the vase. Lay thin pieces of carmine and green clay on top as decoration. Roll the pieces flat and mark with a knife.

3 Press leaves around the roses and put in the vase. Put leaves on the edge. Bake in the oven at 110°C/225°F/Gas ¼ for 30 minutes. When cool, glue on the pin.

ORANGE SLICE EARRINGS

*B*right, jolly earrings to suit the mood of a hot summer's day, or cheer up a dull one. Have fun making the orange slices as realistic as you can – these ones even have pips.

YOU WILL NEED

MATERIALS	EQUIPMENT
polymer clay: pearl, pale orange and dark orange	*craft knife*
	cutting mat
earring findings: eye pins,	*bamboo skewer*
earring hooks and	*rolling pin*
large rings	*old cheese grater*
	round-nosed jewellery pliers

1 Roll a 5 mm/¼ in diameter sausage of pearl clay. Roll the pale orange clay into a sausage of 1.5 cm/⅝ in diameter and cut it lengthways into four triangular segments.

2 Cut lengthways into two of the triangles and insert a skewer. Press the clay together to form a tunnel. Fill the tunnel with the sausage of pearl clay and reform the triangular shape.

3 Roll some dark orange clay and cut 1 cm/½ in strips for between the segments. Arrange to make a semicircle. Roll out a 3 mm/⅛ in layer of pearl and a 2 mm/¹⁄₁₂ in layer of dark orange for the peel and mould around the edge. Make two 1 cm/½ in balls in dark orange and roll on a grater to make them look like oranges. Fit an eye pin through the centre of each. Trim any over-lapping edges from the large segment and roll the peel on a grater. Cut two 5 mm/¼ in slices and make a hole in each for the earring hook. Bake all the pieces at 110°C/225°F/Gas ¼ for 20–30 minutes.

TO ASSEMBLE EACH EARRING
Loop the wire from the small orange and snip off any excess. Put a large ring through the orange slice and attach to the small orange. Attach the earring hook above the small orange.

SUNFLOWER MIRROR

*Y*ou may not always feel cheerful when you look in the mirror, but this sunflower face is sure to lift your spirits. It could grace a dressing table or look good as a decorative object in any room in the house.

YOU WILL NEED

MATERIALS	EQUIPMENT
card	pair of compasses
modelling clay	pencil
small terracotta or plastic	ruler
flowerpot	scissors
8 mm/⅜ in diameter	rolling pin
plaster of Paris	plaster-mixing container
aluminium tubing,	clay-modelling tools
20 cm/8 in	old ballpoint pen
7 cm/2¾ in diameter mirror	paint-mixing container
acrylic paints: yellow,	paintbrush
white, chocolate-brown	
and green	

1 Cut out a circular card template of 12 cm/4¾ in diameter. Cut out a 6 cm/2½ in diameter circle from the centre of this circle. Roll out a sheet of clay to a thickness of 5 mm/¼ in and use the template to cut out two rings.

2 Seal the drainage holes in the bottom of the flowerpot with clay. Mix up the plaster and pour it into the pot. When the plaster is semi-dry, insert the tube in the middle. Allow to dry. Remove the tube. Place the mirror in the centre of one ring and place the tube with one end resting on the bottom edge of the circle. Put the second ring on top. Seal the edges with a wet modelling tool.

3 Roll out another sheet of clay 3 mm/⅛ in thick, in a long oval shape. Cut out regular flower petal shapes.

4 Attach petals all around the back of the mirror, sealing the edges with the tool. Then attach petals to the front, so that they cover the spaces between the back petals. Bend some of the flower petals to make the sunflower look more realistic.

5 Roll two long thin clay "sausages" and flatten them. Put one on top of the join between the petals and the mirror and one at the edge of the mirror. Press the end of a pen into the "sausages" to create little depressions all over.

6 Mix the two yellow and white paints to make a sunny yellow, then paint the sunflower petals yellow with it.

7 Paint the border around the mirror with chocolate-brown. Remove the tube and paint it green. Re-insert the tube in the flowerpot and fit the mirror on top.

HEART BROOCH AND PIN

This little brooch is made from fibreboard and is gilded using a distressed technique. The delicate pin will make the perfect finish to a wedding hat. It is made from modelling clay, gilded and decorated with pretty jewels.

YOU WILL NEED

MATERIALS

fibreboard,
10 x 10 cm/4 x 4 in
pale blue spray paint
water-based size
gold Dutch metal leaf
methylated spirit
acrylic varnishing wax
brooch back
modelling clay
hat pin and cap
gilt cream
plastic jewels

EQUIPMENT

black magic marker
coping saw
sandpaper or chisel
2 bristle brushes
burnishing brush or soft
cloth
steel wool
soft cloth
glue gun and glue sticks
rolling pin
clay-modelling tools

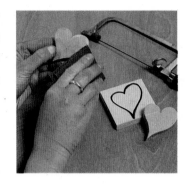

1 Draw a heart shape freehand on to the fibreboard using a black magic marker. Cut out and roughen the edges with sandpaper or a chisel to add texture.

2 Spray both sides of the heart with pale blue spray paint and allow to dry. Paint on a thin, even layer of water-based size and leave for about 20–30 minutes, until it becomes clear and tacky.

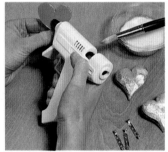

3 Lay the gold leaf on to cover the whole area. Burnish it with a burnishing brush or cloth to remove the excess leaf and bring up a lustre. Gently distress the surface using steel wool and methylated spirit.

4 Seal with acrylic varnishing wax and allow to dry. Buff with a soft cloth. Glue a brooch on to the back of the heart.

5 Warm and roll out the clay to 5 mm/¼ in thick. Cut out a heart shape and round off the edges. Use modelling tools to make indentations and patterns in the clay.

6 Insert the hat pin into the base of the heart. Enlarge the hole slightly by circling the pin, then remove it. Bake the heart in the oven, following the manufacturer's instructions.

7 Rub gilt cream into both sides of the heart and allow to dry, before buffing with a soft cloth.

8 Glue the hat pin into the base of the heart and glue plastic jewels on to the heart.

ABSTRACT HAIRSLIDE

ilver leaf is applied to glow-in-the-dark polymer clay which is then embossed with the spiral patterns of some old earrings to create an intriguing effect. In the dark, a subtle glow emanates from the tiny cracks in the silver leaf.

YOU WILL NEED

MATERIALS

glow-in-the-dark polymer clay
thin card
silver leaf
old jewellery or buttons
dark blue bronze powder
slide clip
varnish
strong glue

EQUIPMENT

rolling pin
pencil
scissors
craft knife
cutting mat
brayer
dust mask
paintbrushes

1 Roll out some clay to a thickness of 5 mm/¼ in. Draw the shape you want freehand on thin card and cut it out. Place the card on the clay and cut out the shape with a craft knife.

2 Apply silver leaf to the clay shape by passing a brayer over it.

3 Create a regular pattern around the edge of the silver-leafed clay by pressing interestingly shaped old jewellery or buttons into it to leave indentations.

4 Fill in the central area of the brooch with a random pattern applied in the same way as in step 3, but using different shapes, if liked.

5 Wearing a dust mask, lightly brush the surface all around the edge with some bronze powder.

6 Slip a small piece of thin card through the full width of the slide clip, then place the decorated clay shape on top. The clay will mould itself to the curved shape of the slide but the card will prevent it sagging too much. Bake it in this position, following the manufacturer's instructions. When it is cool, varnish the surface and glue it back on to the slide clip.

KING OF HEARTS MIRROR

*T*his clay mirror frame is very easy to make, but it looks sophisticated. The heart-shaped cut-away section, outlined with glittering copper wire, makes a really unusual mirror that will be as welcome for its decorativeness as it is for its usefulness.

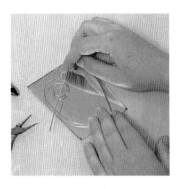

1 Shape a length of wire into a heart with an internal curl to fit within the mirror.

2 Shape two lengths of wire into curls with a right angle at the other end.

3 Roll out the clay to a thickness of 4 mm/³⁄₁₆ in on polythene. Trace the template from the back of the book and cut out a clay "crown" with a wet modelling tool. Cut out a clay rectangle at least 2 cm/¾ in larger than the mirror.

4 Sandwich the mirror between the "crown" and the rectangle. Smooth the clay to get an impression of the mirror. Lift off the rectangle and cut 1 cm/½ in larger than the impression. Replace on the mirror, matching the impression to the mirror outline.

5 With a wet modelling tool, seal the join between the two clay layers.

6 Place the wire heart on top and, with a wet modelling tool, cut around the inside of the heart, revealing the mirror. Carefully insert the wire curls on one side.

7 Mould clay into "buttons" to stick on to the mirror frame under the crown and allow to dry for several days.

8 Give the clay a coat of turquoise paint and allow to dry thoroughly.

9 With a dry brush, cover the frame lightly with gold powder. Finally, give the frame a coat of varnish.

GLOW-IN-THE-DARK CLOCK

*R*ead the time in the dark from this amusing clock
made from special luminous polymer clay.

YOU WILL NEED

MATERIALS
*2¾ blocks glow-in-the-dark
polymer clay
thin card
¼ block polymer clay:
yellow, light and dark blue
and light and dark green
jewellery wire
aluminium foil
jewellery head pins
epoxy resin glue
clock movement
and hands*

EQUIPMENT
*rolling pin
craft knife
cutting mat
metal ruler
pencil
pair of compasses
film canister
smoothing tool
crosshead screw
dressmaker's pin
ballpoint pen
wire-cutters*

1 Roll out the glow-in-the-dark clay to 5 mm/¼ in thick. Cut a 10 x 13 cm/4 x 5 in rectangle. Cut a circular template from thin card, place at one end and cut round to shape the top. Squeeze an empty film canister and stamp an oval near to the bottom.

2 Make templates for a slightly curved strip and for the oval cut out in step 1. Roll some yellow clay and cut out these shapes. Wrap the strip around the oval to form a tapered cup.

3 Fix the cup over the hole in the clockface. Smooth over the join. Mark the hours on the circular template and position on the back plate. Prick through the centre to mark the clockface. Use a tube to stamp a hole for the clock spindle.

4 Cut out two strips of the rolled out glow-in-the-dark clay to 3 cm/1¼ in wide. Make one 31 cm/12¼ in and the other 10 cm/4 in long. Use a very narrow tube to stamp a small hole at the mid-point of the longer strip.

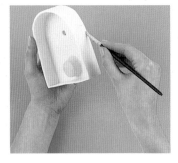

5 Assemble the strips to make the sides of the clockface, smoothing over the joins. Fix the sides to the back of the clockface and smooth over the joins.

6 Roll a marble-size piece of light blue clay into an egg shape. Crumble some dark blue clay and roll the egg in it to speckle the surface.

7 Put two short wires, about 1.5 cm/⅝ in into the egg. Remove the wires and bake the egg in the oven following the manufacturer's instructions.

8 Cut a glow-in-the-dark clay rectangle to cover the bottom section of the back of the clockface. Pack the cavity with foil. Bake the clockface.

9 Twist together some thin strips of yellow and light and dark green clay to create a marbled sausage.

10 Cut the sausage into one long and four short pieces. Join the pieces to make a central stem with four branches. Taper one stem end.

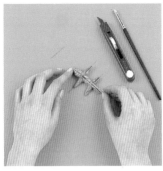

11 Make incisions along the branches and stem and insert wires long enough to protrude from the ends of the branches and the non-tapered end of the stem. Close up the slits and smooth over.

12 Roll out some yellow clay and form a three-petalled flower. Roll out some green clay and shape four leaves. Press patterns on the leaves and flower using the tip of a screw and a pen.

13 Push the flower and the leaves on to the wires of the stem and branches, and bake. When assembled, the tapered stem slots into the hole at the top of the clock.

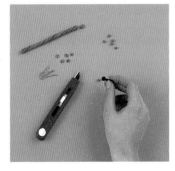

14 Twist together thin strips of light and dark blue clay and slice off 12 discs. Roll these into balls and flatten. Stamp each with the end of a screw and make a hole in the middle. Bake the discs.

15 Push a jewellery head pin through each disc, dab a spot of glue on the back and push the pin into the clockface, at an hour marking. Allow to dry, then snip off the excess wire at the back. Hold the clock movement at the back of the clockface. Push the spindle through the hole from the front and screw together.

TEAPOT CLOCK

*S*alt *dough is easy to prepare and it is so versatile that almost any shape can be sculpted from it. Children, in particular, enjoy working with the medium.*

YOU WILL NEED

MATERIALS

aluminium foil
325 g/8 oz/2¾ cups flour
325 g/8 oz/2¾ cups salt
2 tbsp vegetable oil
200 ml/8 fl oz/1 cup water
baking parchment
florist's wire
acrylic paints: cream and blue
clear acrylic varnish
clock movement and hands

EQUIPMENT

small ovenproof plate
mixing bowl
rolling pin
trefoil-shape cutter
skewer
baking tray
scissors
paintbrushes

1 Turn the plate over and cover the underside with foil, padding out the centre, if necessary, so it is slightly raised.

2 Mix together the flour, salt, oil and water to form the dough. Knead thoroughly and roll out a circle slightly larger than the plate. Lay over the foil, cut a circle in the centre for the spindle and trim to size.

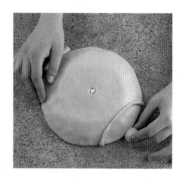

3 Roll sausage shapes for the lid, trim and base. Dampen both dough surfaces before positioning the pieces and press them firmly in place.

4 Shape and add the spout. Mark the flower design with a trefoil cutter and the end of a skewer. Each flower represents a numeral. Prick a dot pattern along the lid and the base.

5 Place on a tray covered in baking parchment and bake for at least five hours at 110°C/225°F/Gas ¼. After one hour take out of the oven and allow to cool. Bend some florist's wire into a handle shape and cover with dough. Fix to the body clock.

6 Return to the oven for about four hours. Allow to cool, then carefully remove the plate. Paint the clock in cream and allow to dry. Paint the flowers pale blue and pick out the details in dark blue.

7 Cover with several coats of clear varnish, allowing it to dry between coats. Fit the clock movement and hands.

SILVER STAR EARRINGS

A clay mould is used to model these eye-catching silver earrings, so it's easy to make as many as you want – as gifts for everyone who admires them on you!

YOU WILL NEED

MATERIALS

*modelling clay
tracing paper
thin card or paper
pair of earring studs
all-purpose glue
black acrylic paint
silver powder
clear varnish*

EQUIPMENT

*rolling pin
pencil
clay-modelling tools
paintbrushes*

1 Roll out a small piece of clay to a thickness of 8 mm/⅜ in.

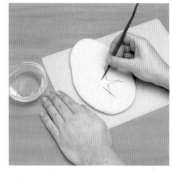

2 Trace the template from the back of the book, enlarging if necessary, and transfer it to thin card or paper. Cut the star out of the clay.

3 Mark a line from the centre of the star to each point where two rays meet and use the flat side of the modelling tool to mould each point to a 90-degree angle. Smooth the star with water, tuck the edges in neatly and allow to dry.

4 Take a small ball of clay and press with your palm until it is about 2 cm/¾ in thick. Press in the hardened clay star, then lift it out carefully without distorting the mould. Allow to dry thoroughly.

5 Use the mould to make further clay stars. Lift them out of the mould and place face up on the work surface.

6 Trim off any excess clay with a modelling tool. Allow to harden.

7 Glue earring studs to the backs of the stars.

8 Paint the stars with black acrylic paint and allow to dry thoroughly.

9 Mix silver powder with varnish and brush over the stars to complete.

SUN AND MOON EARRINGS

These very striking earrings shimmer with a distressed black and gold paint effect that is simple to achieve but looks stunning. The faces are easily modelled out of clay and you only need to leave them to dry thoroughly before you paint them, for a durable finish. The earrings would enhance any formal outfit, or add a touch of glamour to casual clothes.

1 Roll out two pieces of clay to about 5 mm/¼ in thick and 8 cm/3 in in diameter. Use the jar lid as a template to mark an inner circle. With a modelling tool, build up the central area so it is higher than the outer area but still flat.

2 Model the features of your sun with a modelling tool. Mark the rays around the face and cut away any excess clay. Pierce dots in the face and rays. Allow to dry for several days. Model a moon in the same way.

3 Glue the earring backs in position. Sand between the rays for a smoother look. Paint black. Mix the gold powder with the varnish, then paint. With a semi-dry brush, go over the face up and down quickly, so that the black underneath shows through and accentuates the features of the face.

YOU WILL NEED

MATERIALS
modelling clay
strong clear glue
2 earring findings: backs and butterflies
black acrylic paint
gold powder
matt varnish

EQUIPMENT
rolling pin
jar lid
clay-modelling tools
fine-grade sandpaper
fine paintbrushes
paint-mixing container

VALENTINE GIFT BOXES

*S*end your sweetheart
a special gift in one
of these lidded boxes.

YOU WILL NEED

MATERIALS

ovenproof bowl
vegetable fat or cooking oil
1 quantity salt dough (see
Salt Dough Recipe)
baking parchment
acrylic gesso or matt
emulsion (latex) paint
acrylic or craft paints
polyurethane satin varnish

EQUIPMENT

rolling pin
small, sharp knife
baking tray
biscuit cutter
paintbrushes

1 Grease the upturned bowl.
Roll out the dough on
baking parchment to 1 cm/½ in
thick. Mould it over the dish
and cut away any excess.
Smooth with a moistened finger.

2 Roll four balls of dough,
moisten them slightly and
press into the base of the bowl
as "feet". Place the bowl on a
tray and bake for nine hours at
120°C/250°F/Gas ½.

3 Cut out a circle for the lid
and a heart for the handle
from the dough. Bake for about
45 minutes, then leave to cool.
Attach the heart to the lid with
wet dough. Bake for nine hours.

4 Allow all pieces to cool,
then paint an undercoat on
the bowl and lid. Paint on your
own designs and colours and
allow to dry. Seal with five coats
of varnish inside and outside.

TEX MEX CLOCK

*A*dd *a touch of the Wild West to your home with this cheerful "cowboy" wall clock. You can obtain the clock mechanism and hands from craft shops. If you prefer, you could make the clock circular, or even square, and arrange the motifs differently.*

YOU WILL NEED

MATERIALS	EQUIPMENT
tracing paper	*pencil*
thin card	*scissors*
2 quantities of salt dough	*rolling pin*
(see Salt Dough Recipe)	*craft knife*
baking parchment	*cutting mat*
16 silver star studs	*dressmaker's pin*
acrylic or craft paints	*baking tray*
silver craft paint	*paintbrushes*
polyurethane matt varnish	
clock movement and hands	

1 Trace the templates from the back of the book, enlarging if necessary, and transfer them to card. Cut out the shapes. Roll the dough out to 1 cm/½ in thick. Place the clock template on top and cut around the outer edge. Push a pin through the template into the clock at the dots to mark the positions of the hours and the clock centre. Remove the template. Insert the star studs at the hour points and along the lower edge at the marked dots.

2 Cut a hole at the centre large enough for the clockwork spoke to be inserted through it and add an extra 3 mm/⅛ in to the diameter of the hole to allow for painting and varnishing. Roll out the remaining dough on baking parchment to 5 mm/¼ in thick. Use the templates to cut four cacti and a pair of cowboy boots, cutting the boot straps and spurs separately. Pat the cut edges of the piece with a moistened finger. Indent the details with the tip of a knife.

3 Moisten the cowboy boots and place the straps and spurs in place. Emboss a "stud" on each spur with the head of a pin. Place all the pieces on a baking tray and bake for one hour at 110°C/225°F/Gas ¼. Moisten the undersides of the cacti and cowboy boots. Smear sparingly with dough and press in position on the clock. Bake for a further nine hours. Allow to cool, then paint the clock. Use a fine brush to paint the stitching on the boots and paint the clock hands and details with silver paint. Apply five coats of varnish. Assemble the clock movement and hands.

SPIKY NAPKIN RINGS

These eye-catching napkin rings will enliven any table setting – paint the rings to co-ordinate with your china and table linen. Individual names can be painted on the underside of each ring so that no one gets their napkins muddled up! The coats of varnish mean that the rings are easily wiped clean.

YOU WILL NEED

MATERIALS	EQUIPMENT
cardboard tube	*scissors*
½ quantity salt dough (see	*rolling pin*
Salt Dough Recipe)	*chopping board and flour*
acrylic gesso or matt	*baking parchment*
emulsion (flat latex) paint	*(parchment paper)*
acrylic or craft paints	*fine sandpaper*
polyurethane matt varnish	*baking tray*
	paintbrushes

1 Cut 6 cm/2½ in from the cardboard tube. Roll the dough out flat on a lightly floured chopping board or baking parchment (parchment paper) to a thickness of approximately 5 mm/¼ in. Slightly dampen the tube with a little water and cover it inside and out with dough, smoothing down all the joins.

2 To make the spikes, roll nine 2.5 cm/1 in balls of dough. Narrow one end of each ball to make a point, and flatten the other end. Transfer the spikes and the ring on to baking parchment (parchment paper) on a baking tray, and bake in the oven at 120°C/250°F/Gas ½ for 45 minutes until hard.

3 Remove the pieces from the oven. When cool, smear both the spikes and the ring with dough and stick on the spikes. Smooth down any visible seams with a moistened finger. Return to the oven for a further 9 hours and bake until firmly joined.

4 When the napkin ring is cool, lightly sand it all over. Paint on a coat of acrylic gesso or matt emulsion (flat latex) paint and leave it to dry before painting on your own colours and designs. When dry, apply five coats of matt varnish, allowing the varnish to dry between each coat.

WOOD, WIRE AND TINWORK

*W*ood, wire and tin are all everyday materials that can be obtained quite readily. With the recent revival of interest in folk art, wood and tin particularly have had a remarkable resurgence of popularity, and many artefacts, particularly those made from recycled materials, are now being produced in craft workshops throughout the country. Wood, wire and tin can all be formed into products either following a traditional or a contemporary style, and their versatility makes them a popular medium for many craftspeople.

The nature of the materials means that some of the projects require you to wear protective clothing, and some solvents can be very strong, so always work in a well-ventilated area and ensure that children do not get too close.

The projects in this section provide comprehensive instructions if you are a newcomer, but they also aim to inspire the more experienced to experiment and develop the true potential of these exciting craft forms.

MATERIALS AND EQUIPMENT

To complete the projects in this book, you can obtain most of the materials and equipment from craft suppliers and hardware shops. For tin plate, metal foils and sheet metals, you will need to visit a metal supplier or, if you wish to opt for recycled materials, a metal merchant or scrap yard dealer. Sheet metal, whether cut or uncut, is extremely sharp and should only be handled when protective leather gloves and a work shirt are worn. The following lists some of the materials you will need for working with wood, tin and wire.

Epoxy resin glue comes in two parts. Only mix up as much glue one time as it dries very quickly and is wasted otherwise. Once the glue has set firm, which takes as you need at about 24 hours, the join is very strong.

Fine wire is used to join pieces of metal together and as a decoration.

A flux is used during soldering to make the area to be soldered chemically clean. As the flux is heated, it runs along the metal, thus preparing the surface so the solder runs smoothly and adheres properly.

Hammers come in a variety of sizes, so always choose the appropriate hammer to suit the project.

Metal foils are thin sheet metals that usually come on rolls in 15 cm/6 in and 30 cm/12 in wide strips. Metal foil is so thin that it can be cut with a pair of household scissors.

Pliers are useful for holding wire and tin when you are cutting them and also for turning over edges.

Protective clothing such as leather gloves and a work shirt should be worn when cutting metals and wire and sawing wood. A mask and goggles are also needed for soldering. Children should be kept away from this work.

Saws are vital for cutting wood. The most useful varieties are a fretsaw, a coping saw and a jigsaw.

Solder is an alloy, or mixture, of metals. Solder is used to join two pieces of metal together by providing a filler of liquid metal between the surfaces. Always follow the manufacturer's instructions carefully when using solder. Solder is applied with a **soldering iron**.

MATERIALS AND EQUIPMENT

Tin plate is generally used in place of pure tin sheet, which is very expensive. Tin plate is mild sheet steel that has been coated with tin. The tin plating is very bright and will not tarnish in the open air or in humid conditions. Sheet metals come in different thicknesses, or gauges. The higher the gauge, the thinner the metal.

Tin snips and **shears** are needed to cut sheet metal. Try to find a pair with a spring mechanism to open and close the blades.

White spirit is useful for removing excess flux after soldering.

Wire cutters are invaluable for cutting lengths of wire to size.

Wood glue is very strong PVA (white) glue. It is white but becomes clear once it has dried.

OPPOSITE AND BELOW *You'll need quite a few specialist tools for wire and tinwork. But whatever the medium, each project gives clear guidance on the equipment required.*

WOODEN SHEEP SIGN

*P*ainted *signs were a common sight outside shops and taverns in eighteenth-century towns. Here, you can create your own distinct sign.*

YOU WILL NEED

MATERIALS

tracing paper
5 mm/¼ in plywood,
90 x 60 cm/36 x 24 in
off-white emulsion (latex) paint
acrylic paints: burnt umber,
deep grass-green and black
coarse-grade sandpaper
matt water-based varnish
artist's acrylic paints: raw
umber and raw sienna

EQUIPMENT

pencil
coping saw or jigsaw
paintbrushes
stencil brush

1 Trace the template from the back of the book, enlarging to fit your piece of wood. Cut it out with a coping saw or an electric jigsaw.

2 Paint the sheep off-white, using random brushstrokes in all directions.

3 Mix some burnt umber into the off-white to obtain two shades of beige, then apply these with the stencil brush. Paint the grass and the black legs, adding highlights to the legs in dark beige.

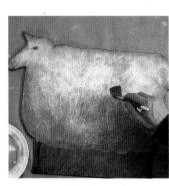

4 Use the darker beige to create the texture of fleece, applying the undiluted paint with a brush. Sand back the paint to reveal a patchy background. Paint an eye and a happy mouth. Apply a coat of varnish tinted with raw umber and raw sienna, and then a coat of clear varnish to finish.

AMISH SEWING BOX

*T*his box, plain and practical, catches the spirit of Amish crafts.

YOU WILL NEED

MATERIALS

plain wood box
emulsion (latex) paints: duck-egg blue, brick-red and beige
clear water-based varnish
acrylic paints: raw sienna and burnt umber
white knob

EQUIPMENT

paintbrushes
cloth
screwdriver

1 Paint the inside of the box with two coats of duck-egg blue. Paint a base coat of red on the outside of the box and beige on the front drawer.

2 Tint the varnish with a small squeeze of raw sienna and burnt umber and paint the outside of the box. Apply it with a thick-bristled brush, using pressure to leave strokes visible.

3 Apply the same varnish over the beige base coat on the drawer and while it is still wet, use a dry thick-bristled brush to lift some of the glaze to imitate woodgrain.

4 Apply a coat of tinted varnish to the inside, and while it is still wet, wipe off patches of it with a damp cloth to imitate wear and tear. Varnish over the whole box.

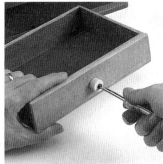

5 Screw on the white knob. If you have bought a new one, try making it look a bit scruffy by scratching on the surface and rubbing it with some burnt umber to age it.

ORNAMENTAL TREE

This tiny ornamental tree will perfume your room with the invigorating aroma of lemon oil.

YOU WILL NEED

MATERIALS

*florist's medium stub wires
brown florist's tape
modelling clay
yellow acrylic paint
fine brass wire
green crepe paper
tracing paper
thin card
PVA (white) glue
4 small wooden beads
dark green gloss paint*

*sand or gravel
cotton wool
pure lemon oil
orange and lemon peel*

EQUIPMENT

*wire-cutters or old scissors
paintbrushes
pencil
scissors*

1 Trim 15 pieces of stub wire to a length of 23 cm/9 in. Bind them all together with brown florist's tape for the first 12 cm/4¾ in, then bind each projecting end in turn. Divide the wires into pairs, and bind each pair part way up. Bend them out from the trunk, then inwards to shape the tree.

2 Make tiny lemons from clay, spike them on to wire and paint yellow. When dry, replace the wire supports with a loop of fine brass wire, covering the join with green crepe paper.

3 Trace the template from the back of the book, enlarging if necessary, and transfer to card. Make up the box by folding along the lines. Glue, then glue a bead to each corner. Paint dark green. Make a card tube to fit the trunk and glue into the centre of the box. Fill the box with sand or gravel and top with cotton wool.

4 Cut the leaves out of green crepe paper. Attach the lemons and leaves to the branches. Drip lemon oil on to the cotton wool and cover with orange and lemon peel.

PUNCHED TIN PANEL

*T*in-punching is a satisfying and stylish way to transform a panelled door. The graphic outline of the citrus slices and the pitted texture of the peel make the fruits appropriate motifs for this treatment.

YOU WILL NEED

MATERIALS

tracing paper
small cupboard with
panelled door
3 mm/⅛ in tin sheet, to fit
inside door panel
sheet of card
masking tape
strong clear glue

EQUIPMENT

pencil
scissors
hammer
steel punch

1 Trace the template from the back of the book, enlarging to fit your door panel. Lay the tin sheet on some card and attach the traced design using masking tape.

2 Starting with the square boxes around the fruit, hammer the steel punch every 2 mm/½ in to make a small dent. Hammer the larger dents to either side of the centre lines. Hammer small dents along all the fruit and leaf outlines.

3 Remove the tracing paper and fill in the whole fruit shapes with dents. Fill in the outer rims of the lemon slices with small dents.

4 Spread strong glue over the back of the tin and on the cupboard panel. Leave until tacky, then glue in position.

EXOTIC TABLE DECORATIONS

*M*ake a selection of whole fruit in this design, as well as an ornamental tree in a tub. These table decorations will look lovely underneath a glass bowl or hanging from drinks glasses.

YOU WILL NEED

MATERIALS	EQUIPMENT
tracing paper	*pencil*
PVA (white) glue	*dried-out ballpoint pen*
aluminium foil	*old scissors*
coloured varnish, or clear	*fine paintbrush*
varnish tinted with artist's	
oil colours	
fine wire	

1 Trace the templates from the back of the book, enlarging if necessary. Glue two sheets of foil together, shiny sides outwards. Lay the tracing over the foil and use a pen to draw round the outlines.

2 Cut out the foil shapes using old scissors, then cover with another sheet of tracing paper to protect the foil. Indent the details on the fruit and leaves with the dried-out ballpoint pen.

3 Using a fine paintbrush, paint the foil shapes with coloured varnish. Allow to dry.

4 Crease the leaves along their central veins and wind the stems around a length of fine wire. Glue them to the fruit. Wire the trunk of the tree.

STORAGE CANISTER

*T*ransform canisters by spraying them with paint and painting cheerful sunflowers all over them.

1 Wash the canister to remove any grease and dry thoroughly. Spray the can and lid with the blue paint, building the colour up with several fine layers and allowing each one to dry before applying the next, to prevent the paint from running.

2 Using the acrylic paints, paint in the sunflowers. For each one, paint a yellow circle about 3 cm/1¼ in in diameter and then evenly space the petals around the edge. Repeat the motif, placing it evenly around the canister, until the whole surface is covered. Allow to dry and then apply another layer of paint.

3 Add more colour to the petals, to give a feeling of depth. Paint the centres brown. Paint in the seeds with circles of brown, highlighting with cream. When the paint is dry, spray the canister and lid with an acrylic sealer, to protect the surface. The canister will withstand gentle cleaning, but not the dishwasher.

LOVE AND KISSES SOAP DISH

A novel idea to brighten up the bathroom – a soap dish made of ordinary gardening wire, spelling out the message with a heart and crosses (kisses). Simple to make, it has the practical virtue of keeping the soap from making a mess! The dish can be attached to the wall by inserting a screw through the pencil-size hoop.

YOU WILL NEED

MATERIALS	EQUIPMENT
thick, plastic-coated gardening wire	*wire-cutters pencil pliers*

1 Cut an 88 cm/35 in length of wire and wrap it, at the halfway point, around the pencil. Make a coil, by twisting the pencil a couple of times.

2 Using about 16 cm/6¼ in of wire on each side of the coil, make a heart shape, and then finish off by twisting the wire into a coil again.

3 Using the wire ends left, hook them together and join the ends by crimping them with pliers. Make this loop into an even oval, which will form the rim of the soap dish.

4 Cut four 14 cm/5½ in lengths of wire. Hook over the outside of the oval, making two crosses. Attach a shorter length across the centre.

GALVANIZED TRIVET

A practical accessory *that is made from galvanized wire, and so will co-ordinate with and complement your stainless steel kitchen utensils and your pots and pans.*

YOU WILL NEED

MATERIALS
2 mm/0.078 in galvanized wire

EQUIPMENT
pliers
broom handle

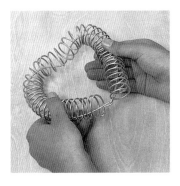

1 Take a 50 cm/20 in length of wire. Using pliers, make a heart shape by bending the wire in the centre, to form the dip in the top of the heart. At the ends, make hooks to join the wires together.

2 Make a coil by tightly and evenly wrapping more wire around a broom handle, about 50 times. Make hooks in the ends in the same way as you did before.

3 Thread the coil over the heart. Connect the ends of the heart by crimping the hooked ends together with pliers. You will need to manipulate the coil to make it sit evenly around the heart shape, before joining and crimping the ends together with pliers.

TIN CAN INSECTS

*T*here's more than one way to recycle empty cans: these light-hearted designs turn cans into insects to crawl up your garden walls. Use beer or lager cans that have the same logos on the front and back so that your insects look symmetrical. Take care not to cut yourself on the sharp edges of the cans.

YOU WILL NEED

MATERIALS	EQUIPMENT
tracing paper	*pencil*
large steel drinks (soda)	*scissors with small points*
can, top and bottom	*large paintbrush with a*
removed	*tapered handle*
masking tape	*small long-nosed pliers*

1 Trace the template on this page, enlarging if necessary. Cut up the side of the can opposite the bar code and open out flat. Place the template in position and secure with tape. Cut round the template carefully with sharp scissors.

2 Place the body of the insect over the tapered handle of a paintbrush, with the fattest part nearest the head. Shape the body by bending it around the handle. Fold the lower wings very slightly under the body and bend the upper wings forward, folding them slightly over the top part of the body.

3 Using some long-nosed pliers, twist the antennae back on themselves and curl the ends to complete.

TIN CANDLEHOLDER

*T*in-punching is an ideal technique to use for creating beautiful candleholders, such as this one. The effect is graphic and yet delicately detailed, and the metallic effect will reflect the warm glow of the candlelight. Take care not to leave burning candles unattended.

YOU WILL NEED

MATERIALS

tracing paper
aluminium or tin sheet
magazine or newspaper
epoxy resin glue
candle

EQUIPMENT

pencil
magic marker
protective gloves
tin snips or sharp scissors
magazine or newspaper
large, strong needle
tack hammer
metal ruler
wire brush

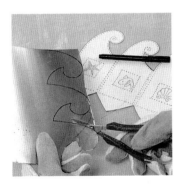

1 Trace the template from the back of the book, enlarging if necessary, and transfer the outline to the metal. Wearing gloves, cut it out, using tin snips or sharp scissors.

2 Lay the template on a magazine or newspaper to protect the work surface. Using a large, strong needle and a hammer, punch the pattern into the metal sheet.

3 Fold the two outer metal panels inwards along the dotted lines, using a metal ruler to crease the sheet cleanly. Do the same with the triangular flaps at the bottom.

4 Overlap the extra lip to secure the triangular shape, and glue it in place. Scratch the surface all over with the wire brush. Put the candle in the bottom of the container.

PIERCED TIN SHELF

*T*in-piercing is a wonderfully cheap and effective form of decoration. Here, it is combined with a traditional quilting pattern to make a small shelf from a recycled cake tin.

YOU WILL NEED

MATERIALS	EQUIPMENT
sheet of paper, to fit tin base	*scissors*
old baking tin	*magic marker*
scrap wood	*tin snips*
	pliers
	tack hammer
	fine, sharp nails

1 Make a pattern for the arch by folding the paper in half and cutting a curve from one half. Select one of the tin's sides and draw the arch above it, using the paper as a guide.

2 Snip 5 mm/¼ in into the raw edges at 2.5 cm/1 in intervals and use pliers to fold it firmly and crimp it until no sharp edges remain exposed.

3 Draw your pattern on to the arch. The pattern used here is an old quilting pattern, but a folk-style embroidery pattern would be just as suitable.

4 Place the tin on a flat piece of scrap wood and use the hammer to tap the nails through the tin and along the dotted lines. The perforations should be quite close to each other without causing the holes to join.

CANDLE COLLARS

YOU WILL NEED

MATERIALS

tracing paper
thin card
masking tape
40 gauge/0.003 in copper foil
wooden block
fine jeweller's wire
glass beads

EQUIPMENT

soft and sharp pencil
scissors
bradawl
ballpoint pen

1 Trace the template on this page, enlarging if necessary. Transfer to thin card and cut out. Tape the template to some copper foil. Draw around the template using a sharp pencil to transfer the design.

2 Remove the template and cut around the outside of the collar. Pierce the centre of the collar using a bradawl. Insert the scissors through the hole and carefully cut out the centre of the collar.

3 Place the collar, face down, on a sheet of thin card. Redraw over the lines of the outer and inner circles with a ballpoint pen. Press dots randomly into the surface of the foil between the two rings. Draw veins on each petal.

4 Place the collar, face up, on some wood. Pierce a hole below the centre of each petal. Thread wire through the first hole in the collar, bending the end back to secure. Thread beads on, twisting the wire at the end to hold in place.

351

PAINTED CHEST

*T*he chest used in this project reflects a combination of Old and New World influences. The shape is English, but the painted decoration was inspired by an old American dowry chest.

YOU WILL NEED

MATERIALS	EQUIPMENT
blanket chest	*paintbrushes*
shellac (optional)	*pencil*
emulsion (latex) paints:	*pair of compasses*
dusky-blue and	*ruler*
regency-cream	*graining comb*
tracing paper	*cloth*
antique pine acrylic	
varnish	

1 If you are starting with bare wood, apply a coat of shellac to seal the surface.

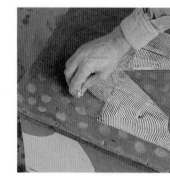

2 Paint the chest with dusky-blue. Trace the templates from the back of the book, enlarging them to fit your box. Use the templates as a guide to position the panels. Draw the panels with a pair of compasses and a ruler.

3 Paint all the panel pieces with cream emulsion (latex) paint.

4 Apply a thick coat of varnish to one panel only.

5 Quickly comb the varnish in a pattern, following the shape of the panel. Make one smooth combing movement into the wet varnish, then wipe off the comb to prevent any build-up of varnish. Complete one panel before repeating steps 4 and 5 for the other panels.

6 Apply a coat of varnish to the whole chest. Immediately, take a just-damp cloth, screw it into a ball and use it to dab off random spots of the varnish.

WOODBURNING

*P*atterns *burnt into wood were a traditional feature of Scandinavian folk art. Nowadays, the specialist tool for the technique is very easily manipulated and gives plenty of scope for creating a pattern to suit every taste.*

YOU WILL NEED

MATERIALS

tracing paper
chalky-based transfer paper
masking tape
woodburning kit, with chisel- and flat-ended tools
clear satin water-based varnish
burnt sienna artist's acrylic paint

EQUIPMENT

hard and soft pencils
paintbrush

1 Trace the template from the back of the book, enlarging to fit your box. Place the transfer paper between the tracing and the box, tape in place and transfer the design, using a soft pencil.

2 Set the woodburner at medium, and follow the lines for the stems and leaf outlines. Use the chisel-ended tool and keep it moving or lift it off the surface as it will burn a deeper hole if held static.

3 Outline the fruit with the flat tool. Fill in the leaf outlines with a pattern of dots using the chisel-ended tool with a prodding movement.

4 Apply two coats of water-based satin varnish tinted with a squeeze of burnt sienna paint, followed by one coat of clear varnish.

WALL SCONCE

These fashionable room accessories were once essential to every household, and nowadays they restore a bit of the romance that electricity has taken out of life.

YOU WILL NEED

MATERIALS

old piece of wood, such as driftwood
brass and black upholstery nails
wood glue
fine nails

EQUIPMENT

saw
hammer

1 Saw through the wood, making two sections to be joined at right angles. Begin the pattern by hammering the upholstery nails in a central line; the pattern can then radiate from it.

2 Form a pattern of arrows, crosses and diamonds, using the contrast between the brass and black nails to enhance the design.

3 Apply a coat of wood glue to the sawn edge of the base. Hammer fine nails through the back into the base.

355

COPPER FRAME

This frame combines two metal foils to create a stunning effect. The embossed shapes and simple nail patterns look very striking indeed.

YOU WILL NEED

MATERIALS

sheet of thin copper foil, 1 cm/½ in wider than frame softwood frame, with sides at least 7 cm/2¾ in deep brass escutcheon pins, 1.5 cm/¾ in and 1 cm/½ in sheet of thin aluminium foil metal polish

EQUIPMENT

*large, soft cloth
ballpoint pen
scissors
bradawl
tack hammer
white china marker
soft cloth*

1 Spread out the cloth and put the copper foil on top. Lay the frame upside down on the foil and draw around the outer and inner edges with a ballpoint pen.

2 Mark on an inner frame 1.5 cm/¾ in deep, to allow for turning around the rebate of the frame. Cut out the outer corners and the middle of foil with scissors.

3 Fold the foil around the outer edges of the frame and make holes with a bradawl. Hammer the longer pins through the holes. Fold the foil around the rebate, mark and pin it with the short pins.

4 Draw simple flower and leaf shapes on the back of the aluminium foil with the china marker. Cut out the shapes with scissors.

5 Place the shapes on the soft cloth and draw decorative patterns on the back of them with a ballpoint pen.

6 Place the flowers and leaves around the frame and prick through both the metals and the wood using a bradawl. Using the long pins, nail the shapes on to the frame through the pricked holes.

7 Further decorate the frame with more long pins hammered in to form star shapes. Finish off by gently rubbing the whole frame with a soft cloth and metal polish.

CHRISTMAS DECORATIONS

*T*hese *twinkly Christmas decorations were inspired by Eastern European architecture and folk art. Stamped and die-cut artefacts were very popular in many European countries throughout the nineteenth century, when there would have been a tin-worker in every village.*

YOU WILL NEED

MATERIALS	EQUIPMENT
tracing paper	*soft and sharp pencils*
thin card	*scissors*
36 gauge/0.005 in	*embroidery scissors*
aluminium foil	*magic marker*
fine wire	*ruler*
	dressmaker's wheel
	ballpoint pen
	wooden block
	bradawl

1 Trace the templates from the back of the book, transfer to thin card and cut out. Cut a small piece of foil and place the template on it. Draw around the outline with a sharp pencil. Using embroidery scissors, cut out the foil shape. Cut it carefully to ensure that there are no rough edges.

2 Using the picture as a guide, mark the basic lines of the design on the back of the decoration using a magic marker and ruler. Place the decoration face down on card. Trace over the lines with a dressmaker's wheel to emboss a row of raised dots at the front. Trace a second line of dots inside the first, in the decoration's centre.

3 Using the picture as a guide, draw the details of the house on the back of the decoration with a pen.

4 Place the decoration face up on a small block of wood. Using a bradawl, make a hole in the top of the decoration, then tie a length of fine wire through the hole to make a hanger.

GILDED CANDLEHOLDER

*T*he gentle glow of candles has an obvious affinity with starlight, and this twelve-pointed star is gilded and studded with copper to reflect the light. Painted in warm, festive colours, it would make a lovely addition to a traditional Christmas table.

YOU WILL NEED

MATERIALS

5 mm/¼ in birch plywood sheet
1 cm/½ in pine sheet
sandpaper
wood glue
white undercoat paint
acrylic paints: dark green, red and gold
matt varnish
6 copper disc rivets, 2 cm/¾ in

EQUIPMENT

pair of compasses
pencil
ruler
fretsaw
paintbrushes
spike
wire-cutters

1 Using a pair of compasses, draw a large circle on the plywood. With the same radius, mark the six points of the star around the circle and join with a ruler. Draw a smaller circle on the pine and mark out the second star in the same way. Draw a circle in the centre to fit your chosen candle size.

2 Cut out the two star shapes and sand any rough edges. Stick together with wood glue to form a twelve-pointed star. Paint with white undercoat and sand lightly when dry. Cover with a base coat of dark green acrylic paint, then paint on the design. Seal with a coat of matt varnish.

3 Using a spike, make six holes for the copper disc rivets. Trim the stems of the rivets with wire-cutters and push into the holes.

GILDED CANDLESTICK

*C*andlelight gives a magical glow to a room, and this shimmering candlestick will really heighten the atmosphere. Both silver and gold are used here, to dramatic effect. The sunflower motif is a relief design built up with layers of gesso, and the depth of the relief enhances the light and shade effect.

YOU WILL NEED

MATERIALS

turned-wood candlestick
red oxide primer
3-hour oil size
aluminium leaf transfer book
acrylic gesso
Dutch gold leaf transfer book
black watercolour paint
methylated spirit-based varnish

EQUIPMENT

medium and fine paintbrushes
large stencil brush
paint-mixing container
rag

1 Prime the candlestick all over with red oxide and allow to dry. Then paint it with size and allow to dry for three hours. When the size is "squeaky", it is ready for gilding. Begin gilding the candlestick with aluminium leaf, rubbing it with a dry stencil brush, so it adheres to the size. Repeat until covered.

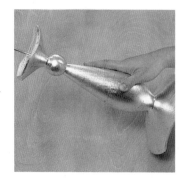

2 Paint a fine layer of acrylic gesso, freehand, in a sunflower shape. Allow to dry. Build up the relief with three or four layers of gesso.

3 Paint lines of gesso in the centre, to make a lattice pattern. Allow to dry.

4 Paint the sunflower with red oxide primer, to seal the surface and to act as a base for the gilding. Allow to dry.

5 Paint the sunflower with size and allow to dry.

6 Once the size is "squeaky", lay a sheet of Dutch gold leaf on the flower.

7 Rub it with the stencil brush, using the bristles to push the metal into the grooves, so it adheres.

8 Put some black paint on to a rag and rub it into the lattice to darken it, giving it an effect of greater depth. Finally, give the whole candlestick a coat of varnish.

SUNFLOWER MAGNET

*T*his sunflower fridge magnet will brighten up the kitchen on the darkest of mornings. In winter, you could consider making a whole row of them, as a reminder of the pleasures of the summer garden.

YOU WILL NEED

MATERIALS	EQUIPMENT
5 mm/¼ in thick birch-faced plywood sheet	pair of compasses
medium- and fine-grade sandpaper	pencil
wood glue	coping saw or fretsaw
white undercoat paint	medium and fine paintbrushes
acrylic paints: yellow, red, green, chocolate-brown and gold	paint-mixing container
gloss varnish	
small magnet	
epoxy resin glue	

1 With a pair of compasses, draw a circle on the plywood for the centre of the flower. Draw in the petals, leaf and stem freehand. Draw another circle the same size on the plywood and cut the shapes out.

2 Sand any rough edges off the flower shape. Sand the circle's edge to a curve. Then glue the circle to the centre of the flower with wood glue.

3 Paint with undercoat. Allow to dry and then sand lightly. Paint in the flower details with acrylic paints. Mix a golden-yellow and paint the petals. Paint the stem and leaves green. Paint the centre brown. When dry, add darker detail on the petals, veining on the leaves and gold dots on the centre. When dry, apply a coat of varnish. When the varnish is dry, stick the magnet on the back of the flower.

GRASSHOPPER ON A STICK

Plant this bold, bright grasshopper in your garden or conservatory, and let it add a splash of colour among the foliage.

YOU WILL NEED

MATERIALS

tracing paper
9 mm/⅜ in pine slat,
5.5 x 23 cm/2¼ x 9 in
2 pieces of 5 mm/¼ in
birch plywood, each
10 x 24 cm/4 x 9½ in
sandpaper
wood glue
5 mm/¼ in dowel,
48 cm/19 in long
white undercoat paint
enamel paints

EQUIPMENT

pencil
fretsaw
double-sided tape
craft knife
5 mm/¼ in drill
medium and fine
paintbrushes
empty wine bottle

1 Trace the templates from the back of the book, enlarging if necessary. Draw the body on the slat and cut out. Stick the plywood pieces together with tape and cut out the legs, sawing through both pieces at once. Cut out the antennae from plywood. Use a craft knife to whittle the edges. Sand all the rough edges.

2 Drill a hole in the underside of the body. Glue the legs and antennae in position on the body and stick the dowel in the hole. Paint with white undercoat and allow to dry, standing in an empty wine bottle. Colour the grasshopper with paints.

STARRY LETTER RACK

*P*ainted *in a lovely midnight-blue with jolly yellow stars, this charming letter rack is quite straightforward to assemble.*

YOU WILL NEED

MATERIALS	EQUIPMENT
tracing paper	*pencil*
5 mm/¼ in birch plywood	*ruler*
sheet	*pair of compasses*
wood glue	*fretsaw*
masking tape	*sandpaper*
4 wooden balls, 15 mm/⅝ in	*paintbrushes*
white undercoat paint	
acrylic paints	
satin varnish	

1 Trace the template from the back of the book, enlarging as required. Mark on the plywood, then cut out and sand all the edges.

2 Glue the pieces together and hold in place with masking tape until the glue has hardened completely.

3 Remove the tape and sand all the edges and corners. Glue the wooden balls to the corners of the base.

4 Paint on a coat of white undercoat, sanding down lightly when dry. Paint the rack and the stars in acrylic paints. Seal with a coat of satin varnish. When the varnish is completely dry, glue the stars in position on the front of the rack.

LEO LETTER RACK

*T*his *jolly letter rack is just the thing to brighten up your desk.*

YOU WILL NEED

MATERIALS

5 mm/¼ in birch plywood sheet, cut as follows:
base 21.5 x 7.3 cm/
8½ x 2⅞ in
sides 13 x 7.3 cm/5 x 2⅞ in
front 23 x 10 cm/9 x 4 in
back 23 x 19 cm/9 x 7½ in
tracing paper
wood glue
masking tape
4 wooden balls, 15 mm/⅝ in
white undercoat paint
acrylic paints: deep cobalt,
deep yellow, cadmium-red,
gold, raw umber and black
matt varnish

EQUIPMENT

pencil
ruler
pair of compasses
fretsaw
sandpaper
paintbrushes
stencil brush

1 Mark out the back, front, base and two sides on the plywood to the sizes listed above. Trace the template from the back of the book, enlarging if necessary, and cut out the back and sides. Cut out the other pieces. Sand the edges.

2 Glue the pieces together and hold in place with tape until the glue has hardened completely. Remove the tape and sand all the edges and corners. Glue the wooden balls to the corners of the base.

3 Paint the letter rack with white undercoat, sanding down lightly when dry. With the stencil brush, stipple the rack with deep cobalt paint.

4 Complete the design in acrylic paints, using the main picture as a guide. Seal with a coat of matt varnish.

LANTERN

*T*his tin can lantern is reminiscent of Moroccan lanterns that have similar curlicues and punched holes. A cold chisel and heavy hammer are used to cut ventilation holes out of the metal on the lantern roof.

YOU WILL NEED

MATERIALS	EQUIPMENT
large tin can	tin opener
thin aluminium sheet	magic marker
sheet of chipboard	protective gloves
scrap of thin tin	tin shears
flux	pliers
fine wire	file
	pair of compasses
	pencil
	protective goggles
	cold chisel
	hammer
	nail or centre punch
	soldering mat
	soldering iron and solder
	protective mask
	wire-cutters

1 Using a tin opener, remove one end of the tin can. Make an aperture for the door by marking a rectangle on to the front of the tin. Wearing gloves, cut out the rectangle.

2 Turn over the door edges with pliers to make the aperture safe. File away any remaining rough edges.

3 To make the lid, draw a semi-circle on a scrap of aluminium sheet. The radius should be equal to the diameter of the tin. Cut out and file the edges smooth.

4 Lay the lid on some chipboard. Wearing goggles, cut ventilation holes in the lid using a cold chisel and hammer. File any rough edges.

5 Using a hammer and nail or centre punch, punch holes around the top edge of the lantern and around the bottom of the curved edge of the lid. File away any rough edges around the holes.

6 To make the candleholder, cut a strip of tin. File the edges and curve the tin around to make a circle. Place the lantern on a soldering mat. Apply flux to the join. Wearing a mask and goggles, solder the holder inside the lantern.

7 Curve the lid around to make a cone. Using a pair of pliers, thread fine wire through the holes in the lid to join the sides together.

8 For the handle, cut a length of fine wire, then cut two shorter pieces. Make a loop in either end of the shorter pieces, then centre them on either side of the longer wire and solder in place. Curve them, then thread the ends through the holes in the top of the lid and twist them into tight spirals inside.

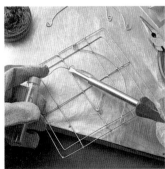

9 Attach the lid to the lantern using fine wire. Pull the wire tight using pliers.

10 For the door, make a decorative rectangular frame from lengths of wire. The frame should be slightly taller and wider than the aperture. Lay the frame on a soldering mat and solder all the sections together. When the door is complete, curve it to the shape of the lantern.

11 To make hinges, bend two short lengths of wire into "U" shapes. Bend each end of the "U" into right angles. Solder one end of each hinge to the lantern. Place the door inside the hinges so that it rests on them and doesn't drop down. Solder the other end of the hinges to the lanterns.

12 For the latch, make a hook and a "U"-shaped catch from short lengths of wire. Solder the catch to the side of the lantern and attach the hook to the door frame.

367

WOODEN DISH

*T*his wooden dish would be good for serving candies or nuts. It's very easy to make, if you take the time to measure, draw, and cut accurately.

YOU WILL NEED

MATERIALS	EQUIPMENT
5 mm/¼ in birch-faced plywood sheet	pencil
2.5 cm/1 in pine slat	fretsaw or coping saw
double-sided tape	ruler
tracing paper	drill, with medium bit
wood filler (optional)	paintbrushes
sandpaper	paint-mixing containers
wood glue	
white undercoat paint	
acrylic paints: red, green, yellow, white and brown	
matt varnish	

1 Attach the plywood to the back of the pine with the double-sided tape. Trace the template on this page, enlarging if necessary. Place the template on the pine and draw around it. Cut out the heart shape from the plywood and pine with the fretsaw or coping saw.

2 Detach the plywood heart. On the pine heart, mark a line 5 mm/¼ in from the edge (make a smaller template and draw around it). Drill a hole for the saw blade. If you can't do this easily, saw through from the side and repair the cut with a little filler. Cut around the inner outline and detach the smaller heart. Sand the two pieces smooth.

3 Line up the plywood heart exactly with the pine one, as a base. Glue it in place and allow to dry. Sand around the edges again. Paint with white undercoat and allow to dry. Lightly sand again, with fine-grade sandpaper, and decorate with acrylic paints. When dry, finish with a coat of varnish.

PAINTED GARDEN STICKS

These cheerful sun and moon faces are very simple to make and will really brighten up the garden. Use them to enhance the festive atmosphere when you are having a barbecue or garden party. You could also put them into a border or bed, or use them to give height and structure to plants in a container.

YOU WILL NEED

MATERIALS
tracing paper
5 mm/¼ in birch-faced
plywood sheet
medium- and fine-grade
sandpaper
garden sticks or canes
white undercoat paint
PVA (white) glue
acrylic paints: red, yellow,
brown, blue and white
gloss varnish

EQUIPMENT
pencil
coping saw or fretsaw
drill
medium and fine
paintbrushes
paint-mixing container

1 Draw the sun and moon shapes freehand on tracing paper and transfer the outlines to the plywood. Cut out the shapes with the saw and sand the edges smooth. Drill a hole in the edge of each shape for the sticks.

2 Paint the sticks and shapes all over with undercoat. Allow to dry. Sand lightly with fine-grade sandpaper. Glue the sticks in place.

3 Decorate the sticks with acrylic paints and allow to dry thoroughly. Finish with a coat of varnish.

WOODEN STAR FRAME

*M*ake your favourite person an instant star by putting their picture in this original frame. Once the photograph is in position, back it with a piece of stiff card cut to size and held in place with tape.

YOU WILL NEED

MATERIALS	EQUIPMENT
picture or photograph	*ruler*
birch plywood sheet,	*pair of compasses*
5 mm/¼ in thick	*pencil*
white undercoat paint	*fretsaw*
acrylic paints	*sandpaper*
satin varnish	*router*
brass triangle picture hook	*paintbrushes*
and pins	*hammer*

1 Measure your picture and subtract 1 cm/½ in from each dimension to work out the size of the frame opening. Mark this on the plywood, then mark out the star pattern from the back of the book around it.

2 Cut out the star shape and inner square and sand down all the edges. On the back, rule a line around the opening 5 mm/¼ in from the edge and make a rebate with the router 3 mm/⅛ in deep.

3 Sand down and then paint the frame with white undercoat, sanding down lightly when dry. Mark out the bands in pencil, then paint the design.

4 Finish with a coat of satin varnish. Finally, pin a triangle hook to the top point of the frame.

DRIFTWOOD FRAME

*T*his frame can be made from any beach finds. Wood that has been smoothed and weathered by the sea is best. Add shells or pebbles for variety. A seascape picture is ideal for a driftwood frame.

YOU WILL NEED

MATERIALS

flat-faced wooden frame
emulsion (latex) paints:
deep and pale blue
wax furniture polish
selection of driftwood
strong glue
shells and beach finds
short piece of old rope
small toy boat

EQUIPMENT

paintbrushes
cloth
fine-grade sandpaper

1 Paint the wooden frame with a base coat of deep blue. Allow to dry, then rub on a layer of wax furniture polish and allow to dry.

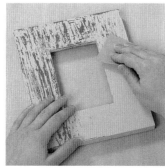

2 Paint on two coats of pale blue, leaving to dry between coats. Sand away the top coat to reveal the base colour in places.

3 Arrange the driftwood pieces around the frame in a pleasing design. Glue in place. Add any shells and beach finds you have got.

4 Glue the old piece of rope on to the back of the frame to act as a hanging hook. Finally, glue the toy boat on to the top of the frame.

WOODEN BEAD NECKLACE

*S*imple wooden balls available from craft shops are transformed by gilding to make this glittering necklace. Experiment with leaf or powders in different colours, and alternate the beads on the string for stunningly original jewellery. This necklace could also make an unusual tie-back.

YOU WILL NEED

MATERIALS	EQUIPMENT
assorted wooden balls	vice
small nails	drill, with fine bit
wood off-cut	hammer
red oxide spray primer	paintbrushes
water-based size	burnishing brush or soft
Dutch metal leaf: gold,	cloth
copper and aluminium	scissors
amber shellac varnish	
acrylic varnishing wax	
leather thongs	

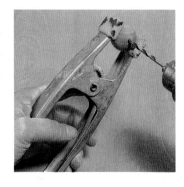

1 Holding each ball in turn in a vice, drill a hole through the centre.

2 Hammer small nails into the off-cut of wood to make a rack. Place the balls on the nails and spray them with red oxide primer. Allow to dry.

3 Paint a thin, even layer of water-based size on to the balls and leave to rest for about 20–30 minutes, until the size becomes clear and tacky.

4 Gild the balls in different colours of metal leaf and burnish with a burnishing brush or soft cloth to remove the excess leaf.

5 Seal the gold balls with amber shellac varnish and the copper and aluminium balls with acrylic varnishing wax. Buff the wax with a soft cloth after several hours to bring up the lustre.

6 Cut lengths of leather thong and thread the balls on to it, alternating each colour. Tie the ends of the thong in a knot.

SUNFLOWER BADGE

This cheerful sunflower face can be worn as a badge or brooch and would enhance a plain black or primary-coloured sweater or jacket.

YOU WILL NEED

MATERIALS

*birch-faced plywood sheet,
5 mm/¼ in thick
wood glue
white undercoat paint
acrylic paints: yellow, red,
chocolate-brown and gold
gloss varnish
brooch pin*

EQUIPMENT

*pencil
pair of compasses
coping saw or fretsaw
medium- and fine-grade
sandpaper
paintbrushes
paint-mixing container*

1 Draw a circle for the flower-centre on the plywood with the pair of compasses. Draw the petals freehand around the centre. Draw another circle the same size as the centre. Cut out these two shapes with a saw.

2 Sand any rough edges on the flower. Sand the circle's edge to a curve. Glue the circle to the centre of the flower shape, with wood glue. Paint with white undercoat and allow to dry. Sand lightly.

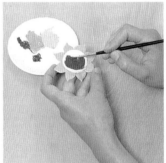

3 Paint in the flower details with the acrylic paints. Mix yellow and red to make a golden-yellow for the petals. Paint the centre brown. When dry, add gold dots to the centre. Apply a coat of gloss varnish. When the varnish is dry, stick the brooch pin on to the back of the badge with wood glue.

SUN AND MOON BADGES

*W*ear one of these jolly badges as a colourful and bold brooch on a plain coat or sweater. Simple to make, these badges are bound to lift everybody's spirits in the early morning.

YOU WILL NEED

MATERIALS

tracing paper
birch-faced plywood sheet,
5 mm/¼ in thick
white undercoat paint
acrylic paints: yellow, red
and blue
gloss varnish
epoxy resin or hot glue
2 brooch pins

EQUIPMENT

pencil
coping saw or fretsaw
medium- and fine-grade
sandpaper
paintbrushes
paint-mixing container

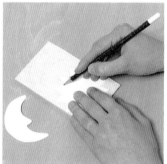

1 Trace the templates from the back of the book, enlarging if necessary, and transfer the outlines to the plywood. Cut out the shapes with the saw and sand the edges smooth.

2 Paint both sides and all the edges of the shapes with white undercoat. When the paint is dry, sand it lightly.

3 Paint the fronts of the sun and moon with acrylic paint and add the features and other details. When the paint is dry, add a coat of varnish and allow to dry. Put a thick line of glue on the back of each badge and press the brooch pin firmly into the glue.

SEAHORSE STORAGE BOX

*D*elicate, swirling brushstrokes create a watery background for this delightful seahorse. The box could be used for storing stationery, pencils, jewellery or even cosmetics.

YOU WILL NEED

MATERIALS

5 mm/¼ in thick pine slat, 68 cm/26½ in long and 3 cm/1¼ in wide
wood glue
masking tape
5 mm/¼ in thick birch-faced plywood sheet, 40 x 40 cm/16 x 16 in
white undercoat paint
acrylic paints: blue, white, green and gold
tracing paper
stencil card or acetate sheet

EQUIPMENT

ruler
coping saw or fretsaw
medium and fine-grade sandpaper
pencil
paintbrush
craft knife
cutting mat
stencil brush

1 Cut two 20 cm/8 in and two 14 cm/5½ in lengths of pine with a saw. Sand the rough edges and glue the pieces together to form the sides of the box. Hold the frame together with masking tape while the glue is drying.

2 Place the frame on the plywood and draw around the inside, to mark out the base of the box. Cut out the base. Repeat the process to make the lid insert. Draw around the outside of the box and cut out to make the lid. Glue the base into the frame. Sand around the lid insert and make sure that it will fit in the box, before gluing it to the lid.

3 Sand the box and then apply a coat of white undercoat paint.

4 When dry, sand the box again, using fine sandpaper. Using two shades of blue acrylic, paint the box with swirling brushstrokes.

5 Trace the template from the back of the book, enlarging if necessary. Transfer it to stencil card or acetate and cut it out.

6 Tape the stencil on to the lid to hold it firmly in place. Stencil the pattern, using a combination of blue and green acrylics. Finish with a light smattering of gold. When the paint is dry, lightly sand the whole box with fine sandpaper.

CORONET PICTURE FRAME

*T*he coronet motif sets off the regal gold and purple of this frame.

YOU WILL NEED

MATERIALS

medium-density fibreboard (MDF), 18 mm/¾ in 18 x 23 cm/7 x 9 in
polyester wadding (batting), 23 x 36 cm/ 9 x 14 in
crimson velvet, 45 x 45 cm/18 x 18 in
double-sided tape
50 cm/20 in gold braid, 2 cm/¾ in wide
50 cm/20 in gold cord
selection of large sequins or filigree buttons
sewing thread
tracing paper
thin card or paper
sheet tin or silver card, 10 x 18 cm/4 x 7 in
diamante or glass gems
mountboard, 18 x 25.5 cm/7 x 10 in
white velvet, 5 x 15 cm/2 x 6 in

EQUIPMENT

dust mask
ruler
pencil
jigsaw
scissors
staple gun
needle
glue gun

1 Wear a dust mask. Using a jigsaw, cut a 9 x 14 cm/3½ x 5½ in rectangle from the centre of the MDF to leave a frame measuring 4.5 cm/1¾ in deep. Cover the front with two layers of polyester wadding (batting) and snip out all of the area in the centre.

2 Cover the frame with a crimson velvet rectangle, 28 x 36 cm/11 x 14 in, fixing it tautly at the back with a staple gun. Make a slit in the centre and snip into the inner corners. Pull the inner edges of the velvet to the back of the frame and staple.

3 Fix double-sided tape to the back of the gold braid. Remove the backing paper and stick around the inside edge of the frame to cover the raw edges. Stick a length of gold cord around the lower edge of the braid.

4 Sew sequins or filigree buttons to the four inside corners of the frame.

5 Trace the template from the back of the book, enlarging it to 15 cm/6 in across, and cut it out of thin card or paper. Draw around it on sheet tin or silver card and cut out. Bend the side tabs inwards and curve the coronet gently. Decorate with diamante or glass gems stuck on with a glue gun.

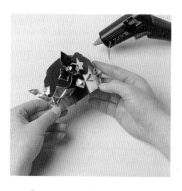

6 Cut an oval shape from the remaining crimson velvet and sew a gathering thread around the edge. Crumple a sheet of paper and place in the centre, then draw up the thread. Fix inside the coronet with a glue gun.

7 Trim the top of the mountboard to fit the frame, leaving a wide tab to support the coronet. Tape the picture to be framed to the back of the opening, then staple the board to the back of the frame.

8 Use the glue gun to fix the coronet to the frame and board. Conceal the join by turning in the raw edges of the white velvet to make a narrow band and gluing it around the base of the coronet.

PAINTED BENCH

Every home should have a bench like this, to squeeze extra guests around the dinner table and to keep by the back door for comfortable boot-changing. This bench is made from reclaimed floorboards which give it just the right rustic feel.

YOU WILL NEED

MATERIALS

bench
shellac
emulsion (latex) paints:
dark blue-grey, deep red
and light blue-green
antique pine colour varnish
clear matt varnish

EQUIPMENT

medium-grade sandpaper
paintbrushes
small piece of sponge

1 Sand the bare wood and seal it with a coat of shellac.

2 Paint the legs in dark blue-grey emulsion (latex) paint, working directly on to the wood.

3 Paint the seat with deep red emulsion (latex) paint.

4 Use the sponge to dab an even pattern of blue-green spots across the whole surface of the seat.

5 When the paint is thoroughly dry, rub the seat and edges with sandpaper to simulate wear and tear.

6 Apply a coat of antique pine varnish to the whole bench. Then apply two coats of matt varnish for a strong finish.

SHOOTING STAR BADGE

*T*his jolly little shooting star will brighten up a plain jumper or jacket. Use pearlized paint for its tail and glossy varnish to make the colours glow.

YOU WILL NEED

MATERIALS

tracing paper
birch-faced plywood sheet,
5 mm/¼ in thick
white undercoat paint
acrylic paints
water-based paints
pearlized paints
gloss varnish
all-purpose glue
brooch pin

EQUIPMENT

pencil
fretsaw
sandpaper

1 Trace the template from the back of the book and transfer to the plywood. Cut out and sand all the edges.

2 Paint with a coat of white undercoat. When dry, sand lightly and mark the remaining points of the star in pencil.

3 Paint on the badge's design in acrylic paints, using pearlized paint for the tail. Protect it with gloss varnish.

4 Glue the brooch pin to the back of the badge.

385

CELESTIAL MOBILE

*S*tars, *the crescent moon and a huge shooting star jostle each other in this amusing mobile. The little star-shaped cut-outs in the meteor's tail can all be joined by saw cuts, so you need drill only one hole through which to pass the saw blade.*

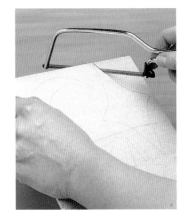

1 Trace the templates from the back of the book, enlarging if necessary, and transfer to the plywood. Cut them out. Drill a small hole inside the circle of the shooting star and through the first cut-out in the tail. Pass the saw blade through each of these to make the internal cuts. With a very small bit, drill holes through the top of each piece and in the marked positions on the hanger. Lightly sand all the pieces.

YOU WILL NEED

MATERIALS	EQUIPMENT
tracing paper	pencil
5 mm/¼ in birch plywood	fretsaw
white undercoat paint	drill
chrome finish spray paint	sandpaper
acrylic paints	paintbrushes
varnish	
fine nylon fishing line	

2 Paint all the pieces with undercoat. Allow to dry, then spray the top of the shooting star and the crescent moon with chrome paint. Complete the decoration using acrylic paints and varnish.

3 Tie the stars to the hanger with thin nylon line. Make sure they do not bump into each other. Add a loop of nylon to the hole at the top.

SPIDER WEB CLOCK

*F*ind gold-coloured *hands for your clock, which will match the gilded spider and contrast prettily with the rich blue background.*

YOU WILL NEED

MATERIALS

5 mm/¼ in birch plywood, about 18 x 18 cm/7 x 7 in white undercoat paint acrylic paints: dark blue, white, black and gold clear matt varnish clock movement and hands

EQUIPMENT

pair of compasses
pencil
ruler
drill
fretsaw or coping saw
sandpaper
paintbrushes
paint-mixing container
white marker pencil

1 Draw a circle on the plywood and divide it into eight segments using a ruler. Draw the looping outline of the web around the edge.

2 Drill a hole in the centre and saw around the edge of the web. Sand, then paint with white undercoat. Allow to dry and sand again.

3 Paint the clockface in dark blue and stipple with a stiff brush while the paint is still wet. Apply a coat of varnish. When dry, draw the web pattern with a white marker pencil.

4 Mix a light grey colour and paint over the web using a fine brush. Paint on the flies and the golden spider. Finish with a coat of matt varnish and attach the clock movement and hands.

BUSY BEE WORKBOX

*Y*ou'll find any number of uses for this handy box. The stylized fretwork bee – the symbol of industry – is both decorative and functional, as it forms the handle of the box.

YOU WILL NEED

MATERIALS

8 mm/⅜ in pine slat,
2 m x 7 cm/6 ft 6 in x 2¾ in
wood glue
tracing paper
carbon paper
5 mm/¼ in birch plywood,
38 x 20 cm/15 x 8 in
panel pins (optional)
light oak wood stain
polyurethane varnish
self-adhesive baize,
38 x 19 cm/15 x 7½ in

EQUIPMENT

tenon saw
pencil
5 mm/¼ in drill
fretsaw
sandpaper
hammer (optional)
paintbrush
fine wire wool
scissors

1 Cut two 38 cm/15 in lengths of pine. Glue the two pieces together to form a single piece.

2 Trace the template from the back of the book, enlarging if necessary, and transfer to the centre of the board using carbon paper.

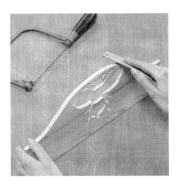

3 Drill a hole through each section of the bee. Pass the saw blade through each hole and saw out the design. Mark and saw the curve of the handle, making the ends 6.5 cm/2½ in deep. Sand.

4 Cut two 39.8 cm/15¾ in and two 20 cm/8 in lengths of pine for the sides of the box. Glue these around the plywood base. You may find it easier to fix the corners with panel pins while the glue dries.

5 Glue the handle section in place. Colour the box with wood stain and allow to dry, then varnish it.

6 Rub the box down with wire wool to achieve a warm lustre. Cut the baize in half and trim to fit in the base.

PHOTOGRAPH FRAME

*B*ecause of its softness, fine-gauge aluminium foil is the perfect material for cladding frames. Coloured and clear glass nuggets combine with the subdued tones of the foil to give this frame a Celtic air, reinforced by a design of repeating circles, a fundamental element in Celtic decorative art.

YOU WILL NEED

MATERIALS

photograph frame
36 gauge/0.005 in
aluminium foil
epoxy resin glue
thin card
coloured and plain
glass nuggets

EQUIPMENT

ruler
scissors
pencil
ballpoint pen

1 Remove the glass and backing from the frame. Measure the four sides and cut strips of foil to cover them, making the foil long enough to wrap over and under, to the back. Mould the foil strips around the frame and glue them in place.

2 Cut pieces of foil to cover the corners. Mould these to the contours of the frame and glue them in place.

3 Draw a circle on to card and cut out to make a template. Draw around the card on to the aluminium foil, using a ballpoint pen. Cut out the foil circles. Draw a design on to one side of each circle. This is now the back of the circle.

4 Turn the foil circles over so that the raised side of the embossing is face up. Glue coloured glass nuggets to the centre fronts of half of the foil circles. Glue plain glass nuggets to the centres of the other half.

5 Glue the foil circles around the photograph frame, spacing them evenly. Alternate the circles so that a coloured glass centre follows one with clear glass. When the glue is dry, replace the glass and backing in the frame.

PAINTED TIN BADGES

A good way to use up small scraps of tin is to make brooches. These can be very simple in construction and made special with painted decorations. The enamel paints are very opaque and they cover previous coats of paint beautifully, so light colours can be painted on top of dark very successfully.

YOU WILL NEED

MATERIALS

scrap of 30 gauge/0.01 in tin
enamel paints
clear gloss polyurethane varnish
epoxy resin glue
brooch fastener

EQUIPMENT

magic marker
work shirt and protective leather gloves
tin snips
bench vice
file
wet and dry sandpaper
china marker
fine paintbrushes

1 To make the brooch front, draw a circle freehand measuring 5 cm/2 in diameter on a piece of tin. Wearing a work shirt and gloves, cut out the circle with tin snips.

2 Clamp the circle in a bench vice and file the edges. Finish off the edges with damp wet and dry paper so that they are completely smooth.

3 Draw the outline of the sun on to one side of the brooch with a china marker. Paint around the outline with enamel paint, then fill in the design. Allow to dry.

4 Paint in the background, then paint the sun's features on top of the first coat of paint, using a fine paintbrush and enamel paint. Set aside and allow to dry.

5 Seal the surface of the brooch with two coats of clear varnish to protect it from scratches. Allow to dry thoroughly between coats.

6 Mix some epoxy resin glue and use it to stick a brooch fastener on to the back. Let the glue dry thoroughly before wearing the brooch.

SPIDER'S WEB BROOCH

*R*eproduce the delicate texture of a web in glittering *copper and silver wire. The resident spider is resplendent in blue and gold and not at all threatening, especially as she has only got six legs and a curly tail!*

YOU WILL NEED

MATERIALS

1 mm/0.039 in copper wire
0.65 mm/0.024 in silver wire
modelling clay
2 small glass beads
strong glue
brooch pin
turquoise acrylic paint
clear varnish
gold powder

EQUIPMENT

wire-cutters
round-nosed jewellery pliers
clay-modelling tool
paintbrush

1 Cut four 8 cm/3 in lengths of copper wire. Curl both ends of each piece into a loop with the pliers.

2 Arrange the pieces to form a star. Wrap the silver wire around the centre. Working outwards in a spiral, twist the silver wire once around each copper wire. Secure and trim.

3 Cut six 6 cm/2½ in lengths of copper wire. Curl one end of each into a loop, then bend into the shape of the spider's legs.

4 Cut an 8 cm/3 in length of wire and bend into a spiral for the tail. Roll two balls of clay for the body and head.

5 Press the two clay balls together, joining securely with the help of the modelling tool. Smooth the surface of the clay with wet fingers or the modelling tool.

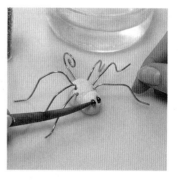

6 Insert the looped ends of the wire legs and tail into the spider's body. Press two glass beads into the head to make the eyes.

7 Press the spider's body on to the wire web. Flatten a small piece of clay and attach it to the spider from underneath the web, using the modelling tool to join it securely. Leave the clay to harden.

8 Glue the brooch pin to the back of the spider and secure the legs and tail with drops of glue. Paint the body and head turquoise and allow to dry. Apply a coat of varnish to seal the paint. Mix gold powder with a little varnish and apply swiftly with a dry brush to leave some of the turquoise paint showing through.

COPPER MOBILE

The glowing warmth of copper catches the light very gracefully as the mobile moves. The mobile looks spectacular and yet is easily worked in wire and thin sheet metal. To help you form the cupid figure, try drawing it out on paper first and then use your drawing as a guide for bending the wires.

YOU WILL NEED

MATERIALS	EQUIPMENT
paper	*pencil*
thin copper sheet,	*scissors*
15 x 4 cm/6 x 1½ in	*tin snips*
thin copper wire, 3 m/3 yd	*wet and dry sandpaper*
medium copper wire,	*hammer and nail*
1 m/1 yd	*round-nosed pliers*
fine gold-coloured wire,	
1 m/1 yd	
epoxy resin glue	

1 Draw a heart and arrow freehand on paper and cut them out. Trace three hearts and one arrow head and flight on to the copper sheet.

2 Cut the shapes out with tin snips and sand the edges smooth to the touch with wet and dry sandpaper.

3 Pierce holes in the hearts by hammering a nail through the metal.

4 Use the pliers to bend a cupid shape from the thin copper wire. In this design the cupid is made in two sections: the head, torso and arm are made from one length of wire, and the legs from another. Bend the medium copper wire into a bow shape.

5 Attach the two parts of the cupid with short lengths of thin wire.

6 Bend three heart shapes from the thin copper wire. Attach the copper hearts to the inside of the wire hearts with lengths of gold-coloured wire.

7 Bend the arrow head to make a groove in which the shaft will lie. Do the same with the flight. Cut a 15 cm/6 in length of medium wire for the shaft and glue it in place.

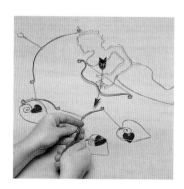

8 Use gold-coloured wire to create the string of the bow and connect it to the bow. Insert the arrow between the cupid's fingers and connect the bow to its chest. Cut two pieces of medium wire, 12 cm/4¾ in and one 25 cm/10 in for the struts. Bend the ends into loops. Assemble the mobile using the gold-coloured wire.

ASTRAL CLOCK

*A**n impressive starburst clock with rays cut out of shining copper. The face is a simple disc of clay, painted in turquoise to give a verdigris effect.*

YOU WILL NEED

MATERIALS
tracing paper
thin card or paper
0.5 mm copper sheet,
10 x 25 cm/4 x 10 in
modelling clay, 450 g/1 lb
acrylic paints: deep
turquoise, lemon-yellow
and white
varnish
gold powder
epoxy resin glue
clock movement and hands

EQUIPMENT
pencil
metal cutters
sandpaper
rolling pin
clay-modelling tools
paintbrush

1 Trace the templates from the back of the book, enlarging if necessary, and cut out of card or paper. Draw the outlines for four large and four small rays on the copper sheet. Cut out with metal cutters and sand the edges.

2 Roll out the clay to a flat sheet 5 mm/¼ in thick.

3 Place the template on the clay and cut out the shape. Trace the inner circle with a modelling tool to impress the shape in the clay.

4 Roll a clay snake and place along the inner circle. Join the ends, then join it to the clockface and smooth with wet fingers. Make a hole in the middle of the face.

5 Press the short rays into the side of the clay and allow to dry completely.

6 Mix turquoise, yellow and white paint and paint the face of the clock.

7 Paint the clockface with a layer of varnish and allow to dry.

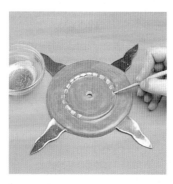

8 Mix the gold powder with varnish and decorate the ridge around the clock with thick gold lines.

9 Bend the bases of the long copper rays to fit over the edge of the face. Fix firmly in position with epoxy resin glue.

10 Fix the movement to the back of the clock and screw the hands on to the front.

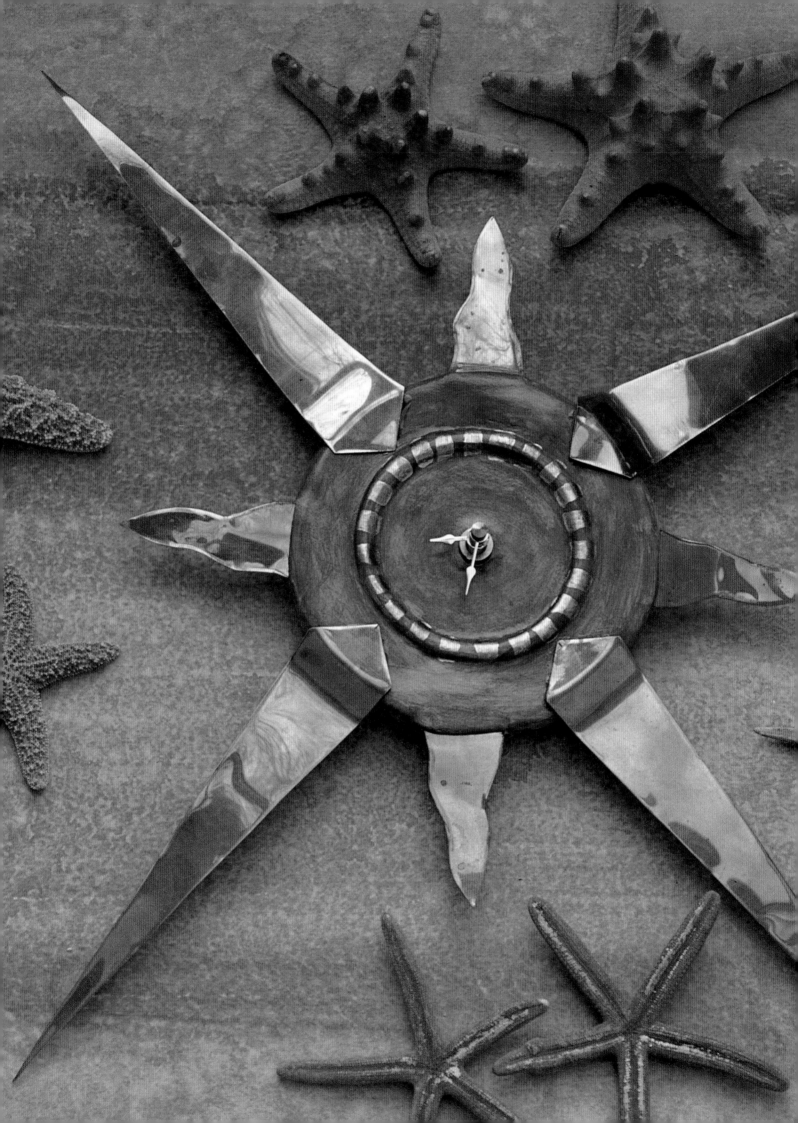

PAINTED TIN

*T*his project does not require you to learn the somewhat specialized brushstrokes used in traditional tin-painting, although the colours and antiquing will ensure that it blends in well with any other painted pieces.

YOU WILL NEED

MATERIALS

metal primer
large metal tin with a lid
emulsion (latex) paints:
black, brick-red
and maize-yellow
tracing paper
masking tape
shellac
clear varnish
raw umber artist's acrylic
paint
clear satin varnish

EQUIPMENT

paintbrushes
hard and soft pencils

1 Prime the tin, then paint the lid black, and the tin brick-red with yellow stripes.

2 Trace the template on this page, enlarging if necessary. Cross-hatch over the back of it with a soft pencil.

3 Tape the pattern in position on the tin and draw over it with a hard pencil to transfer the design.

4 Fill in the main body of the "3" in yellow.

5 Fill in the shadow of the "3" in black.

6 Varnish the tin with shellac to give it a warm glow.

7 Tint the varnish with some raw umber paint and apply it to the tin. Then apply a coat of clear satin varnish to seal the surface.

CRACKLE VARNISHED ANTIQUE

*B*y using antique varnish with a crackle varnish and rubbing raw umber oil paint into the cracks, you can give a frame a wonderful air of aged and distinguished distinction.

YOU WILL NEED

MATERIALS	EQUIPMENT
frame	*paintbrush*
wood filler and wood glue	*soft cloths*
(optional)	
white emulsion (latex) paint	
antique varnish	
crackle varnish	
raw umber oil paint	

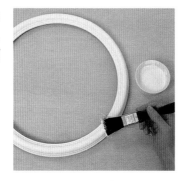

1 If the frame is old, repair it with wood filler and glue. Prepare the frame with one or two coats of white emulsion (latex) paint.

2 Apply one coat of antique varnish to the frame. Allow to dry.

3 Apply a coat of crackle varnish to the frame. The cracks may take a long time to appear, depending on the humidity of the room. To speed up the process, you could place the frame over a heat source for a few moments.

4 When the cracks appear, rub raw umber oil paint into them with a cloth. Allow to dry for 10 minutes. Apply a second coat of antique varnish to seal and protect the finish.

GILDED FRAME

*T*ransform *a plain picture frame with gilded seashells, starfish and seaweed. This would be an ideal frame for a mirror – hang it up to allow the gilding to catch the light.*

YOU WILL NEED

MATERIALS

*flat-faced wooden frame
acrylic gesso
acrylic paints: titanium-
white and raw sienna
clear matt varnish
3-hour oil size
Dutch gold leaf transfer
book*

EQUIPMENT

*decorator's and fine
paintbrushes
paint-mixing container
fine-grade sandpaper
soft pencil
sharp modelling tool*

1 Paint the frame with acrylic gesso and allow to dry. Then make up a creamy wash from diluted white and raw sienna acrylic and paint the frame again. Allow to dry.

2 Lightly sand the frame to distress it slightly and let the wood grain show through. Apply three coats of varnish, allowing each to dry before applying the next.

3 Draw loose, freehand shell, seaweed and starfish shapes in pencil on the frame.

4 Paint size on to the shapes and, when they are tacky, gently press gold leaf on to the size. Brush off any excess. Scratch into the gilded surface with a modelling tool to give additional texture.

SEA CREATURES MOBILE

These creatures will be an instant hit with adults and children.

YOU WILL NEED

MATERIALS

thick galvanized wire, 2 mm/0.078 in, 1.6 mm/0.062 in and 1.2 mm/0.047 in double-sided tape binding wire tracing paper thin card or paper aerosol car paints: red, yellow, aquamarine, blue and green nylon thread

EQUIPMENT

wire-cutters round-nosed pliers half-round jewellery pliers

HANGING THE MOBILE
To balance the mobile, the shapes must be hung from the following lengths of thread: crab 14cm/5½ in, dolphin 8 cm/3 in, seaweed 8 cm/3 in, seahorse 11 cm/4½ in, large fish 12 cm/3¾ in, shell 13 cm/ 5 in, small fish 8 cm/3 in, big starfish 8 cm/3 in, small starfish 8 cm/3 in.

1 To make the small supports, cut two 45 cm/18 in lengths of 2 mm/0.078 in wire. Bend each wire into an arch and form a coil at each end, using round-nosed pliers. Bend a curve in the wire, beside each coil, using half-round pliers. Make two main supports in the same way from 74 cm/29 in lengths of 2 mm/0.078 in wire. Bend waves in the wire, beside coils.

2 Cut a 3 cm/1¼ in length of 2 mm/0.078 in wire. Using the half-round pliers, bend the wire round, to make a ring. Cross the main support wires, so that they meet exactly in the centre and tape them together, with the ring at the top, using double-sided tape. Wrap the binding wire around the join, to secure it, completely covering the double-sided tape.

3 Trace the templates from the back of the book, enlarging them to 300%. Form each creature by shaping the wire around the template. First, cut a 90 cm/35½ in length of 1.6 mm/0.062 in wire. Form it into a seaweed shape, following the template from the book. Join the ends and wrap them with binding wire.

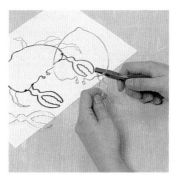

4 Following the template, form the crab's body from a 40 cm/16 in length of 1.6 mm/ 0.062 in wire. Make an eye loop at each end of the wire.

5 Make the front legs from two 29 cm/11½ in lengths of 1.2 mm/0.047 in wire. Twist the ends of the legs around the crab's body and secure.

6 Use a continuous length of binding wire to make the back legs. Wrap the wire around the crab's body, between the legs.

7 Using 1.6 mm/0.062 in wire, make: a shell from 22 cm/8½ in, two starfish from

32 cm/12½ in and 50 cm/19½ in, and a seahorse from 97 cm/ 38 in. Join and wrap the ends with binding wire. Use binding wire to make fins, nipping a point in each arch. Make a small fish from 71 cm/28 in wire, and a large fish from 100 cm/40 in wire. On the large fish, curve the wire across the back. Give each fish a wavy line of wire between head and body, binding the joins. Bend 108 cm/ 42½ in wire around the dolphin outline. Bind the joins.

8 Spray paint the sea creatures in one or two colours. To assemble, follow the finished picture. Attach the sea creatures to the supports with nylon thread.

FOLK ART FRAMES

These simple, graphic frames combine the naïve, hand-painted feel and typical colours of folk art decoration with a boldness that makes them fit for the most sophisticated modern interior.

YOU WILL NEED

MATERIALS	EQUIPMENT
plain, flat-faced wooden frames	*fine-grade sandpaper*
masking tape	*cloth*
acrylic paints: white,	*wide, flat-bristled and*
yellow, black, raw umber,	*fine paintbrushes*
blue and red	*paint-mixing container*
tracing paper	*pencil*
satin polyurethane varnish	

1 Sand the frames to remove any lacquer and to provide a key for the paint. Wipe off any dust with a damp cloth. Mask off the corners of the frames diagonally with tape to prevent any brush marks from over-lapping and lying in the wrong direction. Mix up an "antique" yellow from white and yellow paint, with a touch of black and raw umber. Paint on the background colour on the top and bottom edges; this can be a single, quite thick coat, several coats, or a colour-wash, so that the wood grain shows through. Remove the tape when dry, mask the painted edges at the corners and paint the sides of the frames.

2 Trace the templates from the back of the book, enlarging them if necessary. Paint the templates to try out different colour combinations, if you like. Position the templates on the frames and draw around them with a soft pencil.

3 Paint the design directly on to the frames, adding the circle and star motifs. Varnish the frames to finish.

SUNNY DAISY FRAME

*T*his vibrant painted frame with flowers of childlike simplicity is further enhanced by a charming pattern of gilded swirls.

YOU WILL NEED

MATERIALS

frame
acrylic gesso
acrylic paints: ultramarine,
cobalt-blue, titanium-white
and cadmium-yellow
satin varnish
3-hour oil size
Dutch gold leaf transfer
book

EQUIPMENT

paintbrushes
paint-mixing container
coarse-grade sandpaper
soft cloth

1 Paint the frame with acrylic gesso in thin layers with a damp paintbrush. The gesso takes about 30 minutes to dry between coats and you need to apply at least four coats to form a solid base for the colour.

2 Mix some ultramarine and cobalt-blue paint and paint over the gesso base. Allow to dry, then rub over the frame to give a "sgraffito" look. Buff with a cloth; don't get the gesso wet, or it will dissolve.

3 Paint four freehand daisy flowers in the corners with white and yellow paints. Paint a design of stitches around the edge of the frame in white. Allow to dry. Give the frame a coat of satin varnish and allow to dry.

4 Gild the frame by painting 3-hour size swirls on to it. When the size is tacky, place the gold leaf transfer on top and rub gently with your finger. Allow to dry for 24 hours.

407

CANDLESTICK

Candlesticks are available in many different shapes and sizes and they can be given a rich, aged effect with the use of the various shades of Dutch metal leaf. Don't forget to look for candlesticks in junk shops where you may come across more unusual pieces.

YOU WILL NEED

MATERIALS

wooden candlestick
red oxide spray primer
water-based size
gold Dutch metal leaf
methylated spirit
amber shellac varnish
acrylic paints: red and
yellow-ochre

EQUIPMENT

paintbrushes
burnishing brush or soft
cloth
steel wool
paint-mixing container
soft cloth

1 Spray the candlestick with an even coat of red oxide primer, making sure that all the details and recesses are fully covered. Allow to dry for about 30–60 minutes.

2 Paint on a thin, even layer of water-based size and leave for 20–30 minutes, until it becomes clear and tacky.

3 Carefully lay the gold leaf on to the surface to cover the whole area. Burnish it with a burnishing brush or cloth to remove the excess leaf and bring up a lustre.

4 Dip some steel wool into a little methylated spirit and gently rub the raised areas and details of the candlestick to distress the surface, taking care not to rub too hard.

5 Seal with a thin, even layer of amber shellac varnish and allow to dry for about 45–60 minutes.

6 Mix the red and yellow-ochre paint with some water. Paint it on to the surface and allow to dry for 5 minutes. Rub off most of the paint with a cloth, allowing only a little paint to remain in the areas of detail. Dampen the cloth if the paint has set too much. Allow to dry.

WIRE SUNFLOWER MOBILE

*T*his mobile has a really light and airy feel. Wire can be bent into a variety of interesting and attractive shapes with pliers, and these sunflowers have the pleasing simplicity of a child's drawing. This would make a lovely decoration for a child's room or for any sunny corner.

YOU WILL NEED

MATERIALS

*thick aluminium wire,
2 mm/0.078 in,
1.6 mm/0.062 in and
1 mm/0.039 in
binding wire
tracing paper
paper
aerosol car paints: white
primer, yellow, brown and
green
masking tape
strong green thread
strong clear glue*

EQUIPMENT

*wire-cutters
long ruler
3 round containers, about
6.5 cm/2½ in, 5 cm/2 in
and 2.5 cm/1 in diameter
indelible magic marker
flat-nosed pliers
round-nosed pliers
pencil
scissors*

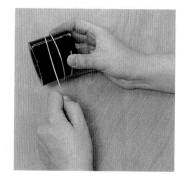

1 Cut lengths of wire for the struts and flowers: large strut, 59 cm/23½ in of 2 mm/0.078 in wire; short ones 2 x 38 cm/15 in of 2 mm/0.078 in wire; small ring, 2 cm/ ¾ in of 2 mm/0.078 in wire; large flower, 104 cm/42 in of 1.6 mm/0.062 in wire; centre circle of large flower, 7 cm/2¾ in of 2 mm/0.078 in wire; medium-size flowers with stems, 2 x 145 cm/57 in of 1.6 mm/0.062 in wire; centre circles of flowers, 2 x 5.5 cm/2¼ in of 2 mm/0.078 in wire; small flowers, 5 x 42 cm/16½ in of 1 mm/0.039 in wire; centre circles of small flowers, 5 x 3 cm/1¼ in of 1.6 mm/0.062 in wire. Bend the wires for the centres of all the flowers around circular containers that are slightly smaller than the centres.

2 For the large flower, mark along the wire with a magic marker 2 cm/¾ in from one end and then at ten intervals of 10 cm/4 in.

3 Bend the wire into folds at every mark.

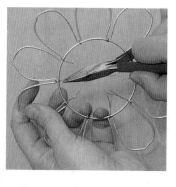

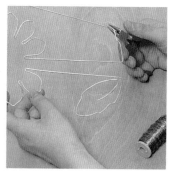

4 Pinch each of the folds together tightly with the flat-nosed pliers.

5 Using round-nosed pliers, bend the centre peaks and curve the petals into shape. Snip off the ends, leaving a small hook for binding the flower to its centre.

6 Bind in the centre circle with binding wire, folding the binding wire over each loop and twisting it tightly, to secure it. Repeat the process for the small flowers, marking the wire at 1 cm/½ in from the end and at ten intervals of 4 cm/1½ in.

7 For the medium-size flowers with stems, mark 35 cm/13¾ in from the end and at ten intervals of 8 cm/3 in apart, leaving another end of 36 cm/14 in. Fold the petals as for the large flower. Use the remaining wire for the leaves.

8 Bind the two stem wires together, using binding wire, to secure the leaves at the base. Bind the centre circle as in step 6. Bend the wires for the struts, using the templates at the back of the book as a guide. Spray everything with white primer. Allow to dry. Spray the pieces in the appropriate colours, masking off any areas as necessary, and leaving to dry between colours. Make up the mobile, securing the threads to the pieces with a knot and a spot of glue.

WASTEPAPER BIN

Complete a baronial look in your sitting-room or study with a suitable ennobled bin.

YOU WILL NEED

MATERIALS

tracing paper
paper
foam or corrugated card,
6 mm/¼ in thick
wood or MDF wastepaper
bin
cotton piping cord
acrylic gesso
thin card
acrylic paints: red, yellow
and dark green
shoe polish: brown, black
and neutral
paper towels
gold size
Dutch gold leaf transfer
book
polyurethane varnish

EQUIPMENT

pencil
scissors
craft knife
cutting mat
glue gun and glue sticks
fine and thick paintbrushes

1 Trace the templates from the back of the book, enlarging them if necessary, and cut out of paper. Draw the shield motif four times on the foam and cut out with a craft knife. Stick the shields on to the sides of the bin with the glue gun. Cut lengths of cotton cord to go around the shields and tie at the bottom in a bow. Stick them on with a glue gun. Paint the whole piece, inside and out, with two coats of acrylic gesso. Paint a piece of thin card with gesso and, when dry, draw around the cross template four times on this. Mix red, yellow and green acrylic paint to resemble red oxide primer and paint the shields and the top edge of the bin.

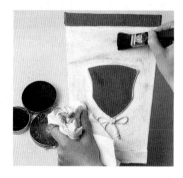

2 Using a large brush in a random sweeping movement, apply patches of brown and black shoe polish, each mixed with neutral to tone them down, over the white gesso, including the string and the cross motifs. Wipe the polish off with paper towels as you go, to build up the desired antiqued effect. Cut out the crosses. Paint a thin layer of gold size on the red oxide areas. When it is nearly dry, gently apply the gold leaf and rub it down through the backing paper with your thumbnail. Rub harder in some areas to reveal the red oxide beneath. Put a spot of gold leaf in the centre of each cross motif. Glue a cross to the centre of each shield. Coat inside and out with polyurethane varnish.

SWAN BOX

*T*he stately swan, with its many regal associations, has long been used for decoration. The long and graceful neck of this heraldic bird is often adorned with the noble insignia of a coronet. This medieval patterned box is decorated with a dignified white swan standing against an ornate blue background.

YOU WILL NEED

MATERIALS

hexagonal box, with lid
acrylic gesso
tracing paper
thin card or paper
craft paints: mid-blue, dark blue, white, black and orange
gold and silver paints
matt acrylic varnish

EQUIPMENT

paintbrushes
pencil
scissors
ruler
coarse-grade sandpaper

1 Prime the box with gesso. Trace the template from the back of the book, enlarging if necessary. Transfer to thin card or paper and cut out. Draw around it on to the lid. Rule a grid of 2 cm/¾ in squares over the background. Paint alternately in mid and dark blue. Paint the swan white, adding black details on the head and wing. Paint the coronet, feet and beak orange and add gold to the coronet.

2 Paint the lid edges and box sides in two shades of blue. When dry, rub very lightly over the whole box with some sandpaper to give a distressed look.

3 Paint silver diamonds over the corners of the background squares and add a tiny gold dot at each corner. Paint gold stars around the edges of the lid. Seal the box with several coats of varnish.

CHERUB BOX

*A*s the trend for paint effects gains momentum, unpainted fibreboard forms are becoming more readily available and can be found in many outlets. This small hinged box has a classic look, which is enhanced by gilding. It is given a baroque appearance by the addition of the cherub.

YOU WILL NEED

MATERIALS

cherub Christmas decoration
small wooden box with hinge
red oxide paint
water-based size
gold Dutch metal leaf
methylated spirit
amber shellac varnish
pink acrylic paint

EQUIPMENT

glue gun and glue sticks
paintbrushes
burnishing brush or soft cloth
steel wool
soft cloth
paint-mixing container

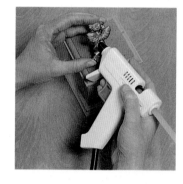

1 Use a glue gun to stick the cherub at an angle on the top of the box. Allow to dry for 10 minutes.

2 Prime the box with red oxide paint and allow to dry for several hours.

3 Paint on a thin, even coat of water-based size and leave for 20–30 minutes until it becomes clear and tacky.

4 Gild the surface with gold Dutch metal leaf, ensuring that the whole area is covered. Burnish with a brush or soft cloth to remove the excess leaf and bring up the lustre.

5 Dip some steel wool into methylated spirit and gently rub to reveal some of the base coat. Seal with a thin even coat of amber shellac and allow to dry for 30–60 minutes.

6 Mix some pink paint with water and paint over the surface. Rub off most of the paint with a cloth, leaving only a little paint in the details. Allow to dry for 30 minutes.

CHILD'S CHAIR

*L*adybirds are always welcome in their paintbox-bright uniforms. Add fun and interest to an ordinary white chair by getting a procession of the little creatures to meander across it. This simple decoration will make it any child's favourite seat.

YOU WILL NEED

MATERIALS

thin card or paper
child's chair
acrylic paints: red and black
oak and clear acrylic varnish

EQUIPMENT

pencil
scissors
fine and decorator's paintbrushes
cloth

1 Draw and cut out a simple template in the shape of a ladybird's head and body from card or paper. Draw around it with a pencil, making the ladybirds trail up and across the child's chair.

2 Using a fine paintbrush, fill in the bodies of the ladybirds with red paint. Allow to dry.

3 Draw around the ladybirds and add the heads, legs and spots using black paint and a fine paintbrush. Allow to dry.

4 Thin the oak varnish with water and paint it on using a decorator's paintbrush. Rub off immediately with a clean cloth. Apply a coat of clear varnish to finish.

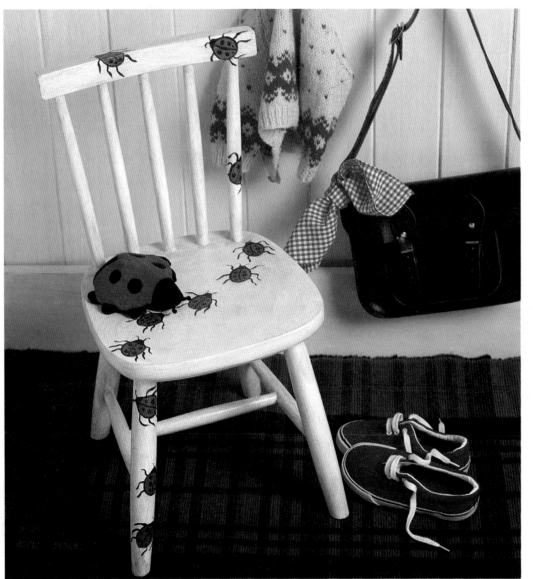

STIPPLED STORAGE TINS

Cheer up a plain set of metal containers to give your kitchen shelves a bright new look. The tins are painted with a stipple technique which gives a textured, sponged effect.

YOU WILL NEED

MATERIALS

*2 metal storage tins
white matt spray paint
acrylic paints: yellow, green
rust-brown, dark brown
and blue
tracing paper
matt spray varnish*

EQUIPMENT

*soft and hard pencils
paintbrushes
paint-mixing container*

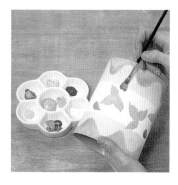

1 Wash the tins and lids, and spray them with several coats of white paint. Mark wavy lines at the top and bottom of each tin. Fill in either side of the lines with yellow and green paint. Use a dry brush and a stippling action, adding some areas of darker colour. You may need to mix colours to achieve the shades you wish.

2 Trace the template from the back of the book, enlarging if necessary, and transfer it to the central panel of the tin. Add extra sections of the design so that it fits all the way around. Paint the large trefoil leaves green and the small leaves rust-brown.

3 Paint a dark brown band on either side of the leaf panel. Add a few blue dots in the spaces. Outline the leaves with darker shades of brown and green, then paint the tendrils brown. Paint the main part of the lid green, picking out the details in brown and blue. Finish off by spraying the tin with a protective matt varnish.

LEAFY FRAME

This picture frame has a very warm autumnal feel about it, and it really would make a nostalgic souvenir of a woodland walk in the beautiful countryside.

YOU WILL NEED

MATERIALS

selection of leaves in various colours
paper towels
wooden frame with a wide, flat moulding
PVA (white) glue
crackle glaze
raw umber oil paint

EQUIPMENT

flower press or heavy book
paintbrush
soft cloth

1 Make sure that all the leaves are thoroughly dry, and then place them between layers of paper towels in a flower press or between the pages of a heavy book. Leave for at least a week to dry completely.

2 Glue the leaves on to the frame, coating them one at a time and waiting for them to dry partly before sticking down. Begin by arranging a row of overlapping leaves around the outer edge of the frame.

3 Make a second round, using different leaf types. Select four large leaves for the corners. Fill gaps with smaller leaves. When the frame is covered, paint it with a layer of PVA (white) glue. Allow to dry.

4 Paint the frame with crackle glaze, following the manufacturer's instructions. When the cracks appear, rub some raw umber oil paint into the surface of the glaze with a soft cloth.

PAW PRINT FRAME

*F*olk art frames were often made from common woods painted and grained to imitate something much grander, such as maple or walnut. The paw print in particular was a popular pattern in which the surface was covered with spots resembling different animal tracks.

YOU WILL NEED

MATERIALS
frame
emulsion (latex) paints:
red-ochre and
pumpkin-yellow
artist's acrylic or stencil
black paint
paper towels
clear water-based varnish
artist's acrylic paints: raw
and burnt sienna

EQUIPMENT
decorator's, stencil and
household paintbrushes
fine-grade steel wool

1 Paint the frame with a base coat of red-ochre, then allow to dry. Apply a coat of pumpkin-yellow.

2 Hold a brush with black paint in a vertical position and push down slightly while twisting it on the frame. Too much paint will "blob", so rub the brush on paper towels between dipping.

3 When the paint is completely dry, rub the edges lightly with steel wool to simulate wear and tear.

4 Tint the clear varnish with a small amount of raw and burnt sienna and apply to the frame. Add a finishing coat of clear varnish.

PAINTED SEWING BOX

*T*his sewing box was inspired by one made by an
Amish woman as a wedding gift. The legs are
aptly made from old wooden cotton reels.

YOU WILL NEED

MATERIALS

*4 wooden cotton reels
wooden box, with hinged
lid
thin nails
wood glue
white emulsion (latex) paint
tracing paper
masking tape
artist's acrylic or stencil
paints: cobalt-blue, raw
umber, emerald-green,
blue, deep and light red,
light blue, yellow-ochre and
white
clear water-based varnish*

EQUIPMENT

*hammer
paintbrushes
paint-mixing container
pencil
scissors
raised wooden batten
(optional)*

1 Attach the cotton reels to
the corners of the box with
nails and some wood glue. Tint
the white paint with a squeeze
of cobalt-blue and raw umber.

2 Apply the emulsion (latex)
paint to the outside of the
box and the inside of the lid.
Allow to dry. Trace the template
from the back of the book,
enlarging if necessary. Cut it out
and transfer it to the box, using
masking tape to hold it in place.

3 The decoration on the box
is very informal and
painterly. Let your brushstrokes
flow and embellish the
decoration to suit yourself.

4 Select initials from the
alphabet and paint them as
solid shapes in blue. Allow
them to dry, then outline the
edges in dark red. Decorate the
letters as shown.

5 Paint thick stripes with red.
It is important to paint
these stripes in a single
brushstroke. It may be helpful
to support your hand on a
raised wooden batten.

6 Allow the stripes to dry,
then use a thin paintbrush
and thinned light blue paint to
outline the red, crossing over to
form boxes in the corners. Tint
the varnish with a squeeze of
raw umber and sienna and then
give a final coat of clear varnish.

GOLD WIRE EARRINGS

*T*hese delicate earrings take the form of tiny sets of scales. The miniature baskets are filled with beads in shades of green and blue. Be sure to thread the same number of beads into each basket so that the scales balance when you are wearing the earrings.

YOU WILL NEED

MATERIALS

fine brass beading wire
selection of small glass
beads: blue and green
4 jump rings
2 split rings
pair of posts with loops
short length of
0.8 mm/0.031 in brass wire
pair of butterfly backs

EQUIPMENT

fine crochet hook
round-ended jewellery
pliers
round-ended pencil
wire-cutters

1 Using the fine beading wire, crochet four round shapes 1 cm/½ in across. On the last round make three 2 cm/¾ in equally spaced loops. Leave a long end of wire. Twist the loops with pliers.

2 Mould each round into a dome shape with a pencil. Thread equal numbers of beads on to the loose end of wire and secure them in each basket. Do not trim the wire yet.

3 Attach a jump ring, then a split ring to each earring fitting. Cut two 4.5 cm/1¾ in lengths of the thicker wire. Twist an upward loop in the centre of each, then bend each end down into two loops from which the baskets will hang. Attach the centre loop to the split ring using another jump ring. Thread the long end of wire on one basket through the top of the twisted loops to bring them together and attach to the bar. Repeat with the other baskets. Trim the ends of wire.

COPPER BIRDBATH

*Y*ou will have endless pleasure watching the birds drinking and washing in this beautiful yet practical birdbath.

YOU WILL NEED

MATERIALS
string
0.9 mm/20 SWG
copper sheet
4 m/13 ft medium
copper wire
cup hook

EQUIPMENT
chinagraph pencil
(china marker)
protective gloves
tin snips
file
blanket or carpet square
hammer
bench vice
hand drill or slow-speed
power drill and
3 mm/⅛ in bit

1 Using a chinagraph pencil (china marker) and a piece of looped string, mark a 45 cm/ 17 in circle on the copper sheet.

2 Wearing protective gloves, cut out the copper circle with a pair of tin snips. Carefully smooth any sharp edges using a file.

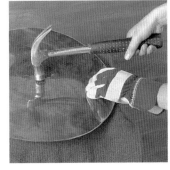

3 Put the copper on a blanket or carpet square and hammer it lightly from the centre. Spread the dips out to the rim. Repeat, starting from the centre each time, to get the required shape.

4 Loop some wire and hold the ends in a vice. Fasten a cup hook into the chuck of the drill, put it through the loop and run to twist the wire. Drill three 3 mm/⅛ in holes around the rim of the bath. Bend a knot in one end of three 1 m/1 yd lengths of wire and thread through the holes from beneath. Slip the twisted wire over two straight wires to form a perch.

ZODIAC MOBILE

*A*n ethereal decoration
inspired by a host of
astrological signs. To
achieve its balance, you
will need to cut the wire
for the various shapes to
the exact lengths as given
in the steps below.

YOU WILL NEED

MATERIALS

soft galvanized wire,
2 mm/0.078 in,
1.6 mm/0.062 in and
1 mm/0.039 in
medium-weight binding
wire
tracing paper
paper
aerosol car paints: white
primer, midnight-blue
and gold

EQUIPMENT

wire-cutters
round-nosed pliers
pencil
flat-nosed pliers

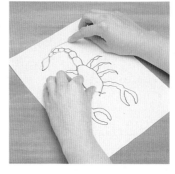

1 Use 2 mm/0.078 in wire for hangers: cut one 76 cm/ 30 in length and two 38 cm/ 15 in lengths. Make a loop in the centre of each. Secure with binding wire. Form waves and coils at each end using pliers. Trace the templates from the back of the book on to paper.

2 Shape wire around the templates to form the motifs. For the scorpion's body, use 64 cm/26 in of 1.6 mm/ 0.062 in wire. Bind the ends at the head and trim. Cut two lengths of 1 mm/0.039 in wire, 33 cm/13 in, for claws. Shape, bind to the body and trim.

3 Following the scorpion template, use binding wire for the back legs and tail detail.

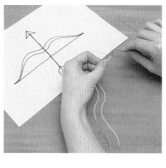

4 For Sagittarius, cut two lengths of 1.6 mm/0.062 in wire, 25 cm/10 in. Bend into the bow shapes and bind ends together, trimming the excess. Make the bow string with binding wire.

5 Bend a 56 cm/22 in length of 1 mm/0/039 in wire into an arrow shape, bind along the shaft and secure to the bow in the centre.

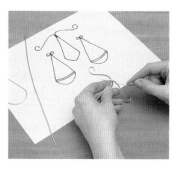

6 For Libra, cut 34 cm/13½ in of 2 mm/0.078 in wire. Bend into a bar shape, coiling the ends into loops. Bend the arms at the centre. For scales, cut two lengths of 1.6 mm/0.039 in wire, 23 cm/9 in. Bend into shape. Use binding wire to outline the dishes and bind to the bar.

7 Follow the templates for Taurus, Leo, Aries and Pisces, binding as shown in the main picture and trimming any excess. You need the following lengths: Taurus: 33 cm/13 in of 1.6 mm/0.062 in wire; the 1 cm/½ in diameter ring is made from the same wire. Leo: 38 cm/ 15 in of 1.6 mm/0.062 in wire; 20 cm/8 in of 1 mm/0.039 in wire for the crown. Aries: 102 cm/40 in of 1.6 mm/ 0.062 in wire. Pisces: 76 cm/ 30 in of 1.6 mm/0.062 in wire.

8 Spray paint the hangers and motifs with white primer and then paint them in the colours as shown.

9 Assemble the mobile by attaching the shapes to the hangers with nylon thread, as shown in the main picture.

SUN-GILDED BOX

A *gilded sun graces the lid of a plain wooden box with a touch of celestial mystery. This luxurious effect is easily achieved using Dutch gold leaf. Delineate the gilding area with size to provide an adhesive background, then apply the Dutch gold as a transfer.*

YOU WILL NEED

MATERIALS

wooden box
acrylic gesso
ultramarine acrylic paint
gloss varnish
Japanese gold size
Dutch gold leaf transfer book
silver leaf transfer book

EQUIPMENT

medium and fine paintbrushes
sandpaper

1 Paint the box, inside and out, with three or more coats of acrylic gesso, using a medium brush (too many coats may stop the lid from closing properly, so be careful). Allow to dry thoroughly.

2 Give the box a coat of ultramarine acrylic paint, using a fine brush. When dry, lightly sand to give a distressed effect. Add a coat of varnish.

3 Paint a freehand sun motif on the lid, using the fine brush and the gold size. When the surface is just tacky, place the gold leaf transfer on top and rub gently with a finger. Using the same technique, paint the side of the lid and loose, freehand moons around the sides of the box. Apply silver leaf transfer and allow to dry.

HAND-PAINTED BOX

*D*ecorate a wooden box with simple paint techniques that produce a wonderful effect reminiscent of inlaid wood patterns or marquetry, and turn it into a real treasure chest. This technique can apply both to old or new wooden furniture, picture frames, or even floors, provided that you strip down to bare wood and lighten with wood bleach, if necessary. The skill lies in developing your own pleasing pattern.

YOU WILL NEED

MATERIALS
bare wooden box, stripped, and bleached, if necessary
waterproof metallic or glossy paint
2 contrasting wood stains, such as brown mahogany and light teak
button polish or clear varnish
wax polish

EQUIPMENT
chalk
pen
small and fine paintbrushes
soft cloths

1 Trace the templates from the back of the book, enlarging to fit your box if necessary. Cover the backs of the templates with chalk, position them and trace around the outlines firmly with a pen.

2 Soak the paintbrushes, to rid them of loose bristles. Paint on the outlines in metallic or glossy paint and allow to dry. Fill in the areas between with the wood stains, flooding them up to the outlines. Be careful not to overload the brush. Allow to dry completely.

3 Coat lightly with button polish or wipe on varnish with a soft cloth. Then apply a few coats of wax polish to bring up the sheen and warmth of the wood.

PUNCHED METAL FRAME

Punched metal work is a colonial craft that was common in early American homes. The metal foil is decorated with naïve motifs, made by punching holes in the foil and the wooden frame.

YOU WILL NEED

MATERIALS

sheet of thin aluminium foil, 1 cm/½ in wider all round than the frame 27 cm/10½ in square softwood frame, with sides 6.5 cm/2½ in deep brass escutcheon pins, 1.5 cm/⅝ in and 1 cm/½ in long, depending on the depth of rebate (rabbet) in frame

EQUIPMENT

*large soft cloth
ballpoint pen
scissors
bradawl
tack hammer
white chinagraph pencil
(china marker)
ruler
soft cloth, for cleaning*

1 Place the aluminium foil on a cloth. Lay the frame upside down on the foil and draw around the outer and inner edges with a ballpoint pen. Mark a further inner frame 1.5 cm/⅝ in deep, to allow for turning around the rebate (rabbet) of the frame.

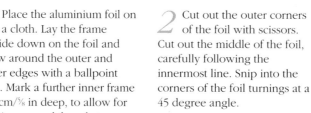

2 Cut out the outer corners of the foil with scissors. Cut out the middle of the foil, carefully following the innermost line. Snip into the corners of the foil turnings at a 45 degree angle.

3 Bring the foil around the frame and make holes with a bradawl. Bang the longer pins in through the holes, using a tack hammer, all around the outer edges of the frame.

4 Fold the foil around the inside of the frame, mark it with holes and pin it to the rebate with the short pins, as you did the outside.

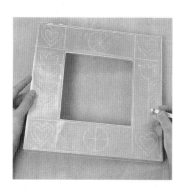

5 Draw lines on the front of the frame with a chinagraph pencil (china marker) and ruler to divide it into squares and rectangles. Draw a heart in each corner and a circle in the top and bottom rectangles. Add star shapes within the circles and outlines within the hearts. Draw a tulip on both sides of the frame. Freehand drawing helps to keep the naïve look associated with punched metal work. The outlines are easily cleaned off with a cloth.

6 Prick all the outlines through the metal and the wood using the bradawl. Wipe off any marks with a slightly soapy soft cloth.

SUNFLOWER SCREEN

*T*he sunflower is an enduring motif in folk art, conveying all that is good and natural. Here, it has been used to bold effect to decorate a small folding screen, which would look wonderful in a corner of a patio or court-yard. It is not intended for children and would not be safe as a play structure.

YOU WILL NEED

MATERIALS
thin white paper
3 panels of 8 mm/⅜ in plywood sheet, each 50 x 112 cm/20 x 48 in
sheet of 4 mm/³⁄₁₆ in birch plywood
water-based wood undercoat
acrylic paints
satin-finish acrylic varnish
wood glue
brass panel pins
2 pairs of hinges

EQUIPMENT
pencil
large dinner plate
scissors
workbench
clamps
protective face mask
coping saw
fine sandpaper
paintbrush
varnish brush
glue brush
tack hammer
drill
screwdriver

1 Make a semicircular paper template by drawing around a large plate. Cut out, place in the centre top of each panel and draw around it. Draw lines from either side to the edges. Clamp each panel in turn firmly to a workbench, and, wearing a face mask, cut out the top with a coping saw.

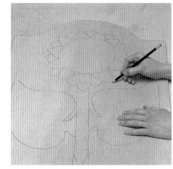

2 Make paper templates for the sunflower shapes and transfer them to the birch plywood. For each panel, you need two pairs of leaves, a stalk and a flower. Clamp the plywood firmly to the workbench and, wearing a face mask, cut out all the pieces.

3 Wearing a face mask, sand the panels and cut-out shapes to remove any rough edges. Paint all the pieces with two coats of undercoat.

4 Sand the panels lightly, then apply a coat of blue paint. Add dark green paint and make crescent-shaped brushstrokes at regular intervals.

5 Paint the sunflowers, leaves and stalks. Leave to dry, then seal the surface of all the shapes and the panels with two coats of varnish. Leave to dry.

6 Glue the shapes to the panels and hold in place with brass panel pins. Hinge the panels together, drilling small pilot holes for the screws first.

EMBOSSED BOOK JACKET

The appearance of a plain notebook or photograph album can be dramatically enhanced with an embossed metal panel. The panel covering this book imitates the ornate leather and metal bindings adorning early bibles and prayer books. Gold lacquer paint has been used to highlight small areas of the embossed pattern to give it a rich, Byzantine feel.

YOU WILL NEED

MATERIALS

sheet of 36 gauge/0.005 in aluminium foil
thin card
gold lacquer paint
epoxy resin glue

EQUIPMENT

scissors
soft marker pen
ruler
ballpoint pen
pencil
fine paintbrush

1 Cut a piece of aluminium foil the same size as the front of the book. Using a soft marker pen and a ruler, draw a 5 mm/¼ in border all the way around the edge of the foil. Divide the rectangle into squares. Using a ruler and ballpoint pen, redraw over the lines to emboss the foil. This is now the back of the jacket.

2 Draw a circle and a rectangle on to card, small enough to fit into the grid squares. Then draw another slightly smaller circle and square. Cut out the shapes. Place the larger round template in the centre of the first square. Carefully draw around it using a ballpoint pen. Repeat with the larger rectangle in the next square. Alternate the shapes to cover the whole jacket.

3 Lay the smaller round template inside the embossed circles and draw around it. Place the smaller rectangle template inside the larger rectangles and draw around it. Emboss all the shapes in the same way.

4 Draw a small double circle and double semicircles inside each circle. Draw a double oval and radiating lines inside each rectangle. Emboss a dotted line around each rectangle and around the edge of the jacket.

5 Turn the jacket over so that it is face up. Using a fine paintbrush, highlight small areas of the design with gold lacquer paint. When the paint is thoroughly dry, glue the jacket to the front of the book with epoxy resin glue.

SPOON RACK

*T*he elegance of this rack will add style to your home and ensure that kitchen implements such as spoons are always close at hand. Garden wire is inexpensive and readily available, and it comes in many different thicknesses and colours. Alternatively, you could use galvanized or tinned copper wire. The clover leaf is a recurrent motif in wirework. It can be formed around cylindrical objects of different sizes such as a wooden spoon, broom handle or rolling pin.

YOU WILL NEED

MATERIALS	EQUIPMENT
thick garden wire	*wire-cutters*
	rolling pin
	round-nosed pliers
	piece of copper piping
	(or similar tube)
	permanent marker pen
	screwdriver
	screws

1 Cut three 1 m/40 in lengths of wire. Wrap one end three times around a rolling pin. Using round-nosed pliers, make a small loop in the coiled end of each wire large enough to take a screw. Shape the coils to make spirals. Bend back the wire from one length at a right angle to make the central stem. To make the spoon-holders, cut three 58 cm/23 in lengths of wire. Bend each wire at a right angle 12 cm/5 in from one end.

2 Make a row of three circles by wrapping another length of wire one and a half times around a piece of copper piping (or similar-sized tube) for each circle.

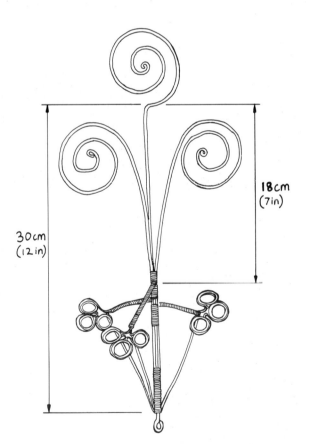

18cm (7in)

30cm (12in)

3 Bend the remaining wire away from the third circle at a right angle. Bend the three circles round to form a clover shape and bind the long end of the wire around the 12 cm/5 in end for 7 cm/2¾ in. Do not cut off the ends. Arrange the three spiralled wires together with the right-angled one in the centre. Measure 30 cm/12 in from the right angle on the central stem and mark this point. Cut a 36 cm/14 in length of wire and make a small loop in one end. Leave 2 cm/¾ in next to the loop, then bind the wire tightly around the spiralled wires upwards from the marked point (see diagram).

4 Measure 18 cm/7 in from the right angle of the central stem. Using the excess wire on one clover shape, bind it on at this point. Bind upwards for 2 cm/¾ in and cut off the wire. Bind on the second clover shape 2 cm/¾ in below the first. Attach the third clover shape below the second, binding downwards for 4 cm/1½ in. Make a bend halfway along the stems of the last two clover shapes to angle them inwards slightly. Bend up the stem wires at the bottom and bind to the neck of one clover shape. Cut off the ends. Screw the spoon rack to the wall through the loops and at the bottom.

DECORATING GLASS AND CERAMICS

*P*ainting glass and ceramics is a straightforward craft that can be as simple or complex as you like. Using a wide range of special paints in different colours and finishes, you can produce a truly varied and dynamic set of glassware, crockery and decorations for around your home, or to give as gifts. Start by experimenting with a single plain tile, then progress as your confidence grows to decorate a whole tea service.

The important thing to remember about this craft is that the surface to be treated must be totally clean and free from grease. Once that has been seen to, you can set to the task of transforming the object to an individual style of your choice. Don't be constrained by the templates and motifs offered here – just follow the steps carefully for the technique, then develop your own personalized style.

MATERIALS AND EQUIPMENT

You probably already have most of the materials and equipment you need for painting glass and ceramics among your household supplies. However, materials such as paints do have to be specially purchased.

As well as considering the aesthetic qualities of a particular type of paint, you should also consider the practicalities; whether, for instance, it can withstand the level of wear and tear it will receive. You should also consider any safety implications, and always read the manufacturer's instructions before applying paint to a surface. This is of the utmost importance if the end product is to be used for food or drink.

A variety of paints can be used on glazed and fired surfaces and specially formulated paint ranges are available from specialist suppliers for application on glassware and ceramics. These include the following.

Solvent-based cold ceramic and glass paints are specially designed for use on ceramics and glass. They are called "cold" because they are not fired. The solvent evaporates, once applied, to leave the colour in place as painted. When painted on to a non-porous surface, such as glazed white tiles, they can be wiped off with a solvent. They take about 24 hours to dry.

Water-based ceramic paints are special paints that are brighter than their solvent-based counterparts, come in a wide range of colours and can be mixed to achieve yet more colours. They have a thermal resin acrylic which, when heated, renders the paint indelible. Though water-based, the paints should not be diluted more than 20 per cent with water. Once the painted object is dry, the object can be baked in the oven to fix the paints. Always follow the manufacturer's instructions.

Acrylic paints A wide range of these can be used on ceramics and glass, though they are not specifically designed for such use. They include rich, opaque colours available in glossy, matt or a pearly finish. Acrylic paints adhere well, but are for decorative use only and are best coated with at least one coat of polyurethane varnish.

Enamel paints work well on glass and ceramics, and they give a hard, smooth covering. However, some of them do contain lead and so are unsuitable for any piece of tableware. They are very durable, with a great range of colours.

Polyurethane varnish and glazes come in matt or gloss finish. Always read the manufacturer's instructions before use and use in a well-ventilated room. Apply the finish evenly, using a large, flat brush and stroking in one direction. The more coats you apply, the more durable and washable the surface, but keep each coat thin, allowing a minimum of four hours' drying time between coats. Polyurethane varnish is unsuitable forsurfaces that may come into contact with food or the mouth.

RIGHT *A selection of tools and materials you'll need to create your own decorative glass and ceramic projects.*

WINSOR & NEWTON
AQUARELLE Fluide artistique de masquage
AQUARELLFARBE Maskiergummi, flüssig
ACUARELA Fluido para enmascarar pintura
WATER COLOUR
Art Masking Fluid
75 ml ℮ 2.5 US fl.oz.

Materials and Equipment

LEMON TILES

You could paint this fresh, graphic design on individual tiles to make focal points on the wall or create a repeating design by setting decorated tiles in groups or rows. Reserve some tiles to paint with a simple "filler" design like the checks used here. Use solvent-based ceramic paints that do not need to be fired.

1 Trace the template on this page, enlarging it to fit your tiles exactly. Copy it on to paper and decorate the border with squares, if liked.

2 Place a sheet of carbon paper on the tile, then the paper template, and secure with masking tape. Draw over the outlines with a sharp pencil to transfer the design.

3 Mix up enough ceramic paint in each colour to complete all the tiles you need, adding ceramic paint medium to give transparency. Paint the tiles, allowing each colour to dry before applying the next.

YOU WILL NEED

MATERIALS

tracing paper
plain white ceramic tiles
paper
carbon paper
masking tape
ceramic paints
transparent ceramic paint medium

EQUIPMENT

pencil
ruler (optional)
scissors
paintbrush

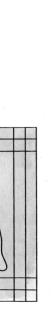

JAPANESE GLASS VASE

*T*ransform a plain vase with some highly effective and attractive stamping in a calligraphic style.

YOU WILL NEED

MATERIALS

high-density foam,
25 x 10 x 5 cm/10 x 4 x 2 in
black acrylic enamel paint
washed plain glass vase

EQUIPMENT

set square
felt-tipped pen
craft knife
plate

1 Using a set square and pen, draw lines 1 cm/½ in apart on the foam. Cut along the lines with a craft knife, then part the foam and cut through.

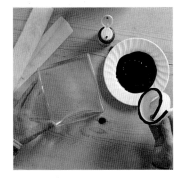

2 Spread an even coating of paint on to a plate. Curl up a strip of foam and dip it into the paint.

3 Curl the foam strip into an open-ended shape. When the curve looks right, press it on to the vase. Lift it off straight away to avoid smudges.

4 Press a straight strip of foam into the paint, then use it to continue the line around the side of the vase.

5 Complete the calligraphic pattern with a series of these straight lines. Applying the pressure unevenly will give a more authentic effect.

SOAP DISH

*I*nspired *by the colours of bright glycerine soap, this dish, with its green, yellow, black and white aquatic theme, adds a fresh and humorous note to a bathroom.*

YOU WILL NEED

MATERIALS

*glazed dish with sides
ceramic paints: yellow,
black and bright green
tracing paper
carbon paper
masking tape*

EQUIPMENT

*paintbrushes
hard and soft pencils*

1 Using ceramic paints, apply a coat of yellow to the base of the dish. Using a fine paintbrush, paint around the inside edge of the base, then use a larger brush to fill the middle. Spread the paint thinly. Fix the paint following the manufacturer's instructions.

2 Trace the template on this page, enlarging if necessary. Place some carbon paper on the underside of the tracing, position on the dish and tape downsecurely. Trace around the frog, then move the carbon and retrace to create a triangle of frogs.

3 Using a fine paintbrush, paint the frogs black from the outline in, spreading the paint thinly to achieve a watery effect. Fix the paints as before.

4 Paint the inner sides of the dish green. Start from the yellow edge, working the strokes along and up and stopping where the sides curve above the rim. Allow to dry. Paint green dots randomly over the yellow base.

5 Paint the outer sides of the dish green. Paint along the edge under the top rim, working the strokes along and down, and tackling a small area at a time. Allow to dry. Fix the paints as before.

6 Using a fine paintbrush, paint a black outline around the frogs, leaving small gaps of yellow here and there. If you like, paint circles with central black dots for a frog spawn effect.

7 Using a soft pencil, mark a stripe motif at the four corners on the rim, then complete the rim pattern one section at a time, following the photograph. Paint the stripe motif in black. Allow to dry, then fix the paints as before.

GILDED FRUIT BOWL

*T*he colours of the fruit really glow in transparent glass paints. Relief gold outliner defines the design like the leading in a stained-glass window.

YOU WILL NEED

MATERIALS
glass bowl
gold glass-painting outliner
solvent-based glass paints:
red, green and yellow

EQUIPMENT
methylated spirit
paper towels
packing material or
bean-bag
paintbrushes

1 Wash the bowl in hot, soapy water and dry thoroughly. Wipe over the surface with methylated spirit to remove any remaining traces of grease.

2 After a few practice runs, draw the design carefully with the gold outliner. It is easiest to do this in sections, leaving each section to dry for at least 12 hours before moving on to the next.

3 Prop the bowl on its side, supported by packing material to keep the section that you are painting horizontal so that the paint does not run. Apply the glass paint thickly to avoid streaky brushstrokes.

4 Leave each section to dry overnight before beginning the next. If you are a beginner, stick to single blocks of colour. More experienced glass painters could try blending two or more colours into each other to achieve an attractive effect.

CANDLE JAR

A straight-sided jar is a good shape to choose if you haven't tried painting glass before, as the flow of the paint is easiest to control on a flat, level surface. As the candle burns down inside the jar, the jewelled colours of the design will really start to glow.

YOU WILL NEED

MATERIALS	EQUIPMENT
glass jar, with a candle	*methylated spirit*
gold glass-painting outliner	*paper towels*
solvent-based glass paints:	*paintbrushes*
red, green and purple	*white spirit*

1 Wash the jar in hot, soapy water and dry thoroughly. Wipe over the surface with methylated spirit to remove any remaining traces of grease.

2 Lay the jar down on its side. After a few practice runs on an old jam jar, draw the design carefully with the gold outliner. Allow this to harden for at least 12 hours before starting to colour your design.

3 When painting the background, apply the glass paint thickly to avoid streaky brushstrokes. Be careful not to allow the paint to run down the sides of the jar: if it does, wipe off immediately with paper towels and white spirit. Complete the design and leave it to dry for at least 12 hours before starting on the next side.

LOW-RELIEF JUG

Ceramics with low-relief decorative motifs are ideal for beginners to paint. Like children's colouring books, the shapes are all set out for you to colour in, and as there are no clearly defined outlines, minor mistakes are not noticeable. Reproduction Victorian white relief pattern and contemporary Portuguese pottery make the ideal base for this work.

YOU WILL NEED

MATERIALS	EQUIPMENT
white glazed low-relief jug	*paintbrushes*
ceramic paints: acid-	
yellow, golden-yellow and	
light, medium and dark	
green	
polyurethane varnish	

1 Paint some lemons on the jug in acid-yellow. Vary them to give one group two acid-yellow lemons, the next group one, and so on. Leave a narrow white line around each lemon and leave the seed cases and small circles at the base of the fruit white. Allow to dry.

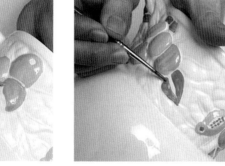

2 Work your way around the relief pattern, painting the remaining fruit a rich golden-yellow. Leave a narrow white line around each fruit. Allow to dry thoroughly.

3 Use the three shades of green for the leaves. Start with the palest green, painting roughly a third of the leaves, evenly spaced apart. Leave the central mid-rib of each leaf white and a narrow white line around each leaf. Allow to dry.

4 Paint a third of the leaves medium green, again spacing them evenly around the jug. Paint the narrow base of the jug green, and allow to dry once more.

5 Paint the remaining leaves dark green and allow to dry. Fix the paints according to the manufacturer's instructions.

6 Paint the rim or the handle in acid-yellow, leaving a narrow white line at the lower line. Once dry, varnish the jug.

STAR-SIGN BOTTLE

*C*reate a container fit for a magic potion using glowing glass paints to enhance a gilded design. This beautiful bottle would look stunning catching the light on a bathroom windowsill, but make sure the contents don't obscure the jewel-like colours.

YOU WILL NEED

MATERIALS

flat-sided glass bottle
gold glass-paint outliner
scrap paper
solvent-based glass paints:
red, blue, green and yellow

EQUIPMENT

methylated spirit
paper towels
paintbrush

1 Wash the bottle in hot, soapy water and dry thoroughly. Wipe over the surface with methylated spirit to remove any remaining traces of grease.

2 Practise using the gold outliner on paper before drawing the outline design (as seen in the picture) on one side of the bottle. Allow to dry for at least 24 hours.

3 Apply the glass paint between the outlines, brushing it on thickly to achieve an even coating. Leave the bottle on its side to dry for at least 24 hours.

4 Using the gold outliner, draw the astrological symbols (see template section) around the design. Allow to dry completely before repeating the design on the other side of the bottle.

GILDED BOTTLE

A corner of a star forms the motif on this lovely, glowing bottle.

YOU WILL NEED

MATERIALS

*flat-sided glass bottle or jar
gold glass-painting outliner
solvent-based glass paints:
red, blue, green and yellow*

EQUIPMENT

*methylated spirit
paper towels
paper
paintbrushes*

1 Wash the bottle or jar in hot, soapy water and dry thoroughly. Wipe over the surface with methylated spirit to remove any remaining traces of grease.

2 Lay the bottle or jar on its side. Practise with the gold outliner on a piece of paper first, then draw on the design from the back of the book. Allow to dry for 12 hours.

3 Apply the glass paint between the outlines, brushing it on thickly to avoid streaky brushstrokes. Leave the bottle or jar, lying on its side, to dry for at least 36 hours before starting the next side.

ITALIANATE TILES

*T*hese *Florentine-style tiles are based on ceramic decoration of the Renaissance. They are painted with easy-to-use enamel paints that are fixed in the oven. A single tile could be a focal point in a bathroom, but when several are arranged together, interesting repeat patterns are formed. Adapt the colours to fit in with your own decor.*

YOU WILL NEED

MATERIALS
tracing paper
washed white square tiles
masking tape
enamel paints: mid-green,
dark blue-green, rust-red
and dark blue

EQUIPMENT
soft and hard pencils
paintbrushes
paint-mixing container

1 Trace the template on this page, enlarging it to fit your tiles. Trace off the main motif (and the border if you wish) and rub over the back of the tracing with a soft pencil. Position the tracing on each tile, secure with masking tape, and draw over the outline with a hard pencil.

2 Paint the leaf in mid-green enamel paint and allow to dry. You may need to mix colours to achieve the shades you wish. Using a dark blue-green, paint over the outline and mark in the veins. Paint a dot in each corner of the tile in the same colour.

3 With a fine brush, paint a border of rust-coloured leaves and a slightly larger leaf in each corner. Paint a curved scroll to either side of the large leaf in dark blue. Repeat with the remaining tiles. When the paint is dry, fix it following the manufacturer's instructions.

WHISKY GLASS

*T*he fleur-de-lys was the heraldic emblem of the kings of France from the twelfth century. Use the template to make two sizes of fleur-de-lys. Paint each motif in a different combination of colours, matching them with small motifs on the opposite side.

YOU WILL NEED

MATERIALS	EQUIPMENT
whisky glass	*methylated spirit*
black cerne relief outliner	*paper towels*
tracing paper	*pencil*
masking tape	*fine black pen*
solvent-based glass paints:	*paintbrushes*
red, blue and yellow	*craft knife*

1 Wash the glass in hot, soapy water and dry thoroughly. Wipe over the surface with methylated spirit to remove any remaining traces of grease. Divide the base of the glass into three equal sections and mark them with cerne relief.

2 Trace the template from the back of the book, enlarging if necessary, and tape it inside the glass. Draw the design with the black pen in each of the three sections. Leave each section to dry for at least 12 hours before moving on to the next. Outline small motifs opposite in this way.

3 Colour the first large motif, using different colours for each section, and allow to dry overnight before turning the glass for the next motif. Paint each small fleur-de-lys in colours matching the motif on the opposite side of the glass. When you have finished, scrape off the reference marks on the base and allow the paint to dry before washing.

DECORATED TEA SERVICE

*I*f you are bored with your plain tea cups and saucers, why not cheer yourself up with some pretty stamped patterns in vibrant colours?

YOU WILL NEED

MATERIALS
tracing paper
paper or thin card
spray adhesive
white china tea service
ceramic paints: orange,
blue and black

EQUIPMENT
pencil
eraser
craft knife
cutting mat
piece of glass

1 Trace the template from this page, enlarging it if desired, and transfer to paper or thin card. Spray the template with adhesive and stick it on the end of an eraser.

2 Cut around the outline of the star, making sure that the points are sharp.

3 Cut horizontally into the eraser, to meet the outline cuts, and remove the excess. The star shape must have points of even lengths, so make a test print and adjust any obvious flaws with a craft knife before you work on the china.

4 Spread an even coating of orange paint on to the glass and press the star stamp into it. Make a test print to ensure that the stamp is not overloaded, then begin stamping widely spaced stars. The inked stamp will tend to slide on the glazed surface, so compensate for this by dotting it on and removing it directly.

5 Stamp blue stars in the same way, leaving space for the final colour.

6 Stamp black stars in the spaces so that the three colours form an all-over pattern. Allow to dry, then fix the paints according to the manufacturer's instructions.

SUN JUG

A good way to brighten up a plain jug is to use china paints to apply a vivid and bold motif. This cheerful sun face would be particularly welcome on the breakfast table. The colours could be adapted to suit your other china.

YOU WILL NEED

MATERIALS

tracing paper
washed white ceramic jug
masking tape
ceramic paints: black,
bright yellow, ochre, blue,
red and white

EQUIPMENT

soft and hard pencils
scissors
fine paintbrushes
hairdryer (optional)

1 Trace the template from the back of the book, enlarging if necessary. Cut it out roughly and rub over the back with a soft pencil. Make several cuts around the edge of the circle, so that the template will lie flat against the jug, and tape it in place. Draw over the outlines with a hard pencil to transfer the design.

2 Using and mixing the paints according to the manufacturer's instructions, paint the sun. Go over the outline for the features in black first of all and allow the paint to dry completely; a hairdryer can speed up the drying process. Paint the main face and the inner rays in bright yellow and then paint the cheeks and the other parts of the rays in ochre.

3 Paint the background in blue and then add fine details to the sun face, to give it a sense of depth. Finish off by painting a white dot as a highlight in each eye. Fix the paints according to the manufacturer's instructions.

454

HANDPAINTED FLORAL TILES

This is a great idea for decorating plain ceramic tiles, which could then be framed and hung on the wall.

YOU WILL NEED

MATERIALS

tracing paper
masking tape
washed white glazed tiles
ceramic paints: green, yellow, red and blue

EQUIPMENT

soft and hard pencils
scissors
paintbrushes
paint-mixing container

1 Trace the template from the back of the book, enlarging if necessary. Turn the paper over and rub over the outline with a soft pencil. Tape the transfer to the tile. Draw over the main flower outline with a hard pencil, to transfer the motif to the tile.

2 Using a medium brush and thin layers of paint, colour in the leaves and petals. Fix the paints according to the manufacturer's instructions.

3 With a fine brush and blue paint, draw in the outline and detail of the petals, leaves and stalk. Paint tiny dots in the centre of the flower. Transfer the four corner motifs in the same way and with a fine brush, paint them blue. Fix the paint as before.

FROSTED JUG

If you love the effect of frosted glass but don't like the rather banal designs often found in shops, this technique is for you. You can use the same technique to make a set of glasses to go with the jug.

YOU WILL NEED

MATERIALS	EQUIPMENT
paper	*pencil*
sticky-backed plastic	*scissors*
washed glass jug	*soft paintbrush*
etching fluid cream	*rubber gloves*

1 Draw a cupid and star freehand on to paper and cut out. Trace around the shapes on to sticky-backed plastic and cut out.

2 Peel the backing off the plastic and stick the shapes around the jug.

3 Follow the manufacturer's instructions to paint the etching fluid cream on to the outside of the jug, avoiding the handle. Leave to stand for about ten minutes.

4 Wearing rubber gloves, wash the cream off the jug in warm water and leave it to dry. If there are any unfrosted patches on the glass where the cream hasn't taken, simply repeat step 3. When you are satisfied with the frosted finish, peel off the shapes.

Rosebud Jug

If you are a beginner at painting on glass, you might find it easier to trace the template (see back of book) on to paper and fit the paper inside the jug. Then trace the design with the outliner.

You Will Need

Materials	Equipment
tracing paper	*methylated spirit*
glass jug	*paper towels*
old jam jar	*pencil*
gold glass-painting outliner	*packing material or*
solvent-based glass paints:	*bean bag*
red and green	*paintbrush*
	white spirit

1 Wash the jug in hot, soapy water and dry thoroughly. Wipe over the surface with methylated spirit to remove any remaining traces of grease.

2 Controlling the flow of the outliner can be tricky, so have a few practice runs on an old jam jar. Draw your design on to the jug. This is easiest to do in sections and each section should be left to harden for at least 12 hours before you begin the next.

3 To fill in the design, prop the jug up on its side on the packing material or bean bag. Try to keep the area that you are painting horizontal, to stop the paint from running. Carefully paint in a section, applying the glass paint thickly, to prevent streaky brushstrokes. Remove any excess paint with the brush. Leave each section to dry overnight before turning the jug to do the next section. Clean the brush with white spirit each time.

MOSAIC DRAGONFLY PLAQUE

Very effective mosaics can be made using broken china, then fixing the pieces with ceramic adhesive and grouting just as you would when laying tiles. The old, chipped plates you were going to throw out may be just the colours you need.

YOU WILL NEED

MATERIALS
tracing paper
plywood, 51 x 51 cm/ 20 x 20 in
PVA (white) glue
acrylic primer
dark green acrylic paint
electric cable
selection of china
tile adhesive
coloured tile grout

EQUIPMENT
pencil
fretsaw or coping saw
bradawl
paintbrush
sandpaper
cable strippers
tile nippers
rubber gloves
nail brush
cloth

1 Trace the template from the back of the book, enlarging if necessary. Transfer it to the plywood. Cut out the dragonfly and make two holes at the top of the body with a bradawl. Seal the front surface with diluted PVA (white) glue and the back with acrylic primer. Allow to dry. Sand the back surface and paint green.

2 Strip some electric cable and cut a short length of wire. Push this through the holes on the dragonfly and twist together securely.

3 Cut the china into regular shapes using tile nippers. Dip each piece into the tile adhesive, scooping up a thick layer, and press down securely. Allow to dry overnight.

4 Press the grout into the gaps between the china. Allow to dry for five minutes, then brush off the excess. Leave for another five minutes, then polish with a cloth.

MOSAIC SHIELD PLAQUE

This plaque uses simple square tiles to build up the design. By carefully mixing light and dark shades, you can give the impression of the curved edge of a shield without having to cut the glass pieces.

YOU WILL NEED

MATERIALS

*5 mm/¼ in medium-density
fibreboard, 23 x 30 cm/
9 x 12 in
tracing paper
PVA (white) glue
glass mosaic squares,
2.5 x 2.5 cm/1 x 1 in
white grouting
2 screw eyes
picture wire, 20 cm/8 in*

EQUIPMENT

*pencil
ruler
paintbrush
damp cloth
soft, dry cloth*

1 Draw a line 2.5 cm/1 in in from each edge of the board. Rule a line down the centre of the board. Draw a horizontal line 11.5 cm/4½ in from the top, then mark in a gentle curve in each lower quarter. Trace a shield shape on to tracing paper as a base for working out the design. Take time to find a satisfying arrangement of colours.

2 Paint a thick layer of glue in a top quarter of the shield and stick on your chosen tiles. Surround these with a single row of white around the outside edge, and a darker colour along the centre lines. Repeat with the remaining quarters of the shield.

3 Leave overnight for the glue to harden, then fill in the spaces between the tiles with white grouting. Wipe off the surplus with a damp cloth and, when dry, polish with a soft cloth. Fix the screw eyes into the back and attach the wire for hanging.

PAINTED VASE

*P*ainted glassware was a popular folk art from Europe, with bright figures used to adorn bottles of spirit and drinking tumblers from France to Hungary. Try to find old glasses in junk or antique shops for this project as imperfections won't show.

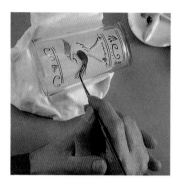

YOU WILL NEED

MATERIALS	EQUIPMENT
tracing paper	*pencil*
glass	*scissors*
masking tape	*cloth*
enamel paints: red, green,	*paintbrushes*
yellow, blue and black	*paint-mixing containers*
enamel paint thinner	*elastic band*

1 Trace the template from the back of the book, enlarging it to fit inside your glass. Cut out and secure it with masking tape.

2 Rest the glass on a cloth and support your painting hand with your other hand as you paint. Make sure the paints are thinned enough to make them flow nicely as you paint the pattern on.

3 Add the dots and motifs to suit your glass. Allow to dry, then place an elastic band around the glass to guide you as you paint stripes of colour.

4 Introduce some individuality by adding embellishments of your own, perhaps just a few squiggles, some dots or even your initials.

SEQUINNED ROSE BOTTLE

This ingenious technique could be used to decorate any kind of container, but it is particularly suited to a tall, narrow bottle, which might otherwise be hard to work on. The rose motif shown here would make a very suitable decoration for a special gift bottle of fragrant rosewater.

YOU WILL NEED

MATERIALS

glass bottle
tights
matching thread
invisible thread
sequins
bugle beads
glass beads

EQUIPMENT

needle
dressmaker's scissors
beading needle
fabric marker

1 Place the bottle in the toe of one leg of the tights. Thread a needle, wrap it around the neck of the bottle, secure it and trim away the excess fabric.

2 Thread the beading needle with invisible thread and work the rose motif: firstly, thread a sequin and then a bugle bead, bring the needle down and then up next to the first stitch and continue working like this.

3 Draw the stripes with the marker and fill them with sequins and glass beads, in the same way.

FRUIT BOWL

*T*his is a freehand project, and the loosely drawn oranges, leaves and flowers do not demand sophisticated artistic skill. You can substitute apples, pears, pineapples or lemons for the oranges.

YOU WILL NEED

MATERIALS

white-glazed bowl
ceramic paints: orange,
lilac, lime-green, dark
green, burgundy and black
polyurethane varnish

EQUIPMENT

black magic marker
paintbrushes

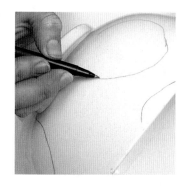

1 Draw four or five whole oranges on to the bowl, leaving space for the leaves and flowers. Draw four or five cut-off oranges along the top rim and base.

2 Paint the oranges, spreading the paint thinly. Allow to dry.

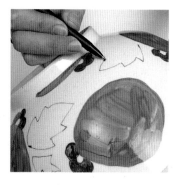

3 Draw flowers peeping out from behind the oranges, as shown, and paint them lilac, leaving the centres white.

4 Draw leaves, one small and one large, for each orange. Space them so there are no big gaps in the background. Draw half leaves going off the bowl.

5 Paint the small leaves in lime-green and the large leaves in dark green.

6 Paint the background burgundy, leaving a thin white outline around the motifs. Spread the paint thinly so the brushstrokes remain visible for textural variety.

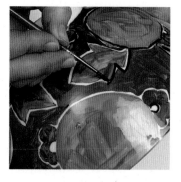
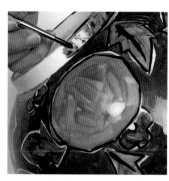

7 Paint loosely around the motifs in black. Vary the pressure on the brush so the line is sometimes thick and sometimes thin. Paint the midribs in the leaves and the circular centres in the flowers.

8 Paint the rim at the bottom in dark green, spreading the paint thinly to emphasize the hand-painted quality of the design. Allow to dry, then varnish the bowl.

HOLLY PLATTER

*D*isplay *this festive painted plate heaped high with Christmas tree balls, repeating the chosen colour scheme, or a mixture of tree balls and pine cones, spray-painted in metallic colours or left natural. For a children's party, heap the platter with sweets and wrapped chocolate coins.*

YOU WILL NEED

MATERIALS	EQUIPMENT
white-glazed plate	*pencil*
masking tape	*craft knife*
paper or thin card	*cutting mat*
ceramic paints: green, red,	*paintbrushes*
maroon and gold	
gold spray	
polyurethane varnish	

1 Mask off the centre of the plate with masking tape, leaving the outer rim clear.

2 Draw two or three holly leaves on to paper or thin card. Cut out the leaves and their centres.

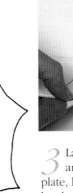

3 Lay the leaf stencils to fit around the rim of the plate, leaving space for a border, if liked. Mark on where the first stencil starts, then trace the leaves on to the plate.

4 Add some straight and curved stems to the leaves. Some can be single, and others should join to form sprigs. Fill the gaps with berries.

5 Paint the leaves and stems green, leaving the central mid-rib white. Allow to dry, then add touches of green to highlight. Allow to dry, then paint the berries red.

6 Paint the background maroon, using a fine brush to go around the motifs first.

7 Paint a gold outline around the leaves and berries and along one side of the stems. Try to leave as much white outline as possible. Use the edge of a craft knife to remove the masking tape from the plate.

8 Lightly spray the plate gold, then paint a narrow red band around the rim, if liked. Allow to dry, then coat with a layer of varnish.

SUNFLOWER MOSAIC

*S*hards of china and mirror wink in the sun on *this attractive and unusual wall decoration. Collect bright fragments of china in a harmonious blend of colours for your design.*

YOU WILL NEED

MATERIALS	EQUIPMENT
plywood sheet, 5 mm/¼ in	*pencil*
electric cable	*coping saw or fretsaw*
masking tape	*medium- and fine-grade*
PVA (white) glue	*sandpaper*
white undercoat paint	*bradawl*
china fragments	*wire-cutters*
mirror strips	*paintbrush*
tile adhesive	*tile nippers*
grout	*rubber gloves and dust*
cement dye	*mask*
	grout-mixing container
	nailbrush
	soft cloth

1 Draw out the sunflower on the plywood. Cut it out with a saw and sand any rough edges. Make two holes with a bradawl. Strip the cable and cut a short length of wire. Push the ends of the wire through the holes from the back and fix the ends with masking tape at the front. Seal the front with diluted PVA (white) glue and the back with white undercoat.

2 Cut the china and mirror strips into irregular shapes, using the tile nippers. Stick them to the plywood, using tile adhesive. Dip each fragment in the adhesive and scoop up enough to cover the sticking surface; the adhesive should squelch out around the edge of the mosaic, to make sure it adheres securely. Allow to dry thoroughly overnight.

3 Wearing rubber gloves and a dust mask, mix up the grout with cement dye, following the manufacturer's instructions. Press a small amount of wet grout into the gaps. Allow to dry for about five minutes. Brush off any excess with a nailbrush. Leave again for five minutes and then polish with a clean, soft cloth. Allow to dry overnight.

ORIENTAL BOWL

Blue and white ceramics are a centuries-old tradition with the classic Oriental willow garden pattern and its many variations being the most famous. Use this bowl to display a bunch of fresh flowers or some pot-pourri.

YOU WILL NEED

MATERIALS

*white glazed bowl
ceramic paints: light, medium and dark blue
polyurethane varnish*

EQUIPMENT

*magic marker
ruler
paintbrushes
paint-mixing container
craft knife
damp cloth*

1 Mark a horizontal line 6 cm/2½ in down from the rim of the bowl. Draw decorative scrolls above the line. To create an overall pattern, draw parts of motifs cut off by the rim and base.

2 Paint the scrolls in light blue. Try to keep the tone evenly flat and dense. Allow to dry, then paint medium blue over all the remaining area above the horizontal line. Allow to dry.

3 Scratch around the edges of the light blue with a craft knife to reveal the white below. Paint a dark blue line around each scroll. Leave as much of the white as visible as possible. Allow to dry.

4 Using dark blue, paint the base up to its rim. Leave the rim white. Aim for a flat, solid tone. Allow to dry, then varnish the bowl to finish.

MARITIME TILES

*F*our plain ceramic tiles combine to make a striking mural design, reminiscent of Japanese crafts in its graphic simplicity and clear, calm blue and white colour scheme. There are many different brands of ceramic paint available. Some are fixed by baking in the oven, while others can just be left to dry.

YOU WILL NEED

MATERIALS

tracing paper
masking tape
4 white glazed tiles,
15 x 15 cm/6 x 6 in
ceramic paints: mid-blue,
dark blue and black

EQUIPMENT

soft and hard pencils
china marker
small and fine paintbrushes
paint-mixing container

1 Trace the template from the back of the book, enlarging if necessary. Tape the tracing to the tiles, positioning it centrally. Transfer the outline to the tiles with a hard pencil.

2 Trace over the outline again with the china marker. Draw the border freehand, and add any extra details to the fish. Follow the finished picture as a guide.

3 Using the ceramic paints, fill in the fish shape. First, paint the main part of the fish in mid-blue.

4 Paint the detail and the border with dark blue. Highlight the scales with black. Fix the paint following the manufacturer's instructions. The tiles should withstand gentle cleaning.

MAJOLICA-STYLE TILES

*M*ajolica is glazed or enamelled earthenware, noted for its bright colours. These tiles imitate the style very effectively, making use of ceramic paints on crisp, white ceramic tiles.

YOU WILL NEED

MATERIALS	EQUIPMENT
tracing paper	*pencil*
4 white square ceramic	*fine paintbrushes*
tiles	*paint-mixing container*
ceramic paints: dark blue,	
yellow and red	

1 Trace the template from the back of the book, enlarging it to fit your tiles. Transfer a quarter of the design on to each tile.

2 With a fine brush and dark blue paint, paint over the main outline on each tile. Fix the paint according to the manufacturer's instructions.

3 Fill in the wings, hair and drapery with yellow. Allow the colour to dry. Mix the colours to add darker tones, using the finished picture as a guide. Fix the paints again, to prevent the colours smudging.

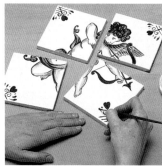

4 With diluted blue paint, mark in the shadows on the cupid's face and body. Go over any areas that need to be defined with more blue paint. Paint the corner motifs freehand and then fix for the final time.

CANDLE POT

*T*here is nothing like candlelight and, for a room with a natural or maritime theme, this candle pot is the perfect finishing touch.

YOU WILL NEED

MATERIALS

florist's tape
thick candle
mossing pins or stub wires
oasis
flowerpot
dried moss
seashells
starfish
dried flowerheads

EQUIPMENT

craft knife
glue gun and glue sticks

1 Stick tape all around the base of the candle. Then hold three evenly spaced mossing pins or bent stub wires against the tape and tape over them, to hold in position.

2 Trim the oasis to fit tightly in the flowerpot. Push it in and secure it firmly with some of the leftover pieces. Push the pins into the oasis to hold the candle firmly.

3 Glue the dried moss around the candle. Then add the shells all around. Place them evenly and keep standing back to check the balance.

4 Add the more delicate materials, such as the starfish and dried flowerheads, to the top to finish off.

PAINTED FLOWERPOTS

Terracotta flowerpots have a chunky robust quality which makes them ideal for holding candles. Use them in their natural state to make lovely impromptu container candles for alfresco evenings, with friends and family.

YOU WILL NEED

MATERIALS
flowerpots
acrylic paints: yellow, gold and blue

EQUIPMENT
flat and fine paintbrushes

1 Using a broad, flat paintbrush, paint the flowerpot yellow both outside and inside.

2 Paint the inside of the pot with one layer of gold.

3 Using a very fine brush, decorate the outside of the pot with blue paint.

GLASS GAZEBO BIRD FEEDER

*U*sing recycled tin cans and small pieces of glass, this converted lantern will sparkle jewel-like amongst the foliage. Take care when using a soldering iron: the solder sets in a matter of seconds, but the metal will remain hot for some time.

YOU WILL NEED

MATERIALS	EQUIPMENT
glass lantern	*chinagraph pencil*
thin glass (optional)	*(china marker)*
shiny tin can (not	*glass cutter*
aluminium), washed and	*ruler*
dried	*protective gloves*
flux	*tin snips*
solder	*soldering iron*
fine wire mesh	*try-square (optional)*

1 If the lantern requires extra glass, measure the areas required and reduce by 5 mm/ ¼ in. Using a chinagraph pencil (china marker), mark the measurements on the glass, then cut out by running a glass cutter in a single pass along a ruler. Tap along the line to break the glass.

2 Wearing protective gloves, cut 8 mm/³⁄₈ in strips from a tin can using tin snips. Wrap a strip around each edge of each glass panel. Trim, then smear a little soldering flux on to the mating surfaces of each corner.

3 To solder the corner joints of each panel, heat with a soldering iron and apply solder until it flows between the surfaces to be joined.

4 Measure the openings for the hoppers. Fold sections of metal to suit, using a try-square or ruler to keep the lines straight. Solder the meeting points of each hopper. Cut a platform from wire mesh. Solder the lantern together.

SUNFLOWER PLATTER

These hand-painted flowerheads give a truly exuberant decorative finish to a plain terracotta flowerpot base. You could also use the same idea to decorate a matching pot for a floral container display. Ceramic pots and bases come in many different sizes and they are ideal for painting on. Use ceramic paints for a translucent quality, or acrylics for a brighter, bolder look.

YOU WILL NEED

MATERIALS

*ceramic flowerpot base
white undercoat paint
acrylic paints: red, yellow,
brown and green
matt varnish*

EQUIPMENT

*paintbrushes
pencil
paint-mixing container*

1 Apply undercoat to the flowerpot base. Sketch out your pattern freehand in pencil. Fill in the background in red acrylic paint and fill in the flowers in yellow.

2 Use a fine paintbrush to draw the outlines for the detail in the central flower.

3 With a fine brush, fill in the detail in the central and other flowers, in brown and green. When dry, give the whole platter two or three coats of varnish, leaving to dry well between coats.

473

MARINEWARE

*I*ntroduce an extra dimension to a plain glass carafe by painting stunning seaside scenes directly on to the glass. Seaweed, shells and starfish are all suitable images. If you want to create a special setting for a dinner party, simply paint on the images with white emulsion (latex) paint and they can be washed off at the end of the evening. Alternatively, use glass paint as here. Do not restrict yourself to just one carafe – make a display of matching glassware with a variety of glasses and pitchers in all shapes and sizes.

YOU WILL NEED

MATERIALS

carafe
alcohol
paper
tracing paper
masking tape
white glass paint

EQUIPMENT

lint-free cotton
pencil
carbon paper
sharp felt tip marker pen
paintbrush

1 Wipe the surface of the glass with lint-free cotton and alcohol to make the surface absolutely clean.

2 Draw simple seashore motifs on paper, then transfer them to tracing paper.

3 Using masking tape, stick your designs around the carafe, placing a piece of carbon paper underneath the tracing paper. Draw around the outline with a sharp felt tip pen so the outline is transferred to the glass.

4 First paint the outlines, then fill in the designs with white glass paint.

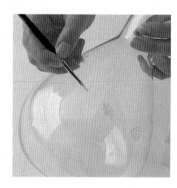

5 Alternatively, you can place the design inside the carafe or on the other side of the glass and paint the image through the glass.

PAINTED SEASHORE CHINA

Jazz up a plain white dinner set with some hand-painted motifs. With ceramic paint, tableware can be decorated permanently. For a special occasion, embellish extra plates using emulsion (latex) paint — although these items cannot be used for food.

YOU WILL NEED

MATERIALS

paper
tracing paper
white china plates and soup bowls
alcohol
masking tape
blue ceramic paint

EQUIPMENT

pencil
scissors
lint-free cotton
ruler
carbon paper
fine paintbrush

1 Draw simple seashore motifs on paper, then transfer them on to tracing paper. Cut the shapes out with sharp scissors.

2 Wipe the surface of the plate with lint-free cotton and alcohol to make the surface absolutely clean.

3 Find and mark the middle of the plate with a ruler and pencil.

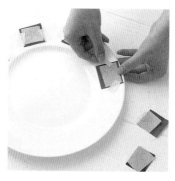

4 Section a plate into eight equal parts and mark up the eight sections. Try various options with your seashore designs to see which one you find the most pleasing.

5 Place pieces of carbon paper under the designs on the plate and stick them down with masking tape to secure in position.

6 Trace around the outlines with a sharp pencil, then remove the masking tape and the designs.

7 Paint in the shapes carefully using ceramic paint. Leave to dry thoroughly.

8 Mark, trace and paint the design in the centre of a soup bowl in the same way.

9 Add small dots on the handles of the bowl. Leave to dry thoroughly.

10 Remove the pencil marks from the china before using.

NUGGET JAR

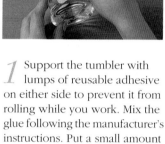

*G*lass nuggets have a myriad of different uses. They look effective scattered around an ornament, stacked up in a glass bowl, or even made into jewellery. Here, they are stuck randomly to the sides of a tumbler, giving an unusual combination of colours at every turn. The tumbler is suitable for drinking from, flowers look wonderful in it, or it can be used as a storage container.

YOU WILL NEED

MATERIALS	EQUIPMENT
glass tumbler	*reusable adhesive*
double epoxy resin glue	*scissors*
glass nuggets in assorted	*washing-up liquid*
colours	
masking tape	

1 Support the tumbler with lumps of reusable adhesive on either side to prevent it from rolling while you work. Mix the glue following the manufacturer's instructions. Put a small amount on the back of each nugget, and begin to stick them randomly on one side of the tumbler.

2 As you stick the nuggets on, secure each one with a small strip of masking tape to hold it in place while the glue dries – this should take about 10 minutes.

3 Turn the tumbler as you complete each section, sticking on nuggets until the whole glass is evenly covered.

4 When the glue is dry on all the nuggets, remove the masking tape. Gently wash the glass to remove any sticky traces of glue.

MEXICAN TUMBLERS

*M*exican designs, with their strong colours and bold images, are extremely popular. Once you have perfected drawing chillies and cacti on paper, copy your designs on to the glass with black contour paste to give a strong outline. The glasses should only be cleaned with a warm, wet cloth.

YOU WILL NEED

MATERIALS

paper
glass tumblers
black contour paste
glass paints: red and green
clear varnish

EQUIPMENT

pen or pencil
bench
small paintbrush

1 Draw some ideas on paper first, to get used to drawing the shapes.

2 Draw the outlines of your designs on the glass with black contour paste. Leave to dry for 10–15 minutes.

3 Carefully colour in the image areas with red and green glass paints.

4 When the paint is completely dry, varnish over the image areas only.

POEM VASE

*T*he next time you give flowers, why not present them in this unusual scratchwork vase? Scratchwork is the technique of creating patterns by removing paint. It works well with free-style paintwork in which the colours are allowed to blend. Instead of lettering, you could try scratching an image or decorative border into the paint, or using a combination of contour paste and scratchwork. A cocktail stick (toothpick) is ideal for fine lines, but why not see what effects you can achieve with other household implements?

1 First create a pair of "ribbon" lines to contain the paint. Mark two dots on the vase with a marker pen. Fill the vase with water to the lower mark, and carefully apply gold contour paste, following the water level. Work in short sections and turn the vase as you work. Add more water and repeat for the top line. Allow the contour paste to dry before you pour the water out.

2 Prepare your palette, as you will have to work quickly. Apply a thin wash of clear varnish between the two lines, then brush the colours lightly into the varnish. Work quickly and apply the paint lightly to prevent it from running. When you have finished painting, hold the vase over a candle and turn for a couple of minutes until the paint has dried.

3 Scratch the words of your poem, or a decorative pattern, into the paint with a cocktail stick. Clean the cocktail stick regularly with a piece of paper towel. Leave to dry. If the paint has flowed over the contour paste lines, clean it off with a piece of paper towel dipped in white spirit, and apply a thin coating of gold contour paste to the "ribbon" lines where necessary.

YOU WILL NEED

MATERIALS

glass vase
gold contour paste
clear varnish
glass paints: pink, orange,
yellow, green, turquoise
and violet
white spirit

EQUIPMENT

felt tip marker pen
mixing palette
paintbrush
candle
cocktail stick (toothpick)
paper towels

MEDIEVAL TRAY

The delicate golden tracery on this piece of glass is an attractive complement to a wooden tray. Toughened glass has been used to protect it from hot cups and plates. The pattern is worked on the reverse side using a gold permanent marker and acrylic paint over the top.

YOU WILL NEED

MATERIALS

wooden tray
toughened glass to fit tray base
paper
gold permanent marker pen
acrylic paints: dark green and light green

EQUIPMENT

pen
reusable adhesive
decorator's paintbrush
2 small paintbrushes

1 Ask a glazier to cut the toughened glass to fit the base of your tray. Draw a tracery design on a piece of paper the same size as the glass. Lay it under the glass. Secure with reusable adhesive. Trace over the lines of the template with a gold marker pen.

2 Wait for the markings to dry. Using a decorator's paintbrush, paint over the gold lines with dark green paint.

3 Immediately scribe lines into the paint as shown, using the ends of two small paintbrushes held together.

4 Leave to dry, then paint over the dark green scribed paint with light green paint. Leave to dry.

TILED TRAY

*T*ile mosaic need not always be random and multicoloured. In this elegant design, the intense blue border is made from whole tiles and the centre panel is covered with crazy mosaic in plain white. Use tiles of the same thickness, for a flat surface. The tiles should have a matt-glazed finish instead of being highly glazed, which would make them too slippery for practical use.

YOU WILL NEED

MATERIALS

unvarnished pine tray
PVA (white) glue
blue matt-glazed ceramic border tiles
plain white matt-glazed ceramic tiles
flexible, cement-based tile adhesive

EQUIPMENT

brush for glue
craft knife
set square
pencil
large scissors (optional)
protective leather gloves
safety goggles
piece of heavy sacking
hammer
rubber gloves
notched spreader
sponge
protective face mask
sanding block

1 Seal all surfaces of the tray with diluted PVA (white) glue. When the wood is dry, key (scuff) the surface with a craft knife.

2 Lay the blue border tiles around the inside edge of the tray. If they do not fit, move the border in and leave a narrow space around the outside Mark the border position with a set square.

3 If necessary, cut the border tiles into strips. Wearing protective leather gloves and goggles, wrap each white tile separately in sacking and break with a hammer to make the mosaic pieces.

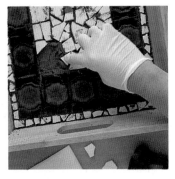

4 Wearing rubber gloves and using the notched edge of a spreader, apply tile adhesive over the border area. Set the blue tiles in position. Fill in the outside and the centre panel with white mosiac. Leave to dry.

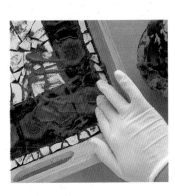

5 Spread more tile adhesive over the mosaic, making sure sharp edges are covered. Press uneven pieces down firmly, and press the adhesive down among the pieces.

6 Remove excess adhesive with a damp sponge, then leave the tray to dry for 24 hours. Wearing a face mask, use a sanding block to remove any remaining adhesive.

DOOR NUMBER PLAQUE

A mosaic door plaque adds a distinctive personal touch and will withstand all weathers. Plan the design carefully so that you have space between the numbers and the border to fit neatly cut tesserae. In the "indirect" method of mosaic, tesserae are glued face-down on to paper and then applied to another surface when the design is complete. When using this method, you can work at your own pace without worrying that the adhesive will set before you have finished.

YOU WILL NEED

MATERIALS

craft paper
floor tile
mosaic tesserae: turquoise,
black and yellow
PVA (white) glue
cement-based powdered
grout
flexible, waterproof,
cement-based tile adhesive

EQUIPMENT

scissors
pencil
ruler
brush for glue
protective leather gloves
safety goggles
mosaic nippers
protective face mask
rubber gloves
notched spreader
sponge
lint-free cloth

1 Cut a piece of craft paper the same size as the tile. Mark the border and numbers in reverse on the shiny side. Allow room between the border and numbers to insert a quarter-tessera.

2 Dilute the PVA (white) glue 50/50 with water. Glue the flat sides of the turquoise tesserae on top of the paper border, with a black tessera at each corner.

3 Wearing protective leather gloves and goggles, cut some black tesserae with mosaic nippers to make rectangles. Glue the black rectangles flat-side down over the paper numbers.

4 Wearing protective gloves and goggles, cut yellow tesserae into quarter-squares. Lay around the straight edges of the numerals, cutting to size as necessary. Glue flat-side down. Also place around the curved edges, cutting as necessary.

5 Wearing a face mask, goggles and rubber gloves, mix the grout. Apply with the spreader, removing the excess with a damp sponge. Leave to dry. Spread tile adhesive over the tile and key (scuff) with the notched edge of the spreader.

6 Place the grouted mosaic paper-side down on a flat surface. Place the tile on top, matching the corners and edges. Press the tile down, wipe away excess adhesive and leave to dry.

7 Using a sponge and water, soak the paper on the front of the mosaic. Leave for 15 minutes.

8 Lift one corner of the paper to see if it comes away cleanly. If it does, peel off, otherwise leave to soak. Wipe away any surplus glue.

9 Wearing rubber gloves, re-grout the plaque, including the sides. Remove the excess with a damp sponge, then polish with a dry cloth.

JACOB'S LADDER

*T*he blue summer sky is the inspiration for this series of wall-mounted picture frames. Pressed foliage and flowers are positioned on coloured glass and clear glass is placed on top. The wire wound around each pair of glass rectangles is both structural and decorative. Opaque blue glass is particularly effective with green leaves, and the colour shows well if hung on a wall. However, if hung in a window, the plant shapes will be silhouetted. The postcard-sized pieces of glass would suit pictures and photographs as well.

YOU WILL NEED

MATERIALS

6 pieces each of coloured glass and matching-sized clear glass
dried, pressed foliage
instant bonding adhesive
masking tape
1 mm/¹⁄₃₂ in copper wire

EQUIPMENT

tweezers
scissors
wire-cutters
ruler
round-nosed pliers
straight-nosed pliers

1 Ask a glazier to cut your chosen coloured glass to size. Lay it on the work surface and, using tweezers, position pressed leaves on to the glass, using a small dab of instant bonding adhesive.

2 Place the clear glass over the leaves and apply masking tape over the edges to hold the two pieces of glass together temporarily.

3 Cut a piece of copper wire 32 cm/12½ in long. Gripping the middle with round-nosed pliers, bend the ends down and twist together with straight-nosed pliers.

4 Bend out two ends of the wire horizontally, then make an "elbow" on both sides to fit over the edges of the glass as shown.

5 Position the wire around the glass and, using your fingers, bend the two ends over the edge. Use straight-nosed pliers to twist and close.

6 With round-nosed pliers, bend the two ends up into loops, forming a strong split ring. Trim off the excess wire to 2 cm/¾ in.

7 Cut a piece of wire 18 cm/7 in long and repeat steps 3 to 6. Link the second panel by sliding the top loop into the split ring. Remove the temporary masking tape.

8 Taking great care, lay the completed Jacob's Ladder face down, and make sure all of the wires are aligned. Press strips of masking tape over the wire to hold it in place.

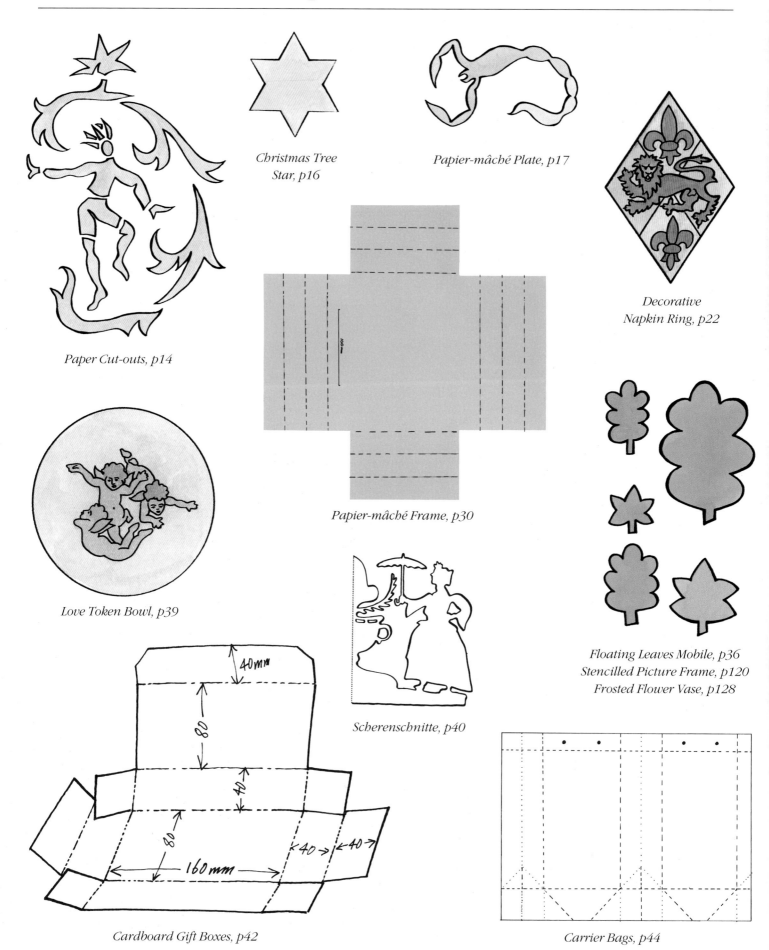

Paper Cut-outs, p14

Christmas Tree
Star, p16

Papier-mâché Plate, p17

Decorative
Napkin Ring, p22

Love Token Bowl, p39

Papier-mâché Frame, p30

Floating Leaves Mobile, p36
Stencilled Picture Frame, p120
Frosted Flower Vase, p128

Scherenschnitte, p40

Cardboard Gift Boxes, p42

Carrier Bags, p44

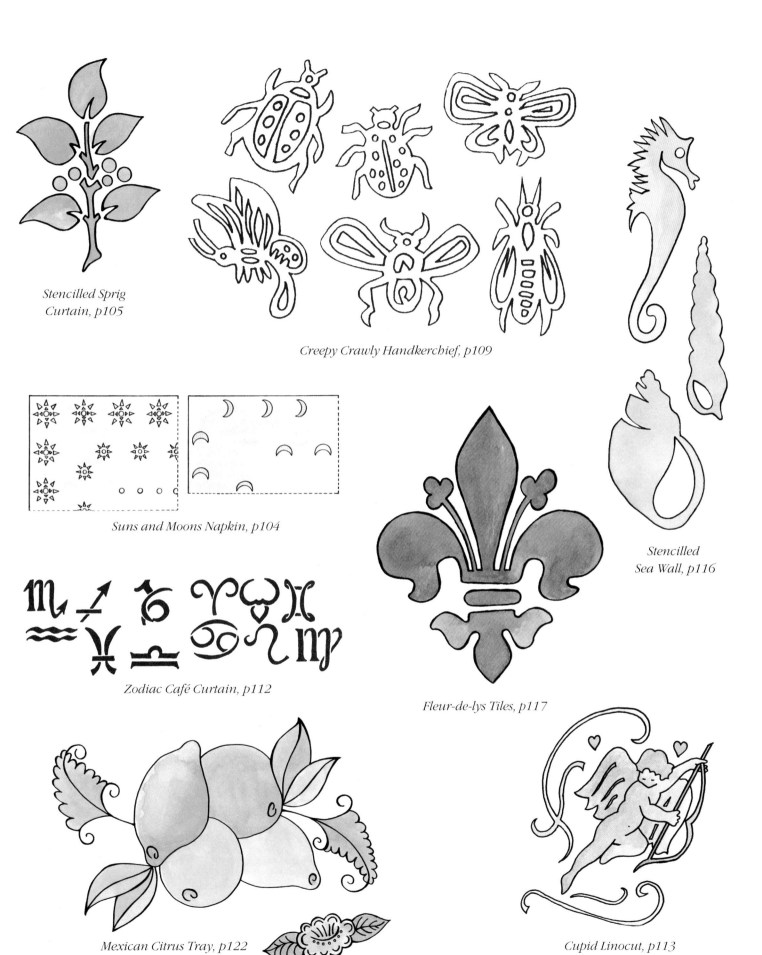

Stencilled Sprig
Curtain, p105

Creepy Crawly Handkerchief, p109

Suns and Moons Napkin, p104

Stencilled
Sea Wall, p116

Zodiac Café Curtain, p112

Fleur-de-lys Tiles, p117

Mexican Citrus Tray, p122

Cupid Linocut, p113

Medieval Cork Tiles, p124

Gilded Wall Border, p126

Art Nouveau Rose Box, p137

Country-style Shelf, p130

Lemon Slice Napkins, p170

Beaded Orange Purse, p172

Embroidered Insect Display, p169

start

Fleur-de-lys Shoe Bag, p171

Sparkling Ivy Garland, p174

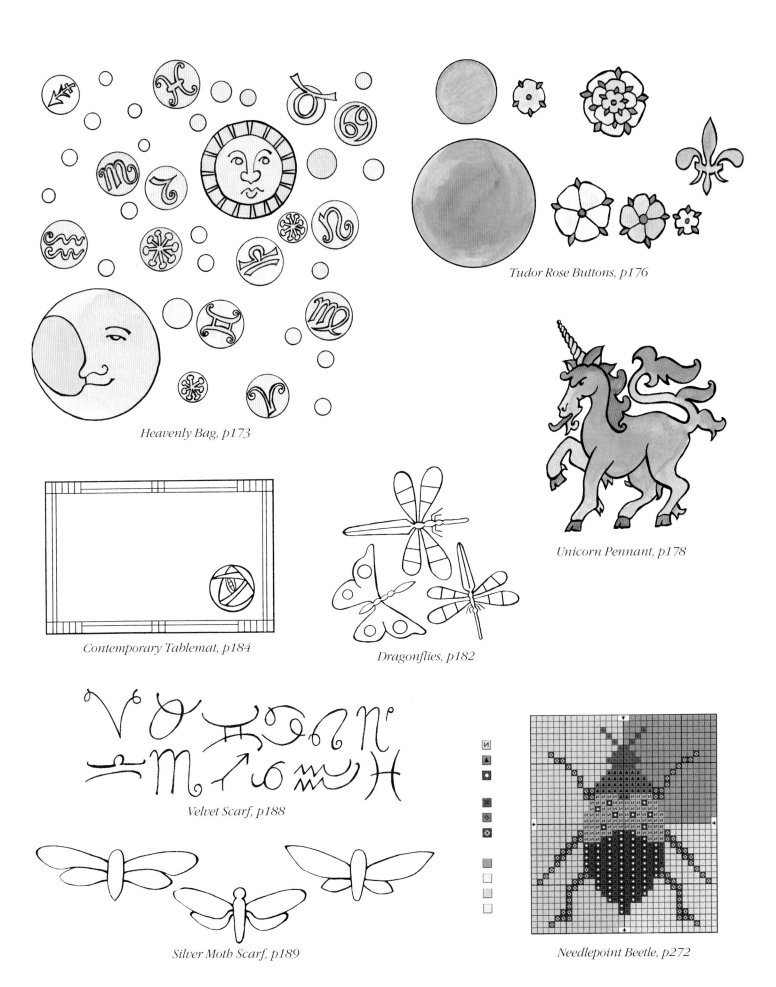

Heavenly Bag, p173

Tudor Rose Buttons, p176

Unicorn Pennant, p178

Contemporary Tablemat, p184

Dragonflies, p182

Velvet Scarf, p188

Silver Moth Scarf, p189

Needlepoint Beetle, p272

Baby Suit, p187
Bridal Heart, p193

Decorative Pincushion, p191

Cupid Camisole, p192

Oak Leaf Potholder, p221

Heraldic Tablemat, p220

Appliquéd
Sunflower Card, p224

Star Patchwork Sachet, p225

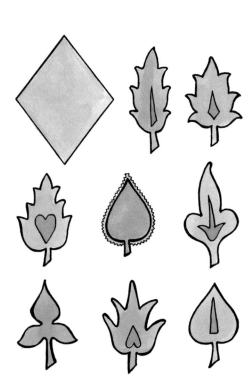

Matisse Outfit, p222

Rose Appliqué Bag, p228

Fleur-de-lys Tieback, p230

Cradle Quilt, p232

Appliqué Throw, p226

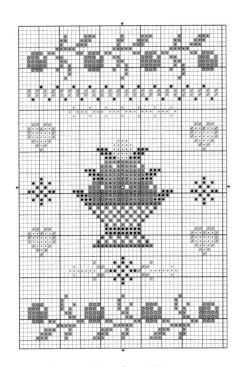

Orange Sampler, p231

726	yellow
832	light olive
729	ochre
722	light orange
801	chocolate brown
720	orange
730	dark olive
☆	Middle point

Star-spangled Banner, p240
Spice-scented Pot Stand, p242

Star-spangled Scarf, p239

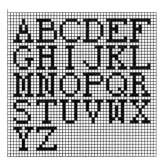

Oranges Tea Towel, p244

Seashell Beach Bag, p236

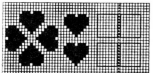

Shaker Towel, p245

Appliqué
Star Card, p247

Appliqué Notebook, p248

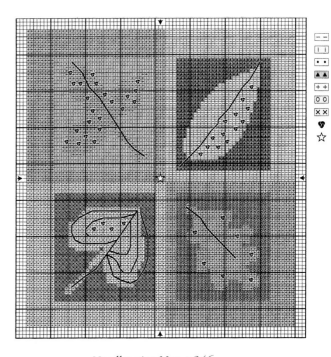

Needlepoint Mat, p246

Hand Towel
and Washcloth, p248

Appliquéd Sheet and Pillowcase, p250

Child's T-shirt, p251

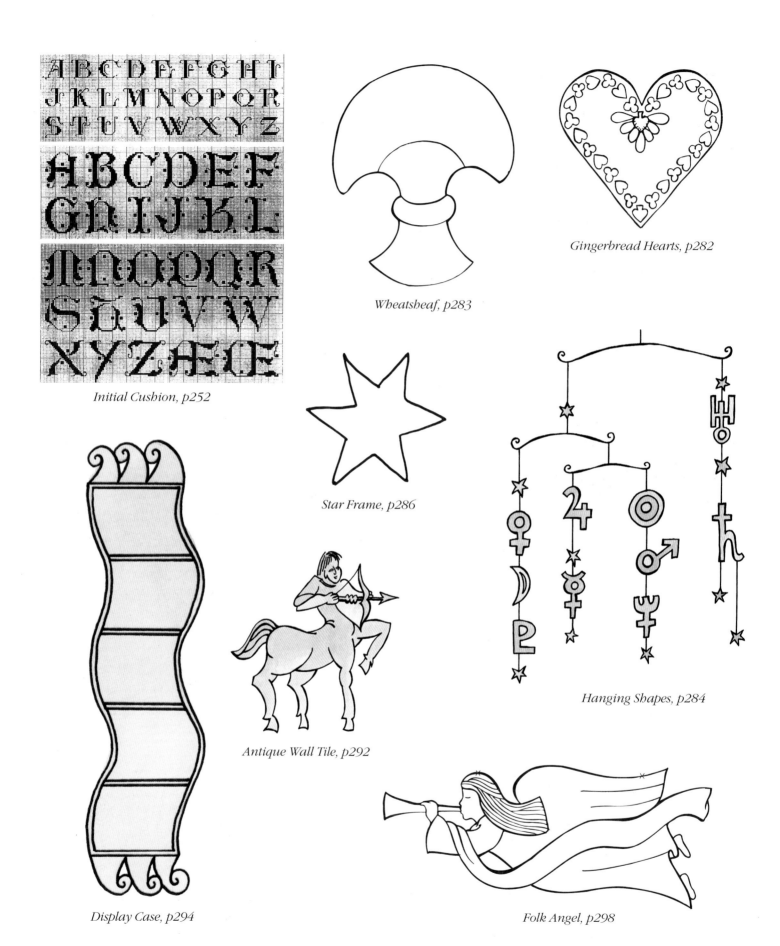

Initial Cushion, p252

Wheatsheaf, p283

Gingerbread Hearts, p282

Star Frame, p286

Hanging Shapes, p284

Display Case, p294

Antique Wall Tile, p292

Folk Angel, p298

Winged Heart, p302

Love Bug, p304

Wall Decoration, p305

Cornucopia, p306

Checkered Heart, p307

Gingerbread Cupids, p309

Punched Tin Panel, p343

Ornamental Tree, p342

Exotic Table Decorations, p344

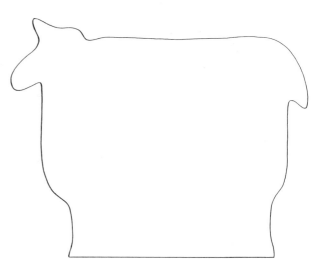

Wooden Sheep Sign, p340

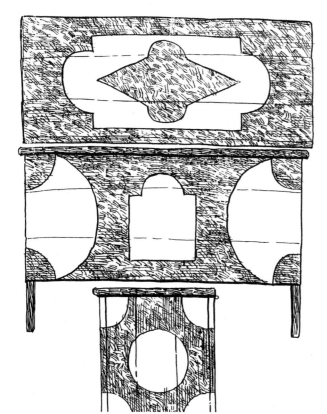

Painted Chest, p352

Tin Candleholder, p349

Woodburning, p354

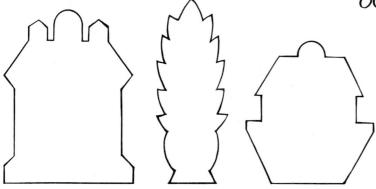

Christmas Decorations, p358

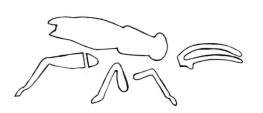

Grasshopper on a Stick, p363

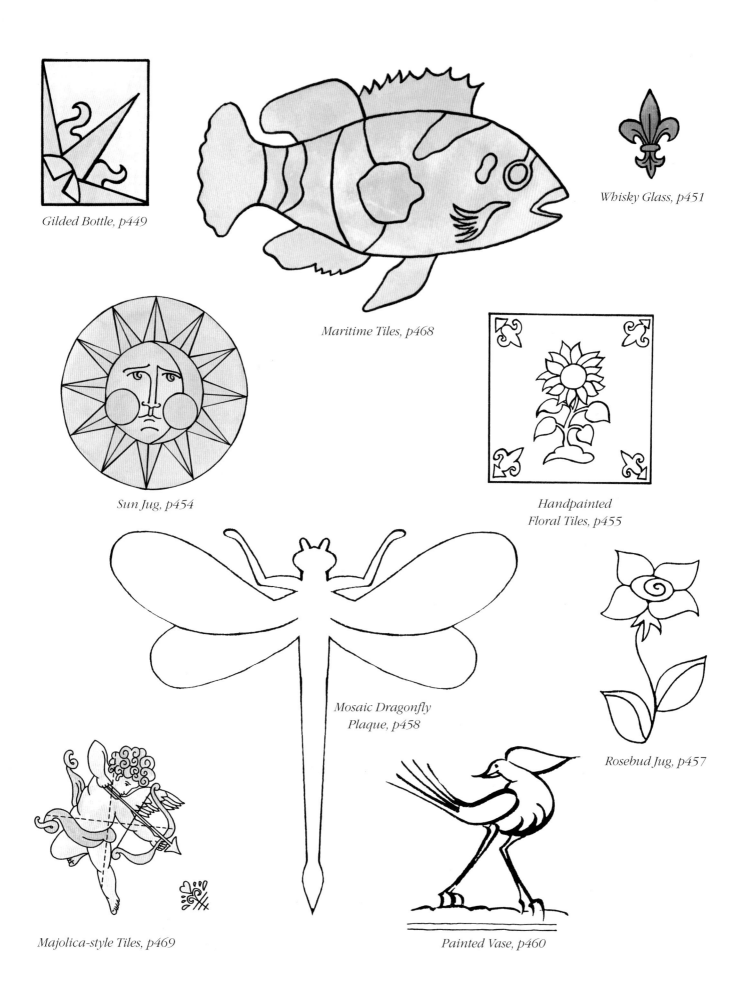

Gilded Bottle, p449

Whisky Glass, p451

Maritime Tiles, p468

Sun Jug, p454

Handpainted
Floral Tiles, p455

Mosaic Dragonfly
Plaque, p458

Rosebud Jug, p457

Majolica-style Tiles, p469

Painted Vase, p460

Papier-mâché Mirror, p46

Folk Art Frames, p406

Coronet Picture Frame, p378

Seashell Mirror, p47

King of Hearts Mirror, p324

Wooden Star Frame, p370

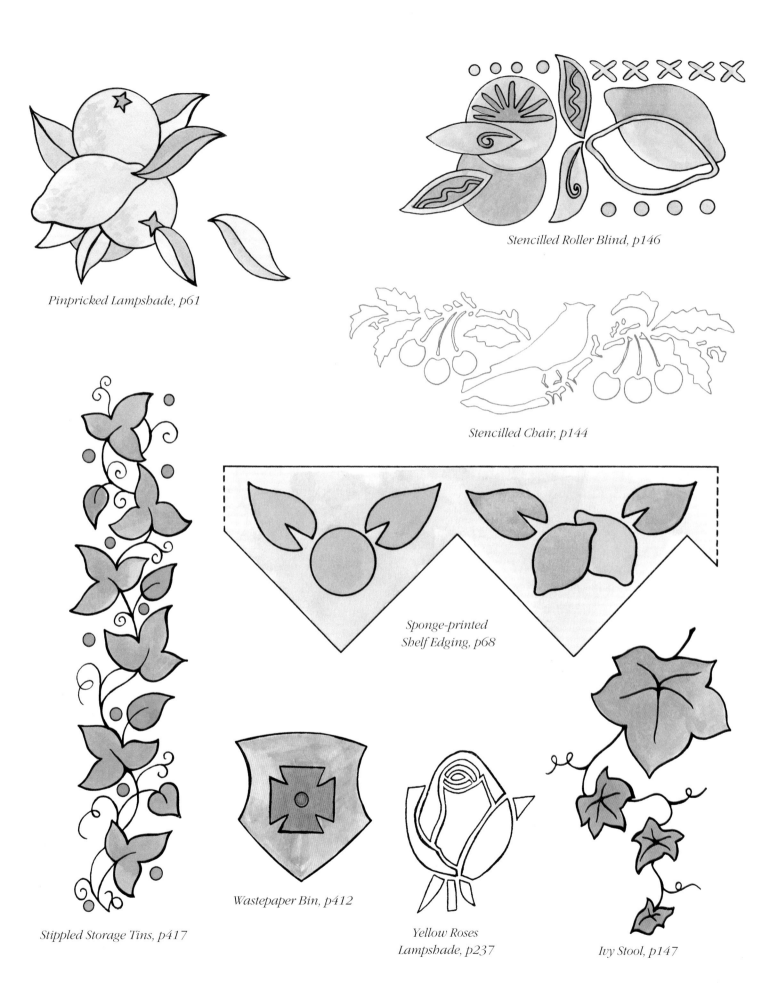

Pinpricked Lampshade, p61

Stencilled Roller Blind, p146

Stencilled Chair, p144

Sponge-printed
Shelf Edging, p68

Stippled Storage Tins, p417

Wastepaper Bin, p412

Yellow Roses
Lampshade, p237

Ivy Stool, p147

Fruity Bracelet, p49

Winged Cupid Brooch, p71

Shooting Star Badge, p385

Sun and Moon Badges, p375

Silver Star Earrings, p330

Embroidered Jewellery, p198

Jewellery Pouch, p211

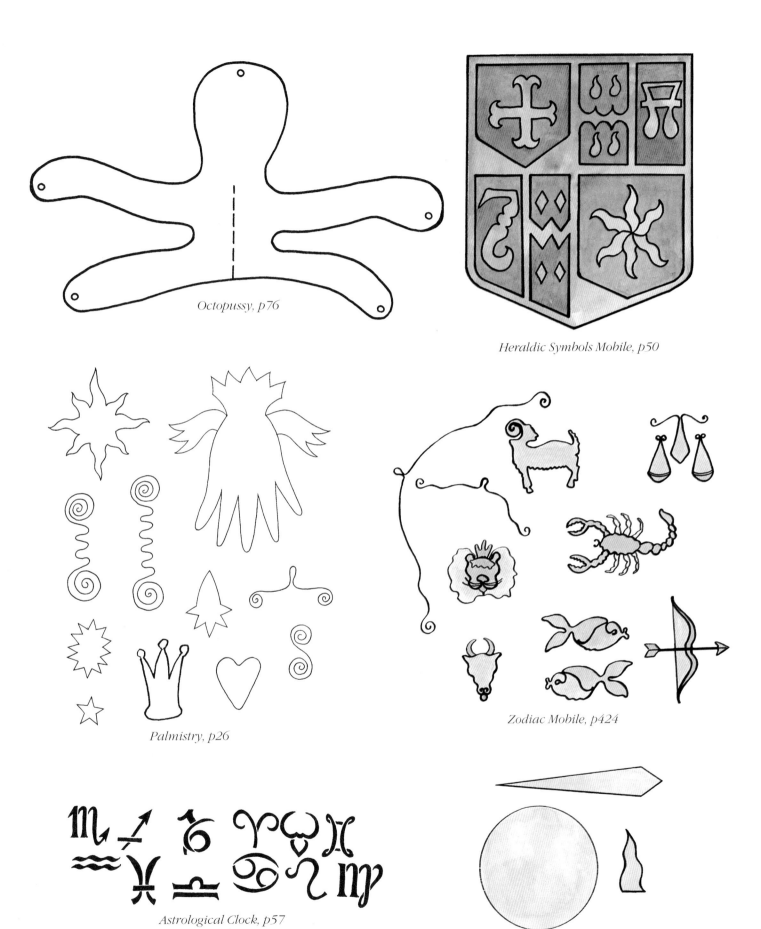

Octopussy, p76

Heraldic Symbols Mobile, p50

Palmistry, p26

Zodiac Mobile, p424

Astrological Clock, p57
Star-sign Bottle, p446

Astral Clock, p398

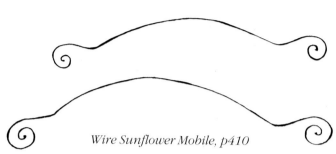

Wire Sunflower Mobile, p410

Sea Creatures Mobile, p404

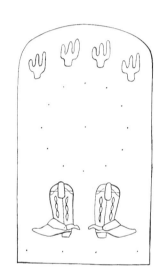

Tex Mex Clock, p334

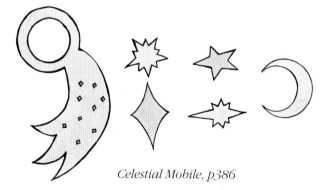

Celestial Mobile, p386

Papier-mâché Mobile, p72

Sunburst Clock, p202

Seahorse Storage Box, p376

Confetti Box, p63

Dancing Bees Box, p89

Folk Art Box, p75

Découpage Valentine Box, p88
Romantic Gift Wrap, p157

Swan Box, p413

Dragonfly Print Box, p155

Cancer Crab Box, p383

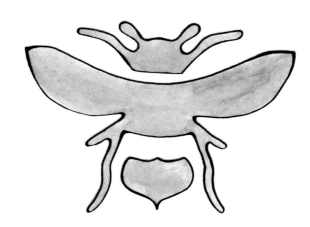

Fleur-de-lys Box, p204

Busy Bee Workbox, p388

Painted Sewing Box, p420

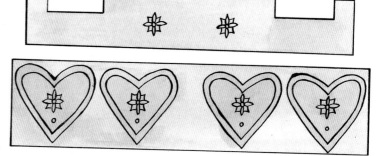

Hand-painted Box, p427

TEMPLATES ·

English Lion Cushion, p209

Stencilled Tablecloth, p150

Fruity Appliqué Cushion, p264

Astrological Cushion, p208

Muslin (Cheesecloth)
Curtain, p253

Sea Pillowcase, p201

Scented Cushion, p214

Peg Bag, p156

Nursery Cushion, p215

Quilted Cushion, p200

Needlepoint Cushion, p258

Embroidered Tablecloth, p213

Cushion with Seashells, p194

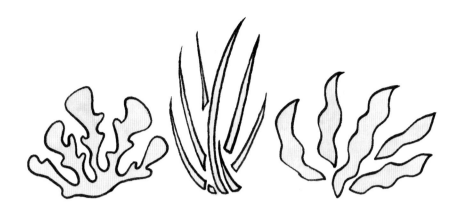

Seaweed Gift Wrap, p163

Embossed Cards, p65

Woodland Gift Wrap, p66

Collage Gift Wrap, p69
Xmas Tree Gift Tags, p70

Flower-stencilled Wrap, p135

Butterfly Gift Wrap, p142

Rose-stamped Stationery, p160

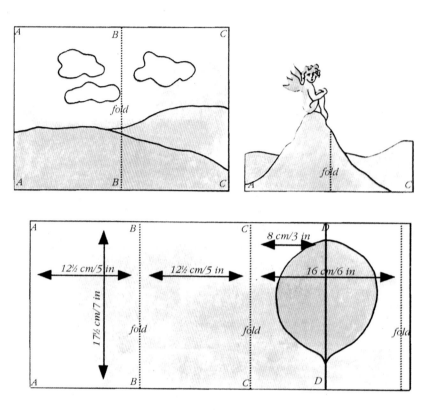

Contemplative Cupid Card, p78

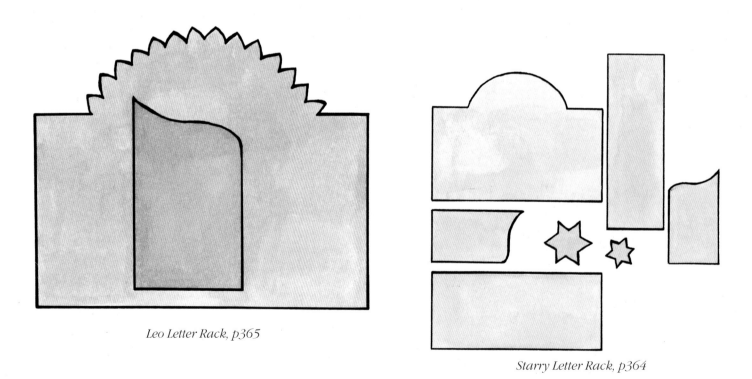

Leo Letter Rack, p365

Starry Letter Rack, p364

A

Abstract Hairslide 322–323

B

Badges
  Painted Tin Badges 392–393
  Shooting Star Badge 385, 500
  Sun and Moon Badges 375, 500
  Sunflower Badge 374
Bags
  Carrier Bags 44–45, 488
  Crepe Paper Bags 44–45
  Fleur-de-lys Shoe Bag 171, 490
  Heavenly Bag 173, 491
  Peg Bag 156, 506
  Rose Appliqué Bag 228–229, 492
  Seashell Beach Bag 236, 493
Beaded Orange Purse 172, 490
Bed-linen
  Appliquéd Sheet and Pillowcase 250, 493
  Child's Blanket 262
  Country-style Pillowcase 255

Cradle Quilt 232–233, 492
Sea Pillowcase 201, 505
Stamped Bedlinen 114–115
Bottles
  Gilded Bottle 449, 497
  Sequinned Rose Bottle 461
  Star-sign Bottle 448, 501
Bowls
  Fruit Bowl 462–463
  Gilded Fruit Bowl 444
  Gold-rimmed Bowl 35
  Love Token Bowl 39, 488
  Metal Embedded Bowl 310–311
  Orange Bowl 23
  Oriental Bowl 467
  Sunburst Bowl 24–25
Boxes
  Amish Sewing Box 341
  Art Nouveau Rose Box 137, 490
  Busy Bee Workbox 388–389, 504
  Cancer Crab Box 383, 504
  Cardboard Gift Boxes 42–43, 488
  Cherub Box 414–415
  Confetti Box 63, 503
  Crepe Paper Gift Box 62
  Dancing Bees Box 89, 503
  Decorated Box 38
  Découpage Oak Leaf Box 74
  Découpage Valentine Box 88, 503
  Dragonfly Print Box 155, 503
  Fleur-de-lys Box 204–205, 504
  Folk Art Box 7
  Hand-painted Box 427, 504
  Insect Storage Box 82–83
  Leaf Box 382
  Mirrored Keepsake Box 37
  Oak Leaf Box 154
  Painted Sewing Box 420–421, 504
  Seahorse Storage Box 376–377, 503
  Sun Hatbox 80–81
  Sun-gilded Box 426
  Swan Box 413, 503
  Toy Box 148–149
  Valentine Gift Boxes 333
  Woodburning 354, 496
Bridal Heart 193, 492
Buttons
  Spider Buttons 287
  Tudor Rose Buttons 176, 491

C

Candles
  Candle Collars 351
  Candle Jar 445
  Candle Pot 470
  Candlestick 408–409
  Gilded Candleholder 359
  Gilded Candlestick 360–361
  Gothic Candelabra 94–95
  Tin Candleholder 349, 496
Cards
  Appliqué Star Card 247, 493
  Appliquéd Sunflower Card 224, 492
  Contemplative Cupid Card 78–79, 508
  Embossed Cards 65, 507
  Paper Cut-outs 14, 488
  Seashore Cards 91
  Valentine's Card 161
Chairs
  Child's Chair 416
  Ivy Stool 147, 499
  Painted Bench 380–381
  Stencilled Chair 144–145, 499
Checkered Heart 307, 495
Child's Strip Patchwork Rucksack 260–261
Christmas Decorations 358, 496
Christmas Tree Star 16, 488
Clocks
  Astral Clock 398–399, 501
  Astrological Clock 57, 501
  Gilded Timepiece 56
  Glow-in-the-dark Clock 326–327
  Spider Web Clock 387
  Sunburst Clock 202–203, 502
  Teapot Clock 328–329
  Tex Mex Clock 334, 502

Clothes
  Baby Suit 187, 492
  Child's T-shirt 251, 493
  Cupid Camisole 192, 492
  Embroidered Dress 185
  Garden Apron 259
  Heavenly Hat 181
  Matisse Outfit 222–223, 492
Cookie Hearts 308
Copper Birdbath 423
Cornucopia 306, 495
Crackle-glazed Print 32–33
Creepy Crawly Handkerchief 109, 489
Cross stitches 218
Cupid Linocut 113, 489
Curtains
  Muslin (Cheesecloth) Curtain 253, 505
  Sprigged Calico Curtains 136
  Stencilled Sprig Curtain 105, 489
  Zodiac Cafe Curtain 112, 489
Cushions
  Astrological Cushion 208, 505
  Baroque Velvet Cushion 238
  Cushion with Seashells 194–195, 506

ACKNOWLEDGEMENTS

PROJECTS OFER ACOO, MADELEINE ADAMS, DINAH ALAN-SMITH, DEBORAH ALEXANDER, HELEN BAIRD, MICHAEL BALL, BETTY BARNDEN, EVELYN BENNETT, DEENA BEVERLEY, AMANDA BLUNDEN, PETRA BOASE, PENNY BOYLAN, JANET BRIDGE, AL BROWN, LOUISE BROWNLOW, ESTHER BURT, JUDY CLAYTON, GILL CLEMENT, LILLI CURTISS, MARION ELLIOT, SOPHIE EMBLETON, LUCINDA GANDERTON, LOUISE GARDAM, LISA GILCHRIST, ANDREW GILMORE, DAWN GULYAS, SANDRA HADFIELD, DAVID HANCOCK, JILL HANCOCK, LESLEY HARLE, ALISON HARPER, STEPHANIE HARVEY, BRIDGET HINGE, LABEENA ISHAQUE, SAMEENA ISHAQUE, PAUL JACKSON, MARY MAGUIRE, RACHEL HOWARD MARSHALL, ABIGAIL MILL, TERENCE MOORE, IZZY MOREAU, JACK MOXLEY, OLIVER MOXLEY, CLEO MUSSIE, SARBJITT NATT, ANDREW NEWTON-COX, CHERYL OWEN, EMMA PETITT, POLLY PLOUVIEZ, LIZZIE REAKES, KIM ROWLEY, DEBORAH SCHNEEBELI-MORRELL, DEBBIE SINISKA, TANYA SINISKA, KERRY SKINNER, THOMASINA SMITH, ANDREA SPENCER, ISABEL STANLEY, ADELE TIPLER, KELLIE-MARIE TOWNSEND, KAREN TRIFFITT, LIZ WAGSTAFF, SALLY WALTON, STEWART WALTON, ANGELA WHEELER, EMMA WHITFIELD, JOSEPHINE WHITFIELD, SUE WHITING, MELANIE WILLIAMS, DOROTHY WOOD

PHOTOGRAPHY STEVE DALTON, JAMES DUNCAN, MICHELLE GARRETT, TIM IMRIE, LUCY MASON, GLORIA NICOL, DAVID PARMITER, DEBBIE PATTERSON, SPIKE POWELL, STEVE TANNER, ADRIAN TAYLOR, PETER WILLIAMS, POLLY WREFORD

the food of
CHINA

Photography by Jason Lowe
Recipes by Deh-Ta Hsiung and Nina Simonds

MURDOCH
B O O K S

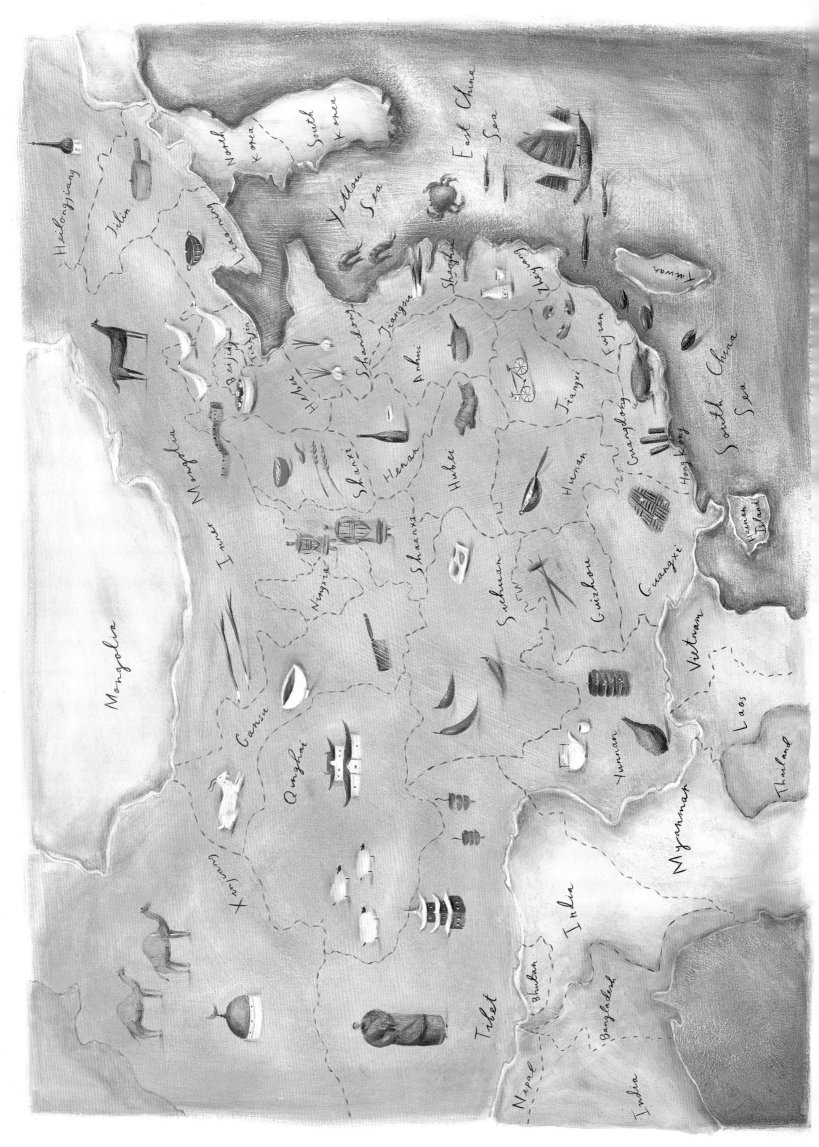

CONTENTS

FOOD JOURNEYS IN CHINA

the food of
CHINA

AN ENORMOUS COUNTRY, WITH A LARGE POPULATION
TO FEED AND A DIVERSE GEOGRAPY AND CLIMATE,
CHINA HAS ONE OF THE GREAT CUISINES OF THE
WORLD AND EATING PLAYS A MAJOR ROLE IN DAILY
LIFE AND IN RITUALS AND FESTIVITIES.

Chinese meals are always centered around a staple, or fan,
such as rice, wheat, corn or millet. Rice, always white and
polished, is the food most associated with China and is
usually steamed, while wheat grows well in the harsh climate
of the North and is made into breads and noodles. In poorer
areas, millet is more common, eaten as porridge. The staple
is then accompanied by secondary dishes, or cai, of meat,
seafood or vegetables, pickles and condiments. Snacks,
from dumplings to spicy bowls of noodles, are eaten all day
long, both as sustenance and to satisfy the taste buds.

INGREDIENTS

The most important factor is freshness: poultry and seafood
are bought live, and a cook may make more than one trip to
the market in a day. Chinese cuisine developed around the
foods available—often there was little meat, poultry or fish,
so rice and vegetables are particularly important. However,
many of the foods we associate with China today, such as
chiles, bell peppers, corn and cilantro all came to China via
trading routes. The Chinese also incorporate a lot of
preserved vegetables and dried foods, particularly seafood,
into their diet, which is especially important in areas where
the climate and terrain make growing enough food a struggle.

FLAVORS

Chinese cooking tries to reach a balance between tastes:
sweet and sour, hot and cold, plain and spicy. At the heart
of Chinese food is a trinity of flavors: ginger, scallions and
garlic which, though by no means included in all Chinese
dishes, contribute to a flavor that is seen as being

Snacking on noodles in the street, or feasting on steamed dumplings in a restaurant, are part of the Chinese enjoyment of food. A new sign goes up in Chengdu and a panda eats breakfast in Sichuan. Bean curd and chives are used in many dishes, while fried fish rolls served at a banquet and fried bread sold in the market, both use the same cooking technique.

In the North, wheat flour is made into staples like noodles, dumplings and breads. New Year is China's most important festival, celebrated with lanterns and food, including these sweet round dumplings. In Guangxi, cormorants are still used to catch fish. All parts of the pig are sold in Chinese markets, and scallions are one of Chinese cooking's most essential ingredients.

quintessentially "Chinese". Soy bean products are another essential flavouring, and fermented bean curd, soy sauce and bean sauces are tastes that define Chinese food, along with vinegars and sesame oil. In the West of the country, chiles and Sichuan pepper add heat to ingredients that are usually more simply cooked.

COOKING STYLES

A wok is without doubt the central item in a Chinese kitchen, and wok cooking, either stir-frying or deep-frying, is at the heart of China's quick style of cooking. Other techniques, such as steaming, poaching and braising, cook food a little slower. Few families own an oven, and foods that need to be oven-roasted, such as roast ducks or char siu, are instead bought from special restaurants. All food is "prepared" in China, salads and raw foods are not eaten, and ingredients are cooked, however briefly, or preserved. A good Chinese meal will include a mix of cooking-styles so all the dishes can be ready at the same time.

EATING

A Chinese meal will also consist of a number of dishes, all made to share, that are fully prepared in the kitchen (not even carving is done at the table) and can be picked up and eaten with chopsticks. Not only must the ingredients be fresh; the finished food must also be fresh. Stir-fried dishes should be served immediately so they still have wok hei or the breath of the wok about them, indicating that they have been cooked at exactly the right heat to exactly the right timing.

BANQUET FOOD

Food eaten at banquets is created to be the very opposite of the everyday diet of grains. The point of a banquet is eating for pleasure, not sustenance, thus rice or noodles are served only at the end, and may be left untouched. Banquet food is often symbolic and as extravagant as can be afforded with dishes such as abalone, shark's fin and whole fish.

MEDICAL

In no other cuisine is the medicinal nature of food so tied to even everyday cooking. Achieving balance at every meal is an essential part of Chinese food. Every ingredient is accorded a nature—hot, warm, cool and neutral—and a flavor—sweet, sour, bitter, salty and pungent—and these are matched to a person's imbalances: a cooling food for a fever, warming food after childbirth. Along with the use of everyday ingredients, are more exotic foods, such as dried lizards, wolf berries and black silky chickens, which are often cooked in special soups and preparations.

THE FOOD OF THE NORTH

The cuisine of the North, centered around Beijing, comes from an area that is generally inhospitable with, apart from Shandong, little fertile land, harsh long winters and short scorching summers. Historically the region has swung between drought and flooding from the Yellow River, "China's Sorrow", though dams and irrigation schemes have improved things in recent years. The main crops have thus always been hardy ones: wheat and millet are eaten as noodles, breads and porridge, while in the winter, vegetables such as turnips and cabbage are supplied to the capital by farmers from neighboring provinces, who drive in trucks to Beijing's markets and live on them until their load of vegetables has been sold. Shandong on the coast is the most fertile area and it has become a source of fruit and vegetables for the capital, as well as providing plentiful seafood.

Flavors are strong, with salty bean pastes and soy sauces, vinegar, scallions and garlic all being important ingredients. Winter vegetables are preserved or pickled, while spicy or piquant condiments are eaten with bowls of steaming noodles or rice when little else is available

The main outside influence on the region has been the Muslim cooking of the Mongol and Manchu invaders who crossed the Great Wall from the North. Mutton and, in spring and summer, lamb, is sold as barbecued skewers on the street and stir-fried and wrapped in wheat pancakes. Steaming Mongolian hotpots and Mongolian barbecues cooked on a grill are seen everywhere.

Peking Duck, however, remains Beijings most famous dish, and is cooked in specialty restaurants all over the city. Beggar's chicken is another local specialty, wrapped in lotus leaves and baked for hours in hot ashes.

In stark contrast to the comforting dumplings and hotpots of Beijing's streets is the imperial cuisine created inside the Forbidden City. The presence of the court not only encouraged a huge diversity of cooking styles in the city from every province in China, but also elevated cooking to a standard probably never seen elsewhere in the world. Food was as important to the myth surrounding the Emperor as his armies, and he employed hundreds if not thousands in his kitchens. This elaborate cuisine is no longer reproduced in its entirety, but is remembered as a set of skills, recipes and flavor combinations important today in both banquet and everyday cooking.

A little girl eats ice cream, old men play Chinese checkers, and visitors climb the steps to the Temple of Heaven despite the cold of a Beijing winter. Steaming hot buns are a staple of the North, along with cabbage, huge winter melons, red carrots and pickled vegetables. Barbecued skewers of lamb and the ubiquitous pot noodles are sold as warming street snacks.

11

Hangzhou is famous for its serene tea houses, while in Shanghai a woman poses for a photo in front of frantic Yuyuan Gardens, known for its snacks and Heart of the Lake Tea House, where tea comes with an orange and a memento. High-rise Pudong towers over old Shanghai, in whose alleys a woman makes lunch and a man walks under New Year lanterns. Fish and bok choy are sold in markets.

THE FOOD OF THE EAST

Though the huge port city of Shanghai now dominates the East, the city is very much a modern one and it is difficult to talk of a real "Shanghai cuisine." Rather, the city's food reflects that of the agriculturally rich provinces that surround it on the fertile plains of the Yangtze Delta. Together they have given this area the nickname "the land of fish and rice."

With a warmer climate than the North and an all-year-round growing season, the cuisine has been shaped by the variety of available ingredients, from rice and wheat to a whole array of vegetables—bok choy, bamboo, beans and squash, as well as some of China's finest fish—freshwater carp from the tributaries of the Yangtze, Shanghai's infamous hairy crabs and fresh seafood from the coast. Duck, chicken and pork from this region are also considered particularly good and a cured ham from Jinhua rivals that of Yunnan.

The cusine is based on slow-braising rather than steaming or stir-frying, and thus has a reputation for being more oily than other regions. Shaoxing wine, an amber rice wine produced for both drinking and cooking in the city of Shaoxing, flavors many dishes, as does black vinegar from Chinkiang and ginger and garlic. A pinch of sugar is often added to balance these flavors, and it is in this region that sweet-and-sour dishes are most expertly cooked. Much of China's soy sauce is produced in the East, and red-cooking is a favored cooking technique using a soy sauce and rice wine stock to braise the area's fine meat and poultry, which is also presented in the form of a mixed cold platter that begins most formal meals. Though many of the region's flavorings are strong, vegetables, fish and seafood tend to be treated simply.

The area is abundant in regional specialties, including spareribs from Wuxi cooked in soy sauce and rice wine; lion's head meatballs from Yangzhou; pressed ducks from Nanjing; and West-lake carp from Hangzhou, which also grows China's finest green tea, Dragon Well, that is sometimes used as an ingredient. The people of Shanghai love their fish and seafood, particularly the freshwater hairy crabs so associated with the city, and available for little over a month every autumn.

Snacking is an obsession, especially in Shanghai, with jiaozi, steamed buns and noodle dishes found everywhere. While rice is grown in the region, filling wheat-based breads, dumplings and noodles are favored, particularly in winter.

13

THE FOOD OF THE WEST

The cooking of China's central and western heartlands is dominated by the spice of Sichuan, whose fertile plains are fed by the Yangtze River and its tributaries. It is famous for its hot cuisine and the sheer variety of its cooking-styles, summed up in the phrase "one hundred dishes and one hundred flavors".

Chiles are not indigenous to China, and in fact came to Asia from South America with the Portuguese. It was therefore probably Buddhist traders and missionaries from the West who brought Indian spices and cooking techniques into Sichuan, and also left the legacy of an imaginative Buddhist vegetarian cuisine.

Sichuan pepper is the dominant spice in many dishes. Not related to Western black and white pepper, it is hot and pungent, leaving a numb sensation in the mouth. The use of chile peppers and ginger adds additional layers of heat. Red (chile) oil, sesame oil, various bean pastes and vinegars are common, as are nuts and sesame seeds in dishes like bang bang chicken. These flavors are uniquely Sichuan, and quite different from those in the rest of China.

Cooking styles are also unusual. "Fish flavored" (Yuxiang) sauces are made from ginger, garlic, vinegar, chiles and scallions, usually served with vegetables like eggplant, but never with even a hint of fish present. Other tastes include hot-and-sour (Cuan La), such as in the famous soup, and a numb-chile flavor (Ma La), such as in the beancurd dish ma po dofu with its fiery sauce. Sichuan also has its own version of the hotpot, the Chongqing hot pot, which is heavily flavored by chile and oil and, true to the style of the region, is red-hot.

Chiles are widely used in other areas of the West, particularly in neighboring Hunan and Guangxi, whose Guilin chile sauce is eaten all over China. Guangxi is also a major rice-growing region, with vast stepped terraces covering its hills.

Southwest China has the most varied mix of ethnic minorities in the country, and it is the only area in which dairy products such as goat cheese are used. Muslim influences are also apparent and goat meat and dried beef are available. Yunnan ham is a whole ham cured in a sweet style, and Yunnan specialties include steampot chicken, cooked with medicinal ingredients, and crossing-the-bridge noodles, cooked in a bowl of boiling hot broth.

Modern Chengdu bustles round a statue of Mao, while a Naxi girl represents one of Yunnan's ethnic minorities. Bean curd is sold on the street and used in ma po dofu, and spicy noodles are a familiar snack. Mushrooms from the mountains, red chile bean paste, bamboo shoots and eggplant are all part of a rich diet. Rice grows in Guilin and sheep live under the mountains of Yunnan.

Dried food stores are found all over Hong Kong and sell many kinds of dried seafood, which is also sold fresh in the markets. Dim sum is enjoyed in Hong Kong at old-fashioned tea houses and at the famous Luk Yu Tea House, with its smart waiters, while egg noodles, steamed whole fish, oyster sauce and bowls of freshly steamed rice are all part of the varied Cantonese diet.

THE FOOD OF THE SOUTH

The food of the South, and especially that of Guangdong (Canton), is renowned both within and outside China as the country's finest. Guangdong has a subtropical climate that sustains rice crops and many vegetables and fruit virtually all year round, while an extensive coastline and inland waterways provide the freshest fish and shellfish.

The area also prides itself on its well-trained chefs, whose restaurants have always catered to the rich merchants of Guangzhou and Hong Kong. They insist on high quality ingredients, which they cook in numerous ways: stir-fried, steamed or boiled, but which are usually kept simple and cooked with little oil to enhance the food's fresh flavor.

The flavors of the South are relatively simple, emphasizing the freshness of the food with just a delicate base of ginger, garlic and scallions. Unlike the rest of China, spicy or fragrant condiments are often served with dishes, particularly bean pastes and sauces, so the diner can add their own flavorings. The area is responsible for the invention of oyster, hoisin, black bean and XO sauces.

Guangzhou is known for its wonderful fish and seafood dishes, served in every restaurant. Always fresh, the customer picks from a large fish tank and specifies the cooking technique. The favored meat of the South is without a doubt pork—roasted or babecued (char siu) and bought from the carry-out counters of roast-meat restaurants, who hang up their wares to tempt customers. Ducks are another favorite, bred all over the South and roasted until crispy. Dim sum is a specialty of Guangzhou and Hong Kong and these snacks, served in tea houses or dim sum restaurants, are universally popular.

The Cantonese are also known for eating just about anything—from shark's fin and snakes to monkeys and dogs. The people of this region are certainly knowledgeable and adventerous about food, though many of the more esoteric ingredients are served only at specialized restaurants or are eaten mostly for their medicinal qualities.

As well as the Cantonese cooking of Guangdong, the South is also home to the food of the Hakka people, China's gypsies, whose cooking is an earthier version of Cantonese, and Chiu Chow food from the east coast of the province, with its emphasis on seafood, goose and sauces. There are also specialties from Fujian and Taiwan.

APPETIZERS

Fold the dumplings as shown, handling the wrappers carefully so they don't tear and making sure they don't get too wet. Squeeze the pleats firmly or they will come undone as they cook.

JIAOZI

PERHAPS NO OTHER FOOD TYPIFIES THE HEARTY CHARACTERISTICS OF NORTHERN HOME-STYLE COOKING MORE THAN THESE MEAT DUMPLINGS. YOU CAN PURCHASE GOOD-QUALITY DUMPLING WRAPPERS AT ASIAN MARKETS, WHICH MAKES THESE A QUICK, EASY SNACK TO PREPARE.

FILLING
6 cups Chinese (Napa) cabbage, finely chopped
1 teaspoon salt
1 lb ground pork
2 cups Chinese garlic chives, finely chopped
2 1/2 tablespoons light soy sauce
1 tablespoon Shaoxing rice wine
2 tablespoons roasted sesame oil
1 tablespoon finely chopped ginger
1 tablespoon cornstarch

50 round wheat dumpling wrappers
red rice vinegar or a dipping sauce (page 282)

MAKES 50

TO MAKE the filling, put the cabbage and salt in a bowl and toss lightly to combine. Allow to stand for 30 minutes. Squeeze all the water from the cabbage and put the cabbage in a large bowl. Add the pork, garlic chives, soy sauce, rice wine, sesame oil, ginger and cornstarch. Stir until combined and drain off any excess liquid.

PLACE a heaping teaspoon of the filling in the center of each wrapper. Spread a little water along the edge of the wrapper and fold the wrapper over to make a half-moon shape. Use your thumb and index finger to form small pleats along the sealed edge. With the other hand, press the 2 opposite edges together to seal. Place the dumplings on a baking sheet that has been lightly dusted with cornstarch. Do not allow the dumplings to sit for too long or they will go soggy.

BRING a large saucepan of water to a boil. Add half the dumplings, stirring immediately to prevent them from sticking together, and return to a boil. For the traditional method of cooking dumplings, add 1 cup cold water and continue cooking over high heat until the water boils. Add another 3 cups cold water and cook until the water boils again. Alternatively, cook the dumplings in the boiling water for 8–9 minutes. Remove the saucepan from the heat and drain the dumplings. Repeat with the remaining dumplings.

THE DUMPLINGS can also be fried. Heat 1 tablespoon oil in a frying pan, add a single layer of dumplings and cook for 2 minutes, shaking the pan to make sure they don't stick. Add 1/3 cup water, cover and steam for 2 minutes, then uncover and cook until the water has evaporated. Repeat with the remaining dumplings.

SERVE with red rice vinegar or a dipping sauce.

SPRING ROLLS

THE FAT, SOLID SPRING ROLLS FOUND IN MANY WESTERN RESTAURANTS ARE QUITE DIFFERENT FROM THE SLENDER AND REFINED SPRING ROLLS THAT ARE TRADITIONALLY MADE TO CELEBRATE CHINESE NEW YEAR. HERE'S AN EASY RENDITION OF THE CLASSIC.

FILLING
5 tablespoons light soy sauce
2 teaspoons roasted sesame oil
3¹/₂ tablespoons Shaoxing rice
   wine
1¹/₂ teaspoons cornstarch
1 lb center-cut pork loin, trimmed
   and cut into very thin strips
6 dried Chinese mushrooms
¹/₂ teaspoon freshly ground
   black pepper
4 tablespoons oil
1 tablespoon finely chopped ginger
3 garlic cloves, finely chopped
3 cups Chinese (Napa) cabbage,
   finely shredded
1 cup carrots, finely shredded
²/₃ cup Chinese garlic chives, cut
   into 1 inch pieces
2 cups bean sprouts

1 egg yolk
2 tablespoons all-purpose flour
20 square spring roll wrappers
oil for deep-frying
hoisin sauce

MAKES 20

TO MAKE the filling, combine 2 tablespoons of the soy sauce and half the sesame oil with 1¹/₂ tablespoons of the rice wine and 1 teaspoon of the cornstarch. Add the pork and toss to coat. Marinate in the fridge for 20 minutes. Meanwhile, soak the dried mushrooms in boiling water for 30 minutes, then drain and squeeze out any excess water. Remove and discard the stems and shred the caps. Combine the remaining soy sauce, sesame oil and cornstarch with the black pepper.

HEAT a wok over high heat, add half the oil and heat until very hot. Add the pork mixture and stir-fry for 2 minutes, or until cooked. Remove and drain. Wipe out the wok.

REHEAT the wok over high heat, add the remaining oil and heat until very hot. Stir-fry the mushrooms, ginger and garlic for 15 seconds. Add the cabbage and carrots and toss lightly. Pour in the remaining rice wine, then stir-fry for 1 minute. Add the garlic chives and bean sprouts and stir-fry for 1 minute, or until the sprouts are limp. Add the pork mixture and soy sauce mixture and cook until thickened. Transfer to a colander and drain for 5 minutes, tossing occasionally to remove the excess liquid.

COMBINE the egg yolk, flour and 3 tablespoons water. Place 2 tablespoons of filling on the corner of a wrapper, leaving the corner itself free. Spread some of the yolk mixture on the opposite corner. Fold over one corner and start rolling, but not too tightly. Fold in the other corners, roll up and press to secure. Repeat with the remaining wrappers.

FILL a wok one quarter full with oil. Heat the oil to 375°F, or until a piece of bread fries golden brown in 10 seconds when dropped in the oil. Cook the spring rolls in 2 batches, turning constantly, for 5 minutes, or until golden. Remove and drain on paper towels. Serve with hoisin sauce.

Spring rolls should look elegant rather than chunky, so use a small amount of filling in each and roll them neatly. Don't roll them too tightly or they may burst open as they cook.

Luk Yu Tea House,
Hong Kong

Gather in the tops of the buns as neatly as you can to make round balls. Bear in mind that they will open slightly as they cook to show their filling.

CHAR SIU BAU

MANTOU, OR STEAMED BUNS, ARE A FILLING STAPLE EATEN ALL OVER CHINA, BUT ESPECIALLY IN THE NORTH. HOWEVER, THESE FILLED, SLIGHTLY SWEET BUNS MADE WITH BARBECUED PORK (CHAR SIU) ARE A CANTONESE SPECIALTY, ENJOYED IN EVERY DIM SUM RESTAURANT.

1 teaspoon oil
8 oz barbecued pork (char siu), diced
3 teaspoons Shaoxing rice wine
1 teaspoon roasted sesame oil
2 tablespoons oyster sauce
2 teaspoons light soy sauce
3 teaspoons sugar
1 quantity basic yeast dough (page 278)
chili sauce

MAKES 12 LARGE OR
24 SMALL BUNS

HEAT the oil in a wok. Add the pork, rice wine, sesame oil, oyster sauce, soy sauce and sugar and cook for 1 minute. Allow to cool.

DIVIDE the dough into 12 or 24 portions, depending on how large you want the buns to be, and cover with a kitchen towel. Working with 1 portion at a time, press the dough into circles with the edges thinner than the center. Place 1 teaspoon of filling on the dough for a small bun or 3 teaspoons for a large bun. Draw the sides in to enclose the filling. Pinch the top together and put each bun on a square of waxed paper. When you get more proficient at making these, you may be able to get more filling into the buns, which will make them less doughy. Ensure that you seal them properly. The buns can also be turned over, then cooked the other way up so they look like round balls.

ARRANGE the buns well spaced in 3 steamers. Cover and steam over simmering water in a wok, reversing the steamers halfway through, for 15 minutes, or until the buns are well risen and a skewer inserted into the centre comes out hot. Serve with some chili sauce.

荷叶糯米团

STEAMED GLUTINOUS RICE IN LOTUS LEAVES

LOR MAI GAI ARE A DIM SUM CLASSIC THAT ALSO MAKE GOOD SNACKS. WHEN STEAMED, THE RICE TAKES ON THE FLAVORS OF THE OTHER INGREDIENTS AND OF THE LOTUS LEAVES THEMSELVES. THE PACKAGES CAN BE MADE AHEAD AND FROZEN, THEN STEAMED FOR 40 MINUTES.

1 1/4 lb glutinous rice
4 large lotus leaves

FILLING
2 tablespoons dried shrimp
4 dried Chinese mushrooms
2 tablespoons oil
12 oz skinned, boneless chicken
    breasts, cut into 1/2 inch cubes
1 garlic clove, crushed
2 Chinese sausages (lap cheong),
    thinly sliced
2 scallions, thinly sliced
1 tablespoon oyster sauce
3 teaspoons light soy sauce
3 teaspoons sugar
1 teaspoon roasted sesame oil
1 tablespoon cornstarch
chili sauce

MAKES 8

PLACE the rice in a bowl, cover with cold water and allow to soak overnight. Drain in a colander and place the rice in a bamboo steamer lined with a kitchen towel. Steam, covered, over simmering water in a wok for 30–40 minutes, or until the rice is cooked. Cool slightly before using.

SOAK the lotus leaves in boiling water for 1 hour, or until softened. Shake dry and cut the leaves in half to give 8 equal pieces.

TO MAKE the filling, soak the dried shrimp in boiling water for 1 hour, then drain. Soak the dried mushrooms in boiling water for 30 minutes, then drain and squeeze out any excess water. Remove and discard the stems and finely chop the caps.

HEAT a wok over high heat, add half the oil and heat until very hot. Stir-fry the chicken for 2–3 minutes, or until browned. Add the shrimp, mushrooms, garlic, sausage and scallions. Stir-fry for another 1–2 minutes, or until aromatic. Add the oyster sauce, soy sauce, sugar and sesame oil and toss well. Combine the cornstarch with 3/4 cup water, add to the sauce and simmer until thickened.

WITH WET hands, divide the rice into 16 balls. Place the lotus leaves on a work surface, put a ball of rice in the center of each leaf and flatten the ball slightly, making a slight indentation in the middle. Spoon one eighth of the filling onto each rice ball, top with another slightly flattened rice ball and smooth into one ball. Wrap up firmly by folding the leaves over to form an envelope.

PLACE the packages in 3 steamers. Cover and steam over simmering water in a wok, reversing the steamers halfway through, for 30 minutes. To serve, open up each leaf and eat straight from the leaf while hot with some chili sauce.

Enclose the filling in the rice as much as possible, then neatly fold over the leaves. The leaves seal in the flavor and hold the rice in shape while cooking.

Rock sugar is sold loose in a market in Sichuan.

Chickens are bought live and prepared on the spot in Beijing market to make sure they are really fresh.

燜鸡翅

BRAISED CHICKEN WINGS

THESE DEEP-FRIED, CRISP WINGS ARE A FAVORITE SNACK FOR THE CHINESE. THIS RECIPE IS A SIMPLE ONE THAT MAKES A GOOD SNACK OR FIRST COURSE. YOU'LL NEED TO HAND OUT FINGER BOWLS FOR YOUR GUESTS.

24 chicken wings
2 tablespoons rock sugar
1 tablespoon dark soy sauce
1 tablespoon light soy sauce
1 tablespoon Shaoxing rice wine
oil for deep-frying
2 teaspoons finely chopped ginger
1 scallion, finely chopped
2 tablespoons hoisin sauce
1/2 cup chicken stock (page 281)

SERVES 6

DISCARD the tip of each chicken wing. Cut each wing into 2 pieces through the joint. Put the wing pieces in a bowl.

PUT the rock sugar, dark soy sauce, light soy sauce and rice wine in a small pitcher or bowl. Mix until combined, breaking the sugar down as much as you can. Pour the mixture over the chicken wings. Marinate in the fridge for at least 1 hour, or overnight.

DRAIN the chicken wings, reserving the marinade. Fill a wok one quarter full of oil. Heat the oil to 350°F, or until a piece of bread fries golden brown in 15 seconds when dropped in the oil. Cook the chicken wings in batches for 2–3 minutes, or until they are well browned. Drain on paper towels.

CAREFULLY POUR the oil from the wok, reserving 1 tablespoon. Reheat the wok over high heat, add the reserved oil and heat until very hot. Stir-fry the ginger and scallion for 1 minute. Add the hoisin sauce, reserved marinade and chicken wings and cook for 1 minute, then add the stock and bring to a boil. Reduce the heat, cover the wok and cook gently for 8–10 minutes, or until the chicken wings are cooked through and tender.

INCREASE the heat and bring the sauce to a boil, uncovered. Cook until the sauce reduces to a sticky coating.

Traveling by truck in Yunnan.

蒸 米 粉 卷

STEAMED RICE NOODLE ROLLS

A DIM SUM FAVORITE, THESE SILKY RICE NOODLES CAN BE FILLED WITH BARBECUED PORK (CHAR SIU),

SHRIMP OR VEGETABLES. THE NOODLES ARE SOLD AS A LONG SHEET FOLDED INTO A ROLL. DO NOT

REFRIGERATE THEM—THEY MUST BE USED AT ROOM TEMPERATURE OR THEY WILL BREAK.

Put the filling on the piece of noodle roll closest to you. Roll up carefully so you don't tear it, keeping the filling tucked inside.

PORK FILLING
11 oz Chinese barbecued pork
    (char siu), chopped
3 scallions, finely chopped
2 tablespoons chopped cilantro

OR

SHRIMP FILLING
8 oz shrimp
1 tablespoon oil
3 scallions, finely chopped
2 tablespoons finely chopped
    cilantro

OR

VEGETABLE FILLING
1 bunch (about 3/4 lb) Chinese
    broccoli (gai lan)
1 teaspoon light soy sauce
1 teaspoon roasted sesame oil
2 scallions, finely chopped

4 fresh rice noodle rolls
oyster sauce

MAKES 4

TO MAKE the pork filling, combine the pork with the scallions and cilantro.

TO MAKE the shrimp filling, peel and devein the shrimp. Heat a wok over high heat, add the oil and heat until very hot. Stir-fry the shrimp for 1 minute, or until they are pink and cooked through. Season with salt and white pepper. Add the scallions and cilantro and mix well.

TO MAKE the vegetable filling, wash the Chinese broccoli well. Discard any tough-looking stems and chop the rest of the stems. Put on a plate in a steamer, cover and steam over simmering water in a wok for 3 minutes, or until all the and leaves are just tender. Combine the broccoli with the soy sauce, sesame oil and scallions.

CAREFULLY UNROLL the rice noodle rolls (don't worry if they crack or tear a little at the sides). Trim each one into a neat rectangle 6 x 7 inches (you may be able to get 2 rectangles out of 1 roll if they are very large). Divide the filling among the rolls, then reroll the noodles. Put the rolls on a plate in a large steamer, cover and steam over simmering water in a wok for 5 minutes. Serve the rolls cut into pieces and drizzled with the oyster sauce.

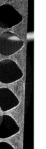

香辣椒盐排骨

SPICY SALT AND PEPPER SPARERIBS

2 lb Chinese-style pork spareribs
1 egg, beaten
2–3 tablespoons all-purpose flour
oil for deep-frying
2 scallions, finely chopped
2 small red chiles, finely chopped

MARINADE
1/2 teaspoon ground Sichuan
   peppercorns
1/2 teaspoon five-spice powder
1/2 teaspoon salt
1 tablespoon light soy sauce
1 tablespoon Shaoxing rice wine
1/4 teaspoon roasted sesame oil

SERVES 4

ASK the butcher to cut the slab of spareribs crosswise into thirds that measure 1 1/2–2 inch in length, or use a cleaver to do so yourself. Cut the ribs between the bones to separate them.

TO MAKE the marinade, combine the ingredients in a bowl. Add the ribs and toss lightly. Marinate in the fridge for at least 3 hours, or overnight.

MIX the egg, flour and a little water to form a smooth batter with the consistency of heavy cream. Fill a wok one quarter full of oil. Heat the oil to 350°F, or until a piece of bread fries golden brown in 15 seconds when dropped in the oil. Dip the ribs in the batter and fry in batches for 5 minutes until they are crisp and golden, stirring to separate them, then remove and drain. Reheat the oil and fry the ribs for 1 minute to darken their color. Remove and drain on paper towels.

SOAK the scallions and chiles in the hot oil (with the heat off) for 2 minutes. Remove with a wire strainer or slotted spoon and place on top of the ribs.

A cleaver is the only knife heavy enough to easily cut through the bones of spareribs.

烤排骨

BARBECUED SPARERIBS

3 lb Chinese-style pork spareribs

MARINADE
1/2 cup hoisin sauce
3 tablespoons light soy sauce
3 tablespoons Shaoxing rice wine
2 tablespoons sugar
3 tablespoons tomato ketchup
4 garlic cloves, finely chopped
3 tablespoons finely chopped
   ginger

SERVES 6

ASK the butcher to cut the slab of spareribs crosswise into thirds that measure 1 1/2–2 inch in length, or use a cleaver to do so yourself.

PLACE the spareribs in a large clay pot, braising pan or saucepan and cover with water. Bring to a boil, then reduce the heat to a simmer. Cook for 20 minutes, drain and allow the ribs to cool. Cut the ribs between the bones to separate them.

TO MAKE the marinade, combine the ingredients in a bowl. Add the ribs and toss lightly. Marinate in the fridge for at least 3 hours, or overnight.

PREHEAT the oven to 350°F. Put the ribs and marinade on a baking sheet lined with aluminium foil. Bake for 45 minutes, turning once, until golden.

BARBECUED SPARERIBS

HAR GAU

HAR GAU are the benchmark dim sum for any restaurant. The filling of prawns and minced water chestnuts or bamboo is folded into wrappers made from wheat starch. Each wrapper is filled as it is made because the pastry is hard to handle. The wrapper is then pleated, sealed and the dim sum placed in a steamer. As the har gau cook they turn from an opaque white to translucent, showing the filling inside.

SIU MAI

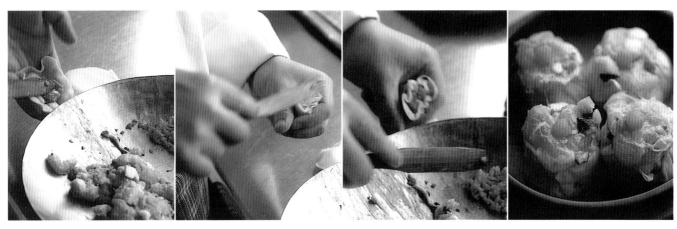

SIU MAI means 'cook and sell' because of their unsurpassed popularity. Egg noodle wrappers are filled with a mixture of pork, prawns and Chinese mushrooms or water chestnuts. The round wrapper is held in one hand and the filling is placed in the middle. The wrapper is then squeezed up around the filling and the top levelled off. Siu mai are usually dotted with a small blob of duck egg yolk or crab roe.

SWEET DIM SUM

BO LOH BAU sweet yellow cream pastries encased in a glazed yeast dough and baked.

LIN YUNG BAU sweet chewy buns filled with lotus seed paste. The red dot indicates it is sweet.

DAN TA these rich, golden egg custard tarts are set in a flaky pastry and are served warm.

LAI WONG restaurants often invent their own 'signature' dim sum, like these sweet rabbits.

CITY HALL CHINESE RESTAURANT is one of Hong Kong's busiest dim sum restaurants, appealing to the building's civil servants during the week and long queues of families at the weekends. The dim sum are stacked on trolleys that are wheeled from table to table, and are also found at 'stations' throughout the room, such as the one above frying turnip cake and noodles to order.

DIM SUM

DIM SUM ARE SNACKS AND DUMPLINGS THAT 'TOUCH THE HEART' AND ARE CENTRAL TO THE CANTONESE TEA HOUSE TRADITION OF YUM CHA. YUM CHA MEANS SIMPLY 'TO DRINK TEA', BUT EATING DIM SUM, READING NEWSPAPERS AND CATCHING UP WITH FRIENDS AND FAMILY ARE ALL PART OF THE EXPERIENCE.

The Chinese love to snack and each region has its favourites, from mantou and jiaozi in the North to little spicy Sichuan dishes. But it is in Guangzhou and Hong Kong's tea houses that dim sum—China's most famous snacks—are found.

TEA HOUSES

Traditional tea houses are almost like a pub. Regulars, mostly older men, spend their early mornings sipping tea, eating just a few dim sum and reading the newspapers. In a few tea houses, the men are accompanied by their song birds, whose cages are hung up around the room. Today, most tea houses are bright, dim sum palaces. Often huge, multi-level restaurants, they work at a frantic, noisy pace, with office workers or families eating a whole meal of dim sum.

EATING DIM SUM

Dim sum is usually eaten mid-morning, but it can be found at any time, and even enjoyed as a midnight snack in busy Hong Kong. The meal begins by choosing a tea, usually pu-er (a black tea), jasmine or chrysanthemum. In fact, yum cha is the only meal where the tea is drunk with the food rather than before or afterwards. Anyone from the table can top up

THIS TRADITIONAL TEA HOUSE in Sham Shui Po, Hong Kong, opens as early as 5 o'clock in the morning for its regulars, almost all of whom are men. The dim sum are brought around in trays hung from the server's neck and are mostly large and filling. Just one or two items are chosen to supplement the important business of tea drinking, gossiping and catching up on the racing form.

the tea cups during the meal, and they are thanked by tapping your fingers on the table, expressing gratitude even when mouths are full. To get the pot refilled, the lid is lifted to the side so the waiters can see that it is empty.

Sometimes dim sum is ordered from a menu, but in the most busy places it is usually taken around the tables in trays or trolleys hot from the kitchen. Servers shout out the name of the dishes they have and people lift up the lids to peak at what is on offer. There may also be 'stations' where noodles are fried and vegetables cooked. Dim sum mostly come in small steamers or dishes, usually three servings to a portion.

Dim sum are rarely made at home and restaurants prize their chefs, who make everything by hand. These chefs undergo an apprenticeship of 3 years, and take another 5 years on average to become fully qualified dim sum chefs.

THE BILL for a dim sum meal is calculated from a card kept on each table. Each time a dish is ordered, the server marks the card with a stamp called a chop.

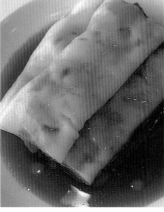

NGAU YUK KAO beef balls shaped from minced beef, seasoned with coriander and soy sauce and steamed. They may also contain pork and are served on thin bean curd sheets.

CHEUNG FAN sheets of silky rice noodles wrapped around a filling such as barbecue pork or prawns, then steamed. A soy and sesame oil sauce is poured over just before serving.

PAI GWAT meaning 'fat ribs', these are spareribs, usually pork, which are fried and then steamed, often with a black bean or chilli sauce.

WU GOK a mashed taro pastry wrapped around a filling such as prawn or pork and deep-fried. The pastry flakes up to give a crispy appearance.

LOH BAK GOH a turnip cake made from grated Chinese turnip, a sort of daikon radish, flavoured with Chinese bacon or sausage, steamed, cut in slices and fried to order until crispy.

FUNG JAU meaning 'phoenix claws', these are in fact chickens' feet, steamed in a black bean or soy chilli sauce. The feet are eaten whole, the flavour sucked out, and the bones spat out.

NIANG QING JIAO green peppers stuffed with a minced fish or shrimp stuffing and then deep-fried. Aubergine pieces are treated in a similar way.

JAI GAU glutinous rice wrappers with a vegetarian filling such as garlic chives, ginger and spinach. The dumplings are steamed until the wrappers turn translucent and their filling shows through.

LUO MAI GAI parcels of sticky rice mixed with dried shrimp, Chinese sausage and cubed chicken, wrapped in lotus leaves and steamed. The leaves add flavour, but are not eaten.

HOM SUI GOK these sticky torpedo-shaped dumplings are made from a rice dough filled with a mixture of dried shrimp, pork and Chinese mushrooms. The dumplings are deep-fried.

CHAR SIU BAU steamed buns made from a slightly sweet yeast dough filled with barbecue pork, oyster and soy sauces. The best crack open a little at the top to reveal the filling.

YU CHI GAU a large dumpling filled with shark's fin and served in a broth. The dumpling can contain other fillings and the whole dish is steamed.

HAR GAU

HAR GAU ARE THE BENCHMARK DIM SUM BY WHICH RESTAURANTS ARE MEASURED AND THEY ARE
NOT EASY TO MAKE. THE WHEAT STARCH DOUGH IS HARD TO HANDLE AND NEEDS TO BE KEPT WARM
WHILE YOU WORK WITH IT, BUT THE RESULTS ARE VERY SATISFYING.

FILLING
1 lb shrimp
1 1/2 oz pork or bacon fat (rind
    removed), finely chopped
1/4 cup fresh or canned bamboo
    shoots, rinsed, drained and
    finely chopped
1 scallion, finely chopped
1 teaspoon sugar
3 teaspoons light soy sauce
1/2 teaspoon roasted sesame oil
1 egg white, lightly beaten
1 teaspoon salt
1 tablespoon cornstarch

WRAPPER DOUGH
1 1/2 cups wheat starch
3 teaspoons cornstarch
2 teaspoons oil

soy sauce, chili sauce or a dipping
    sauce (page 282)

MAKES 24

TO MAKE the filling, peel and devein the shrimp
and cut half of them into 1/2 inch chunks. Chop
the remaining shrimp very finely. Combine all the
shrimp in a large bowl. Add the pork or bacon
fat, bamboo shoots, scallion, sugar, soy sauce,
sesame oil, egg white, salt and cornstarch. Mix
well and drain off any excess liquid.

TO MAKE the dough, put the wheat starch,
cornstarch and oil in a small bowl. Add 1 cup
boiling water and mix until well combined. Add a
little extra wheat starch if the dough is too sticky.

ROLL the dough into a long cylinder, divide it into
24 pieces and cover with a hot damp kitchen
towel. Working with 1 portion at a time, roll out
the dough using a rolling pin or a well-oiled
cleaver. If using a rolling pin, roll the dough into
a 3 1/2–4 inch round between 2 pieces of greased
plastic wrap. If using a cleaver, place the blade
facing away from you and gently press down
on the flat side of the blade with your palm,
squashing the dough while twisting the handle
at the same time to form a round shape. Fill each
wrapper as you make it.

PLACE a heaping teaspoon of the filling in the
center of each wrapper. Spread a little water
along the wrapper edge and fold the wrapper
over to make a half-moon shape. Use your thumb
and index finger to form small pleats along the top
edge. With the other hand, press the 2 opposite
edges together. Place in 4 steamers lined with
waxed paper punched with holes. Cover the
har gau as you make them.

COVER AND steam the har gau over simmering
water in a wok, reversing the steamers halfway
through, for 6–8 minutes, or until the wrappers
are translucent. Serve with soy sauce, chili sauce
or a dipping sauce.

Har gau pastry is more delicate
to handle than noodle-type
wrappers. To make it easier,
keep the pastry warm and pliable
while you are working with it.

TURNIP CAKE

ONE OF THE MORE COMMON DIM SUM, TURNIP CAKE IS SOLD BY WOMEN PUSHING HOT PLATES ON

CARTS. EACH PORTION OF THE TURNIP CAKE IS FRESHLY FRIED TO ORDER. SERVE WITH LIGHT SOY

SAUCE OR A CHILI SAUCE FOR DIPPING.

2 lb Chinese turnip, grated
1 oz dried shrimp
1 1/3 cups dried Chinese
    mushrooms
5 oz Chinese sausage
    (lap cheong)
1 tablespoon oil
3 scallions, thinly sliced
3 teaspoons sugar
3 teaspoons Shaoxing rice wine
1/4 teaspoon freshly ground
    white pepper
2 tablespoons finely chopped
    cilantro
1 2/3 cups rice flour
oil for frying

MAKES 6

PLACE the turnip in a large bowl and cover with boiling water for 5 minutes. Drain, reserving any liquid, then allow the turnip to drain in a colander. When it is cool enough to handle, squeeze out any excess liquid. Place in a large bowl.

SOAK the dried shrimp in boiling water for 1 hour, then drain, adding any soaking liquid to the reserved turnip liquid.

SOAK the dried mushrooms in boiling water for 30 minutes, then drain, adding any soaking liquid to the reserved turnip liquid. Squeeze out any excess water from the mushrooms. Remove and discard the stems and finely dice the caps.

PLACE the sausage on a plate in a steamer. Cover and steam over simmering water in a wok for 10 minutes, then finely dice it.

HEAT a wok over high heat, add the oil and heat until very hot. Stir-fry the sausage for 1 minute, then add the shrimp and mushrooms and stir-fry for 2 minutes, or until fragrant. Add the scallions, sugar, rice wine and pepper, then add the turnip, cilantro and rice flour and toss to combine. Pour in 2 cups of the reserved liquid and mix well.

PLACE the mixture in a greased and lined 10 inch square cake pan (or in 2 smaller dishes if your steamers are small). Place the pan in a steamer. Cover and steam over simmering water in a wok for 1 1/4–1 1/2 hours, or until firm, replenishing with boiling water during cooking. Remove the pan and cool in the fridge overnight. Take the cake from the pan and cut into 2 inch squares that are 1/2 inch thick.

HEAT a wok over high heat, add 2 tablespoons of the oil and heat until very hot. Cook the turnip cakes in batches, adding more oil between batches if necessary, until golden and crispy.

In dim sum restaurants, turnip cake is always fried to order.

SCALLION PANCAKES

ONE OF THE MOST POPULAR SNACKS IN NORTHERN CHINA IS CRISP SCALLION PANCAKES EATEN
STRAIGHT FROM THE HOT OIL. SOME RESTAURANTS ALSO MAKE BIG, THICK PANCAKES THAT THEY CUT
INTO WEDGES AND SERVE AS AN ACCOMPANIMENT TO A MEAL.

2 cups all-purpose flour
1/2 teaspoon salt
1 tablespoon oil
3 tablespoons roasted sesame oil
2 scallions, green part only, finely
  chopped
oil for frying

MAKES 24

PLACE the flour and salt in a mixing bowl and stir
to combine. Add the oil and 3/4 cup boiling water
and, using a wooden spoon, mix to a rough
dough. Turn the dough out onto a lightly floured
surface and knead for 5 minutes, or until smooth
and elastic. If the dough is very sticky, knead in a
little more flour. Cover the dough with a cloth and
let it rest for 20 minutes.

ON a lightly floured surface, use your hands to
roll the dough into a long cylinder. Divide the
dough into 24 pieces. Working with 1 portion of
dough at a time, place the dough, cut edge
down, on the work surface. Using a small rolling
pin, roll it out to a 4 inch circle. Brush the surface
generously with the sesame oil and sprinkle with
some scallion. Starting with the edge closest to
you, roll up the dough and pinch the ends to seal
in the scallion and sesame oil. Lightly flatten the
roll, then roll it up again from one end like a snail,
pinching the end to seal it. Repeat with the
remaining dough, sesame oil and scallion. Let
the cylinders rest for 20 minutes.

PLACE EACH roll flat on the work surface and
press down with the palm of your hand. Roll out
to a 4 inch circle and place on a lightly floured
baking sheet. Stack the pancakes between lightly
floured sheets of waxed paper and allow to rest
for 20 minutes.

HEAT a frying pan over medium heat, brush the
surface with oil, and add 2 or 3 of the pancakes
at a time. Cook for 2–3 minutes on each side,
turning once, until the pancakes are light golden
brown and crisp. Remove and drain on paper
towels. Serve immediately.

YOU CAN reheat the pancakes, wrapped in
aluminium foil, in a 350°F oven for 15 minutes.

Spread the scallion through the
dough by first rolling up the
pancake and scallion, then rolling
this into a snail shape, and finally
by rolling the snail into a pancake
shape again.

Folding sesame oil into the dough means that when the breads are steamed, the layers will spring open.

STEAMED BREADS

THE BASIC YEAST DOUGH CAN BE USED TO MAKE LOTS OF DIFFERENT STEAMED BUNS, CALLED "MANTOU" IN CHINA. FLOWER ROLLS ARE ONE OF THE SIMPLEST SHAPES, WHILE SILVER THREAD ROLLS REQUIRE MORE DEXTERITY. THESE BREADS ARE DELICIOUS WITH MEATS INSTEAD OF RICE.

1 quantity basic yeast dough
 (page 278)
3 tablespoons roasted sesame oil

MAKES 12 FLOWER ROLLS
OR 6 SILVER THREAD LOAVES

CUT the dough in half and, on a lightly floured surface, roll out each half to form a 12 x 4 inch rectangle. Brush the surface of the rectangles liberally with the sesame oil. Place one rectangle directly on top of the other, with both oiled surfaces facing up. Starting with one of the long edges, roll up the dough jelly-roll style. Pinch the 2 ends to seal in the sesame oil.

LIGHTLY FLATTEN the roll with the heel of your hand and cut the roll into 2 inch pieces. Using a chopstick, press down on the center of each roll, holding the chopstick parallel to the cut edges. (This will cause the ends to "flower" when they are steamed.) Arrange the shaped rolls well spaced in 4 steamers lined with waxed paper punched with holes. Cover and let rise for 15 minutes.

COVER AND steam each steamer separately over simmering water in a wok for 15 minutes, or until the rolls are light and springy. Keep the rolls covered until you are about to eat them to make sure they stay soft.

THE DOUGH can also be shaped in other ways, one of the most popular being silver thread bread. Divide the dough in half and roll each half into a sausage about 1¼ inches in diameter, then cut each sausage into 6 pieces. Roll 6 of the pieces into rectangles 8 x 4 inches and set aside. Roll the remaining pieces into rectangles 8 x 4 inches, brush each with a little sesame oil and fold in half to a 4 inch square. Brush with more sesame oil and fold in half again. Cut into thin strips crosswise. Place one of the rectangles on the work surface and stretch the strips so they fit down the center. Fold the ends and sides in to completely enclose the strips. Repeat with the remaining dough until you have 6 loaves. Steam as for the flower rolls for 20–25 minutes.

Steaming mantou being sold in the streets in Beijing.

TEA EGGS

TEA EGGS, BRAISED IN A FRAGRANT TEA AND SOY SAUCE MIXTURE, ARE EASY TO MAKE AND GREAT FOR SNACKS—THEY CAN BE REHEATED AND TASTE EQUALLY GOOD HOT OR COLD. IN CHINA, THEY ARE FOUND IN TEA HOUSES AND ROADSIDE STANDS, OFTEN BUBBLING AWAY IN VATS FULL OF HOT TEA.

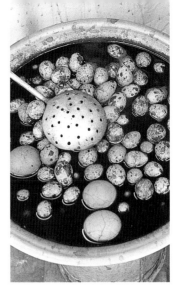

Tea eggs sold warm as a snack.

10 very fresh eggs or 20 quail eggs

TEA COOKING MIXTURE
3 tablespoons light soy sauce
3 tablespoons Shaoxing rice wine
1 star anise
1 tablespoon sugar
1 cinnamon stick
3 slices ginger, smashed with the
 flat side of a cleaver
3 tablespoons Chinese black
 tea leaves

MAKES 10 EGGS OR
20 QUAIL EGGS

PLACE the eggs in a saucepan with enough cold water to cover. Bring the water to a boil, then reduce the heat to low and let the eggs simmer for 10 minutes, or until they are hard-boiled. Refresh the eggs in cold water. Drain the eggs and lightly tap and roll the shells on a hard surface to crack them. Do not remove the shells.

PUT the tea cooking mixture ingredients in a heavy-bottomed clay pot, braising pan or saucepan with 4 cups water and heat until boiling. Reduce the heat to low and simmer for 20 minutes. Add the cooked eggs and simmer for another 45 minutes. Turn off the heat and let the eggs sit in the tea mixture until cool enough to handle. Remove the shells and serve the eggs warm or cold, cut into wedges, with some of the cooking mixture on top.

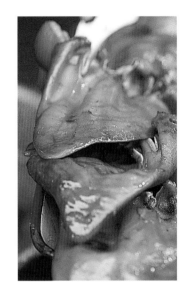

CRISPY FRIED PIG'S EAR

EVERY PART OF THE PIG IS USED IN ONE WAY OR ANOTHER IN CHINESE COOKING. HERE PIG'S EARS ARE SLOW-COOKED WHOLE TO BRING OUT THEIR MELTING, GELATINOUS QUALITIES, THEN SHREDDED AND FRIED TO GIVE THEM A CRISP COATING. EAT AS A SNACK WITH DRINKS OR AS AN APPETIZER.

1 pig's ear
1 tablespoon Shaoxing rice wine
1 tablespoon oil
2 garlic cloves, crushed
4 scallions, thinly sliced
2 tablespoons light soy sauce
1/2 teaspoon salt
2 teaspoons chili oil
2 teaspoons roasted sesame oil

SERVES 4 AS A SNACK

SCRAPE the pig's ear to get rid of any bristles and rinse. Put it in a clay pot, braising pan or saucepan, cover with water, add the rice wine and bring to the boil. Reduce the heat and simmer for 40 minutes, or until tender. Drain and allow to cool.

SLICE the ear diagonally into thin strips and finely shred the strips. Heat a wok over high heat, add the oil and heat until very hot. Cook the strips until very crisp. Add the garlic and scallions and toss together. Add the soy sauce, salt and chili and sesame oils and toss together. Serve immediately.

CRISPY FRIED PIG'S EAR

A wide variety of hot pickles are sold in the markets in Sichuan.

CANTONESE PICKLED
VEGETABLES

四川腌黄瓜

SICHUAN PICKLED CUCUMBER

THE COMPLEXITY OF FLAVORS IN THIS SIMPLE PICKLE IS UNUSUAL. THE SEASONINGS COMBINE TO CREATE

A TASTE THAT IS SIMULTANEOUSLY SWEET, SOUR, HOT AND NUMBING.

1/2 lb cucumbers
1/2 teaspoon salt
1 1/2 tablespoons finely shredded
 ginger
1/2 small red chile, seeded and
 finely shredded
3 tablespoons roasted sesame oil
1/2 teaspoon Sichuan peppercorns
6 dried chiles, seeded and cut into
 1/4 inch pieces
1 1/2 tablespoons clear rice vinegar
1 1/2 tablespoons sugar

SERVES 6 AS A SNACK

CUT the cucumbers in half lengthwise, remove the seeds, and cut into 2 1/2 inch long, 3/4 inch thick slices. Place in a bowl, add the salt, toss lightly and allow to sit for 30 minutes. Place the ginger in a bowl and soak in cold water for 20 minutes.

POUR OFF any water that has accumulated with the cucumbers, rinse the cucumbers lightly, then drain thoroughly and pat dry. Place the cucumber in a bowl with the drained ginger and chiles.

HEAT a wok over high heat, add the sesame oil and heat until very hot. Add the peppercorns and stir-fry for 15 seconds until fragrant. Add the dried chiles and stir-fry for 15 seconds, or until dark. Pour into the bowl with the cucumbers, toss lightly and allow to cool. Add the vinegar and sugar, toss to coat, then keep in the fridge for at least 6 hours or overnight. Serve cold or at room temperature.

广东腌菜

CANTONESE PICKLED VEGETABLES

VARIATIONS OF PICKLED VEGETABLE SALADS ARE FOUND ALL OVER CHINA. THIS SWEET-AND-SOUR

VERSION FROM THE SOUTH IS GOOD ALONE OR WITH SWEET-AND-SOUR SHRIMP OR PORK.

1/2 lb Chinese turnip, peeled
2 carrots
1 cucumber
1/2 teaspoon salt
1/3 cup sugar
1/3 cup clear rice vinegar
5 thin slices ginger, smashed with
 the flat side of a cleaver

SERVES 6 AS A SNACK

CUT the turnip in half lengthwise, then cut lengthwise into thirds and diagonally cut into 3/4 inch pieces. Diagonally cut the carrots into 3/4 inch pieces. Cut the cucumber in half lengthwise, remove any seeds and cut lengthwise into thirds. Diagonally cut into 3/4 inch pieces. Place the vegetables in a bowl, add the salt, toss lightly, and allow to sit for 1 hour. Dry thoroughly.

COMBINE the sugar and vinegar and stir until the sugar has dissolved. Add to the vegetables with the ginger and toss lightly to coat. Keep in the fridge for at least 6 hours, or overnight.

盐水蚕豆

SALTED SOY BEAN PODS

3/4 lb fresh soy bean pods
1 tablespoon coarse sea salt
4 star anise

SERVES 4 AS A SNACK

TRIM both ends of the soy bean pods, then place in a bowl with the salt and rub some of the fuzz off the skin. Rinse the pods. Place in a saucepan of salted water with the star anise and bring to a boil. Reduce the heat and simmer for 20 minutes, or until tender. Drain and allow to cool.

TO EAT, suck the beans out of the pods and throw the pods away. Serve as a snack.

SALTED SOY BEAN PODS

油炸花生米

FRIED PEANUTS

1 tablespoon Sichuan peppercorns
4 star anise
1 tablespoon sugar
1 teaspoon salt
2 lb shelled peanuts with skins on
3 tablespoons roasted sesame oil

SERVES 8 AS A SNACK

PUT 3 cups water in a saucepan with the spices, sugar and salt and bring to a boil. Add the peanuts and simmer for 5 minutes. Turn off the heat and allow the peanuts to cool in the liquid.

DRAIN and dry the peanuts, removing the whole spices. Heat the sesame oil in a wok and fry the peanuts until brown. Serve warm or cold as a snack.

鲁味核桃仁

CANDIED WALNUTS

1 cup sugar
4 1/2 cups shelled walnut halves
oil for deep-frying

SERVES 8 AS A SNACK

DISSOLVE the sugar in 1/2 cup water, then bring to a boil and cook for 2 minutes.

BLANCH the walnuts in a saucepan of boiling water briefly, then drain. Put immediately into the syrup, stirring to coat. Cool for 5 minutes; drain.

FILL a wok one quarter full of oil. Heat the oil to 375°F, or until a piece of bread fries golden brown in 10 seconds when dropped in the oil. Add the walnuts in batches, stirring to brown evenly. As soon as they brown, remove with a wire strainer or slotted spoon and lay on some aluminium foil, making sure they are well spaced. Do not touch as they will be hot. When cool, drain on paper towels. Serve as a snack or at the start of a meal.

FRIED PEANUTS

CANDIED WALNUTS

SOUPS

Stripping corn cobs in Yunnan.

CHICKEN AND
MUSHROOM SOUP

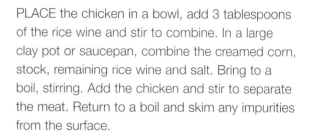

CANTONESE CORN SOUP

THIS DELECTABLE SOUP IS A CANTONESE CLASSIC. YOU NEED TO USE A GOOD-QUALITY CAN OF CREAMED CORN WITH A SMOOTH TEXTURE, OR ALTERNATIVELY, IF IT IS QUITE COARSE, QUICKLY BLEND A CAN OF CREAMED CORN IN A BLENDER OR FOOD PROCESSOR TO MAKE IT EXTRA SMOOTH.

1 lb skinned boneless chicken
  breasts, ground
1/2 cup Shaoxing rice wine
1 2/3 cups canned creamed corn
6 cups chicken stock (page 281)
1 teaspoon salt
2 1/2 tablespoons cornstarch
2 egg whites, lightly beaten
1 teaspoon roasted sesame oil

SERVES 6

PLACE the chicken in a bowl, add 3 tablespoons of the rice wine and stir to combine. In a large clay pot or saucepan, combine the creamed corn, stock, remaining rice wine and salt. Bring to a boil, stirring. Add the chicken and stir to separate the meat. Return to a boil and skim any impurities from the surface.

COMBINE the cornstarch with enough water to make a paste, add to the soup and simmer until thickened. Remove from the heat. Mix 2 tablespoons water into the egg white, then slowly add to the clay pot or saucepan in a thin stream around the edge of the saucepan. Stir once or twice, then add the sesame oil. Check the seasoning, adding more salt if necessary. Serve immediately.

CHICKEN AND MUSHROOM SOUP

FOR THIS SOUP YOU CAN USE EITHER BUTTON OR CHINESE MUSHROOMS. CHINESE MUSHROOMS ARE USUALLY LABELLED SHIITAKE (THE JAPANESE NAME FOR THEM) WHEN FRESH AND WILL ADD MORE FLAVOR TO THE FINISHED SOUP.

2 tablespoons cornstarch
3–4 egg whites, beaten
4 oz skinned, boneless chicken
  breasts, thinly sliced
3 cups chicken and meat stock
  (page 281)
1/4 lb fresh button or Chinese
  mushrooms, thinly sliced
1 teaspoon roasted sesame oil
chopped scallion

SERVES 4

COMBINE the cornstarch with enough water to make a paste. Mix 1 teaspoon each of the egg white and cornstarch paste and a pinch of salt with the chicken. Blend the remaining egg white and cornstarch mixture to a smooth paste.

BRING the stock to a rolling boil in a large clay pot or saucepan. Add the chicken and return to a boil, then add the mushrooms and salt. Return to the boil then, very slowly, pour in the egg white and cornstarch mixture, stirring constantly. As soon as the soup has thickened, add the sesame oil. Serve sprinkled with the chopped scallion.

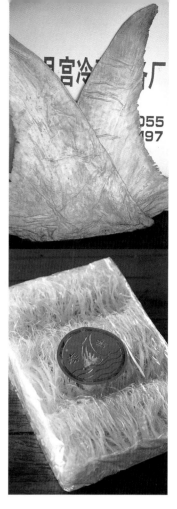

鱼 翅 汤

SHARK'S FIN SOUP

ONE OF THE MOST EXPENSIVE AND PRIZED OF ALL CHINESE DELICACIES, SHARK'S FIN IS SERVED ON
SPECIAL OCCASIONS AND AT BANQUETS. IF POSSIBLE, MAKE THE STOCK A DAY IN ADVANCE AND STORE
IN THE FRIDGE. THIS WILL IMPROVE THE FLAVORS AND ALLOW ANY FAT TO EASILY BE SKIMMED OFF.

10 oz prepackaged shark's fin
13 oz bacon or ham bones
1 lb chicken bones
1 lb beef bones
4 slices ginger
10 oz skinned boneless chicken
  breasts, ground
1 egg white, lightly beaten
4 tablespoons cornstarch
1 tablespoon light soy sauce
red rice vinegar

SERVES 6

PLACE the shark's fin in a large bowl and cover
with cold water. Allow to soak overnight. Strain
the shark's fin and rinse gently to remove any
remaining sand and sediment. Bring a stockpot
of water to a boil. Add the shark's fin, reduce the
heat and simmer, covered, for 1 hour. Strain and
set aside.

PLACE the bacon or ham bones, chicken bones
and beef bones in a large stockpot with the ginger
slices and 8 cups water. Bring to a boil, then
reduce the heat and simmer, covered, for 2 hours.
Skim off any impurities and fat during cooking.
Strain the stock, discarding the bones. Measure
the stock—you will need 6–7 cups. If you have
more, return the stock to the stockpot and reduce
it further until you have the correct amount.

COMBINE the chicken, egg white and 1 tablespoon
of the cornstarch. Set aside in the fridge.

PUT the prepared shark's fin and stock in a large
braising pan or saucepan and simmer, covered,
for 30 minutes. Add the chicken mixture and stir
to separate the meat. Simmer for 10 minutes, or
until the chicken is cooked.

SEASON the soup with the soy sauce and some
salt and white pepper. Combine the remaining
cornstarch with 1/2 cup water, add to the soup
and simmer until thickened.

SERVE the soup with some red rice vinegar,
which can be added to the soup to taste.

Shark's fin comes prepackaged,
usually compressed and shrink-
wrapped. It needs to be soaked
and simmered to soften it before
you use it.

To see if they have been fertilized, eggs are checked at the market by placing them above a light.

Scalding the tomatoes in boiling water makes it very easy to peel off their skins.

番茄蛋花湯

TOMATO AND EGG SOUP

THIS DELICIOUS AND NUTRITIOUS SOUP IS SIMPLICITY ITSELF AND IS SOMETIMES KNOWN AS EGG DROP SOUP BECAUSE THE EGG IS SLOWLY POURED IN NEAR THE END OF COOKING. MAKE SURE YOU USE RIPE TOMATOES OR BOTH THE COLOR AND FLAVOR WILL BE INSIPID.

1 lb firm ripe tomatoes
2 eggs
1 scallion, finely chopped
1 tablespoon oil
4 cups vegetable or chicken and
    meat stock (page 281)
1 tablespoon light soy sauce
1 tablespoon cornstarch

SERVES 4

SCORE a cross in the bottom of each tomato. Plunge into boiling water for 20 seconds, then drain and peel the skin away from the cross. Cut into slices or thin wedges, trimming off the core. Beat the eggs with a pinch of salt and a few pieces of scallion.

HEAT a wok over high heat, add the oil and heat until very hot. Stir-fry the scallion for a few seconds to flavor the oil, then pour in the stock and bring to a boil. Add the tomatoes and return to a boil. Add the soy sauce and very slowly pour in the beaten eggs, stirring as you pour. Return to a boil.

COMBINE the cornstarch with enough water to make a paste, add to the soup and simmer until thickened.

TOMATO AND EGG SOUP

豆腐菠菜湯

BEAN CURD AND SPINACH SOUP

THIS SIMPLE BUT BEAUTIFUL SOUP IS ALSO KNOWN AS "EMERALD AND WHITE JADE SOUP" IN CHINESE. IT IS A CLEAR SOUP, WHICH REQUIRES A VERY GOOD STOCK FOR FLAVOR, WHILE PIECES OF SOFT BEAN CURD ADD TEXTURE AND THE SPINACH ADDS COLOR AND FLAVOR.

1/4 lb soft bean curd, drained
2 cups baby spinach leaves
4 cups chicken and meat stock
    (page 281)
1 tablespoon light soy sauce

SERVES 4

CUT the bean curd into small slices about 1/4 inch thick. Chop the baby spinach leaves roughly if they are large.

BRING the stock to a rolling boil in a large clay pot or saucepan, then add the bean curd slices and soy sauce. Return to a boil, then reduce the heat and simmer gently for 2 minutes. Skim any impurities from the surface. Add the spinach and cook for 1–2 minutes. Season with salt and white pepper. Serve hot.

BEAN CURD AND SPINACH SOUP

冬瓜火腿汤

WINTER MELON AND HAM SOUP

ALTHOUGH IT LOOKS LIKE A WATERMELON, A WINTER MELON IS REALLY A MARROW OR WAX GOURD. IT IS SAID THAT WINTER MELONS WITH A GOOD COVERING OF WHITE POWDER ARE BEST. THE DELICATE FLESH BECOMES ALMOST TRANSLUCENT WHEN COOKED AND TASTES A LITTLE LIKE MARROW.

1 tablespoon dried shrimp
1/2 lb winter melon, rind and seeds removed
3 cups chicken and meat stock (page 281)
5 oz Chinese ham or prosciutto, chopped

SERVES 4

SOAK the dried shrimp in boiling water for 1 hour, then drain. Cut the winter melon into small pieces.

BRING the stock to a rolling boil in a large clay pot or saucepan. Add the shrimp, winter melon and ham. Return to a boil, then reduce the heat and simmer for 2 minutes. Season with salt and white pepper. Serve hot.

什锦菜汤

MIXED VEGETABLE SOUP

ALMOST ANY TYPE OF VEGETABLE CAN BE USED FOR THIS SOUP. CHOOSE THREE OR FOUR DIFFERENT ITEMS FROM THE INGREDIENTS LIST DEPENDING ON WHAT'S IN SEASON, BEARING IN MIND THAT THEY SHOULD CREATE A HARMONY OF COLOR AND TEXTURES.

1 lb mixed vegetables, such as carrots, baby corn, bamboo shoots, Chinese (shiitake) or button mushrooms, asparagus, spinach leaves, lettuce, cucumber, Chinese (Napa) cabbage or tomatoes
1/4 lb soft bean curd, drained
3 cups vegetable or chicken stock (page 281)
1 tablespoon light soy sauce
1/2 teaspoon roasted sesame oil
chopped scallion or chives

SERVES 4

CUT YOUR selection of vegetables and the bean curd into a roughly uniform shape and size. You can cut into shreds, cubes or slices, but the pieces should be small enough for a spoonful of soup to include several at once, giving a balance of flavors.

BRING the stock to a rolling boil in a large clay pot or saucepan. Add your selection of the carrots, corn, bamboo shoots and mushrooms first and cook for 2–3 minutes, then add any other vegetables and the bean curd and cook for 1 minute. Do not overcook the vegetables or they will become soggy and lose their crispness and delicate flavor.

SEASON WITH salt and white pepper. Add the soy sauce, drizzle with the sesame oil and sprinkle with the chopped scallion or chives.

WINTER MELON AND HAM SOUP

Using a cornstarch mixture to coat seafood before cooking is called "velveting." The coating adds a silky texture to the cooked food while protecting it and keeping it moist.

鱼片香菜汤

SLICED FISH AND CILANTRO SOUP

THE CHINESE OFTEN USE A CHICKEN AND MEAT STOCK WHEN COOKING SEAFOOD. HOWEVER, IF YOU PREFER, YOU CAN USE A VEGETABLE OR FISH STOCK FOR THIS RECIPE.

1/2 lb firm white fish fillets, such as cod, halibut or monkfish, skin removed
2 teaspoons egg white, beaten
1 teaspoon Shaoxing rice wine
2 teaspoons cornstarch
3 cups chicken and meat stock (page 281)
1 tablespoon light soy sauce
1 1/3 cups cilantro leaves

SERVES 4

CUT the fish into 3/4 x 1 1/4 inch slices. Blend the egg white, rice wine and cornstarch to make a smooth paste, and use it to coat each fish slice.

BRING the stock to a rolling boil in a large clay pot or saucepan. Add the fish slices one by one, stir gently and return to a boil. Reduce the heat and simmer for 1 minute, then add the soy sauce and cilantro leaves. Return to a boil, season with salt and white pepper and serve immediately.

西湖牛肉汤

WEST LAKE BEEF SOUP

THERE IS A WEST LAKE (AND OFTEN A NORTH, SOUTH OR EAST LAKE) IN MOST CITIES IN CHINA, SO THIS SOUP IS MORE LIKELY NAMED AFTER A LAKE IN ITS PROVINCE OF ORIGIN, GUANGZHOU, THAN THE FAMOUS WEST LAKE OF HANGZHOU.

5 oz beef top round steak
1 teaspoon salt
1 teaspoon sugar
1 tablespoon light soy sauce
1 tablespoon Shaoxing rice wine
2 tablespoons cornstarch
1/2 teaspoon roasted sesame oil
3 cups chicken and meat stock (page 281)
3/4 cup peas, fresh or frozen
1 egg, lightly beaten
chopped scallion

SERVES 4

TRIM the fat off the steak and cut the steak into small pieces, about the size of the peas. Combine the beef with a pinch of the salt, about half the sugar, 1 teaspoon each of the soy sauce, rice wine and cornstarch and the sesame oil. Marinate in the fridge for at least 20 minutes.

BRING the stock to a rolling boil in a large clay pot or saucepan. Add the beef and stir to separate the meat, then add the peas and the remaining salt, sugar, soy sauce and rice wine. Return to a boil, then stir in the egg. Combine the remaining cornstarch with enough water to make a paste, add to the soup and simmer until thickened. Garnish with the chopped scallion.

WEST LAKE BEEF SOUP

十宝炖汤

TEN-TREASURE SOUP

THIS MEAL-IN-ONE SOUP IS ALMOST A KIND OF STEW, WHERE THE INGREDIENTS SIMMER TOGETHER SO THAT THE FLAVORS MIX. TRADITIONALLY THIS SOUP HAS TEN MAIN INGREDIENTS, BUT THE EXACT NUMBER DOES NOT MATTER AND YOU CAN VARY THE INGREDIENTS DEPENDING ON WHAT'S AVAILABLE.

9 cups Chinese (Napa) cabbage
2 tablespoons oil
4 garlic cloves, smashed with the
    flat side of a cleaver
$1/2$ cup Shaoxing rice wine
6 cups chicken stock (page 281)
1 teaspoon salt
$1/2$ lb center-cut pork loin, trimmed
2 teaspoons light soy sauce
$1/2$ teaspoon roasted sesame oil
1 lb shrimp
3 slices ginger, smashed with the
    flat side of a cleaver
1 oz bean thread noodles
6 dried Chinese mushrooms
1 lb firm bean curd, drained and cut
    into 1 inch squares
2 carrots, cut into $3/4$ inch pieces
$41/2$ cups baby spinach leaves
3 scallions, green part only, cut
    diagonally into $1/2$ inch pieces

SERVES 6

Use the flat side of a cleaver to smash the garlic cloves and the blade for cutting the carrots.

REMOVE the stems from the cabbage and cut the leaves into 2 inch squares. Separate the hard cabbage pieces from the leafy ones. Heat a wok over high heat, add the oil and heat until very hot. Add the hard cabbage pieces and the garlic. Toss lightly over high heat, adding 1 tablespoon of the rice wine. Stir-fry for several minutes, then add the leafy cabbage pieces. Stir-fry for 1 minute, then add 4 tablespoons of the rice wine, the stock and half of the salt. Bring to a boil, then reduce the heat to low and cook for 30 minutes. Transfer to a clay pot or saucepan.

CUT the pork against the grain into slices about $1/8$ inch thick. Place the pork in a bowl, add the soy sauce and sesame oil, and toss lightly. Marinate in the fridge for 20 minutes.

PEEL and devein the shrimps, then place in a bowl with the ginger, remaining rice wine and salt and toss lightly. Marinate in the fridge for 20 minutes. Remove and discard the ginger.

SOAK the bean thread noodles in hot water for 10 minutes, then drain and cut into 6 inch pieces. Soak the dried mushrooms in boiling water for 30 minutes, then drain and squeeze out any excess water. Remove and discard the stems.

ARRANGE the pork slices, bean curd, mushrooms, noodles and carrots in separate piles on top of the cabbage in the casserole, leaving some space in the center for the shrimps and spinach. Cover and cook over medium heat for 20 minutes. Arrange the shrimps and spinach in the center and sprinkle with the scallions. Cover and cook for 5 minutes, or until the shrimp are pink and cooked through. Season with salt if necessary. Serve directly from the clay pot.

酸辣汤

HOT-AND-SOUR SOUP

THIS SOUP SHOULD NOT CONTAIN HOT CHILES—THE HOTNESS COMES FROM GROUND WHITE PEPPER, WHICH, IN ORDER TO GET A GOOD FLAVOR, MUST BE VERY FRESHLY GROUND.

Adding the egg to the hot soup forms egg drops. Pour it in in an even stream.

4 dried Chinese mushrooms
2 tablespoons dried black fungus
  (wood ears)
4 oz lean pork, thinly shredded
1 tablespoon cornstarch
4 oz firm bean curd, drained
1/4 cup fresh or canned bamboo
  shoots, rinsed and drained
4 cups chicken and meat stock
  (page 281)
1 teaspoon salt
1 tablespoon Shaoxing rice wine
2 tablespoons light soy sauce
1–2 tablespoons Chinese black
  rice vinegar
2 eggs, beaten
1–2 teaspoons freshly ground
  white pepper
chopped scallion

SERVES 4

SOAK the dried mushrooms in boiling water for 30 minutes, then drain and squeeze out any excess water. Remove and discard the stems and shred the caps. Soak the dried black fungus in cold water for 20 minutes, then drain and squeeze out any excess water. Shred the black fungus.

COMBINE the pork, a pinch of salt and 1 teaspoon of the cornstarch. Thinly shred the bean curd and bamboo shoots to the same size as the pork.

BRING the stock to a boil in a large clay pot or saucepan. Add the pork and stir to separate the meat, then add the mushrooms, bean curd and bamboo. Return to a boil and add the salt, rice wine, soy sauce and vinegar. Slowly pour in the egg, whisking to form thin threads, and cook for 1 minute. Combine the remaining cornstarch with enough water to make a paste, add to the soup and simmer until thick. Put the pepper in a bowl, pour in the soup and stir. Garnish with scallion.

LAMB AND CUCUMBER SOUP

羊肉黄瓜汤

LAMB AND CUCUMBER SOUP

1/2 lb lamb steak
1 tablespoon Shaoxing rice wine
1 tablespoon light soy sauce
1 teaspoon roasted sesame oil
1/2 cucumber
3 cups chicken and meat stock
  (page 281)
2 teaspoons Chinese black rice
  vinegar, or to taste
cilantro leaves

SERVES 4

CUT the lamb into very thin slices and combine with the rice wine, soy sauce and sesame oil. Marinate in the fridge for at least 15 minutes. Halve the cucumber lengthwise, discarding the seeds, and cut it into thin slices.

BRING the stock to a rolling boil in a large clay pot or saucepan. Add the lamb and stir to separate the meat. Return to a boil, then add the cucumber and rice vinegar, and season with salt and white pepper. Return to a boil. Serve garnished with the cilantro leaves.

FISH & SEAFOOD

Remove the meat from the abalone by severing the muscle that holds it to the shell. Trim off any hard patches.

New Year fireworks over Beijing.

极品海鲜（鲍鱼、焖荷兰豆和凤尾菇）

ABALONE, SNOW PEAS AND OYSTER MUSHROOMS

ABALONE IS EATEN IN CHINA AT FESTIVAL TIMES, ESPECIALLY AT NEW YEAR AS THE CHINESE NAME FOR ABALONE, "BAU YU," SOUNDS JUST LIKE THE WORDS FOR "GUARANTEED WEALTH." DRIED ABALONE IS OFTEN USED IN CHINA, BUT FRESH OR TINNED ABALONE IS MUCH EASIER TO PREPARE.

2³/4 lb fresh abalone (1 lb prepared weight) or 1 lb canned abalone
³/4 lb snow peas, ends trimmed
¹/4 lb oyster mushrooms
2 tablespoons oil
2 garlic cloves, finely chopped
2 teaspoons finely chopped ginger
2 tablespoons oyster sauce
2 teaspoons light soy sauce
1 teaspoon sugar
3 teaspoons cornstarch

SERVES 4

PREPARE the fresh abalone by removing the meat from the shell using a sharp knife. Wash the meat under cold running water, rubbing well to remove any dark-colored slime. Trim off any hard outer edges and the mouth as well as any hard patches on the bottom of the foot. Pound the meat with a mallet for 1 minute to tenderize it, but be careful not to break the flesh.

PLACE the fresh abalone in a saucepan of simmering water and cook, covered, for 2 hours, or until the meat is tender (test it by seeing if a fork will pierce the meat easily). Drain the abalone and, when it is cool enough to handle, cut it into thin slices.

IF YOU are using canned abalone, simply drain, reserving the juice, and cut into thin slices.

CUT any large snow peas in half diagonally. Halve any large oyster mushrooms.

HEAT a wok over medium heat, add the oil and heat until hot. Stir-fry the snow peas and mushrooms for 1 minute. Add the garlic and ginger and stir for 1 minute, or until aromatic.

REDUCE the heat slightly and add the oyster sauce, soy sauce, sugar and the sliced abalone. Stir well to combine. Combine the cornstarch with enough water (or the reserved abalone juice if using canned abalone) to make a paste, add to the sauce and simmer until thickened.

Test if the flesh of the fish is cooked by pressing it to see if it feels or looks flaky—you can use either a pair of chopsticks or your fingers.

CANTONESE-STYLE STEAMED FISH

ALL CHINESE COOKS, BUT PARTICULARLY THE CANTONESE, DEMAND THE FRESHEST INGREDIENTS. THE LUSH LAND OF GUANGZHOU PROVIDES FRESH VEGETABLES, AND SINCE THE REGION IS BORDERED BY THE SEA AND HAS MANY RIVERS AND LAKES, FISH IS SOLD LIVE AND KILLED JUST BEFORE COOKING.

1 1/2–2 lb whole fish, such as carp, porgy, grouper or sea bass
2 tablespoons Shaoxing rice wine
1 1/2 tablespoons light soy sauce
1 tablespoon finely chopped ginger
1 teaspoon roasted sesame oil
2 tablespoons oil
2 scallions, finely shredded
3 tablespoons finely shredded ginger
1/4 teaspoon freshly ground black pepper

SERVES 4

IF YOU do manage to buy a live fish, then ask the fishmonger to gut it through the gills. This is harder than gutting through the stomach, but leaves the fish looking whole. If you are gutting the fish yourself, make a cut from the throat to the tail and pull out the guts through the stomach. Remove any scales with a fish scaler or the back of a knife. Check that the gills have been cut out, then rinse the fish under cold, running water and drain thoroughly in a colander.

PLACE the fish in a large bowl. Add the rice wine, soy sauce, chopped ginger and sesame oil, and toss lightly to coat. Cover with plastic wrap and allow to marinate in the fridge for 10 minutes.

ARRANGE the fish on a flameproof plate, with the marinade, and place in a steamer. Steam over simmering water in a covered wok for 5–8 minutes, or until the fish flakes when the skin is pressed firmly or the dorsal fin pulls out easily. Remove the fish from the steamer and place on a flameproof platter.

HEAT a wok over high heat, add the oil and heat until smoking. Sprinkle the steamed fish with the shredded scallions, shredded ginger and pepper, and slowly pour the hot oil over the fish. This will cause the skin to crisp, and cook the garnish.

豆豉蒸蚌

STEAMED MUSSELS WITH BLACK BEAN SAUCE

MUSSELS ARE NOT EATEN AS MUCH IN CHINA AS CLAMS, HOWEVER, THEY ARE ENJOYED IN SEASIDE

AREAS. THIS RECIPE WORKS EQUALLY WELL WITH CLAMS IF YOU PREFER.

Scrub off any barnacles from the mussels, then remove the beards (byssus) by tugging on them firmly.

2 lb mussels
1 tablespoon oil
1 garlic clove, finely chopped
1/2 teaspoon finely chopped ginger
2 scallions, finely chopped
1 red chile, chopped
1 tablespoon light soy sauce
1 tablespoon Shaoxing rice wine
1 tablespoon salted, fermented
    black beans, rinsed and mashed
2 tablespoons chicken and meat
    stock (page 281)
few drops of roasted sesame oil

SERVES 4

SCRUB the mussels, remove any beards, and throw away any that do not close when tapped on the work surface.

PLACE the mussels in a large dish in a steamer. Steam over simmering water in a covered wok for 4 minutes, discarding any that do not open after this time.

MEANWHILE, HEAT the oil in a small saucepan. Add the garlic, ginger, scallions and chile and cook, stirring, for 30 seconds. Add the remaining ingredients, and blend well. Bring to a boil, then reduce the heat and simmer for 1 minute.

TO SERVE, remove and discard the top shell of each mussel, pour 2 teaspoons of the sauce into each mussel and serve on the shell.

豆醬焖蛤

CLAMS IN YELLOW BEAN SAUCE

CLAMS ARE IMMENSELY POPULAR IN CHINA AND ARE SEEN AS A SYMBOL OF GOOD FORTUNE AS THEIR

SHELLS ARE SAID TO LOOK LIKE COINS. THIS IS A VERY SIMPLE RECIPE FOR THEM.

CLAMS IN YELLOW
BEAN SAUCE

3 lb hard-shelled clams
1 tablespoon oil
2 garlic cloves, crushed
1 tablespoon grated ginger
2 tablespoons yellow bean sauce
1/2 cup chicken stock (page 281)
1 scallion, sliced

SERVES 4

WASH the clams in several changes of cold water, leaving them for a few minutes each time to remove any grit. Scrub the clams well, discarding any that remain open. Drain well.

HEAT a wok over high heat, add the oil and heat until very hot. Stir-fry the garlic and ginger for 30 seconds, then add the bean sauce and clams and toss together. Add the stock and stir for 3 minutes until the clams have opened, discarding any that do not open after this time. Season with salt and white pepper. Transfer the clams to a plate and sprinkle with the scallion.

The Li River in Guangxi.

SMOKED FISH

IN FACT, THE FISH IN THIS DISH IS NOT SMOKED AT ALL. INSTEAD IT ACQUIRES A SMOKY FLAVOR FROM BEING MARINATED AND BRAISED IN A SPICY SAUCE, THEN BEING DEEP-FRIED AND MARINATED IN THE SAUCE ONCE MORE BEFORE SERVING.

2 tablespoons light soy sauce
1 tablespoon dark soy sauce
3 tablespoons Shaoxing rice wine
2 tablespoons rock sugar
2 teaspoons five-spice powder
1 scallion, finely chopped
2 teaspoons finely chopped ginger
1 lb firm white fish fillets, such as monkfish, rock cod or sea bass, with skin
1¼ cups chicken and meat stock (page 281)
oil for deep-frying
cilantro leaves

SERVES 6

MIX together the soy sauces, rice wine, sugar, five-spice powder, scallion and ginger. Pat dry the fish and leave in the marinade for 1 hour. Transfer the fish and marinade to a clay pot or saucepan. Add the stock and bring to a boil. Reduce the heat and simmer gently for 10 minutes, or until the fish is cooked through, then drain the fish, reserving the marinade.

FILL a wok one quarter full of oil. Heat the oil to 375°F, or until a piece of bread fries golden brown in 10 seconds when dropped in the oil. Carefully cook the fish in batches for 3–4 minutes, or until golden and crisp (it will spit a little). Remove the fish from the oil and return it to the marinade. Allow to cool for 2–3 hours.

REMOVE the fish from the marinade and allow to dry for a few minutes. Cut the fish into thin slices and serve cold, sprinkled with cilantro leaves.

THE MARINADE can be reused as a "Master Sauce" (see page 290).

Fishermen on the Li River use tame cormorants to catch fish.

油炸椒盐苏东

DEEP-FRIED SQUID FLOWERS WITH SPICY SALT

1 lb squid bodies
1 teaspoon ginger juice (page 285)
1 tablespoon Shaoxing rice wine
oil for deep-frying
2 teaspoons spicy salt and pepper
  (page 285)
cilantro leaves

SERVES 4

OPEN UP the squid bodies and scrub off any soft jelly-like substance, then score the inside of the flesh with a fine crisscross pattern, making sure you do not cut all the way through. Cut the squid into 1¹/₄ x 2 inch pieces.

BLANCH the squid in a saucepan of boiling water for 25–30 seconds—each piece will curl up and the crisscross pattern will open out, hence the name "squid flower." Remove, refresh in cold water, then drain and dry. Marinate in the ginger juice and the rice wine for 25–30 minutes.

FILL a wok one quarter full of oil. Heat the oil to 350°F, or until a piece of bread fries golden brown in 15 seconds when dropped into the oil. Cook the squid for 35–40 seconds, then carefully remove and drain well. Sprinkle with the spicy salt and pepper and toss to coat. Serve sprinkled with the cilantro.

Score the inside of the squid with fine lines in a crisscross pattern before cutting into pieces.

STIR-FRIED SQUID FLOWERS WITH PEPPERS

辣椒炒苏东

STIR-FRIED SQUID FLOWERS WITH PEPPERS

13 oz squid bodies
3 tablespoons oil
2 tablespoons salted, fermented
  black beans, rinsed and mashed
1 small onion, cut into small cubes
1 small green pepper, cut into small
  cubes
3–4 small slices ginger
1 scallion, cut into short lengths
1 small red chile, chopped
1 tablespoon Shaoxing rice wine
¹/₂ teaspoon roasted sesame oil

SERVES 4

OPEN UP the squid bodies and scrub off any soft jelly-like substance, then score the inside of the flesh with a fine crisscross pattern, making sure you do not cut all the way through. Cut the squid into 1¹/₄ x 2 inch pieces.

BLANCH the squid in a saucepan of boiling water for 25–30 seconds—each piece will curl up and the crisscross pattern will open out, hence the name "squid flower." Remove and refresh in cold water, then drain and dry well.

HEAT a wok over high heat, add the oil and heat until very hot. Stir-fry the black beans, onion, green pepper, ginger, scallion and chile for 1 minute. Add the squid and rice wine, mix together and stir for 1 minute. Sprinkle with the sesame oil.

WEST LAKE FISH

HANGZHOU IN THE EAST OF CHINA IS FAMOUS FOR ITS REFINED CUISINE AND EXQUISITE SCENERY. A SPECIALTY OF THIS REGION IS WEST LAKE FISH MADE WITH FRESHWATER CARP. THE POACHING METHOD IS UNIQUE AND QUITE INGENIOUS AS THE FISH IS COOKED OFF THE HEAT.

3¹/₂ lb whole fish, such as carp, porgy, grouper or sea bass
4 tablespoons Shaoxing rice wine
2 teaspoons salt
4 slices ginger, smashed with the flat side of a cleaver
4 scallions, sliced and smashed with the flat side of a cleaver
1 tablespoon oil
2 tablespoons finely shredded ginger
1 scallion, finely shredded
1 red chile, seeded and finely shredded
¹/₂ teaspoon freshly ground white pepper
2¹/₂ tablespoons light soy sauce
2 tablespoons sugar
2 tablespoons Chinese black rice vinegar
1 tablespoon cornstarch

SERVES 6

IF YOU do manage to buy a live fish, then ask the fishmonger to gut it through the gills. This is harder than gutting through the stomach, but leaves the fish looking whole. If you are gutting the fish yourself, make a cut from the throat to the tail and pull out the guts through the stomach. Remove any scales with a fish scaler or the back of a knife. Check that the gills have been cut out, then rinse the fish under cold, running water and drain thoroughly in a colander.

DIAGONALLY score both sides of the fish, cutting through as far as the bone at intervals of ³/₄ inch.

COMBINE 1 tablespoon of the rice wine, 1 teaspoon of the salt, the ginger slices and smashed scallions. Pinch the ginger slices and the scallions in the marinade repeatedly for several minutes to impart their flavors into the marinade. Rub the marinade all over the outside of the fish and into the slits. Allow the fish to marinate in the refrigerator for 30 minutes.

BRING 16 cups water to a boil in a wok with the oil and remaining rice wine. Gently lower the fish into the poaching liquid and return to a boil. Turn off the heat, cover, and allow to sit for 20 minutes, or until the fish flakes when the skin is pressed firmly or the dorsal fin pulls out easily. If the fish is not cooked through, cook over low heat for 5 minutes. Using slotted spoons, carefully transfer the fish to a platter. Reserve 1¹/₂ cups of the poaching liquid. Sprinkle the ginger, shredded scallion, chile and white pepper over the fish.

ADD the soy sauce, remaining salt, sugar and black vinegar to the liquid. Heat the wok over high heat, add the liquid and bring to a boil. Combine the cornstarch with enough water to make a paste, add to the sauce and simmer until thickened. Pour the sauce over the fish.

Rinse the fish thoroughly, making sure that all the scales are washed off—scales left on will be hard and unpalatable. Marinating the fish not only adds flavor but also makes it aromatic and less "fishy" tasting.

青菜炒干贝

STIR-FRIED SCALLOPS WITH CHINESE GREENS

THIS DISH EMPHASIZES THE FRESHNESS AND DELICATE SEASONING THAT GIVE CANTONESE CUISINE ITS REPUTATION, WHILE A HIGH HEAT AND SHORT COOKING TIME ARE ALSO ESSENTIAL TO ITS SUCCESS. CHINESE BROCCOLI OR BOK CHOY IS TRADITIONALLY USED, BUT YOU COULD USE REGULAR BROCCOLI.

11 oz scallops, roe removed
2 tablespoons Shaoxing rice wine
1 tablespoon roasted sesame oil
1 teaspoon finely chopped ginger
1/2 scallion, finely chopped
1 bunch (about 1/2 lb) Chinese
    broccoli (gai lan) or bok choy
1/3 cup chicken stock (page 281)
1/2 teaspoon salt
1/4 teaspoon sugar
1/4 teaspoon freshly ground white
    pepper
1 teaspoon cornstarch
1 tablespoon oil
1 tablespoon finely shredded ginger
1 scallion, finely shredded
1 garlic clove, very thinly sliced

SERVES 6

SLICE the small, hard white muscle off the side of each scallop and pull off any membrane. Rinse the scallops and drain. Holding a knife blade parallel to the cutting surface, slice each scallop in half horizontally. Place the scallops in a bowl with 1 tablespoon of the rice wine, 1/4 teaspoon of the sesame oil and the chopped ginger and scallion. Toss lightly, then leave to marinate for 20 minutes.

WASH the broccoli well. Discard any tough-looking stems and diagonally cut into 3/4 inch pieces through the stem and the leaf. Blanch the Chinese broccoli in a pan of boiling water for 2 minutes, or until the stems and leaves are just tender, then refresh in cold water and dry thoroughly.

COMBINE the chicken stock, salt, sugar, white pepper, cornstarch and the remaining rice wine and sesame oil.

HEAT a wok over high heat, add the oil and heat until very hot. Add the scallops and stir-fry for 30 seconds, then remove. Add the shredded ginger, shredded scallion and garlic and stir-fry for 10 seconds. Add the stock mixture and cook, stirring constantly, until the sauce thickens. Add the Chinese broccoli and scallops. Toss lightly to coat with the sauce.

Slice the white muscle off the side of each scallop—these will be hard and rubbery if left on and cooked. Stir-fry the scallops in the sauce for only a few seconds just to heat them through; if they overcook they can be tough.

青菜炒干贝

A fresh produce market in Sichuan.

酸甜素菜拌虾

SWEET-AND-SOUR SHRIMP WITH VEGETABLES

SWEET AND SOUR IS PROBABLY ONE OF THE MOST ABUSED CHINESE DISHES, BUT WHEN WELL DONE IT CAN BE ONE OF THE MOST PLEASING. THE KEY IS THE SAUCE, WHICH HAS EQUAL AMOUNTS OF RICE VINEGAR AND SUGAR TO GIVE IT ITS SWEET-AND-SOUR FLAVOR.

Bottles of condiments and sauces for sale in a grocery shop in Beijing.

1¹/₂ lb shrimp
2 tablespoons Shaoxing rice wine
2 slices ginger, smashed with the
    flat side of a cleaver
3 teaspoons roasted sesame oil
1¹/₂ tablespoons cornstarch
¹/₂ cup oil
2 scallions, white part only, finely
    chopped
1 tablespoon finely chopped ginger
2 garlic cloves, finely chopped
1 red pepper, diced
1 green pepper, diced
2¹/₂ tablespoons tomato ketchup
2 tablespoons clear rice vinegar
2 tablespoons sugar
1 teaspoon light soy sauce
¹/₂ teaspoon salt

SERVES 6

PEEL the shrimp, score each one along the length of the back so the shrimp will "butterfly" when cooked, and devein them. Place the shrimp in a bowl and add the rice wine, ginger, 2 teaspoons of the sesame oil and 1 tablespoon of the cornstarch. Pinch the ginger slices in the marinade repeatedly for several minutes to impart the flavor into the marinade. Toss lightly, then allow to marinate for 20 minutes. Discard the ginger slices and drain the shrimp.

HEAT a wok over high heat, add 2 tablespoons of the oil and heat until very hot. Add half the shrimp and toss lightly over high heat for about 1¹/₂ minutes, or until the shrimp turn pink and curl up. Remove with a wire strainer or slotted spoon and drain. Repeat with another 2 tablespoons of the oil and the remaining shrimp. Pour out the oil and wipe out the wok.

REHEAT the wok over high heat, add the remaining oil and heat until very hot. Add the scallion, ginger and garlic and stir-fry for 15 seconds, or until fragrant. Add the red and green pepper and stir-fry for 1 minute. Combine the tomato ketchup, rice vinegar, sugar, soy sauce, salt and the remaining sesame oil and cornstarch with ¹/₂ cup water, add to the sauce and simmer until thickened. Add the shrimp and toss lightly to coat.

芙蓉龙虾

LOBSTER FU RONG

THE WORDS "FU RONG" MEAN EGG WHITES AND IN RECIPES DENOTE A CLASSIC CANTONESE COOKING METHOD, THOUGH THE TERM IS OFTEN ASSOCIATED WITH THE QUITE DIFFERENT EGG FOO YOUNG OF WESTERN CHINESE RESTAURANTS. THIS DISH CAN BE MADE WITH ANY KIND OF SEAFOOD.

1 lb lobster meat
3 tablespoons Shaoxing rice wine
3 teaspoons finely chopped ginger
1 1/2 teaspoons salt
12 egg whites
1/2 teaspoon cream of tartar
oil for deep-frying
1/2 cup chicken stock (page 281)
1/4 teaspoon freshly ground white
  pepper
1 teaspoon roasted sesame oil
1 teaspoon cornstarch
2 scallions, finely chopped
2 scallions, green part only, sliced

SERVES 6

CUT the lobster meat into pieces, put in a bowl with 1 tablespoon of the rice wine, 1 teaspoon of the ginger and 1/2 teaspoon of the salt and toss lightly to coat. Beat the egg whites and cream of tartar using a hand whisk or electric mixer until stiff. Fold the lobster into the egg white mixture.

FILL a wok one quarter full of oil. Heat the oil to 375°F, or until a piece of bread fries golden brown in 10 seconds when dropped in the oil. Pour the lobster into the wok in batches—do not stir, otherwise it will scatter, but gently stir the oil from the bottom of the wok so that the "fu rong" rises to the surface. Remove each batch as soon as it is set, without letting it go too brown, and drain well. Pour the oil out, reserving 2 tablespoons.

COMBINE the chicken stock, remaining rice wine and salt, white pepper, sesame oil and cornstarch.

REHEAT the reserved oil over high heat until very hot and stir-fry the finely chopped scallion and the remaining ginger for 10 seconds, or until fragrant. Add the stock mixture and cook, stirring constantly to prevent lumps, until thickened. Add the cooked lobster mixture and carefully toss it in the sauce. Transfer to a serving platter, sprinkle with the sliced scallions and serve.

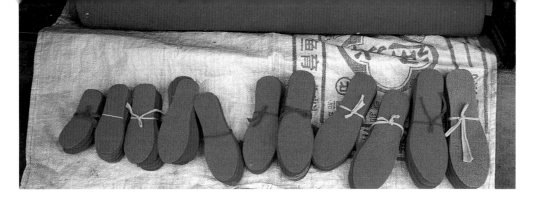

JELLYFISH AND CHICKEN SALAD

JELLYFISH ARE ONLY EVER EATEN ONCE THEY HAVE BEEN PRESERVED AND DRIED. THEY HAVE A CRUNCHY TEXTURE AND ARE NOT LIKE JELLY. YOU CAN BUY THEM DRIED, CUT INTO STRIPS OR WHOLE, AND ALSO ALREADY RECONSTITUTED IN VACUUM PACKS. THE LATTER ARE MUCH EASIER TO USE.

12 oz dried or prepackaged jellyfish
2³/₄ lb chicken
2 celery stalks, cut into 2 inch
　pieces and finely shredded
1 carrot, cut into 2 inch pieces
　and finely shredded
1 tablespoon oyster sauce
2 teaspoons light soy sauce
2 teaspoons roasted sesame oil
³/₄ cup cilantro leaves
3 teaspoons sesame seeds

DRESSING
³/₄ cup clear rice vinegar
¹/₄ cup sugar
1 tablespoon finely chopped ginger
3 scallions, thinly sliced

SERVES 8

TO PREPARE dried jellyfish, remove from the package, cover with tepid water and soak overnight. Drain, then rinse to remove any sand and sediment. Drain well. Cut into strands using a pair of scissors, then cut any long strands into shorter pieces. If you are using vacuum-packed jellyfish, remove it from the package and rinse.

RINSE the chicken, drain, and remove any fat from the cavity opening and around the neck. Cut off and discard the tail. Bring a large saucepan of water to a boil. Add the chicken and bring the water to a gentle simmer. Cook, covered, for 25–30 minutes, or until the chicken is cooked through. Remove the chicken from the saucepan and plunge into cold water. When cool enough to handle, remove the skin and bones from the chicken and finely shred the meat.

PLACE the chicken in a large bowl and add the jellyfish, celery, carrot, oyster sauce, soy sauce, sesame oil and cilantro. Mix well to combine.

TO MAKE the dressing, place the vinegar and sugar in a bowl and stir until dissolved. Stir in the ginger and scallions.

TOAST the sesame seeds by dry-frying in a pan until brown and popping. Sprinkle the salad with the sesame seeds and serve cold with the dressing on the side.

It is easiest to cut the jellyfish using a pair of scissors. Make sure you keep the strands roughly the same width.

Cut the last 2 joints off all the crab legs as these don't contain much meat.

辣椒螃蟹

CHILI CRAB

4 x ¹/₂ lb live crabs
3 tablespoons oil
1 tablespoon Guilin chili sauce
2 tablespoons light soy sauce
3 teaspoons clear rice vinegar
4 tablespoons Shaoxing rice wine
¹/₂ teaspoon salt
2 tablespoons sugar
2 tablespoons chicken stock
  (page 281)
1 tablespoon grated ginger
2 garlic cloves, crushed
2 scallions, finely chopped

SERVES 4

TO KILL the crabs humanely, put them in the freezer for 1 hour. Bring a large saucepan of water to a boil. Plunge the crabs into boiling water for about 1 minute, then rinse them in cold water. Twist off and discard the upper shell, and remove and discard the spongy grey gill tissue from inside the crab. Rinse the bodies and drain well. Cut away the last two hairy joints of the legs. Cut each crab into 4 to 6 pieces, cutting so that a portion of the body is attached to 1 or 2 legs. Crack the crab claws using crab crackers or the back edge of a cleaver—this will help the flavoring penetrate the crab meat.

HEAT a wok over high heat, add 1 tablespoon of the oil and heat until very hot. Add half the crab and fry for several minutes to cook the meat right through. Remove and drain. Repeat with another tablespoon of the oil and the remaining crab.

COMBINE the chili sauce, soy sauce, rice vinegar, rice wine, salt, sugar and stock.

REHEAT the wok over high heat, add the remaining oil and heat until very hot. Stir-fry the ginger, garlic and scallions for 10 seconds. Add the sauce mixture to the wok and cook briefly. Add the crab pieces and toss lightly to coat with the sauce. Cook, covered, for 5 minutes, then serve immediately.

CRAB IS best eaten with your hands, so supply finger bowls as well as special picks to help remove the meat from the crab claws.

AT A WEDDING BANQUET food is often presented in pairs, like these dumplings and wrapped lettuce parcels, to symbolize marriage. Ducks represent fidelity in Chinese culture because mandarin ducks live in couples for their whole lives. They are used to symbolize a pair that is not identical but belongs together. Here two egg white ducks float on top of a soup.

BANQUET

FOOD PLAYS AN IMPORTANT PART IN THE CHINESE FESTIVALS THAT MARK THE PASSING OF THE YEAR AND LIFE ITSELF, FROM CHINESE NEW YEAR TO THE MOON FESTIVAL, AND FROM BIRTH THROUGH TO MARRIAGE AND EVEN DEATH.

A banquet can be a social or commercial event to celebrate anything from a graduation to a successful business deal. Dishes are chosen carefully as different foods symbolize instantly recognizable meanings to the guests, while the number of courses and even the colour of the food (red and yellow are particularly lucky colours) are important.

Banquets can consist of 10 to 15 courses or even more, though often eight dishes are served as in Chinese the word 'eight' sounds like the word for prosperity and success, or sometimes nine as this word sounds like long-lasting. As each course is served, the host respectfully offers the choice pieces to the honoured guest or perhaps the eldest. The banquet traditionally starts with a beautifully arranged cold platter of sliced meats, seafood and nuts, to be picked at during the toasts. This is followed by some deep-fried, steamed or stir-fried dishes, then shark's fin or another special soup. Next come the main dishes featuring the most expensive and prestigious ingredients: poultry, usually whole, or possibly a roast suckling pig. At New Year, a fish course will be served last so that some may remain on the table for the start of the next year. Simple rice and noodle dishes come at the end to fill up any gaps. Finally fresh fruit, a sweet soup or the equivalent of petits fours are served.

THE LUNAR NEW YEAR is welcomed in with a huge family feast—each dish promising good luck and happiness for the year to come. Shops and homes are decorated in red and yellow and on New Year's Day, envelopes of lucky money and tangerines are exchanged with family and friends. The Lantern Festival marks the end of the festivities, with tiny dumplings and fireworks.

BIRTHDAYS AND MARRIAGES

A child's first celebration occurs at a month old and is a big family affair, with healing dishes of chicken and pig's trotters for the mother. Birthdays are then only celebrated enthusiastically after the age of 60 and every decade thereafter. A marriage is usually an extravagant affair, with a banquet following the ceremony that may involve hundreds of guests. The couple traditionally perform a tea ceremony for their parents.

FESTIVALS

The New Year is the most important festival: houses are cleaned, debts paid and special food prepared. The New Year's Eve meal is a family affair at home, after which the festival continues with 2 weeks of visiting family and friends and eating. The Qing Ming and Hungry Ghosts Festivals honour the dead, offering food to placate the spirits, and moon cakes, pastries filled with egg yolk, are eaten at the Moon Festival.

DURING CHINESE NEW YEAR gods are pasted on the doors of houses along with sayings that wish for happiness, wealth, longevity and fertility, the most longed-for states.

A market stall in Sichuan.

川式焖虾

SICHUAN-STYLE BRAISED SHRIMP

ALSO KNOWN AS CHILI OR SPICY SHRIMP, THIS IS ONE OF THE MOST POPULAR DISHES IN CHINESE RESTAURANTS. USE UNCOOKED, UNPEELED SHRIMP WITH THEIR HEADS AND TAILS STILL ATTACHED FOR THE BEST RESULTS, AS THE SHELLS ADD FLAVOR TO THE SAUCE.

16 large prawns
oil for deep-frying
1 tablespoon oil, extra
1 garlic clove, finely chopped
1/2 teaspoon finely chopped ginger
1 tablespoon light soy sauce
1 tablespoon Shaoxing rice wine
1 tablespoon chile bean paste
  (toban jiang)
1 teaspoon sugar
3–4 tablespoons chicken and meat
  stock (page 281)
1 teaspoon clear rice vinegar
1 scallion, finely chopped
2 red chiles, finely chopped
1/4 teaspoon roasted sesame oil
2 teaspoons cornstarch
cilantro leaves

SERVES 4

PULL OFF the legs from the shrimp, but leave the body shells on. Using a pair of scissors, cut each shrimp along the back to devein it.

FILL a wok one quarter full of oil. Heat the oil to 375°F, or until a piece of bread fries golden brown in 10 seconds when dropped in the oil. Cook the shrimp in batches for 2 minutes, or until they turn bright orange. Remove and drain. It is important to keep the oil hot for each batch or the shells with not turn crisp. Pour out the oil and wipe out the wok.

REHEAT the wok over high heat, add the extra oil and heat until very hot. Cook the garlic and ginger for a few seconds to flavor the oil. Add the soy sauce, rice wine, chile bean paste, sugar and stock. Stir to combine, then bring to a boil. Add the shrimp and cook for 1 minute, then add the rice vinegar, scallion, chiles and sesame oil, stirring constantly. Combine the cornstarch with enough water to make a paste, add to the sauce and simmer until thickened. Serve sprinkled with the cilantro leaves, and provide finger bowls.

Loosen the shrimp's dark, vein-like digestive tract with the point of some scissors, then gently pull it out.

上海式五柳鱼

SHANGHAI-STYLE FIVE-WILLOW FISH

THIS IS A VARIATION ON THE CLASSIC SWEET-AND-SOUR FISH (SEE PAGE 117). THE "FIVE-WILLOW" REFERS TO THE FIVE SHREDDED VEGETABLES USED FOR THE SAUCE, WHILE THE AROMATICS TRADITIONALLY REMOVED ANY "FISHY" TASTE FROM THE FRESHWATER FISH.

3–4 dried Chinese mushrooms
1 1/2–2 lb whole fish, such as carp, porgy, grouper or sea bass
1 teaspoon salt
oil for deep-frying
2 tablespoons oil, extra
1 tablespoon shredded ginger
2 scallions, shredded
1/2 small carrot, shredded
1/2 small green pepper, shredded
1/2 celery stalk, shredded
2 red chiles, seeded and finely shredded
2 tablespoons light soy sauce
3 tablespoons sugar
3 tablespoons Chinese black rice vinegar
1 tablespoon Shaoxing rice wine
1/2 cup chicken and meat stock (page 281)
1 tablespoon cornstarch
1/2 teaspoon roasted sesame oil

SERVES 4

SOAK the dried mushrooms in boiling water for 30 minutes, then drain and squeeze out any excess water. Remove and discard the stems. Finely shred the caps.

IF YOU do manage to buy a live fish, then ask the fishmonger to gut it through the gills. This is harder than gutting through the stomach, but leaves the fish looking whole. If you are gutting the fish yourself, make a cut from the throat to the tail and pull out the guts through the stomach. Remove any scales with a fish scaler or the back of a knife. Check that the gills have been cut out, then rinse the fish under cold, running water and drain thoroughly in a colander.

DIAGONALLY score both sides of the fish, cutting through as far as the bone at intervals of 3/4 inch. Rub the salt all over the inside and outside of the fish and into the slits.

FILL a wok one quarter full of oil. Heat the oil to 375°F, or until a piece of bread fries golden brown in 10 seconds when dropped in the oil. Holding the fish by its tail, gently and carefully lower it into the oil. Cook the fish for 3–4 minutes on each side, or until the fish flakes when the skin is pressed firmly or the dorsal fin pulls out easily. Remove from the wok and drain on paper towels, then place on a dish and keep warm in a low oven. Pour out the oil and wipe out the wok.

REHEAT the wok over high heat, add the extra oil and heat until very hot. Stir-fry the mushrooms, ginger, scallion, carrot, green pepper, celery and chiles for 1 1/2 minutes. Add the soy sauce, sugar, rice vinegar, rice wine and stock, and bring to a boil. Combine the cornstarch with enough water to make a paste, add to the sauce and simmer until thickened. Add the sesame oil, blend well and spoon over the fish.

The Oriental Pearl Tower in Pudong, Shanghai.

SEA CUCUMBER WITH MUSHROOMS

SEA CUCUMBER, OR BECHE-DE-MER, IS SOLD DRIED OR RECONSTITUTED. THE DRIED TYPE NEEDS A LOT

OF SOAKING TO REHYDRATE AND BECOMES GELATINOUS IN TEXTURE. SEA CUCUMBER HAS NO FLAVOR

OF ITS OWN, BUT ABSORBS FLAVORS FROM WHATEVER IT IS COOKED WITH.

3 dried or reconstituted
  sea cucumbers
24 dried Chinese mushrooms
4 tablespoons oil
1 skinned, boneless chicken breast,
  cut into 3/4 inch cubes
1 egg white
3–4 tablespoons cornstarch
1 tablespoon light soy sauce
3 tablespoons oyster sauce
3 teaspoons sugar
2 scallions, cut into 3/4 inch pieces

SERVES 4

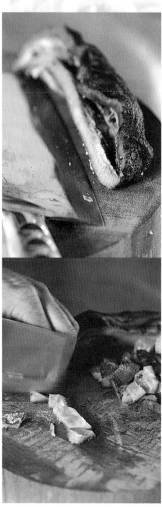

TO PREPARE the dried sea cucumbers, allow up to 4 days for them to rehydrate. On the first day, soak the cucumbers in water overnight. Drain and cook in a saucepan of simmering water for 1 hour, then drain again. Re-soak overnight and repeat the cooking and soaking process at least 3 times to allow the sea cucumbers to soften. Once softened, cut the sea cucumbers in half lengthwise, scrape out and discard the insides and cut into chunks. If you are using reconstituted sea cucumbers, they only need to be rinsed, drained and have the insides discarded before cutting into chunks.

PLACE the dried mushrooms in a saucepan and add 2 cups water and half the oil. Cover, bring to a boil, then reduce the heat and simmer for 1 hour. Drain the mushrooms, reserving 1 cup of the liquid. Remove and discard the stems.

COMBINE the chicken with the egg white and 1 tablespoon of the cornstarch until it is completely coated. Heat a wok over high heat, add the remaining oil and heat until very hot. Stir-fry the chicken pieces in batches for 3 minutes, or until browned. Return all the chicken to the wok and add the sea cucumber, mushrooms, reserved liquid, soy sauce, oyster sauce, sugar and scallions. Stir to combine, then cook for 2 minutes.

COMBINE the remaining cornstarch with enough water to make a paste, add to the sauce and simmer until thickened.

Slice the sea cucumber in half and scrape out the insides, leaving the cavity clean. Cut the sea cucumber into chunks.

鸳鸯大虾

LOVE BIRDS SHRIMP

THE CHINESE NAME FOR THIS DISH, YUAN YANG XIA, REFERS TO MANDARIN DUCKS KNOWN AS "LOVE BIRDS" BECAUSE THEY ARE ALWAYS SEEN TOGETHER, SYMBOLIZING AFFECTION AND HAPPINESS. DISHES WITH ONE MAIN INGREDIENT PRESENTED IN TWO WAYS OFTEN REPRESENT THIS IN CHINESE COOKING.

1¼ lb large shrimp
1 tablespoon cornstarch
¹/₂ egg white, beaten
oil for deep-frying
¹/₄ lb snow peas, ends trimmed
¹/₂ teaspoon salt
¹/₂ teaspoon sugar
1 scallion, finely chopped
1 teaspoon finely chopped ginger
1 tablespoon light soy sauce
1 tablespoon Shaoxing rice wine
¹/₂ teaspoon roasted sesame oil
1 tablespoon chile bean paste
   (toban jiang)
1 tablespoon tomato paste

SERVES 4

PEEL and devein the shrimp, leaving the tails intact. Combine the cornstarch with enough water to make a paste. Stir in the egg white and a pinch of salt, then stir in the shrimp.

FILL a wok one quarter full of oil. Heat the oil to 350°F, or until a piece of bread fries golden brown in 15 seconds when dropped in the oil. Cook the shrimp for 1 minute, stirring to separate them. Remove the shrimp from the wok with a wire strainer or slotted spoon as soon as the color changes, then drain. Pour the oil out, reserving 1 tablespoon.

REHEAT the reserved oil over high heat until very hot and stir-fry the snow peas with the salt and sugar for 1¹/₂ minutes. Remove and place in the center of a serving platter.

REHEAT the wok again and stir-fry the scallion and ginger for a few seconds. Add the shrimps, soy sauce and rice wine, blend well and stir-fry for about 30 seconds, then add the sesame oil. Transfer about half of the shrimp to one end of the serving platter.

ADD the chile bean paste and tomato purée to the remaining shrimps, blend well, tossing to coat the shrimp, then transfer the shrimp to the other end of the platter.

A theatrical wedding in progress in Hangzhou.

SWEET-AND-SOUR FISH FILLETS

THIS SWEET-AND-SOUR DISH IS SUBTLY VINEGARY AND HAS JUST A FAINT TOUCH OF SWEETNESS.

SWEET-AND-SOUR FISH IS EATEN ALL OVER CHINA, OFTEN USING A WHOLE DEEP-FRIED FISH, BUT

THIS RECIPE COMES FROM THE SOUTH-EAST AND IS A GREAT WAY TO COOK FISH FILLETS.

1 lb firm white fish fillets, such as
  monkfish, rock cod or sea bass,
  skin removed
1/2 teaspoon salt
1 1/2 tablespoons Shaoxing rice
  wine
1 egg, beaten
3–4 tablespoons all-purpose flour
oil for deep-frying
1/2 teaspoon chopped ginger
1 scallion, finely chopped
1/3 cup chicken and meat stock
  (page 281)
2 tablespoons light soy sauce
1 tablespoon sugar
2 tablespoons clear rice vinegar
1 red chile, finely chopped (optional)
1 tablespoon cornstarch
1/2 teaspoon roasted sesame oil
cilantro leaves

SERVES 4

PAT DRY the fish, cut into 1 1/4 inch cubes and marinate with the salt and 2 teaspoons of the rice wine for about 15–20 minutes.

MEANWHILE, blend the egg and flour with a little water to form a smooth batter with the consistency of heavy cream. Coat the fish cubes with the batter.

FILL a wok one quarter full of oil. Heat the oil to 350°F, or until a piece of bread fries golden brown in 15 seconds when dropped in the oil. Carefully lower the pieces of fish, one by one, into the hot oil and stir gently to make sure they do not stick together. Cook for about 3 minutes, or until golden. Remove and drain well on crumpled paper towels. Pour out the oil, reserving 1 tablespoon, and wipe out the wok.

REHEAT the reserved oil over high heat until very hot and add the ginger, scallion, stock, soy sauce, remaining rice wine, sugar and half the rice vinegar. Bring to a boil, then reduce the heat and simmer for 30 seconds. Add the fish pieces and cook for 2 minutes. Add the chile, if using, and the remaining rice vinegar. Combine the cornstarch with enough water to make a paste, add to the sauce and simmer until thickened.

SPRINKLE the fish with the sesame oil and the cilantro leaves to serve.

You can use your wok for deep-frying, but make sure that it is really steady on the wok burner. A wire strainer drains away more oil than a slotted spoon and leaves the batter less greasy.

Dried fish in the market in Guangzhou.

Carefully lower the whole fish into the hot oil. If you like you can gently hold the fish open with a fish lifter so the oil can get inside the cavity easily.

A girl in a traditional headdress in Dali, Yunnan.

豆酱金目鲈

WHOLE FISH WITH YELLOW BEAN SAUCE

1¹/₂–2 lb whole fish, such as carp, porgy, grouper or sea bass
1 tablespoon light soy sauce
1 tablespoon Shaoxing rice wine
oil for deep-frying
1 tablespoon shredded ginger
2 scallions, thinly shredded
1 teaspoon sugar
1 tablespoon dark soy sauce
2 tablespoons yellow bean sauce
¹/₂ cup chicken and meat stock (page 281)
¹/₂ teaspoon roasted sesame oil

SERVES 4

IF YOU do manage to buy a live fish, then ask the fishmonger to gut it through the gills. This is harder than gutting through the stomach, but leaves the fish looking whole. If you are gutting the fish yourself, make a cut from the throat to the tail and pull out the guts through the stomach. Remove any scales with a fish scaler or the back of a knife. Check that the gills have been cut out, then rinse the fish under cold, running water and drain thoroughly in a colander.

DIAGONALLY score both sides of the fish, cutting through as far as the bone at intervals of ³/₄ inch. Place the fish in a shallow dish with the light soy sauce and rice wine and allow to marinate for 10–15 minutes, then drain off any liquid, reserving the marinade.

FILL a wok one quarter full of oil. Heat the oil to 375°F, or until a piece of bread fries golden brown in 10 seconds when dropped in the oil. Holding the fish by its tail, gently and carefully lower it into the oil, bending the body so that the cuts open up. Cook for 5 minutes, or until golden brown, tilting the wok so that the entire fish is cooked in the oil. Remove and drain on crumpled paper towels and keep warm in a low oven. Pour the oil from the wok, leaving 1¹/₂ tablespoons.

REHEAT the reserved oil over high heat until very hot. Add the ginger, scallions, sugar, dark soy sauce, yellow bean sauce and reserved marinade. Stir for a few seconds, add the stock, bring to a boil and add the fish. Cook for 4–5 minutes, basting constantly and turning the fish once after 2 minutes.

TURN the fish over and sprinkle with the sesame oil. Serve with the sauce poured over.

STEAMED SHRIMP CUSTARDS

4 eggs
1¼ cups chicken stock (page 281)
16 shrimp
1 scallion, finely chopped
1 tablespoon light soy sauce
1 tablespoon oil

SERVES 4

BEAT the eggs and chicken stock together and season with salt and white pepper. Peel and devein the shrimp, then roughly chop the shrimp meat.

DIVIDE the shrimp among 4 small flameproof bowls. Pour the egg and stock mixture over the shrimp. Put the bowls in a steamer, and steam over simmering water in a covered wok for 10 minutes. The custards should be just set. Shake them gently to see if the center is set. If you overcook them they will be rubbery.

SPRINKLE the custards with the scallion and soy sauce. Heat the oil in a wok until very hot and pour a little over each custard (it will spit as it hits the surface). Serve immediately.

STEAMED MUSSEL CUSTARDS

1 lb mussels
2 tablespoons Shaoxing rice wine
1 tablespoon finely chopped ginger
6 eggs
1 teaspoon salt

SERVES 6

SCRUB the mussels, remove any beards, and throw away any that do not close when tapped on the work surface. Put the mussels in a wok with 1 cup water, the rice wine and ginger. Cook, covered, over high heat for 1 minute, or until the mixture is boiling. Reduce the heat to low and cook, covered, for 2 minutes, or until the mussels have opened, shaking the pan so that they cook evenly. Discard any that do not open after 2 minutes.

REMOVE the mussels with a wire strainer or slotted spoon, reserving the liquid, and allow to cool. Remove the mussels from their shells and divide among 6 small flameproof bowls. Lightly beat the eggs, salt and 250 ml of the reserved liquid, then pour over the mussels.

PUT the bowls in a steamer and steam over simmering water in a covered wok for 10 minutes. The custards should be just set. Shake them gently to see if the center is set. If you overcook them they will be rubbery. Serve immediately.

STEAMED MUSSEL CUSTARDS

STEAMED SHRIMP CUSTARDS

川式辣焖鱼

SICHUANESE BRAISED FISH IN SPICY SAUCE

1 x 3¹/₂ lb whole fish, such as carp, porgy, grouper or sea bass
2¹/₂ tablespoons Shaoxing rice wine
2¹/₂ tablespoons finely chopped ginger
¹/₂ teaspoon salt
¹/₂ oz dried black fungus (wood ears)
oil for deep-frying
2 scallions, finely chopped
4 garlic cloves, finely chopped
1¹/₂ teaspoons chile bean paste (toban jiang)
2 cups chicken stock (page 281)
1¹/₂ tablespoons light soy sauce
2 teaspoons sugar
1 tablespoon Chinese black vinegar
1 tablespoon cornstarch
2 scallions, green part only, finely chopped

SERVES 6

IF YOU do manage to buy a live fish, then ask the fishmonger to gut it through the gills. This is harder than gutting through the stomach, but leaves the fish looking whole. If you are gutting the fish yourself, make a cut from the throat to the tail and pull out the guts through the stomach. Remove any scales with a fish scaler or the back of a knife. Check that the gills have been cut out, then rinse the fish under cold, running water and drain thoroughly in a colander.

DIAGONALLY score both sides of the fish, cutting through as far as the bone at intervals of ³/₄ inch. Combine 1 tablespoon of rice wine, 2 teaspoons of ginger and the salt. Place the fish in a dish and rub the mixture all over the outside of the fish and into the slits. Marinate for 30 minutes, then drain.

SOAK the dried fungus in cold water for 20 minutes, drain, squeeze out any excess water, and shred.

FILL a wok one quarter full of oil. Heat the oil to 375°F, or until a piece of bread fries golden brown in 10 seconds when dropped in the oil. Holding the fish by its tail, gently and carefully lower it into the oil, bending the body so that the cuts open up. Cook for 5 minutes, or until golden brown, tilting the wok so that the entire fish is cooked in the oil. Remove and drain on crumpled paper towels and keep warm in a low oven. Pour the oil from the wok, leaving 1¹/₂ tablespoons.

REHEAT the reserved oil over high heat until very hot and stir-fry the scallions, remaining ginger, garlic and chile bean paste for 10 seconds. Toss in the fungus, then the remaining rice wine, stock, soy sauce, sugar and vinegar and bring to a boil. Add the fish, return to a boil, then reduce the heat and cook, covered, for 12 minutes, or until the fish flakes when the skin is pressed firmly or the dorsal fins pulls out easily. Remove the fish.

SKIM ANY impurities from the sauce and bring to a boil. Combine the cornstarch with enough water to make a paste, add to the sauce and simmer until thickened. Pour over the fish with the scallions.

Scoring the fish through the flesh allows the heat to penetrate much more easily.

Renmin Park in Chengdu.

椒盐软壳蟹

SALT AND PEPPER SOFT-SHELL CRABS

THESE CRABS ARE A DELIGHT TO EAT AS YOU CAN DEVOUR THE ENTIRE CREATURE—SHELLS AND ALL.

THEY ARE EATEN WHEN THEY HAVE JUST SHED THEIR OLD SHELL AND BEFORE A NEW SHELL HARDENS.

4 soft-shell crabs
1 teaspoon spicy salt and pepper
  (page 285)
1 tablespoon Shaoxing rice wine
1 egg, beaten
1 tablespoon all-purpose flour
oil for deep-frying
1 scallion, chopped
2 small red chiles, chopped

SERVES 4

TO KILL the crabs humanely, put them in the freezer for 1 hour. Bring a large saucepan of water to a boil. Plunge the crabs into boiling water for about 1 minute, then rinse them in cold water. Marinate in the spicy salt and pepper and rice wine for 10–15 minutes, then coat with the egg and dust with the flour.

FILL a wok one quarter full of oil. Heat the oil to 375°F, or until a piece of bread fries golden brown in 10 seconds when dropped in the oil. Cook the crabs for 3–4 minutes, or until golden. Remove and drain, reserving the oil. Cut each crab in half and arrange on a serving plate.

SOAK the scallion and chiles in the hot oil (with the heat turned off) for 2 minutes. Remove with a wire strainer or slotted spoon and sprinkle over the crabs.

芙蓉蟹肉

CRABMEAT FU RONG

1/2 lb crabmeat, picked over
1/2 teaspoon salt
4 egg whites, beaten
1 tablespoon cornstarch
4 tablespoons milk
oil for deep-frying
1/2 cup chicken and meat stock
  (page 281)
1/2 scallion, finely chopped
1/2 teaspoon grated ginger
2 tablespoons peas
1 teaspoon Shaoxing rice wine
1/4 teaspoon roasted sesame oil
cilantro leaves

SERVES 4

FLAKE the crabmeat and mix with the salt, egg white, cornstarch and milk. Blend well.

FILL a wok one quarter full of oil and heat to 375°F, or until a piece of bread fries golden brown in 10 seconds when dropped in the oil. Pour the crabmeat into the wok in batches—do not stir, otherwise it will scatter, but gently stir the oil from the bottom of the wok so that the "fu rong" rises to the surface. Remove each batch as soon as it is set, without letting it go too brown, and drain. Pour out the oil and wipe out the wok.

REHEAT the wok over high heat until very hot, add the stock, bring to a boil and add the scallion, ginger, peas and rice wine. Add the sesame oil. Pour over the fu rong and sprinkle with cilantro.

CRABMEAT FU RONG

酱油炒干贝

SCALLOPS WITH BLACK BEAN SAUCE

2 lb large scallops
2 tablespoons salted, fermented
  black beans, rinsed and mashed
2 garlic cloves, crushed
3 teaspoons finely chopped ginger
2 teaspoons sugar
2 teaspoons light soy sauce
2 tablespoons oyster sauce
2 tablespoons oil
2 scallions, cut into 3/4 inch pieces

SERVES 6

SLICE the small, hard white muscle off the side of each scallop and pull off any membrane. Rinse the scallops and drain.

PLACE the black beans, garlic, ginger, sugar, and soy and oyster sauces in a bowl and mix together.

HEAT a wok over high heat, add the oil and heat until very hot. Stir-fry the scallops and roes for 2 minutes, or until the scallops are cooked through and opaque. Just before the scallops are cooked, add the scallions. Drain the mixture in a strainer.

REHEAT the wok over medium heat. Stir-fry the black bean mixture for 1–2 minutes, or until aromatic. Return the scallops and scallions to the wok and toss together to combine.

SCALLOPS WITH BLACK
BEAN SAUCE

海鲜沙锅

SEAFOOD CLAY POT

8 scallops
12 shrimp
12 hard-shelled clams
8 oysters, shucked
4 slices ginger
2 tablespoons Shaoxing rice wine
1 teaspoon roasted sesame oil
4 1/2 oz bean thread noodles
1 small head (about 1/4 lb) Chinese
  (Napa) cabbage
1 scallion, thinly sliced
1 1/4 cups chicken stock (page 281)
cilantro sprigs

SERVES 4

SLICE the small, hard white muscle off the side of each scallop and pull off any membrane. Rinse the scallops and drain. Peel and devein the shrimp. Wash the clams in several changes of cold water, leaving them for a few minutes each time to remove any grit. Scrub the clams well, discarding any that remain open. Drain well.

PUT the scallops, shrimp, clams and oysters in a bowl with the ginger, rice wine and sesame oil. Marinate for 30 minutes. Soak the bean thread noodles in hot water for 10 minutes, then drain.

CUT the cabbage into small squares, put in a clay pot or flameproof casserole with the scallion and place the noodles on top. Remove the ginger from the marinade and put the seafood and marinade on top of the noodles. Pour the stock over. Slowly bring to a boil, then simmer, covered, for 10 minutes. Stir once, season and cook for 8 minutes. Serve from the dish, sprinkled with cilantro.

SWEET-AND-SOUR FISH

PEOPLE TEND TO THINK THAT SWEET-AND-SOUR DISHES ARE CANTONESE, BUT IN FACT COOKS IN THE YELLOW RIVER VALLEY INVENTED THEM TO SUPPRESS THE MUDDY TASTE OF CARP FROM THE YELLOW RIVER. THIS RECIPE REPRESENTS WHAT MAY BE THE ORIGINAL "SWEET-AND-SOUR SAUCE".

1¹/₂–2 lb whole fish, such as sea bass, carp, grouper or porgy
1 teaspoon salt
2 tablespoons all-purpose flour
³/₄ oz dried black fungus (wood ears)
3–4 peeled water chestnuts
oil for deep-frying
2 tablespoons oil, extra
¹/₂ teaspoon chopped garlic
1 tablespoon shredded ginger
2 scallions, shredded
¹/₄ cup fresh or canned bamboo shoots, rinsed and drained, shredded
3 tablespoons rice vinegar
¹/₂ cup chicken and meat stock (page 281)
3 tablespoons sugar
2 tablespoons light soy sauce
2 tablespoons Shaoxing rice wine
2 teaspoons cornstarch
cilantro leaves

SERVES 4

IF YOU do manage to buy a live fish, then ask the fishmonger to gut it through the gills. This is harder than gutting through the stomach, but leaves the fish looking whole. If you are gutting the fish yourself, make a cut from the throat to the tail and pull out the guts through the stomach. Remove any scales with a fish scaler or the back of a knife. Check that the gills have been cut out, then rinse the fish under cold, running water and drain thoroughly in a colander.

DIAGONALLY score both sides of the fish, cutting through as far as the bone at intervals of ³/₄ inch. Rub a little salt, then a little flour, all over the outside of the fish and into the slits. Put the remaining flour in a dish and coat the whole fish, from head to tail on both sides, with flour. Soak the dried black fungus in cold water for 20 minutes then drain, squeeze out any excess water, and shred. Blanch the water chestnuts in a pan of boiling water for 1 minute, then refresh in cold water. Drain, pat dry and roughly chop them.

FILL a wok one quarter full of oil. Heat the oil to 375°F, or until a piece of bread fries golden brown in 10 seconds when dropped in the oil. Holding the fish by the tail, carefully lower it into the oil, bending the body so that the cuts open up. Cook the fish for 5 minutes, or until golden brown. Remove and drain on crumpled paper towels and keep warm in a low oven. Pour off the oil and wipe out the wok.

REHEAT the wok over high heat, add the extra oil and heat until very hot. Stir-fry the garlic, ginger, scallions, bamboo shoots, water chestnuts and black fungus for 30 seconds, then add the vinegar, stock, sugar, soy sauce and rice wine. Combine the cornstarch with enough water to make a paste, add to the sauce and simmer until thickened. Pour over the fish and sprinkle with cilantro.

Peeling water chestnuts with a cleaver requires some dexterity.

Coating the fish in flour soaks up any moisture and gives it a very crisp surface when fried.

A rice wine store in Beijing.

米酒蘑菇蒸比目鱼

SOLE WITH MUSHROOMS AND RICE WINE

THIS DISH IS SURPRISINGLY SIMILAR TO THE FRENCH SOLE BONNE FEMME (SOLE WITH MUSHROOMS

AND WINE SAUCE), THOUGH THE CHINESE VERSION IS MUCH SIMPLER TO MAKE. YOU COULD USE ANY

WHITE FISH INSTEAD OF THE FLAT FISH.

1 lb flat fish fillets, such as sole,
    plaice, flounder or brill
1 egg white, beaten
1 tablespoon cornstarch
1/2 lb button mushrooms
oil for deep-frying
1 garlic clove, thinly shredded
2 scallions, thinly shredded
1 teaspoon shredded ginger
1 teaspoon salt
1 teaspoon sugar
1 tablespoon light soy sauce
2 tablespoons Shaoxing rice wine
1 tablespoon Chinese spirit
    (Mou Tai) or brandy
1/2 cup chicken and meat stock
    (page 281)
1/2 teaspoon roasted sesame oil
cilantro leaves

SERVES 4

TRIM the soft bones along the edges of the fish, but leave the skin on. Cut each fillet into 3 or 4 slices if large, 2 or 3 if small. Mix the egg white with half the cornstarch and 1 teaspoon of water. Add the fish slices and toss to coat thoroughly. Thinly slice the mushrooms.

FILL a wok one quarter full of oil. Heat the oil to 350°F, or until a piece of bread fries golden brown in 15 seconds when dropped in the oil. Cook the fish slices for 1 minute, or until golden brown. Stir gently to make sure the slices do not stick together. Remove and drain on paper towels and keep warm in a low oven. Pour the oil out, reserving 2 tablespoons.

REHEAT the reserved oil over high heat until very hot and stir-fry the garlic, scallions, ginger and mushrooms for 1 minute. Add the salt, sugar, soy sauce, wine, Chinese spirit and stock, and bring to a boil. Return the fish slices to the sauce, blend well and simmer for 1 minute.

COMBINE the remaining cornstarch with enough water to make a paste, add to the sauce and simmer until thickened. Sprinkle the fish with the sesame oil and cilantro leaves.

Posters of the gods are pasted on front doors over the New Year period to bring good luck and good fortune.

POULTRY

云 南 气 锅 鸡

YUNNAN POT CHICKEN

A YUNNAN POT IS AN EARTHENWARE SOUP POT WITH A CHIMNEY. THE POT COOKS FOOD BY "CLOSED STEAMING," WHICH GIVES A CLEARER, MORE INTENSELY FLAVORED STOCK THAN ORDINARY STEAMING. INSTEAD OF A YUNNAN POT, YOU CAN USE A CLAY POT OR BRAISING PAN INSIDE A STEAMER.

25 jujubes (dried Chinese dates)
3 lb chicken
6 wafer-thin slices dang gui (dried angelica)
6 slices ginger, smashed with the flat side of a cleaver
6 scallions, ends trimmed, smashed with the flat side of a cleaver
1/4 cup Shaoxing rice wine
1/2 teaspoon salt

SERVES 6

SOAK the jujubes in hot water for 20 minutes, then drain and remove the pits.

RINSE the chicken, drain, and remove any fat from the cavity opening and around the neck. Cut off and discard the tail. Using a cleaver, cut the chicken through the bones into square 1 1/2 inch pieces. Blanch the chicken pieces in a saucepan of boiling water for 1 minute, then refresh in cold water and drain thoroughly.

ARRANGE the chicken pieces, jujubes, dang gui, ginger and scallions in a clay pot or braising pan about 10 inches in diameter. Pour the rice wine and 4 cups boiling water over the top and add the salt. Cover the clay pot or casserole tightly, adding a layer of wet cheesecloth, if necessary, between the pot and lid to form a good seal, then place it in a steamer.

STEAM over simmering water in a covered wok for about 2 hours, replenishing with boiling water during cooking.

REMOVE the pot from the steamer and skim any fat from the surface of the liquid. Discard the dang gui, ginger and scallions. Taste and season if necessary. Serve directly from the pot.

Dried jujubes, or Chinese dates.

Chopping ginger outside a shop in Chengdu.

STIR-FRIED SQUAB IN LETTUCE LEAVES

THIS DISH IS A CANTONESE CLASSIC, SOMETIMES CALLED SAN CHOY BAU, AND THE LITTLE PACKAGES, WITH THE CONTRAST BETWEEN THEIR WARM FILLING AND THE COLD LETTUCE, ARE WONDERFUL. IF SQUAB IS UNAVAILABLE, CHICKEN MAY BE USED INSTEAD.

Like all poultry, pigeons are sold live in the markets so there is no doubt as to how fresh they are.

12 soft lettuce leaves, such as
  butterhead lettuce
8 oz squab meat
1 lb center-cut pork loin, trimmed
1/3 cup light soy sauce
3 1/2 tablespoons Shaoxing rice
  wine
2 1/2 teaspoons roasted sesame oil
8 dried Chinese mushrooms
1 1/2 cups peeled water chestnuts
1/2 cup oil
2 scallions, finely chopped
2 tablespoons finely chopped
  ginger
1 teaspoon salt
1 teaspoon sugar
1 teaspoon cornstarch

SERVES 6

RINSE the lettuce and separate the leaves. Drain thoroughly, then lightly pound each leaf with the flat side of a cleaver. Arrange the flattened leaves in a basket or on a platter and set aside.

GRIND the squab meat in a food processor or chop very finely with a sharp knife. Grind the pork to the same size as the squab. Place the squab and pork in a bowl with 2 tablespoons of the soy sauce, 1 1/2 tablespoons of the rice wine and 1 teaspoon of the sesame oil, and toss lightly. Marinate in the fridge for 20 minutes.

SOAK the dried mushrooms in boiling water for 30 minutes, then drain and squeeze out any excess water. Remove and discard the stems and chop the caps. Blanch the water chestnuts in a saucepan of boiling water for 1 minute, then refresh in cold water. Drain, pat dry and roughly chop them.

HEAT a wok over high heat, add 3 tablespoons of the oil and heat until very hot. Stir-fry the meat mixture, mashing and separating the pieces, until browned. Remove and drain. Reheat the wok, add 3 tablespoons more of the oil and heat until very hot. Stir-fry the scallions and ginger, turning constantly, for 10 seconds, or until fragrant. Add the mushrooms and stir-fry for 5 seconds, turning constantly. Add the water chestnuts and stir-fry for 15 seconds, or until heated through. Add the remaining soy sauce, rice wine and sesame oil with the salt, sugar, cornstarch and 1/2 cup water. Stir-fry, stirring constantly, until thickened. Add the cooked meat mixture and toss lightly.

TO SERVE, place some of the stir-fried meat in a lettuce leaf, roll up and eat.

A restaurant in Beijing.

Preparing scallions in a kitchen in Beijing.

Selling vegetables in Yunnan.

香菇蒸鸡

STEAMED CHICKEN WITH MUSHROOMS

THIS DISH IS TRADITIONALLY COOKED USING PIECES OF CHICKEN WITH BOTH THE BONE AND SKIN STILL ATTACHED, BUT YOU CAN ALSO USE CHICKEN FILLET, IN WHICH CASE THE THIGH MEAT HAS MORE FLAVOR THAN BREAST MEAT.

1 lb skinned, boneless chicken thighs or 3 lb chicken
1 teaspoon salt
1/2 teaspoon sugar
1 tablespoon Shaoxing rice wine
1 teaspoon cornstarch
3–4 dried Chinese mushrooms
1 tablespoon shredded ginger
a pinch of ground Sichuan peppercorns
1 teaspoon roasted sesame oil

SERVES 4

CUT the chicken thighs into bite-size pieces. If using a whole chicken, rinse, drain, and remove any fat from the cavity opening and around the neck. Cut off and discard the tail. Using a cleaver, cut the chicken through the bones into square 1 1/2 inch pieces. Combine with the salt, sugar, rice wine and cornstarch.

SOAK the dried mushrooms in boiling water for 30 minutes, then drain and squeeze out excess water. Discard the stems and shred the caps.

GREASE a shallow flameproof dish and place the chicken pieces on the plate with the mushrooms, ginger, Sichuan peppercorns and sesame oil on top. Put the plate in a steamer. Steam over simmering water in a covered wok for 20 minutes.

芹菜炒鸡丝

SHREDDED CHICKEN WITH CELERY

8 oz skinned, boneless chicken breasts
1/4 egg white, beaten
2 teaspoons cornstarch
3 Chinese celery or celery stalks
1 2/3 cups oil
1 tablespoon shredded ginger
2 scallions, shredded
1 red chile, shredded (optional)
1 teaspoon salt
1/2 teaspoon sugar
1 tablespoon light soy sauce
1 tablespoon Shaoxing rice wine
2 tablespoons chicken and meat stock (page 281)
1/4 teaspoon roasted sesame oil

SERVES 4

CUT the chicken into matchstick-size shreds. Combine with a pinch of salt, the egg white and cornstarch. Shred the celery.

HEAT a wok over high heat. Add the oil and heat until hot, then turn off the heat. Blanch the chicken in the oil for 1 minute. Stir to separate the shreds, then remove and drain. Pour the oil from the wok, leaving 2 tablespoons.

REHEAT the reserved oil over high heat until very hot and stir-fry the ginger, scallion, celery and chile for 1 minute. Add the salt and sugar, blend well, then add the chicken with the soy sauce, rice wine and stock. Stir thoroughly and stir-fry for 1 minute. Sprinkle with the sesame oil to serve.

Roast meat stall in Kunming.

CRISPY SKIN DUCK

NORTHERN CHEFS HAVE THEIR FAMOUS PEKING DUCK, BUT IN SICHUAN, CRISPY SKIN DUCK IS EQUALLY POPULAR. THIS DISH CAN ALSO BE MADE WITH BONELESS DUCK BREASTS, JUST ADJUST THE COOKING TIMES. SERVE THE DUCK WITH MANDARIN PANCAKES OR STEAMED FLOWER ROLLS.

4 1/2 lb duck
8 scallions, ends trimmed, smashed with the flat side of a cleaver
8 slices ginger, smashed with the flat side of a cleaver
3 tablespoons Shaoxing rice wine
2 tablespoons salt
2 teaspoons Sichuan peppercorns
1 star anise, smashed with the flat side of a cleaver
2 tablespoons light soy sauce
1 cup cornstarch
oil for deep-frying
hoisin sauce
Mandarin pancakes (page 277) or steamed breads (page 46)

SERVES 6

RINSE the duck, drain, and remove any fat from the cavity opening and around the neck. Cut off and discard the tail. Combine the scallions, ginger, rice wine, salt, Sichuan peppercorns and star anise. Rub the marinade all over the inside and outside of the duck. Place, breast side down, in a bowl with the remaining marinade and keep in the fridge for at least 1 hour. Put the duck and the marinade, breast side up, on a flameproof plate in a steamer, or cut into halves or quarters and put in several steamers.

STEAM over simmering water in a covered wok for 1 1/2 hours, replenishing with boiling water during cooking. Remove the duck, discard the marinade, and let cool. Rub the soy sauce over the duck and then dredge in the cornstarch, pressing lightly to make it adhere to the skin. Let the duck dry in the fridge for several hours until very dry.

FILL a wok one quarter full of oil. Heat the oil to 375°F, or until a piece of bread fries golden brown in 10 seconds when dropped in the oil. Lower the duck into the oil and fry, ladling the oil over the top, until the skin is crisp and golden.

DRAIN the duck and, using a cleaver, cut the duck through the bones into pieces. Serve plain or with hoisin sauce and pancakes or bread.

Steaming the duck and then frying it keeps the meat very moist and allows the marinade flavors to penetrate. For serving, poultry is traditionally chopped into bite-size pieces, rather than jointed, so that the pieces can be picked up with chopsticks.

Cook the spinach for just a short amount of time so that it keeps its rich color.

Roasting seeds for the sesame oil outside a shop where it is sold in Chengdu.

宫保鸡丁

KUNG PAO CHICKEN

KUNG PAO IS ONE OF THE MOST CLASSIC HOT-AND-SOUR SICHUANESE SAUCES, AND CAN BE STIR-FRIED WITH SEAFOOD, PORK OR VEGETABLES AS WELL AS CHICKEN. THE SEASONINGS ARE FRIED IN OIL OVER HIGH HEAT, INTENSIFYING THE SPICINESS AND FLAVORING THE OIL.

11 oz skinned, boneless chicken breasts
3 tablespoons light soy sauce
3 tablespoons Shaoxing rice wine
2 teaspoons roasted sesame oil
1 tablespoon cornstarch
3/4 cup peeled water chestnuts
3 tablespoons oil
10 cups baby spinach leaves
1/2 teaspoon salt
3 garlic cloves, finely chopped
3/4 cup unsalted peanuts
1 scallion, finely chopped
1 tablespoon finely chopped ginger
1 teaspoon chili sauce
1 tablespoon sugar
1 teaspoon Chinese black rice vinegar
1/4 cup chicken stock (page 281)

SERVES 6

CUT the chicken into 1 inch cubes. Place the cubes in a bowl, add 2 tablespoons of the soy sauce, 2 tablespoons of the rice wine, 1 teaspoon of the sesame oil and 2 teaspoons of the cornstarch, and toss lightly. Marinate in the fridge for at least 20 minutes.

BLANCH the water chestnuts in a saucepan of boiling water, then refresh in cold water. Drain, pat dry and cut into thin slices.

HEAT a wok over high heat, add 1 teaspoon of the oil and heat until very hot. Stir-fry the spinach, salt, 2 teaspoons of the garlic and 2 teaspoons of the rice wine, turning constantly, until the spinach is just becoming limp. Remove the spinach from the wok, arrange around the edge of a platter, cover and keep warm.

REHEAT the wok over high heat, add 1 tablespoon of the oil and heat until very hot. Stir-fry half the chicken pieces, turning constantly, until the meat is cooked. Remove with a wire strainer or slotted spoon and drain. Repeat with 1 tablespoon of oil and the remaining chicken. Wipe out the pan.

DRY-FRY the peanuts in the wok or a saucepan until browned.

REHEAT the wok over high heat, add the remaining oil and heat until very hot. Stir-fry the scallion, ginger, remaining garlic and the chili sauce for 10 seconds, or until fragrant. Add the sliced water chestnuts and stir-fry for 15 seconds, or until heated through. Combine the sugar, black vinegar, chicken stock and remaining soy sauce, rice wine, sesame oil and cornstarch, add to the sauce and simmer until thickened. Add the cooked chicken and the peanuts. Toss lightly to coat with the sauce. Transfer to the center of the platter and serve.

海 南 鸡 饭

HAINAN CHICKEN

HAINAN CHICKEN IS A MEAL OF CHICKEN, RICE AND SOUP, EATEN WITH A SCALLION OR CHILI SAUCE. ORIGINALLY FROM HAINAN ISLAND IN THE SOUTH OF CHINA, THIS DISH WAS BROUGHT TO SINGAPORE BY IMMIGRANTS AND IS NOW A SINGAPOREAN CLASSIC.

2^1/$_4$ lb chicken
2 scallions, cut into 2 inch pieces
5 cilantro sprigs
^{3}/$_4$ teaspoon salt
4 slices ginger, smashed with the
    flat side of a cleaver
^{1}/$_4$ teaspoon black peppercorns
finely chopped scallion

DIPPING SAUCES
2 scallions, sliced
1 tablespoon finely grated ginger
1 teaspoon salt
3 tablespoons oil
3 tablespoons light soy sauce
1–2 red chiles, sliced

SERVES 4

RINSE the chicken, drain, and remove any fat from the cavity opening and around the neck. Cut off and discard the tail. Place the chicken in a large clay pot or braising pan. Add the scallion, cilantro, salt, ginger, peppercorns and enough water to cover the chicken. Cover and bring to a boil, then reduce the heat and simmer very gently for 30 minutes. Turn off the heat and allow the chicken to sit for 10 minutes. Remove the chicken from the pot and drain well. Skim off any impurities from the liquid and strain the liquid.

TO MAKE the dipping sauces, combine the scallions, ginger and salt in one small heatproof or metal bowl.

HEAT a wok over high heat, add the oil and heat until smoking. Allow it to cool slightly, then pour over the scallion mixture. The mixture will splatter. Stir well. Combine the soy sauce and chiles in another small bowl.

USING a cleaver, cut the chicken through the bones into bite-size pieces. Pour the stock into soup bowls, sprinkle with the finely chopped scallion, and serve with the chicken along with bowls of rice and the dipping sauces.

Carve the duck so that each slice has some crispy skin and tender meat. The skin can also be eaten separately, wrapped in the pancakes, while the meat is used in a stir-fry.

Commercially made pancakes are available in Asian markets, fresh or frozen, or from restaurants that sell carry-out ducks and barbecued meat.

北京烤鸭

PEKING DUCK

THIS DISH OWES ITS REPUTATION NOT SO MUCH TO THE WAY IT IS COOKED, BUT TO THE WAY IT IS THEATRICALLY CARVED AND EATEN ROLLED INTO PANCAKES. IN RESTAURANTS, THE DUCK IS COOKED IN A SPECIAL OVEN, BUT THIS RECIPE HAS BEEN MODIFIED FOR THE HOME KITCHEN.

5 lb duck
2 tablespoons maltose or honey,
    dissolved in 2 tablespoons water
1/2 cup hoisin sauce or plum sauce
24 Mandarin pancakes (page 277)
6–8 scallions, shredded
1/2 cucumber, shredded

SERVES 6

CUT the wing tips off the duck with a pair of poultry shears. Rinse the duck, drain, and remove any fat from the cavity opening and around the neck. Cut off and discard the tail. Plunge the duck into a pot of boiling water for 2–3 minutes to tighten the skin. Remove and drain, then dry thoroughly.

WHILE the skin is still warm, brush the duck all over with the maltose or honey and water solution, then hang it up to dry in a cool and airy place for at least 6 hours, or overnight, or keep it, uncovered, in the fridge.

PREHEAT the oven to 400°F. Place the duck, breast side up, on a rack in a roasting pan, and roast without basting or turning for 1 1/2 hours. Check to make sure the duck is not getting too dark and, if it is, cover it loosely with aluminum foil.

TO SERVE, remove the crispy duck skin in small slices by using a sharp carving knife, then carve the meat, or carve both together. Arrange on a serving plate.

TO EAT, spread about 1 teaspoon of the hoisin sauce or plum sauce in the center of a pancake, add a few strips of scallions, cucumber, duck skin and meat, roll up the pancake and turn up the bottom edge to prevent the contents from falling out.

THE QUANJUDE ROAST DUCK RESTAURANTS are perhaps the most famous Peking duck restaurants in Beijing. Established as early as 1864, the name Quanjude means 'everything is included'. More than just Peking duck restaurants, these restaurants specialize in all-duck dinners. Originally the menu included just four items: roast duck, stuffed duck neck, duck soup and stir-fried duck, but at the Quanjude

PEKING DUCK

DUCK DISHES HAVE ALWAYS BEEN CLASSICS OF THE CHINESE KITCHEN: ROASTED IN GUANGZHOU, CAMPHOR AND TEA-SMOKED IN SICHUAN, AND PRESSED IN NANJING, BUT IT IS IN THE CAPITAL THAT PEKING DUCK, PERHAPS CHINA'S MOST FAMOUS DISH, ORIGINATED.

True Peking duck must be made with a white-feathered mallard called a Peking duck. These ducks are bred on farms around Beijing and fattened up with grain for a few months to produce tender meat.

MAKING PEKING DUCK

The dish is prepared in different ways by different restaurants, though there are some principles that remain the same. After the duck is plucked, air is pumped in between the skin and body to inflate the bird, then the duck is blanched in boiling water. The crispy skin is formed by washing the duck with a maltose solution and leaving it to dry in a cool, dry place. The maltose, made from fermented barley, turns a dark reddish brown when cooked to give the bird a lacquered effect.

The duck is filled with boiling water to steam it from the inside and roasted in a specially made kiln-like oven. Inside the oven, the ducks are hung vertically or spit-roasted over fruit wood at very high temperatures for a relatively short time—this produces a truly crisp skin, but prevents the meat from drying out.

today you can order from more than 200 duck dishes, using every conceivable part of the duck, from deep-fried hearts to webs with mustard sauce and stewed tongues. The branch in Wangfujing has two duck kitchens, two pancake kitchens and two general kitchens for a restaurant that seats 800. The chefs are trained at the Beijing Culinary Institute for 3 years before working their way up through the kitchens.

PERFECT PEKING DUCK

The quality of the ingredients is paramount to the flavour of Peking duck. The Peking duck is specially bred to be plump and tender and is reared on a grain diet. Some restaurants add flavourings to the duck by varying the ingredients of the maltose solution or adding flavourings to the boiling water inside the cavity. However, Peking duck should not have a spicy or sweet aroma, instead the natural flavour of the duck juices and crispy skin should dominate.

Crispy skin is the true test of perfect Peking duck. This is achieved by separating the skin from the flesh, then drying the skin thoroughly before the duck is cooked. The wood-fired oven uses its high heat to cook the skin quickly, which also causes most of the fat to melt and run out, while the liquid that has been put inside the duck heats up and steams the flesh from the inside, keeping the meat moist.

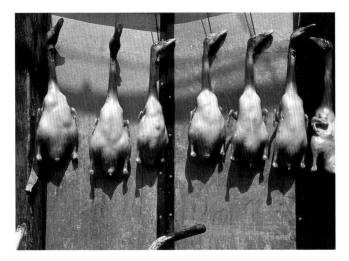

THE WEATHER can be an important factor with Peking and roast ducks, and ducks can be seen hanging up outside all over China when it is cold and dry. To form a really crisp skin, the ducks must be thoroughly dried in air with a low humidity until the skin is like paper.

盐焗鸡

SALT-BAKED CHICKEN

THIS IS ANOTHER CANTONESE SPECIALTY THAT EMPLOYS A RATHER UNUSUAL COOKING METHOD. THE WHOLE CHICKEN IS WRAPPED IN CLOTH AND BAKED IN SALT, WHICH ACTS LIKE AN OVEN, KEEPING IN THE HEAT TO PRODUCE VERY SUCCULENT CHICKEN MEAT.

3 lb chicken
2 tablespoons light soy sauce
4 lb sea salt or coarse salt

FILLING
1 scallion, chopped
1 teaspoon grated ginger
2 star anise, crushed
1/2 teaspoon salt
4 tablespoons Mei Kuei Lu Chiew
   or brandy

DIPPING SAUCE
1 tablespoon oil
1 scallion, chopped
1 teaspoon chopped ginger
1/2 teaspoon salt
1/4 cup chicken and meat stock
   (page 281)

SERVES 4

RINSE the chicken, drain, and remove any fat from the cavity opening and around the neck. Cut off and discard the tail. Blanch the chicken in a saucepan of boiling water for 2–3 minutes, then refresh under cold water and dry well. Brush the chicken with the soy sauce and hang it up to dry in a cool and airy place for a couple of hours, or keep it, uncovered, in the fridge.

MEANWHILE, TO make the filling, combine the scallion, ginger, star anise, salt and Mei Kuei Lu Chiew. Pour the filling into the cavity of the chicken. Wrap the chicken tightly with a large sheet of cheesecloth.

HEAT the salt in a large clay pot or braising pan very slowly until very hot, then turn off the heat and remove and reserve about half the salt. Make a hole in the center of the salt and place the chicken in it, breast side up, then cover with the salt removed earlier so that the chicken is completely buried. Cover the clay pot or braising pan and cook over medium heat for 15–20 minutes, then reduce the heat to low and cook for 45–50 minutes. Allow to sit for at least 15–20 minutes before taking the chicken out. (The salt can be reused.)

TO MAKE the dipping sauce, heat the oil in a small wok or saucepan. Fry the scallion and ginger for 1 minute, then add the salt and stock. Bring to a boil, then reduce the heat and simmer for a couple of minutes.

REMOVE the chicken from the casserole and unwrap it. Using a cleaver, cut the chicken through the bones into bite-size pieces. Arrange on a serving dish and serve hot or cold with the dipping sauce.

Make sure every part of the chicken is covered in salt to seal in the flavor completely. The salt does not affect the flavor of the chicken as the wrapping and skin keep it from coming into contact with the flesh.

Table tennis played at an outside recreation area in Beijing.

RED-COOKED CHICKEN

RED-COOKED CHICKEN

RED-COOKING LIQUID
2 cinnamon or cassia sticks
1¹/₂ star anise
2 pieces dried tangerine or orange
    peel, about 2 inches long
¹/₂ teaspoon fennel seeds
1¹/₂ cups dark soy sauce
¹/₂ cup sugar
¹/₂ cup Shaoxing rice wine

3 lb chicken
1 tablespoon roasted sesame oil

SERVES 6

TO MAKE the red-cooking liquid, place all the ingredients in a clay pot or braising pan with 6 cups water, bring to a boil, then simmer for 30 minutes.

RINSE the chicken, drain, and remove any fat from the cavity opening and around the neck. Cut off and discard the tail. Place the chicken, breast side down, in the cooking liquid and cook for 1¹/₂ hours, turning 2 or 3 times. Turn off the heat and leave in the liquid for 30 minutes, then remove. Brush the chicken with the sesame oil then, using a cleaver, cut the chicken through the bones into bite-size pieces. Spoon over a little liquid and serve hot or cold.

THE SAUCE can be reused as a "Master Sauce" (see page 290).

SOY CHICKEN

3 lb chicken
1 tablespoon ground Sichuan
    peppercorns
2 tablespoons grated ginger
2 tablespoons sugar
3 tablespoons Shaoxing rice wine
1¹/₄ cups dark soy sauce
³/₄ cup light soy sauce
2¹/₂ cups oil
1³/₄ cups chicken and meat stock
    (page 281)
2 teaspoons roasted sesame oil

SERVES 4

RINSE the chicken, drain, and remove any fat from the cavity opening and around the neck. Cut off and discard the tail. Rub the Sichuan peppercorns and ginger all over the inside and outside of the chicken. Combine the sugar, rice wine and soy sauces, add the chicken and marinate in the fridge for at least 3 hours, turning occasionally.

HEAT a wok over high heat, add the oil and heat until very hot. Drain the chicken, reserving the marinade, and fry for 8 minutes until browned. Put in a clay pot or braising pan with the marinade and stock. Bring to a boil, then simmer, covered, for 35–40 minutes. Take off the heat for 2–3 hours, transferring to the fridge when cool. Drain the chicken, brush with oil and refrigerate for 1 hour.

USING a cleaver, chop the chicken through the bones into bite-size pieces, pour over a couple of tablespoons of sauce and serve.

THE SAUCE can be reused as a "Master Sauce" (see page 290).

The soy sauce and sugar in the marinade turn the chicken skin a rich dark brown when cooked.

椒盐炸鹌鹑

DEEP-FRIED QUAILS WITH SPICY SALT

FRESH QUAILS ARE BEST FOR THIS RECIPE BECAUSE ONCE FROZEN, QUAIL CAN BECOME QUITE DRY
AND BLAND, AND TENDERNESS AND SUCCULENCE ARE THE MAIN CHARACTERISTICS OF THIS DISH.

4 quails
1 teaspoon spicy salt and pepper
  (page 285)
1 teaspoon sugar
1 tablespoon light soy sauce
1 tablespoon Shaoxing rice wine
2–3 tablespoons all-purpose flour
oil for deep-frying
1 scallion, finely chopped
1 red chile, finely chopped

SERVES 4

SPLIT EACH quail in half down the middle and
clean well. Marinate with the spicy salt and
pepper, the sugar, soy sauce and rice wine for
2–3 hours in the fridge, turning frequently. Coat
each quail piece in the flour.

FILL a wok one quarter full of oil. Heat the oil to
375°F, or until a piece of bread fries golden brown
in 10 seconds when dropped in the oil. Reduce
the heat and fry the quail for 2–3 minutes on
each side. Remove from the wok and drain on
paper towels.

SOAK the scallion and chile in the hot oil (with the
heat turned off) for 2 minutes. Remove with a wire
strainer or slotted spoon and drain, then sprinkle
over the quail pieces. Serve hot.

Erhai Lake in Yunnan.

Marinate the quail long enough
for the flavors to penetrate
the meat.

油烧乳鸽

LACQUERED SQUAB

THIS COOKING METHOD GIVES THE SKIN OF THE SQUAB A SHINY, DEEP REDDISH-BROWN GLAZE. THE
SIMMERING GIVES THE FLAVOR AND THE FINAL DEEP-FRYING CRISPS THE SKIN.

2 x 1 lb squab
4 slices ginger
4 scallions, cut into short pieces
4 tablespoons light soy sauce
3 tablespoons dark soy sauce
3 tablespoons Shaoxing rice wine
4 tablespoons rock sugar or dark
  brown sugar
1 teaspoon salt
2 cinnamon sticks
2 star anise
4 cups chicken stock (page 281)
oil for deep-frying

SERVES 4

BLANCH the squab in a saucepan of boiling
water for 2 minutes, then remove and drain.

COMBINE the remaining ingredients except the
oil in a clay pot or braising pan and bring to a
simmer. Add the squab, cover and simmer for
20 minutes. Remove from the heat, take out the
squab and allow to dry for at least 1 hour.

FILL a wok one quarter full of oil. Heat the oil to
375°F, or until a piece of bread fries golden brown
in 10 seconds when dropped in the oil. Fry the
squab until they are very crisp and brown. Drain
well and sprinkle with salt. Using a cleaver, cut the
squabs through the bones into bite-size pieces.

LACQUERED SQUAB

A chicken seller in Chengdu.

In China, rice wine can be bought directly out of the earthenware pots it is matured in.

柠檬鸡

LEMON CHICKEN

LEMON CHICKEN IS A POPULAR CANTONESE DISH OF FRIED CHICKEN GLAZED WITH A TART, LEMONY SAUCE. HERE THE LEMON SAUCE IS HOMEMADE AND QUITE UNLIKE THE THICK SAUCES OFTEN SERVED WITH THIS DISH. CHICKEN WINGS OR DUCK ARE ALSO DELICIOUS PREPARED THIS WAY.

1 lb skinned, boneless chicken
   breasts
1 tablespoon light soy sauce
1 tablespoon Shaoxing rice wine
1 scallion, finely chopped
1 tablespoon finely chopped ginger
1 garlic clove, finely chopped
1 egg, lightly beaten
3/4 cup cornstarch
oil for deep-frying

LEMON SAUCE
2 tablespoons lemon juice
2 teaspoons sugar
1/2 teaspoon salt
1/2 teaspoon toasted sesame oil
3 tablespoons chicken stock
   (page 281) or water
1/2 teaspoon cornstarch

SERVES 6

CUT the chicken into slices. Place in a bowl, add the soy sauce, rice wine, scallion, ginger and garlic, and toss lightly. Marinate in the fridge for at least 1 hour, or overnight.

ADD the egg to the chicken mixture and toss lightly to coat. Drain any excess egg and coat the chicken pieces with the cornstarch. The easiest way to do this is to put the chicken and cornstarch in a plastic bag and shake it.

FILL a wok one quarter full of oil. Heat the oil to 375°F, or until a piece of bread fries golden brown in 10 seconds when dropped in the oil. Add half the chicken, a piece at a time, and fry, stirring constantly, for 3¹/₂–4 minutes, or until golden brown. Remove with a wire strainer or slotted spoon and drain. Repeat with the remaining chicken. Reheat the oil and return all the chicken to the wok. Cook until crisp and golden brown. Drain the chicken. Pour off the oil and wipe out the wok.

TO MAKE the lemon sauce, combine the lemon juice, sugar, salt, sesame oil, stock and cornstarch.

REHEAT the wok over medium heat until hot, add the lemon sauce and stir constantly until thickened. Add the chicken and toss lightly in the sauce.

醉鸡

DRUNKEN CHICKEN

THERE ARE SEVERAL VERSIONS OF THIS POPULAR DISH, BUT IN THIS SIMPLE RECIPE, THE CHICKEN IS STEAMED IN THE "DRUNKEN" SAUCE, WHICH IS THEN POURED OVER TO SERVE.

3 lb chicken
1/2 cup Shaoxing rice wine
3 tablespoons Chinese spirit (Mou Tai) or brandy
3 slices ginger
3 scallions, cut into short pieces
2 teaspoons salt
1/4 teaspoon freshly ground black pepper
cilantro leaves

SERVES 4

RINSE the chicken, drain, and remove any fat from the cavity opening and around the neck. Cut off and discard the tail. Blanch the chicken in a saucepan of boiling water for 2–3 minutes, then refresh in cold water.

PLACE the chicken, breast side down, in a bowl. Add the rice wine, Chinese spirit, ginger, scallion and half the salt. Place the bowl in a steamer. Cover and steam over simmering water in a wok for 1 1/2 hours, replenishing with boiling water during cooking. Transfer the chicken to a dish, breast side up, reserving the cooking liquid.

POUR half the liquid into a wok or saucepan and add the remaining salt and the pepper. Bring to a boil, then pour the sauce over the chicken. Using a cleaver, cut the chicken through the bones into bite-size pieces. Garnish with the cilantro.

DRUNKEN CHICKEN

三杯鸡

THREE-CUP CHICKEN

THREE-CUP CHICKEN IS SO CALLED BECAUSE THE ORIGINAL RECIPE USES ONE CUP EACH OF RICE WINE, SOY SAUCE AND LARD. CHRISTINE YAN OF YMING RESTAURANT IN LONDON MODIFIED IT WITH THIS RECIPE THAT REPLACES THE LARD WITH STOCK, AND THE RESULT IS A MUCH HEALTHIER DISH.

1 lb skinned, boneless chicken thighs
1 tablespoon cornstarch
1 tablespoon oil
2 scallions, cut to short pieces
4 small pieces ginger
3 tablespoons Shaoxing rice wine
3 tablespoons light soy sauce
1/2 cup chicken and meat stock (page 281)
1/2 teaspoon toasted sesame oil

SERVES 4

CUT the chicken into 3/4 inch cubes. Combine the cornstarch with enough water to make a paste and toss the chicken cubes in the paste to coat.

HEAT the oil in a small clay pot or braising pan, lightly brown the chicken with the scallion and ginger, then add the rice wine, soy sauce and stock. Bring to a boil, then reduce the heat and simmer, covered, for 20–25 minutes. There should be a little liquid left—if there is too much, boil it off. Add the sesame oil and serve the chicken hot from the pot.

泰式泡凤爪

A sign proclaims "Thai-style chicken feet" for sale at an outside stall in Chengdu.

A shopping street in central Shanghai.

上海醬鴨

SHANGHAI SOY DUCK

THIS DUCK, SIMILAR TO CANTONESE SOY CHICKEN, IS TRADITIONALLY SERVED AT ROOM TEMPERATURE AS A FIRST COURSE, THOUGH THERE IS NO REASON WHY IT CAN'T BE SERVED AS A MAIN COURSE, HOT OR COLD. YOU CAN ALSO USE JOINTED PIECES OR DUCK BREASTS, JUST REDUCE THE COOKING TIME.

4¹/₂ lb duck
2 teaspoons salt
4 scallions, each tied in a knot
4 x ¹/₂ inch slices ginger, smashed
  with the flat side of a cleaver
6 star anise
3 cinnamon or cassia sticks
1 tablespoon Sichuan peppercorns
¹/₂ cup Shaoxing rice wine
³/₄ cup light soy sauce
¹/₂ cup dark soy sauce
3 oz rock sugar

SERVES 4

RINSE the duck, drain, and remove any fat from the cavity opening and around the neck. Cut off and discard the tail. Blanch the duck in a saucepan of boiling water for 2–3 minutes, then refresh in cold water, pat dry and rub the salt inside the cavity.

PLACE the duck, breast side up, in a clay pot or braising pan, and add the scallions, ginger, star anise, cinnamon, peppercorns, rice wine, soy sauces, rock sugar and enough water to cover. Bring to a boil, then reduce the heat and simmer, covered, for 40–45 minutes. Turn off the heat and allow the duck to cool in the liquid for 2–3 hours, transferring the clay pot to the fridge once it is cool enough. Keep in the fridge until completely cold (you can keep the duck in the liquid overnight and serve it the next day).

TO SERVE, remove the duck from the liquid and drain well. Using a cleaver, cut the duck through the bones into bite-size pieces.

TRADITIONALLY this dish is served at room temperature, but if you would like to serve it hot, put the clay pot with the duck and the liquid back on the stove and bring it to a boil. Simmer for 10 minutes, or until the duck is completely heated through.

THE SAUCE can be reused as a "Master Sauce" (see page 290).

Ducks hanging up to dry after they have been plucked.

棒棒鸡

BANG BANG CHICKEN

THIS CLASSIC SICHUAN STYLE COLD PLATTER IS MADE FROM CHICKEN, CUCUMBER AND BEAN THREAD NOODLES, MIXED IN A SESAME OR PEANUT SAUCE. THE SESAME DRESSING IS THE AUTHENTIC ONE BUT THE PEANUT VERSION IS ALSO VERY GOOD.

1¹/2 cucumbers
1 teaspoon salt
1 oz bean thread noodles
1 teaspoon toasted sesame oil
8 oz cooked chicken, cut into
   shreds
2 scallions, green part only, finely
   sliced

SESAME DRESSING
¹/4 teaspoon Sichuan peppercorns
3 garlic cloves
³/4 inch piece ginger
¹/2 teaspoon chili sauce
3 tablespoons toasted sesame paste
2 tablespoons toasted sesame oil
2¹/2 tablespoons light soy sauce
1 tablespoon Shaoxing rice wine
1 tablespoon Chinese black rice
   vinegar
1 tablespoon sugar
3 tablespoons chicken stock
   (page 281)

OR

PEANUT DRESSING
¹/2 cup smooth peanut butter
1 teaspoon light soy sauce
1¹/2 tablespoons sugar
2 teaspoons Chinese black rice
   vinegar
1 tablespoon Shaoxing rice wine
1 tablespoon toasted sesame oil
1 scallion, finely chopped
1 tablespoon finely chopped ginger
1 teaspoon chili sauce
2¹/2 tablespoons chicken stock
   (page 281)

SERVES 6

SLICE the cucumbers lengthwise and remove most of the seeds. Cut each half crosswise into thirds, then cut each piece lengthwise into thin slices that are 2 inches long and ³/4 inch wide. Place the slices in a bowl, add the salt, toss lightly, and set aside for 20 minutes. Pour off the water that has accumulated.

TO MAKE the sesame dressing, put the Sichuan peppercorns in a frying pan and cook over medium heat, stirring occasionally, for 7–8 minutes, or until golden brown and very fragrant. Cool slightly, then crush into a powder. Combine the garlic, ginger, chili sauce, sesame paste, sesame oil, soy sauce, rice wine, vinegar, sugar and stock in a blender, food processor or mortar and pestle. Blend to a smooth sauce the consistency of heavy cream. Stir in the Sichuan peppercorn powder. Pour into a bowl and set aside.

TO MAKE the peanut dressing, combine the peanut butter, soy sauce, sugar, vinegar, rice wine, sesame oil, scallion, ginger, chili sauce and stock in a blender, food processor or mortar and pestle. Blend until the mixture is the consistency of heavy cream, adding a little water if necessary. Pour into a bowl and set aside.

SOAK the bean thread noodles in hot water for 10 minutes, then drain and cut into 3 inch pieces. Blanch the noodles in a saucepan of boiling water for 3 minutes, then refresh in cold water and drain again. Toss the noodles in the sesame oil and arrange them on a large platter. Arrange the cucumber slices on top. Place the chicken shreds on top of the cucumber. Just before serving, pour the sesame or peanut dressing over the chicken. Sprinkle with the chopped scallions and serve.

Peeling garlic in Sichuan.

WHITE CUT CHICKEN

"WHITE CUT" IS A POACHING METHOD USED ALL OVER CHINA, WHERE A WHOLE CHICKEN IS COOKED IN A RELATIVELY SHORT TIME IN A WATER-BASED BROTH, THEN THE HEAT IS TURNED OFF AND THE RETAINED HEAT CARRIES OUT THE REMAINDER OF THE COOKING.

$2^1/_2$ lb chicken
2 scallions, each tied in a knot
3 slices ginger, smashed with the
    flat side of a cleaver
3 tablespoons Shaoxing rice wine
1 tablespoon salt

DIPPING SAUCE
4 tablespoons dark soy sauce
1 tablespoon sugar
1 scallion, finely chopped
1 garlic clove, finely chopped
1 teaspoon finely chopped ginger
1 teaspoon roasted sesame oil

SERVES 4

RINSE the chicken, drain, and remove any fat from the cavity opening and around the neck. Cut off and discard the tail. Bring 6 cups water to a rolling boil in a clay pot or braising pan, and gently lower the chicken into the water with the breast side up. Add the scallions, ginger and rice wine, return to a boil, then add the salt and simmer, covered, for 15 minutes.

TURN OFF the heat and allow the chicken to cool in the liquid for 5–6 hours, without lifting the lid.

ABOUT 30 minutes before serving time, remove and drain the chicken. Using a cleaver, cut the chicken through the bones into bite-size pieces.

TO MAKE the dipping sauce, combine the soy sauce, sugar, scallion, garlic, ginger and sesame oil with a little of the cooking liquid. Divide the sauce among small saucers, one for each person. Each piece of the chicken is dipped before eating.

ALTERNATIVELY, pour the sauce over the chicken before serving, but use light soy sauce instead of dark soy sauce so as not to spoil the "whiteness" of the chicken.

Old men take their song birds out with them to the park when they meet their friends. The cages are hung up so the birds can sing together while their owners chat.

MEAT

木薯炒肉

MU SHU PORK

SINCE WHEAT IS THE STAPLE CROP IN NORTHERN CHINA, MEAT AND VEGETABLE DISHES ARE COMMONLY SERVED THERE WITH STEAMED BREAD OR PANCAKES INSTEAD OF RICE. THIS BEIJING DISH IS SERVED ROLLED IN MANDARIN PANCAKES, WHICH ARE FIRST SPREAD WITH HOISIN SAUCE.

You may find it easier to cut the meat into thin slices if you freeze it for 15 minutes first to firm it up.

8 oz center-cut pork loin, trimmed
1/4 cup light soy sauce
1/4 cup Shaoxing rice wine
1/2 teaspoon roasted sesame oil
2 teaspoons cornstarch
5 dried Chinese mushrooms
3/4 oz dried black fungus
   (wood ears)
4 tablespoons oil
2 eggs, lightly beaten
4 garlic cloves, finely chopped
2 tablespoons finely chopped
   ginger
1 leek, white part only, finely
   shredded
1/4 small Chinese cabbage,
   shredded, stem sections and
   leafy sections separated
1/2 teaspoon sugar
1/4 teaspoon freshly ground black
   pepper
1/3 cup hoisin sauce
12 Mandarin pancakes (page 277)

SERVES 4

CUT the pork against the grain into slices about 1/4 inch thick, then cut into thin, matchstick-size shreds about 3/4 inch long. Put the shreds in a bowl, add 1 tablespoon of the soy sauce, 1 tablespoon of the rice wine, the sesame oil and 1 teaspoon of the cornstarch, and toss lightly to coat. Cover with plastic wrap and marinate in the fridge for 30 minutes.

SOAK the dried mushrooms in boiling water for 30 minutes, then drain and squeeze out any excess water. Remove and discard the stems and shred the caps. Soak the dried black fungus in cold water for 20 minutes, then drain and squeeze out any excess water. Shred the black fungus.

HEAT a wok over high heat, add 2 tablespoons of the oil and heat until very hot. Stir-fry the pork mixture for 2–3 minutes, until the meat is brown and cooked. Remove with a wire strainer or slotted spoon and drain. Rinse and dry the wok.

REHEAT the wok over high heat, add 1 tablespoon of the oil and heat until hot. Stir-fry the egg to scramble, then move to the side of the wok. Add 1 tablespoon of oil, heat until very hot, and stir-fry the garlic, ginger, mushrooms and black fungus for 10 seconds, or until fragrant. Add the leek and toss lightly for 1 1/2 minutes, then add the cabbage stems and stir-fry for 30 seconds. Add the leafy cabbage sections, and cook for 1 minute, or until the vegetables are just tender. Combine 1 1/2 tablespoons of the soy sauce, the remaining rice wine and cornstarch, the sugar, black pepper and the meat, add to the sauce and simmer until thickened.

COMBINE the hoisin sauce, remaining soy sauce and 1 1/2 tablespoons water in a small bowl. Serve the pork with the pancakes and sauce.

Harvesting bok choy in Liugan.

狮子头肉丸

LION'S HEAD MEATBALLS

THIS DISH IS SO NAMED BECAUSE THE LARGE MEATBALLS ARE SAID TO LOOK LIKE LION'S HEADS SURROUNDED BY A MANE OF BOK CHOY. ORIGINALLY THE MEATBALLS TENDED TO BE MADE FROM PORK AND PORK FAT AND WERE COARSER IN TEXTURE.

1 lb ground pork
1 egg white
4 scallions, finely chopped
1 tablespoon Shaoxing rice wine
1 teaspoon grated ginger
1 tablespoon light soy sauce
2 teaspoons sugar
1 teaspoon roasted sesame oil
1/2–3/4 lb bok choy
1 tablespoon cornstarch
oil for frying
2 cups chicken and meat stock
　(page 281)

SERVES 4

PUT the pork and egg white in a food processor and process briefly until you have a fluffy mixture, or mash the ground pork in a large bowl and gradually stir in the egg white, beating the mixture well until it is fluffy. Add the scallion, rice wine, ginger, soy sauce, sugar and sesame oil, season with salt and white pepper, and process or beat again briefly. Fry a small portion of the mixture and taste it, reseasoning if necessary. Divide the mixture into walnut-size balls.

SEPARATE the boy choy leaves and place in the bottom of a clay pot or braising pan.

DUST the meatballs with cornstarch. Heat a wok over high heat, add 1/2 inch oil and heat until very hot. Cook the meatballs in batches until they are browned all over. Drain well and add to the clay pot in an even layer. Pour off the oil and wipe out the wok.

REHEAT the wok over high heat until very hot, add the chicken stock and heat until it is boiling. Pour over the meatballs. Cover and bring very slowly to a boil. Simmer gently with the lid slightly open for 1 1/2 hours, or until the meatballs are very tender. Serve the meatballs in the dish they were cooked in.

Roll the mixture into balls using the palms of your hands, then dust with cornstarch to prevent them from sticking when you cook them.

A pickle stall in Sichuan.

Deep-frying the pork gives it a crispy, well-browned outside while keeping the meat inside very tender.

酸甜肉

SWEET-AND-SOUR PORK

ALTHOUGH SWEET-AND-SOUR PORK IS OFTEN THOUGHT OF AS A WESTERN INVENTION, IT IS IN FACT CHINESE. IN THE ORIGINAL VERSION, THE PORK IS LIGHT AND CRISPY AND SERVED IN A PIQUANT SWEET-AND-SOUR SAUCE. IF YOU LIKE IT WITH PINEAPPLE, ADD 2 CUPS CUBED PINEAPPLE.

1 1/4 lb center-cut pork loin, trimmed
1 egg
3/4 cup cornstarch
1 tablespoon oil
1 onion, cubed
1 red pepper, cubed or cut into
  small triangles
2 scallions, cut into 3/4 inch pieces
2/3 cup Chinese pickles
1 cup clear rice vinegar
1/3 cup tomato ketchup
1 1/4 cups sugar
oil for deep-frying

SERVES 4

CUT the pork into 3/4 inch cubes and put it in a bowl with the egg, 1/2 cup of the cornstarch and 2 teaspoons water. Stir to coat all of the pieces of pork.

HEAT a wok over high heat, add the oil and heat until very hot. Stir-fry the onion for 1 minute. Add the pepper and scallions and cook for 1 minute. Add the pickles and toss together to combine. Add the rice vinegar, tomato ketchup and sugar and stir over low heat until the sugar dissolves. Bring to a boil, then simmer for 3 minutes.

COMBINE the remaining cornstarch with 1/4 cup water, add to the sweet-and-sour mixture and simmer until thickened. Set aside.

FILL a wok one quarter full of oil. Heat the oil to 350°F, or until a piece of bread fries golden brown in 15 seconds when dropped in the oil. Cook the pork in batches until golden brown and crispy. Return all of the pork to the wok, cook until crisp again, then remove with a wire strainer or slotted spoon and drain well. Add the pork pieces to the sauce, stir to coat, and reheat until bubbling.

红烧排骨

RED-COOKED PORK

RED-COOKING, OR BRAISING IN A SOY-SAUCE BASED LIQUID, IS A TECHNIQUE USED ALL OVER CHINA

TO MAKE CHICKEN, MEAT OR FISH VERY TENDER WITH LITTLE EFFORT.

3 lb pork leg or fresh ham, with
   bone in and rind on
4 scallions, each tied in a knot
4 slices ginger, smashed with the
   flat side of a cleaver
$3/4$ cup dark soy sauce
4 tablespoons Shaoxing rice wine
1 teaspoon five-spice powder
2 oz rock sugar

SERVES 8

SCRAPE the pork rind to make sure it is free of any bristles. Blanch the pork in a saucepan of boiling water for 4–5 minutes. Rinse the pork and place in a clay pot or braising pan with $2^{1}/_{2}$ cups water, the scallions, ginger, soy sauce, rice wine, five-spice powder and sugar. Bring to a boil, then reduce the heat and simmer, covered, for $2^{1}/_{2}$–3 hours, turning several times, until the meat is very tender and falling from the bone.

IF THERE is too much liquid, remove the pork and reduce the sauce by boiling it for 10–15 minutes. Slice the pork and serve with the sauce poured over it.

RED-COOKED PORK

东坡肉

DONG PO PORK

NAMED AFTER A GOURMET STATESMAN OF THE SONG DYNASTY, THE PORK IS FRIED TO GIVE THE SKIN

A GOOD COLOR AND TEXTURE, THEN SLOW COOKED TO MELTINGLY TENDER.

2 lb belly pork, rind on
2 tablespoons oil
6 scallions, sliced
8 slices ginger
3 oz rock sugar
$1/4$ cup dark soy sauce
$1/4$ cup light soy sauce
$1/2$ cup Shaoxing rice wine

SERVES 6

SCRAPE the pork rind to make sure it is free of any bristles. Blanch the pork in a saucepan of boiling water for 10 minutes, then drain well and dry thoroughly with paper towels.

HEAT a wok over high heat, add the oil and heat until very hot. Cook the pork until well browned and the skin is crisp and brown. Drain the pork.

PUT the scallions, ginger, sugar, soy sauces, rice wine and $1/2$ cup water in a clay pot or braising pan. Bring to a boil, stirring until the sugar has dissolved. Add the pork, cover and simmer for $2^{1}/_{2}$–3 hours, or until very tender. Remove the pork and drain, straining the liquid. Cut the pork into very thin slices and serve with the sauce.

Make sure that the pork is very well browned and that the skin is crisp, otherwise it will be soggy after the second stage of cooking.

Hanging the char siu to roast above a tray of water creates a steamy atmosphere which helps keep the meat moist. Generally in China, char siu is bought from carry-out restaurants as most homes do not have an oven.

CHAR SIU

CHAR SIU, OR BARBECUED PORK, IS A CANTONESE SPECIALTY THAT CAN BE SEEN HANGING IN CHINESE RESTAURANTS. CHAR SIU MEANS "SUSPENDED OVER FIRE" AND IS TRADITIONALLY DYED A RED COLOR.

MARINADE
1 tablespoon rock sugar
1 tablespoon yellow bean sauce
1 tablespoon hoisin sauce
1 tablespoon oyster sauce
1 tablespoon fermented red bean curd
1 tablespoon Chinese spirit (Mou Tai) or brandy
1/2 teaspoon roasted sesame oil

1 1/2 lb center-cut pork loin, trimmed
2 tablespoons maltose or honey, dissolved with a little water

SERVES 4

TO MAKE the marinade, combine the ingredients. Cut the pork into 4 x 8 inch strips, add to the marinade and keep in the fridge for at least 6 hours.

PREHEAT the oven to 425°F. Put a baking dish filled with 2 1/2 cups boiling water in the bottom of the oven. Drain the pork, reserving the marinade. Put an S-shaped meat hook through one end of each strip and hang from the top rack.

ROAST FOR 10–15 minutes, then baste with the marinade. Reduce the heat to 350°F and roast for 8–10 minutes. Cool for 2–3 minutes, then brush with the maltose and lightly brown under a broiler for 4–5 minutes, turning to give a charred look around the edges.

CUT the meat into slices. Pour 3/4 cup liquid from the dish into the marinade. Bring to a boil and cook for 2 minutes. Strain and pour over the pork.

SPICY CRISPY PORK

SPICY CRISPY PORK

1 1/2 lb pork belly, rind on
1 teaspoon salt
1 teaspoon five-spice powder

DIPPING SAUCE
2 tablespoons light soy sauce
1 tablespoon dark soy sauce
1 tablespoon chili sauce (optional)

SERVES 6

SCRAPE the pork rind to make sure it is free of any bristles. Dry, then rub with the salt and five-spice powder. Keep uncovered in the fridge for at least 2 hours.

TO MAKE the dipping sauce, combine all of the ingredients.

PREHEAT the oven to 475°F. Place the pork, skin side up, on a rack in a roasting pan. Roast for 20 minutes, reduce the heat to 400°F and roast for 40–45 minutes until crispy. Cut into pieces and serve with the sauce.

芥菜焖三尘肉

BRAISED PORK BELLY WITH MUSTARD CABBAGE

MEAT FROM THE BELLY IS A CUT OF MEAT THAT NEEDS LONG, SLOW COOKING TO MAKE IT TENDER. THE

RED BEAN CURD AND PRESERVED MUSTARD CABBAGE TEMPER THE RICHNESS OF THE MEAT BECAUSE

THEY ARE BOTH STRONGLY FLAVORED.

8 oz preserved mustard cabbage
2 lb pork belly, rind on
2 tablespoons dark soy sauce
oil for frying

SAUCE
1^1/$_2$ pieces fermented red bean
   curd
1 tablespoon yellow bean sauce
1^1/$_2$ tablespoons oyster sauce
2 tablespoons dark soy sauce
2 teaspoons sugar
4 star anise
2 tablespoons oil
2 garlic cloves, bruised
4 slices ginger, smashed with the
   flat side of a cleaver

SERVES 6

SOAK the preserved mustard cabbage in cold water for 4 hours. Drain and wash well in a sink full of water until the water is clear of grit. Drain again, then cut the cabbage into ^{3}/$_4$ inch pieces.

SCRAPE the pork rind to make sure it is free of any bristles. Bring a large clay pot or braising pan full of water to a boil and add the pork belly. Simmer, covered, for 40 minutes, or until tender. Drain the pork and, when cool enough to handle, prick holes over the skin with a fork. Rub the soy sauce over the skin.

HEAT a wok with a lid over medium heat, add ^{3}/$_4$ inch of the oil and heat until hot. Add the pork belly, skin side down, and cook for 5–8 minutes, or until the skin is crispy, then turn over to brown the meat. Cover the wok slightly with the lid to protect you from the fat—the pork will sizzle violently as it cooks. Place the pork in a bowl of hot water for 30 minutes to make the skin bubble up and soften. Remove the pork from the bowl and cut it into ^{3}/$_4$ inch wide strips. Set aside.

TO MAKE the sauce, put the fermented bean curd, yellow bean sauce, oyster sauce, soy sauce, sugar and star anise in a bowl. Heat a wok over medium heat, add the oil and heat until hot. Cook the garlic for 30 seconds, then add the sauce mixture and the ginger. Cook for 1–2 minutes, or until aromatic.

ADD the pork and coat with the sauce, then add 3 cups water and mix well. Cover and bring to a boil, then reduce the heat and simmer for 40 minutes. Add the mustard cabbage and cook for 15 minutes. If the sauce is too thin, boil it, uncovered, for a few minutes, until it thickens.

A cured meat shop in Guangzhou.

煱猪蹄

PICKLED PIG'S FEET

THIS RECIPE IS TRADITIONALLY SERVED TO NEW MOTHERS—THE GINGER IS SAID TO BE RESTORATIVE AND THE DISH SUPPOSEDLY HELPS MOTHERS PRODUCE PLENTY OF MILK FOR THEIR BABIES. THE HARD-BOILED EGGS ARE A SYMBOL OF LIFE AND CAN BE EATEN WITH THE MEAT.

1 lb young ginger, peeled and cut into 1 inch pieces
3 lb pig's feet or hocks, front and back legs
4 cups Chinese black rice vinegar
4 oz rock sugar
6 hard-boiled eggs (optional)

SERVES 6

PUT the ginger in a bowl of water. Bring a wok or saucepan of water to a boil, add the feet, return to a boil, then drain. Scrape the rind to make sure it is free of any bristles. Using a cleaver, cut each foot through the bone into 3 or 4 pieces.

DRAIN the ginger and lightly smash each piece with the side of a cleaver. Blanch the ginger in a saucepan of boiling water for 2 minutes, refresh in cold water and allow to cool.

PUT the vinegar and sugar in a wok or saucepan and bring to a boil, stirring to dissolve the sugar. Add the feet and ginger and simmer, covered, for 2 hours, then simmer, uncovered, for 1–2 hours until tender. Add the unpeeled eggs and cook for 5 minutes. Allow to cool, then refrigerate overnight. Remove any fat and bring to a boil. Serve hot or cold.

Pig's feet need to be cooked for several hours in order to break down all the connective tissue and make them tender.

水晶猪肉

CRYSTAL-BOILED PORK

2 lb pork leg, bone removed and rind on
2 garlic cloves, finely chopped
1 scallion, finely chopped
1 teaspoon sugar
4 tablespoons light soy sauce
1 teaspoon roasted sesame oil
1 teaspoon chile oil (optional)

SERVES 8

SCRAPE the pork rind to make sure it is free of any bristles. Tie up like a package to hold its shape, then place in a clay pot or braising pan of boiling water, return to a boil and skim off any impurities. Simmer, covered, for 45–50 minutes.

TURN OFF the heat and cool the pork in the water, without taking off the lid, for at least 4 hours, transferring the pot or braising pan to the fridge once it is cool enough. Remove the pork from the liquid and drain, rind side up, for 2–3 hours.

CUT OFF the rind, leaving a thin layer of fat. Cut the pork against the grain into thin slices. Combine the remaining ingredients and pour over the pork.

CRYSTAL-BOILED PORK

A meat stand in an outdoor market in Sichuan.

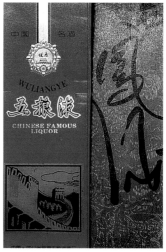

Chinese spirits are sold in fancy packaging. The Wuliangye shown here is made from five grains: sorghum, corn, wheat and two kinds of rice.

酸 甜 红 烧 排 骨

SPARERIBS WITH SWEET-AND-SOUR SAUCE

THIS DELICIOUS DISH IS CANTONESE IN ORIGIN. THE SAUCE SHOULD BE BRIGHT AND TRANSLUCENT, THE MEAT TENDER AND SUCCULENT, AND THE FLAVOR NEITHER TOO SWEET NOR TOO SOUR. IF YOU PREFER YOU CAN USE A BONELESS CUT OF PORK SUCH AS LOIN.

1 lb Chinese-style pork spareribs
1/4 teaspoon salt
1/4 teaspoon freshly ground black pepper
1 teaspoon sugar
1 tablespoon Chinese spirit (Mou Tai) or brandy
1 egg yolk, beaten
1 tablespoon cornstarch
oil for deep-frying

SAUCE
1 tablespoon oil
1 small green pepper, shredded
3 tablespoons sugar
2 tablespoons clear rice vinegar
1 tablespoon light soy sauce
1 tablespoon tomato paste
1/4 teaspoon roasted sesame oil
1/4 cup chicken and meat stock (page 281)
2 teaspoons cornstarch

SERVES 4

ASK the butcher to cut the slab of spareribs crosswise into thirds that measure 1 1/2–2 inches in length, or use a cleaver to do so yourself. Cut the ribs between the bones to separate them. Put the pieces in a bowl with the salt, pepper, sugar and Chinese spirit. Marinate in the fridge for at least 35 minutes, turning occasionally.

MEANWHILE, blend the egg yolk with the cornstarch and enough water to make a thin batter. Remove the spareribs from the marinade and coat them with the batter.

FILL a wok one quarter full of oil. Heat the oil to 350°F, or until a piece of bread fries golden brown in 15 seconds when dropped in the oil. Fry the spareribs in batches for 5 minutes until they are crisp and golden, stirring to separate them, then remove and drain. Reheat the oil and fry the spareribs again for 1 minute to darken their color. Remove and drain well on crumpled paper towels. Keep warm in a low oven.

TO MAKE the sauce, heat a wok over high heat, add the oil and heat until very hot. Stir-fry the green pepper for a few seconds, then add the sugar, rice vinegar, soy sauce, tomato paste, sesame oil and stock, and bring to a boil. Combine the cornstarch with enough water to make a paste, add to the sauce and simmer until thickened. Add the spareribs and toss to coat them with the sauce. Serve hot.

A tea seller in Guangzhou.

豆瓣炒牛肉

BEEF WITH PEPPERS AND BLACK BEAN SAUCE

LEAN STEAK IS A PARTICULARLY GOOD CUT OF BEEF FOR STIR-FRYING. THE TRADITIONAL VERSION OF THIS CANTONESE DISH CALLS FOR JUST GREEN PEPPERS, BUT THIS RECIPE USES ALL DIFFERENT COLORS TO MAKE A MORE ATTRACTIVE DISH.

1 1/2 lb beef top round steak, trimmed
1 tablespoon light soy sauce
2 teaspoons Shaoxing rice wine
1/2 teaspoon roasted sesame oil
1 teaspoon cornstarch
1 cup oil

BLACK BEAN SAUCE
1 tablespoon oil
1/4 cup finely chopped scallions
1 tablespoon finely chopped garlic
1 tablespoon salted, fermented black beans, rinsed and coarsely chopped
1 tablespoon finely chopped ginger
1 green pepper, shredded
1 red pepper, shredded
1 orange or yellow pepper, shredded
2 teaspoons light soy sauce
1 tablespoon Shaoxing rice wine
1 teaspoon sugar
2 1/2 tablespoons chicken stock (page 281)
1/2 teaspoon roasted sesame oil
2 teaspoons cornstarch

SERVES 6

CUT the beef against the grain into very thin slices. Cut each slice of beef into thin strips and place in a bowl. Add the soy sauce, rice wine, sesame oil, cornstarch and 1 tablespoon water, toss lightly to combine, then marinate in the fridge for 30 minutes. Drain the beef.

HEAT a wok over high heat, add the oil and heat until almost smoking. Add a third of the beef and cook, stirring constantly, for 1 minute, or until the pieces brown. Remove with a wire strainer or slotted spoon, then drain. Repeat with the remaining beef.

TO MAKE the black bean sauce, heat a wok over high heat, add the oil and heat until very hot. Stir-fry the scallions, garlic, black beans and ginger for 10 seconds, or until fragrant. Add the peppers and stir-fry for 1 minute, or until cooked.

COMBINE the soy sauce, rice wine, sugar, stock, sesame oil and cornstarch, add to the sauce and simmer until thickened. Add the beef and toss lightly to coat with the sauce.

红烧牛肉

RED-COOKED BEEF

THIS IS BASICALLY A STEW, SLOW-COOKED IN AN EQUAL MIXTURE OF SOY SAUCE, RICE WINE AND GINGER. THIS DISH IS A VERY HOME-STYLE ONE, MORE LIKELY FOUND IN SOMEONE'S KITCHEN THAN ON A RESTAURANT MENU.

1 lb boneless stewing beef, such as chuck or bottom round, trimmed
3 tablespoons Shaoxing rice wine
3 slices ginger
3 tablespoons dark soy sauce
2 oz rock sugar
$^3/_4$ lb carrots
1 teaspoon salt

SERVES 4

CUT the beef into $^5/_8$ inch cubes and put in a clay pot or braising pan with enough water to cover. Add the rice wine and ginger, bring to a boil, skim off any impurities, then simmer, covered, for 35–40 minutes. Add the soy sauce and sugar and simmer for 10–15 minutes.

CUT the carrots into pieces roughly the same size as the beef, add to the saucepan with the salt and cook for 20–25 minutes.

RED-COOKED BEEF

五香牛肉

FIVE-SPICE BEEF

THIS IS A DELICIOUS BEEF RECIPE THAT IS VERY SIMPLE TO PREPARE. THE LIQUID IN WHICH THE BEEF HAS BEEN COOKED CAN BE REUSED FOR COOKING OTHER TYPES OF MEAT OR POULTRY, AND IS KNOWN AS LUSHUI ZHI—A "MASTER SAUCE."

1$^1/_2$ lb boneless stewing beef, such as chuck or bottom round, trimmed
2 scallions, each tied in a knot
3 slices ginger, smashed with the flat side of a cleaver
4 tablespoons Chinese spirit (Mou Tai) or brandy
6 cups chicken and meat stock (page 281)
1 teaspoon salt
4 tablespoons light soy sauce
3 tablespoons dark soy sauce
1 tablespoon five-spice powder
5 oz rock sugar
1 scallion, finely sliced
1 teaspoon roasted sesame oil

SERVES 8

CUT the beef into 2–3 long strips and place in a clay pot or braising pan with the scallions, ginger, Chinese spirit and stock. Bring to a boil and skim off any impurities. Simmer, covered, for 15–20 minutes.

ADD the salt, soy sauces, five-spice powder and sugar to the beef, return to a boil, then simmer, covered, for 25–30 minutes.

ALLOW the beef to cool in the liquid for 1 hour, then remove, drain, and continue to cool for 3–4 hours. Just before serving, slice thinly against the grain and sprinkle with the chopped scallion and sesame oil.

THE SAUCE can be reused as a "Master Sauce" (see page 290).

Tying the scallions into knots bruises the flesh and allows more flavor to come out.

蒙古火锅

MONGOLIAN HOTPOT

THE HOTPOT WAS INTRODUCED TO NORTHERN CHINA BY THE MONGOLIANS, BUT IT SOON BECAME SO POPULAR THAT REGIONAL VARIATIONS EVOLVED. TRADITIONALLY LAMB OR BEEF IS USED, AS IN THIS SLIGHTLY ADAPTED VERSION OF THE NORTHERN CLASSIC.

The Great Wall of China.

A hotpot restaurant in Yunnan.

11 oz beef top round steak, trimmed
1 tablespoon light soy sauce
1/3 cup Shaoxing rice wine
1/2 teaspoon roasted sesame oil
1/2 lb Chinese (Napa) cabbage, stems removed and leaves cut into 2 inch squares
1 tablespoon oil
2 garlic cloves, smashed with the flat side of a cleaver
3 cups chicken stock (page 281)
1/2 teaspoon salt
1 oz bean thread noodles
1/2 lb Chinese mushrooms (shiitake) or button mushrooms
4 cups baby spinach

DIPPING SAUCE
2 tablespoons light soy sauce
1 tablespoon Shaoxing rice wine
1 teaspoon Chinese black rice vinegar
1 teaspoon sugar
1/2 teaspoon chili sauce or dried chili flakes (optional)
1/2 scallion, finely chopped
1 teaspoon finely chopped ginger
1 garlic clove, finely chopped

SERVES 6

CUT the beef against the grain into paper-thin slices. Place in a bowl and add the soy sauce, 1 tablespoon of the rice wine and the sesame oil, toss lightly, and arrange the slices on a platter.

SEPARATE the hard cabbage pieces from the leafy ones. Heat a wok over high heat, add the oil and heat until very hot. Stir-fry the hard cabbage pieces and garlic for several minutes, adding 1 tablespoon of water. Add the leafy cabbage pieces and stir-fry for several minutes. Add the remaining rice wine, chicken stock and salt, and bring to a boil. Reduce the heat and simmer for 20 minutes.

SOAK the bean thread noodles in hot water for 10 minutes, then drain and cut into 6 inch pieces. Arrange the mushrooms, spinach and noodles on several platters and place on a table where a heated Mongolian hotpot has been set up. (If you do not have a Mongolian hotpot, use an electric frying pan or an electric wok.)

COMBINE the dipping sauce ingredients and divide among 6 bowls. Put a bowl of dipping sauce at each diner's place.

POUR the cabbage soup mixture into the hotpot and bring to a boil. To eat, each diner takes a slice of meat, dips it into the hot stock until the meat is cooked, then dips the meat into the dipping sauce, and eats. The mushrooms, noodles and spinach are cooked in the same way and dipped in the sauce before eating. Supply small wire strainers to cook the noodles so they stay together. The mushrooms and noodles should cook for 5 to 6 minutes, but the spinach should only take about 1 minute. Once all the ingredients have been eaten, the soup is eaten.

香脆牛肉片

CRISPY SHREDDED BEEF

THE ORIGINS OF THIS DISH ARE A BIT OBSCURE, THOUGH SOME CLAIM THAT IT IS FROM SICHUAN OR HUNAN, PROBABLY BECAUSE IT IS SPICY. MAKE SURE THE BEEF IS REALLY CRISPY WHEN YOU FRY IT.

13 oz beef top round steak,
    trimmed
2 eggs, beaten
1/2 teaspoon salt
4 tablespoons cornstarch
oil for deep-frying
2 carrots, finely shredded
2 scallions, shredded
1 garlic clove, finely chopped
2 red chiles, shredded
4 tablespoons superfine sugar
3 tablespoons Chinese black rice
    vinegar
2 tablespoons light soy sauce

SERVES 4

CUT the beef into thin shreds. Combine the eggs, salt and cornstarch, then coat the shredded beef with the batter. Mix well.

FILL a wok one quarter full of oil. Heat the oil to 350°F, or until a piece of bread fries golden brown in 15 seconds when dropped in the oil. Cook the beef for 3–4 minutes, stirring to separate, then remove and drain. Cook the carrots for 1 1/2 minutes, then remove and drain. Pour out the oil, reserving 1 tablespoon.

REHEAT the reserved oil over high heat until very hot and stir-fry the scallion, garlic and chiles for a few seconds. Add the beef, carrots, sugar, vinegar and soy sauce and stir to combine.

CRISPY SHREDDED BEEF

青葱炒牛肉

STIR-FRIED BEEF WITH SCALLIONS

THIS NORTHERN DISH COMBINES DELICIOUSLY TENDER BEEF WITH A LIGHT GLAZE OF SOY SAUCE AND SUGAR AND FRIED SCALLIONS. YOU CAN SERVE IT WITH MANDARIN PANCAKES OR RICE.

1 lb beef top round steak, trimmed
2 garlic cloves, finely chopped
2 tablespoons light soy sauce
1 tablespoon Shaoxing rice wine
2 teaspoons sugar
1 tablespoon cornstarch
3 tablespoons oil
5 scallions, green part only,
    cut into thin strips

SAUCE
3 tablespoons light soy sauce
2 teaspoons sugar
1/2 teaspoon roasted sesame oil

SERVES 6

CUT the beef against the grain into slices 3/4 inch thick, then cut into bite-size pieces. Combine in a bowl with the garlic, soy sauce, rice wine, sugar and cornstarch. Marinate in the fridge for at least 1 hour. Drain.

TO MAKE the sauce, combine all the ingredients.

HEAT a wok over high heat, add the oil and heat until very hot. Cook the beef in 2 batches for 1 1/2 minutes, or until brown. Remove and drain. Pour out the oil, reserving 1 tablespoon.

REHEAT the reserved oil over high heat until very hot and stir-fry the scallion for 1 minute. Add the beef and the sauce. Toss well.

STIR-FRIED BEEF WITH SCALLIONS

蚝油炒牛肉

BEEF WITH OYSTER SAUCE

10 oz beef top round steak,
   trimmed
1 teaspoon sugar
1 tablespoon dark soy sauce
2 teaspoons Shaoxing rice wine
2 teaspoons cornstarch
4 dried Chinese mushrooms
oil for deep-frying
4 slices ginger
1 scallion, cut into short pieces
3/4 cup snow peas, ends trimmed
1 small carrot, thinly sliced
1/2 teaspoon salt
2–3 tablespoons chicken and meat
   stock (page 281)
2 tablespoons oyster sauce

SERVES 4

CUT the beef against the grain into thin bite-size slices. Combine with half the sugar, the soy sauce, rice wine, cornstarch and 2 tablespoons water. Marinate in the fridge for several hours, or overnight.

SOAK the dried mushrooms in boiling water for 30 minutes, then drain and squeeze out any excess water. Remove and discard the stems and cut the caps in half, or quarters if large.

FILL a wok one quarter full of oil. Heat the oil to 180°C (350°F), or until a piece of bread fries golden brown in 15 seconds when dropped in the oil. Cook the beef for 45–50 seconds, stirring to separate the pieces, and remove as soon as the color changes. Drain well in a colander. Pour out the oil, reserving 2 tablespoons.

REHEAT the reserved oil over high heat until very hot and stir-fry the ginger and scallion for 1 minute. Add the snow peas, mushrooms and carrot and stir-fry for 1 minute, then add the salt, stock and remaining sugar and stir-fry for 1 minute. Toss with the beef and oyster sauce.

蒸面粉牛肉

STEAMED BEEF WITH RICE FLOUR

1 lb beef top round steak, trimmed
2 tablespoons soy sauce
1 tablespoon chile bean paste
   (toban jiang)
1 tablespoon Shaoxing rice wine
1 tablespoon finely chopped ginger
1/4 teaspoon freshly ground white
   pepper
1 tablespoon oil
3/4 cup glutinous rice flour
1/2 teaspoon ground cinnamon
1 teaspoon roasted sesame oil
1 scallion, shredded

SERVES 4

CUT the beef into 3/4 inch slices and cut the slices into bite-size pieces. Combine with the soy sauce, chile bean paste, rice wine, ginger, pepper and oil. Marinate in the fridge for 30 minutes.

DRY-FRY the rice flour in a wok until it is brown and smells roasted. Add the cinnamon. Drain the beef and toss in the rice flour to coat the slices.

PLACE the beef slices in a steamer lined with waxed paper punched with holes. Cover and steam over simmering water in a wok for 20 minutes. Sprinkle with the sesame oil and garnish with the shredded scallion.

STEAMED BEEF WITH RICE
FLOUR

蒙古羊肉

MONGOLIAN LAMB

10 oz lamb steak
2 teaspoons finely chopped ginger
1 scallion, chopped
2 teaspoons ground Sichuan
   peppercorns
1 teaspoon salt
2 tablespoons light soy sauce
1 tablespoon yellow bean sauce
1 tablespoon hoisin sauce
1 teaspoon five-spice powder
2 tablespoons Shaoxing rice wine
oil for deep-frying
crisp lettuce leaves
1/3 cup hoisin sauce, extra
1/2 cucumber, shredded
6 scallions, shredded

SERVES 4

CUT the lamb along the grain into 6 long strips. Combine with the ginger, scallion, pepper, salt, soy sauce, yellow bean and hoisin sauces, five-spice powder and rice wine. Marinate in the fridge for at least 2 hours. Put the lamb and marinade in a flameproof dish in a steamer. Cover and steam for 2 1/2–3 hours over simmering water in a wok, replenishing with boiling water during cooking. Remove the lamb from the liquid and drain well.

FILL a wok one quarter full of oil. Heat the oil to 350°F, or until a piece of bread fries golden brown in 15 seconds when dropped in the oil. Cook the lamb for 3–4 minutes, then remove and drain. Cut the lamb into bite-size shreds.

TO SERVE, place some lamb in the lettuce leaves with some hoisin sauce, cucumber and scallions and roll up into a package.

Making bread and pancakes at a street stall in Beijing.

韭菜炒羊肉

STIR-FRIED LAMB AND LEEKS

10 oz lamb steak
1/4 teaspoon ground Sichuan
   peppercorns
1/2 teaspoon sugar
1 tablespoon light soy sauce
2 teaspoons Shaoxing rice wine
2 teaspoons cornstarch
1/2 teaspoon roasted sesame oil
3 tablespoons dried black fungus
   (wood ears)
2 1/2 cups oil
4 small pieces ginger
1 1/2 cups young leeks, white part
   only, cut into short lengths
2 tablespoons yellow bean sauce

SERVES 4

CUT the lamb into thin slices and combine with the Sichuan peppercorns, sugar, soy sauce, rice wine, cornstarch and sesame oil. Marinate in the fridge for at least 2 hours.

SOAK the dried black fungus in cold water for 20 minutes, then drain and squeeze out any excess water.

HEAT a wok over high heat, add the oil and heat until very hot. Stir-fry the lamb for 1 minute, or until the color changes. Remove and drain. Pour out the oil, reserving 2 tablespoons.

REHEAT the reserved oil over high heat until very hot and stir-fry the ginger, leeks and black fungus for 1 minute, then add the yellow bean sauce, blend well, and add the lamb. Continue stirring for 1 minute.

STIR-FRIED LAMB AND LEEKS

BEAN CURD

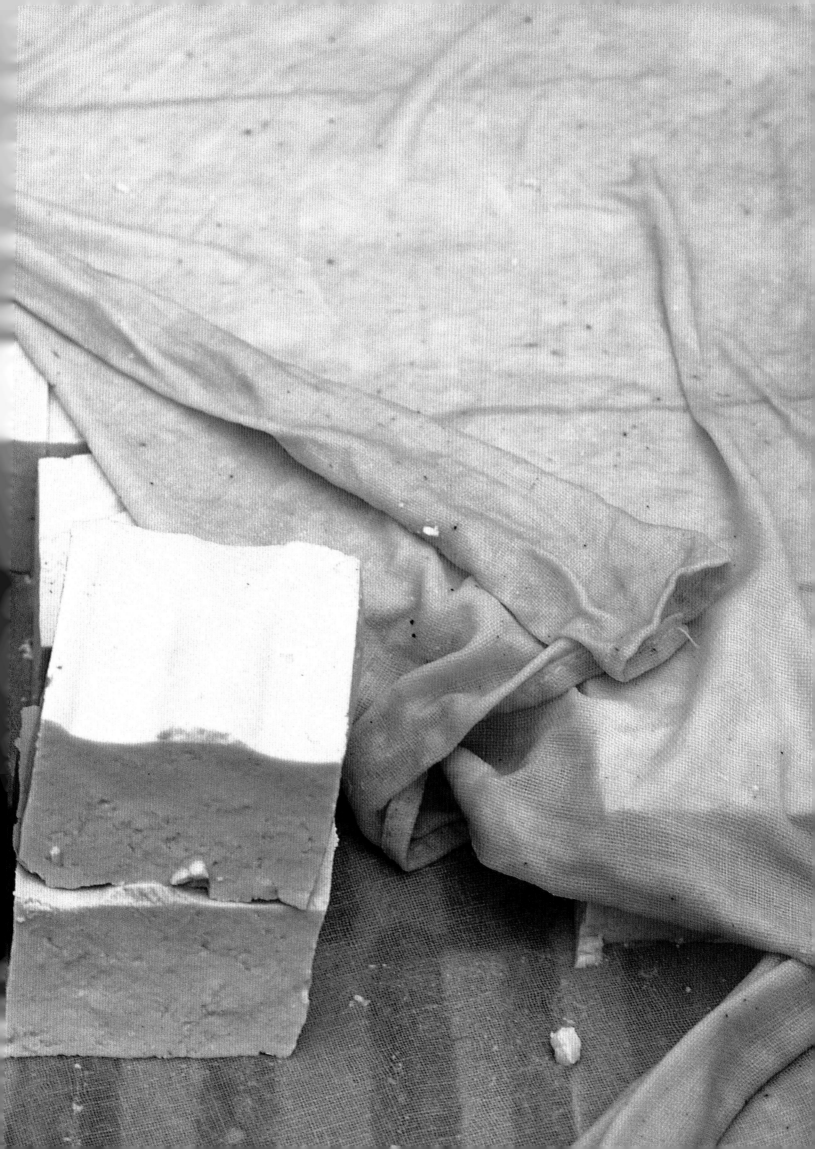

香菇焖豆腐

BRAISED BEAN CURD WITH CHINESE MUSHROOMS

SOME PEOPLE FIND BEAN CURD BLAND, BUT BY COOKING IT WITH STRONGLY FLAVORED MUSHROOMS, YOU HAVE A WELL-BALANCED DISH WITH A CONTRAST IN COLOR, AROMA, FLAVOR AND TEXTURE.

10 oz firm bean curd, drained
1 3/4 oz dried Chinese mushrooms
4 tablespoons oil
1 teaspoon salt
1 teaspoon sugar
1 tablespoon Shaoxing rice wine
1/2 teaspoon roasted sesame oil
1 teaspoon cornstarch
1 tablespoon light soy sauce

SERVES 4

CUT the bean curd into strips. Soak the dried mushrooms in boiling water for 30 minutes, then drain, reserving the soaking liquid, and squeeze out any excess water. Remove and discard the stems. Cut the caps in half.

HEAT a wok over high heat, add the oil and heat until very hot. Stir-fry the mushrooms for 35 seconds, then add 1/2 cup of the reserved liquid and bring to a boil. Add the bean curd, salt, sugar and rice wine, and stir very gently to blend well. Braise for 2 minutes, making sure there is enough liquid to prevent the bean curd from sticking to the wok, then sprinkle with the sesame oil.

COMBINE the cornstarch and soy sauce with enough of the reserved liquid to make a paste. Add to the sauce and simmer to form a clear, light glaze.

青菜炒腐酱

FERMENTED BEAN CURD WITH ASIAN GREENS

USE ANY SELECTION OF ASIAN GREENS THAT YOU WISH—CHOY SUM, BOK CHOY, CHINESE CABBAGE, CHINESE BROCCOLI AND WATER SPINACH ARE ALL SUITABLE. FERMENTED WHITE BEAN CURD IS STRONG, ESPECIALLY IF IT CONTAINS CHILES, SO DON'T BE TEMPTED TO ADD ANY MORE TO THE RECIPE.

FERMENTED BEAN CURD WITH
ASIAN GREENS

1 1/4 lb choy sum
1/2 lb bok choy
1 tablespoon oil
3 garlic cloves, crushed
3 tablespoons fermented white
  bean curd
1 teaspoon light soy sauce
3 tablespoons oyster sauce
2 teaspoons sugar
1 teaspoon roasted sesame oil

SERVES 4

CUT the choy sum horizontally into thirds and the bok choy into thirds and then quarters. Trim off any roots that may hold the pieces together, then wash well and dry thoroughly.

HEAT a wok over high heat, add the oil and heat until very hot. Stir-fry the garlic and bean curd for 1 minute. Add the choy sum stems and stir-fry for 1 minute, then add the leaves and bok choy and stir-fry for 1–2 minutes, or until the vegetables just start to wilt. Add the soy and oyster sauces, sugar and sesame oil and toss everything together.

Selling snacks in Yunnan.

麻婆豆腐

MA PO DOUFU

A QUINTESSENTIAL SICHUAN-STYLE DISH, SUPPOSEDLY NAMED AFTER AN OLD WOMAN WHO SERVED THIS IN HER RESTAURANT AND WHOSE POCKMARKED COMPLEXION LED TO THE DISH BEING CALLED MA PO DOUFU, "POCKMARKED GRANDMOTHER'S DOUFU." SOFT BEAN CURD IS TRADITIONALLY USED.

1¹/₂ lb soft or firm bean curd, drained
¹/₂ lb ground beef or pork
2 tablespoons dark soy sauce
1¹/₂ tablespoons Shaoxing rice wine
¹/₂ teaspoon roasted sesame oil
2 teaspoons Sichuan peppercorns
1 tablespoon oil
2 scallions, finely chopped
2 garlic cloves, finely chopped
2 teaspoons finely chopped ginger
1 tablespoon chile bean paste (toban jiang), or to taste
1 cup chicken and meat stock (page 281)
1¹/₂ teaspoons cornstarch
1 scallion, finely shredded

SERVES 6

CUT the bean curd into cubes. Place the meat in a bowl with 2 teaspoons of the soy sauce, 2 teaspoons of the rice wine and the sesame oil, and toss lightly. Dry-fry the Sichuan peppercorns in a wok or frying pan until brown and aromatic, then crush lightly.

HEAT a wok over high heat, add the oil and heat until very hot. Stir-fry the meat until browned, mashing and chopping to separate the pieces. Remove the meat with a wire strainer or slotted spoon and heat the oil until any liquid from the meat has evaporated. Add the scallions, garlic and ginger and stir-fry for 10 seconds, or until fragrant. Add the chile bean paste and stir-fry for 5 seconds.

COMBINE the stock with the remaining soy sauce and rice wine. Add to the wok, bring to a boil, then add the bean curd and meat. Return to a boil, reduce the heat to medium and cook for 5 minutes, or until the sauce has reduced by a quarter. If you are using soft bean curd, do not stir or it will break up.

COMBINE the cornstarch with enough water to make a paste, add to the sauce and simmer until thickened. Season if necessary. Serve sprinkled with the scallion and Sichuan peppercorns.

Fresh bean curd and chile pastes are readily available at the markets in China.

BRAISED BEAN CURD

Soft bean curd is sold by shops and traveling carts and is eaten as a snack. Here it is dressed with honey.

焖豆腐

BRAISED BEAN CURD

BEAN CURD PICKS UP ITS FLAVOR FROM THE INGREDIENTS IT IS COOKED WITH. THE VEGETABLES SHOULD BE COOKED THROUGH, BUT NOT SO MUCH THAT THEY ARE SOFT AND MUSHY.

8 dried Chinese mushrooms
3¹/₃ cups Chinese cabbage or choy sum
7 oz firm bean curd, drained
¹/₄ lb carrots
¹/₄ lb baby corn
3–4 tablespoons oil
2 tablespoons light soy sauce or oyster sauce
1 teaspoon salt
¹/₂ teaspoon sugar
1 tablespoon Shaoxing rice wine
2 scallions, cut into short pieces
1 teaspoon roasted sesame oil

SERVES 4

SOAK the dried mushrooms in boiling water for 30 minutes, then drain, reserving the liquid, and squeeze out any excess water. Remove and discard the stems and cut the caps in half.

CUT the cabbage into large pieces and the bean curd into 12 cubes. Diagonally cut the carrots. Leave the corn whole if small, or cut into pieces.

LINE a clay pot, braising pan or saucepan with the Chinese cabbage and pour in ¹/₄ cup of the reserved liquid. Heat a wok over high heat, add half the oil and heat until very hot. Lightly brown the bean curd for 2–3 minutes, transfer to the pot and add the soy or oyster sauce.

REHEAT the wok over high heat, add the remaining oil and heat until very hot. Stir-fry the carrots, corn and mushrooms for 1 minute. Add the salt, sugar and rice wine, blend well, then transfer to the pot. Bring to a boil, place the scallions on top, then simmer, covered, for 15–20 minutes. Sprinkle with the sesame oil.

小葱辣椒拌豆腐

SOFT BEAN CURD WITH CHILE AND SCALLIONS

THIS RECIPE PERFECTLY SETS OFF THE SOFT, COOL SMOOTHNESS OF THE BEAN CURD BY ADDING A HOT, HIGHLY SPICED DRESSING. SERVE WITH RICE AND STIR-FRIED GREENS FOR A HEALTHY MEAL.

¹/₂ lb soft bean curd, drained
2 scallions, thinly sliced
1 red chile, thinly sliced
2 tablespoons chopped cilantro
2 tablespoons soy sauce
¹/₃ cup oil
1 teaspoon roasted sesame oil

SERVES 4

CUT the bean curd into cubes and put it on a flameproof plate.

SCATTER the scallions, chile, cilantro and soy sauce over the bean curd. Put the oils in a small saucepan and heat until they are smoking, then immediately pour the oils over the bean curd.

Transporting bean curd in Hangzhou.

NORTHERN-STYLE BEAN CURD

THIS DISH WAS APPARENTLY A FAVORITE OF DOWAGER EMPRESS TZU-HSI IN THE NINETEENTH CENTURY, AND IT'S STILL A POPULAR CLASSIC IN CHINA TODAY. THE BEAN CURD IS FIRST FRIED, THEN SIMMERED SO THAT IT MELTS IN YOUR MOUTH.

The Temple of Heaven in Beijing.

2 lb firm bean curd, drained
oil for deep-frying
1 cup cornstarch
2 eggs, lightly beaten
1 tablespoon finely chopped ginger
1$^1/_3$ cups chicken stock (page 281)
2 tablespoons Shaoxing rice wine
1 teaspoon salt, or to taste
$^1/_2$ teaspoon sugar
1$^1/_2$ teaspoons roasted sesame oil
2 scallions, green part only, finely
    chopped

SERVES 6

HOLDING a cleaver parallel to the cutting surface, slice each bean curd cake in half horizontally. Cut each piece into 1$^1/_4$ inch squares.

FILL a wok one quarter full of oil. Heat the oil to 375°F, or until a piece of bread fries golden brown in 10 seconds when dropped in the oil. Coat each piece of bean curd in the cornstarch, then dip in the beaten egg to coat. Cook the bean curd in batches for 3–4 minutes on each side, or until golden brown. Remove with a wire strainer or slotted spoon and drain in a colander. Pour out the oil, reserving 1 teaspoon.

REHEAT the reserved oil over high heat until very hot and stir-fry the ginger for 5 seconds, or until fragrant. Add the stock, rice wine, salt and sugar, and bring to a boil. Add the fried bean curd and pierce the pieces with a fork so that they will absorb the cooking liquid. Cook over medium heat for 20 minutes, or until all the liquid is absorbed. Drizzle the sesame oil over the bean curd, toss carefully to coat, sprinkle with the scallions and serve.

An outdoor haircut in Beijing.

豆干包

STUFFED BEAN CURD

SEVERAL VERSIONS EXIST OF THIS HIGHLY POPULAR DISH, WHICH IS THOUGHT TO BE A HAKKA RECIPE FROM THE SOUTHEAST OF CHINA. THE STUFFING HERE IS A MIXTURE OF SHRIMP AND PORK AND THOUGH THE RECIPE MAY APPEAR RATHER COMPLICATED, IT IS WORTH THE EFFORT.

Push the stuffing fairly firmly into the slit in the bean curd—the pocket should be open at one end and the stuffing showing.

6 x 2 inch square cakes firm bean curd, drained
2 dried Chinese mushrooms
2 oz shrimp
2 oz ground pork
a pinch of salt
1/2 egg white, beaten
1 teaspoon Shaoxing rice wine
1 teaspoon light soy sauce
1–2 teaspoons cornstarch
3–4 tablespoons oil
1/4 cup chicken and meat stock (page 281)
2 tablespoons oyster sauce
1 scallion, sliced

SERVES 4

PARBOIL the bean curd in a saucepan of lightly salted boiling water for 2–3 minutes to harden, then drain. Cut each cake into 2 triangular pieces and make a slit at the bottom of each triangle.

SOAK the dried mushrooms in boiling water for 30 minutes, then drain and squeeze out any excess water. Remove and discard the stems and finely chop the caps. Peel and devein the shrimp and chop them finely until they are almost a paste. Put the mushrooms and shrimp in a bowl with the pork, salt, egg white, rice wine, soy sauce and enough cornstarch to hold the mixture together. Fill the slit of each bean curd piece with stuffing (the pieces will gape open and show the stuffing).

HEAT a wok over high heat, add the oil and heat until very hot. Cook the stuffed bean curd for 2 minutes on each side, or until golden. Pour off any excess oil. Add the stock and oyster sauce, bring to a boil and braise for 5–6 minutes. Sprinkle with the scallion.

STIR-FRIED BEAN CURD IN YELLOW BEAN SAUCE

豆瓣醬炒豆腐

STIR-FRIED BEAN CURD IN YELLOW BEAN SAUCE

3/4 lb firm bean curd, drained
2 tablespoons oil
1 garlic clove, crushed
11/2 tablespoons yellow bean sauce
2 teaspoons oyster sauce
2 teaspoons sugar
2 teaspoons cornstarch
1 scallion, cut into 3/4 inch lengths
5 cilantro sprigs

SERVES 4

CUT the bean curd into bite-size pieces. Heat the wok over medium heat, add the oil and heat until hot. Cook the bean curd until it is golden brown on both sides.

ADD the garlic, yellow bean sauce, oyster sauce and sugar and toss until well combined. Combine the cornstarch with 2/3 cup water, add to the sauce with the scallion and simmer until the sauce has thickened and the scallion has softened slightly. If the sauce is still a little thick, add a little water. Garnish with cilantro sprigs.

Wash the gluten thoroughly under running water to get rid of the starch. You should end up with a firm, sliceable piece of gluten.

焖 面 筋

BRAISED GLUTEN

GLUTEN IS A WHEAT FLOUR DOUGH THAT HAS HAD THE STARCH WASHED AWAY SO IT IS SPONGY AND POROUS, SIMILAR TO BEAN CURD, BUT MUCH FIRMER. IN CHINA, GLUTEN IS USED AS A MOCK MEAT AS IT CAN BE COOKED IN THE SAME WAY. YOU CAN USE 10 OZ STORE-BOUGHT GLUTEN IN THIS RECIPE.

2 lb all-purpose flour
$1^{1}/_{2}$ teaspoons salt
oil for deep-frying
1 teaspoon sugar
1 tablespoon light soy sauce
3–4 tablespoons vegetable stock
   (page 281)
$^{1}/_{4}$ teaspoon roasted sesame oil

SERVES 4

SIFT the flour into a bowl with 1 teaspoon of the salt and gradually add $2^{1}/_{2}$ cups warm water to make a dough. Knead until smooth, then cover with a damp cloth and allow to rest in a warm place for 55–60 minutes.

RINSE the dough under cold water and wash off all the starch by pulling, stretching and squeezing the dough with your hands. You should have about 10 oz gluten after 10–15 minutes of washing and squeezing. Extract as much water as you can by squeezing the dough hard, then cut the dough into bite-size pieces. Dry thoroughly.

FILL a wok one quarter full of oil. Heat the oil to 350°F, or until a piece of bread fries golden brown in 15 seconds when dropped in the oil. Cook the gluten pieces for 3 minutes, or until golden. Remove and drain. Pour the oil from the wok, leaving 1 teaspoon.

REHEAT the reserved oil over high heat until very hot and add the gluten, remaining salt, sugar, soy sauce and stock, bring to a boil and braise for 2–3 minutes, or until the liquid has evaporated. Sprinkle with the sesame oil. Serve hot or cold.

A Buddhist temple in Sichuan.

Incense and temple offerings are on sale at stores in the streets around temples.

MOCK DUCK

GLUTEN IS USED IN VEGETARIAN CHINESE COOKING TO TAKE THE PLACE OF MEAT IN RECIPES. RATHER THAN RESEMBLING DUCK, THIS DISH IS COOKED AS DUCK WOULD BE COOKED. YOU CAN MAKE THE GLUTEN OR USE 10 OZ STORE-BOUGHT GLUTEN—PLAIN OR SHAPED LIKE PIECES OF DUCK.

2 lb all-purpose flour
1 teaspoon salt
1¹/₂ tablespoons cornstarch
2 tablespoons oil
1 green pepper, diced
¹/₃ cup vegetable stock (page 281)
2 tablespoons light soy sauce
2 teaspoons Shaoxing rice wine
1 teaspoon sugar
1 teaspoon roasted sesame oil

SERVES 4

SIFT the flour into a bowl with the salt and gradually add 2¹/₂ cups warm water to make a dough. Knead until smooth, then cover with a damp cloth and allow to rest in a warm place for 55–60 minutes.

RINSE the dough under cold water and wash off all the starch by pulling, stretching and squeezing the dough with your hands. You should have about 10 oz gluten after 10–15 minutes of washing and squeezing. Extract as much water as you can by squeezing the dough hard, then cut the dough into bite-size pieces. Dry thoroughly.

TOSS the gluten in 1 tablespoon of the cornstarch. Heat a wok over high heat, add the oil and heat until very hot. Quickly stir-fry the gluten until it is browned all over, then remove from the wok. Stir-fry the pepper until it starts to brown around the edges, then remove. Pour off any excess oil.

ADD the stock, soy sauce, rice wine and sugar to the wok and bring to a boil. Return the gluten and pepper and simmer for 1 minute.

COMBINE the remaining cornstarch with enough water to make a paste, add to the sauce and simmer until thickened. Sprinkle with the sesame oil and serve.

VEGETABLES

Lighting candles at a
Buddhist temple.

Tiger lily buds, or golden
needles, are dried unopened
lilies. When reconstituted they
resemble limp bean sprouts.

佛跳墙

BUDDHA'S DELIGHT

THE ORIGINAL RECIPE FOR THIS WELL-KNOWN VEGETARIAN DISH USED NO LESS THAN EIGHTEEN
DIFFERENT INGREDIENTS TO REPRESENT THE EIGHTEEN BUDDHAS. NOWADAYS, ANYTHING BETWEEN
SIX TO EIGHT INGREDIENTS IS USUAL PRACTICE.

Bean curd puffs are cubes of
deep-fried bean curd. They have
a spongy interior that soaks up
liquid and flavors well.

1/4 cup tiger lily buds
6–8 dried Chinese mushrooms
1/4 oz dried black fungus (wood
  ears)
5 oz braised gluten (page 198)
  or store-bought braised gluten,
  drained
2 oz bean curd puffs
1 cup bean sprouts
1 carrot
4 tablespoons oil
1/2 cup snow peas, ends trimmed
1 teaspoon salt
1/2 teaspoon sugar
4 tablespoons vegetable stock
  (page 281)
2 tablespoons light soy sauce
1/2 teaspoon roasted sesame oil

SERVES 4

SOAK the tiger lily buds in boiling water for
30 minutes. Rinse and drain the tiger lily buds,
and trim off any roots if they are hard. Soak the
dried mushrooms in boiling water for 30 minutes,
then drain and squeeze out any excess water.
Remove and discard the stems and cut the caps
in half (or quarters if large). Soak the dried black
fungus in cold water for 20 minutes, then drain
and squeeze out any excess water. Cut any large
pieces of fungus in half.

CUT the gluten and bean curd into small pieces.
Wash the bean sprouts, discarding any husks and
straggly end pieces, and dry thoroughly.
Diagonally cut the carrot into thin slices.

HEAT a wok over high heat, add the oil and heat
until very hot. Stir-fry the carrot for 30 seconds,
then add the snow peas and bean sprouts.
Stir-fry for 1 minute, then add the gluten, bean
curd, tiger lily buds, mushrooms, black fungus,
salt, sugar, stock and soy sauce. Toss everything
together, then cover and braise for 2 minutes at
a gentle simmer.

ADD the sesame oil, toss it through the mixture
and serve hot or cold.

炒生菜

STIR-FRIED LETTUCE

LETTUCE IS GENERALLY EATEN COOKED IN CHINA AND LOTS OF DIFFERENT VARIETIES ARE AVAILABLE. LETTUCE IS ADDED TO SOUPS, STIR-FRIES AND CASSEROLES, AS WELL AS COOKED ON ITS OWN AS A VEGETABLE. YOU CAN USE ANY CRISP LETTUCE FOR THIS RECIPE.

1 1/2 lb iceberg or Romaine lettuce
1 tablespoon oil
4 tablespoons oyster sauce
1 teaspoon roasted sesame oil

SERVES 4

CUT the lettuce in half and then into wide strips, trimming off any roots that may hold the pieces together. Wash well and dry thoroughly (if too much water clings to the lettuce it will cause it to steam rather than fry).

HEAT a wok over high heat, add the oil and heat until very hot. Toss the lettuce pieces around the wok until they start to wilt, then add the oyster sauce and toss everything together. Sprinkle with the sesame oil, season and serve.

炒豆芽

BEAN SPROUTS STIR-FRY

BEAN SPROUTS CAN MEAN EITHER SOY BEAN SPROUTS OR MUNG BEAN SPROUTS AND BOTH ARE USED IN THIS RECIPE. SOY BEAN SPROUTS ARE SLIGHTLY BIGGER AND MORE ROBUST FOR COOKING, AS WELL AS BEING MORE COMMONLY FOUND IN CHINA.

2 1/2 cups mung bean sprouts
3 cups soy bean sprouts
1 tablespoon oil
1 red chile, finely chopped
1 scallion, finely chopped
2 tablespoons light soy sauce

SERVES 4

WASH the bean sprouts, discarding any husks and straggly end pieces, and drain thoroughly.

HEAT a wok over high heat, add the oil and heat until very hot. Stir-fry the chile and scallion for 30 seconds, add the bean sprouts and toss until they start to wilt. Add the soy sauce and toss for 1 minute, then season and serve.

BEAN SPROUTS STIR-FRY

炒双冬

STIR-FRIED TWIN WINTER

THIS SIMPLE DISH IS CALLED "TWIN WINTER" BECAUSE BOTH MUSHROOMS AND BAMBOO SHOOTS ARE AT THEIR BEST IN THE WINTER MONTHS. ANOTHER VERSION OF THIS DISH, TRIPLE WINTER, USES BAMBOO SHOOTS AND MUSHROOMS WITH CABBAGE.

Fresh bamboo shoots.

12 dried Chinese mushrooms
1¼ cups fresh or canned bamboo
  shoots, rinsed and drained
3 tablespoons oil
2 tablespoons light soy sauce
2 teaspoons sugar
2 teaspoons cornstarch
½ teaspoon roasted sesame oil

SERVES 4

SOAK the dried mushrooms in boiling water for 30 minutes, then drain, reserving the liquid, and squeeze out any excess water. Remove and discard the stems and cut the caps in half (or quarters if large). Cut the bamboo shoots into small pieces the same size as the mushrooms.

HEAT a wok over high heat, add the oil and heat until very hot. Stir-fry the mushrooms and bamboo shoots for 1 minute. Add the soy sauce and sugar, stir a few times, then add ½ cup of the reserved liquid. Bring to a boil and braise for 2 minutes, stirring constantly.

COMBINE the cornstarch with enough water to make a paste, add to the sauce and simmer until thickened. Sprinkle with the sesame oil, blend well and serve.

STIR-FRIED CHINESE CABBAGE

炒包菜

STIR-FRIED CHINESE CABBAGE

CHINESE CABBAGE IS A COOL-WEATHER CROP, BUT IT CAN NOW BE BOUGHT ALL YEAR ROUND. THERE ARE TWO KINDS; ONE HAS A GREEN, FINE LEAF, THE OTHER IS YELLOW AND TIGHTLY CURLED.

1 oz dried shrimp
1 tablespoon oil
¾ lb Chinese (Napa) cabbage,
  cut into ½ inch strips
1 tablespoon light soy sauce
2 teaspoons sugar
1 tablespoon clear rice vinegar
2 teaspoons roasted sesame oil

SERVES 4

SOAK the dried shrimp in boiling water for 1 hour, then drain.

HEAT a wok over high heat, add the oil and heat until very hot. Toss the Chinese cabbage for 2 minutes, or until wilted. Add the shrimp, soy sauce, sugar and rice vinegar and cook for 1 minute. Sprinkle with the sesame oil and serve.

Preserved mustard cabbage *(bottom, second from left)* for sale in Beijing.

回锅长豆

DOUBLE-COOKED YARD-LONG BEANS

THIS SICHUAN-STYLE RECIPE IS SO NAMED BECAUSE THE BEANS, AFTER BEING FRIED UNTIL TENDER, ARE THEN COOKED AGAIN WITH SEASONINGS AND A SAUCE. TRADITIONALLY YARD-LONG, OR SNAKE, BEANS ARE USED. THESE ARE AVAILABLE IN CHINESE MARKETS, BUT HARICOT VERTS ARE ALSO DELICIOUS.

2 lb yard-long (snake) beans or haricot verts, trimmed
6 oz ground pork or beef
2 tablespoons light soy sauce
1 1/2 tablespoons Shaoxing rice wine
1/2 teaspoon roasted sesame oil
oil for deep-frying
5 tablespoons finely chopped preserved mustard cabbage
3 scallions, finely chopped
1 1/2 teaspoons sugar

SERVES 6

DIAGONALLY cut the beans into 2 inch pieces. Lightly chop the ground meat with a cleaver until it becomes slightly fluffy. Put the meat in a bowl, add 1 teaspoon of the soy sauce, 1 teaspoon of the rice wine and the sesame oil and stir vigorously to combine.

FILL a wok one quarter full of oil. Heat the oil to 350°F, or until a piece of bread fries golden brown in 15 seconds when dropped in the oil. Add 1/3 of the beans, covering the wok with the lid as they are placed in the oil to prevent the oil from splashing. Cook for 3 1/2–4 minutes, stirring constantly, until they are tender and golden brown at the edges. Remove with a wire strainer or slotted spoon and drain. Reheat the oil and repeat with the remaining beans. Pour the oil from the wok, leaving 1 tablespoon.

REHEAT the reserved oil over high heat until very hot, add the ground meat and stir-fry until the color changes, mashing and chopping to separate the pieces of meat. Push the meat to the side and add the preserved mustard cabbage and scallions. Stir-fry over high heat for 15 seconds, or until fragrant. Add the beans with the remaining soy sauce and rice wine, sugar and 1 tablespoon water, and return the meat to the center of the pan. Toss lightly to coat the beans with the sauce.

Meat, such as this pork, is ground by hand using two cleavers at a market.

CHINESE BROCCOLI IN OYSTER SAUCE

CHINESE BROCCOLI DIFFERS FROM ITS WESTERN RELATIVE IN THAT THE STEMS ARE LONG, THE FLORETS ARE TINY, AND THE FLAVOR IS SLIGHTLY BITTER. SOME VERSIONS ARE PURPLE IN COLOR. CHINESE BROCCOLI IS AVAILABLE IN CHINESE MARKETS.

2 lb Chinese broccoli (gai lan)
1¹/₂ tablespoons oil
2 scallions, finely chopped
1¹/₂ tablespoons grated ginger
3 garlic cloves, finely chopped
3 tablespoons oyster sauce
1¹/₂ tablespoons light soy sauce
1 tablespoon Shaoxing rice wine
1 teaspoon sugar
1 teaspoon roasted sesame oil
¹/₂ cup chicken stock (page 281)
2 teaspoons cornstarch

SERVES 6

WASH the broccoli well. Discard any tough-looking stems and diagonally cut into ³/₄ inch pieces through the stem and the leaf. Blanch the broccoli in a saucepan of boiling water for 2 minutes, or until the stems and leaves are just tender, then refresh in cold water and dry thoroughly.

HEAT a wok over high heat, add the oil and heat until very hot. Stir-fry the scallions, ginger and garlic for 10 seconds, or until fragrant. Add the broccoli and cook until the broccoli is heated through. Combine the remaining ingredients, add to the wok, stirring until the sauce has thickened, and toss to coat the broccoli.

SICHUAN-STYLE SPICY EGGPLANT

THE TENDER FLESH OF THE EGGPLANT ABSORBS FLAVORS AND IT IS THE PERFECT CARRIER FOR BOTH SPICY AND DELICATE SAUCES. THIS RECIPE USES THIN EGGPLANTS (USUALLY REFERRED TO AS JAPANESE EGGPLANT), BUT IF THEY ARE UNAVAILABLE, USE SMALL, TENDER WESTERN ONES.

1 lb thin eggplants
¹/₂ teaspoon salt
3 tablespoons light soy sauce
1 tablespoons Shaoxing rice wine
1 tablespoon roasted sesame oil
2 teaspoons clear rice vinegar
1 teaspoon sugar
1 scallion, finely chopped
2 garlic cloves, finely chopped
1 teaspoon chile bean paste
  (toban jiang)

SERVES 6

PEEL the eggplants and trim off the ends. Cut the eggplants in half lengthwise and cut each half into strips ³/₄ inch thick. Cut the strips into 2 inch pieces. Place the epplants in a bowl, add the salt and toss lightly, then set aside for 1 hour. Pour off any water that has accumulated.

ARRANGE the eggplant on a flameproof plate and place in a steamer. Cover and steam over simmering water in a wok for 20 minutes, or until tender. Combine the remaining ingredients in a bowl, then pour the sauce over the eggplant, tossing lightly to coat.

SICHUAN-STYLE SPICY
EGGPLANT

蒜爆炒豆苗

STIR-FRIED PEA SHOOTS WITH GARLIC

PEA SHOOTS ARE THE DELICATE LEAVES AT THE TOP OF PEA PLANTS. THEY ARE PARTICULARLY GOOD WHEN STIR-FRIED SIMPLY WITH A LITTLE OIL AND GARLIC. IF UNAVAILABLE, SPINACH OR ANY OTHER LEAFY GREEN MAY BE SUBSTITUTED.

3/4 lb pea shoots
1 teaspoon oil
2 garlic cloves, finely chopped
1 1/2 tablespoons Shaoxing rice wine
1/4 teaspoon salt

SERVES 6

TRIM the tough stems and wilted leaves from the pea shoots. Wash well and dry thoroughly.

HEAT a wok over high heat, add the oil and heat until very hot. Add the pea shoots and garlic and toss lightly for 20 seconds, then add the rice wine and salt, and stir-fry for 1 minute, or until the shoots are slightly wilted, but still bright green. Transfer to a platter, leaving behind most of the liquid. Serve hot, at room temperature, or cold.

Selling pea shoots in Dali.

炒莲藕

STIR-FRIED LOTUS ROOT

THE LOTUS IS A SYMBOL OF PURITY IN BUDDHIST CULTURE AS THE ROOTS, WHICH GROW IN MUD, ARE CLEAN AND PURE DESPITE THEIR MUDDY ORIGINS. LOTUS ROOT CAN BE EATEN RAW OR COOKED AND HAS A CRISP, CRUNCHY TEXTURE.

1 lb fresh lotus root or 3/4 lb pre-packaged lotus root
1 tablespoon oil
1 garlic clove, thinly sliced
10 very thin slices ginger
2 scallions, finely chopped
2 oz Chinese ham, rind removed, diced
1 tablespoon Shaoxing rice wine
1 tablespoon light soy sauce
1 teaspoon sugar

SERVES 4

IF USING fresh lotus root, peel, cut into slices, wash well and drain thoroughly. Pre-packaged lotus root just needs to be washed, sliced and drained thoroughly.

HEAT a wok over high heat, add the oil and heat until very hot. Stir-fry the garlic and ginger for 30 seconds. Add the scallion, ham and lotus root and stir-fry for 1 minute, then add the rice wine, soy sauce and sugar and cook for 2–3 minutes, or until the lotus root is tender but still crisp.

STIR-FRIED LOTUS ROOT

Market crops near Guilin.

番茄炒蛋

STIR-FRIED EGGS AND TOMATOES

THIS IS A SIMPLE DISH OF SCRAMBLED EGGS FLAVORED WITH TOMATOES, SCALLIONS AND SESAME

OIL, WHICH CAN BE EATEN ON ITS OWN OR AS A SIDE DISH. YOU CAN MAKE THIS IN A WOK OR IN A

NONSTICK FRYING PAN.

STIR-FRIED EGGS AND
TOMATOES

4 eggs
2 teaspoons roasted sesame oil
1 tablespoon oil
2 scallions, finely chopped
2 very ripe large tomatoes, roughly
chopped

SERVES 4

BEAT the eggs with the sesame oil and season
with salt. Heat a wok or nonstick frying pan over
high heat, add the oil and heat until very hot.
Stir-fry the scallions for 30 seconds, then add
the tomatoes and stir-fry for 30 seconds. Add
the eggs and stir until the eggs are set.

Chinese celery is similar to celery
but has darker stems and a more
pronounced flavor.

芹菜沙律

CELERY SALAD

YOU CAN OMIT THE DRIED SHRIMP USED AS A GARNISH FROM THIS DELICIOUS SALAD IF YOU ARE A

VEGETARIAN. USE YOUNG CELERY THAT DOES NOT HAVE STRINGS RUNNING THROUGH IT IF YOU CAN,

OTHERWISE PULL OUT THE STRINGS BEFORE SLICING.

2 tablespoons dried shrimp
2 tablespoons Shaoxing rice wine
8 Chinese celery or celery stalks
1 tablespoon light soy sauce
1 tablespoon sugar
1 tablespoon clear rice vinegar
1 teaspoon roasted sesame oil
1 tablespoon finely chopped ginger

SERVES 4

SOAK the dried shrimp in the rice wine for 1 hour.

CUT the celery into thin slices and blanch in a
saucepan of boiling water for 1–2 minutes, then
refresh in cold water and dry thoroughly. Arrange
the celery on a serving dish.

COMBINE the soaked shrimp and rice wine with
the soy sauce, sugar, rice vinegar, sesame oil and
ginger. Blend well and pour over the celery just
before serving.

釀苦瓜炒豆瓣醬

STUFFED BITTER MELON IN BLACK BEAN SAUCE

BITTER MELON LIVES UP TO ITS NAME—IT REALLY IS BITTER, AND SOMETHING OF AN ACQUIRED TASTE. BUY RIPER MELONS, WHICH ARE MORE YELLOW IN COLOR, AS THESE ARE A LITTLE SWEETER. BLANCHING THE MELON IN BOILING WATER ALSO GETS RID OF A LITTLE BITTERNESS.

BLACK BEAN SAUCE
2 tablespoons salted, fermented
   black beans, rinsed and coarsely
   chopped
2 garlic cloves, finely chopped
2 teaspoons finely chopped ginger
2–3 small red chiles, seeded and
   thinly sliced
2 teaspoons oyster sauce
2 teaspoons soy sauce
3 teaspoons sugar

3 bitter melons
1 lb firm white fish fillets, such
   as cod, halibut or monkfish,
   skin removed
3 teaspoons finely chopped ginger
3 teaspoons light soy sauce
1 teaspoon roasted sesame oil
3/4 oz finely chopped cilantro
2 scallions, thinly sliced
1/4 teaspoon freshly ground white
   pepper
2 1/2 tablespoons cornstarch
2 tablespoons oil

SERVES 4

TO MAKE the black bean sauce, combine the black beans, garlic, ginger, chiles, oyster sauce, soy sauce and sugar in a small bowl. Set aside.

SLICE the bitter melons into rings about 1 inch wide. Remove the seeds and membranes and blanch the pieces in a saucepan of boiling water for 2–3 minutes, then refresh in cold water and dry thoroughly.

FINELY CHOP the fish fillets with a cleaver or in a food processor and place in a bowl with the ginger, soy sauce, sesame oil, cilantro, scallions, pepper and 1 tablespoon of the cornstarch, stirring to combine. Set aside in the fridge for up to 1 hour to allow the flavors to develop.

LIGHTLY COAT the bitter melon in 1 tablespoon of the cornstarch to help the stuffing stick to it. Fill the center of each piece with the fish mixture. Heat a wok over high heat, add the oil and heat until very hot. Cook the bitter melon in batches, without turning, until golden brown. Remove from the wok and keep warm.

ADD the black bean sauce to the wok and stir-fry over medium heat for 1 minute. Add the stuffed melon pieces and coat with the sauce.

COMBINE the remaining cornstarch with about 1/2 cup water, add to the sauce and simmer until thickened.

Press the filling firmly into the hollow in each piece of melon so that it stays intact when the melon is fried.

CHINESE BROCCOLI WITH SOY SAUCE

CHINESE BROCCOLI (GAI LAN) IS A QUICK AND EASY VEGETABLE TO PREPARE. ALTHOUGH IT CAN BE USED IN STIR-FRIES OR WITH MORE COMPLICATED SAUCES, IT GOES EQUALLY WELL WITH A SIMPLE DRIZZLE OF OYSTER SAUCE AND SOY SAUCE.

Chinese broccoli (gai lan) comes in both the more common green and a dark reddish-purple variety.

3/4–1 lb Chinese broccoli
  (gai lan)
2 tablespoons oil
1 tablespoon oyster sauce
2 tablespoons light soy sauce

SERVES 4

WASH the broccoli well. Discard any tough-looking stems and cut the rest of the stems in half. Blanch the broccoli in a saucepan of boiling water for 2 minutes, or until the stems and leaves are just tender, then refresh in cold water and dry thoroughly. Arrange in a serving dish.

HEAT a wok over high heat, add the oil and heat until very hot. Carefully pour the hot oil over the Chinese broccoli (it will splatter). Gently toss the oil with the Chinese broccoli and drizzle with the oyster sauce and soy sauce. Serve hot.

STIR-FRIED BOK CHOY

BOK CHOY COMES IN SEVERAL VARIETIES AND SIZES. SOME TYPES HAVE LONG WHITE STEMS AND VERY GREEN LEAVES, OTHERS, SUCH AS BABY BOK CHOY, HAVE SHORTER PALE-GREEN STEMS AND LEAVES. ALL TYPES ARE INTERCHANGEABLE IN RECIPES.

CHINESE BROCCOLI WITH
SOY SAUCE

3/4 lb bok choy
2 tablespoons oil
2 garlic cloves, smashed with the
  flat side of a cleaver
3 thin slices ginger, smashed with
  the flat side of a cleaver
3 tablespoons chicken stock
  (page 281)
1 teaspoon sugar
salt or light soy sauce, to taste
1 teaspoon roasted sesame oil

SERVES 4

CUT the bok choy into 2–3 inch pieces. Trim off any roots that may hold the pieces together, then wash well and dry thoroughly.

HEAT a wok over high heat, add the oil and heat until very hot. Stir-fry the garlic and ginger for 30 seconds. Add the bok choy and stir-fry until it begins to wilt, then add the stock and sugar and season with the salt or soy sauce. Simmer, covered, for 2 minutes, or until the stems and leaves are tender but still green. Add the sesame oil and serve hot.

酸辣包心菜

HOT-AND-SOUR CABBAGE

THIS SPICY PICKLE OR SIDE DISH IS WELL LOVED IN MANY PARTS OF CHINA, ALTHOUGH IT IS ESPECIALLY POPULAR IN HANGZHOU, A CITY IN EAST CHINA THAT BOASTS GREAT FOOD. IT MAY BE MADE WITH OTHER VEGETABLES BESIDES CABBAGE AND CAN BE EATEN HOT, WARM OR COLD.

1 small Chinese (Napa) cabbage
3 tablespoons light soy sauce
$^1/_2$ teaspoon salt
2 tablespoons sugar
4 tablespoons Chinese black rice vinegar
1 tablespoon oil
1 red chile, finely chopped
2$^1/_2$ tablespoons finely chopped ginger
1$^1/_2$ red peppers, cut into $^1/_4$ inch dice
1$^1/_2$ tablespoons Shaoxing rice wine
1 teaspoon roasted sesame oil

SERVES 6

SEPARATE the cabbage leaves and trim off the stems. Cut the leaves lengthwise into $^1/_2$ inch wide strips, separating the stem sections from the leafy sections.

COMBINE the soy sauce, salt, sugar and Chinese black vinegar and set aside.

HEAT a wok over high heat, add the oil and heat until very hot. Stir-fry the red chile and ginger for 15 seconds. Add the red peppers and stir-fry for 30 seconds, then add the rice wine and stir-fry for 30 seconds. Add the stem sections of the cabbage, toss lightly and cook for 1 minute. Add the leafy sections and toss lightly, then pour in the soy sauce mixture, tossing lightly to coat. Cook for 30 seconds, then add the sesame oil. Serve hot, at room temperature, or cold.

Chinese cabbages for sale in a Beijing market. The cabbages are often covered in blankets to protect them from frost.

黑椒炒白菜

FLAT CABBAGE WITH BLACK PEPPER

FLAT CABBAGE (TAT SOI) HAS SMALL, DARK-GREEN, SHINY LEAVES WITH A WHITE STEM. IT IS SOMETIMES CALLED ROSETTE CABBAGE. THE LEAVES NEED TO BE WASHED THOROUGHLY BEFORE THEY ARE USED AS THEY HARBOR A LOT OF DIRT.

1 flat cabbage (tat soi)
1 tablespoon oil
2 garlic cloves, sliced
$^1/_4$ teaspoon freshly ground black pepper
2 teaspoons Shaoxing rice wine
light soy sauce, to taste
2 teaspoons roasted sesame oil

SERVES 4

SEPARATE the cabbage leaves, wash well and dry thoroughly.

HEAT a wok over high heat, add the oil and heat until very hot. Stir-fry the garlic for a few seconds. Add the cabbage leaves and stir-fry until they have just wilted. Add the pepper and rice wine and toss together. Season with the soy sauce and add the sesame oil.

FLAT CABBAGE WITH BLACK PEPPER

芥末白菜卷

CABBAGE ROLLS WITH MUSTARD

MUSTARD SEEDS COME FROM PLANTS BELONGING TO THE CABBAGE FAMILY, WHICH HAVE GROWN IN CHINA FOR CENTURIES. ALTHOUGH IT WAS TRADITIONALLY GROWN FOR ITS LEAVES, MUSTARD IS ALSO SOMETIMES USED AS A SPICE IN ITS GROUND FORM, OR MADE UP INTO A PASTE AS A CONDIMENT.

1 Chinese (Napa) cabbage
3 tablespoons English mustard
  powder
1 tablespoon light soy sauce
1 tablespoon clear rice vinegar
1 teaspoon roasted sesame oil

SERVES 4

SEPARATE the cabbage leaves and blanch them in a saucepan of boiling water for 1 minute, then refresh in cold water and dry thoroughly.

COMBINE the mustard powder, soy sauce, rice vinegar and sesame oil, then add enough cold water to make a stiff but spreadable paste.

TRIM the cabbage leaves into long strips about 2 inch wide. For each roll, use 3 strips. Lay a bottom strip on the work surface and cover with a thin layer of mustard, lay another strip on top covered with a layer of mustard, finish with a final strip and some mustard, then roll up. Repeat with the remaining cabbage to make four rolls. Put the rolls, standing upright, on a flameproof plate in a steamer. Cover and steam over simmering water in a wok for 20 minutes.

Blanching the leaves first makes them easier to roll. Make sure you only spread a thin layer of mustard on each.

虾酱炒菠菜

STIR-FRIED WATER SPINACH WITH SHRIMP SAUCE

2 lb water spinach (ong choy)
2 1/2 tablespoons oil
2 teaspoons Chinese shrimp paste
3 garlic cloves, crushed
1–2 red chiles, seeded and
  chopped
2 teaspoons oyster sauce
2 teaspoons sugar

SERVES 4

WASH the water spinach well and dry thoroughly. Remove any tough lower stalks and only use the young stems and leaves.

HEAT a wok over high heat, add 1 1/2 tablespoons of the oil and heat until very hot. Stir-fry the water spinach for 1 minute, or until it begins to wilt. Drain in a colander.

ADD the remaining oil to the wok with the shrimp paste, garlic and chiles, and toss over medium heat to release the flavors for 30 seconds to 1 minute. Add the water spinach, oyster sauce and sugar and toss for 1 minute.

STIR-FRIED WATER SPINACH
WITH SHRIMP SAUCE

RICE & NOODLES

EGG FRIED RICE

IN CHINA, PLAIN COOKED RICE IS SERVED WITH EVERYDAY MEALS, WHILE FRIED RICE IS ONLY EATEN AS A SNACK ON ITS OWN OR AT BANQUETS, WHEN IT IS SERVED AT THE END OF THE MEAL. THIS VERSION IS HOWEVER QUITE SIMPLE, SO IT WOULD GO WELL AS A SIDE DISH.

4 eggs
1 scallion, chopped
2 oz fresh or frozen peas (optional)
3 tablespoons oil
1 quantity cooked rice (page 274)

SERVES 4

BEAT the eggs with a pinch of salt and 1 teaspoon of the scallion. Cook the peas in a saucepan of simmering water for 3–4 minutes for fresh or 1 minute for frozen.

HEAT a wok over high heat, add the oil and heat until very hot. Reduce the heat, add the eggs and lightly scramble. Add the rice before the eggs are set too hard, increase the heat and stir to separate the rice grains and break the eggs into small bits. Add the peas and the remaining scallion and season with salt. Stir constantly for 1 minute.

EGG FRIED RICE

YANGZHOU FRIED RICE WITH SHRIMP

THIS WELL-KNOWN FRIED RICE DISH HAILS FROM YANGZHOU, A CITY IN THE EAST. IT CAN BE SERVED BY ITSELF AS A LIGHT MEAL OR WITH SOUP. THE SECRET TO NON-LUMPY FRIED RICE IS USING COOKED RICE THAT HAS BEEN CHILLED, THEN LEFT OUT TO REACH ROOM TEMPERATURE.

4 oz cooked shrimp
1 cup fresh or frozen peas
1 tablespoon oil
3 scallions, finely chopped
1 tablespoon finely chopped ginger
2 eggs, lightly beaten
1 quantity cooked rice (page 274)
1 1/2 tablespoons chicken stock
  (page 281)
1 tablespoon Shaoxing rice wine
2 teaspoons light soy sauce
1/2 teaspoon salt, or to taste
1/2 teaspoon roasted sesame oil
1/4 teaspoon freshly ground black
  pepper

SERVES 4

PEEL the shrimp and cut then in half through the back, removing the vein. Cook the peas in a saucepan of simmering water for 3–4 minutes for fresh or 1 minute for frozen.

HEAT a wok over high heat, add the oil and heat until hot. Stir-fry the scallions and ginger for 1 minute. Reduce the heat, add the eggs and lightly scramble. Add the shrimp and peas and toss lightly to heat through, then add the rice before the eggs are set too hard, increase the heat and stir to separate the rice grains and break the eggs into small bits.

ADD the stock, rice wine, soy sauce, salt, sesame oil and pepper, and toss lightly.

PEARL BALLS

THIS FAMOUS DISH ORIGINATED IN HUNAN PROVINCE, ONE OF CHINA'S MAJOR RICE BASINS. ONCE STEAMED, THE STICKY RICE THAT FORMS THE COATING FOR THESE MEATBALLS TURNS INTO PEARL-LIKE GRAINS. TRADITIONALLY, GLUTINOUS OR SWEET RICE IS USED, BUT YOU COULD USE RISOTTO RICE.

1³/₄ cups glutinous or sweet rice
8 dried Chinese mushrooms
1 cup peeled water chestnuts
1 lb ground pork
1 small carrot, grated
2 scallions, finely chopped
1¹/₂ tablespoons finely chopped
   ginger
2 tablespoons light soy sauce
1 tablespoon Shaoxing rice wine
1¹/₂ teaspoons roasted sesame oil
2¹/₂ tablespoons cornstarch
soy sauce

SERVES 6

PUT the rice in a bowl and, using your fingers as a rake, rinse under cold running water to remove any dust. Drain the rice in a colander, then place it in a bowl with enough cold water to cover. Set aside for 1 hour. Drain the rice and transfer it to a baking sheet in an even layer.

SOAK the dried mushrooms in boiling water for 30 minutes, then drain and squeeze out any excess water. Remove and discard the stems and chop the caps.

BLANCH the water chestnuts in a saucepan of boiling water for 1 minute, then refresh in cold water. Drain, pat dry and finely chop them.

PLACE the pork in a bowl, add the mushrooms, water chestnuts, carrot, scallions, ginger, soy sauce, rice wine, sesame oil and cornstarch. Stir the mixture vigorously to combine.

ROLL the mixture into ³/₄ inch balls, then roll each meatball in the glutinous rice so that it is completely coated. Lightly press the rice to make it stick to the meatball. Arrange the pearl balls well spaced in 3 steamers lined with waxed paper punched with holes or some damp cheesecloth. Cover and steam over simmering water in a wok, reversing the steamers halfway through, for 25 minutes. If the rice is still *al dente*, continue to cook for a little longer until it softens. Serve with the soy sauce.

Roll the meatballs so they are completely coated in the glutinous rice, then press the rice on firmly so it sticks.

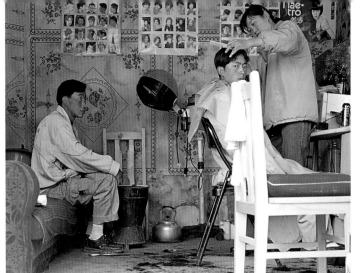

A haircut in Lijiang.

蒸鸡腊肠饭

STEAMED CHICKEN AND SAUSAGE RICE

THIS WARMING CANTONESE DISH IS TRADITIONALLY COOKED IN SMALL CLAY POTS SO THERE IS ONE POT FOR EACH INDIVIDUAL. CHINESE SAUSAGE (LAP CHEONG) TASTES A LITTLE LIKE A SWEET SALAMI, BUT IT MUST BE COOKED BEFORE EATING.

4 dried Chinese mushrooms
8 oz skinned boneless chicken
   thighs
1 teaspoon Shaoxing rice wine
2 teaspoons cornstarch
3 Chinese sausages (lap cheong)
1 cup long-grain rice
1 scallion, chopped

SAUCE
2 tablespoons light soy sauce
1 tablespoon Shaoxing rice wine
1/2 teaspoon superfine sugar
1/2 garlic clove, chopped (optional)
1/2 teaspoon chopped ginger
1/2 teaspoon roasted sesame oil

SERVES 4

SOAK the dried mushrooms in boiling water for 30 minutes, then drain and squeeze out any excess water. Remove and discard the stems and shred the caps.

CUT the chicken into bite-size pieces and combine with a pinch of salt, the rice wine and cornstarch.

PLACE the sausages on a plate in a steamer. Cover and steam over simmering water in a wok for 10 minutes, then thinly slice on the diagonal.

PUT the rice in a bowl and, using your fingers as a rake, rinse under cold running water to remove any dust. Drain the rice in a colander. Place in a large clay pot or braising pan and add enough water so that there is 3/4 inch of water above the surface of the rice. Bring the water slowly to a boil, stir, then place the chicken pieces and mushrooms on top of the rice, with the sausage slices on top of them. Cook, covered, over very low heat for 15–18 minutes, or until the rice is cooked.

TO MAKE the sauce, combine the soy sauce, rice wine, sugar, garlic, ginger and sesame oil in a small saucepan and heat until nearly boiling. Pour the sauce over the chicken and sausage and garnish with the chopped scallion.

白粥加各样小菜

PLAIN CONGEE WITH ACCOMPANIMENTS

CONGEE IS EATEN IN CHINA FOR BREAKFAST OR AS AN ALL-DAY SNACK. PLAIN CONGEE IS SERVED WITH LOTS OF DIFFERENT CONDIMENTS TO SPRINKLE OVER IT AND OFTEN A FRIED DOUGH STICK.

1 cup short-grain rice
9 cups litres chicken stock
   (page 281) or water
light soy sauce, to taste
sesame oil, to taste

TOPPINGS
3 scallions, chopped
4 tablespoons chopped cilantro
1 oz sliced pickled ginger
4 tablespoons finely chopped
   preserved turnip
4 tablespoons roasted peanuts
2 one-thousand-year-old eggs, cut
   into slivers
2 tablespoons toasted sesame
   seeds
2 fried dough sticks, diagonally sliced

SERVES 4

PUT the rice in a bowl and, using your fingers as a rake, rinse under cold running water to remove any dust. Drain the rice in a colander. Place in a clay pot, braising pan or saucepan and stir in the stock or water. Bring to a boil, then reduce the heat and simmer very gently, stirring occasionally, for 1³/₄–2 hours, or until it has a porridge-like texture and the rice is breaking up.

ADD a sprinkling of soy sauce, sesame oil and white pepper to season the congee. The congee can be served plain, or choose a selection from the toppings listed and serve in bowls alongside the congee for guests to help themselves.

Fried dough sticks are available in Chinese markets and are sold as long thin sticks, best eaten fresh on the day they are made, or broiled until crisp again.

鱼粥

FISH CONGEE

EVERYDAY CONGEE, OR RICE PORRIDGE, IS USUALLY SERVED WITH A FEW SIMPLE ACCOMPANIMENTS, BUT IT IS SOMETIMES COOKED INTO A MORE SUBSTANTIAL MEAL BY ADDING FISH OR MEAT.

1 cup short-grain rice
9 cups chicken stock (page 281)
   or water
¹/₂ lb firm white fish fillets, such as
   cod, halibut or monkfish, skin
   removed and cut into small cubes
1 tablespoon finely shredded ginger
light soy sauce, to taste
2 scallions, chopped

SERVES 4

PUT the rice in a bowl and, using your fingers as a rake, rinse under cold running water to remove any dust. Drain the rice in a colander. Place in a clay pot, braising pan or saucepan and stir in the stock or water. Bring to a boil, then reduce the heat and simmer very gently, stirring occasionally, for 1³/₄–2 hours, or until it has a porridge-like texture and the rice is breaking up.

ADD the fish, ginger and a little soy sauce and bring to a boil for 1 minute. Garnish with the chopped scallions.

FISH CONGEE

Rice terraces at Longsheng.

A game of mahjong in Chengdu.

什锦粥

RAINBOW CONGEE

TO THE CHINESE, CONGEE IS A VERSATILE DISH. IT IS A FAVORITE COMFORT FOOD, A DISH PREPARED FOR CONVALESCENTS BECAUSE IT IS SO SOOTHING TO EAT, AND A FILLING AND FLAVORFUL SNACK.

1 cup short-grain rice
2 dried Chinese mushrooms
3/4 cup snow peas, ends trimmed
2 Chinese sausages (lap cheong)
2 tablespoons oil
1/4 red onion, finely diced
1 carrot, cut into 1/2 inch dice
8–9 cups chicken stock
   (page 281) or water
1/4 teaspoon salt
3 teaspoons light soy sauce

SERVES 6

PUT the rice in a bowl and, using your fingers as a rake, rinse under cold running water to remove any dust. Drain the rice in a colander.

SOAK the dried mushrooms in boiling water for 30 minutes, then drain and squeeze out any excess water. Remove and discard the stems and chop the caps into 1/4 inch dice. Cut the snow peas into 1/2 inch pieces.

PLACE the sausages on a plate in a steamer. Cover and steam over simmering water in a wok for 10 minutes, then cut them into 1/4 inch pieces.

HEAT a wok over medium heat, add the oil and heat until hot. Stir-fry the sausage until it is brown and the fat has melted out of it. Remove with a wire strainer or slotted spoon and drain. Pour out the oil, reserving 1 tablespoon.

REHEAT the reserved oil over high heat until very hot. Stir-fry the red onion until soft and transparent. Add the mushrooms and carrot and stir-fry for 1 minute, or until fragrant.

PUT the mushroom mixture in a clay pot, braising pan or saucepan and stir in 8 cups of stock or water, the salt, soy sauce and the rice. Bring to a boil, then reduce the heat and simmer very gently, stirring occasionally, for 13/4–2 hours, or until it has a porridge-like texture and the rice is breaking up. If it is too thick, add the remaining stock and return to a boil. Toss in the snow peas and sausage, cover and let stand for 5 minutes before serving.

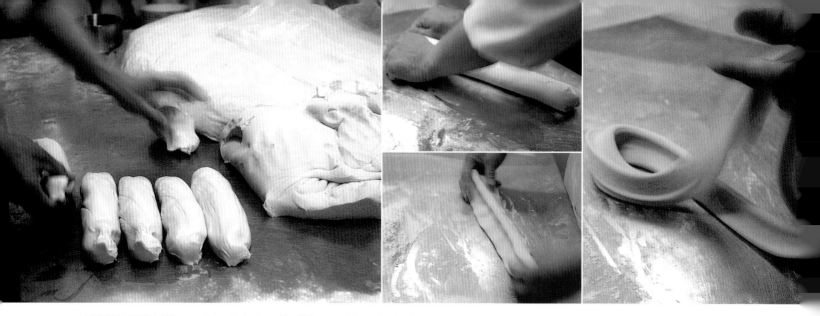

WHEAT NOODLES are still made by hand in China, and these 'pulled' or 'hand-drawn' noodles are an ancient art. At the Malan restaurants in Beijing, they follow a century-old recipe from Lanzhou in northwestern China. First, a large batch of dough is made from strong wheat flour, water and a little vegetable oil (to make the dough soft), left to rest, then worked to stretch the gluten. Portions are rolled into tubes and pulled

NOODLES

NOODLES GEOGRAPHICALLY DIVIDE CHINA, FROM THE COOL NORTH, WHERE HARDY WHEAT IS A STAPLE MADE INTO *MIAN*— WHEAT-FLOUR NOODLES—DOWN TO THE WARM, HUMID SOUTH, WHERE GROUND RICE IS TURNED INTO RICE NOODLES—*FEN*.

Though both kinds of noodles are now eaten all over China, noodles remain more of a staple in the North than the South, where a bowl of rice is the usual accompaniment to a meal.

TYPES OF NOODLES

Mian is the name for noodles made from wheat and barley, though it is often used as the general name for all noodles across China. They can be dried or fresh, made by machine

or hand, and eggs can be added to the flour and water paste to make egg noodles, a Cantonese speciality.

Fen is the Chinese word for the flour made from millet and rice, and also refers to noodles made from ground rice. Popular in the South, they are also known as Sha He noodles after a town near Guangzhou, renowned for the quality of its noodles. Fresh rice noodles are formed in sheets and cut up after steaming to make the soft white noodles often found in dim sum. Dried rice noodles come in various thicknesses, from flat rice sticks to strand-like vermicelli, and are usually machine-made.

Fen also refers to non-grain noodles that are not regarded as 'true' noodles made from a staple ingredient such as wheat or rice. *Fen si,* or bean thread noodles, are made of mung bean flour, and their translucent appearance is reflected in their English names of cellophane or glass noodles. *Gan si* are made from pressed bean curd.

amount of strands until the required thickness of noodle is reached (noodles for men are traditionally thicker than for women to provide more 'energy'). The thicker end of the noodles (the lump of dough that forms as the noodles are folded) is twisted off and the noodles gathered into a skein. The noodles must now be handled quickly and gently. They are dropped into a continually boiling pot of water and cooked for a couple of

horizontally to arm's length, folded back and stretched again until the dough is soft and elastic. The noodle-maker then starts to let the dough stretch to the floor in an arc, folding it just before it touches so the dough twists up like a coiled rope. Now strong enough to be split into strands, the dough is folded over and over, keeping each folded piece separate by dusting it in the flour on the work surface. Every fold doubles the

EATING NOODLES

Noodles are most often served up in bowls of soup or as roadside snacks in China, especially in the South, where they are rarely served in restaurants and are considered a home-cooking style dish. In the North, noodles are served with meals, and are also found in small restaurants or stalls dedicated to just a few noodle dishes, where the noodles are often hand-thrown to order, then boiled in large pots.

Noodles are a symbol of longevity in Chinese gastronomy and are sometimes eaten on special occasions. Very long, they are rarely cut as to do this may bring bad luck.

Most areas of China have a special noodle dish associated with the region. In Beijing, these are *la mian,* the pulled noodles *(shown above)* that are also known as Dragon's whiskers. In Sichuan, crossing-the-bridge noodles and ants climbing trees are favourite dishes, while fried Singapore noodles are actually from Fujian.

COOKING NOODLES

NOODLES IN SOUP the most common way to eat noodles, dropped into broth, sometimes topped with a little meat, vegetables or seafood, and always eaten as a snack, never as a soup or main course.

BRAISED NOODLES noodles in a thick sauce (which they may have been cooked in), with meat, vegetables or seafood.

FRIED NOODLES crisp- or soft-fried noodles, tossed with meat, vegetables or seafood and flavourings. Stir-fried noodles may be eaten as part of a meal—usually at home, as they are considered home-cooking style dishes. The Chinese name for fried noodles is *chao mian,* corrupted in English to *chow mein.*

TOSSED NOODLES plain boiled noodles, served with a meat sauce and fresh vegetables to mix through, and often eaten cold in the summer.

WON TONS made from an egg noodle dough, won ton wrappers are usually filled with meat and the dumplings poached in soup or fried.

minutes, then lifted out with chopsticks into a bowl. Malan's special recipe is based on five different colours. The broth (transparent) is made with beef and chicken stock, chinese herbs and a little MSG and is poured over the noodles. To this are added sliced turnip (white), chilli (red), coriander and spring onion (green) and noodles (yellow)—the colours are thought to influence the taste. A little cooked beef finishes the dish.

FRESH NOODLES WITH BEEF AND GARLIC CHIVES

1/2 lb beef top round steak, trimmed
2 large garlic cloves, crushed
3 tablespoons oyster sauce
2 teaspoons sugar
1 tablespoon dark soy sauce
3 teaspoons cornstarch
1/4 teaspoon roasted sesame oil
3 tablespoons oil
1 red pepper, thinly sliced
1/4 lb Chinese garlic chives, cut into
   2 inch pieces
2 lb fresh rice noodle rolls, cut into
   3/4 inch thick slices and separated
   slightly
chili sauce

SERVES 6

CUT the beef against the grain into thin bite-size strips. Combine with the garlic, 1 tablespoon of the oyster sauce, 1 teaspoon of the sugar, 2 teaspoons of the soy sauce, the cornstarch and sesame oil. Marinate in the fridge for at least 30 minutes, or overnight.

HEAT a wok over high heat, add the oil and heat until very hot. Stir-fry the pepper for 1–2 minutes, or until it begins to soften. Add the beef and toss until it changes color. Add the garlic chives and noodles and toss for 1–2 minutes, or until they soften. Add the remaining oyster sauce, sugar and soy sauce and toss well until combined.

SERVE with some chili sauce on the side.

Slice the fresh noodle roll into thick slices, which will unroll and separate into noodles.

COLD TOSSED NOODLES

THIS IS A SUMMER DISH THAT PROVIDES A VERY REFRESHING SNACK FOR A HOT AFTERNOON OR EVENING. THE DRESSING CAN BE VARIED ACCORDING TO PERSONAL PREFERENCE BY ADDING MORE OR LESS CHILI SAUCE OR PRESERVED TURNIP. OMIT THE SHRIMP FOR A VEGETARIAN DISH.

DRESSING
3/4 oz dried shrimp
3 tablespoons Shaoxing rice wine
3 tablespoons light soy sauce
2 tablespoons clear rice vinegar
1 teaspoon chili sauce
1 tablespoon finely chopped ginger
2 tablespoons chopped preserved
   turnip
1 teaspoon roasted sesame oil

1 lb fresh or 3/4 lb dried egg
   noodles
1 tablespoon oil
2 scallions, finely shredded

SERVES 6

TO MAKE the dressing, soak the dried shrimp in boiling water for 1 hour, then drain, coarsely chop and soak in the rice wine for 15 minutes. Combine the shrimp, soy sauce, rice vinegar, chili sauce, ginger, preserved turnip and sesame oil.

COOK the noodles in a saucepan of salted boiling water for 2–3 minutes if fresh and 10 minutes if dried, then drain and rinse in cold water. Combine with the oil and spread the noodles out on a dish.

POUR the dressing over the top of the noodles and sprinkle with the shredded scallions. Toss at the table before serving.

COLD TOSSED NOODLES

荷兰豆炒牛肉烩炸面

CRISPY NOODLES WITH BEEF AND SNOW PEAS

THIS CANTONESE DISH IS A FAVORITE ACROSS THE GLOBE. THE CRISP NOODLES WITH THEIR BEEF AND

SNOW PEA TOPPING ARE DRENCHED IN A VELVETY OYSTER SAUCE.

A pot of boiling water for cooking noodles in Chengdu.

9 oz fresh or 6 oz dried egg
  noodles
1¹/₂ teaspoons roasted sesame oil
³/₄ lb beef top round steak, trimmed
1 tablespoon dark soy sauce
2 teaspoons Shaoxing rice wine
¹/₂ teaspoon sugar
1 garlic clove, finely chopped
1 teaspoon cornstarch
1 cup snow peas, ends trimmed
3 tablespoons oil

SAUCE
1 tablespoon finely chopped ginger
1 scallion, finely chopped
1¹/₄ cups chicken stock (page 281)
3 tablespoons oyster sauce
1 tablespoon Shaoxing rice wine
¹/₂ teaspoon dark soy sauce
1 teaspoon sugar
¹/₂ teaspoon roasted sesame oil
1¹/₂ tablespoons cornstarch

SERVES 4

COOK the noodles in a saucepan of salted boiling water for 2–3 minutes if fresh and 10 minutes if dried, then drain and combine with 1 teaspoon of the sesame oil. Place the noodles in 4 small cake pans or flat-bottomed bowls and allow to cool.

CUT the beef against the grain into slices about ¹/₈ inch thick, then cut into 1¹/₂ inch squares. Combine the beef, soy sauce, rice wine, sugar, garlic, cornstarch and the remaining seame oil and toss lightly. Marinate in the fridge for at least 1 hour.

BLANCH the snowpeas in a saucepan of boiling water for 15 seconds. Drain and refresh immediately in cold water. Dry thoroughly.

HEAT a wok over high heat, add 2 tablespoons of the oil and heat until almost smoking. Invert the noodle cakes, one at a time, into the wok and fry on both sides until golden brown, swirling the pan from time to time to move the noodles so that they cook evenly. Put the noodles on a plate and keep warm and crisp in a low oven.

REHEAT the wok over high heat, add the remaining oil and heat until very hot. Drain the beef and stir-fry in batches for 1 minute, or until the beef changes color. Remove with a wire strainer or slotted spoon, and drain. Pour out the oil, reserving 2 tablespoons.

TO MAKE the sauce, reheat the reserved oil over high heat until very hot and stir-fry the ginger and scallion for 10 seconds, or until fragrant. Add the remaining sauce ingredients, except the cornstarch, and bring to a boil. Combine the cornstarch with enough water to make a paste, add to the sauce and simmer until thickened.

ADD the beef and snow peas, toss to coat with the sauce, and pour the mixture over the noodles.

新加坡炒面

SINGAPORE NOODLES

10 oz rice vermicelli
2 tablespoons dried shrimp
4 oz barbecued pork (char siu)
1 cup bean sprouts
4 tablespoons oil
2 eggs, beaten
1 onion, thinly sliced
1 teaspoon salt
1 tablespoon Chinese curry powder
2 tablespoons light soy sauce
2 scallions, shredded
2 red chiles, shredded

SERVES 4

SOAK the noodles in hot water for 10 minutes, then drain. Soak the dried shrimp in boiling water for 1 hour, then drain. Thinly shred the pork. Wash the bean sprouts and drain thoroughly.

HEAT a wok over high heat, add 1 tablespoon of the oil and heat until very hot. Pour in the egg and make an omelet. Remove from the wok and cut into small pieces.

REHEAT the wok over high heat, add the remaining oil and heat until very hot. Stir-fry the onion and bean sprouts with the pork and shrimp for 1 minute, then add the noodles, salt, curry powder and soy sauce, blend well and stir for 1 minute. Add the omelet, scallions and chiles and toss to combine.

SINGAPORE NOODLES

担担面

DAN DAN MIAN

A COMMON STREET FOOD SNACK IN SICHUAN, THIS DISH IS NOW POPULAR ALL OVER THE NORTH OF CHINA AND THE RECIPE VARIES FROM STAND TO STAND.

1 tablespoon Sichuan peppercorns
7 oz ground pork
2 oz preserved turnip, rinsed and
  finely chopped
2 tablespoons light soy sauce
2 tablespoons oil
2 garlic cloves, crushed
2 tablespoons grated ginger
4 scallions, finely chopped
2 tablespoons sesame paste or
  smooth peanut butter
2 tablespoons light soy sauce
2 teaspoons chile oil
3/4 cup chicken stock (page 281)
3/4 lb thin wheat flour noodles

SERVES 4

DRY-FRY the Sichuan peppercorns in a wok or frying pan until brown and aromatic, then crush lightly. Combine the pork with the preserved turnip and soy sauce and allow to marinate for a few minutes. Heat a wok over high heat, add the oil and heat until very hot. Stir-fry the pork until crisp and browned. Remove and drain well.

ADD the garlic, ginger and scallions to the wok and stir-fry for 30 seconds, then add the sesame paste, soy sauce, chile oil and stock and simmer for 2 minutes.

COOK the noodles in a saucepan of salted boiling water for 4–8 minutes, then drain well. Divide among 4 bowls, ladle the sauce over the noodles, then top with the crispy pork and Sichuan peppercorns.

Making wheat noodles by pulling them by hand. The noodles are made fresh for each customer and cooked immediately.

Lunch in Chengdu.

Make sure you separate all the ground meat as it cooks, or it will form large lumps and not resemble ants at all.

蚂 蚁 上 树

ANTS CLIMBING TREES

THE UNUSUAL NAME OF THIS SPICY SICHUAN-STYLE DISH IS SUPPOSED TO COME FROM THE FACT THAT IT BEARS A RESEMBLANCE TO ANTS CLIMBING TREES, WITH LITTLE PIECES OF GROUND PORK COATING LUSTROUS BEAN THREAD NOODLES.

4 oz pork or beef
1/2 teaspoon light soy sauce
1/2 teaspoon Shaoxing rice wine
1/2 teaspoon roasted sesame oil
4 oz bean thread noodles
1 tablespoon oil
2 scallions, finely chopped
1 tablespoon finely chopped ginger
1 garlic clove, finely chopped
1 teaspoon chile bean paste
 (toban jiang), or to taste
2 scallions, green part only, finely
 chopped

SAUCE
1 tablespoon light soy sauce
1 tablespoon Shaoxing rice wine
1/2 teaspoon salt
1/2 teaspoon sugar
1/2 teaspoon roasted sesame oil
1 cup chicken stock (page 281)

SERVES 4

COMBINE the ground meat with the soy sauce, rice wine and sesame oil. Soak the bean thread noodles in hot water for 10 minutes, then drain.

HEAT a wok over high heat, add the oil and heat until very hot. Stir-fry the ground meat, mashing and separating it, until it changes color and starts to brown. Push the meat to the side of the wok, add the scallions, ginger, garlic and chile bean paste and stir-fry for 5 seconds, or until fragrant. Return the meat to the center of the pan.

TO MAKE the sauce, combine all the ingredients. Add the sauce to the meat mixture and toss lightly. Add the noodles and bring to a boil. Reduce the heat to low and cook for 8 minutes, or until almost all the liquid has evaporated. Sprinkle with the chopped scallions.

Making noodle dishes at a market in Yunnan.

RAINBOW NOODLES

THIS DISH OF SHRIMP, BEAN SPROUTS AND THIN RICE NOODLES IS ENLIVENED WITH A TOUCH OF CHINESE CURRY POWDER. MUCH MILDER THAN ITS INDIAN COUNTERPART AND SIMILAR TO FIVE-SPICE POWDER, YOU COULD USE A MILD INDIAN CURRY POWDER INSTEAD.

7 oz shrimp
1 tablespoon Shaoxing rice wine
$2^1/_2$ tablespoons finely chopped
  ginger
1 teaspoon roasted sesame oil
10 oz rice vermicelli
2 leeks, white part only
4 tablespoons oil
$1^1/_2$ tablespoons Chinese curry
  powder
$2^1/_4$ cups bean sprouts
$^1/_4$ cup chicken stock (page 281)
  or water
2 tablespoons light soy sauce
1 teaspoon salt
$^1/_2$ teaspoon sugar
$^1/_2$ teaspoon freshly ground black
  pepper

SERVES 4

PEEL the shrimp, leaving the tails intact. Using a sharp knife, score lengthwise along the back of each and remove the vein. Place in a bowl, add the rice wine, 2 teaspoons of the ginger and the sesame oil, and toss to coat.

SOAK the noodles in hot water for 10 minutes, then drain. Cut the leeks into roughly 2 inch pieces and shred finely. Wash well and dry thoroughly.

HEAT a wok over high heat, add 1 tablespoon of the oil and heat until very hot. Stir-fry the shrimp in batches for $1^1/_2$ minutes, or until they turn opaque. Remove with a wire strainer or slotted spoon and drain. Pour out the oil and wipe out the wok.

REHEAT the wok over high heat, add the remaining oil and heat until very hot. Stir-fry the curry powder for a few seconds, or until fragrant. Add the leeks and remaining ginger and stir-fry for $1^1/_2$ minutes. Add the bean sprouts and cook for 20 seconds, then add the shrimp, stock or water, soy sauce, salt, sugar and pepper, and stir to combine.

ADD the noodles and toss until they are cooked through and have absorbed all the sauce. Transfer to a serving dish and serve.

Chinese, or black, mushrooms are also known as shiitake mushrooms. They can be bought fresh when in season and dried all year round.

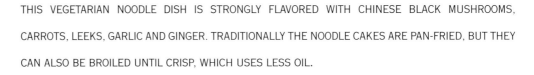

BLACK MUSHROOM NOODLES

THIS VEGETARIAN NOODLE DISH IS STRONGLY FLAVORED WITH CHINESE BLACK MUSHROOMS, CARROTS, LEEKS, GARLIC AND GINGER. TRADITIONALLY THE NOODLE CAKES ARE PAN-FRIED, BUT THEY CAN ALSO BE BROILED UNTIL CRISP, WHICH USES LESS OIL.

9 oz fresh or 6 oz dried egg
   noodles
1 1/2 teaspoons roasted sesame oil
5 dried Chinese mushrooms
2 leeks, white part only
2 carrots
1 tablespoon oil
2 garlic cloves, finely chopped
1 tablespoon finely chopped ginger
2 tablespoons Shaoxing rice wine
2 tablespoons light soy sauce
1 tablespoon oyster sauce
1/4 teaspoon freshly ground black
   pepper
1 1/2 tablespoons cornstarch

SERVES 4

COOK the noodles in a saucepan of salted boiling water for 2–3 minutes if fresh and 10 minutes if dried, then drain and combine with 1/2 teaspoon of the sesame oil.

PREHEAT the broiler, shape the noodles into 4 loose mounds on a lightly greased baking sheet and broil for 10 minutes on each side, turning once, until golden brown. Keep warm in a low oven.

SOAK the dried mushrooms in boiling water for 30 minutes, then drain, reserving the soaking liquid, and squeeze out any excess water. Remove and discard the stems and shred the caps. Cut the leeks into 2 inch pieces, then into 1/2 inch wide strips. Wash well and dry thoroughly. Cut the carrots to the same size as the leeks.

HEAT a wok over high heat, add the oil and heat until very hot. Stir-fry the garlic and ginger until fragrant. Add the leeks and carrots and stir-fry for 1 minute. Add the rice wine and mushrooms and cook for 1 minute.

ADD the soy and oyster sauces, pepper, remaining sesame oil and 1/3 cup of the reserved liquid. Combine the cornstarch with enough water to make a paste, add to the sauce and simmer until thickened. Put the noodles on a plate and spoon over with the sauce.

彩桥面

CROSSING-THE-BRIDGE NOODLES

LEGEND HAS IT THAT THIS DISH WAS INVENTED BY A WOMAN WHO HAD TO TAKE HER HUSBAND'S FOOD
TO HIM EACH DAY. TO KEEP THE SOUP HOT FOR THE LONG JOURNEY, SHE FLOATED OIL ON TOP. THE
SOUP MUST BE SERVED CLOSE TO BOILING AS YOU COOK THE FOOD IN IT.

¹/₄ lb shrimp
¹/₄ lb skinned boneless chicken
  breasts
¹/₄ lb squid bodies
¹/₄ lb Chinese ham, thinly sliced
8 dried Chinese mushrooms
1¹/₃ cups bean sprouts
11 oz fresh rice noodles or
  8 oz rice stick noodles
chili sauce
light soy sauce
4 cups chicken stock (page 281)
4 scallions, finely chopped

SERVES 4

PEEL the shrimp and cut them in half through the
back, removing the vein. Slice the shrimp and the
chicken breast thinly on the diagonal.

OPEN up the squid bodies by cutting down one
side, scrub off any soft jelly-like substance and
slice thinly on the diagonal. Arrange the shrimp,
chicken, squid and ham on a plate, cover and
refrigerate until needed.

SOAK the dried mushrooms in boiling water for
30 minutes, then drain and squeeze out any
excess water. Remove and discard the stems.
Add the mushrooms to the plate. Wash the bean
sprouts and drain thoroughly. Add to the plate.

SEPARATE the rice noodles into 4 bundles. If you
are using dried rice noodles, soak in hot water for
10 minutes, then drain.

GIVE EACH guest a small saucer of chili sauce
and a saucer of soy sauce. Place the ingredients
and dipping sauces on the table. Heat 4 soup
bowls either in a low oven or by running them
under very hot water for a few minutes. Put
the chicken stock in a clay pot, braising pan
or saucepan with the scallions and bring to a boil.
When the stock has reached a rolling boil,
fill the soup bowls.

GIVE EACH guest a hot bowl filled with stock and
let them cook the meat, vegetables and noodles
in the stock. You can be authentic and add a
dash of oil to each bowl to seal in the heat, but it
isn't really necessary.

A canal running through Lijiang.

CINNAMON BEEF NOODLES

1 teaspoon oil
10 scallions, cut into 1¹/₂ inch
  pieces, lightly smashed with the
  flat side of a cleaver
10 garlic cloves, thinly sliced
6 slices ginger, smashed with the
  flat side of a cleaver
1¹/₂ teaspoons chile bean paste
  (toban jiang)
2 cassia or cinnamon sticks
2 star anise
¹/₂ cup light soy sauce
2 lb chuck steak, trimmed and cut
  into 1¹/₂ inch cubes
¹/₂ lb rice stick noodles
¹/₂ lb baby spinach
3 tablespoons finely chopped
  scallion

SERVES 6

HEAT a wok over medium heat, add the oil and heat until hot. Stir-fry the scallions, garlic, ginger, chile bean paste, cassia and star anise for 10 seconds, or until fragrant. Transfer to a clay pot, braising pan or saucepan. Add the soy sauce and 9 cups water. Bring to a boil, add the beef, then return to a boil. Reduce the heat and simmer, covered, for 1¹/₂ hours, or until the beef is very tender. Skim the surface occasionally to remove impurities and fat. Remove and discard the ginger and cassia.

SOAK the noodles in hot water for 10 minutes, then drain and divide among 6 bowls. Add the spinach to the beef and bring to a boil. Spoon the beef mixture over the noodles and sprinkle with the chopped scallion.

In China, cassia bark (*middle*) is more often used than cinnamon to make this recipe.

LONGEVITY NOODLES

NOODLES SYMBOLIZE A LONG LIFE BECAUSE OF THEIR LENGTH AND ARE THEREFORE SERVED AT SPECIAL OCCASIONS SUCH AS BIRTHDAYS AND FEAST DAYS. THE NOODLES FOR THIS DISH ARE PARTICULARLY LONG AND CAN BE BOUGHT LABELED AS LONGEVITY NOODLES.

¹/₂ lb precooked longevity or dried
  egg noodles
1 cup bean sprouts
¹/₃ cup fresh or canned bamboo
  shoots, rinsed and drained
1 tablespoon oil
1 tablespoon finely chopped ginger
4 scallions, thinly sliced
1 tablespoon light soy sauce
1 teaspoon roasted sesame oil
¹/₄ cup chicken stock (page 281)

SERVES 4

IF USING dried egg noodles, cook in a saucepan of salted boiling water for 10 minutes, then drain. Wash the bean sprouts and drain thoroughly. Shred the bamboo shoots.

HEAT a wok over high heat, add the oil and heat until very hot. Stir-fry the ginger for a few seconds, then add the bean sprouts, bamboo shoots and scallions and stir-fry for 1 minute. Add the soy sauce, sesame oil and stock and bring to a boil. Add the longevity or dried egg noodles and toss together until the sauce is absorbed.

LONGEVITY NOODLES

叉烧面/汤

CHAR SIU NOODLE SOUP

NOODLES IN SOUP ARE FAR MORE POPULAR THAN FRIED NOODLES (CHOW MEIN) IN CHINA. LIKE FRIED

RICE, NOODLE DISHES ARE EATEN AS SNACKS RATHER THAN SERVED AS PART OF AN EVERYDAY MEAL.

THIS IS A BASIC RECIPE—YOU CAN USE DIFFERENT INGREDIENTS FOR THE TOPPING.

4 dried Chinese mushrooms
7 oz barbecue pork (char siu)
1/3 cup fresh or canned bamboo
   shoots, rinsed and drained
2 cups green vegetable, such as
   spinach, bok choy or Chinese
   (Napa) cabbage
2 scallions
14 oz fresh or 11 oz dried egg
   noodles
4 cups chicken and meat stock
   (page 281)
2–3 tablespoons oil
1 teaspoon salt
1/2 teaspoon sugar
1 tablespoon light soy sauce
1 teaspoon Shaoxing rice wine
1/4 teaspoon roasted sesame oil

SERVES 4

SOAK the dried mushrooms in boiling water for 30 minutes, then drain and squeeze out any excess water. Remove and discard the stems and shred the caps. Thinly shred the pork, bamboo shoots, green vegetable and scallions.

COOK the noodles in a saucepan of salted boiling water for 2–3 minutes if fresh and 10 minutes if dried, then drain and place in 4 bowls. Bring the stock to a boil, then reduce the heat to simmering.

HEAT a wok over high heat, add the oil and heat until very hot. Stir-fry the pork and half the scallions for 1 minute, then add the mushrooms, bamboo shoots and green vegetable and stir-fry for 1 minute. Add the salt, sugar, soy sauce, rice wine and sesame oil and blend well.

POUR the stock over the noodles and top with the meat mixture and the remaining scallions.

烧鸭面/汤

ROAST DUCK NOODLE SOUP

THIS IS A QUICK AND EASY SNACK OR MEAL. CANTONESE-STYLE ROAST DUCK CAN BE BOUGHT AT

CHINESE AND CARRY-OUT RESTAURANTS. ASK FOR IT TO BE CHOPPED INTO BITE-SIZE PIECES.

ROAST DUCK NOODLE SOUP

1 lb fresh or 11 oz dried egg
   noodles
4 cups chicken stock or chicken
   and meat stock (page 281)
3/4 lb roast duck, chopped
1/4 lb bok choy, shredded
2 tablespoons soy sauce
1/4 teaspoon roasted sesame oil

SERVES 4

COOK the noodles in a saucepan of salted boiling water for 2–3 minutes if fresh and 10 minutes if dried, then drain and place in 4 bowls. Bring the stock to a boil, then reduce the heat and keep at simmering point.

TOP EACH bowl with the duck, bok choy, soy sauce and sesame oil. Pour over the stock.

Rice noodles being sold in a market in Yunnan.

Shred the steamed scallops into pieces. They have a strong flavor and are best eaten in small pieces.

干贝海鲜面

NOODLES WITH SEAFOOD AND DRIED SCALLOPS

THIS NOODLE DISH IS RATHER GRAND TO BE A SIMPLE SNACK. NOT ONLY DOES IT INCLUDE FRESH SEAFOOD, IT ALSO HAS DRIED SCALLOPS AS AN ADDED FLAVORING. DRIED SCALLOPS, ALSO KNOWN AS CONPOY, ARE REGARDED AS A DELICACY AND HAVE A RICH FLAVOR.

4 dried scallops (conpoy)
12 shrimp
7 oz squid bodies
13 oz thin rice stick noodles
1 tablespoon oil
2 tablespoons shredded ginger
2 scallions, thinly sliced
3 cups Chinese (Napa) cabbage, finely shredded
1 cup chicken stock (page 281)
2 tablespoons light soy sauce
2 tablespoons Shaoxing rice wine
1 teaspoon roasted sesame oil

SERVES 4

PUT the dried scallops in a flameproof bowl with 1 tablespoon water and put them in a steamer. Cover and steam over simmering water in a wok for 30 minutes, or until they are completely tender. Remove the scallops and shred the meat.

PEEL the shrimp and cut them in half through the back, removing the vein.

OPEN up the squid bodies by cutting down one side, scrub off any soft jelly-like substance, then score the inside of the flesh with a fine crisscross pattern, making sure you do not cut all the way through. Cut the squid into 3 x 2 inch pieces.

SOAK the noodles in hot water for 10 minutes, then drain.

HEAT a wok over high heat, add the oil and heat until very hot. Stir-fry the ginger and scallions for 1 minute, then add the shrimp and squid and stir-fry until just opaque. Add the scallops and Chinese cabbage and toss together. Pour in the stock, soy sauce and rice wine and boil for 1 minute. Add the noodles and sesame oil, toss together and serve.

WON TON SOUP

WON TON LITERALLY TRANSLATED MEANS "SWALLOWING A CLOUD". WON TONS, KNOWN AS HUN TUN

OUTSIDE OF GUANGZHOU, ARE CATEGORIZED AS NOODLES AS THEY USE THE SAME DOUGH AS EGG

NOODLES. WON TON SOUP CAN ALSO INCLUDE EGG NOODLES—ADD SOME IF YOU LIKE.

^{1}/$_2$ lb shrimp
^{1}/$_2$ cup peeled water chestnuts
^{1}/$_2$ lb lean ground pork
3^1/$_2$ tablepoons light soy sauce
3^1/$_2$ tablespoons Shaoxing rice
  wine
1^1/$_2$ teaspoons salt
1^1/$_2$ teaspoons roasted sesame oil
^{1}/$_2$ teaspoon freshly ground black
  pepper
1 teaspoon finely chopped ginger
1^1/$_2$ tablespoons cornstarch
30 square or round won ton
  wrappers
6 cups chicken stock (page 281)
1 lb spinach, trimmed (optional)
2 scallions, green part only, finely
  chopped

SERVES 6

PEEL AND devein the shrimp. Place in a kitchen towel and squeeze out as much moisture as possible. Grind the shrimp to a coarse paste using a sharp knife or a food processor.

BLANCH the water chestnuts in boiling water for 1 minute, then refresh in cold water. Drain, pat dry and roughly chop them. Place the shrimp, water chestnuts, pork, 2 teaspoons of the soy sauce, 2 teaspoons of the rice wine, ^{1}/$_2$ teaspoon of the salt, ^{1}/$_2$ teaspoon of the sesame oil, the black pepper, ginger and cornstarch in a mixing bowl. Stir vigorously to combine.

PLACE a teaspoon of filling in the center of one won ton wrapper. Brush the edge of the wrapper with a little water, fold in half and then bring the two folded corners together and press firmly. Place the won tons on a cornstarch-dusted baking sheet.

BRING a saucepan of water to a boil. Cook the won tons, covered, for 5–6 minutes, or until they have risen to the surface. Using a wire strainer or slotted spoon, remove the won tons and divide them among 6 bowls.

PLACE the stock in a saucepan with the remaining soy sauce, rice wine, salt and sesame oil, and bring to a boil. Add the spinach and cook until just wilted. Pour the hot stock over the won tons and sprinkle with the chopped scallions.

The easiest way to make the won tons is to shape them in the same way as tortellini.

DESSERTS

生姜布丁

GINGER PUDDING

THIS DESSERT CAN ALSO BE EATEN AS A SNACK. THE GINGER JUICE CAUSES THE HOT MILK TO COAGULATE AND FORMS A GINGER-FLAVORED PUDDING WITH A SLIPPERY SMOOTH TEXTURE. IT IS IMPORTANT TO USE YOUNG, SWEET FRESH GINGER OR THE FLAVOR WILL BE TOO HARSH.

7 oz young ginger
1 tablespoon sugar
2 cups milk

SERVES 4

GRATE the ginger as finely as you can, collecting any juice. Place it in a piece of cheesecloth, twist the top hard and squeeze out as much juice as possible. You will need 4 tablespoons. Alternatively, push the ginger through a juicer.

PUT 1 tablespoon of ginger juice and 1 teaspoon of sugar each into 4 bowls. Put the milk in a saucepan and bring to a boil, then divide among the bowls. Allow to set for 1 minute (the ginger juice will cause the milk to solidify). Serve warm.

Squeeze the juice out of the ginger by twisting it up in a piece of cheesecloth.

杏仁豆腐（加水果）

ALMOND BEAN CURD WITH FRUIT

DURING HOT WEATHER IN CHINA, REFRESHING FRUIT SALADS MADE FROM PINEAPPLE, MANGO, PAPAYA, MELON, LYCHEE AND LOQUAT ARE POPULAR SNACKS. THE MILKY SQUARE OF ALMOND JELLY THAT GOES WITH THIS FRUIT SALAD IS SAID TO RESEMBLE BEAN CURD, HENCE THE NAME.

2$^1/_2$ tablespoons powdered gelatin
  or 6 gelatin sheets
$^1/_3$ cup superfine sugar
2 teaspoons almond extract
$^1/_2$ cup condensed milk
13 oz can lychees in syrup
13 oz can loquats in syrup
$^1/_2$ papaya, cut into cubes
$^1/_2$ melon, cut into cubes

SERVES 6

PUT $^1/_2$ cup water in a saucepan. If you are using powdered gelatin, sprinkle it on the water and let it dissolve for 1 minute. If you are using sheets, soak in the water until floppy. Heat the mixture slightly, stirring constantly to dissolve the gelatin.

PLACE the sugar, almond extract and condensed milk in a bowl and stir to combine. Slowly add 5$^1/_2$ cups water, stirring to dissolve the sugar. Stir in the dissolved gelatin. Pour into a chilled 9 inch square pan. Chill for at least 4 hours, or until set.

DRAIN HALF the syrup from the lychees and the loquats. Place the lychees and loquats with their remaining syrup in a large bowl. Add the cubed papaya and melon. Cut the almond bean curd into diamond-shaped pieces and arrange on plates, then spoon the fruit around the bean curd.

ALMOND BEAN CURD
WITH FRUIT

NEW YEAR SWEET DUMPLINGS

THESE GLUTINOUS SWEET DUMPLINGS ARE MADE FOR THE CHINESE NEW YEAR AND ARE OFTEN EATEN IN A SWEET SOUP. THEY CAN BE FILLED WITH A NUT OR BEAN PASTE.

1/4 cup black sesame paste, red bean paste or smooth peanut butter
4 tablespoons superfine sugar
1 1/2 cups glutinous rice flour
1 oz rock sugar

MAKES 24

COMBINE the sesame paste with the sugar.

SIFT the rice flour into a bowl and stir in 3/4 cup boiling water. Knead carefully (the dough will be very hot) to form a soft, slightly sticky dough. Dust your hands with extra rice flour, roll the dough into a cylinder, then divide it into cherry-size pieces. Cover the dough with a kitchen towel and, using one piece at a time, form each piece of dough into a flat round, then gather it into a cup shape. The dough should be fairly thin.

FILL EACH cup shape with 1 teaspoon of paste and fold the top over, smoothing the dough so you have a round ball with no visible seams.

BRING 4 cups water to a boil, add the rock sugar and stir until dissolved. Return to a boil, add the dumplings in batches and simmer for 5 minutes, or until they rise to the surface. Serve warm with a little of the syrup.

New Year dumplings are widely available in the markets and night markets of China during the New Year celebrations.

FRIED FRAGRANT BANANAS

1/2 cup self-rising flour
2 tablespoons milk
1 tablespoon butter, melted
1 tablespoon superfine sugar
4 apple or lady finger bananas, or 3 ordinary bananas
oil for deep-frying
honey (optional)

SERVES 4

COMBINE the flour, milk, butter and sugar, then add enough water to make a thick batter.

CUT the bananas into 1 1/4 inch chunks.

FILL a wok one quarter full of oil. Heat the oil to 350°F, or until a piece of bread fries golden brown in 15 seconds when dropped in the oil. Dip the banana pieces, a few at a time, into the batter and then fry them for 3 minutes, or until they are well browned on all sides. Drain on paper towels. Serve the bananas drizzled with honey for extra sweetness.

FRIED FRAGRANT BANANAS

Packaged eight-treasure rice.

Fresh longans.

Eight-treasure rice can be made in any round dish. If you want it to sit higher on the plate, then choose a deep bowl. Remember that the pattern you make on the bottom will come out on top.

八宝饭

EIGHT-TREASURE RICE

THIS CHINESE RICE PUDDING IS A FAVORITE AT BANQUETS AND CHINESE NEW YEAR. THE EIGHT TREASURES VARY, BUT CAN ALSO INCLUDE OTHER PRESERVED FRUITS.

12 whole blanched lotus seeds
12 jujubes (dried Chinese dates)
20 fresh or canned gingko nuts, shelled
1 cup glutinous rice
2 tablespoons sugar
2 teaspoons oil
1 oz slab sugar
8 candied cherries
6 dried longans, pitted
4 almonds or walnuts
1 cup red bean paste

SERVES 8

SOAK the lotus seeds and jujubes in bowls of cold water for 30 minutes, then drain. Remove the pits from the jujubes. If using fresh gingko nuts, blanch in a saucepan of boiling water for 5 minutes, then refresh in cold water and dry thoroughly.

PUT the glutinous rice and 1^1/$_4$ cups water in a heavy-bottomed saucepan and bring to a boil. Reduce the heat to low and simmer for 10–15 minutes. Stir in the sugar and oil.

DISSOLVE the slab sugar in ^{3}/$_4$ cup water and bring to a boil. Add the lotus seeds, jujubes and gingko nuts and simmer for 1 hour, or until the lotus seeds are soft. Drain, reserving the liquid.

GREASE a 4-cup flameproof bowl and decorate the bottom with the lotus seeds, jujubes, gingko nuts, cherries, longans and almonds. Smooth ^{2}/$_3$ of the rice over this to form a shell on the surface of the bowl. Fill with the bean paste, cover with the remaining rice and smooth the surface.

COVER the rice with greased aluminum foil and put the bowl in a steamer. Cover and steam over simmering water in a wok for 1–1^1/$_2$ hours, replenishing with boiling water during cooking.

TURN the pudding out onto a plate and pour the reserved sugar liquid over the top. Serve hot.

STEAMED PEARS IN HONEY

THIS RECIPE COMBINES SWEET PEARS WITH JUJUBES, SMALL RED DATES THAT ARE THOUGHT TO HAVE MEDICINAL BENEFITS. THEY ARE SOLD DRIED, BUT CAN BE LEFT OUT IF THEY ARE UNAVAILABLE.

3/4 cup jujubes (dried Chinese
  dates)
6 nearly ripe pears
6 tablespoons honey

SERVES 6

SOAK the jujubes in hot water for 1 hour, changing the water twice. Drain, remove pits and cut crosswise into strips.

CUT a slice off the bottom of each pear so that it will sit flat. Cut a 1 inch piece off the top and set it aside. Using a fruit corer or knife, remove the cores without cutting right through to the bottom.

ARRANGE the pears upright on a flameproof plate. Place 1 tablespoon of honey and some jujubes into the cavity of each pear. Replace the tops and, if necessary, fasten with cocktail sticks.

PUT the plate in a steamer. Cover and steam over simmering water in a wok for 30 minutes, or until tender when pierced with a knife. Serve hot or cold.

STEAMED PEARS IN HONEY

ALMOND COOKIES

ALMONDS ARE USED FOR SWEET RATHER THAN SAVORY DISHES IN CHINA. THESE COOKIES MAKE GREAT SNACKS AND CAN ALSO BE SERVED ALONGSIDE DESSERTS SUCH AS ALMOND BEAN CURD.

1/2 cup unsalted butter, softened
3/4 cup sugar
1 egg, lightly beaten
1 1/2 cups all-purpose flour
1/2 teaspoon baking powder
1/2 teaspoon salt
1 cup finely chopped almonds
1 teaspoon almond extract
1 egg, lightly beaten, extra
25 whole blanched almonds

MAKES 25

PREHEAT the oven to 350°F. Lightly grease a baking sheet. Cream the butter and sugar for 5 minutes. Add the egg and beat until smooth. Sift together the flour, baking powder and salt and slowly add to the butter, stirring until smooth. Add the almonds and extract and stir until smooth.

DROP tablespoons of the mixture onto the baking sheet, spacing them about 1 1/4 inches apart. Dip your thumb into some flour and make an indentation in the center of each cookie. Brush each cookie with the beaten egg and place an almond in the center of each indentation. Bake for 10–12 minutes, or until the cookies are golden and puffed. Cool slightly, then transfer to a rack to cool completely.

Dip your thumb in some flour and make an indent in each cookie to hold the almonds.

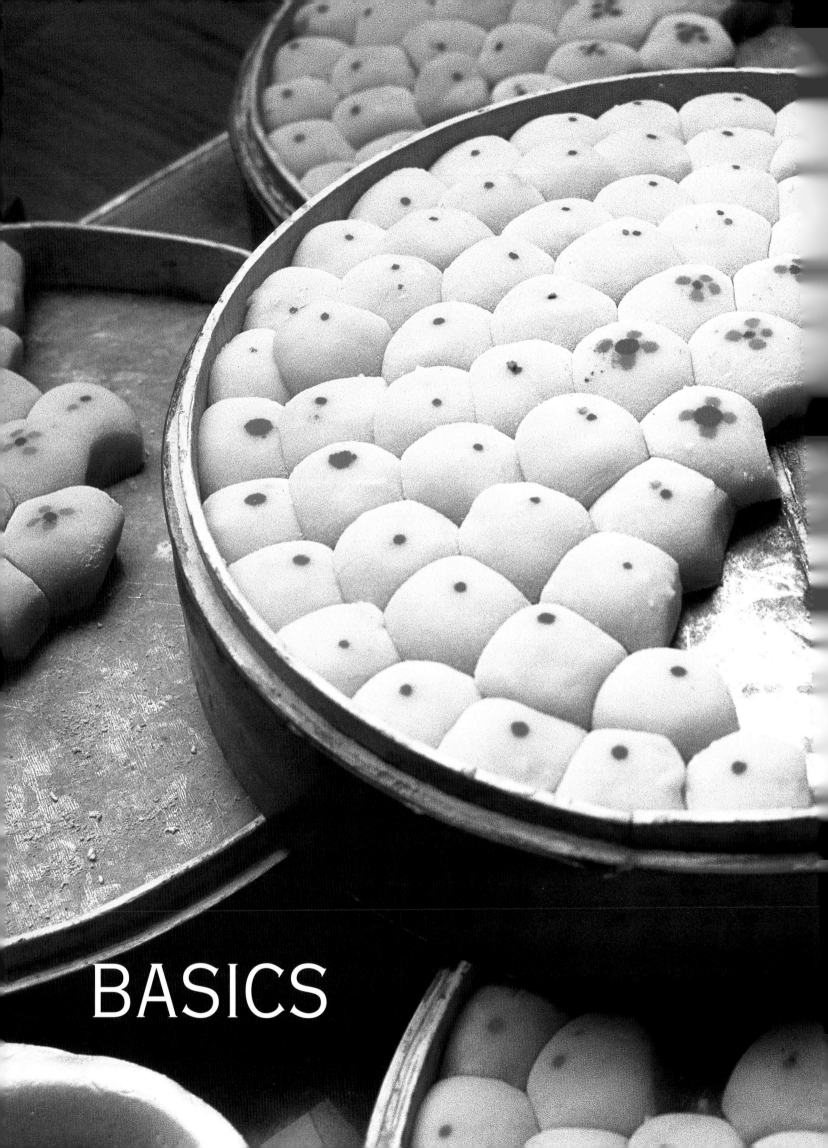

BASICS

BOILED OR STEAMED RICE

1 cup white long-grain rice

SERVES 4

PUT the rice in a bowl and, using your fingers as a rake, rinse under cold running water to remove any dust. Drain the rice in a colander.

TO BOIL the rice, put the rice and 1²/₃ cups water in a heavy-bottomed saucepan and bring to a boil. Reduce the heat to low and simmer, covered, for 15–18 minutes, or until the water has evaporated and craters appear on the surface.

TO STEAM the rice, spread the rice in a steamer lined with waxed paper punched with holes or damp cheesecloth. Cover and steam over simmering water in a wok for 35–40 minutes, or until tender.

FLUFF the rice with a fork to separate the grains. Serve or use as directed.

For steamed rice, line a steamer with waxed paper punched with holes or cheesecloth to let in the steam. Spread out the rice in an even layer.

CRISPY RICE

CRISPY RICE IS A GREAT WAY TO USE UP LEFTOVER RICE, ALTHOUGH YOU CAN MAKE IT FROM SCRATCH, AS HERE. THE DEEP-FRIED RICE IS PUT IN THE BOTTOM OF BOWLS AND A SOUP SUCH AS TOMATO AND EGG (PAGE 60) OR MIXED VEGETABLE (PAGE 63) IS POURED OVER IT TO MAKE THE RICE SIZZLE.

²/₃ cup white long-grain rice

SERVES 4

PUT the rice in a bowl and, using your fingers as a rake, rinse under cold running water to remove any dust. Drain the rice in a colander.

PUT the rice and ³/₄ cup water in a heavy-bottomed saucepan and bring to the boil. Reduce the heat to low and simmer, covered, for 15–18 minutes.

CONTINUE to cook uncovered until the rice has formed a cake that comes loose from the saucepan. Allow to cool. Turn the cake out and dry completely.

FILL a wok one quarter full of oil. Heat the oil to 350°F, or until a piece of bread fries golden brown in 15 seconds when dropped in the oil. Cook the rice cake until it is brown and crisp.

CRISPY RICE

MANDARIN PANCAKES

THESE THIN PANCAKES ARE ALSO CALLED DUCK PANCAKES AND ARE USED FOR WRAPPING PEKING

DUCK (PAGE 134) AND OTHER NORTHERN DISHES, SUCH AS CRISPY SKIN DUCK (PAGE 129), MU SHU

PORK (PAGE 156) AND MONGOLIAN LAMB (PAGE 183).

3¹/₃ cups all-purpose flour
1¹/₄ cups boiling water
1 teaspoon oil
roasted sesame oil

MAKES 24–30

SIFT the flour into a bowl, slowly pour in the boiling water, stirring as you pour, then add the oil and knead into a firm dough. Cover with a damp kitchen towel and set aside for 30 minutes.

TURN the dough out onto a lightly floured surface and knead for 8–10 minutes, or until smooth. Divide the dough into 3 equal portions, roll each portion into a long cylinder, then cut each cylinder into 8 to 10 pieces.

ROLL EACH piece of dough into a ball and press into a flat round with the palm of your hand. Brush one round with a little sesame oil and put another round on top. Using a rolling pin, flatten each pair of rounds into a 6 inch pancake.

HEAT an ungreased wok or frying pan over high heat, then reduce the heat to low and place the pairs of pancakes, one at a time, in the pan. Turn over when brown spots appear on the underside. When the second side is cooked, lift the pancakes out and carefully peel them apart. Fold each pancake in half with the cooked side facing inwards, and set aside under a damp cloth.

JUST BEFORE serving, put the pancakes on a plate in a steamer. Cover and steam over simmering water in a wok for 10 minutes.

TO STORE the pancakes, put them in the fridge for 2 days or in the freezer for several months. Reheat the pancakes either in a steamer for 4–5 minutes or a microwave for 30–40 seconds.

Mandarin pancakes are always rolled and cooked as a pair; the two pancakes are separated by a layer of sesame oil.

BASIC YEAST DOUGH

CHINESE CHEFS USE TWO TYPES OF BREAD DOUGH FOR MAKING STEAMED BREADS, ONE MADE WITH YEAST AS HERE, THE OTHER MADE WITH A YEAST STARTER DOUGH.

3 tablespoons sugar
1 cup warm water
1 1/2 teaspoons dried yeast
3 1/4 cups all-purpose flour
2 tablespoons oil
1 1/2 teaspoons baking powder

MAKES 1 QUANTITY

DISSOLVE the sugar in the water, then add the yeast. Stir lightly, then set aside for 10 minutes, or until foamy.

SIFT the flour into a bowl and add the yeast mixture and the oil. Using a wooden spoon, mix the ingredients into a rough dough. Turn the mixture out onto a lightly floured surface and knead for 8–10 minutes, or until the dough is smooth and elastic. If it is very sticky, knead in a little more flour—the dough should be soft. Lightly grease a bowl with the oil. Place the dough in the bowl and turn it so that all sides of the dough are coated. Cover the bowl with a damp cloth and set aside to rise in a draft-free place for 3 hours.

UNCOVER the dough, punch it down, and turn it out onto a lightly floured surface. If you are not using the dough right away, cover it with plastic wrap and refrigerate.

WHEN YOU are ready to use the dough, flatten it and make a well in the center. Place the baking powder in the well and gather up the edges to enclose the baking powder. Pinch the edges to seal. Lightly knead the dough for several minutes to evenly incorporate the baking powder, which will activate immediately.

USE the prepared dough as directed.

This bread dough is twice risen, first with yeast and then with baking powder, which is kneaded into the dough, making it very light and fluffy.

CHICKEN STOCK

3 lb chicken carcasses, necks and feet
1 cup Shaoxing rice wine
6 slices ginger, smashed with the flat side of a cleaver
6 scallions, ends trimmed, smashed with the flat side of a cleaver
16 cups water

MAKES 2½ QUARTS

REMOVE ANY excess fat from the chicken, then chop into large pieces and place in a stockpot with the rice wine, ginger, scallions and water and bring to a boil. Reduce the heat and simmer gently for 3 hours, skimming the surface to remove any impurities.

STRAIN through a fine strainer, removing the solids, and skim the surface to remove any fat. If the stock is too weak, reduce it further. Store in the fridge for up to 3 days or freeze in small portions.

CHICKEN AND MEAT STOCK

CHICKEN AND MEAT STOCK

1 lb 5 oz chicken carcasses, necks and feet
1 lb 5 oz pork spareribs or veal bones
4 scallions, each tied into a knot
12 slices ginger, smashed with the flat side of a cleaver
16 cups water
⅓ cup Shaoxing rice wine
2 teaspoons salt

MAKES 2½ QUARTS

REMOVE ANY excess fat from the chicken and meat, then chop into large pieces and place in a stockpot with the scallions, ginger and water and bring to a boil. Reduce the heat and simmer gently for 3½–4 hours, skimming the surface to remove any impurities.

STRAIN through a fine strainer, removing the solids, and skim the surface to remove any fat. Return to the pot with the rice wine and salt. Bring to a boil and simmer for 3–4 minutes. Store in the fridge for up to 3 days or freeze in small portions.

VEGETABLE STOCK

VEGETABLE STOCK

1 lb fresh soy bean sprouts
10 dried Chinese mushrooms
6 scallions, each tied into a knot (optional)
16 cups water
3 tablespoons Shaoxing rice wine
2 teaspoons salt

MAKES 2½ QUARTS

DRY-FRY the sprouts in a wok for 3–4 minutes. Place the sprouts, mushrooms, scallions and water in a stockpot and bring to the boil. Reduce the heat and simmer for 1 hour.

STRAIN through a fine strainer, removing the solids (keep the mushrooms for another use). Return to the stockpot with the rice wine and salt. Bring to a boil and simmer for 3–4 minutes. Store in the fridge for up to 3 days or freeze in small portions.

SOY AND VINEGAR

SOY, VINEGAR AND CHILI

SOY, CHILI AND SESAME

酱醋调味酱

SOY AND VINEGAR DIPPING SAUCE

SIMPLE DIPPING SAUCES ARE SERVED WITH FOODS SUCH AS STEAMED DUMPLINGS. THE ADDITION OF
VINEGAR GIVES A MORE ROUNDED FLAVOR THAN USING JUST SOY SAUCE.

1/2 cup light soy sauce
3 tablespoons Chinese black rice
  vinegar

MAKES 1 CUP

COMBINE the soy sauce and vinegar with
2 tablespoons water in a small bowl, then
divide among individual dipping bowls. This
dipping sauce goes well with jiaozi (page 20) or
dim sum like siu mai (page 38).

酱醋辣酱

SOY, VINEGAR AND CHILI DIPPING SAUCE

1/2 cup light soy sauce
2 tablespoons Chinese black rice
  vinegar
2 red chiles, thinly sliced

MAKES 3/4 CUP

COMBINE the soy sauce, vinegar and chiles in a
small bowl, then divide among individual dipping
bowls. This dipping sauce goes well with jiaozi
(page 20) or dim sum like har gau (page 41) or
bean curd rolls (page 35).

红醋调味酱

RED VINEGAR DIPPING SAUCE

1/2 cup red rice vinegar
3 tablespoons shredded ginger

MAKES 1 CUP

COMBINE the rice vinegar, 2 1/2 tablespoons water
and the ginger in a small bowl, then divide among
individual dipping bowls. This dipping sauce goes
well with jiaozi (page 20).

酱辣芝麻调味酱

SOY, CHILI AND SESAME DIPPING SAUCE

1/2 cup light soy sauce
1/4 cup chile oil
1 tablespoon roasted sesame oil
1 scallion, finely chopped

MAKES 3/4 CUP

COMBINE the soy sauce, chile oil, sesame oil
and scallion in a small bowl, then divide among
individual dipping bowls. This dipping sauce goes
well with jiaozi (page 20) and steamed breads
(page 46).

MAKING GREEN TEA

GREEN TEA is served in glasses so its colour and the leaves themselves can be appreciated. The glasses are warmed, then tea added with a little freshly boiled water (spring water is considered best). The glasses are topped up by pouring in more water from a height, known as flushing, to aerate the water for a better infusion. The tea is drunk very hot and the leaves briefly steeped compared to black teas.

MAKING OOLONG TEA

OOLONG is made here by the *gong fu* method. The cups and pot are warmed, then the leaves are rinsed with boiling water, strained into a jug and topped up with more water. Water is poured over the pot to keep it warm while the tea brews, then when dry, the tea is poured back and forth over tall smelling cups to ensure an even strength. The aroma is taken in from the tall cups after the tea is tipped into small cups to taste.

TEA SEASONS

TEA is seasonal: spring teas are the finest, while winter teas have an enticing aroma but are rare as there is little harvesting. For Dragon Well tea, the first and best quality picking of the year is the *nu'er* (daughter) tea *(left)*. The second is known as *Qing Ming (middle)* as it is picked around the time of that festival in April. The last picking is called *gu yu (right)* and is picked in the season of this name between spring and summer.

TEA HOUSES are popular all over China. Some are a male domain where business is conducted, such as at this one in Yuyuan Bazaar, Shanghai *(top)*, while others, like this one at Wenshu Monastery, Chengdu *(bottom right)*, are family-orientated and allow patrons to sit all day over a constantly refilled cup of tea. Tea houses also offer snacks to accompany the tea, from melon seeds or oranges to more ornate sweet offerings *(bottom left)*.

TEA

TEA HAS BEEN POPULAR IN CHINA SINCE AT LEAST THE SIXTH CENTURY BC, AND IT WAS FROM CHINA THAT TEA TRAVELLED TO JAPAN, EUROPE AND INDIA. INTEGRAL TO FESTIVALS, A SIGN OF HOSPITALITY, A MEDICINE, AND STEEPED IN TRADITION, TEA IS BOTH A DRINK AND A PART OF CHINESE CULTURE ITSELF.

For the Chinese, tea is a drink to be savoured on its own or before or after a meal. The exception is tea with yum cha, which means to 'drink tea' and originated as a few snacks to complement the tea at tea houses, rather than the full meal

it often is today. In China, hot water is provided in hotels, waiting rooms and on trains for people to make tea using their own screwtop jar or in a large cup with a lid that can be slid back just enough to drink the tea without the leaves coming too. Carrying a receptacle for tea is not a statement of class or rank, everyone does it.

ORIGINS OF TEA

Tea plants (*Camellia sinensis*) are native to the mountains of Southwest China, and are now grown all over the South, and in the East and North where conditions are favourable. Teas from Yunnan and Fujian are particularly treasured. Tea is made from the two top leaves and bud, picked every 7–10 days to gather the young shoots and to encourage more shoots to sprout, known as a flush. These small leaves are more prized than too large or broken leaves. Fannings (tea dust and broken leaves) are the lowest grades of all.

DRAGON WELL TEA is China's finest green tea, grown around the West Lake of Hangzhou, especially in the village of Longjing (Dragon Well). Here, the Wen family runs a small tea estate producing three pickings a year. The tea buds are hand-picked, then dried by rubbing the leaves around a heated metal basin to arrest any fermentation. The Wen family teas are sold by weight from their house in the village.

VARIETIES OF TEA

Tea is categorized by the different methods of its production:
GREEN an unfermented tea made by firing (drying) fresh leaves in a kind of wok to prevent them oxidizing (fermenting). The tea is usually rolled and twisted to uncurl in boiling water.
OOLONG the leaves are semi-fermented before firing to produce a tea halfway between green and black. The most famous oolong teas are from Fujian and Taiwan.
BLACK a fully fermented tea where the leaves are wilted and bruised by rolling, then fermented and dried.
WHITE a very rare, totally unfermented green tea from Fujian.

Chinese teas can also be categorized by other factors:
BRICK usually pu-er teas from Yunnan compressed into blocks. A piece is sliced off to make tea.
SCENTED tea leaves mixed with scented flowers.
FLOWER petal teas, which are not true teas but tisanes.

BRICK TEA a compressed tea, usually made from Yunnan pu'er, which was originally devised to carry tea easily and was even used as a form of currency. The character on the tea is for wealth.

CLOUD AND MIST (*Yun Wu*) a green tea grown on mountain sides and cliffs, appreciated for its colour and fine clear flavour. It is a legendary 'monkey pick' tea, said to be harvested by monkeys.

IRON GODDESS (*Tie Guan Yin*) a strong, bitter oolong tea, also called Iron Buddha, drunk before and after a meal from a tiny cup. It is often served with Chiu Chow cuisine to balance the rich food.

FLOWER TEA made from chrysanthemum flowers, wolf berries and peppermint sugar, this is not strictly a tea, but is served in tea houses as a medicinal tonic.

QIMEN RED TEA this prized mild, sweet and aromatic black tea from the Huangshan mountains in Anhui is known in the West as Keemun. A gong fu tea, meaning that it is precisely prepared.

LYCHEE TEA made from black tea leaves that are processed with lychee juice, this tea has a fragrant sweet flavour that is very palate cleansing. It is also called lychee red.

DRAGON WELL (*Long Jing*) this fragrant, sweet green tea from Hangzhou in the East is considered the best in China. The leaves are flat, not rolled, and stand up when infused.

WHITE TEA (*Chai Tou Yu Ming*) this fine white tea is named after a hair ornament. White tea is made from hand-picked buds, dried in the sun to create a silvery tea with a very pure taste.

JASMINE TEA a light, fragrant tea of green or black leaves mixed with jasmine flowers. Jasmine is renowned as a good digestive after a rich meal and contains little caffeine.

CHRYSANTHEMUM TEA a flower tea with a mixture of whole chrysanthemum and tea or just chrysanthemum. It is regarded as cooling and its mild flavour goes well with dim sum.

CAKE TEA also known as bowl tea, this is the round form of compressed pu'er. This variety is called gold melon. It symbolizes a blessing and is a gift for a couple's families after their wedding.

PU'ER, or Bou Lei, is a popular black tea from Yunnan that often accompanies dim sum as it is said to aid the digestion of fats (and ease hangovers). Pu'er is sold loose or as a cake or brick.

Chinese chives Garlic chives have a long, flat leaf and are green and very garlicky, or yellow with a milder taste. Flowering chives are round-stemmed with a flower at the top, which can be eaten. Both are used as a vegetable rather than as a herb.

Chinese curry powder A strong and spicy version of five-spice powder, with additional spices including turmeric and coriander which lend the curry flavour.

Chinese ham A salted and smoked ham with a strong flavor and dry flesh. Yunnan and Jinhua hams are the best known, and outside China, Yunnan ham can be bought in cans. You can substitute prosciutto if you can't find it.

Chinese mushrooms The fresh version, found as shiitake mushrooms, is cultivated by the Japanese. The Chinese, however, usually use dried ones, which have a strong flavor and aroma and need to be soaked to reconstitute them before they are used. The soaking liquid can be used to add flavor to dishes. These are widely available.

Chinese pickles These can be made from several types of vegetables, preserved in a clear brine solution or in a soy-based solution, which is called jiang cai. Both can be used where Chinese pickles are called for in a recipe. They are available in packages and jars from Chinese markets.

Chinese sausage There are two kinds of Chinese sausage: a red variety, lap cheong or la chang, which is made from pork and pork fat and dried; and a brown variety, yun cheung or xiang chang, which is made from liver and pork and also dried. Chinese sausages have to be cooked before eating.

Chinese shrimp paste Very pungent pulverized shrimp. Refrigerate after opening.

Chinese spirits Distilled from grains, these vary in strength but generally are stronger than Western spirits. Spirits are used for drinking and cooking and Mou Tai is a common brand. Brandy can be substituted.

Chinese-style pork spareribs These are the shorter, fatter ribs known as pai gwat and are cut into short pieces. If unavailable, use any spareribs but trim off any excess fat.

Chinese turnip Looking like a huge white carrot, this is actually a type of radish and is also called Chinese white radish. It has a crisp, juicy flesh and mild radish flavor. It is also known as mooli, or by the Japanese name daikon, and is widely available.

choy sum A green vegetable with tender pale-green stalks, small yellow flowers and dark-green leaves. It has a mild flavor and is often just blanched and eaten with a simple flavoring like garlic or oyster sauce.

clay pot Also known as a sand pot, these earthenware, lidded pots are used for braised dishes, soups and rice dishes that need to be cooked slowly on the stove. The pots come in different shapes: the squatter ones are for braising and the taller ones for soups and rice. The pots can be fragile and should be heated slowly, preferably with a liquid inside.

cleaver A large, oblong, flat-bladed knife. In China, different cleavers are used for all chopping and cutting, but heavy-duty ones are good for chopping through bones as they are very robust. They can be bought in Chinese markets and at specialty stores.

dang gui A bitter Chinese herb that is a relation of European Angelica and is valued for its medicinal properties. It looks like small bleached pieces of wood, and is generally added to braised dishes and soups. Buy it in Chinese markets or Chinese herb shops.

dried scallops (conpoy) Scallops dried to thick amber disks. They need to be soaked or steamed until soft and are often shredded before use. They have a strong flavor so you don't need many, and as they are expensive they are mostly eaten at banquets.

dried shrimp These are tiny, orange, saltwater shrimp that have been dried in the sun. They come in different sizes and the really small ones have their heads and shells still attached. Dried shrimp need to be soaked in water or rice wine to soften them before use and are used as a seasoning, not as a main ingredient.

dumpling wrappers Used for jiaozi, wheat wrappers, also called Shanghai wrappers or wheat dumpling skins, are white and can be round or square. Egg wrappers for siu mai are yellow and may also be round or

square. They are sometimes labeled gow gee wrappers or egg dumpling skins. All are found in the refrigerated section in Chinese markets and good supermarkets and can be frozen until needed.

fermented bean curd A marinated bean curd that is either red, colored with red rice, or white, and may also be flavored with chiles. It is sometimes called preserved bean curd or bean curd cheese and is used as a condiment or flavoring. It can be found in jars in Chinese markets.

five-spice powder A Chinese mixed spice generally made with star anise, cassia, Sichuan pepper, fennel seeds and cloves, which gives a balance of sweet, hot and aromatic flavors. Five-spice may also include cardamom, coriander, dried orange peel and ginger. Used ground together as a powder or as whole spices tied in muslin.

flat cabbage (tat soi) Also known as a rosette cabbage, this is a type of bok choy. It looks like a giant flower with pretty, shiny, dark-green leaves that grow out flat.

gingko nuts These are the nuts of the maidenhair tree. The hard shells are cracked open and the inner nuts soaked to loosen their skins. The nuts are known for their medicinal properties and are one of the eight treasures in dishes like eight-treasure rice. Shelled nuts can be bought in cans in Chinese markets and are easier to use.

glutinous rice A short-grain rice that, unlike other rice, cooks to a sticky mass and is used in dishes where the rice is required to hold together. Glutinous rice is labeled as such and has plump, highly polished and shiny grains. Black or red glutinous rice, used mainly in desserts, is slightly different.

Guilin chili sauce From the southwest of China, this sauce is made from salted, fermented yellow soy beans and chiles. It is used as an ingredient in cooking. If it is unavailable, use a thick chili sauce instead.

hoisin sauce This sauce is made from salted, yellow soy beans, sugar, vinegar, sesame oil, red rice for coloring and spices such as five-spice or star anise. It is generally used as a dipping sauce, for meat glazes or in barbecue marinades.

jujubes Also known as Chinese or red dates, jujubes are an olive-sized dried fruit with a red, wrinkled skin, thought to build strength. They need to be soaked and are used in eight-treasure or tonic-type dishes. They are thought to be lucky because of their red color.

longans From the same family as lychees, these are round with smooth, buff-colored skins, translucent sweet flesh and large brown seeds. Available fresh, canned or dried.

lotus leaves The dried leaves of the lotus, they need to be soaked before use and are used for wrapping up food like sticky rice to hold it together while it is cooking. They are sold in packages in Chinese markets.

lotus root The rhizome of the Chinese lotus, the root looks like a string of three cream-colored sausages, but when cut into it has a beautiful lacy pattern. Available fresh (which must be washed), canned or dried. Use the fresh or canned version as a fresh vegetable and the dried version in braised dishes.

lotus seeds These seeds from the lotus are considered medicinal and are used in eight-treasure dishes as well as being toasted, salted or candied and eaten as a snack. Lotus seeds are also made into a sweet paste to fill buns and pancakes. Fresh and dried lotus seeds are both available and dried seeds need to be soaked before use.

maltose A sweet liquid of malted grains used to coat Peking duck and barbecued meats. It is sold in Chinese markets, but honey can be used instead.

master sauce This is a basic stock of soy sauce, rice wine, rock sugar, scallions, ginger and star anise. Additional ingredients vary according to individual chefs. Meat, poultry or fish is cooked in the stock, then the stock is reserved so it matures, taking on the flavors of everything that is cooked in it. The spices are replenished every few times the sauce is used. Master sauce spices can be bought as a mix, or a ready-made liquid version. Freeze between uses.

Mei Kuei Lu Chiew A fragrant spirit known as Rose Dew Liqueur. Made from sorghum and rose petals. It is used in marinades, but brandy can be used instead.

noodles Egg noodles come fresh and dried in varying thicknesses. In recipes they are interchangeable, so choose a brand that you like and buy the thickness appropriate to the dish you are making. Wheat noodles are also available fresh and dried and are interchangeable in recipes. Rice noodles are made from a paste of ground rice and water and can be bought fresh or as dried rice sticks or vermicelli. The fresh noodles are white and can be bought in a roll.

one-thousand-year-old eggs Also known as one-hundred-year old or century eggs, these are eggs that have been preserved by coating them in a layer of wood ash, slaked lime and then rice husks. The eggs are left to mature for 40 days to give them a blackish-green yolk and amber white. To eat, the coating is scraped off and the shell peeled. These eggs are eaten as an hors d'oeuvre or used to garnish congee.

oyster sauce A fairly recent invention, this is a soy-based sauce flavored with oyster extract. Add to dishes at the end of cooking or use as part of a marinade.

pepper Used as an ingredient rather than as a condiment, most hot dishes were originally flavored with copious quantities of pepper rather than the chiles used now. White pepper is used rather than black.

plum sauce This comes in several varieties, with some brands sweeter than others and some adding chile, ginger or garlic. It is often served with Peking duck rather than the true sauce and is a good dipping sauce.

preserved ginger Ginger pickled in rice vinegar and sugar, which is typically used for sweet-and-sour dishes. Japanese pickled ginger could be used as a substitute.

preserved mustard cabbage Also called Sichuan pickle or preserved vegetables, this is the root of the mustard cabbage preserved in chile and salt. It is available whole and shredded in jars or cans, or vacuum-packed from Chinese markets.

preserved turnip This is Chinese turnip, sliced, shredded or grated, and usually preserved in brine. It has a crunchy texture and needs to be rinsed before using so it is less salty.

red bean paste Made from crushed adzuki beans and sugar, this sweet paste is used in soups and to fill dumplings and pancakes. There is a richer black version and this can be used instead.

rice flour This is finely ground rice, often used to make rice noodles. Glutinous rice flour, used for making sweet things, makes a chewier dough. Obtainable from Chinese markets or supermarkets.

rice vinegar Made from fermented rice, Chinese vinegars are milder than Western ones. Clear rice vinegar is mainly used for pickles and sweet-and-sour dishes. Red rice vinegar is a mild liquid used as a dipping sauce and served with shark's fin soup. Black rice vinegar is used in stews, especially in northern recipes—Chinkiang (Zhenjiang) vinegar is a good label. Rice vinegars can last indefinitely but may lose their aroma, so buy small bottles. If you can't find them, use cider vinegar instead of clear and balsamic instead of black.

rock sugar Yellow rock sugar comes as uneven lumps of sugar, which may need to be further crushed before use if very big. It is a pure sugar that produces a clear syrup and makes sauces it is added to shiny and clear. You can use sugar lumps instead.

salted, fermented black beans Very salty black soy beans that are fermented using the same molds as are used for making soy sauce. Added to dishes as a flavoring, they must be rinsed before use and are often mashed or crushed. They are available in jars or bags from specialist shops. You can also use a black bean sauce made with black beans and garlic.

sea cucumber A slug-like sea creature related to the starfish, available dried or vacuum-packed. When sold dried, it needs to be reconstituted by soaking. It has a gelatinous texture and no flavor .

sesame oil (roasted) Chinese sesame oil is made from roasted white sesame seeds and is a rich amber liquid, unlike the pale unroasted Middle Eastern sesame oil. Buy small bottles as it loses its aroma quickly. It does not fry well as it smokes at a low temperature, but sprinkle it on food as a seasoning or mix it with other oils for stir-frying.

sesame paste Made from ground, toasted white sesame seeds, this is a fairly dry paste. It is more aromatic than tahini, which can be used instead by mixing it with a little Chinese sesame oil. Black sesame paste is used for sweets like New Year's dumplings.

Shaoxing rice wine Made from rice, millet, yeast and Shaoxing's local water, this is aged for at least three years, then bottled either in glass or decorative earthenware bottles. Several varieties are available. As a drink, rice wine is served warm in small cups. Dry sherry is the best substitute.

shark's fin Prized for its texture more than for its flavor, shark's fin is very expensive. Preparing a dried fin takes several days, so using the prepackaged version is much easier as it just needs soaking and then cooking. It looks like very thin dried noodles.

Sichuan (Szechwan) peppercorns Not a true pepper, but the berries of a shrub called the prickly ash. Sichuan pepper, unlike ordinary pepper, has a pungent flavor and the aftertaste, rather than being simply hot, is numbing. The peppercorns should be crushed and dry-roasted to bring out their full flavor.

slab sugar Dark brown sugar with a caramel flavor sold in a slab. Soft brown sugar can be used instead.

soy sauce Made from fermented soy beans, soy sauce comes in two styles: light soy sauce, which is also known as just soy sauce or superior soy sauce, and is used with fish, poultry and vegetables, and dark soy sauce, which is more commonly used with meats. Chinese soy sauce, unlike Japanese, is not used as a condiment except with Cantonese cuisine. As it is not meant to be a dipping sauce, it is best to mix a tablespoon of dark with two tablespoons of light to get a good flavor for a condiment. It does not last forever so buy small bottles and store it in the fridge.

soy beans These are oval, pale green beans. The fresh beans are cooked in their fuzzy pods and served as a snack. The dried beans can be yellow or black, and the yellow ones are used to make soy milk by boiling and then puréeing the beans with water before straining off the milk. Dried beans need to be soaked overnight.

spring roll wrappers Also called spring roll skins, these wrappers are made with egg and are pale or dark yellow. They are found in the refrigerated section of Chinese markets and supermarkets and can be frozen until needed.

star anise An aromatic ingredient in Chinese cooking, this is a star-shaped dried seed pod containing a flat seed in each point. It has a similar flavor and aroma to fennel seed and aniseed. It is used whole in braised dishes or ground into five-spice powder.

steaming A method of cooking food in a moist heat to keep it tender and preserve its flavor. Bamboo steamers fit above a saucepan or wok and a 10 inch steamer is the most useful, although you will need a bigger one for whole fish. Use as many as you need, stacked on top of each other, and reverse them halfway through cooking to ensure the cooking is even. Metal steamers are available, but bamboo ones are preferred in China as they absorb the steam, making the food a little drier.

stir-frying A method of cooking in a wok that only uses a little oil and cooks the food evenly and quickly, retaining its color and texture. Everything to be cooked needs to be prepared beforehand, cut to roughly the same shape, dry and at room temperature. The wok is heated, then the oil added and heated before the ingredients are thrown in. Stir-frying should only take a couple of minutes, the heat should be high and the ingredients continually tossed.

tangerine peel Dried tangerine or orange peel is used as a seasoning. It looks like dark-brown strips of leather with a white underside, and is used mostly in braised dishes or master sauces. It is not soaked first but is added straight to the liquid in the dish. Sold in bags in Chinese markets.

tiger lily buds Sometimes called golden needles, these aren't from tiger lilies but are the unopened flowers from another type of lily. The buds are bought dried and then soaked. They have an earthy flavor and are used mainly in vegetarian dishes.

water chestnuts These are the rhizomes of a plant that grows in paddy fields in China. The nut has a dark-brown shell and a crisp white interior. The raw nuts need to be peeled with a knife and blanched, then stored in water. Canned ones need to be drained and rinsed. Freshly peeled nuts are sometimes available from Chinese markets.

water spinach Called ong choy in Chinese, this vegetable has long, dark-green pointed leaves and long hollow stems. Often cooked with shrimp paste.

wheat starch A powder-like flour made by removing the protein from wheat flour. It is used to make dumpling wrappers.

winter melon A very large dark green gourd or squash that looks like a watermelon. The skin is dark green, often with a white waxy bloom, and the flesh is pale green. You can usually buy pieces of it in Chinese markets.

wok A bowl-shaped cooking vessel that acts as both a frying pan and a saucepan in the Chinese kitchen. Choose one made from carbon steel about 14 inch in diameter. To season it, scrub off the layer of machine oil, then heat with two tablespoons of oil over low heat for several minutes. Rub the inside with paper towels, changing the paper until it comes out clean. The inside will continue to darken as it is used and only water should be used for cleaning. Use a different wok for steaming, as boiling water will strip off the seasoning. A metal spatula (charn) is perfect for moving ingredients around the wok.

won ton wrappers Also called won ton skins, these are square and yellow and slightly larger than dumpling wrappers. They can be found in the refrigerated section in Chinese markets and good supermarkets and can be frozen until needed.

yard-long beans Also called snake or long beans, these are about 16 inches long. The darker green variety has a firmer texture.

yellow bean sauce This is actually brown in color and made from fermented yellow soy beans, which are sweeter and less salty than black beans, mixed with rice wine and dark brown sugar. It varies in flavor and texture (some have whole beans in them) and is sold under different names—crushed yellow beans, brown bean sauce, ground bean sauce and bean sauce. It is mainly used in Sichuan and Hunan cuisine.

INDEX